Criminal Law Casebook

4th edition

Edited by Michael T Molan

BA, LLM (Lond), Barrister
Senior Lecturer at South Bank University

HLT Publications

HLT PUBLICATIONS
200 Greyhound Road, London W14 9RY

First published 1988
4th edition 1992

© The HLT Group Ltd 1992

ISBN 0 7510 0128 7

British Library Cataloguing-in-Publication.
A CIP Catalogue record for this book is
available from the British Library.

Acknowledgement

The publishers and author would like to
thank the Incorporated Council of Law
Reporting for England and Wales for kind
permission to reproduce extracts from the
Weekly Law Reports.

The publishers and editor would like to
thank Professor J C Smith and Di Birch
and Sweet & Maxwell for granting
permission for the reproduction of
copyright material from the *Criminal Law
Review*.

Material from the *Criminal Appeal Reports*
© Sweet & Maxwell.

The publishers and editor would like to
thank Sweet & Maxwell for granting
permission for the reproduction of material
from the *Criminal Appeal Reports*.

Printed and bound in Great Britain

CONTENTS

CONTENTS

PREFACE

This HLT casebook can be used as a companion volume to the HLT *Criminal Law Textbook*, but also comprises an invaluable reference tool in itself. Its aim is to supplement and enhance students' understanding and interpretation of this particular area of the law, and to provide essential background reading. The book is divided into chapters and for ease of reference cases are arranged alphabetically within each chapter.

Many new cases have been added to this new edition, notably *R* v *Savage*; *R* v *Parmenter* (mens rea for statutory assaults), *R* v *Cheshire* (causation in homicide), *R* v *Burgess* (sleepwalking as insanity), *R* v *Gomez* (appropriation in theft). In addition, the scope of this casebook has been extended to include s20 of the Theft Act 1968, procuring the execution of a valuable security by deception.

The *Criminal Law Casebook* aims to state the law as of 1st March 1992.

TABLE OF CASES

1   CRIME AND PUNISHMENT

GENERAL NOTE

It is not the purpose of this chapter to provide detailed materials on sentencing policy and practice. For an excellent survey of materials relevant to that topic see *Criminal Law: Cases and Materials* by Clarkson & Keating (Sweet & Maxwell, 1990).

The materials included in this chapter illustrate the sources of criminal law, some of the policy considerations that judges have to weigh in the balance when developing the principles of criminal liability, and some of the more significant procedural matters that students of criminal law should be aware of.

A-G v Able [1984] QB 795 Queen's Bench Division (Woolf J)

Use of the civil courts to determine a criminal matter

Facts

The respondent was a member of the executive committee of the organisation 'EXIT', which promoted euthanasia. The society had published a booklet entitled 'A guide to self deliverance', which gave advice on how those who wished to commit suicide might successfully do so. The Attorney-General adopted the view that the publication might constitute an offence under s2(1) of the Suicide Act 1961, but instead of instigating a criminal prosecution against members of the society's executive committee, he sought a declaration in the High Court that the publication would be a violation of the criminal law. The respondents argued that this was an inappropriate procedure where a point of criminal law was in question.

Held

The civil courts should exercise great restraint in granting declarations on points of criminal law, so as to avoid usurping the function of the criminal courts. Where there was evidence that the booklet in question was supplied to a person who was known to be contemplating suicide, with the intention that this should encourage the commission of the suicide, and that suicide did result, the supply of the booklet could amount to an offence of aiding and abetting suicide. In the present case there was no evidence to suggest that the booklet was to be supplied in such circumstances, hence the declaration would be refused.

Woolf J:

'The House of Lords has recently dealt with the question of the propriety of the civil courts granting declaratory relief in cases involving the criminal law in *Imperial Tobacco Ltd* v *Attorney-General* [1981] AC 718. In that case it was the company which sought the declaratory relief and the Attorney-General who opposed the grant of it. Before the matter came before the High Court, criminal proceedings had already been commenced. Giving the leading speech, Viscount Dilhorne said, at p742: "My Lords, it is not necessary in this case to decide whether a declaration as to the criminality or otherwise of future conduct can ever properly be made by a civil court. In my opinion it would be a very exceptional case in which it would be right to do so. In my opinion it cannot be right to grant a declaration that an accused is innocent after a prosecution has started."

That there can be circumstances where it is appropriate to give declaratory relief I accept. Indeed, in *Royal College of Nursing of the United Kingdom* v *Department of Health and Social Security* [1981] AC 800, I gave such relief, and my decision to do so was not subject to criticism in either the Court of Appeal or the House of Lords. Furthermore, if it is open to a private individual, in exceptional circumstances, to obtain such relief, it is certainly open to the Attorney-General to do so, since his right to seek the assistance of the civil courts in upholding the criminal law has been fully recognised by the courts: see *Attorney-General* v *Bastow* [1957] 1 QB 514.

The position of the Attorney-General in this respect was also dealt with by the House of Lords in *Gouriet* v *Union of Post Office Workers* [1978] AC 435. Lord Fraser of Tullybelton said, at p523:

"It seems to me entirely appropriate that responsibility for deciding whether to initiate preventive proceedings for injunction or declaration in the public interest should be vested in a public officer, and for historical reasons that officer is the Attorney-General. It is well established that he is not bound to prosecute in every case where there is sufficient evidence, but that when a question of public policy may be involved the Attorney-General has the duty of deciding whether prosecution would be in the public interest, see the statement by Sir Hartley Shawcross in 1951 in *Edwards on The Law Officers of the Crown* (1964), p223. It seems even more necessary that similar consideration should be given to the public interest before initiating preventive proceedings for injunction or declaration."

There are, however, differences between this case and other cases where declaratory relief has been granted in aid of the criminal law. Declarations are being sought that certain conduct is criminal, not that certain conduct is not criminal. The declarations are addressed to future distributions of the booklet and it is a real possibility that if a declaration is granted, but despite this further distributions take place, there could be a criminal prosecution. This makes it particularly important that this court should bear in mind the danger of usurping the jurisdiction of the criminal courts.

In this connection, I do not accept in full the submission by counsel for the respondents that because the proceedings are brought by the Attorney-General, it will only be appropriate exceptionally to refuse declaratory relief. It is true, as he contends, that in effect the Attorney-General is in a position to obtain declarations as to the law from the Court of Appeal (Criminal Division) on an Attorney-General's reference. However, while the court's decision on such references frequently clarifies the law, the court does so in relation to specific facts which are before it, in exactly the same way as it would in the case of an ordinary appeal against conviction. Furthermore, if a court declares what conduct will be criminal, it may be performing exactly the task which the jury would have to perform at a criminal trial. However, if the court rules that conduct is not criminal, it is performing a similar function to the judge at a criminal trial who stops the case on a submission of no case to answer. While of course recognising the advantages of the application of the law being clear in relation to future conduct, it would only be proper to grant a declaration if it is clearly established that there is no risk of it treating conduct as criminal which is not clearly in contravention of the criminal law.

Adopting this standard, I consider it appropriate to proceed to consider whether, on the evidence which is before me, the Attorney-General has established that he is entitled to the declaratory relief which he seeks.'

Commentary

See further chapter 9, for extracts dealing with accessorial liability.

DPP for Northern Ireland v Lynch [1975] AC 653 House of Lords

This authority is further discussed in chapter 13 under *R* v *Howe*.

Policy considerations in judicial law making

Held

Lord Kilbrandon:

'It is my misfortune that while I agree with those of your Lordships who consider that the law is in a very unsatisfactory state, and is in urgent need of restatement, I remain convinced that the grounds on which the majority propose that conviction of the appellant be set aside involve changes in the law which are outside the proper functions of your Lordships in your judicial capacity. If duress per minas has never been admitted as a defence to a charge of murder, and if the proposal that it should now be so admitted be approved, it seems to me that your Lordships, in countenancing a defence for many years authoritatively (though not in your Lordships' House) denied, would be doing what in the converse, was firmly and properly disapproved in *R* v *Knuller*. . . Instead of, for reasons of public policy, declaring criminal for the first time conduct until then not so described, your Lordships would be for the first time declaring the existence of a defence to a criminal charge which had up to now by judges, text writers, and law teachers throughout the common law world, been emphatically repudiated ...

An alteration in a fundamental doctrine of law, such as this appeal proposes, could not properly by given effect to save after the widest reference to interests, both social and intellectual, far transcending those available in the judicial committee of your Lordships' House. Indeed general public opinion is deeply and properly concerned. It will not do to claim that judges have the duty – call it the privilege – of seeing to it that the common law expands and contracts to meet what the judges conceive to be the requirement of modern society. Modern society rightly prefers to exercise that function for itself, and this it conveniently does through those who represent it in Parliament. And its representatives nowadays demand, or should demand, that they be briefed by all those who can qualify an interest to advise them. The fascinating discussions of policy which adorn the speeches of your Lordships – and to which I intend to make a short and undistinguished addition – are themselves highly illustrative of what I mean. They may perhaps be taken as the ultimate in the distillation of legal policy-opinion, but that is not enough. I will not take time to enumerate the various other disciplines and interests whose views are of equal value in deciding what policy should inform the legislation, necessary if reform of the law is really called for, giving effect to the defence of duress per minas in all crimes including murder. In the absence of such consultations I do not think it would be right to decide an appeal in such a way as to set aside the common understanding of the law ...'

Commentary

See further *R* v *Howe* [1987] AC 417, chapters 9 and 13.

Shaw v DPP [1962] AC 220 House of Lords (Viscount Simmonds, Lord Reid, Lord Tucker, Lord Morris of Borth-y-Gest and Lord Hodson)

Creation of new offence by the judiciary: policy considerations in judicial law making

Facts

The appellant published a circular known as the 'Ladies' Directory' which was in effect a 'contact magazine' for prostitutes and their potential clients. He was convicted, inter alia, for conspiring to corrupt public morals. He appealed unsuccessfully to the Court of Appeal on the ground that there was no such offence known to law. He appealed further to the House of Lords.

Held   (Lord Reid dissenting)

The appeal would be dismissed

Viscount Simmonds:

[Having indicated that he was not an advocate of judicial law making]

'... I am at a loss to understand how it can be said either that the law does not recognise a conspiracy to corrupt public morals or that, though there may not be an exact precedent for such a conspiracy as this case reveals, it does not fall fairly within the general words by which it is described. I do not propose to examine all the relevant authorities. That will be done by my noble and learned friend. The fallacy in the argument that was addressed to us lay in the attempt to exclude from the scope of general words acts well calculated to corrupt public morals just because they had not been committed

3

or had not been brought to the notice of the court before. It is not thus that the common law has developed. We are, perhaps, more accustomed to hear this matter discussed on the question whether such and such a transaction is contrary to public policy. At once the controversy arises. On the one hand it is said that it is not possible in the twentieth century for the court to create a new head of public policy, on the other it is said that this is but a new example of a well-established head. In the sphere of criminal law, I entertain no doubt that there remains in the courts of law a residual power to enforce the supreme and fundamental purpose of the law, to conserve not only the safety and order but also the moral welfare of the state, and that it is their duty to guard it against attacks which may be the more insidious because they are novel and unprepared for. That is the broad head (call it public policy if you wish) within which the present indictment falls. It matters little what label is given to the offending act. To one of your Lordships it may appear an affront to public decency, to another, considering that it may succeed in its obvious intention of provoking libidinous desires, it will seem a corruption of public morals. Yet others may deem it aptly described as the creation of a public mischief or the undermining of moral conduct. The same act will not in all ages be regarded in the same way. The law must be related to the changing standards of life, not yielding to every shifting impulse of the popular will, but having regard to fundamental assessments of human values and the purposes of society. Today a denial of the fundamental Christian doctrine, which in past centuries would have been regarded by the ecclesiastical courts as heresy and by the common law as blasphemy, will no longer be an offence if the decencies of controversy are observed. When Lord Mansfield, speaking long after the Star Chamber had been abolished, said [in *Delaval* (1763) 3 Burr 1434 at 1438] that the Court of King's Bench was the custos morum of the people and had the superintendency of offences contra bonos mores, he was asserting, as I now assert, that there is in that court a residual power, where no statute has yet intervened to supersede the common law, to superintend those offences which are prejudicial to the public welfare. Such occasions will be rare, for Parliament has not been slow to legislate when attention has been sufficiently aroused. But gaps remain and will always remain since no one can foresee every way in which the wickedness of man may disrupt the order of society. Let me take a single instance to which my noble and learned friend, Lord Tucker, refers. Let it be supposed that, at some future, perhaps, early, date homosexual practices between adult consenting males are no longer a crime. Would it not be an offence if, even without obscenity, such practices were publicly advocated and encouraged by pamphlet and advertisement? Or must we wait until Parliament finds time to deal with such conduct? I say, my Lords, that if the common law is powerless in such an event, then we should no longer do her reverence. But I say that her hand is still powerful and that it is for Her Majesty's judges to play the part which Lord Mansfield pointed out to them.

I have so far paid little regard to the fact that the charge here is of conspiracy. But, if I have correctly described the conduct of the appellant, it is an irresistible inference that a conspiracy between him and others to do such acts is indictable. It is irrelevant to this charge that s2(4) of the Obscene Publications Act 1959, might bar proceedings against him if no conspiracy were alleged. It may be thought superfluous, where that Act can be invoked, to bring a charge also of conspiracy to corrupt public morals, but I can well understand the desirability of doing so where a doubt exists whether obscenity within the meaning of the Act can be proved ...

The appeal on both counts should, in my opinion, be dismissed.'

Lord Reid (dissenting):

'... there are two competing views. One is that conspiring to corrupt public morals is only one facet of a still more general offence, conspiracy to effect public mischief; and that, like the categories of negligence, the categories of public mischief are never closed. The other is that, whatever may have been done two or three centuries ago, we ought not now to extend the doctrine further than it has already been carried by the common law courts. Of course I do not mean that it should only be applied in circumstances precisely similar to those in some decided case. Decisions are always authority for other cases which are reasonably analogous and are not properly distinguishable. But we ought not to extend the doctrine to new fields. I agree with R.S.Wright, when he says (*Law of Criminal Conspiracies and Agreements*, p86):

"there appear to be great theoretical objections to any general rule that agreement may make punishable that which ought not to be punished in the absence of agreement."

And I think, or at least I hope, that it is now established that the courts cannot create new offences by individuals. So far at least I have the authority of Lord Goddard CJ, in delivering the opinion of the court in *Newland* [[1954] 1 QB 158 at 167; [1953] 2 All ER 1067 at 1072] ...

Every argument against creating new offences by an individual appears to me to be equally valid against creating new offences by a combination of individuals. But there is this historical difference. The judges appear to have continued to extend the law of conspiracy after they had ceased to extend offences by individuals. Again I quote from R.S.Wright (*Law of Criminal Conspiracies and Agreements*, p88):

"In an imperfect system of criminal law the doctrine of criminal agreements for acts not criminal may be of great practical value for the punishment of persons for acts which are not, but which ought to be made, punishable irrespectively of agreement."

Even if there is still a vestigial power of this kind, it ought not, in my view, to be used unless there appears to be general agreement that the offence to which it is applied ought to be criminal if committed by an individual. Notoriously there are wide differences of opinion today how far the law ought to punish immoral acts which are not done in the face of the public. Some think that the law already goes too far, some that it does not go far enough. Parliament is the proper place, and I am firmly of opinion the only proper place, to settle that. When there is sufficient support from public opinion, Parliament does not hesitate to intervene. Where Parliament fears to tread it is not for the courts to rush in ...

In my judgment, the House is in no way bound and ought not to sanction the extension of "public mischief" to any new field, and certainly not if such extension would be in any way controversial. Public mischief is the criminal counterpart of public policy, and the criminal law ought to be even more hesitant than the civil law in founding on it some new aspect ... as I understood counsel for the Crown, he did not argue that these advertisements were obscene libels, and that must mean that merely reading them does not tend to deprave or corrupt – if it did, they would be obscene libels by virtue of the definition in the Act, conspiracy to publish them would obviously be a crime, and the point now in controversy would never have arisen. So, any depraving and corrupting must be the result of resorting to the prostitutes. Prostitution is not an offence; it is not said that the woman or any man resorting to her is guilty of any offence. The argument is that, if two or more persons (who may include the prostitute herself) combine to issue such an invitation to members of the public, they are guilty of an offence. It could not matter whether the invitation was made by words or in some other way. So both Pearce and Brooks in *Pearce v Brooks* [(1866) LR 1 Exch 213] would today be guilty of an indictable offence by reason of having acted in concert to enable Brooks to attract men for the purpose of prostitution. That seems to me to be novel doctrine. It hardly seems to accord with views expressed in the *Mogul* series of cases [[1892] AC 25] to which I referred earlier, and I cannot believe that it is right.

But the advertisements also contain much more objectionable matter. The particulars refer to inducing readers to take part in "other disgusting and immoral acts" and with this I think there must be coupled the reference in the intent charge to "inordinate" desires. The evidence shows that the invitations were to resort to certain of the prostitutes for the purpose of certain forms of perversion. That I would think to be an offence for a different reason. I shall not examine the authorities, because I think that they establish that it is an indictable offence to say or do or exhibit anything in public which outrages public decency, whether or not it also tends to corrupt and deprave those who see or hear it. It my view, it is open to a jury to hold that a public invitation to indulge in sexual perversion does so outrage public decency as to be a punishable offence. If the jury in this case had been properly directed, they might well have found the appellant guilty for this reason. And the offence would be the same whether the invitation was made by an individual or by several people acting in concert. But it appears to me to be impossible to say the same with regard to ordinary prostitution. The common law has never treated the appearance of a prostitute in public as an indictable offence, however obvious her purpose might be, and an Act of Parliament has been found necessary to stop the nuisance of prostitutes parading in the public street ... '

Commentary

See further *Knuller* v *DPP* [1972] 2 All ER 898; and generally chapter 10.

Woolmington v DPP [1935] AC 462 House of Lords (Lord Sankey LC, Lord Hewart CJ, Lord Atkin, Lord Tomlin and Lord Wright)

Burden of proof in criminal trials

Facts

The defendant had been convicted of murdering his wife by firing a sawn off shotgun at her. He claimed that it had gone off accidentally. The trial judge had directed the jury as follows:

'Once it is shown to a jury that somebody has died through the act of another, that is presumed to be murder, unless the person who has been guilty of the act which causes the death can satisfy a jury that what happened was something less, something which might be alleviated, something which might be reduced to a charge of manslaughter, or was something which was accidental, or was something which could be justified.

[At the end of his summing up the trial judge added:]

The Crown has got to satisfy you that this woman, Violet Woolmington, died at the prisoner's hands. They must satisfy you of that beyond any reasonable doubt. If they satisfy you of that, then he has to show that there are circumstances to be found in the evidence which has been given from the witness-box in this case which alleviate the crime so that it is only manslaughter, or which excuse the homicide altogether by showing that it was a pure accident.'

The defendant appealed unsuccessfully to the Court of Appeal. He then appealed to the House of Lords.

Held

The appeal would be allowed. The burden of proving guilt in a criminal trial always rests with the Crown.

Lord Sankey LC:

'It is true, as stated by the Court of Criminal Appeal, that there is apparent authority for the law as laid down by the learned judge. But your Lordships' House has had the advantage of a prolonged and exhaustive inquiry dealing with the matter in debate from the earliest times, an advantage which was not shared by either of the courts below. Indeed your Lordships were referred to legal propositions dating as far back as the reign of King Canute (944-1035). I do not think it is necessary for the purpose of this opinion to go as far back as that. Rather would I invite your Lordships to begin by considering the proposition of law which is contained in *Foster's Crown Law*, written in 1762, and which appears to be the foundation for the law as laid down by the learned judge in this case. It must be remembered that Sir Michael Foster, although a distinguished judge, is for this purpose to be regarded as a textbook writer, for he did not lay down the doctrine in any case before him, but in an article which is described as "The Introduction to the Discourse of Homicide". In the folio edition, published at Oxford at the Clarendon Press in 1762, at p255, he states:

"In every charge of murder, the fact of killing being first proved, all the circumstance of accident, necessity, or infirmity, are to be satisfactorily proved by the prisoner, unless they arise out of the evidence produced against him; for the law presumeth the fact to have been founded in malice until the contrary appeareth. And very right it is, that the law should so presume. The defendant in this instance standeth upon just the same foot that every other defendant doth: the matters tending to justify, excuse, or alleviate must appear in evidence before he can avail himself of them."

Now the first part of this passage appears in nearly every textbook or abridgment which has been since written ...

The question arises: Is that statement correct law? Is it correct to say, and does Sir Michael Foster mean to lay down, that there may arise in the course of a criminal trial a situation at which it is incumbent upon the accused to prove his innocence? To begin with, if that is what Sir Michael Foster meant, there is no previous authority for his proposition, and I am confirmed in this opinion by the fact that in all the textbooks no earlier authority is cited for it ...

If at any period of a trial it was permissible for the judge to rule that the prosecution had established its case and that the onus was shifted on the prisoner to prove that he was not guilty, and that, unless he discharged that onus, the prosecution was entitled to succeed, it would be enabling the judge in such a case to say that the jury must in law find the prisoner guilty and so make the judge decide the case and not the jury, which is not the common law. It would be an entirely different case from those exceptional instances of special verdicts where a judge asks the jury to find certain facts and directs them that on such facts the prosecution is entitled to succeed. Indeed, a consideration of such special verdicts shows that it is not till the end of the evidence that a verdict can properly be found and that at the end of the evidence it is not for the prisoner to establish his innocence, but for the prosecution to establish his guilt. Just as there is evidence on behalf of the prosecution so there may be evidence on behalf of the prisoner which may cause a doubt as to his guilt. In either case, he is entitled to the benefit of the doubt. But while the prosecution must prove the guilt of the prisoner, there is no such burden laid on the prisoner to prove his innocence, and it is sufficient for him to raise a doubt as to his guilt; he is not bound to satisfy the jury of his innocence.

This is the real result of the perplexing case of *Abramovitch* (1912) 7 Cr App 145 which lays down the same proposition, although, perhaps, in somewhat involved language. Juries are always told that, if conviction there is to be, the prosecution must prove the case beyond reasonable doubt. This statement cannot mean that in order to be acquitted the prisoner must "satisfy" the jury. This is the law as laid down in the Court of Criminal Appeal in *Davies* [1913] 1 KB 573 the head-note of which correctly states that where intent is an ingredient of a crime there is no onus on the defendant to prove that the act alleged was accidental. Throughout the web of the English criminal law one golden thread is always to be seen – that it is the duty of the prosecution to prove the prisoner's guilt subject to what I have already said as to the defence of insanity and subject also to any statutory exception. If, at the end of and on the whole of the case, there is a reasonable doubt, created by the evidence given by either the prosecution or the prisoner, as to whether the prisoner killed the deceased with a malicious intention, the prosecution has not made out the case and the prisoner is entitled to an acquittal. No matter what the charge or where the trial, the principle that the prosecution must prove the guilt of the prisoner is part of the common law of England and no attempt to whittle it down can be entertained. When dealing with a murder case the Crown must prove (a) death as the result of a voluntary act of the accused and (b) malice of the accused. It may prove malice either expressly or by implication. For malice may be implied where death occurs as the result of a voluntary act of the accused which is (i) intentional and (ii) unprovoked. When evidence of death and malice has been given (this is a question for the jury) the accused is entitled to show by evidence or by examination of the circumstances adduced by the Crown that the act on his part which caused death was either unintentional or provoked. If the jury are either satisfied with his explanation or, upon a review of all the evidence, are left in reasonable doubt whether, even if his explanation be not accepted, the act was unintentional or provoked, the prisoner is entitled to be acquitted. It is not the law of England to say, as was said in the summing up in the present case, "if the Crown satisfy you that this woman died at the prisoner's hands, then he has to show that there are circumstances to be found in the evidence which has been given from the witness-box in this case which alleviate the crime so that it is only manslaughter or which excuse the homicide altogether by showing it was a pure accident."'

Commentary

Note that if the law ever places a legal burden of proof on a defendant in a criminal matter, such as establishing insanity or diminished responsibility, the defendant only has to satisfy the civil standard of proof, ie the balance of probabilities.

Chief Constable of Avon and Somerset v **Shimmen** (1987) 84 Cr App R 7 Court of Appeal Criminal Division (Watkins LJ and Taylor J)

Recklessness - gap between *Caldwell* and *Cunningham*

Facts (as stated by Taylor J)

'The charge against the defendant was that on 15 February 1985 in the city of Bristol, without lawful excuse, he destroyed property belonging to Maskreys Ltd., namely a plate glass window of the value of £495, intending to destroy such property or being reckless as to whether such property would be destroyed, contrary to section 1(1) of the Criminal Damage Act 1971. The justices found the following facts ... [T]he defendant had, on the relevant evening, been in the company of four friends. They had been in a public house and later they went to a club. During the evening, the defendant consumed a quantity of alcohol. He and his four friends left the club together and made their way along the road to a position outside Maskrey's shop. There the defendant and one of his friends, David Woodhouse, were laughing, joking, and larking around. Woodhouse pushed the defendant who then started flailing his arms and legs, contriving not to make any contact with Mr. Woodhouse. Mr. Woodhouse issued a warning to the defendant that he might one day hurt someone. The defendant assured Woodhouse that he had everything under control and, to prove it, he made as if to strike the window with his foot. His foot, however, did make contact with the window and broke it. The defendant was the holder of a green belt and yellow belt in the Korean art of self-defence. He was a skilled and experienced practitioner of that art. It was conceded that he had no intent to break the window. But the prosecutor's contention was that his act amounted to recklessness and that he ought to be convicted on that ground. The defendant contended that by reason of the skill which he had, he had satisfied himself that the window would not break and that he was, in those circumstances, not reckless.'

The justices found that the defendant had perceived there could have been a risk of damage, but after considering such risk he concluded that no damage would result. They dismissed the charge.

The prosecutor appealed.

The question posed for the court by the justices was:

Were we correct in law to decide that the defendant should not be regarded as reckless as to whether or not property would be destroyed or damaged if he does an act which in fact creates an obvious risk that property will be destroyed or damaged and having considered the circumstances subjectively concludes that no damage will result from that act?

Taylor J:

'The court was, as one would expect, referred to the leading authorities on the nature of recklessness. They are two decisions of the House of Lords. The first is *R* v *Caldwell* (1981) 73 Cr App R 13; [1982] AC 341. The second is *R* v *Lawrence* (1981) 73 Cr App R 1; [1982] AC 510. The defendant relied particularly on a passage in the speech of Lord Diplock in *R* v *Lawrence* p11 and p527 respectively. The passage reads as follows:

"If satisfied that an obvious and serious risk was created by the manner of the defendant's driving, the jury are entitled to infer that he was in one or other of the states of mind required to constitute the offence and will probably do so; but regard must be given to any explanation he gives as to his state of mind which may displace the inference."

Relying upon that passage, it was suggested that the explanation which had been given by the defendant in this case, that he had taken what he considered to be the necessary steps to avoid any risk of damage, entitled him to be acquitted. The two states of mind which were referred to by Lord Diplock were those which he himself described in the earlier case of *Caldwell* at p20 and p354F respectively. He put the matter in the following way:

"In my opinion, a person charged with an offence under section 1(1) of the Criminal Damage Act 1971 is "reckless as to whether any such property would be destroyed or damaged if (l) he does an act which in fact creates an obvious risk that property will be destroyed or damaged and (2) when he does the act he either has not given any thought to the possibility of the being any such risk or has recognised that there was some risk involved and has nonetheless gone on to do it.""

The justices were also referred to Smith and Hogan's textbook on Criminal Law (5th ed) at p55, where the following passage appears:

"Once the obvious risk is proved, it matters not whether the defendant realised there was a risk and decided to take it or never considered whether there was a risk or not. Either way, he is guilty. He can escape only if he considered the matter and decided that there was no risk."

It was that last sentence upon which particular reliance was placed by the defendant ... The two decisions in *R* v *Caldwell* (supra) and *R* v *Lawrence* (supra) have been followed by a considerable volume of academic writing. It was conceded on behalf of the prosecutor here that a number of the writers have expressed the view that between the two possible states of mind constituting recklessness as defined in *R* v *Caldwell*, there exists or could exist a lacuna, that is a state of mind which fell into neither of the two alternative categories posed by Lord Diplock. The way in which the matter is put is perhaps most helpfully, in the circumstances of this case, illustrated by an article "Reckless Damage and Reckless Driving: Living with Caldwell and Lawrence" in the Criminal Law Review of 1981 at p743 by Professor Griew. At p748, he cited two hypothetical cases under the heading "The conscientious but inefficient actor." The Professor said:

"The following cases are outside the terms of the model direction in *Caldwell*. (a) M does give thought to whether there is a risk of damage to another's property attending his proposed act. He mistakenly concludes that there is no risk; or he perceives only a risk such as would in the circumstances be treated as negligible by the ordinary prudent individual. He missed the obvious and substantial risk. (b) N's case is a more likely one. He is indeed aware of the kind of risk that will attend his act if he does not take adequate precautions. He takes precautions that are intended and expected to eliminate the risk (or to reduce it to negligible proportions). But the precautions are plainly, though not plainly to him, inadequate for this purpose. These appear not to be cases of recklessness. Evidence of conscientiousness displaces what would otherwise be an available inference of recklessness, (to use the language of Lord Diplock in *Lawrence*, ... The position of the person doing his best is further considered in the special context of reckless driving)."

He then went on to refer to *R* v *Lawrence* (supra). Those two examples which were given by Professor Griew seem to me not to be "on all fours." In the first example, it may well be arguable that the lacuna exists because it is not a case where M failed to give any consideration to the possibility of a risk. It is a case where he did give consideration to the possibility of the risk and concluded, albeit mistakenly, that there was no risk. In terms, therefore, of Lord Diplock's definition, he has not recognised that there was some risk involved. He therefore is outside the second possible state of mind referred to in *R* v *Caldwell* (supra). A different situation, however, seems to me to apply in the case of N posed by Professor Griew. He was aware of the kind of risk which would attend his act if he did not take adequate precautions. He seeks to rely upon the fact that he did take precautions which were intended, and by him expected, to eliminate the risk. He was wrong, but the fact that he was conscientious to the degree of trying to minimise the risk does not mean that he falls outside the second limb of Lord Diplock's test. Lord Diplock's second limb is simply whether or not he has recognised that there was some risk. It seems clear to me that in the case of N, as posed by Professor Griew, N certainly did recognise that there was some risk and went on to do the act. In my judgment, therefore, the second example given by Professor Griew does not constitute any lacuna in the definition given by Lord Diplock. Applying those examples to the present case, it seems to me that on the findings of the justices and more particularly, as I shall indicate in a moment, on the evidence which they exhibited to their case, this defendant did recognise the risk. It was not a case of his considering the possibility and coming to the conclusion that there was no risk. What he said to the justices in cross-examination should be quoted. He said: "I thought I might break the window but then I thought I will not break the window ... I thought to myself, the window is not going to break." A little later on he said: "I weighed up the odds and thought I had eliminated as much risk as possible by missing by two inches instead of two millimetres." The specific finding of the justices ... was as follows:

"... the defendant perceived there could be a risk of damage but after considering such risk concluded that no damage would result." It seems to me that what this case amounts to is as follows; that this defendant did perceive, which is the same as Lord Diplock's word "recognise", that there could be a risk, but by aiming off rather more than he normally would in this sort of display, he thought he had minimised it and therefore no damage would result. In my judgment, that is far from saying that he falls outside the state of mind described by Lord Diplock in these terms, "... has recognised that there was some risk involved and has nonetheless gone on to do it."

In my judgment, therefore, whatever may be the situation in a hypothetical case such as that of M as detailed by Professor Griew, which may need to be considered on another occasion, so far as this case is concerned, the justices were wrong in coming to the conclusion that this was not recklessness by reason of what the defendant had put forward. I should say that I have considerable sympathy with the justices when there is so much academic discussion of this particular test and where, as I have indicated, some of that discussion does not seem to result in accurate conclusions. However that may be, I, for my part, would allow this appeal and send the case back to the justices and require them to convict.'

Commentary

See *R* v *Reid,* below.

R v Church [1966] 1 QB 59

See chapter 8 and *R* v *Le Brun,* below.

Commissioner of Police of the Metropolis v Caldwell [1982] AC 341 House of Lords (Lords Wilberforce, Diplock, Edmund-Davies, Keith of Kinkel, and Roskill)

Objective recklessness

Facts

The defendant, who had been sacked from his employment at an hotel, became drunk and returned at night to the hotel, setting it on fire. There were ten people resident in the hotel at the time, but the fire was discovered and extinguished before any serious harm could be caused. The defendant pleaded guilty to a charge under s1(1) of the Criminal Damage Act 1971, but pleaded not guilty to the charge under s1(2) of the 1971 Act, which alleged criminal damage with intent to endanger life or recklessness as to whether life would be endangered. His contention was that due to his drunken state it had never crossed his mind that people's lives might be endangered by his actions, he had simply set fire to the hotel because of his grudge against his former employer. The trial judge directed the jury that self-induced intoxication was no defence to a charge under s1(2), and the defendant was convicted. On appeal, the Court of Appeal quashed his conviction for the offence under s1(2), but upheld the sentence of three years' imprisonment in respect of the s1(1) charge. The prosecutor appealed to the House of Lords, the following question being certified for the opinion of their Lordships -

'Whether evidence of self-induced intoxication can be relevant to the following questions - (a) Whether the defendant intended to endanger the life of another; and (b) Whether the defendant was reckless as to whether the life of another would be endangered, within the meaning of section 1(2)(b) of the Criminal Damage Act 1971.'

Held

(Lords Wilberforce and Edmund-Davies dissenting):

Self-induced intoxication can provide a defence under s1(2) of the 1971 Act where the basis of the charge against the defendant is that he intended to endanger life. Self-induced intoxication would not, however, avail a defendant who was alleged to have been reckless as to whether life would be endangered.

Lords Diplock, Roskill and Keith of Kinkel further expressed the view that a defendant was to be regarded as reckless where he created an obvious risk of a particular type of harm occurring, and either went on to take that risk, or failed to give any thought to its existence.

Lord Diplock [explaining the type of recklessness involved in the offence of criminal damage]:

'My Lords, the Criminal Damage Act 1971 replaced almost in their entirety the many detailed provisions of the Malicious Damage Act 1861. Its purpose, as stated in its long title, was to *revise* the law of England and Wales, as to offences of damage to property. As the brevity of the Act suggests, it must have been hoped that it would also simplify the law.

In the Act of 1861, the word consistently used to describe the mens rea that was a necessary element in the multifarious offences that the Act created was "maliciously" – a technical expression, not readily intelligible to juries, which became the subject of considerable judicial exegesis. This culminated in a judgment of the Court of Criminal Appeal in *R v Cunningham* [1957] 2 QB 396, 399 which approved, as an accurate statement of the law, what had been said by Professor Kenny in the first edition of his *Outlines of Criminal Law* published in 1902:

"In any statutory definition of a crime, malice must be taken … as requiring either (1) an actual intention to do the particular kind of harm that in fact was done; or (2) recklessness as to whether such harm should occur or not (ie, the accused has foreseen that the particular kind of harm might be done and yet has gone on to take the risk of it)."

My Lords, in this passage Professor Kenny was engaged in defining for the benefit of students the meaning of "malice" as a term of art in criminal law. To do so he used ordinary English words in their popular meaning. Among the words he used was "recklessness," the noun derived from the adjective "reckless," of which the popular or dictionary meaning is: careless, regardless, or heedless, of the possible harmful consequences of one's acts. It presupposes that if thought were given to the matter by the doer before the act was done, it would have been apparent to him that there was a real risk of its having the relevant harmful consequences; but, granted this, recklessness covers a whole range of states of mind from failing to give any thought at all to whether or not there is any risk of those harmful consequences, to recognising the existence of the risk and nevertheless deciding to ignore it. Conscious of this imprecision in the popular meaning of recklessness as descriptive of a state of mind. Professor Kenny, in the passage quoted, was, as it seems to me, at pains to indicate by the words in brackets the particular species within the genus reckless states of mind that constituted "malice" in criminal law. This parenthetical restriction on the natural meaning of recklessness was necessary to an explanation of the meaning of the adverb "maliciously" when used as a term of art in the description of an offence under the Malicious Damage Act 1861 (which was the matter in point in *R v Cunningham* [1957] 2 QB 396); but it was not directed to and consequently has no bearing on the meaning of the adjective "reckless" in section 1 of the Criminal Damage Act 1971. To use it for that purpose can, in my view, only be misleading.

My Lords, the restricted meaning that the Court of Appeal in *R v Cunningham* had placed upon the adverb "maliciously" in the Malicious Damage Act 1861 in cases where the prosecution did not rely upon an actual intention of the accused to cause the damage that was in fact done, called for a meticulous analysis by the jury of the thoughts that passed through the mind of the accused at or before the time he did the act that caused the damage, in order to see on which side of a narrow dividing line they fell. If it had crossed his mind that there was a risk that someone's property might be damaged but, because his mind was affected by rage or excitement or confused by drink, he did not appreciate the seriousness of the risk or trusted that good luck would prevent its happening, this state of mind would amount to malice in the restricted meaning placed upon that term by the Court of Appeal; whereas if, for any of these reasons, he did not even trouble to give his mind to the question whether there was any risk of damaging the property, this state of mind would not suffice to make him guilty of an offence under the Malicious Damage Act 1861.

Neither state of mind seems to me to be less blameworthy than the other; but if the difference between the two constituted the distinction between what does and what does not in legal theory amount to a guilty state of mind for the purpose of a statutory offence of damage to property, it would not be a practicable distinction for use in a trial by jury. The only person who knows what the accused's mental processes were is the accused himself – and probably not even he can recall them accurately when the rage or excitement under which he acted has passed, or he has sobered up if he were under the influence of drink at the relevant time. If the accused gives evidence that because of his rage, excitement or drunkenness the risk of particular harmful consequences of his acts simply did not occur to him, a jury would find it hard to be satisfied beyond reasonable doubt that his true mental process was not that, but was the slightly different mental process required if one applies the restricted meaning of "being reckless as to whether" something would happen, adopted by the Court of Appeal in *R* v *Cunningham*.

My Lords, I can see no reason why Parliament when it decided to revise the law as to offences of damage to property should go out of its way to perpetuate the fine and impracticable distinctions such as these between one mental state and another. One would think that the sooner they were got rid of, the better.

When cases under section 1(1) of the new Act, in which the prosecution's case was based upon the accused having been "reckless as to whether ... property would be destroyed or damaged," first came before the Court of Appeal, the question as to the meaning of the expression "reckless" in the context of that subsection appears to have been treated as soluble simply by posing and answering what had by then, unfortunately, become an obsessive question among English lawyers: Is the test of recklessness "subjective" or "objective"? The first two reported cases, in both of which judgments were given off the cuff, are first *R* v *Briggs* (*Note*) [1977] 1 WLR 605 which is reported in a footnote to the second, *R* v *Daryl Parker* [1977] 1 WLR 600. Both classified the test of recklessness as "subjective." This led the court in *R* v *Briggs* (*Note*) [1977] 1 WLR 605, 608 to say: "A man is reckless in the sense required when he carries out a deliberate act knowing that there is some risk of damage resulting from that act but nevertheless continues in the performance of that act." This leaves over the question whether the risk of damage may not be so slight that even the most prudent of men would feel justified in taking it, but it excludes that kind of recklessness that consists of acting without giving any thought at all to whether or not there is any risk of harmful consequences of one's act, even though the risk is great and would be obvious if any thought were given to the matter by the doer of the act. *R* v *Daryl Parker* [1977] 1 WLR 600, 604, however, opened the door a chink by adding as an alternative to the actual knowledge of the accused that there is some risk of damage resulting from his act and his going on to take it, a mental state described as "closing his mind to the obvious fact" that there is such a risk.

R v *Stephenson* [1979] QB 695, the first case in which there was full argument, though only on one side, and a reserved judgment, slammed the door again upon any less restricted interpretation of "reckless" as to whether particular consequences will occur than that originally approved in *R* v *Briggs* (*Note*) [1977] 1 WLR 605. The appellant, a tramp, intending to pass the night in a hollow in the side of a haystack, had lit a fire to keep himself warm; as a result of this the stack itself caught fire. At his trial, he was not himself called as a witness but a psychiatrist gave evidence on his behalf that he was schizophrenic and might not have had the same ability to foresee or appreciate risk as a mentally normal person. The judge had given to the jury the direction on the meaning of reckless that had been approved in *R* v *Daryl Parker* [1977] 1 WLR 600. The argument for the appellant on the appeal was that this let in an "objective" test whereas the test should be entirely "subjective."   It was buttressed by copious citation from previous judgments in civil and criminal cases where the expressions "reckless" or "recklessness" had been used by judges in various contexts. Counsel for the Crown expressed his agreement with the submissions for the appellant. The judgment of the court contains an analysis of a number of the cited cases, mainly in the field of civil law. These cases do not disclose a uniform judicial use of the terms; and as respects judicial statements made before the current vogue for classifying all tests of legal liability as either "objective" or "subjective" they are not easily assignable to one of those categories rather than the other. The court, however, reached its final conclusion by a different route. It made the assumption that although Parliament in replacing the Act of 1861 by the Act of 1971 had discarded the word "maliciously" as descriptive of the mens rea of the offences of which the actus reus is damaging property, in favour of the more explicit phrase "intending to destroy or damage any such property or being reckless as to whether any such property would be destroyed," it nevertheless intended the words to be interpreted in precisely the same sense as that in which the single adverb "maliciously" had been construed by Professor Kenny in the passage that received the subsequent approval of the Court of Appeal in *R* v *Cunningham* [1957] 2 QB 396.

My Lords, I see no warrant for making any such assumption in an Act whose declared purpose is to revise the then existing law as to offences of damage to property, not to perpetuate it. "Reckless" as used in the new statuatory definition of the mens rea of these offences is an ordinary English word. It had not by 1971 become a term of legal art with some more limited esoteric meaning than that which it bore in ordinary speech – a meaning which surely includes not only deciding to ignore a risk of harmful consequences resulting from one's acts that one has recognised as existing, but also failing to give any thought to whether or not there is any such risk in circumstances where, if any thought were given to the matter, it would be obvious that there was.

If one is attaching labels, the latter state of mind is neither more nor less "subjective" than the first. But the label solves nothing. It is a statement of the obvious; mens rea is, by definition, a state of mind of the accused himself at the time he did the physical act that constitutes the actus reus of the offence; it cannot be the mental state of some non-existent, hypothetical person.

Nevertheless, to decide whether someone has been "reckless" as to whether harmful consequences of a particular kind will result from his act, as distinguished from his actually intending such harmful consequences to follow, does call for some consideration of how the mind of the ordinary prudent individual would have reacted to a similar situation. If there were nothing in the circumstances that ought to have drawn the attention of an ordinary prudent individual to the possibility of that kind of harmful consequence, the accused would not be described as "reckless" in the natural meaning of that word for failing to address his mind to the possibility; nor if the risk of the harmful consequences was so slight that the ordinary prudent individual upon due consideration of the risk would not be deterred from treating it as negligible, could the accused be described as "reckless" in its ordinary sense if, having considered the risk, he decided to ignore it. (In this connection the gravity of the possible harmful consequences would be an important factor. To endanger the life must be one of the most grave). So to this extent, even if one ascribes to "reckless" only the restricted meaning, adopted by the Court of Appeal in *R* v *Stephenson* [1979] QB 695 and *R* v *Briggs* (*Note*) [1977] 1 WLR 605, of foreseeing that a particular kind of harm might happen and yet going on to take the risk of it, it involves a test that would be described in part as "objective" in current legal jargon. Questions of criminal liability are seldom solved by simply asking whether the test is subjective or objective.

In my opinion, a person charged with an offence under section 1(1) of the Criminal Damage Act 1971 is "reckless as to whether any such property would be destroyed or damaged" if (1) he does an act which in fact creates an obvious risk that property will be destroyed or damaged and (2) when he does the act he either has not given any thought to the possibility of there being any such risk or has recognised that there was some risk involved and has nonetheless gone on to do it. That would be a proper direction to the jury; cases in the Court of Appeal which held otherwise should be regarded as overruled.

Where the charge is under section 1(2) the question of the state of mind of the accused must be approached in stages, corresponding to paragraphs (a) and (b). The jury must be satisfied that what the accused did amounted to an offence under section 1(1), either because he actually intended to destroy or damage the property or because he was reckless (in the sense that I have described) as to whether it might be destroyed or damaged. Only if they are so satisfied must the jury go on to consider whether the accused also either actually intended that the destruction or damage of the property should endanger someone's life or was reckless (in a similar sense) as to whether a human life might be endangered.'

Lord Edmund-Davies [dissenting]:

(1)   Recklessness

'The words "intention" and "recklessness" have increasingly displaced in statutory crimes the word "maliciously," which has frequently given rise to difficulty in interpretation. In *R* v *Cunningham* [1957] 2 QB 396, Byrne J in the Court of Criminal Appeal cited with approval at pp399-400 the following passage which has appeared in *Kenny's Outlines of Criminal Law* from its first edition in 1902 onwards:

"In any statutory definition of a crime, malice must be taken not in the old, vague sense of wickedness in general, but as requiring either (1) an actual intention to do the particular kind of harm that in fact was done; or (2) recklessness as to whether such harm should occur or not (ie, the accused has foreseen that the particular kind of harm might be done and yet has gone on to take the risk of it). It is neither limited to nor does it indeed require any ill towards the person injured."

Byrne J's comment at p400 was laconic and unqualified: "We think that this is an accurate statement of the law … In our opinion the word 'maliciously' in a statutory crime postulates foresight of consequence." My Lords, my noble and learned friend, Lord Diplock, somewhat dismissively describes Professor Kenny as having been "engaged in defining for the benefit of students the meaning of 'malice' as a term of art in criminal law," adding, ante, p351D-G.

"To do so he used ordinary English words in their *popular* meaning. Among the words he used was 'recklessness,' the noun derived from the adjective 'reckless,' of which the popular dictionary meaning is: careless, regardless, or heedless, of the possible harmful consequences of one's acts. It presupposes that *if* thought were given to the matter by the doer before the act was done, *it would have been apparent to him* that there was a real risk of its having the relevant consequences … [The] parenthetical restriction on the natural meaning of recklessness was necessary to an explanation of the meaning of the adverb 'maliciously' when used as a term of art in the description of an offence under the Malicious Damage Act 1861 (which was the matter in point *R* v *Cunningham* [1957] 2 QB 396); but it was not directed to and consequently has no bearing on the meaning of the adjective 'reckless' in section 1 of the Criminal Damage Act 1971." (Emphasis added).

I have to say that I am in respectful, but profound, disagreement. The law in action compiles its own dictionary. In time, what was originally the common coinage of speech acquires a different value in the pocket of the lawyer than when in the layman's purse. Professor Kenny used lawyers' words in a lawyer's sense to express his distillation of an important part of the established law relating to mens rea, and it did so in a manner accurate not only in respect of the law as it stood in 1902 but also as it has been applied in countless cases ever since, both in the United Kingdom and in other countries where the common law prevails: see for example, in Western Australia, *Lederer* v *Hutchins* [1961] WAR 99, and, in the United States of America, *Jethro Brown's General Principles of Ciminal Law,* 2nd ed (1960), p115. And it is well known that the Criminal Damage Act 1971 was in the main the work of the Law

Commission, who, in their Working Paper No 31, Codification of the Criminal Law, General Principles, The Mental Element in Crime (issued in June 1970), defined recklessness by saying, at p52:

"A person is reckless if, (a) knowing that there is a risk that an event may result from his conduct or that a circumstance may exist, he takes that risk, and (b) it is unreasonable for him to take it, having regard to the degree and nature of the risk which he knows to be present."

It was surely with this contemporaneous definition and the much respected decision of *R v Cunningham* [1957] 2 QB 396 in mind that the draftsman proceeded to his task of drafting the Criminal Damage Act 1971.

It has therefore to be said that, unlike negligence, which has to be judged objectively, recklessness involves foresight of consequences, combined with an objective judgment of the reasonableness of the risk taken. And recklessness in vacuo is an incomprehensible notion. It *must* relate to foresight of risk of the particular kind relevant to the charge preferred, which, for the purpose of section 1(2), is the risk of endangering life and nothing other than that.

So if a defendant says of a particular risk, "It never crossed my mind," a jury could not on those words alone properly convict him of recklessness simply because they considered that the risk *ought* to have crossed his mind, though his words might well lead to a finding of negligence. But a defendant's admission that he "closed his mind" to a particular risk could prove fatal, for, "A person cannot, in any intelligible meaning of the words, close his mind to a risk unless he first realises that there is a risk; and if he realises that there is a risk, that is the end of the matter": see *Glanville Williams, Textbook of Criminal Law* (1978), p79.

In the absence of exculpatory factors, the defendant's state of mind is therefore all-important where recklessness is an element in the offence charged ...

[His Lordship then referred to s8 of the Criminal Justice Act 1967, and continued]

My Lords, it is unnecessary to examine at length the proposition that ascertainment of the state of mind known as "recklessness" is a *subjective* exercise, for the task was expansively performed by Geoffrey Lane LJ in *R v Stephenson* [1977] QB 695. And, indeed, that was the view expressed by the learned recorder herself in the instant case when, citing *R v Briggs* (*Note*) [1977] 1 WLR 605, 608, she directed the jury at one stage in these terms:

"It may be the most useful function that I can perform if I read to you the most recent (I hope) definition of 'recklessness' ... by a superior court ... 'A man is reckless ... when he carries out a deliberate act, knowing that there is some risk of damage resulting from that act, but nevertheless continues in the performance of that act' ... That came, in fact, in a case of straight arson and damage to property, but in this case you would probably feel that you had to add after the words to fit this section of the Act, 'some risk of damage to life,' ... because that is what we are concerned with. I see both counsel nod assent to that. So, we can stay on common ground ... "

Commentary

For extracts from both speeches dealing with the availability of the defence of self-induced intoxication, see chapter 12.

R v Cunningham [1957] 2 QB 396 Court of Criminal Appeal (Byrne, Slade, and Barry JJ)

Subjective recklessness

Facts

The defendant had entered the basement of a building and ripped a gas meter from the wall in order to remove the money that it contained. In his efforts the defendant ruptured the gas supply pipes with the result that gas escaped and seeped through the porous basement wall into an adjoining property, which was occupied by a Mrs Wade and her husband. The defendant was convicted of maliciously administering a noxious substance, contrary to s23 of the Offences Against the Person Act 1861, following a direction from the trial judge that the jury were to convict if they were satisfied that the defendant's action had been 'wicked'. The defendant appealed to the Court of Appeal.

Held

The appeal would be allowed.

Byrne J:

' ... the following principle which was propounded by the late Professor C.S. Kenny in the first edition of his Outlines of Criminal Law published in 1902 and repeated in 1952: "In any statutory definition of a crime, malice must be taken not in the old vague sense of wickedness in general but as requiring either (1) An actual intention to do the particular kind of harm that in fact was done; or (2) recklessness as to whether such harm should occur or not (ie, the accused has foreseen that the particular kind of harm might be done and yet has gone on to take the risk of it). It is neither limited to nor does it indeed require any ill will towards the person injured." The same principle is repeated by Mr Turner in his 10th edition of Russell on Crime at p1592.

We think that this is an accurate statement of the law. It derives some support from the judgments of Lord Coleridge CJ and Blackburn J in *Pembliton's* case (1874) LR 2 CCR 119. In our opinion the word "maliciously" in a statutory crime postulates foresight of the consequence...

With the utmost respect to the learned judge, we think it is incorrect to say that the word "malicious" in a statutory offence merely means wicked. We think the judge was, in effect, telling the jury that if they were satisfied that the appellant had acted wickedly – and he had clearly acted wickedly in stealing the gas meter and its contents – they ought to find that he had acted maliciously in causing the gas to be taken by Mrs Wade so as thereby to endanger her life.

In our view it should have been left to the jury to decide whether, even if the appellant did not intend the injury to Mrs Wade, he foresaw that the removal of the gas meter might cause injury to someone but nevertheless removed it. We are unable to say that a reasonable jury, properly directed as to the meaning of the word "maliciously" in the context of section 23, would without doubt have convicted.

In these circumstances this court has no alternative but to allow the appeal and quash the conviction.'

R v Deller (1952) 36 Cr App R 184 Court of Appeal (Criminal Division) (Hilbery, McNair and Streatfield JJ)

Actus reus must be proved

Facts

The defendant sold a car which he wrongly believed to be the subject of a hire purchase agreement in respect of which payments were still outstanding. In fact the car was free from all encumbrances. He was charged with what is now the offence of obtaining property by deception. He appealed against his conviction on the basis that as the car was free from all encumbrances, he had been telling the truth when he had told the purchaser this, even though he had thought he was lying.

Held

The conviction would be quashed. As the car was free from encumbrances the defendant had not deceived the purchaser, hence the actus reus of deception was absent. The fact that the defendant had thought he was committing an offence, ie he had mens rea, was insufficient on its own for liability.

Hilbery J:

'It has been argued that, because a document was in existence purporting to represent as between the parties an agreement of hire and purchase, the false pretence was established when the appellant said that it was his car and not encumbered, because he must have believed that and known that there was in existence this agreement. It is to be observed that the false pretence which was alleged was not that he falsely pretended that there was not in existence any hire purchase agreement in respect of the car; and that in fact he made no such representation was clearly established in the cross-examination of Mr Clarke when before the magistrates, as appears from the depositions.

In those circumstances, if the direction given to the jury was a clear direction that, in the event of their finding that this was in truth a loan transaction on the security of the car and not a genuine sale with a hiring back, the right verdict would be Not Guilty, the verdict of Guilty by the jury would be tantamount to a finding by them that the transaction was not one merely of loan but was in fact a genuine transaction of sale and hiring back to the man who had, prior to that sale, been the owner of the car. Unfortunately whereas the issue that the jury had to try was correctly put in the summing-up, there was matter later on in the summing-up which, in our opinion, prevents us from taking that view of the verdict and vitiates the summing-up, having regard to the exact terms of the false pretences alleged in the indictment ...

[His Lordship referred to the trial judge's direction to the jury, and continued]

... Of course, once the jury came to the conclusion that in fact the transaction was one of loan and not of sale of the car, but loan on the attempted security of the car, the documents as a matter of law were void documents, and that the learned Deputy Chairman must have known. But in one and the same breath he was asking the jury to say, if they thought it was a loan, to look upon the documents as being the security for the loan and saying to the jury that, whatever they thought about the strict ownership of the car, when they came to the representation that it was unencumbered, here were these documents which were a charge upon the car. In truth, if they came to the conclusion that the transaction was a loan, as a matter of law the documents were void; they were no more than pieces of paper. The charge to the jury ought to have been: if they came to the conclusion that the documents represented only a transaction of loan on the security of the car, then the documents were all void and of no effect, and the falsity of every one of the alleged representations was not proved because, it may be quite accidentally and, strange as it may sound, dishonestly, the appellant had told the truth. In the circumstances, it seems to us to be quite clear that the jury may well have thought that, although these were documents to cloak a loan transaction and to give a loan transaction the colour of a sale and hiring back, yet none the less they were a charge on the car, and to say it was unencumbered became a false pretence. Having regard, therefore, to the indictment and the direction in the summing-up, we are of opinion that this conviction must be quashed.'

Commentary

See further *R* v *Shivpuri*, chapter 11.

Elliot v C [1983] 1 WLR 939 Divisional Court (Robert Goff LJ and Glidewell J)

Objective recklessness

Facts

The defendant was an educationally sub-normal 14 year old schoolgirl. She had entered a neighbour's garden shed, poured white spirit on the floor and ignited it. The defendant fled as the shed burst into flames. The magistrates dismissed a charge under s1(1) of the Criminal Damage Act 1971, on the basis that the defendant would not have been aware of the risk of damage to property even if she had given thought to the matter. The prosecution appealed by way of case stated to the Divisional Court.

The questions stated for the Divisional Court by the justices were:

'1. Whether properly directing ourselves and upon a true construction of section 1(1) of the Criminal Damage Act 1971 we were correct in our interpretation of the meaning of reckless, namely, that a defendant should only be held to have acted recklessly by virtue of his failure to give any thought to an obvious risk that property would be destroyed or damaged, where such risk would have been obvious to him if he had given any thought to the matter?

2. Whether properly directing ourselves on the evidence we could properly have come to our decision that the [defendant] had acted neither intentionally nor recklessly in destroying by fire the shed and its contents?'

Held

Both questions would be answered in the negative, and the appeal would be allowed. The court was constrained by the decisions of the House of Lords in both *Caldwell* and *Lawrence*. There was no scope for introducing a subjective element into the defintion of recklessness propounded by Lord Diplock in those cases.

Glidewell J had referred to the issues raised in this appeal as follows:

'The questions posed by the case were "1. Whether properly directing themselves and upon a true construction of section 1(1) of the Criminal Damage Act 1971 the justices were correct in their interpretation of the meaning of reckless, namely, that a defendant should only be held to have acted recklessly by virtue of his failure to give any thought to an obvious risk that property would be destroyed or damaged, where such risk would have been obvious to him if he had given any thought to the matter?

2. Whether properly directing themselves on the evidence the justices could properly have come to their decision that the defendant had acted neither intentionally nor recklessly in destroying by fire the shed and its contents?"

He then stated that he would answer 'no' to both questions.

Robert Goff LJ:

'I agree with the conclusion reached by Glidewell J but I do so simply because I believe myself constrained to do so by authority. I feel moreover that I would be lacking in candour if I were to conceal my unhappiness about the conclusion which I feel compelled to reach. In my opinion, although of course the courts of this country are bound by the doctrine of precedent, sensibly interpreted, nevertheless it would be irresponsible for judges to act as automata, rigidly applying authorities without regard to consequences.

I turn next to the crime with which she was charged, *viz* that she without lawful excuse destroyed by fire the shed and contents, intending to destroy such property or being reckless as to whether such property would be destroyed, contrary to section 1(1) of the Criminal Damage Act 1971. The case advanced against her was not that she intended to destroy the property, but that she was reckless as to whether the property would be destroyed.

Plainly, she did destroy the shed and its contents by fire; plainly too, she did so without lawful excuse. But was she reckless as to whether the shed and its contents would be destroyed? Here I turn, as Glidewell J has done, to authority; and in the decision of the House of Lords in *R* v *Caldwell* (1981) 73 Cr App R 13; [1982] AC 341, I find an authority, binding upon this Court, which was concerned with the interpretation of the word "recklessness" as used in the very subsection under which the respondent was charged. In that case, although the House was divided, the ratio decidendi of the decision of the House is to be found in the speech of Lord Diplock, with which both Lord Keith and Lord Roskill agreed. Lord Diplock analysed the word "reckless" as used in this subsection, and his analysis culminated in the conclusion, expressed at pp20 and 354 of the respective reports, which reads as follows: "In my opinion, a person charged with an offence under section 1(1) of the Criminal Damage Act 1971 is 'reckless as to whether any such property would be destroyed or damaged' if (1) he does an act which in fact creates an obvious risk that property will be destroyed or damaged and (2) when he does the act he either has not given any thought to the possibility of there being any such risk or has recognised that there was some risk involved and has nonetheless gone on to do it. That would be a proper direction to the jury; cases in the Court of Appeal which held otherwise should be regarded as overruled."

Now, if that test is applied literally in the present case, the conclusion appears inevitable that, on the facts found by the justices, the defendant was reckless whether the shed and contents would be destroyed; because first she did an act which created an obvious risk that the property would be destroyed, and second she had not given any thought to the possibility of there being any such risk.

Yet, if I next pause (as I have done, in accordance with what I conceive to be my proper function) and ask myself the question – would I, having regard only to the ordinary meaning of the word, consider this girl to have been, on the facts found, *reckless* whether the shed and contents would be destroyed, my answer would I confess, be in the negative. This is not a case where there was a deliberate disregard of a known risk of damage or injury of a certain type or degree; nor is it a case where there was a mindless indifference to a risk of such damage or injury, as is expressed in common speech in the context of motoring offences (though not, I think, of arson as "blazing on regardless": nor is it even a case where failure to give thought to the possibility of the risk was due to some blameworthy cause, such as intoxication. This is a case where it appears that the only basis upon which the accused might be held to have been reckless would be if the appropriate test to be applied was purely objective – a test which might in some circumstances be thought justifiable in relation to certain conduct (eg reckless driving), particularly where the word "reckless" is used simply to characterise the relevant conduct. But such a test does not appear at first sight to be appropriate to a crime such as that under consideration in the present case, especially as recklessness in that crime has to be related to a particular consequence. I therefore next ask myself the question whether I can, consistently with the doctrine of precedent, sensibly interpreted, legitimately construe or qualify the principle stated by Lord Diplock in *R* v *Caldwell* (supra) so as to accommodate what I conceive to be the appropriate result on the facts of the present case, bearing in mind that those facts are very different from the facts under consideration by the House of Lords in *R* v *Caldwell* (supra), where the defendant had set fire to a hotel when in a state of intoxication.

Here again, it would be unrealistic if I were to disguise the fact that I am well aware that the statement of principle by Lord Diplock in *R* v *Caldwell* (*supra*) has been the subject of comment, much of it critical, in articles written by jurists; and that I have studied certain of these articles with interest. I find it striking that the justices, in reaching their conclusion in the present case, have done so (no doubt in response to an argument advanced on the defendant's behalf) by imposing upon Lord Diplock's statement of principle a qualification similar to one considered by Professor Glanville Williams in his article "Recklessness Redefined" in [1981] CLJ 252, 270-271. This is that a defendant should only be regarded as having acted recklessly by virtue of his failure to give any thought to an obvious risk that property would be destroyed or damaged, where such risk would have been obvious *to him* if he had given any thought to the matter. However, having studied Lord Diplock's speech, I do not think it would be consistent with his reasoning to impose any such qualification. I say that not only because this qualification does not appear in terms in his conclusion which I have already quoted, but also because, when considering earlier in his speech Professor Kenny's definition of recklessness (which he rejected as being too narrow), Lord Diplock expressly adverted to the fact that the definition presupposed that "if thought were given to the matter by the doer before the act was done, it would have been apparent *to him* that there was a real risk of its having the relevant harmful consequences."

It seems to me that, having expressly considered that element in Professor Kenny's test, and having (as I think) plainly decided to omit it from his own formulation of the concept of recklessness, it would not now be legitimate for an inferior court, in a case under this particular subsection, to impose a qualification which had so been rejected by Lord Diplock himself. It follows that for that reason alone I do not feel able to uphold the reasoning of the magistrates in the present case. But I wish to add that, for my part, I doubt whether this qualification can be justified in any event. Where there is no thought of the consequences, any further inquiry necessary for the purposes of establishing guilt should prima facie be directed to the question why such thought was not given, rather than to the purely hypothetical question of what the particular person would have appreciated had he directed his mind to the matter.

We were referred to the decision of the Court of Appeal in *Pigg* (1982) 74 Cr App R 352; [1982] 1 WLR 762, a case decided after *R* v *Caldwell* (supra) and the related decision of the House of Lords in *R* v *Lawrence* (1981) 73 Cr App R 1; [1982] AC 510, but concerned not with section 1(1) of the Criminal Damage Act 1971 but with section 1 of the Sexual Offences (Amendment) Act 1976. The defendant had been convicted of rape; and one ground of appeal was concerned with a direction given by the judge to the jury on the question whether he knew that the complainant did not consent to intercourse or was reckless as to whether she consented or not. The judgment of the Court of Appeal was delivered by the Lord Chief Justice. He referred to the decision of the House of Lords in *R* v *Caldwell* (supra) and in *R* v *Lawrence* (supra) and quoted extensively from the speeches of Lord Diplock in both cases. He then said at pp362 and 772 of the respective reports: "Of course it is plain that the opinion cannot, so to speak, be lifted bodily and applied to rape. There has to be a modification in certain of the matters which are there dealt with. But, in the end it seems to us that in the light of that decision, so far as rape is concerned, a man is reckless if either he was indifferent and gave no thought to the possibility that the woman might not be consenting in circumstances where there was a risk she was not, or, that he was aware of the possibility that she might not be consenting but nevertheless persisted regardless of whether she consented or not."

Now it cannot be disguised that the addition of the words "was indifferent and" constituted a gloss upon the defintion of recklessness proposed by Lord Diplock in *R* v *Caldwell* (supra). Furthermore, if it were legitimate so to interpret Lord Diplock's speech in relation to a case arising not under section 1(1) of the Criminal Damage Act 1971, the effect would be that the second question posed by the magistrates in the case now before this court would be answered in the affirmative, and the appeal would be dismissed; because there is no finding of fact that this defendant in the case before us was indifferent to the risk of destruction by fire of the shed and its contents. This is an approach which I would gladly adopt, if I felt that I was free to do so. However, I do not consider that it is open to this court, in a case arising under the very subsection to which Lord Diplock's speech was expressly directed, to impose this qualification, which I feel would in this context constitute too substantial a departure from the test proposed by him.

Both these possible avenues are, I believe, closed to the Court in the present case. I have considered anxiously whether there is any other interpretation which the Court could legitimately place upon Lord Diplock's statement of principle in *R* v *Caldwell* (supra) which would lead to the conclusion which I would prefer to reach, that the defendant was not reckless whether the shed and contents would be destroyed by fire. I have discovered none which would not involve what I would regard as constituting, in relation to the relevant offence, an illegitimate departure from that statement of principle.

In these circumstances, I agree that the questions must be answered as proposed by Glidewell J and that the appeal must be allowed.'

R v Hancock and Shankland [1986] 2 WLR 257 House of Lords (Lords Scarman, Keith of Kinkel, Roskill, Brightman and Griffiths)

Intention based on foresight: mens rea for murder.

Facts

The defendants were miners in South Wales who were on strike. They had taken up position on a bridge over a motorway, knowing that miners who were not willing to come out on strike would be using the road and passing under the bridge. When a taxi carrying a working miner approached, the defendants dropped two large blocks of concrete over the bridge. One of the blocks fell through the windscreen of the car and killed its driver. The defendants were convicted of murdering the taxi driver, and appealed on the ground that it had been their intention to block the road, not to cause death. The Court of Appeal quashed the conviction, in a decision which was somewhat critical of the previous House of Lords decision in R v Moloney [1985] AC 905 (considered below in the extract from the speech of Lord Scarman). The Crown appealed to the House of Lords.

Held

The appeal would be dismissed. The Moloney guidelines on the relationship between foresight and intention were unsatisfactory in that they were likely to mislead a jury.

Lord Scarman:

' ... My Lords, in this case the Director of Public Prosecutions appeals against the decision of the Court of Appeal (Criminal Division) [1985] 3 WLR 1014 quashing the respondents' convictions of murder and substituting verdicts of manslaughter. The appeal is brought to secure a ruling from the House upon the refusal of the Court of Appeal to accept as sound the guidelines formulated by this House in a recent case in which the House gave guidance as to the direction appropriate to be given by the judge to the jury in a murder trial in which the judge considers it necessary to direct the jury upon the issue of intent by reference to foresight of consequences. The case is *R v Moloney* [1985] AC 905, and the guidance was in these terms, at p929:

"In the rare cases in which it is necessary to direct a jury by reference to foresight of consequences, I do not believe it is necessary for the judge to do more than invite the jury to consider two questions. First, was death or really serious injury in a murder case (or whatever relevant consequences must be proved to have been intended in any other case) a natural consequence of the defendant's voluntary act? Secondly, did the defendant foresee that consequence as being a natural consequence of his act? The jury should then be told that if they answer yes to both questions it is a proper inference for them to draw that he intended that consequence."

In the present case, the trial judge having based his direction to the jury on the guidance which I have quoted, the two accused (respondents to this appeal) were convicted of murder. The Court of Appeal quashed the convictions on the ground that the judge's guidance may well have misled the jury. The court refused leave to appeal but certified the following point of general public importance:

"Do the questions to be considered by a jury set out in the speech of Lord Bridge of Harwich in *R v Moloney* [1985] AC 905, 929 as a model direction require amplification?"

[His Lordship considered the facts of the case, and continued]

In the Court of Appeal Lord Lane CJ delivered the judgment of the court. The court found itself driven to the conclusion that the use by the judge of *Moloney* guidelines may have misled the jury. The guidelines offered the jury no assistance as to the relevance or weight of the probability factor in determining whether they should, or could properly, infer from foresight of a consequence (in this case, of course, death or serious bodily harm) the intent to bring about that consequence. This was, in the court's view, a particularly serious omission because the case law, as Lord Bridge of Harwich in *Moloney* [1985] A.C. 905, 925H had recognised, indicated "that the probability of the consequence taken to have been foreseen must be little short of overwhelming before it will suffice to establish the necessary intent." In the court's view the judge's failure to explain the factor of probability was because he faithfully followed *Moloney* : "[he] was unwittingly led into misdirecting he jury by reason of the way in which the guidelines in Moloney were expressed." [1985] 3 WLR 1014, 1018H.

The question for the House is, therefore, whether the *Moloney* guidelines are sound. In *Moloney's* case the ratio decidendi was that the judge never properly put to the jury the defence, namely that the accused was unaware that the gun was pointing at his stepfather. The House, however, held it necessary in view of the history of confusion in this branch of the law to attempt to clarify the law relating to the establishment of the mental element necessary to constitute the crime of murder and to lay down guidelines for assisting juries to determine in what circumstances it is proper to infer intent from foresight. The House certainly clarified the law. First, the House cleared away the confusions which had obscured the law during the last 25 years laying down authoritatively that the mental element in murder is a specific intent, the intent to kill or to inflict serious bodily harm. Nothing less suffices: and the jury must be sure that the intent existed when the act was done which resulted in death before they can return a verdict of murder.

Secondly, the House made it absolutely clear that foresight of consequences is no more than evidence of the existence of the intent; it must be considered, and its weight assessed, together with all the evidence in the case. Foresight does not necessarily imply the existence of intention, though it may be a fact from which when considered with all the other evidence a jury might think it right to infer the necessary intent. Lord Hailsham of St Marylebone LC put the point succinctly and powerfully in his speech in *R* v *Moloney* [1985] AC 905, 913:

"I conclude with the pious hope that your Lordships will not again have to decide that <u>foresight and foreseeability are not the same thing as intention although either may give rise to an irresistible inference of such</u>, and that matters which are essentially to be treated as matters of inference for a jury as to a subjective state of mind will not once again be erected into a legal presumption. They should remain what they always should have been, part of the law of evidence and inference to be left to the jury after a proper direction as to their weight, and not part of the substantive law."

Thirdly, the House emphasised that the probability of the result of an act is an important matter for the jury to consider and can be critical in their determining whether the result was intended.

These three propositions were made abundantly clear by Lord Bridge of Harwich. His was the leading speech and received the assent of their other Lordships, Lord Hailsham of St. Marylebone LC, Lord Fraser of Tullybelton, Lord Edmund-Davies, and Lord Keith of Kinkel. His speech has laid to rest ghosts which had haunted the case law ever since the unhappy decision of your Lordships' House in *R* v *Smith* [1961] AC 290 and which were given fresh vigour by the interpretation put by some upon the speeches of members of this House in *R* v *Hyam* [1975] AC 55.

It is only when Lord Bridge of Harwich turned to the task of formulating guidelines that difficulty arises. It is said by the Court of Appeal that the guidelines by omitting any express reference to probability are ambiguous and may well lead a jury to a wrong conclusion. The omission was deliberate. Lord Bridge omitted the adjective "probable" from the time-honoured formula "foresight of the natural and probable consequences of his acts" because he thought that "if a consequence is natural, it is really otiose to speak of it as also being probable" [1985] AC 905, 902B. But is it?

Lord Bridge of Harwich did not deny the importance of probability. He put it thus, at p925:

"But looking on their facts at the decided cases where a crime of specific intent was under consideration, including *R* v *Hyam* [1975] AC 55 itself, they suggest to me that <u>the probability of the consequence taken to have been foreseen must be little short of overwhelming before it will suffice to establish the necessary intent.</u>"

In his dicussion of the relationship between foresight and intention, Lord Bridge of Harwich reviewed the case law since the passing of the Homicide Act 1957 and concluded, at p928:

"foresight of consequences, as an element bearing on the issue of intention in murder, or indeed any other crime of specific intent, belongs, not to the substantive law, but to the law of evidence."

He referred to the rule of evidence that a man is presumed to intend the natural and probable consequences of his acts, and went on to observe that the House of Lords in *Smith's* case [1961] AC 290 had treated the presumption as irrebuttable, but that Parliament intervened by section 8 of the Criminal Justice Act 1967 to return the law to the path from which it had been diverted, leaving the presumption as no more than an inference open to the jury to draw if in all the circumstances it appears to them proper to draw it.

Yet he omitted any reference in his guidelines to probability. He did so because he included probability in the meaning which he attributed to "natural." My Lords, I very much doubt whether a jury without further explanation would think that "probable" added nothing to "natural." I agree with the Court of Appeal that the probability of a consequence is a factor of sufficient importance to be drawn specifically to the attention of the jury and to be explained. In a murder case where it is necessary to direct a jury on the issue of intent by reference to foresight of consequences, the probability of death or serious injury resulting from the act done may be critically important. Its importance will depend on the degree of probability: if the likelihood that death or serious injury will result is high, the probability of that result may, as Lord Bridge of Harwich noted and the Lord Chief Justice emphasised, be seen as overwhelming evidence of the existence of the intent to kill or injure. Failure to explain the relevance of probability may, therefore, mislead a jury into thinking that it is of little or no importance and into concentrating exclusively on the causal link between the act and its consequence. In framing his guidelines Lord Bridge of Harwich [1985] AC 905, 929G, emphasised that he did not believe it necessary to do more than to invite the jury to consider his two questions. Neither question makes any reference (beyond the use of the word "natural") to probability. I am not suprised that when in this case the judge faithfully followed this guidance the jury found themselves perplexed and unsure. In my judgment, therefore, the *Moloney* guidelines as they stand are unsafe and misleading. They require a reference to probability. They also require an explanation that the greater the probability of a consequence the more likely it is that the consequence was foreseen and that if the consequence was foreseen the greater the probability is that the consequence was also intended. But juries also require to be reminded that the decision is theirs to be reached upon a consideration of all the evidence.

Accordingly, I accept the view of the Court of Appeal that the *Moloney* guidelines are defective. I am, however, not persuaded that guidelines of general application, albeit within a limited class of case, are wise or desirable. Lord Lane CJ formulated in this case [1985] 3 WLR 1014, 1019, guidelines for the assistance of juries but for the reason which follows, I would not advise their use by trial judges when summing up to a jury.

I fear that their elaborate structure may well create difficulty. Juries are not chosen for their understanding of a logical and phased process leading by question and answer to a conclusion but are expected to exercise practical common sense. They want help on the practical problems encountered in evaluating the evidence of a particular case and reaching a conclusion. It is better, I suggest, notwithstanding my respect for the comprehensive formulation of the Court of Appeal's guidelines, that the trial judge should follow the traditional course of summing up. He must explain the nature of the offence charged, give directions as to the law applicable to the particular facts of the case, explain the incidence and burden of proof, put both sides' cases making especially sure that the defence is put; he should offer help in understanding and weighing up all the evidence and should make certain that the jury understand that whereas the law is for him the facts are for them to decide. Guidelines, if given, are not to be treated as rules of law but as a guide indicating the sort of approach the jury may properly adopt to the evidence when coming to their decision on the facts.

In a case where foresight of a consequence is part of the evidence supporting a prosecution submission that the accused intended the consequence, the judge, if he thinks some general observations would help the jury, could well, having in mind section 8 of the Criminal Justice Act 1967, emphasise that the probability, however high, of a consequence is only a factor, though it may in some cases be a very significant factor, to be considered with all the other evidence in determining whether the accused intended to bring it about. The distinction between the offence and the evidence relied on to prove it is vital. Lord Bridge's speech in *Moloney* made the distinction crystal clear: it would be a disservice to the law to allow his guidelines to mislead a jury into overlooking it.

For these reasons I would hold that the *Moloney* guidelines are defective and should not be used as they stand without further explanation. The laying down of guidelines for use in directing juries in cases of complexity is a function which can be usefully exercised by the Court of Appeal. But it should be done sparingly, and limited to cases of real difficulty. If it is done, the guidelines should avoid generalisation so far as is possible and encourage the jury to exercise their common sense in reaching what is their decision on the facts. Guidelines are not rules of law: judges should not think they must use them. A judge's duty is to direct the jury in law and to help them upon the particular facts of the case.

Accordingly, I would answer the certified question in the affirmative and would dismiss the appeal.'

Commentary

See *R* v *Nedrick* below.

R v Instan [1893] 1 QB 450 Court for Crown Cases Reserved

Common law duty to act

Facts

The defendant lived with her aunt who was an elderly woman. The aunt developed gangrene in her leg and was unable to look after herself. The defendant was the only person who knew of her condition, but failed to provide her aunt with food (despite having been given money by her for this purpose) or medical assistance. After 12 days of suffering the aunt died. The defendant was convicted of manslaughter, and appealed.

Held

The conviction would be upheld.

Lord Coleridge CJ:

'We are all of opinion that this conviction must be affirmed. It would not be correct to say that every moral obligation involves a legal duty; but every legal duty is founded on a moral obligation. A legal common law duty is nothing else than the enforcing by law of that which is a moral obligation without legal enforcement. There can be no question in this case that it was the clear duty of the prisoner to impart to the deceased so much as was necessary to sustain life of the food which she from time to time took in, and which was paid for by the deceased's own money for the purpose of the maintenance of herself and the prisoner; it was only through the instrumentality of the prisoner that the deceased could get the food. There was, therefore, a common law duty imposed upon the prisoner which she did not discharge.

Nor can there be any question that the failure of the prisoner to discharge her legal duty at least accelerated the death of the deceased, if it did not actually cause it. There is no case directly in point; but it would be a slur upon and a discredit to the administration of justice in this country if there were any doubt as to the legal principle, or as to the present case being within it. The prisoner was under a moral obligation to the deceased from which arose a legal duty towards her; that legal duty the prisoner has wilfully and deliberately left unperformed, with the consequence that there has been an acceleration of the death of the deceased owing to the non-performance of that legal duty. It is unnecessary to say more than that upon the evidence this conviction was most properly arrived at.'

R v Larsonneur (1933) 97 JP 206 Court of Criminal Appeal (Lord Hewart CJ, Avory and Humphreys JJ)

Absence of a freely willed actus reus: absolute liability

Facts

The defendant, a French national, entered the United Kingdom lawfully, but was given only a restricted power to remain in the country. Her passport stated that she had to leave the United Kingdom on 22 March 1933. On that day the defendant left England, not to return to France, but to travel to the Irish Free State. The Irish authorities made a deportation order against her, and she was forcibly removed from Ireland and returned to the United Kingdom mainland at Holyhead. On arrival at Holyhead the defendant was charged, under the Aliens Order 1920, with 'being found' in the United Kingdom whilst not having permission to enter the country. The defendant was convicted, and appealed on the basis that her return to the United Kingdom had not been of her own free will, in that she had been forcibly taken to Holyhead by the immigration authorities.

Held

The appeal would be dismissed.

Lord Hewart CJ:

'The fact is, as the evidence shows, that the appellant is an alien. She has a French passport, which bears this statement under the date March 14, 1933, "Leave to land granted at Folkestone this day on condition that the holder does not enter any employment, paid or unpaid, while in the United Kingdom," but on March 22 that condition was varied and one finds these words: "The condition attached to the grant of leave to land is hereby varied so as to require departure from the United Kingdom not later than March 22, 1933." Then follows the signature of an Under Secretary of State. In fact, the appellant went to the Irish Free State and afterwards, in circumstances which are perfectly immaterial, so far as this appeal is concerned, came back to Holyhead. She was at Holyhead on April 21, 1933, a date after the day limited by the condition on her passport.

In these circumstances, it seems to be quite clear that Art. 1(4) of the Aliens Order, 1920 (as amended by the Orders of March 12, 1923, and August 11, 1931), applies. The Article is in the following terms: "An immigration officer, in accordance with the general or special directions of the Secretary of State, may, by general order or notice or otherwise, attach such conditions as he may think fit to the grant of leave to land, and the Secretary of State may at any time vary such conditions in such manner as he thinks fit, and the alien shall comply with the conditions so attached or varied. An alien who fails to comply with any conditions so attached or varied, and an alien who is found in the United Kingdom at any time after the expiration of the period limited by any such conditions, shall for the purposes of this Order be deemed to be an alien to whom leave to land has been refused."

The appellant was, therefore, on April 12, 1933, in the position in which she would have been if she had been prohibited from landing by the Secretary of State and, that being so, there is no reason to interfere with the finding of the jury. She was found here and was, therefore, deemed to be in the class of persons whose landing had been prohibited by the Secretary of State, by reason of the fact that she had violated the condition on her passport. The appeal, therefore, is dismissed and the recommendation for deportation remains.'

Commentary

See further *R* v *Winzar*, below, and generally chapter 24.

R v Latimer (1886) 17 QBD 359 Court for Crown Cases Reserved (Lord Coleridge CJ, Lord Esher MR, Bowen LJ, Field and Manisty JJ)

Transferred malice

Facts

The defendant struck a blow with his belt at Horace Chapple which glanced off him, severely injuring an innocent bystander, Ellen Rolston. The defendant was convicted of maliciously wounding the woman, and appealed on the ground that it had never been his intention to hurt her.

Held

The conviction would be affirmed. The defendant had committed the actus reus of the offence with the necessary mens rea, ie he acted maliciously. There was no requirement in the relevant Act that his mens rea should relate to a named victim.

Lord Coleridge CJ:

'We are of opinion that this conviction must be sustained. It is common knowledge that a man who has an unlawful and malicious intent against another, and, in attempting to carry it out, injures a third person, is guilty of what the law deems malice against the person injured, because the offender is doing an unlawful act, and has that which the judges call general malice, and that is enough ... So, but for *R* v *Pembliton* [below], there would not have been the slightest difficulty. Does that case make any difference? I think not, and, on consideration, that it was quite rightly decided. But it is clearly distinguishable, because the indictment in *R* v *Pembliton* was on the Act making unlawful and malicious injury to property a statutory offence punishable in a certain way, and the jury expressley negatived, the facts expressly negatived, any intention to do injury to property, and the court held that under the Act making it an offence to injure any property there must be an intent to injure property. *R* v *Pembliton,* therefore, does not govern the present case, and on no other ground is there anything to be said for the prisoner.'

Commentary

See *R* v *Pembliton* below.

R v Lawrence [1982] AC 510 House of Lords (Lords Hailsham, Diplock, Fraser, Roskill and Bridge)

Objective recklessness

Facts

The defendant motor cyclist had collided with and killed a pedestrian. He was convicted of causing death by reckless driving contrary to s1 of the Road Traffic Act 1972. The conviction was quashed by the Court of Appeal, and the prosecution appealed to the House of Lords.

Held

The appeal would be dismissed

Lord Diplock:

'My Lords, this House has very recently had occasion in *R* v *Caldwell* [1982] AC 341 to give close consideration to the concept of recklessness as constituting mens rea in criminal law. The conclusion reached by the majority was that the adjective "reckless" when used in criminal statute, ie the Criminal Damage Act 1971, had not acquired a special meaning as a term of legal art, but bore its popular or dictionary meaning of careless, regardless, or heedless of the possible harmful consequences of one's act. The same must be true of the adverbial derivative "recklessly."

The context in which the word "reckless" appears in section 1 of the Criminal Damage Act 1971 differs in two respects from the context in which the word "recklessly" appears in sections 1 and 2 of the Road Traffic Act 1972 as now amended. In the Criminal Damage Act 1971 the actus reus, the physical act of destroying or damaging property belonging to another, is in itself a tort. It is not something that one does regularly as part of the ordinary routine of daily life, such as driving a car or a motor cycle. So there is something out of the ordinary to call the doer's attention to what he is doing and its possible consequences, which is absent in road traffic offences. The other difference in context is that in section 1 of the Criminal Damage Act 1971 the mens rea of the offences is defined as being reckless as to whether particular harmful consequences would occur, whereas in sections 1 and 2 of the Road Traffic Act 1972, as now amended, the possible harmful consequences of which the driver must be shown to have been heedless are left to be implied from the use of the word "recklessly" itself. In ordinary usage "recklessly" as descriptive of a physical act such as driving a motor vehicle which can be performed in a variety of different ways, some of them entailing danger and some of them not, refers not only to the state of mind of the doer of the act when he decides to do it but also qualifies the manner in which the act itself is performed. One does not speak of a person acting "recklessly," even though he has given no thought at all to the consequences of his act, unless the act is one that presents a real risk of harmful consequences which anyone acting with reasonable prudence would recognise and give heed to. So the actus reus of the offences under sections 1 and 2 is not simply driving a motor vehicle on a road, but driving it in a manner which in fact creates a real risk of harmful consequences resulting from it. Since driving in such a manner as to do no worse than create a risk of causing inconvenience or annoyance to other road users constitutes the lesser offence under section 3, the manner of driving that constitutes the actus reus of an offence under sections 1 and 2 must be worse than that; it must be such as to create a real risk of causing physical injury to someone else who happens to be using the road or damage to property more substantial than the kind of minor damage that may be caused by an error of judgment in the course of parking one's car …

I turn now to the mens rea. My task is greatly simplified by what has already been said about the concept of recklessness in criminal law in *R v Caldwell* [1982] AC 341. Warning was there given against adopting the simplistic approach of treating all problems of criminal liability as soluble by classifying the test of liability as being either "subjective" or "objective." Recklessness on the part of the doer of an act does pre-suppose that there is something in the circumstances that would have drawn the attention of an ordinary prudent individual to the possibility that his act was capable of causing the kind of serious harmful consequences that the section which creates the offence was intended to prevent, and that the risk of those harmful consequences occuring was not so slight that an ordinary prudent individual would feel justified in treating them as negligible. It is only when this is so that the doer of an act is acting "recklessly" if before doing the act, he either fails to give any thought to the possibility of there being any such risk or, having recognised that there was such risk, he nevertheless goes on to do it.

In my view, an appropriate instruction to the jury on what is meant by driving recklessly would be that they must be satisfied of two things:

First, that the defendant was in fact driving the vehicle in such a manner as to create an obvious and serious risk of causing physical injury to some other person who might happen to be using the road or of doing substantial damage to property; and

Second, that in driving in that manner the defendant did so without having given any thought to the possibility of there being any such risk or, having recognised that there was some risk involved, had nonetheless gone on to take it.

It is for the jury to decide whether the risk created by the manner in which the vehicle was being driven was both obvious and serious and, in deciding this, they may apply the standard of the ordinary prudent motorist as represented by themselves.

If satisfied that an obvious and serious risk was created by the manner of the defendant's driving, the jury are entitled to infer that he was in one or other of the states of mind required to constitute the offence and will probably do so; but regard must be given to any explanation he gives as to his state of mind which may displace the inference.'

R v Le Brun [1991] 3 WLR 653 Court of Appeal (Criminal Division) (Lord Lane CJ, Auld and Judge JJ)

Coincidence of actus reus and mens rea

Facts

The appellant hit his wife during an argument. He did not intend to cause her serious harm. She was knocked unconscious by the blow. The appellant attempted to move her body, and in the course of so doing dropped her, causing her head to strike the pavement. His wife sustained fractures to the skull that proved fatal. The appellant was convicted of manslaughter following a direction from the trial judge to the effect that the jury could convict of either murder or manslaughter if they were sure that having committed the first assault the appellant had accidentally caused the fractures to the skull in attempting to move her body.

Held

The appeal would be dismissed.

Lord Lane CJ:

'The main thrust of his (counsel for the appellant's) argument is to be found in ground 3 of the notice of appeal which I will now read:

"The judge erred in law in directing the jury that they could convict the appellant of murder or manslaughter (depending on the intention with which he had previously assaulted the victim) if they were sure that, having committed the assault with no serious injury resulting, the appellant had accidentally dropped the victim causing her death whilst either: (a) attempting to move her to her home against her wishes, including any wishes she may have expressed prior to the previous assault, and/or (b) attempting to dispose of her body or otherwise cover up the previous assault."

Problems of causation and remoteness of damage are never easy of solution. We have had helpful arguments from both counsel on this point, the point in the present case being, to put it in summary before coming to deal with it in more detail, that the intention of the appellant to harm his wife one way or another may have been separated by a period of time from the act which in fact caused the death, namely, the fact of her falling to the ground and fracturing her skull. That second incident may have taken place without any guilty mind on the part of the appellant.

The authors of *Smith & Hogan, Criminal Law*, 6th ed (1988), p320, say:

"An intervening act by the original actor will not break the chain of causation so as to excuse him, where the intervening act is part of the same transaction, but it is otherwise if the act which causes the actus reus is part of a completely different transaction. For example, D, having wounded P, visits him in hospital and accidentally infects him with smallpox of which he dies."

The problem in the instant case can be expressed in a number of different ways, of which causation is one. Causation on the facts as the jury in this case must have found them - I say at the best from the point of view of the appellant - is in one sense clear. Death was caused by the victim's head hitting the ground as she was being dragged away by the appellant. The only remoteness was that between the initial unlawful blow and the later moment when the skull was fractured causing death.

The question can be perhaps framed in this way. There was here an initial unlawful blow to the chin delivered by the appellant. That, again on what must have been the jury's finding, was not delivered with the intention of doing really serious harm to the wife. The guilty intent accompanying that blow was sufficient to have rendered the appellant guilty of manslaughter, but not murder, had it caused death. But it did not cause death. What caused death was the later impact when the wife's head hit the pavement. At the moment of impact the appellant's intention was to remove her, probably unconscious, body to avoid detection. To that extent the impact may have been accidental. May the earlier guilty intent be joined with the later non-guilty blow which caused death to produce in the conglomerate a proper verdict of manslaughter?

It has usually been in the previous decisions in the context of murder that the problem has arisen. We have had our attention directed to a Privy Council case, *Meli* v *The Queen* [his Lordship referred to the passage from the speech of Lord Reid, extracted later in this chapter, and also cited *R* v *Moore* [1975] Crim LR 229 and continued] ... It will be observed that the present case is different from the facts of those two cases in that death here was not the result of a preconceived plan which went wrong, as was the case in those two decisions which we have cited. Here the death, again assuming the jury's finding to be such as it must have been, was the result of an initial unlawful blow, not intended to cause serious harm, in its turn causing the appellant to take steps possibly to evade the consequences of his unlawful act. During the taking of those steps he commits the actus reus but without the mens rea necessary for murder or manslaughter. Therefore the mens rea is contained in the initial unlawful assault, but the actus reus is the eventual dropping of the head on to the ground.

Normally the actus reus and mens rea coincide in point of time. What is the situation when they do not? Is it permissible, as the prosecution contend here, to combine them to produce a conviction for manslaughter?'

His Lordship referred to *R v Church* (referred to earlier in this chapter) and continued:

'It seems to us that where the unlawful application of force and the eventual act causing death are parts of the same sequence of events, the same transaction, the fact that there is an appreciable interval of time between the two does not serve to exonerate the defendant from liability. That is certainly so where the appellant's subsequent actions which caused death, after the initial unlawful blow, are designed to conceal his commission of the original unlawful assault.

It would be possible to express the problem as one of causation. The original unlawful blow to the chin was a causa sine qua non of the later actus reus. It was the opening event in a series which was to culminate in death: the first link in the chain of causation, to use another metaphor. It cannot be said that the actions of the appellant in dragging the victim away with the intention of evading liability broke the chain which linked the initial blow with the death.

In short, in circumstances such as the present, which is the only concern of this court, the act which causes death, and the necessary mental state to constitute manslaughter, need not coincide in point of time.

We now turn to the summing up given by the judge to the jury in order to see whether the judge, in the way he put the matter to the jury, fell within those principles which we have endeavoured to state.'

His Lordship then considered at some length the trial judge's direction to the jury, which included the following:

' "If you are sure that it has been proved that the defendant unlawfully attacked his wife and whatever he did to her caused her to fall and sustain in the fall fatal brain damage then he is guilty of murder or manslaughter depending on the intent with which he assaulted her. If you are sure that it has been proved that the defendant unlawfully attacked his wife and that it was whatever he did to her that rendered her unconscious or helpless even though that did not cause fatal brain damage he would still be guilty if the fatal brain damage (resulted) from his dropping her or dropping her head while trying to manoeuvre her up the steps and towards the house, if he was doing that because he was determined to make her come home even though she had refused to do so, or because having injured her he was in panic and wanted to conceal what he had done and to avoid detection and not because he was trying to assist her."

[The trial judge's summing up continued]

"In such a case he would be guilty of murder, if the initial attack was with the intention of causing really serious harm; or, if you are not sure that was his intent, of manslaughter. But if the fatal injury happened in the course of well-intentioned efforts to help her he would not be guilty of murder or manslaughter."

Finally, in answer to a question from the jury, the judge said:

"… if the fatal injury happened in the course of, and we come to the phrase again, well intentioned efforts to help her, he would be guilty neither of murder nor of manslaughter and I hope I have said enough to show you the distinction that I am drawing between as it were an extension or a furtherance or a continuation of the unlawful conduct and a different tack where whatever he has done to her before he is trying his best to help or comfort her even if in a misguided way, even in a way in which other people might think it was foolish to act." '

His Lordship then returned to the submissions made by counsel for the appellant:

'The argument advanced on behalf of the appellant is this. There has to be shown by the prosecution in order to succeed a continuing transaction, or, an unbroken chain of causation between the act which proved the mens rea and the final incident which resulted in death before it can be said that there is a sufficient connection between the mens rea and the actus reus. The mere fact that this man attempts to get his wife home when she is unconscious, it is argued, coupled with her earlier unwillingness to go home, is not enough to show a continuing transaction of an unbroken chain as has to be shown.

In every case, and this is no exception, the summing up has to be read against the background of fact which lies behind the whole of the case. Part of the background is, as we have already indicated when trying to set out the facts of the case, that the dispute between the two was certainly in part, and probably very largely, abut whether she was going to go home or not. If one looks where the judge is dealing with Mrs Luke's (a witness) evidence, this is what he said:

"She said: 'The man was swearing and wanted the woman to get in the house, he sounded very angry and she was saying: 'Get off you fucking bastard.' She said she had heard domestic arguments from time to time but this was different. She said the woman seemed scared and wanted the man to get away and the argument was very heated and very aggressive and she spoke of hearing a woman's footsteps hurrying alone."

Again Mr Hislop (another witness), as already cited:

"the man was shouting 'Get on home.' The woman was saying 'Get off me.' they were saying that sort of thing repeatedly and there was a lot of swearing from both of them ..."

The second matter which has to be borne in mind when viewing a summing up is that it must be read as a whole and not merely one passage taken out of its context. If one reads the whole of the passage to which attention has been primarily directed, it runs as follows:

"if he was doing that because he was determined to make her come home even though she had refused to do so, or because having injured her he was in panic and wanted to conceal what he had done and to avoid detection and not because he was trying to assist her."

The judge was drawing a sharp distinction between actions by the appellant which were designed to help his wife and actions which were not so designed: on the one hand that would be a way in which the prosecution could establish the connection if he was not trying to assist his wife; on the other hand if he was trying to assist his wife, the chain of causation would have been broken and the nexus between the two halves of the prosecution case would not exist.

That is emphasised if one turns to another passage altogether later on in the summing up. There the judge said:

"May it be true that having attacked her his attitude changed and all that followed was done with good intentions, he feeling that what he was doing was appropriate to get her to the comfort of her own home, or are you sure that what he did was not well intentioned but a product of his anger and impatience, his continued determination to get her home or his fear of discovery? If you are sure of that, he would be guilty of murder or manslaughter depending upon the intention with which the initial attack was made. If you conclude that you may be sure that he deliberately inflicted the chin wound and you were impressed with some of Mr Wilson-Smith's submissions on that part of the case, I suggest you will readily conclude that you cannot be sure that he had the intent necessary for murder when he carried out the initial attack if that is what he did. If that was your view then if you conclude that he was not well intentioned in what he did subsequently of trying to get her home for other purposes or was trying to conceal what he had done or escape detection, he would be guilty, not of murder but of manslaughter."

We say, in order to provide completeness to the argument, that the jury came back after having been in retirement for a short time and asked the judge to assist them again on this somewhat difficult point of the chain of causation and the nexus between the original assault and the eventual fracture of the skull. What he did there was to repeat what he had earlier said which we have already read.

Having said that, we conclude that the direction of the judge taken as a whole was satisfactory. It was satisfactory in so far, and only in so far as the directions related to manslaughter. In that respect, in our judgment, they comply with the view of the law which we have endeavoured to set out by reference to the authorities. In short the criticisms of the judge's treatment of submissions and the criticisms of the summing up are not justified.

In our judgment, accordingly, the appeal fails and must be dismissed.'

R v Miller [1983] 2 AC 161 House of Lords (Lords Diplock, Keith, Bridge, Brandon and Brightman)

Failure to prevent harm caused by an accidental act

Facts

The defendant, a vagrant, had been occupying an empty house. One evening he lay on a mattress and lit a cigarette. He fell asleep and the lighted cigarette set fire to the mattress. The defendant was awoken by the flames, but instead of putting the fire out, he simply got up and went into an adjoining room where he found another mattress, and went back to sleep. As a result, the house was substantially damaged by fire, and the defendant was convicted of criminal damage. He appealed on the point that he had not committed any positive act which had caused harm.

Held

The appeal would be dismissed. The defendant's initial setting fire to the mattress may not have been a culpable act in that he was asleep at the time, but once he awoke and realised what had happened, he came under a responsibility to limit the harmful effects of the fire. His failure to discharge this responsibility provided the basis for the imposition of liability.

Lord Diplock:

'The first question is a pure question of causation; it is of fact to be decided by the jury in a trial on indictment. It should be answered No if, in relation to the fire during the period starting immediately before its ignition and ending with its extinction, the role of the accused was at no time more than that of a passive bystander. In such a case the subsequent questions to which I shall be turning would not arise. The conduct of the parabolical priest and Levite on the road to Jericho may have been indeed deplorable, but English law has not so far developed to the stage of treating it as criminal; and if it ever were to do so there would be difficulties in defining what should be the limits of the offence.

If, on the other hand the question, which I now confine to: "Did a physical act of the accused start the fire which spread and damaged property belonging to another?", is answered "Yes", as it was by the jury in the instant case, then for the purpose of the further questions the answers to which are determinative of his guilt of the offence of arson, the conduct of the accused, throughout the period from immediately before the moment of ignition to the completion of the damage to the property by the fire, is relevant; so is his state of mind throughout that period.

Since arson is a result-crime the period may be considerable, and during it the conduct of the accused that is causative of the result may consist not only of his doing physical acts which cause the fire to start or spread but also of his failing to take measures that lie within his power to counteract the danger that he himself created. And if his conduct, active or passive, varies in the course of the period, so may his state of mind at the time of each piece of conduct. If, at the time of any particular piece of conduct by the accused that is causative of the result, the state of mind that actuates his conduct falls within the description of one or other of the states of mind that are made a necessary ingredient of the offence of arson by s 1 (1) of the Criminal Damage Act 1971 (ie intending to damage property belonging to another or being reckless whether such property would be damaged), I know of no principle of English criminal law that would prevent his being guilty of the offence created by that subsection. Likewise I see no rational ground for excluding from conduct capable of giving rise to criminal liability conduct which consists of failing to take measures that lie within one's power to counteract a danger that one has oneself created, if at the time of such conduct one's state of mind is such as constitutes a necessary ingredient of the offence. I venture to think that the habit of lawyers to talk of "actus reus", suggestive as it is of action rather than inaction, is responsible for any erroneous notion that failure to act cannot give rise to criminal liability in English law.

No one has been bold enough to suggest that if, in the instant case, the accused had been aware at the time that he dropped the cigarette that it would probably set fire to his mattress and yet had taken no steps to extinguish it he would have not been guilty of the offence of arson, since he would have damaged property of another being reckless whether any such property would be damaged.

I cannot see any good reason why, so far as liability under criminal law is concerned, it should matter at what point of time before the resultant damage is complete a person becomes aware that he has done a physical act which, whether or not he appreciated that it would at the time when he did it, does in fact create a risk that property of another will be damaged, provided that, at the moment of awareness, it lies within his power to take steps, either himself or by calling for the assistance of the fire brigade if this be necessary, to prevent or minimise the damage to the property at risk …

My Lords, in the instant case the prosecution did not rely on the state of mind of the accused as being reckless during that part of his conduct that consisted of his lighting and smoking a cigarette while lying on his mattress and falling asleep without extinguishing it. So the jury were not invited to make any finding as to this. What the prosecution did rely on as being reckless was his state of mind during that part of his conduct after he awoke to find that he had set his mattress on fire and that it was smouldering, but did not then take any steps either to try to extinguish it himself or to send for the fire brigade, but simply went into the other room to resume his slumbers, leaving the fire from the already smouldering mattress to spread and to damage that part of the house in which the mattress was.

The recorder, in his lucid summing up to the jury (they took 22 minutes only to reach their verdict), told them that the accused, having by his own act started fire in the mattress, which, when he became aware of its existence, presented an obvious risk of damaging the house, became under a duty to take some action to put it out. The Court of Appeal upheld the conviction, but its ratio decidendi appears to be somewhat different from that of the recorder. As I understand the judgment, in effect it treats the whole course of conduct of the accused, from the moment at which he fell asleep and dropped the cigarette onto the mattress until the time the damage to the house by fire was complete, as a continuous act of the accused, and holds that it is sufficient to constitute the statutory offence of arson if at any stage in that course of conduct the state of mind of the accused, when he fails to try to prevent or minimise the damage which will result from his initial act, although it lies within his power to do so, is that of being reckless whether property belonging to another would be damaged ...'

Commentary

See *R* v *Ahmad* [1986] Crim LR 739.

R v Nedrick [1986] Crim LR 742 Court of Appeal (Criminal Division) (Lord Lane CJ, Leggatt and Kennedy JJ)

Foresight necessary for intention: mens rea of murder

Facts

'The appellant was convicted of murder on a majority verdict. He had a grudge against a woman whom he had threatened to "burn out." Early one morning he poured paraffin through her letter box and onto the front door and ignited it. He gave no warning. A child in the house died as a result of the fire. To the police the appellant admitted starting the fire saying he had not wanted anyone to die but had only wanted to frighten the woman. At his trial his defence was that he had neither started the fire nor made any admissions. He appealed against conviction on the ground of misdirection as to the intent necessary to establish murder.

Held

Substituting a verdict of manslaughter (and imposing a sentence of 15 years' imprisonment) the judge's direction had been based on the passage in Archbold (42nd ed., at para. 17-13) subsequently disapproved in Moloney [1985] AC 905. In the light of Moloney and Hancock [1986] 2 WLR 357 the direction was plainly wrong. The jury has to decide whether the defendant intended to kill or do serious bodily harm. In order to reach that decision they must pay regard to all the relevant circumstances, including what the defendant said and did. In the great majority of cases that direction will be enough. In some cases such as the present, the defendant does an act which is manifestly dangerous and as a result someone dies, and the primary desire or motive may not have been to harm that person. In that situation, it may be advisable first to explain to the jury that a man may intend to achieve a certain result whilst at the same time not desiring it to come about. In determining whether the defendant had the necessary intent, it may be helpful for the jury to ask themselves (1) How probable was the consequence which resulted from the defendant's voluntary act? (2) Did he foresee that consequence? If he did not appreciate that death or really serious harm was likely to result from his act, he cannot have intended to bring it about. If he did, but thought that the risk was only slight, then it may be easy for the jury to conclude that he did not intend to bring about that result. On the other hand, if the jury are satisfied that at the material time the defendant recognised that death or serious harm would be virtually certain (barring some unforeseen intervention) to result from his voluntary act, then that is a fact from which they may find it easy to infer that he intended to kill or do serious bodily harm, even though he may not have had any desire to achieve that result. The jury should be directed that they are not entitled to infer the necessary intention unless they feel sure that death or serious bodily harm was a virtual certainty (barring some unforeseen intervention) as a result of the defendant's actions and that the defendant appreciated that such was the case.'

[Reported by Lynne Knapman, Barrister]

See further *R* v *Walker and Hayles* Chapter 11.

R v Pembliton (1874) LR 2 CCR 119 Court for Crown Cases Reserved (Lord Coleridge CJ, Blackburn and Lush JJ, Pigott and Cleasby BB)

Transferred malice

Facts

The defendant threw a stone at another person during an argument. The stone missed the intended victim, but instead broke a nearby window. The defendant was charged with malicious damage to property, and although the jury found as a special fact that he had not intended to break the window, he was convicted. The defendant appealed.

Held

The conviction would be quashed. The doctrine of transferred malice was inapplicable where the defendant's intention had not been to cause the type of harm that actually materialised. His intention to assault another person could not be used as the mens rea for the damage that he had caused to the window.

Lord Coleridge CJ:

'I am of the opinion that the evidence does not support the conviction. The indictment is under [section 51, Malicious Damage Act 1861] which deals with malicious injuries to property, and the section expressly says that the act is to be unlawful and malicious. There is also the fifty-eighth section, which makes it immaterial whether the offence has been committed from malice against the owner of the property or otherwise, that is, from malice against someone not the owner of the property. In both these sections it seems to me that what is intended by the statute is wilful doing of an intentional act. Without saying that if the case had been left to them in a different way the conviction could not have been supported, if, on these facts, the jury had come to a conclusion that the prisoner was reckless of the consequences of his act, and might reasonably have expected that it would result in breaking the window, it is sufficient to say that the jury have expressly found the contrary...'

R v Reid [1991] Crim LR 269 Court of Appeal (Criminal Division) (Mustill LJ, Nolan and Saville JJ)

Recklessness - whether a lacuna in *Cunningham/Caldwell* tests

Facts

'The appellant was convicted of causing death by reckless driving. While on the inside lane of a dual carriageway he tried to overtake a vehicle on its nearside. His car struck a taxi drivers' rest hut which protruded six feet into the carriageway and his passenger received fatal injuries. He appealed against conviction on the ground that the judge has misdirected the jury as to the ingredients of the offence. The judge had directed in terms of Lord Diplock's speech in *Lawrence* [1982] AC 510. Counsel for the applicant submitted that a consequence of *Lawrence* was two different states of mind relevant to a charge of reckless driving: for complete inadvertence the test followed the general principle that there must be an obvious and serious risk of causing physical injury to the person or damage to property, whereas for the defendant who has actually given some thought to the matter the test is some risk, whether serious or not, short of *de minims*. That must be a mistake and the adoption of two different subjective standards for the same specific offence did not make sense. The first test made sense and the second should be rejected. In following the direction for reckless driving word for word the court has chosen the wrong part of *Lawrence* to follow.

Held

Dismissing the appeal, (1) In the circumstances of the present case the theoretical problem of pitching the subjective assessment of risk at the right level never arose. The appellant was not saying that he recognised the existence of a risk and assessed it as negligible or that he assessed it as less than serious. So far as he was concerned there was no risk. Although it was not surprising in the light of *Madigan* (1982) Cr App R 145 that the judge thought it best to give a full *Lawrence* direction, with hindsight it could be seen that the elaborate exposition that entailed served only to complicate what was really a very simple case.

(2) The Court of Appeal was obliged to follow the decision in *Lawrence*. The House of Lords has furnished answers to the questions asked of it; those answers established the constituents of the mens rea in cases of recklessness. The speech of Lord Diplock may be taken into account to elucidate the answers if their meaning is said to be unclear. It was not permissible for the Court of Appeal to entertain the possibility of holding that the reasoning does not lead to the conclusion and so discard the conclusion. Only the House of Lords could properly take that course if the logic of the situation demanded.

Obiter

It was inconceivable that Lord Diplock should by design have changed the requirements of the mens rea in the course of a few lines of his speech and even less conceivable that he should have done so by accident. Counsel's argument in the present case had pre-supposed three levels of risk. At one extreme a serious, ie really substantial risk, at the other a negligible risk and, in between, a risk which is not so slight as to be negligible and yet not so grave as to rank as "serious." In those terms the proposed solution would be to posit that "some risk" in the direction suggested by Lord Diplock means "some such risk." The test for both heads of the subjective element would be the same, so that the prosecution must prove a risk high enough to rank as serious, in the ordinary sense of that word. It may be that the premise on which this interpretation is based may be wrong. Instead of there being three degrees of risk, perhaps there are only two, interpreting "serious" not as indicating something close to "grave", but rather as "to be taken seriously." On this view there is no difference between the two degrees of risk. This interpretation would have the advantage, not only of eliminating the apparent conflict between the two limbs of the subjective stage of the enquiry, but also, since "to be taken seriously" is roughly synonymous with "not negligible," of reconciling the answers given by the House of Lords to the certified questions with the discussion in the speech of Lord Diplock.'

[*Reported by Lynne Knapman, Barrister*]

R v Satnam; R v Kewal (1984) 78 Cr App R 149 Court of Appeal (Criminal Division) (Dunn LJ, Bristow J and Sir John Thompson)

Recklessness as the mens rea in rape

Facts

The defendants were both convicted of the rape of a 13 year old girl, on the basis that she had not consented to the intercourse and the defendants had been reckless as to whether she was consenting. The trial judge had directed the jury that they should convict if they were satisfied that the defendants had failed to give any thought to an obvious risk that the girl had not been consenting to intercourse. The defendant appealed to the Court of Appeal.

Held

The appeal would be allowed.

Bristow J:

[Having considered the facts of the case]

'The judge rightly pointed out that there was no dispute that sexual intercourse had in fact taken place. He went on to deal impeccably with the elements of consent by the girl and the knowledge of the appellants which was relevant to the counts on which they were acquitted. He then turned to the element of recklessness and said this: "Members of the jury, a person is reckless in this context; if there was an obvious reason, in the circumstances as the jury find them to be, if there was an obvious reason that the girl was not in fact willing to have sexual intercourse, that is to say, obvious to every ordinary observer, and the defendant either did not apply his mind to that reason at all, for whatever reason, or applied his mind to the reason, but carried on having sexual intercourse with her, or trying to, that is recklessness." He then repeated that direction and gave no further direction as to the necessary elements to be proved in the crime of reckless rape.

Two grounds of appeal were relied on in this Court. (1) That the judge should have directed the jury that a genuine though mistaken belief that the girl was consenting offered a defence to a charge of reckless rape; (2) that the judge erred in referring to an "ordinary observer" in his direction as to recklessness, and that he should have directed the jury that it was necessary to prove that each appellant was actually aware of the possibility that the girl was not consenting before they could find him reckless.

So far as the first ground was concerned, it was accepted by Mr Smith for the Crown that he could not support the summing-up in the absence of a direction as to belief. In *Thomas* (1983) 77 Cr App R 63 Lord Lane CJ said, at p65: "In this particular case, the judge should spelt out in terms that a

2 ACTUS REUS AND MENS REA

mistaken belief that the woman was consenting, however unreasonable it may appear to have been, is an answer to the charge, and that it is for the prosecution to eliminate the possibility of such a mistake if they are to succeed. He should then have gone on to deal with the matters set out in section 1(2) of the 1976 Act. As it was the jury were left without any guidance on the matter." The same situation arose here. The jury were left without any guidance on the matter of belief and on that ground alone we would allow the appeal.

We turn now to consider the second ground, ie the direction as to recklessness. Strictly it may be said that this point has already been decided in *Bashir* (1983) 77 Cr App R 59, 62 where Watkins LJ said: "As recently as the fifth of this month, Lord Lane CJ in *Thomas* (supra) restated the defintion of 'reckless' as applied to the offence of rape. He said (1983) 77 Cr App R 63, 66: 'A man is reckless if either he was indifferent and gave no thought to the possibility that the woman might not be consenting, in circumstances where, if any thought had been given to the matter, it would have been obvious that there was a risk she was not, or, he was aware of the possibility that she might not be consenting but nevertheless persisted, regardless of whether she consented or not.' He was in almost exact form repeating the definition of 'reckless' in relation to rape which he had provided in the case of *Pigg* (1982) 74 Cr App R 352. It will be noted that the definition allows none other than a subjective approach to the state of mind of a person of whom it is said he acted recklessly in committing a crime. It was incumbent therefore on the trial judge in the present case to ensure that he provided the jury with this kind of defintion of the word 'reckless.' "

Mr Tayler on behalf of the appellants submitted, in his able argument, that the use of the word "obvious" in its context in both *Pigg* (supra) and *Thomas C* (supra) gives rise to a possible ambiguity. "Obvious" to whom? If it meant obvious to any reasonable person that would introduce an objective test, and Mr Tayler submitted that the authorities properly understood do not warrant such a conclusion. He invited us in effect to clarify the situation which has developed since *Caldwell* (supra) and *Lawrence* (supra), as he said that the judges up and down the country are now in a state of some confusion as to the state of the law. He submitted that the direction of recklessness in *Pigg* (supra) was in any event obiter.

As Robert Goff LJ said in *Elliott* v *C (A Minor)* (1983) 77 Cr App R 103, 119; [1983] 1 WLR 939, 950, with reference to the suggested direction in *Pigg* (supra): "Now it cannot be disguised that the addition of the words 'was indifferent and' constituted a gloss upon the definition of recklessness proposed by Lord Diplock in *R* v *Caldwell* (supra). Furthermore, if it were legitimate so to interpret Lord Diplock's speech in relation to a case arising not under section 1(1) of the Criminal Damage Act 1971, the effect would be that the second question posed by the magistrates in the case now before this court would be answered in the affirmative, and the appeal would be dismissed; because there is no finding of fact that this defendant in the case before us was indifferent to the risk of destruction by fire of the shed and its contents. This is an approach which I would gladly adopt, if I felt that I was free to do so. However, I do not consider that it is open to this Court, in a case arising under the very subsection to which Lord Diplock's speech was expressly directed, to impose this qualification, which I feel would in this context constitute too substantial a departure from the text proposed by him."

The instant case, unlike *Elliott* (supra), is not concerned with the Criminal Damage Act 1971 but with the Sexual Offences (Amendment) Act 1976, and the Court is considering recklessness in the context of rape and not in the context of criminal damage. We feel we are therefore free to review the situation so far as it is governed by relevant authority, and accepting as we do that there is an ambiguity in the suggested direction in *Pigg*, which was in any event obiter.

Mr Tayler took as his starting point *Director of Public Prosecutions* v *Morgan* (1975) 61 Cr App R 136; [1976] AC 182, a decision of the House of Lords on the very question of rape, which was not overruled by either *Caldwell* or *Lawrence* and is binding on this Court. Lord Hailsham said at p151 and p215 of the respective reports: " I am content to rest my view of the instant case on the crime of rape by saying that it is my opinion that the prohibited act is and always has been intercourse without consent of the victim and the mental element is and always has been the intention to commit that act, or the equivalent intention of having intercourse willy-nilly not caring whether the victim consents or no. A failure to prove this involves an acquittal because the intent, an essential ingredient, is lacking. It matters not why it is lacking if only it is not there, and in particular it matters not that the intention is lacking only because of a belief not based on reasonable grounds."

In the Report of the Advisory Group on the Law of Rape (The Heilbron Committee) Command Paper 6352 1975, the following "Recommendations for declaratory legislation" were made:

"81. Notwithstanding our conclusions that *Morgan's* case (supra) is right in principle, we nevertheless feel that legislation is required to clarify the law governing intention in rape cases, as it is now settled. We think this for two principal reasons. The first is that it would be possible in future cases to argue that the question of recklessness did not directly arise for decision in *Morgan's* case, in view of the form of the question certified: to avoid possible doubts the ruling on recklessness needs to be put in statutory form.

82. Secondly, it would be unfortunate if a tendency were to rise to say to the jury 'that a belief, however unreasonable, that the woman consented, entitled the accused to acquittal.' Such a phrase might tend to give an undue or misleading emphasis to one aspect only and the law, therefore, should be statutorily restated in a fuller form which would obviate the use of those words.

83. We think that there would be advantage if this matter could also be dealt with by a statutory provision which would—(i) declare that (in cases where the question of belief is raised) the issue which the jury have to consider is whether the accused at the time when sexual intercourse took place believed that she was consenting, and (ii) make it clear that, while there is no requirement of law that such a belief must be based on reasonable grounds, the presence or absence of such grounds is a relevant consideration to which the jury should have regard, in conjunction with all other evidence, in considering whether the accused genuinely had such a belief."

There followed the Sexual Offences (Amendment) Act 1976, section 1 of which is in the following terms: "(1) For the purpose of section 1 of the Sexual Offences Act 1956 (which relates to rape) a man commits rape if—(a) he has unlawful sexual intercourse with a woman who at the time of the intercourse does not consent to it; and (b) at that time he knows that she does not consent to the intercourse or he is reckless as to whether she consents to it; ... (2) It is hereby declared that if at a trial for a rape offence the jury has to consider whether a man believed that a woman was consenting to sexual intercourse, the presence or absence of reasonable grounds for such a belief is a matter to which the jury is to have regard, in conjunction with any other relevant matters, in considering whether he so believed."

We think that in enacting those provisions Parliament must have accepted the recommendations of the Heilbron Committee, so that the provisions are declaratory of the existing law as stated in *DDP* v *Morgan* (supra).

Any direction as to the definition of rape should therefore be based upon section 1 of the 1976 Act and upon *DPP* v *Morgan* (supra), without regard to *R* v *Caldwell* (supra) or *R* v *Lawrence* (supra), which were concerned with recklessness in a different context and under a different statute.

The word "reckless" in relation to rape involves a different concept to its use in relation to malicious damage or, indeed in relation to offences against the person. In the latter cases the foreseeability, or possible foreseeability is as to the consequences of the criminal act. In the case of rape the foreseeability is as to the state of mind of the victim.

A practical definition of recklessness in sexual offences was given in *Kimber* (1983) 77 Cr App R 225; [1983] 1 WLR 1118, where the Court was concerned with how far an honest belief in consent constituted a defence to a charge of indecent assault. The defendant said in evidence: "I was not really interested in Betty's" (the victim's) "feelings at all." Lawton LJ said at p230 and p1123 of the respective reports: "We have already set out in this judgment the admissions which he is alleged to have made to the police and the relevant parts of his own evidence. In our judgment a reasonable jury would inevitably have decided that he had no honest belief that Betty was consenting. His own evidence showed that his attitude to her was one of indifference to her feelings and wishes. This state of mind is aptly described in the colloquial expression, 'couldn't care less.' In law this is recklessness."

In summing-up a case of rape which involves the issue of consent, the judge should, in dealing with the state of mind of the defendant, first of all direct the jury that before they could convict of rape the Crown had to prove either that the defendant knew the woman did not want to have sexual intercourse, or was reckless as to whether she wanted to or not. If they were sure he knew she did not want to they should find him guilty of rape knowing there to be no consent. If they were not sure about that, then they would find him not guilty of such rape and should go on to consider reckless rape. If they thought he might genuinely have believed that she did not want to, even though he was mistaken in his belief, they would find him not guilty. In considering whether his belief was genuine, they should take into account all the relevant circumstances (which could at that point be summarised) and ask themselves whether, in the light of those circumstances, he had reasonable grounds for such a belief. If, after considering those circumstances, they were sure he had no genuine belief that she wanted to, they would find him guilty. If they came to the conclusion that he could not care less whether she wanted to or not, but pressed on regardless, then he would have been reckless and could not have believed that she wanted to, and they would find him guilty of reckless rape.'

R v Seymour [1983] 2 AC 493

See chapter 8.

R v Shivpuri [1986] 2 WLR 988

See chapter 11.

R v Speck (1977) 65 Cr App R 161 Court of Appeal (Criminal Division) (The Lord Chief Justice, Caulfield and Gibson JJ)

Distinguishing positive acts from omissions

Facts

The defendant was convicted of an offence under s1 of the Indecency with Children Act 1960. An 8 year old girl had approached him and placed her hand on his penis. He allowed her hand to remain there for approximately five minutes, during which time he had an erection. He appealed against his conviction on the basis that he had not committed any ... act of gross indecency with or towards a child under the age of fourteen ...

Held

The appeal would be dismissed. The defendant's inactivity in failing to remove the hand of the little girl could amount to an invitation to the child to undertake the act.

Widgery LCJ [having referred to the details of the offence, continued]:

'The ... point of course was whether, having regard to the inactivity of the appellant himself, it could fairly be said that what had passed between him and the child constituted an act of gross indecency with or towards the child.

In considering whether that was or was not so the learned recorder had regard to the well-known principle that in general mere inactivity, mere absence of movement or action, does not amount to a criminal offence. . .

In supporting this appeal today it has been said that the inactivity which I have described was not something prohibited by the section, and that in view of the sheer inactivity there was no proof of the essentials of the offence. . .

Getting to the essential features of this problem, and accepting that for present purposes there was inactivity on the part of the appellant at all material times, we think that such inactivity can nevertheless amount to an invitation to the child to undertake the act. If a fair view of the facts be that the appellant has in any sense invited the child to do what she did, then the mere fact that the appellant himself remained inactive is no defence to it ...

Since in our opinion the element of invitation is important, and that is an element which the jury ultimately would have to consider, the ruling in law should have been that the conduct described by the learned recorder could be an offence if the jury took the view that it amounted to an invitation from the male to the child, either to start, to stop, or to continue this activity.'

R v Stone and Dobinson [1977] 1 QB 354 Court of Appeal (Criminal Division) (Geoffrey Lane LJ, Nield and Croom-Johnson JJ)

Liability for failure to act based upon reliance

Facts

The defendants lived as common law man and wife. The man was quite elderly; he had greatly impaired senses of sight, smell, and hearing. His common law wife was described as 'weak' and ineffectual. It was accepted that both defendants were of low intelligence and not particularly 'worldly' in character. One day they were visited by Fanny, the sister of the husband, a somewhat eccentric woman who was described as being morbidly anxious about becoming overweight. The defendants took Fanny in and provided her with a bed, but over the following weeks Fanny's condition worsened. She did not eat properly, developed bed sores, and eventually died of blood poisoning when the sores became infected. The defendants had known of her condition but had failed to obtain medical help for her. The defendants were convicted of manslaughter, in the form of killing by gross negligence, and appealed to the Court of Appeal.

Held

The appeal would be dismissed. The defendants had been under a common law duty to care for Fanny. This duty had arisen from their voluntarily assuming the responsibility for looking after her, knowing that she was relying on them. The defendants' failure to discharge this duty was the cause of the victim's death.

Geoffrey Lane LJ:

[On the question of liability for failing to act]

'The prosecution alleged that in the circumstances the appellants had undertaken the duty of caring for Fanny who was incapable of looking after herself, that they had, with gross negligence, failed in that duty, that such failure caused her death and that they were guilty of manslaughter.

[Counsel for the appellant] suggests that the situation here is unlike any reported case. Fanny came to this house as a lodger. Largely, if not entirely due to her own eccentricity and failure to look after herself or feed herself properly, she became increasingly infirm and immobile and eventually unable to look after herself. Is it to be said, asks [counsel for the appellant] rhetorically, that by the mere fact of becoming infirm and helpless in these circumstances she casts a duty on her brother and the appellant Dobinson to take steps to have her looked after or taken into hospital? The suggestion is that, heartless though it may seem. this is one of those situations where the appellants were entitled to do nothing; where no duty was cast upon them to help, any more than it is cast upon a man to rescue a stranger from drowning, however easy such a rescue might be.

This court rejects that proposition. Whether Fanny was a lodger or not she was a blood relation of the appellant Stone; she was occupying a room in his house; the appellant Dobinson had undertaken the duty of trying to wash her, of taking such food as she required. There was ample evidence that each appellant was aware of the poor condition she was in by mid-July. It was not disputed that no effort was made to summon an ambulance or the social services or the police despite the entreaties of Mrs Wilson and Mrs West [neighbours of the defendants]. A social worker used to visit Cyril [the defendant's son]. No word was spoken to him. All these were matters which the jury were entitled to take into account when considering whether the necessary assumption of a duty to care for Fanny had been proved.

This was not a situation analogous to the drowning stranger. They did make efforts to care. They tried to get a doctor; they tried to discover the previous doctor. The appellant Dobinson helped with the washing and the provision of food. All these matters were put before the jury in terms which we find it impossible to fault. The jury were entitled to find that the duty had been assumed. They were entitled to conclude that once Fanny became helplessly infirm, as she had by July 19, the appellants were in the circumstances, obliged either to summon help or else to care for Fanny themselves.'

Thabo Meli v R [1954] 1 WLR 228 Privy Council (Lord Goddard CJ, Lord Reid and Mr LMD de Silva)

Coincidence of actus reus and mens rea

Facts

The defendants took their intended victim to a hut and plied him with drink so that he became intoxicated, they then hit the victim around the head, intending to kill him. In fact the defendants only succeeded in knocking him unconscious, but believing him to be dead, they threw the victim's body over a cliff. The victim died some time later of exposure. The defendants were convicted of murder, and appealed to the Privy Council on the ground that there was no coincidence of the mens rea and actus reus of murder. The defendants' submissions were that when they had acted with the intention of killing the victim by striking him on the head, they had failed to kill him. On the other hand, when they did actually cause his death, by throwing him over the cliff, they lacked the mens rea for murder as they believed he was already dead.

Held

The appeal would be dismissed. The correct view of what the defendants had done was to treat the chain of events as a continuing actus reus. The actus reus of causing death started with the victim being struck on the head and continued until he died of exposure. It was sufficient for the prosecution to establish that at some time during that chain of events the defendants had acted with the requisite mens rea for murder.

Lord Reid:

'The point of law which was raised in this case can be simply stated. It is said that two acts were done: - first, the attack in the hut: and, secondly, the placing of the body outside afterwards - and that they were separate acts. It is said that, while the first act was accompanied by mens rea, it was not the cause of death; but that the second act, while it was the cause of death, was not accompanied by mens rea; and on that ground, it is said that the accused are not guilty of murder, though they may have been guilty of culpable homicide. It is said that the mens rea necessary to establish murder is an intention to kill, and that there could be no intention to kill when the accused thought that the man was already dead, so their original intention to kill had ceased before they did the act which caused the man's death. It appears to their Lordships impossible to divide up what was really one series of acts in this way. There is no doubt that the accused set out to do all these acts in order to achieve their plan, and as parts of their plan; and it is much too refined a ground of judgment to say that, because they were under a misapprehension at one stage and thought that their guilty purpose had been achieved before, in fact, it was achieved, therefore they are to escape the penalties of the law… Their crime is not reduced from murder to a lesser crime merely because the accused were under some misapprehension for a time during the completion of their criminal plot.'

Commentary

See further *R* v *Le Brun*, above.

W (A Minor) v Dolbey [1983] Crim LR 681 Divisional Court (Robert Goff LJ and Forbes J)

Recklessness under s20 Offences Against the Persons Act 1861

Facts

'The defendant, who was 15, took out his brother's air rifle and, having spent some time shooting at bottles, went to a nearby farm. There he met R, standing in the doorway of a barn. The defendant lay down and pointed the gun at R, who told him to put the gun down. The defendant told R "there is nothing in the gun; I have got no pellets." He fired the gun. There was a pellet in the gun, and it hit R between the eyes, wounding him. The defendant was charged with unlawfully and maliciously wounding R contrary to section 20 of the Offences against the Person Act 1861. The justices found as facts (i) that the defendant believed the gun to have been unloaded, because he thought he had used the last pellet whilst shooting at the bottles; (ii) that he had not opened the gun before aiming it at R; and (iii) that he had ignored the risk that the gun might be loaded. The justices concluded that the defendant had been reckless, and that that was sufficient to constitute the malicious intent required by the 1861 Act. They convicted the defendant, who appealed by case stated to the Queen's Bench Divisional Court.

Held

Allowing the appeal and quashing the conviction, that in order to establish that a defendant had acted maliciously it had to be shown that, on the facts known to him at the time, he actually foresaw that a particular kind of harm might be done to his victim. In *Caldwell* [1982] AC 341, Lord Diplock, after referring to the definition of malice given by Professor Kenny in his *Outlines of Criminal Law* (1st ed., 1902), was careful to distinguish recklessness from malice. It was clear that no guidance could be derived from the meaning of recklessness in order to define malice, and that in respect of the latter the definition in *Cunningham* [1957] 2 QB 396 still stood. Accordingly, if the defendant honestly believed that the gun was not loaded then, whether or not he was reckless in pointing it at someone without first checking it, he did not foresee the physical harm done to R, and therefore he was not malicious.'

[*Reported by Paul Magrath, Barrister.*]

Winzar v Chief Constable of Kent (1983) The Times 28 March Divisional Court (Goff LJ and McNeill J)

Absence of a freely willed actus reus

Facts

The defendant had been admitted to a hospital on a stretcher. Upon examination he was found to be drunk and was told to leave. Later he was found in a corridor of the hospital and the police were called to remove him. The police officers took the defendant outside onto the roadway, then placed him in a police car and drove him to the police station where he was charged with 'being found drunk in a public highway'. The defendant was convicted, and appealed on the ground that he had not been on the public road of his own volition.

Held

Conviction affirmed.

Robert Goff LJ:

'Does the fact that the Appellant was only momentarily on the highway and not there of his own volition, prevent his conviction of the offence of being found drunk in a highway?...

In my judgment, looking at the purpose of this particular offence, it is designed ... to deal with the nuisance which can be caused by persons who are drunk in a public place. This kind of offence is caused quite simply when a person is found drunk in a public place or in a highway ... [A]n example ... illustrates how sensible that conclusion is. Suppose a person was found as being drunk in a restaurant or a place of that kind and was asked to leave. If he was asked to leave, he would walk out of the door of the restaurant and would be in a public place or in a highway of his own volition. He would be there of his own volition because he had responded to a request. However, if a man in a restaurant made a thorough nuisance of himself, was asked to leave, objected and was ejected, in those circumstances, he would not be in a public place of his own volition because he would have been put there either by a gentleman on the door of the restaurant, or by a police officer, who might have been called to deal with the man in question. It would be nonsense if one were to say that the man who responded to the plea to leave could be said to be found drunk in a public place or in a highway, whereas the man who had been compelled to leave could not.

This leads me to the conclusion that a person is "found to be drunk in a public place or in a highway," within the meaning of those words as used in the section, when he is perceived to be drunk in a public place. It is enough for the commission of the offence if (1) a person is in a public place or a highway, (2) he is drunk, and (3) in those circumstances he is perceived to be there and to be drunk. Once those criteria have been fulfilled, he is liable to be convicted of the offence of being found drunk in a highway. Finally, I turn to the question: Does it matter if the Appellant was only momentarily in the highway? In my judgment, it makes no difference. A man may be perceived to be drunk in the highway for five minutes, for one minute or for ten seconds. However short the period of time, if a man is perceived to be drunk in a highway, he is guilty of the offence under the section. Of course, if the period of time is very short, the penalty imposed may be minimal, indeed in such circumstances a police officer, using his discretion, may think it unnecessary to charge the man. The point is simply that the offence is committed if a person is perceived to be drunk in a public place or in the highway. Once that criterion is fulfilled, then the offence is committed.'

Commentary

See *R* v *Larsonneur*, above.

3   CRIMINAL DAMAGE

R v **Appleyard** [1985] Crim LR 723 Court of Appeal (Criminal Division) (Lord Lane CJ, Skinner and MacPherson JJ)

Destruction of company property by managing director

Facts

'The appellant was convicted on three counts – conspiracy to obtain property by deception, conspiracy to steal and arson. It was alleged that he, with another who was acquitted, set fire to a store belonging to a limited company of which he was the managing director. The appellant appealed against conviction for arson on the ground that he must be taken to have been entitled to consent to the damage. Counsel relied upon *Denton* (1982) 74 Cr App R 81.

Held

Dismissing the appeal, the point at issue in the present case was not that at issue in *Denton*. The point in *Denton* concerned an employee and it was merely a concession for the purposes of argument in that case that the employer was entitled to consent to the damage. To seek to base a proposition of law upon that concession was a fruitless exercise.'

[*Reported by Lynne Knapman, Barrister.*]

R v **Ashford and Smith** [1988] Crim LR 682 Court of Appeal (Criminal Division) Glidewell LJ, Gatehouse and Pill JJ

Criminal Damage Act 1971 s5 - lawful excuse - objective test

Facts

'The appellants were convicted of two counts of possession of an article with intent to damage property. They had tried to cut the wire fence surrounding an Air Force base as part of a demonstration of opposition to nuclear weapons. They sought to call evidence that they had a lawful excuse. The judge ruled that the cutting of the wire to draw attention to the undesirability of nuclear weapons and to a reduction in nuclear weapons to protect the property of persons abroad and, by lessening the risk of retaliation, of persons in England did not fall within the definition of a lawful excuse and therefore that no evidence to that effect could be called. The appellants were acquitted on two counts of attempting to damage the wire fence. They appealed against conviction on the grounds that the judge erred in law and, in the alternative, that the verdicts were inconsistent.

Held

Dismissing the appeal, the reasoning in *Hunt* (1978) 66 Cr App R 105 applied. The question whether or not an act was done or made in order to protect property belonging to another must be, on the true construction of the statute, an objective test. The judge had ruled correctly. There was an inconsistency in the verdicts. However, it was clear on the view taken by the Court on the issue of lawful excuse that the jury were logically bound to convict on both counts and it would merely compound the error to allow the appeals against conviction. *Hunt* [1968] 2 QB 433; *Drury* (1972) 56 Cr App R 104; *Segal* [1976] RTR 319 considered.'

[*Reported by Lynne Knapman, Barrister.*]

R v **Caldwell** [1982] AC 341

See chapters 2 and 12.

Chief Constable of Avon and Somerset v **Shimmen** [1986] Crim LR 800

See chapter 2.

Cox v **Riley** [1986] Crim LR 460 Divisional Court (Stephen Brown LJ and McCullough J)

Erasure of a computer program as criminal damage

Facts

'The appellant was convicted of damaging a plastic circuit card of a computerised saw, contrary to section 1(1) of the Criminal Damage Act 1971. He had erased the programmes, rendering the saw inoperable save for limited manual operation. The justices found that the printed card was property within section 10(1) of the 1971 Act in that it was tangible and could be programmed; and that the appellant had caused damage as the card required reprogramming to operate the saw. The appellant appealed by way of case stated.

Held

Dismissing the appeal, the card was undoubtedly property of a tangible nature within section 10(1). The erasure of the programmes from a printed circuit card used to operate the saw constituted damage. The Court applied the reasoning of the Court of Appeal Criminal Division in *Henderson and Battley* (unrep. November 29, 1984) in which the unauthorised dumping of waste on a cleared building site was held to be damage – the site's usefulness was impaired and work and expenditure were required to restore it to its former state. The Court considered *Fisher* (1865) LR 1 CCR 7.'

[*Reported by Lynne Knapman, Barrister.*]

R v **Dudley** [1989] Crim LR 57 Court of Appeal (Criminal Division) (Staughton LJ, Otton and Steyn JJ)

Criminal Damage Act 1971 s1(2) - relevance of actual damage done.

Facts

'D who had a grievance against the J family, consumed drink and drugs, went to their house and, using an accelerant, threw a fire bomb at the house, causing a high sheet of flame outside the glass door. The fire was extinguished by the J family and only trivial damage was caused. He was charged with arson under section 1(1) and (2) of the Criminal Damage Act 1971; he pleaded guilty to simple arson and a trial proceeded on the counts laid under section 1(2). At the close of the prosecution case D's counsel submitted that there was no case to answer because the jury could not properly find that the actual damage caused was intended to endanger life or was likely to do so; and he relied on *R* v *Steer* [1988] AC 111. The trial judge rejected the submission and D thereupon changed his plea to guilty to the count of arson being reckless as whether life would be endangered. He appealed against conviction, submitting that the judge's ruling was wrong in law.

Held

The appeal would be dismissed. The words "destruction or damage" in section 1(2)(*b*)of the Act (endangering life) referred back to the destruction or damage intended, or as to which there was recklessness, in section 1(2)(*a*) (damaging property). The words did not refer to the destruction or damage actually caused; if they did, injustice would be done in the converse case where someone was reckless only as to trivial damage but by some mishap caused danger to life. *R* v *Steer* [1988] AC 111 was distinguishable because the House of Lords in that case was considering a different question, *viz* whether the danger to life had to be caused by the destruction or damage to property or by the act of the defendant (in firing a rifle at a window); and in that case the actual damage and the intended damage coincided. In the present case the judge's ruling was correct and D changed his plea, no doubt after advice, on the basis of his state of mind.'

[*Reported by Tom Rees, Barrister.*]

Elliot v C [1983] 1 WLR 939

See chapter 2.

Hardman v Chief Constable of Avon and Somerset Constabulary [1986] Crim LR 330, Bristol Crown Court (His Honour Judge Llewellyn-Jones and JJs)

Graffiti as criminal damage

Facts

'The appellants were convicted by the Justices of causing criminal damage to a pavement. They appealed. They were members of the Campaign for Nuclear Disarmament. On August 6, 1985 (which was the fortieth anniversary of the Hiroshima bombing) they painted human silhouettes on an asphalt pavement to represent vaporised human remains. The "paint" was a fat free unstable whitewash, which was soluble in water. It was specially mixed in the expectation that rainwater would wash away the markings. The evidence suggested that this was correct and that rainwater and pedestrian traffic would eventually eradicate the markings. However, the Local Authority had acted before this happened and a "Graffiti Squad" was employed to clean the pavement using high pressure water jets. It was contended by the appellants that following *"A" (a Juvenile)* v *The Queen* (1978) Crim LR 689, there was no "damage" within the meaning of section 1 of the Criminal Damage Act 1971.

Held

Notwithstanding the fact that the markings could be washed away there had nonetheless been damage, which had caused expense and inconvenience to the Local Authority. An unduly narrow definition of damage was not appropriate. The approach of Walters J in S*amuels* v *Stubbs*, 4 SASR 200 was approved when he said at p203:

> "It seems to me that it is difficult to lay down any very general and, at the same time, precise and absolute rule as to what constitutes 'damage'. One must be guided in a great degree by the circumstances of each case, the nature of the article, and the mode in which it is affected or treated.

> Moreover, the meaning of the word 'damage' must as I have already said, be controlled by its context. The word may be used in the sense of 'mischief done to property'." '

R v Hill; R v Hall (1989) 89 Cr App R 74 Court of appeal (Criminal Division) (Lord Lane CJ, McCullough J, and Kennedy J)

Criminal damage - defence of lawful excuse

Facts

Both defendants were convicted of possession of an article with intent to damage property, contrary to section 3 of the Criminal damage Act 1971. The article in question in each case was a hacksaw blade. Each defendant had intended to use such a blade to damage the perimeter fences of airforce bases, as part of a larger campaign of protest at the presence of nuclear missiles on British soil. Both defendants sought to rely on the 'lawful excuse' defence provided by section 5(2) of the 1971 Act, which provides inter alia:

'A person charged with an offence to which this section applies shall, whether or not he would be treated for the purposes of this Act as having a lawful excuse apart from this subsection, be treated for those purposes as having a lawful excuse ... (b) if he ... intended to use or cause or permit the use of something to destroy or damage [the property], in order to protect property belonging to himself or another or a right or interest in property which was or which he believed to be vested in himself or another, and at the time of the act or acts alleged to constitute the offence he believed (i) that the property, right or interest was in immediate need of protection ....' Subsection (3) reads: 'For the purposes of this section it is immaterial whether belief is justified or not if it is honestly held.'

The Lord Chief Justice summarised the nature of the defendants' 'excuse' in referring to the case of Valerie Hill:

'[She] believed that the purpose of [the airbase] base was to monitor the movements of Soviet submarines, that in the event of hostilities breaking out between the United States and the Soviets or the Soviets and ourselves, the base would be the subject of a nuclear strike with devastation in that area. She lived about 40 miles away from the base. Consequently her property and the property of friends and neighbours of hers in Pembrokeshire would be put at risk, to say the least, should there be any such nuclear strike. There was an alternative limb to this particular argument, and that was this that the Soviets might select the site at Brawdy as a target for a sudden nuclear strike in order to indicate that they, the Soviets, did not want all-out nuclear war, but were in a position to protect their submarines in the Atlantic if they so wished, and so to maintain the nuclear threat which those submarines posed to the United States. That latter limb, so to speak, was the subject of evidence by a gentleman called Dr Cox, whose qualifications seemed to us, if we may say so respectfully, to fall far short of entitling him to speak about these matters as an expert which he purported to be. However that may be, the way in which the matter presented itself to Valerie Hill was this, that if enough people took a hacksaw blade and did as she intended to do, namely cut a strand of the perimeter wire, the Americans might come to the conclusion that it was no longer possible to maintain the safety and integrity of their base: it would be too insecure to be maintained. They accordingly might remove their base. Thereby they would have removed the reason for any nuclear attack to be made by the Soviet forces; or else possibly the United Kingdom government would take steps to remove the need for such places by abandoning the idea of nuclear defence. Thus, goes the reasoning that at the end of these hypothetical events, the property, whether it was her own property or the property of neighbours in Pembrokeshire, would avoid destruction. It seems that this was part of a concerted campaign by the Campaign for Nuclear Disarmament. Broadly speaking that was the background to these two cases.'

The defendants now appealed against the trial judge's directions to the jury in relation to subsections 5(2) and (3)

Held

The appeals would be dismissed.

Per Lord Lane CJ

[Having recited the facts and the provisions of subsections 5(2) and (3), his Lordship continued]

'The learned judge, as I have already indicated, directed the jury to convict on two bases. The first basis was this, that what the applicant did or proposed to do could not, viewed objectively, be said to have been done to protect her own or anyone else's property under section 5(2)(b) which I have just read. It is simply, he concluded, part of a political campaign aimed at drawing attention to the base and to the risks as she described them raised by the presence of the base in Pembrokeshire. It aimed further at having the base removed. He came to the conclusion that the causative relationship between the acts which she intended to perform and the alleged protection was so tenuous, so nebulous, that the acts could not be said to be done to protect viewed objectively. The second ground was with reference to the provision that the lawful excuse must be based upon an immediate need for protection. In each case the judge came to the same conclusion that on the applicant's own evidence the applicant could not be said to have believed under the provisions of section 5(2)(b)(i) that the property was in immediate need of protection... The judge in each case relied upon a decision of this Court in *Hunt* (1978) 66 Cr App R 105. We have the advantage also of having that report in transcript. We also have before us a more recent decision of this Court in *Ashford and Smith* (unreported) decided on May 26, 1988, in which very similar considerations were raised to those which exist in the present case. It also has the advantage of having set out the material findings of the Court in *Hunt* which were delivered by Roskill LJ. I am referring to p4 of the transcript in *Ashford and Smith,* and it will help to set out the basis of the decision not only in *Ashford and Smith* but also in *Hunt* if I read the passage. It runs as follows:

> "The judge relied very largely upon the decision of this Court in *Hunt* (1978) 66 Cr App R 105. That was a case in which the appellant set fire to a guest room in an old people's home. He did so, he said, to draw attention to the defective fire alarm system. He was charged with arson, contrary to section 1(1) of the Criminal Damage Act 1971. He sought to set up the statutory defence under section 5(2) by claiming to have had a lawful excuse in doing what he did and that he was not reckless whether any such property would be destroyed. The trial judge withdrew the defence of lawful excuse from the jury and left the issue of recklessness for them to determine. The jury by a majority verdict convicted the appellant. On appeal, held that, applying the objective test, the trial judge had ruled correctly because what the appellant had done was not an act which in itself did protect or was capable of protecting property; but in order to draw attention to what in his view was an immediate need for protection by repairing the alarm system; thus the statutory defence under section 5(2) of the Act was not open to him; accordingly, the appeal would be dismissed."

Giving the judgment of the Court Roskill LJ said, at p108:

> "Mr. Marshall-Andrews' submission can be put thus: if this man honestly believed that that which he did was necessary in order to protect this property from the risk of fire and damage to the old people's home by reason of the absence of a working fire alarm, he was entitled to set fire to that bed and so to claim the statutory defence accorded by section 5(2). I have said we will assume in his favour that he possessed the requisite honest belief. But in our view the question whether he was entitled to the benefit of the defence turns upon the meaning of the words in order to protect property belonging to another. It was argued that those words were subjective in concept, just like the words in the latter part of section 5(2)(b) which are subjective. We do not think that is right. The question whether or not a particular act of destruction or damage or threat of destruction or damage was done or made in order to protect property belonging to another must be, on the true construction of the statute, an objective test. Therefore we have to ask ourselves whether, whatever the state of this man's mind and assuming an honest belief, that which he admittedly did was done in order to protect this particular property, namely the old peoples home in Hertfordshire? If one formulates the question in that way, in the view of each member of this Court, for the reason Slynn J gave during the argument, it admits of only one answer: this was not done in order to protect property; it was done in order to draw attention to the defective state of the fire alarm. It was not an act which in itself did protect or was capable of protecting property."

Then the judgment in *Ashford and Smith,* delivered by Glidewell LJ continued as follows:

> "In our view that reasoning applies exactly in the present case. *Hunt* is, of course, binding upon us. But even if it were not, we agree with the reasoning contained in it. Now it is submitted by Mr Bowyer [for the applicants] to us that the decision in *Hunt* and the decision in *Ashford and Smith* were wrong and that the test is a subjective test. In other words the

submission is that it was a question of what the applicant believed and accordingly it should have been left to the jury as a matter of fact to decide what it was the applicant did believe."

We are bound by the decision in *Hunt* just as the Court in *Ashford and Smith* were bound, unless that case can be demonstrated to have been wrongly decided in the light of previous authority. Mr Bowyer endeavoured to persuade us that the decision which I have read of Roskill LJ flew in the face of the decision of the House of Lords in *Chandler v Director of Public Prosecutions* (1962) 46 Cr App R 347, [1964] AC 763. That was a case which bore certain superficial resemblances to the present case, because the appellants there were members of the Committee of 100, who were set to further the aims of the campaign for nuclear disarmament by demonstrations of civil disobedience, and they picked on Wethersfield Airfield, which was a prohibited place under the Official Secrets Act 1911, in order to mount a rally. It was occupied at the material time by certain US Air Force Squadrons. The idea was that demonstrators would take up positions outside the entrances to the airfield and would remain sitting there for five hours while others would enter and sit in front of the aircraft in order to prevent them operating. We have examined the speeches in this case with some particularity. I hope we will not give offence if we say we are unable to derive any assistance whatsoever from the case of *Chandler v DPP* so far as the decisions in *Hunt* and *Ashford and Smith* are concerned. It certainly does not have the effect of casting any doubt upon the validity or the accuracy of the decision in those cases.

That leaves us with the fact that we are bound by the decision in *Hunt*. But we add that we think that *Hunt* was correctly decided, for this reason. There are two aspects to this type of question. The first aspect is to decide what it was that the applicant, in this case Valerie Hill, in her own mind thought. The learned judge assumed, and so do we, for the purposes of this decision, that everything she said about her reasoning was true. I have already perhaps given a sufficient outline of what it was she believed to demonstrate what is meant by that. Up to that point the test was subjective. In other words one is examining what is going on in the applicant's mind. Having done that, the judges in the present cases – and the judge particularly in the case of Valerie Hill – turned to the second aspect of the case, and that is this. He had to decide as a matter of law, which means objectively, whether it could be said that on those facts as believed by the applicant, snipping the strand of the wire, which she intended to do, could amount to something done to protect either the applicant's own home or the homes of her adjacent friends in Pembrokeshire. He decided, again quite rightly in our view, that that proposed act on her part was far too remote from the eventual aim at which she was targeting her actions to satisfy the test. It follows therefore, in our view, that the judges in the present two cases were absolutely right to come to the conclusion that they did so far as this aspect of the case is concerned, and to come to that conclusion as a matter of law, having decided the subjective test as the applicants wished them to be decided. The second half of the question was that of the immediacy of the danger. Here the wording of the Act, one reminds oneself, is as follows: She believed that the property ... was in immediate need of protection. Once again the judge had to determine whether, on the facts as stated by the applicant, there was any evidence on which it could be said that she believed there was a need of protection from immediate danger. In our view that must mean evidence that she believed that immediate action had to be taken to do something which would otherwise be a crime in order to prevent the immediate risk of something worse happening. The answers which I have read in the evidence given by this woman (and the evidence given by the other applicant was very similar) drives this Court to the conclusion, as they drove the respective judges to the conclusion, that there was no evidence on which it could be said that there was that belief.'

Jaggard v Dickinson [1981] QB 527 Divisional Court (Donaldson LJ and Mustill J)

Drunkenness as evidence of honest belief in owner's consent to the destruction of property

Facts

The defendant was convicted of criminal damage contrary to s1(1) of the 1971 Act, on facts that showed that she had broken into a house whilst drunk. She had mistaken it for the house of a friend, who she believed would have consented to her causing damage to gain access. She appealed on the ground that the magistrates had erred in refusing to take into account her drunken state as evidence that she had honestly believed she had the consent of the owner to damage the property.

Held

The appeal would be allowed.

Mustill J:

[Referred to ss1(1) and 5(2) of the 1971 Act and continued]

'It is convenient to refer to the exculpatory provisions of s5(2) as if they created a defence while recognising that the burden of disproving the facts referred to by the subsection remains on the prosecution. The magistrates held that the appellant was not entitled to rely on s5(2) since the belief relied on was brought about by a state of self-induced intoxication.

In support of the conviction counsel for the respondent advanced an argument which may be summarised as follows (i) where an offence is one of "basic intent", in contrast to one of "specific intent", the fact that the accused was in a state of self-induced intoxication at the time when he did the acts constituting the actus reus does not prevent him from possessing the mens rea necessary to constitute the offence: see *DPP* v *Morgan* [chapter 15] *DPP* v *Majewski* [chapter 14]. (ii) Section 1(1) of the 1971 Act creates an offence of basic intent: see *R* v *Stephenson* [1979] QB 695. (iii) Section 5 (3) has no bearing on the present issue. It does not create a separate defence, but is no more than a partial definition of the expression "without lawful excuse" in s1(1). The absence of lawful excuse forms an element in the mens rea: see *R* v *Smith* [1974] QB 354 at 360. Accordingly, since drunkenness does not negative mens rea in crimes of basic intent, it cannot be relied on as part of a defence based on s5(2).

Whilst this is an attractive submission, we consider it to be unsound, for the following reasons. In the first place, the argument transfers the distinction between offences of specific and of basic intent to a context in which it has no place. The distinction is material where the defendant relies on his own drunkenness as a ground for denying that he had the degree of intention or recklessness required in order to constitute the offence. Here, by contrast, the appellant does not rely on her drunkenness to displace an inference of intent or recklessness; indeed she does not rely on it at all. Her defence is founded on the state of belief called for by s5(2). True, the fact of the appellant's intoxication was relevant to the defence under s5(2) for it helped to explain what would otherwise have been inexplicable, and hence lent colour to her evidence about the state of her belief. This is not the same as using drunkenness to rebut an inference of intention or recklessness. Belief, like intention or recklessness, is a state of mind; but they are not the same states of mind.

Can it nevertheless be said that, even if the context is different, the principles established by *Majewski* ought to be applied to this new situation? If the basis of the decision in *Majewski* had been that drunkenness does not prevent a person from having an intent or being reckless, then there would be grounds for saying that it should equally be left out of account when deciding on his state of belief. But this is not in our view what *Majewski* decided. The House of Lords did not conclude that intoxication was irrelevant to the fact of the defendant's state of mind, but rather that, whatever might have been his actual state of mind, he should for reasons of policy be precluded from relying on any alteration in that state brought about by self-induced intoxication. The same considerations of policy apply to the intent or recklessness which is the mens rea of the offence created by s1(1) and that offence is accordingly regarded as one of basic intent (see *R* v *Stephenson*). It is indeed essential that this should be so, for drink so often plays a part in offences of criminal damage, and to admit drunkenness as a potential means of escaping liability would provide much too ready a means of avoiding conviction. But these considerations do not apply to a case where Parliament has specifically required the court to consider the defendant's actual state of belief, not the state of belief which ought to have existed. This seems to us to show that the court is required by s5(3) to focus on the existence of the belief, not its intellectual soundness; and a belief can be just as much honestly held if it is induced by intoxication as if it stems from stupidity, forgetfulness or inattention.

It was however, urged that we could not properly read s5(2) in isolation from s1(1), which forms the context of the words "without lawful excuse" partially defined by s5(2). Once the words are put in context, so it is maintained, it can be seen that the law must treat drunkenness in the same way in relation to lawful excuse (and hence belief) as it does to intention and recklessness, for they are all part of the mens rea of the offence. To fragment the mens rea, so as to treat one part of it as affected by drunkenness in one way and the remainder as affected in a different way, would make the law impossibly complicated to enforce.

If it had been necessary to decide whether, for all purposes, the mens rea of an offence under s1(1) extends as far as the intent (or recklessness) as to the existence of a lawful excuse, I should have wished to consider the observations of James LJ, delivering the judgment of the Court of Appeal in *R v Smith* [1974] QB 354 at 360. I do not however find it necessary to reach a conclusion on this matter and will only say that I am not at present convinced that, when these observations are read in the context of the judgment as a whole, they have the meaning which the respondent has sought to put on them. In my view, however, the answer to the argument lies in the fact that any distinctions which have to be drawn as to the relevance of drunkenness to the two subsections arises from the scheme of the 1971 Act itself. No doubt the mens rea is in general indivisible, with no distinction being possible as regards the effect of drunkenness. But Parliament has specifically isolated one subjective element, in the shape of honest belief, and has given it separate treatment and its own special gloss in s5(3). This being so, there is nothing objectionable in giving it special treatment as regards drunkenness, in accordance with the natural meaning of its words.

In these circumstances, I would hold that the magistrates were in error when they decided that the defence furnished to the appellant by s5(2) was lost because she was drunk at the time. I would therefore allow the appeal.'

R v Miller [1983] 2 WLR 539

See chapter 2.

R v Smith [1974] QB 354 Court of Appeal (Criminal Division) (Roskill, James, LJJ and Talbot J)

Mens rea of criminal damage

Facts

The defendant was the tenant of a flat. With the landlord's consent he installed some hi-fi equipment and soundproofing. When given notice to quit the flat, the defendant tore down the soundproofing to gain access to some wires that lay behind. Unknown to the defendant the soundproofing had, as a matter of law, become a fixture of the property and therefore property belonging to the landlord. The defendant was convicted of criminal damage contrary to s1(1) of the 1971 Act, and appealed on the ground that he had honestly believed that the property he had destroyed was his own.

Held

The appeal would be allowed and conviction quashed.

James LJ:

'The offence created includes the elements of intention or recklessness and the absence of lawful excuse. There is in section 5 of the Act a partial "definition" of lawful excuse ...

[After reading Section 5(2), (3), (5), his Lordship continued]

It is argued for the appellant that an honest, albeit erroneous, belief that the act causing damage or destruction was done to his own property provides a defence to a charge brought under section 1 (1). The argument is put in three ways. First, that the offence charged includes the act causing the damage or destruction and the element of mens rea. The element of mens rea relates to all the circumstances of the criminal act. The criminal act in the offence is causing damage to or destruction of "property belonging to another" and the element of mens rea, therefore, must relate to "property belonging to another". Honest belief, whether justifiable or not, that the property is the defendant's own negatives the element of mens rea. Secondly, it is argued that by the terms of section 5, in particular the words of subsection (2), "whether or not he would be treated for the purposes of this Act as having a lawful excuse apart from this subsection", and the words in subsection (5), the appellant had a lawful excuse in that he honestly believed he was entitled to do as he did to property he believed to be his own. This seems is the way the argument was put at the trial. Thirdly, it is argued, with understandable diffidence, that if a defendant honestly believes he is damaging his own property he has a lawful excuse for so doing because impliedly be believes that he is the person entitled to give consent to the damage being done and that he has consented; thus the case falls within section 5 (2) (a) of the Act.

We can dispose of the third way in which it is put immediately and briefly. Mr Gerber for the Crown argues that to apply section 5 (2) (a) to a case in which a defendant believes that he is causing damage to his own property involves a tortuous and unjustifiable construction of the wording. We agree. In our judgment, to hold that those words of section 5 (2) (a) are apt to cover a case of a person damaging the property of another in the belief that it is his own would be to strain the language of the section to an unwarranted degree. Moreover, in our judgment, it is quite unnecessary to have recourse to such a construction.

Mr. Gerber invited our attention to *Cambridgeshire and Isle of Ely County Council* v *Rust* [1972] 2 QB 426, a case under section 127 of the Highways Act 1959, concerning the pitching of a stall on a highway without lawful excuse. The case is cited as authority for the proposition that in order to establish a lawful excuse as a defence it must be shown that the defendant honestly but mistakenly believed on reasonable grounds that the facts were of a certain order, and that if those facts were of that order his conduct would have been lawful. Applying that proposition to the facts of the present case, Mr Gerber argues that the appellant cannot be said to have had a lawful excuse because in law the damaged property was part of the house and owned by the landlord. We have no doubt as to the correctness of the decision in the case cited. The proposition is argued here in relation to the appellant's contention that he had a lawful excuse and does not touch the argument based on absence of mens rea.

It is conceded by Mr Gerber that there is force in the argument that the element of mens rea extends to "property belonging to another". But, it is argued, the section creates a new statutory offence and that it is open to the construction that the mental element in the offence relates only to causing damage to or destroying property. That if in fact the property damaged or destroyed is shown to be another's property the offence is committed although the defendant did not intend or foresee damage to another person's property.

We are informed that so far as research has revealed this is the first occasion on which this court has had to consider the question which arises in this appeal.

It is not without interest to observe that, under the law in force before the passing of the Criminal Damage Act 1971, it was clear that no offence was committed by a person who destroyed or damaged property belonging to another in the honest but mistaken belief that the property was his own or that he had a legal right to do the damage. In *R* v *Twose* (1879) 14 Cox CC 327 the prisoner was indicted for setting fire to furze on a common. Persons living near the common had occasionally burned the furze in order to improve the growth of grass but without the right to do so. The prisoner denied setting fire to the furze and it was submitted that even if it were proved that she did she could not be found guilty if she bona fide believed she had a right to do so whether the right were a good one or not. Lopes J. ruled that if she set fire to the furze thinking she had a right to do so that would not be a criminal offence.

Upon the facts of the present appeal the charge, if brought before the Act of 1971 came into force, would have been laid under section 13 of the Malicious Damage Act 1861, alleging damage by a tenant to a building. It was a defence to a charge under that section that the tenant acted under a claim of right to do the damage.

If the direction given by the deputy judge in the present case is correct, then the offence created by section 1(1) of the Act of 1971 involves a considerable extension of the law in a surprising direction. Whether or not this is so depends upon the construction of the section. Construing the language of section 1(1) we have no doubt that the actus reus is "destroying or damaging any property belonging to another". It is not possible to exclude the words "belonging to another" which describes the "property". Applying the ordinary principles of mens rea, the intention and recklessness and the absence of lawful excuse required to constitute the offence have reference to property belonging to another. It follows that in our judgment no offence is committed under this section if a person destroys or causes damage to property belonging to another if he does so in the honest though mistaken belief that the property is his own, and provided that the belief is honestly held it is irrelevant to consider whether or not it is a justifiable belief.

In our judgment, the direction given to the jury was a fundamental misdirection in law. The consequence was that the jury were precluded from considering facts capable of being a defence to the charge and were directed to convict ...'

R v Steer [1987] 3 WLR 205 House of Lords (Lords Bridge, Griffiths, Ackner, Oliver and Goff)

Aggravated criminal damage - mens rea as to the endangering of life

Facts

The defendant, who had been in dispute with a business partner, fired an automatic rifle at the bedroom window of his partner's house. The bedroom was occupied at the time. The defendant pleaded guilty to s1(1) criminal damage, and following a ruling by the trial judge, pleaded guilty to a charge under s1(2)(b) of causing criminal damage being reckless as to whether life would be endangered. The defendant appealed against the conviction under s1(2)(b), on the ground that he had not intended that the criminal damage to the window should endanger life, and therefore lacked the mens rea for the aggravated offence. The Court of Appeal allowed the appeal, and the prosecutor appealed to the House of Lords. The question certified for consideration by their Lordships was: whether upon a true construction of s1(2) (b) of the Criminal Damage Act 1971, the prosecution are required to prove that the danger to life resulted from the destruction of or damage to the property, or whether it is sufficient for the prosecution to prove that it resulted from the act of the defendant which caused the destruction or damage.

Held

The appeal would be dismissed

Lord Bridge:

'Under both limbs of section 1 of the Act of 1971 it is the essence of the offence which the section creates that the defendant has destroyed or damaged property. For the purpose of analysis it may be convenient to omit reference to destruction and to concentrate on the references to damage, which was all that was here involved. To be guilty under subsection (1) the defendant must have intended or been reckless as to the damage to property which he caused. To be guilty under subsection (2) he must additionally have intended to endanger life or been reckless as to whether life would be endangered "by the damage" to property which he caused. This is the context in which the words must be construed and it seems to me impossible to read the words "by the damage" as meaning "by the damage or by the act which caused the damage." Moreover, if the language of the statute has the meaning for which the Crown contends, the words "by the destruction or damage" and "thereby" in subsection (2)(b) are mere surplusage. If the Crown's submission is right, the only additional element necessary to convert a subsection (1) offence into a subsection (2) offence is an intent to endanger life or recklessness as to whether life would be endangered simpliciter.

It would suffice as a ground for dismissing this appeal if the statute were ambiguous, since any such ambiguity in a criminal statute should be resolved in favour of the defence. But I can find no ambiguity. It seems to me that the meaning for which the respondent contends is the only meaning which the language can bear.

The contrary construction leads to anomalies which Parliament cannot have intended. If A and B both discharge firearms in a public place, being reckless as to whether life would be endangered, it would be absurd that A, who incidentally causes some trifling damage to property, should be guilty of an offence punishable with life imprisonment, but that B, who causes no damage, should be guilty of no offence. In the same circumstances, if A is merely reckless but B actually intends to endanger life, it is scarcely less absurd that A should be guilty of the graver offence under section 1(2) of the Act of 1971, B of the lesser offence under section 16 of the Firearms Act 1968.

Counsel for the Crown did not shrink from arguing that section 1(2) of the Act of 1971 had created, in effect, a general offence of endangering life with intent or recklessly, however the danger was caused, but had incidentally included as a necessary, albeit insignificant, ingredient of the offence that some damage to property should also be caused. In certain fields of legislation it is sometimes difficult to appreciate the rationale of particular provisions, but in a criminal statute it would need the clearest language to persuade me that the legislature had acted so irrationally, indeed perversely, as acceptance of this argument would imply.

It was further argued that to affirm the construction of section 1(2)(b) adopted by the Court of Appeal would give rise to problems in other cases in which it might be difficult or even impossible to distinguish between the act causing damage to property and the ensuing damage caused as the source of danger to life. In particular it was suggested that in arson cases the jury would have to be directed that they could only convict if the danger to life arose from falling beams or similar damage caused by the fire, not if the danger arose from the heat, flames or smoke generated by the fire itself. Arson is, of course, the prime example of a form of criminal damage to property which, in the case of an occupied building, necessarily involves serious danger to life and where the gravity of the consequence which may result as well from recklessness as from a specific intent fully justifies the severity of the penalty which the Act of 1971 provides for the offence. But the argument in this case is misconceived. It is not the match and the inflammable materials, the flaming firebrand or any other inflammatory agent which the arsonist uses to start the fire which causes danger to life, it is the ensuing conflagration which occurs as the property which has been set on fire is damaged or destroyed. When the victim in the bedroom is overcome by the smoke or incinerated by the flames as the building burns, it would be absurd to say that this does not result from the damage to the building.

Counsel for the Crown put forward other examples of cases which he suggested ought to be liable to prosecution under section 1(2) of the Act of 1971 including that of the angry mob of striking miners who throw a hail of bricks through the window of the cottage occupied by the working miner and that of people who drop missiles from motorway bridges on passing vehicles. I believe that the criminal law provides adequate sanctions for these cases without the need to resort to section 1(2) of the Act of 1971. But if my belief is mistaken, this would still be no reason to distort the plain meaning of that subsection.

Some reference was also made to damage caused by explosives. This is the subject of specific provision under the Explosive Substances Act 1883 (46 & 47 Vict c 3) as amended. The offence created by section 3(1)(a) of that Act as substituted by section 7(1) of the Criminal Jurisdiction Act 1975, of doing "any act with intent to cause ... by an explosive substance an explosion of a nature likely to endanger life, or cause serious injury to property" obviates the need to resort to the Act of 1971 when explosives are used.

The trial judge was, it seems, in large part persuaded to rule as he did in reliance on a sentence from the judgment of the Court of Appeal (Criminal Division) delivered by Parker LJ in *R v Hardie* [1985] 1 WLR 64, 67 where he said in reference to the state of mind of a defendant who commits the actus reus of an alleged offence under section 1(2) of the Act of 1971:

"If, when doing that act, he creates an obvious risk both that property will be destroyed and that the life of another will be endangered and gives no thought to the possibility of there being either risk, the requirements of the subsection are in our judgment clearly satisfied."

R v Hardie was concerned solely with the effect of self-administered tranquillising drugs on the state of mind of the defendant. It had nothing whatever to do with the issue of causation arising in the instant case. If I may say so without offence, the judge's error vividly illustrates the danger, which is particularly acute in the field of statutory construction, of reading a judicial dictum entirely out of context and treating the precise words used as relevant to the decision of an issue to which the author of the words had never applied his mind.

I can well understand that the prosecution in this case thought it necessary and appropriate that, even if they could not establish the intent to endanger life necessary to support a conviction under section 16 of the Act of 1968 they should include a count in the indictment to mark in some way the additional gravity of an offence of criminal damage to property in which a firearm is used. But they had no need to resort to section 1(2) of the Act of 1971. A person who, at the time of committing an offence under section 1 of the Act of 1971, has in his possession a firearm commits a distinct offence under section 17(2) of the Act of 1968: see Schedule 1 to the Act of 1968, as amended by section 11(7) of the Act of 1971. If the respondent had been charged with that offence in addition to the offence under section 1(1) of the Act of 1971, he must have pleaded guilty to both and, if the prosecution were content to accept that there was no intent to endanger life, this would have been amply sufficient to mark the gravity of the respondent's criminal conduct in the incident at the Gregory bungalow. I would accordingly dismiss the appeal. The certified question should be answered as follows:

"Upon the true construction of section 1(2)(b) of the Criminal Damage Act 1971 the prosecution are required to prove that the danger to life resulted from the destruction of or damage to property; it is not sufficient for the prosection to prove that it resulted from the act of the defendant which caused the destruction or damage." '

R v Whiteley (1991) The Times 6 February

Computer program - whether property capable of being damaged

Facts

The appellant gained unauthorised access to a computer network, the Joint Academic Network (JANET). Using his skill and knowledge of such systems he created and deleted files, changed the passwords of authorised users, and deleted the user file to remove evidence of his own use of the system. The appellant was convicted on a number of counts of criminal damage. The appellant's main ground of appeal was that the magnetic disks on which the system's files were stored had not themselves been damaged by his activities, hence the only damage was to the information stored on the discs, and this fell outside the scope of the offence as it was intangible property.

Held

The appeal would be dismissed. The magnetic disks on which files were stored were clearly tangible property, and by deleting files, the appellant had interfered with the configuration of magnetic particles on the disks. The result was damage to tangible property.

Commentary

The Lord Chief Justice pointed out that it was wrong to conclude that, because the offence of criminal damage required interference with tangible property, the damage itself had to be tangible, in the sense that it had to be observable to the naked eye, or perceptible by touch. Any alteration to the physical nature of the property would suffice.

It is interesting to note that the jury acquitted the appellant in respect of the prosecution's other allegations of criminal damage, which had been based on the premise that the appellant had damaged the computer system itself as his activities caused it to be shut down for long periods whilst the effects of his interference were rectified. See further, the Computer Misuse Act 1990.

4 NON-FATAL OFFENCES AGAINST THE PERSON I

Attorney-General's Reference (No 6 of 1980) [1981] QB 715 Court of Appeal (Criminal Division) (Lord Lane CJ, Phillips and Drake JJ)

Extent of consent as defence to a charge of assault

Facts

See the extract from the judgment of Lord Lane CJ.

The following point of law was referred to the Court of Appeal upon which the court was asked to provide its opinion:

'Where two persons fight (otherwise than in the course of sport) in a public place can it be a defence for one of those persons to a charge of assault arising out of the fight that the other consented to the fight?'

Held

A fight between two persons would be unlawful, whether in public or private, if it involved the infliction of at least actual bodily harm, or if actual bodily harm or worse was intended. This would make most fights between people wishing to 'settle their differences' in this manner unlawful.

Lord Lane CJ:

'The facts out of which the reference arises are these. The respondent, aged 18, and a youth aged 17 met in a public street and argued together. The respondent and the youth decided to settle the argument there and then by a fight. Before the fight the respondent removed his watch and handed it to a bystander for safe keeping and the youth removed his jacket. The respondent and the youth exchanged blows with their fists and the youth sustained a bleeding nose and bruises to his face caused by blows from the respondent.

Two issues arose at the trial: (1) self defence and (2) consent. The learned judge directed the jury in part as follows: "Secondly, if both parties consent to a fight then that fight may be lawful. In that respect I disagree with Mr Inglis' description of the law. It may well be that a fight on the pavement is a breach of the peace or fighting in public or some other offence but it does not necessarily mean that both parties are guilty of an assault. So that if two people decide to fight it out with their fists then that is not necessarily an assault. If they use weapons or something of that nature, other considerations apply. So you have to consider those two matters in this case. Was [the youth] acting in self-defence? Was this a case of both parties agreeing to fight and using only reasonable force?"

Thus the jury were directed that the respondent would, or might, not be guilty of assault if the victim agreed to fight, and the respondent only used reasonable force. The respondent was acquitted.

At the hearing of the reference, Mr Rougier, QC and Mr Inglis appeared for the Attorney-General. Mr Rougier submitted that this direction was incorrect, that the answer to the point of law was "No," and that if an act (ordinarily constituting an assault) is unlawful *per se*, no amount of consent can render it lawful. Thus an act committed in public might, he submitted, be an assault, even though it would not be if committed in private, since if committed in public it would be a breach of the peace and for that reason unlawful.

Mr Allan Green appeared as *amicus curiae*, and drew the attention of the Court to the relevant authorities and text books. He pointed out that though the conclusions in the cases are reasonably consistent, the reasons for them are not.

For convenience we use the word "assault" as including "battery," and adopt the definition of James J in *Fagan* v *Metropolitan Police Commissioner* (1968) 52 Cr App R 700, 703; [1969] 1 QB 439, 444, namely: "… the actual intended use of unlawful force to another person without his consent," to which we would respectfully add "or any other lawful excuse."

We think that it can be taken as a starting point that it is an essential element of an assault that the act is done contrary to the will and without the consent of the victim; and it is doubtless for this reason that the burden lies on the prosecution to negative consent. Ordinarily, then, if the victim consents, the assailant is not guilty.

But the cases show that the Courts will make an exception to this principle where the public interest requires: *Coney* (1882) 8 QBD 534 (the Prize Fight case). The 11 judges were of opinion that a prize fight is illegal, that all persons aiding and abetting were guilty of assault, and that the consent of the actual fighters was irrelevant. Their reasons varied as follows: Cave J, that the blow was struck in anger and likely to do corporal hurt, as opposed to one struck in sport, not intended to cause bodily harm; Matthew J, the dangerous nature of the proceedings; Stephen J, what was done was injurious to the public, depending on the degree of force and the place used; Hawkins J, the likelihood of a breach of the peace, and the degree of force and injury; Coleridge CJ, breach of the peace and protection of the public.

The judgment in *Donovan* (1934) 24 Cr App R 1; [1934] 2 KB 498 (beating for the purposes of sexual gratification), the reasoning in which seems to be tautologous, proceeds upon a different basis, starting with the proposition that consent is irrelevant if the act complained of is "unlawful … in itself," which it will be if it involves the infliction of bodily harm.

Bearing in mind the various cases and the views of the text book writers cited to us, and starting with the proposition that ordinarily an act consented to will not constitute an assault, the question is: at what point does the public interest require the Court to hold otherwise?

In answering this question the diversity of view expressed in the previous decisions, such as the two cases cited, make some selection and a partly new approach necessary. Accordingly we have not followed the dicta which would make an act (even if consensual) an assault if it occurred in public, on the ground that it constituted a breach of the peace, and was therefore itself unlawful. These dicta reflect the conditions of the times when they were uttered, when there was little by way of an established police force and prize fights were a source of civil disturbance. Today with regular policing, conditions are different. Statutory offences, and indeed bye-laws, provide a sufficient sanction against true cases of public disorder, as do the common law offences of affray, etc. Nor have we followed the Scottish case of *Smart* v *HM Advocate,* 1975 SLT 65, holding the consent of the victim to be irrelevant on a charge of assault, guilt depending upon the "evil intent" of the accused, irrespective of the harm done.

The answer to this question, in our judgment, is that it is not in the public interest that people should try to cause or should cause each other actual bodily harm for no good reason. Minor struggles are another matter. So, in our judgment, it is immaterial whether the act occurs in private or in public; it is an assault if actual bodily harm is intended and/or caused. This means that most fights will be unlawful regardless of consent.

Nothing which we have said is intended to cast doubt upon the accepted legality of properly conducted games and sports, lawful chastisement or correction, reasonable surgical interference, dangerous exhibitions, etc. These apparent exceptions can be justified as involving the exercise of a legal right, in the case of chastisement or correction, or as needed in the public interest, in the other cases.

Our answer to the point of law is No, but not (as the reference implies) because the fight occurred in the public place, but because, wherever it occurred, the participants would have been guilty of assault (subject to self-defence) if (as we understand was the case) they intended to and/or did cause actual bodily harm.

The point of law referred to us by the Attorney-General has revealed itself as having been the subject of much interesting legal and philosophical debate, but it does not seem that the particular uncertainty enshrined in the reference has caused practical inconvenience in the administration of justice during the last few hundred years. We would not wish our judgment on the point to be the signal for unnecessary prosecutions.'

R v Brown [1992] 2 WLR 441 Court of Appeal (Criminal Division) Lord Lane CJ, Rose and Potts JJ)

Extent to which victims consent can negative an assault.

Facts

The appellants were members of a group of sado-masochistic homosexuals. Members of the group carried out acts of violence on each other, from which they derived sexual gratification. The appellants were charged on a number of counts alleging (inter alia) offences under ss47 and 20 of the Offences Against the Person Act 1861. Following the trial judge's ruling that the willing consent by the victim of such assaults did not amount to a defence, the appellants charged their pleas to guilty, and appealed against conviction.

Held

The appeal would be dismissed.

Lord, Lane CJ:

'... It is contended that it was inappropriate to lay charges under the Offences against the Person Act 1861, which, it is said, was not intended to apply to consensual actions in private not causing serious injury, particularly where such actions are merely incidents of private sexual behaviour.

If these events had been merely incidents in the course of private activities, whether homosexual or heterosexual, then no doubt different considerations would have applied. Where, however, as here, there has admittedly been inflicted either wounding or actual bodily harm, it was in our judgment both permissible and correct to lay charges under the Act of 1861 ...

Thirdly, and this is the real nub of the appeal, it is contended that the consent of the victim in these circumstances prevents the prosecution from proving an essential element of the offence whether charged under s20 or s47 of the Act of 1861.'

His Lordship referred to the provisions of s20 and s47 of the 1861 Act, and continued:

'Generally speaking, the prosecution in order to bring home a charge of assault, must prove that the victim did not consent to the defendant's actions, an assault being any unlawful touching of another without that other's consent. There are, however, certain circumstances in which the law does not permit a defendant to rely, so to speak, on the victim's consent. The victim's consent to being killed would provide no excuse for the killer. Where the assault to which consent is given involves permanent injury or maiming - eg the severing of a limb - there is no dispute that the victim's consent is immaterial.

It is however contended that the same considerations do not apply where there is no permanent injury, even though the assault may have amounted to grievous bodily harm or wounding.

The classic authority is *Reg* v *Coney* (1882) 8 QBD 534. That was the prize-fight case in which a number of views were expressed by the 11 judges who heard the case. Cave J said at p539:

"The true view is, I think, that a blow struck in anger, or which is likely to is intended to do corporal hurt, is an assault ... and that, an assault being a breach of the peace and unlawful, the consent of the person struck is immaterial."

The other judges gave varying reasons for holding that the consent of the fighters was immaterial.'

Having referred to *R v Donovan* and *Attorney-General's Reference (No 6 of 1980)*, his Lordship concluded:

'It is sufficient to say, so far as the instant case is concerned, that we agree with the trial judge that the satisfying of sado-masochistic libido does not come within the category of good reason nor can the injuries be described as merely transient or trifling.

It was submitted to us that the facts in that case were so different from those in the instant case that the principle which is expressed in the answer to the Attorney-General's question does not apply to the present circumstances. We disagree. In our judgment the principle as expressed in *Attorney-General's Reference (No 6 of 1980)* [1981] QB 715 does apply. Consequently for those reasons the question of consent was immaterial. The judge's ruling was accordingly correct.

Any attempt to distinguish between offences coming within s18 of the Act of 1861, and those coming within s20 or s47 would, it seems to us, be almost impossible to draw. Miss Worrall, on behalf of the appellant Laskey, at one stage seemed to be arguing for such a distinction, on the basis that absence of consent must be proved in cases under s20 and 47 of the Act, but not in those laid under s18. We gathered that she eventually abandoned that contention.

Many of the s47 charges could equally well have been laid under s20 and the only distinction between s20 and s18 is the intent of the defendant, and not the degree of violence.'

Coffin v Smith (1980) 71 Cr App R 221 Divisional Court (Donaldson LJ and Bristow J)

Scope of a police officer's duty

Facts

The defendant assaulted a police officer who had been called to deal with a group of 'gatecrashers' at a youth club disco. It was accepted that no offences had been committed by the defendant up to this point, but he was nevertheless charged with assaulting a police officer in the execution of his duty. The justices upheld a submission of no case to answer on the basis that the police officer had not been under any duty to compel the defendant to leave the scene. The prosecutor appealed.

Donaldson LJ:

'I am bound to say, speaking for myself, that when I read this case through overnight, I regarded this decision as prima facie perverse and incomprehensible. We have had the advantage today of very full argument from Mr Staddon, for the defendants, who plainly considers, and quite firmly considers, that this case raises an issue of considerable constitutional importance. I can well understand the justices, having been told that there was such an issue involved here and having been exposed to the skill with which his arguments were no doubt deployed there as they were deployed before us, reaching the decision that they did reach. I remain however of opinion that it was wholly and completely wrong. Let me justify that.

The whole basis of Mr Staddon's argument is that a police officer is not in the execution of his duty if he is doing something that he is not compelled by law to do. He relies upon two old cases. The first is *Prebble and Others* (1858) 1 F & F 325, a nisi prius decision briefly reported. There the prisoners were indicted for assaulting a constable in the execution of his duty, and also for common assault. It appears that some persons were drinking at a late hour of the night in a barn attached to a public house and the landlord desired the constable to clear them out. While he was doing so the prisoners assaulted him.

In the words of Bramwell B at pp325, 326 "the people were doing nothing illegal, or contrary to any Act of Parliament, and therefore the constable was not acting in the execution of his duty as such, although what he did may have been very laudable and proper. It would have been otherwise had there been a nuisance or disturbance of the public peace, or any danger of a breach of the peace."

The second is *Roxburgh* (1971) 12 Cox CC 8, a decision of Cockburn J. It appears from the report that "The prisoner had been drinking at a public house and was so much the worse for liquor that the publican desired to get him out and called in a constable. The man had wanted to go to bed, and the publican had assented to this, but the man desired a light, with which, on account of his condition, the publican refused to entrust him. Thereupon the prisoner said he would leave, and then said he would not, and upon this the publican desired the prosecutor to assist in ejecting him which he attempted to do. In resisting him the prisoner inflicted a serious injury, for which he was indicted. The defence was, that the violence used by the prosecutor was unlawful, as he had no right to use force to eject the prisoner, and was acting beyond his duty in doing so ..."

Cockburn J said at p9 that "although, no doubt, the prosecutor might not have been acting – strictly speaking – in the execution of his duty as a police officer, since he was not actually obliged to assist in ejecting the prisoner, yet he was acting quite lawfully in doing so; for the landlord had a right to eject the prisoner under the circumstances, and the prosecutor might lawfully assist him in so doing."

It must of course be appreciated that those decisions were under a different statute, slightly differently worded. They are authorities supporting the proposition for which Mr Staddon contended, but I do not for my part think that they can be regarded as good law today. The modern law on the subject is, I think, to be found in two different cases. The first is a decision of the Court of Criminal Appeal, *Waterfield and Lynn* (1963) 48 Cr App R 42; [1964] 1 QB 164, where Ashworth J delivering the judgment of the Court, at p47 and 170 respectively said: "In the judgment of this court it would be difficult, and in the present case it is unnecessary, to reduce within specific limits the general terms in which the duties of police constables have been expressed. In most cases it is probably more convenient to consider what the police constable was actually doing and in particular whether such conduct was prima facie an unlawful interference with a person's liberty or property. If so, it is then relevant to consider whether (a) such conduct falls within the general scope of any duty imposed by statute or recognised at common law and (b) whether such conduct, albeit within the general scope of such a duty, involved an unjustifiable use of powers associated with the duty."

Applying that basis, it is quite clear that these constables were on duty, they were in uniform and they were not doing anything which was prima facie any unlawful interference with a person's liberty or property.

Further guidance on the scope of the police officer's duty in this context is I think to be derived from the judgment of Lord Parker CJ in *Rice* v *Connolly* [1966] 2 QB 414, and the passage to which I would like to refer is at p419:

"It is also in my judgment clear that it is part of the obligations and duties of a police constable to take all steps which appear to him necessary for keeping the peace, for preventing crime or for protecting property from criminal injury. There is no exhaustive definition of the powers and obligations of the police, but they are at least those, and they would further include the duty to detect crime and to bring an offender to justice."

In a word a police officer's duty is to be a keeper of the peace and to take all necessary steps with that in view. These officers, just like the ordinary officer on the beat, were attending a place where they thought that their presence would assist in the keeping of the peace. I know that Mr Staddon says "Oh no, this is all part and parcel of the assistance which they gave to the youth leader in ejecting these people." Even if that was so, they would have been doing no more than a police officer's duty in all the circumstances. In fact it is clear that there was a break. Both the respondents went away and came back. The officers were in effect simply standing there on their beat in the execution of their duty when they were assaulted. This is a very clear case indeed.'

Hills v Ellis [1983] QB 680 Divisional Court (Griffiths LJ and McCullough J)

Meaning of 'wilful' in the context of s51(3) Police Act 1964

Facts

The defendant had witnessed a fight outside a football ground. He later saw the innocent party in the fight being arrested by a police officer. He grabbed the officer's elbow and shouted at him in order to alert him to what the defendant feared would be a miscarriage of justice. The policeman told the defendant to desist, but he refused. The defendant was convicted under s51(3) of the Police Act 1964, and appealed to the Divisional Court.

Held

The appeal would be dismissed.

Griffiths LJ:

'There can be no doubt in this case that there was an obstruction within the meaning of that definition. The appellant was actually grabbing hold of the officer when in very difficult conditions, at the end of a football match, he was trying to arrest a man. Lord Parker CJ then continues to consider the element of wilfulness in the offence, and he says: "The only remaining ingredient, and the one upon which in my judgment this case revolves, is whether the obstructing of which the defendant was guilty was a wilful obstruction. 'Wilful' in this context not only in my judgment means 'intentional' but something which is done without lawful excuse, and that indeed is conceded by counsel."

What is submitted in this case on behalf of the defendant is that his action was not wilful in the sense of being done without lawful excuse, because he had a moral duty to draw to the attention of the officer that he was arresting the wrong man. I cannot accept that submission. Here was an officer, acting in the course of his duty, arresting a man. It would be quite intolerable if citizens, who may genuinely believe the wrong man was arrested, were entitled to lay hands on the police and obstruct them in that arrest because they thought that some other person should be arrested. One has only got to state the proposition to see the enormous abuse to which any such power on the part of the citizen might be put. A private citizen has no lawful excuse to interfere with a lawful arrest by a police officer. Accordingly, he was acting without lawful excuse within the definition as stated by Lord Parker CJ in *Rice v Connolly* [below]

The only other authority cited in support of the defendant's submission is *Willmott v Atack* [1977] QB 498; [1976] 3 All ER 794. The facts in that case were very different. A police officer was attempting to restrain a man under arrest and to get him into a police car. The defendant intervened, not with the intention of making it more difficult for the police officer to get the man into the police car, but with the intention of helping the officer. But due to the clumsiness of his intervention, the man in fact escaped. There is no doubt that in those circumstances the first part of the definition of "wilfully obstructing" has been fulfilled. The officer had, in fact, been obstructed, but the Court held that it had not been a wilful obstruction. Croom-Johnson J expressed the view of the Court in the following way at pp504 and 800 respectively: "When one looks at the whole context of section 51, dealing as it does with assaults on constables in subsection (1) and concluding in subsection (3) with resistance and wilful obstruction in their execution of their duty, I am of the view that the interpretation of this subsection for which the appellant contends is the right one. It fits the words 'wilfully obstructs' in the context of the subsection, and in my view there must be something in the nature of a criminal intent of the kind which means that it is done with the idea of some form of hostility to the police with the intention of seeing that what is done is to obstruct, and that it is not merely enough to show that he intended to do what he did and that it did, in fact, have the result of the police being obstructed."

The defendant's counsel argues from that passage that as the motive here was merely to correct a policeman's error, it cannot be said that he, the defendant, was acting with any hostility towards the police. But in my view, the phrase "hostility towards the police" in that passage means no more than that the actions of the defendant are aimed at the police. There can be no doubt here that his action in grabbing the policeman's arm was aimed at the policeman. It was an attempt to get that policeman to desist from the arrest that he was making. In my view, this is as clear a case as we can have of obstructing a police officer in the course of his duty, and the justices came to the right decision. But as always, one finds the justices took a very sensible view of the overall circumstances, and being satisfied of the defendant's overall motive, they gave him an absolute discharge.'

McCullough J:

'What is meant by an "intention to obstruct"? I would construe "wilfully obstructs" as doing deliberate actions with the intention of bringing about a state of affairs which, objectively regarded, amount to an obstruction as that phrase was explained by Lord Parker CJ in *Rice* v *Connolly* [1966] 2 QB 414, 419B *ie* making it more difficult for the police to carry out their duty. The fact that the defendant might not himself have called that state of affairs an obstruction is, to my mind, immaterial. This is not to say that it is enough to do deliberate actions which, in fact, obstruct; there must be an intention that those actions should result in the further state of affairs to which I have been referring.

If I may give an example: D interferes while a police officer, P, is arresting X, and delays the arrest. It is not enough that his deliberate actions in fact delay the arrest. If D intends to prevent P from arresting X, then D is guilty because it is his intention to do that which objectively regarded amounts to an obstruction, that is to say, to prevent the arrest. D's motives for wanting to prevent the arrest are immaterial. He is guilty even though he feels no hostility to the officer. He is guilty even though he believes the officer is arresting the wrong man. He is guilty even though he does not appreciate that interfering with the arrest amounts to what would be regarded objectively as an obstruction.

It may very well be that what I have been endeavouring to express would accord with Croom-Johnson J's opinion. I am not certain that May J in his three paragraph judgment was adopting what Croom-Johnson J had said about hostility. But even if he was, I think that what I have said can stand with his judgment. The Lord Chief Justice's judgment is in two sentences. He did not adopt the reasoning of the other two judges. He merely said that the question posed should be answered in the negative. The question is to be found at p502F. It is in the form: "whether it is sufficient for the prosecution to prove that the defendant wilfully did an act which obstructed the police officer in the execution of his duty or must it also be proved that ... ?" It is quite plain that in saying that the question must be answered in the negative, Lord Widgery CJ was referring only to the first part of the question.

The facts found by the Crown Court in *Willmott* v *Atack* are not easy to reconcile with one another. Although it is said, at pp499F and 796C respectively, that Willmott attempted to interfere and in doing so pushed the officer in the throat while he was holding and restraining the other man, Howe, who was under arrest, the Court did not see that as an assault (see p500E and p796H); and although Willmott's actions were found to be deliberate (*ibid*), the court did not anywhere say in terms that he was trying to prevent the arrest or secure the man's release. For these reasons it is, in my judgment, impossible to derive much assistance from the facts of that case.

It is to be noted that in *Green* v *Moore* (1982) 74 Cr App R 250, 262; [1982] QB 1044, 1052, Donaldson LJ in speaking of *Willmott* v *Atack*, and when comparing the facts of the case he was considering with *Willmott* v *Atack*, did not speak in terms of hostility.

When one comes to the facts of this case, all the essentials are present. The defendant deliberately grabs the officer. In so doing be intended to intervene on behalf of the person whom the officer was arresting. He intended to cause the officer to revise his decision to arrest that man. It is therefore clear that he intended to do that which in fact amounted to an obstruction of the officer, namely, to interfere with his actions in arresting and detaining the man. His motive for intending to interfere in this way is irrelevant. The fact that he may have harboured no feeling of hostility towards the officer is likewise irrelevant. So too, it is irrelevant whether or not he realised that interfering with an arrest was an obstruction as that word is generally understood.'

R v Kimber [1983] 1 WLR 1118 Court of Appeal (Criminal Division) (Lawton LJ, Michael Davies and Sheldon J)

Mistake as to the consent of the victim

Facts

The defendant was convicted of indecently assaulting a female patient at a mental hospital contrary to s14 Sexual Offences Act 1956. He appealed on the ground that he had honestly thought she was consenting to his actions.

Held

The appeal would be allowed.

The jury had been misdirected to the extent that the trial judge should have explained to them that if the defendant had honestly believed that the victim was consenting to his actions he would not have had the *mens rea* necessary for the offence. His belief in her consent did not have to be reasonable, merely honest. On the facts, however, it was evident that even if the jury had been properly directed the defendant would still have been convicted, and on that basis the appeal would be dismissed.

Lawton LJ:

'The appeal raise these points. First, can a defendant charged with an indecent assault on a woman raise the defence that he believed she had consented to what he did? The trial judge, Mr Recorder Smyth QC, ruled that he could not. Secondly, if he could, did the jury have to consider merely whether his belief was honestly held or, if it was, did they have to go on to consider whether it was based on reasonable grounds? Another way of putting these points is to ask whether the principles upon which the House of Lords decided *R* v *Morgan* [1976] AC 182, should be applied to a charge of indecent assault on a woman ...

The burden of proving lack of consent rests upon the prosecution ... The consequence is that the prosecution has to prove that the defendant intended to lay hands on his victim without her consent. If he did not intend to do this, he is entitled to be found not guilty; and if he did not so intend because he believed she was consenting, the prosecution will have failed to prove the charge. It is the defendant's belief, not the grounds on which it was based, which goes to negative the intent.

In analysing the issue in this way we have followed what was said by the majority in *R* v *Morgan* ... If, as we adjudge, the prohibited act in indecent assault is the use of personal violence to a woman without her consent, then the guilty state of mind is the intent to do it without her consent. Then, as in rape at common law, the inexorable logic, to which Lord Hailsham referred in *R* v *Morgan*, takes over and there is no room either for a "defence" of honest belief or mistake, or of a "defence" of honest and reasonable belief or mistake ... The application of the *Morgan* principle to offences other than indecent assault on a woman will have to be considered when such offences come before the courts. We do, however, think it necessary to consider two of them because of what was said in the judgments. The first is a decision of the Divisional Court in *Albert* v *Lavin* [1982] AC 546. The offence charged was assaulting a police officer in the execution of his duty, contrary to section 51 of the Police Act 1964. The defendant in his defence contended, inter alia, that he had not believed the police officer to be such and in consequence had resisted arrest. His counsel analysed the offence in the same way as we have done and referred to the reasoning in Morgan. Hodgson J, delivering the leading judgment, rejected this argument and in so doing said, at pp561-562:

"But in my judgment Mr Walker's ingenious argument fails at an earlier stage. It does not seem to me that the element of unlawfulness can properly be regarded as part of the definitional elements of the offence. In defining a criminal offence the word "unlawful" is surely tautologous and can add nothing to its essential ingredients ... And no matter how strange it may seem that a defendant charged with assault can escape conviction if he shows that he mistakenly but unreasonably thought his victim was consenting but not if he was in the same state of mind as to whether his victim had a right to detain him, that in my judgment is the law."

We have found difficulty in agreeing with this reasoning, even though the judge seems to be accepting that belief in consent does entitle a defendant to an aquittal on a charge of assault. We cannot accept that the word "unlawful" when used in a definition of an offence is to be regarded as "tautologous " In our judgment the word "unlawful" does import an essential element into the offence. If it were not there social life would be unbearable, because every touching would amount to a battery unless there was an evidential basis for a defence ...'

Commentary

See further chapter 15.

Lewis v Cox [1984] 3 WLR 875 Divisional Court

(Kerr LJ and Webster J)

Police Act 1964 s51(3) - whether obstruction 'wilful'

Facts

The defendant had been present at the scene of the arrest of another man named Marsh, who had been placed in the back of a police van. The defendant opened the rear doors of the van to inquire of Marsh where he was being taken. The prosecuting officer shut the doors of the van before Marsh was able to reply, whereupon the defendant opened the doors a second time and renewed his inquiries of Marsh. The defendant was thereupon arrested for wilful obstruction of a police officer in the execution of his duty. The defendant was acquitted by the justices, a decision from which the prosecution now appealed.

Held

The appeal would be allowed.

Webster J:

'The justices found as a fact that the opening of the rear door of the van by the defendant was not aimed at the police, and that he did not intend to obstruct the police.

It was accepted by counsel on behalf of the defendant that the arrest of Marsh was lawful, and that the defendant's conduct in opening the door on the second occasion in fact obstructed the police because it prevented the prosecutor from driving the police vehicle away, which he would have done had the defendant not opened the door. The contention before the justices, which was substantially the same as the contention made on his behalf before this court, was that the defendant did not wilfully obstruct the police because his actions were not aimed at the police. The expression "aimed at the police" is an expression taken from the judgment of Griffiths LJ in *Hills* v *Ellis* [1983] QB 680, 685, to which I will refer more fully later in this judgment. The justices considered that the principle laid down by the decision in that case was that a person is guilty of wilful obstruction of a police constable in the execution of his duty if he deliberately does some act which is aimed at the police and if that act, viewed objectively, obstructs the police. They concluded that on the evidence before them the defendant had done no deliberate aggressive act which was aimed at the police but that his sole aim was to ask Marsh where he was to be taken and that, as the actions of the defendant were not aimed at the police the justices were of the opinion that they could not convict him of the offence, and they accordingly dismissed the charge against him.'

The question which they ask for the opinion of this court is whether the principles applied by them were those laid down in *Hills* v *Ellis*; they also ask whether, given the evidence in the case, the decision to dismiss the charge was perverse and unreasonable. For the moment I will consider only the first of those two questions. For my part, I approach this question, in the first place, by disregarding any decision as to the meaning of the words "wilful" or "wilfully" in any context other than that of the section in question. This is because whereas, for instance, this court has held in *Arrowsmith* v *Jenkins* [1963] 2 QB 561 that the wilful obstruction of a highway, contrary to section 121 of the Highways Act 1959, does not import mens rea in the sense that a person will only be guilty of that offence if he knowingly did a wrongful act, there is a line of authority, to which I will turn, that the word "wilfully" in the context of section 51(3) of the Police Act 1964 connotes an element of mens rea. I find it necessary to consider this line of authority, although not every case in it, in some detail because it cannot, in my view confidently be asserted that the test, whether the actions of the defendant are "aimed at the police," is the definitive and authoritative test. It can however, in my view be confidently stated, as I have already mentioned that the word "wilfully" imports an element of mens rea. In *Betts* v *Stevens* [1910] 1 KB 1, a case arising out of the warnings given at the time by Automobile Association patrol men to those who were exceeding the speed limit of the existence of a nearby police trap. Darling J, dealing with the question of intention, said, at p8: "The gist of the offence to my mind lies in the intention with which the thing is done."

In *Willmott* v *Atack* [1977] QB 498, the defendant had intervened and obstructed a police officer while the officer was attempting to restrain a man under arrest and take him to a police car. The justices convicted him of an offence under section 51(3) of the Police Act 1964. Although they found that the defendant had intervened in the belief that he could resolve the situation better than the police, they concluded that his deliberate conduct had obstructed the police, and that he was: therefore guilty of wilful obstruction. This court allowed his appeal against that conviction. Before this court, counsel for the defendant contended, at p500:

"The proper interpretation of 'wilfully obstructs' within section 51(3) of the Police Act 1964 is that there should not merely be an intention on the part of the defendant to do something which happens to result in an obstruction of a police officer in the execution of his duty, but that there should also be an element of hostility and criminal intent towards the police officer:..."

Croom-Johnson J, who gave the first judgment, said, at pp504-505:

"When one looks at the whole context of section 51, dealing as it does with assaults upon constables in subsection (1) and concluding in subsection (3) with resistance and wilful obstruction in the execution of the duty, I am of the view that the interpretation of this subsection for which the defendant contends is the right one. It fits the words 'wilfully obstructs' in the context of the subsection, and in my view there must be something in the nature of a criminal intent of the kind which means that it is done with the idea of some form of hostility to the police with the intention of seeing that what is done is to obstruct, and that it is not enough merely to show that he intended to do what he did and that it did in fact have the result of the police being obstructed."

May J agreed. He observed that the word "wilfully" had been inconsistently interpreted in various statutes which defined criminal offences, and continued, at p505:

"I agree with Croom-Johnson J that when one looks at the judgment of Darling J in *Betts* v *Stevens* [1910] 1 KB 1, 8 ... it is clear that 'wilfully' in this particular statute does import a requirement of mens rea."

Lord Widgery CJ, in a very short judgment, at p505 agreed that the question posed should be answered in the negative, that question being (see p502):

"whether upon a charge of wilfully obstructing a police officer in the execution of his duty it is sufficient for the prosecution to prove that the defendant wilfully did an act which obstructed the police officer in the execution of his duty, or must the prosecution further prove that the defendant intended to obstruct the police officer."

In *Moore* v *Green* [1983] 1 All ER 663, the facts of which are immaterial for present purposes, McCullough J, having cited the passage from the judgment of Croom-Johnson J in *Willmott* v *Atack* [1977] QB 498, 500, which I have just cited, said at p665:

"I do not understand the reference to 'hostility' to indicate a separate element of the offence. I understand the word to bear the same meaning as the phrase which Croom-Johnson J used immediately afterwards, namely 'the intention of seeing that what is done is to obstruct' ..."

Griffiths LJ agreed with the judgment of McCullough J.

Finally, on this aspect of the matter, I return to *Hills* v *Ellis* [1983] 1 QB 680.' [His Lordship referred to the facts of the case, set out elsewhere in this chapter, and continued]

'Griffiths LJ cited the same passage from the judgment of Croom Johnson J in *Willmott* v *Atack* [1977] QB 498 and continued, at p685:

"The defendant's counsel argues from that passage that as the motive here was merely to correct an officer's error, it cannot be said that he, the defendant, was acting with any hostility towards the police. But in my view, the phrase 'hostility to the police' in that passage means no more than that the actions of the defendant are aimed at the police. There can be no doubt here that his action in grabbing the officer's arm was aimed at that officer. It was an attempt to get that officer to desist from the arrest that he was making. In my view, this is as clear a case as we can have of obstructing a police officer in the course of his duty, and the justices came to the right decision."

McCullough J agreed with the judgment of Griffiths LJ and added, at p686:

"I am uncertain what Croom-Johnson J had in mind when he used the word 'hostility' ... Hostility suggests emotion and motive, but motive and emotion are alike irrelevant in criminal law. What matters is intention, that is, what state of affairs the defendant intended to bring about. What motive he had while so intending is irrelevant. What is meant by an intention to obstruct? I would construe 'wilfully obstructs' as doing deliberate actions with the intention of bringing about a state of affairs which, objectively regarded, amount to an obstruction as that phrase was explained by Lord Parker CJ in *Rice* v *Connolly* [1966] 2 QB 414, 419B, that is, making it more difficult for the police to carry out their duty. The fact that the defendant might not himself have called that state of affairs an obstruction is, to my mind, immaterial. That is not to say that it is enough to do deliberate actions which, in fact, obstruct: there must be an intention that those actions should result in the further state of affairs to which I have been referring."

Lord Parker CJ on the same page of his judgment in *Rice* v *Connolly* said that "wilful" in the context of this section "not only in my judgment means 'intentional' but something which is done without lawful excuse "; and his explanation of "wilfully obstructs" as something which makes it more difficult for the police to carry out their duties was taken by him from the judgment of Lord Goddard CJ in *Hinchcliffe* v *Sheldon* [1955] 1 WLR 1207, where Lord Goddard CJ said at p1210: "Obstructing, for the present purpose, means making it more difficult for the police to carry out their duties."

For my part I conclude that, although it may not be unhelpful in certain cases to consider whether the actions of a defendant were aimed at the police, the simple facts which the court has to find are whether the defendant's conduct in fact prevented the police from carrying out their duty, or made it more difficult for them to do so, and whether the defendant intended that conduct to prevent the police from carrying out their duty or to make it more difficult to do so. In the present case the test which the justices applied was whether the defendant had deliberately done some act which was aimed at the police, they found that his actions were not aimed at the police and accordingly dismissed the charge. In my view, for the reasons I have given, the justices did not ask themselves the right question for the purposes of the present case, or the whole of the right question.'

R v Venna (1975) 61 Cr App Rep 310 Court of Appeal (Criminal Division) (James and Ormrod LJJ and Cusack J)

Mens rea for assault and battery

Facts

The defendant was arrested after being involved in a fracas with police officers during which he had lashed out with his foot, fracturing the hand of an officer who was trying to restrain him. The defendant was convicted of (inter alia) assault occasioning actual bodily harm. He appealed on the ground (inter alia) that recklessness was insufficient mens rea for the offence.

Held

James LJ:

[Having considered the first ground of appeal, his Lordship continued]

'The second substantial ground of appeal relates to the conviction of assault occasioning actual bodily harm. Having summed-up to the jury the issue of self defence in relation to the alleged assault, the judge directed them in these terms, and I read from the transcript: "However, you would still have to consider, on this question of assault by Venna, whether it was an accident. If he is lashing out ... Let me put it this way. Mr Woods on behalf of Venna says 'Well, he is not guilty of an assault because it was neither intentional nor reckless. It was a pure accident that he happened to hit the officer,' and that is quite right. If you hit somebody accidentally, it cannot be a criminal offence so you have got to ask yourselves, 'Was this deliberate, or was it reckless?' If it was, then he is guilty. To do an act deliberately hardly needs explanation. If you see somebody in front of you and you deliberately kick him on the knee, that is a deliberate act and, no two ways about it, that is an assault, but it can equally well be an assault if you are lashing out, knowing that there are people in the neighbourhood or that there are likely to be people in the neighbourhood and, in this case, it is suggested that he had two people by his arms and he knew that he was being restrained so as to lead to arrest. If he lashes out with his feet, knowing that there are officers about him and knowing that by lashing out he will probably or is likely to kick somebody or hurt his hand by banging his heel down on it, then he is equally guilty of the offence. Venna can therefore be guilty of the offence in count 3 in the indictment if he deliberately brought his foot down on Police Constable Spencer's hand or if he lashed out simply reckless as to who was there, not caring an iota as to whether he kicked somebody or brought his heel down on his hands."

Mr Woods argued that the direction is wrong in law because it states that the mental element of recklessness is enough, when coupled with the *actus reus* of physical contact to constitute the battery involved in assault occasioning actual bodily harm. Recklessness, it is argued, is not enough; there must be intention to do the physical act the subject matter of the charge. Counsel relied on the case of *Lamb* (1967) 51 Cr App R 417; [1967] 2 QB 981 and argued that an assault is not established by proof of a deliberate act which gives rise to consequences which are not intended.

In *Fagan* v *Commissioner of Metropolitan Police* (1968) 52 Cr App R 700; [1969] 1 QB 439, it was said "An assault is any act which intentionally or possibly recklessly causes another person to apprehend immediate and unlawful personal violence." In *Fagan* (supra) it was not necessary to decide the question whether proof of recklessness is sufficient to establish the mens rea ingredient of assault. That question falls for decision in the present case. Why it was considered necessary for the Crown to put the case forward on the alternative bases of "intention" and "recklessness" is not clear to us. This resulted in the direction given in the summing-up.

On the evidence of the appellant himself one would have thought that the inescapable inference was that the appellant intended to make physical contact with whoever might try to restrain him. Be that as it may, in the light of the direction given, the verdict may have been arrived at on the basis of "recklessness." Mr Woods cited *Ackroyd* v *Barett* (1894) 11 TLR 115 in support of his argument that recklessness, which falls short of intention, is not enough to support a charge of battery, and argued that, there being no authority to the contrary, it is now too late to extend the law by a decision of the courts and that any extension must be by the decision of Parliament.

Mr Woods sought support from the distinction between the offences which are assaults and offences which by statute include the element contained in the word "maliciously," eg unlawful and malicious wounding contrary to section 20 of the Offences Against the Person Act 1861 in which recklessness will suffice to support the charge. See *Cunningham* (1957) 41 Cr App R 155; [1957] 2 QB 396. In so far as the editors of text books commit themselves to an opinion on this branch of the law, they are favourable to the view that recklessness is or should logically be sufficient to support the charge of assault or battery. See Glanville Williams *Criminal Law: The General Part* (2nd ed), para 27, p65; Kenney *Criminal Law* (19th ed), (1966) para 164, p218; *Russell on Crime* (12th ed), p656 and Smith and Hogan (3rd ed), p286.

We think that the decision in *Ackroyd v Barett* (supra) is explicable on the basis that the facts of the case did not support a finding of recklessness. The case was not argued for both sides. The case of *Bradshaw* (1878) 14 Cox CC 83 can be read as supporting the view that unlawful physical force applied recklessly constitutes a criminal assault. In our view the element of mens rea in the offence of battery is satisfied by proof that the defendant intentionally or recklessly applied force to the person of another. If it were otherwise, the strange consequence would be that an offence of unlawful wounding contrary to section 20 of the Offences Against the Person Act 1861, could be established by proof that the defendant wounded the victim either intentionally or recklessly but, if the victim's skin was not broken and the offence was therefore laid as an assault occasioning actual bodily harm contrary to section 47 of the Act, it would be necessary to prove that the physical force was intentionally applied.

We see no reason in logic or in law why a person who recklessly applies physical force to the person of another should be outside the criminal law of assault. In many cases the dividing line between intention and recklessness is barely distinguishable. This is such a case.'

Commentary

Following *R v Savage*; *R v Parmenter* (extracted in chapter 5) it would appear that *R v Venna* is still authority for the type of recklessness needed for assault.

Weight v Long [1986] Crim LR 746 Divisional Court (Watkins LJ and Taylor J)

Police constable - whether acting within the execution of his duty

Facts

'The respondent was charged with assaulting a police officer in the execution of his duty, contrary to section 51(1) of the Police Act 1964. In the early hours the respondent had been arguing with his girlfriend who ran away from him. She was seen by a uniformed officer. He went to ask her if she was all right and gave her directions of how to get home. The respondent approached and the officer spoke to him in order "to check him out in case he was following" the girl, according to the findings of the justices. The respondent did not stop and when the officer again approached him he pushed him aside and punched and kicked him. The justices dismissed the information. In their opinion (1) the respondent had assaulted the officer without justification and (2) in speaking to the respondent the officer was not acting in the execution of his duty because he had no reason to believe that an offence had been or was being, or would be committed; or that the situation represented anything except a tiff between friends. The prosecutor appealed by way of case stated.

Held

Allowing the appeal and remitting the case with a direction to convict, providing the officer's intention in attempting to speak to a person is in pursuit of the preservation of the peace or the prevention of crime or investigation into crime already committed, he acts in the execution of his duty. There was an obvious conflict between the justices' finding of fact as to the officer's purpose and the second part of their opinion.

Per Watkins LJ: Where the facts reveal that there has been by the so-called detaining officer, no use of physical force, the conclusion that there has been a detention merely from words used and demeanour exhibited must not be lightly reached. If they are so to find courts must be sure in such circumstances that conduct by spoken word and demeanour must be so impressive as to lead inevitably to the conclusion that there was a detention by those means. Otherwise the work of the police on the streets will become quite impossible. A police officer who does not in circumstances such as the present case seek to investigate the reason for such an occurrence, far from acting outside his duty in trying to speak to someone else about the matter, would be positively in dereliction of duty unless he sought to discover whether there was something about that person's behaviour or apprehended behaviour which might actually disturb or tend to disturb the peace.'

[*Reported by Lynne Knapman, Barrister.*]

5 NON-FATAL OFFENCES AGAINST THE PERSON II

R v Blaue [1975] 1 WLR 1411

See chapter 6.

R v Bourne [1939] 1 KB 687 Central Criminal Court (MacNaghten J)

Miscarriage procured in good faith - whether an offence under s58 1861 Act

Facts

The defendant doctor performed an abortion upon a 14 year old girl who had been raped. He performed the operation in a hospital, with the consent of the parents, and did not receive any fee. He had formed the view that if the girl was allowed to give birth she might not survive. The defendant was charged under s58 with unlawfully procuring a miscarriage.

Held

Following the direction from the trial judge [detailed below], the jury returned a verdict of not guilty.

MacNaghten J's direction to the jury:

'... A man of the highest skill, openly, in one of our great hospitals, performs the operation. Whether it was legal or illegal you will have to determine, but he performs the operation as an act of charity, without fee or reward, and unquestionably believing that he was doing the right thing, and that he ought, in the performance of his duty as a member of a profession devoted to the alleviation of human suffering, to do it. That is the case that you have to try today.

It is, a case, of first instance, first impression. The matter has never, so far as I know, arisen before for a jury to determine circumstances such as these, and there was, even amongst learned counsel, some doubt as to the proper direction to the jury in such a case as this.

The defendant is charged with an offence against section 58 of the Offences against the Person Act, 1861. That section is a re-enactment of earlier statutes, the first of which was passed at the beginning of the last century in the reign of George III (43 Geo 3, c58, s1). But long before then, before even Parliament came into existence, the killing of an unborn child was by the common law of England a grave crime, see *Bracton*, Book III (*De Corona*), fol. 121. The protection which common law afforded to human life extended to the unborn child in the womb of its mother. But, as in the case of homicide, so also in the case where an unborn child is killed, there may be justification for the act.

Nine years ago Parliament passed an Act called the Infant Life (Preservation) Act, 1929. Section 1, subsection 1, of that Act provides that "any person who, with intent to destroy the life of a child capable of being born alive, by any wilful act causes a child to die before it has an existence independent of its mother, shall be guilt of felony, to wit, of child destruction, and shall be liable on conviction thereof on indictment to penal servitude for life: Provided that no person shall be found guilty of an offence under this section unless it is provided that the act which caused the death of the child was not done in good faith for the purpose only of preserving the life of the mother." It is true ... that this enactment provides for the case where a child is killed by a wilful act at the time when it is being delivered in the ordinary course of nature; but in my view the proviso that it is necessary for the Crown to prove that the act was not done in good faith for the purpose only of preserving the life of the mother is in accordance with what has always been the common law of England with regard to the killing of an unborn child. No such proviso is in fact set out in section 58 of the Offences Against the Person Act, 1861; but the words of that section are that any person who "unlawfully" uses an instrument with intent to procure miscarriage shall be guilty of felony. In my opinion the word "unlawfully" is not, in that section, a meaningless word. I think it imports the meaning expressed by the proviso in section 1, subsection 1, of the Infant Life (Preservation) Act, 1929, and that section 58 of the Offences against the Person Act, 1861, must be read as if the words making it an offence to use an instrument with intent to procure a miscarriage were qualified by a similar proviso.

In this case, therefore, my direction to you in law is this – that the burden rests on the Crown to satisfy you beyond reasonable doubt that the defendant did not procure the miscarriage of the girl in good faith for the purpose only of preserving her life. If the Crown fails to satisfy you of that, the defendant is entitled by the law of this land to a verdict of acquittal. If, on the other hand, you are satisfied that what the defendant did was not done by him in good faith for the purpose only of preserving the life of the girl, it is your duty to find him guilty. It is said, and I think said rightly, that this is a case of great importance to the public and, more especially, to the medical profession; but you will observe that it has nothing to do with the ordinary case of procuring abortion ... In those cases the operation is performed by a person of no skill, with no medical qualifications, and there is no preference that it is done for the preservation of the mother's life. Cases of that sort are in no way affected by the consideration of the question which is put before you today.

What then is the meaning to be given to the words "for the purpose of preserving the life of the mother"? There has been much discussion in this case as to the difference between danger to life and danger to health. It may be that you are more fortunate than I am, but I confess that I have found it difficult to understand what the discussion really meant, since life depends upon health, and it may be that health is so gravely impaired that death results. A question was asked by the learned Attorney-General in the course of his cross-examination of Mr Bourne. "I suggest to you, Mr Bourne," said the Attorney-General, "that there is a perfectly clear line - there may be border-line cases - there is a clear line of distinction between danger to health and danger to life." The answer of Mr Bourne was: "I cannot agree without qualifying it; I cannot say just yes or no. I can say there is a large group whose health may be damaged, but whose life almost certainly will not be sacrificed. There is another group at the other end whose life will be definitely in very great danger." And then he adds: "There is a large body of material between those two extremes in which it is not really possible to say how far life will be in danger, but we find, of course, that the health is depressed to such an extent that life is shortened, such as in cardiac cases, so that you may say that their life is in danger, because death might occur within measurable distance of the time of their labour." If that view commends itself to you, you will not accept the suggestion that there is a clear line of distinction between danger to health and danger to life. Mr Oliver wanted you to give what he called a wide and liberal meaning to the words "for the purpose of preserving the life of the mother." I should prefer the word "reasonable" to the words "wide and liberal." I think you should take a reasonable view of those words.

It is not contended that those words mean merely for the purposes of saving the mother from instant death. There are cases, we are told, where it is reasonably certain that a pregnant woman will not be able to deliver the child which is in her womb and survive. In such a case where the doctor anticipates, basing his opinion upon the experience of the profession, that the child cannot be delivered without the death of the mother, it is obvious that the sooner the operation is performed the better. The law does not require the doctor to wait until the unfortunate woman is in peril of immediate death. In such a case he is not only entitled, but it is his duty to perform the operation with a view to saving her life.

Here let me diverge for one moment to touch upon a matter that has been mentioned to you, the various views which are held with regard to this operation. Apparently there is a great difference of opinion even in the medical profession itself. Some there may be for all I know, who hold the view that the fact that a woman desires the operation performed is a sufficient justification for it. Well, that is not the law: the desire of a woman to be relieved of her pregnancy is no justification at all for performing the operation. On the other hand there are people who, from what are said to be religious reasons, object to the operation being performed under any circumstance. That is not the law either. On the contrary, a person who holds such an opinion ought not to be an obstetrical surgeon, for if a case arose where the life of the woman could be saved by performing the operation and the doctor refused to perform it because of his religious opinions and the woman died, he would be in grave peril of being brought before this court on a charge of manslaughter by negligence. He would have no better defence than a person who, again for some religious reason, refused to call in a doctor to attend his sick child, where a doctor could have been called in and the life of the child could have been saved. If the father, for a so-called religious reason, refused to call in a doctor, he is also answerable to the criminal law for the death of his child. I mention these two extreme views merely to show that the law lies between them. It permits the termination of pregnancy for the purpose of preserving the life of the mother.

As I have said, I think those words ought to be construed in a reasonable sense, and, if the doctor is of opinion, on reasonable grounds and with adequate knowledge, that the probable consequences of the continuance of the pregnancy will be to make the woman a physical or mental wreck, the jury are quite entitled to take the view that the doctor who, under those circumstances and in that honest belief operates, is operating for the purpose of preserving the life of the mother ...'

Commentary

See chapter 13.

C v S [1987] 2 WLR 1108 Court of Appeal (Civil Division) (Sir John Donaldson MR, Stephen Brown and Russell LJJ)

Whether abortion at 18-21 weeks of gestation is an offence under the Infant Life (Preservation) Act 1929.

Facts

The plaintiff sought an injunction to prevent the defendant, who was pregnant with his child, from going ahead with an abortion. He claimed (inter alia) that as the foetus had reached between 18 and 21 weeks of gestation, it was a 'child capable of being born alive' within the meaning of the Infant Life (Preservation) Act 1929. His claim rested on the assertion that an injunction should be granted either to himself, as the prospective father, or to the unborn child, to prevent the commission of what would be an offence under the 1929 Act.

Held at first instance

The application would be refused.

Heilbron J:

'Since the enactment of the Infant Life (Preservation) Act 1929 there have undoubtedly been rapid, extensive and truly remarkable developments in medical science, not least in the field of obstetrics. Some matters have become much clearer, some have remained obscure and difficult to determine; so it is perhaps understandable that the question as to when life begins, as to when a foetus is capable of being born alive, as to when a child is actually alive, are all problems of complexity to even the greatest medical minds. The determination of when life ends is now also a matter of concern and dispute.

Having said that, this case, I remind myself, concerns to some extent the meaning of the phrase "capable of being born alive." Unless Mr Norris's [see below] ... unequivocal assertion that *all* foetuses of 18 weeks' gestation *are* capable of being born alive is taken at face value as credible, then in reality and in the hospital where the decisions are taken it is the doctor (one of a team and probably one not yet designated) who has to make his decision on that problem in respect of Miss S's unborn child. We do not know on what basis he will make his prognosis, for that is what is entailed, or indeed, if by now he has been nominated, whether he has made the decision and on what criteria.

That the phrase *is* ambiguous would seem to follow from the differing points of view as disclosed in the affidavits and the exhibits …

… The word "viable" is, I believe from what I have heard in this case, sometimes used interchangeably and in a number of cases where others might use the words "born alive." In the United States of America, in the Supreme Court, *Roe* v *Wade* (1973) 410 US 113, it was said:

"With respect to the State's important and legitimate interest in potential life, the 'compelling' point is at *viability*. This is so because the foetus then presumably has the capability of meaningful life outside the mother's womb. State regulation protective of foetal life after viability thus has both logical and biological justifications."

As far as the phrase in the Infant Life (Preservation) Act 1929 is concerned, Mr Sheridan [for the defendant] submits, it either contains an ambiguity or the phrase is a technical one. In my view, one or both of those submissions is or are correct. That expression, in my judgment, does not have a clear and plain meaning. It is ambiguous. It is a phrase which is capable of different interpretations; and probably for the reason that it is also a medical concept and, as with the example of earlier days, the expertise of doctors may well be required and gratefully received to assist the court.

Even distinguished medical men have found considerable difficulties but have discovered that it is more helpful to equate that phrase with viability, possibly with the example from the parliamentary draftsman in mind.

I cannot accept Mr Wright's [for the plaintiff] submission that this is not, at any rate in this court, even partly a matter of expert opinion as to the meaning of "alive," for I have to point out that the first expert who produced an affidavit on that very topic was introduced by him, namely Mr Norris. Professor Newton replied later.

Mr Levy on behalf of the Official Solicitor, acting as amicus curiae, submitted that the alleged threatened criminality raised a difficult question of interpretation and pointed out that the phrase in the Abortion Act 1967 itself incorporates the word "viable" in the phrase which refers to "protecting the life of the viable foetus," a section to which I have already referred: see section 5(1). By that date, he argued, Parliament would no doubt be aware of the controversies over the law on abortion and it is possible that the use of that word is some indication that Parliament thought it necessary to use that particular qualifying word. I think that is possible too, though I would not attach too much weight to the parenthesis containing that word as an aid to construction.

Perhaps it is more significant that, though the reference to a foetus of 28 weeks or more being "deemed capable of being born alive" is referable to the burden of proof, it is probably dealing with a foetus of an age that would be known or expected, to be viable in 1929.

Mr Norris, of course, does not limit his statement to a question of presumption. He goes much further and in effect makes his 18 weeks an irrebuttable presumption, thus, at a stroke, as it were, reducing the 28 weeks to 18.

Mr Levy submitted that the court should reject Mr Norris's interpretation of "born alive" as the minimum indicia, without breathing, possibly without circulation and minus a number of indications referred to by Professor Newton.

In considering this submission, I find Mr Norris's statements as to the inevitability of every 18-week foetus being born alive unacceptable. It is not necessary for me, nor would I want, to try to decide on affidavit evidence in a somewhat limited sphere, the answer, which baffles men and women with great scientific expertise, to a very profound question. I would, however, say that I am not greatly attracted to the very limited definition relied upon by Mr Norris and I do not accept it as a realistic one.'

Held on appeal to the Court of Appeal

The appeal would be dismissed.

Sir John Donaldson MR:

'There is more than one way of measuring the duration of a pregnancy, but it is common ground that, however measured, this pregnancy has continued for between 18 and 21 weeks. Shortly after the time when conception must have taken place, the first defendant was prescribed and took medicine designed to prevent pregnancy developing. Later she was prescribed and took anti-depressant drugs. Later still, in ignorance that she was pregnant, she was twice subjected to X-ray examination for a chest infection. On one such occasion there was no shielding to prevent damage to the foetus whose presence was unknown. The pregnancy was revealed by a later body scan.

All these treatments could damage a foetus and the first defendant wishes to terminate the pregnancy. It is common ground that all the steps required by the Abortion Act 1967 as a pre-condition to such a termination have been taken and, in particular, that in accordance with section 1(1) (a) of that Act it has been certified by two doctors that in their opinion the continuance of the pregnancy would involve risk of injury to the physical or mental health of the first defendant greater than if the pregnancy were terminated.

What is said by Mr Wright is that termination of a pregnancy at this stage will necessarily involve the commission of a criminal offence under section 1(1) of the Infant Life (Preservation) Act 1929, the provisions of which are unaffected by the Abortion Act 1967. That subsection is in the following terms:

[His Lordship detailed the subsection and continued]

The key words for present purposes are "destroy the life of a child capable of being born alive."

We have received affidavit evidence from three doctors, none of whom has examined the first defendant. Their evidence is thus necessarily directed at the stage in the development of a foetus which can normally be expected to have been reached by the 18th to 21st week. On this, as one would expect, they are in substantial agreement. At that stage the cardiac muscle is contracting and a primitive circulation is developing. Thus the foetus could be said to demonstrate real and discernible signs of life. On the other hand, the foetus, even if then delivered by hysterotomy, would be incapable ever of breathing either naturally or with the aid of a ventilator. It is not a case of the foetus requiring a stimulus or assistance. It cannot and will never be able to breathe. Where the doctors disagree is as to whether a foetus, at this stage of development, can properly be described as "a child capable of being born alive" within the meaning of the Act of 1929. That essentially depends upon the interpretation of the statute and is a matter for the courts.

We have no evidence of the state of the foetus being carried by the first defendant, but if it has reached the normal stage of development and so is incapable ever of breathing, it is not in our judgment "a child capable of being born alive" within the meaning of the Act and accordingly the termination of this pregnancy would not constitute an offence under the Infant Life (Preservation) Act 1929.'

R v Cato (1976) 62 Cr App R 41

See chapter 8.

R v Clarence (1888) 22 QBD 23 Court for Crown Cases Reserved

Whether 'infliction' of grievous bodily harm contrary to s20 of the Offences Against the Person Act 1861 requires proof of an assault

Facts

The defendant had sexual intercourse with his wife whilst suffering from venereal disease. He had been aware of his condition but his wife had not. There was evidence that his wife would not have consented to intercourse if she had known of his condition. The defendant was convicted under both s47 and s20 of the 1861 Act, and appealed against conviction contending that as his wife had consented to intercourse she had not been assaulted, and in the absence of an assault he could not be held to have inflicted any harm upon her.

Held

By a majority of nine to four, both convictions would be quashed.

Stephen J:

'I now come to the construction of the precise words of the statute ... is there an "infliction of bodily harm either with or without any weapon or instrument?" I think not for the following reasons.

The words appear to me to mean the direct causing of some grievous injury to the body itself with a weapon, as by a cut with a knife, or without a weapon, as by a blow with the first or by pushing a person down. Indeed, though the word "assault" is not used in the section, I think the words imply an assault and battery of which a wound or grievous bodily harm is the manifest immediate and obvious result. This is supported by ... 14 and 15 Vict c19 s4 of which the present section is a re-enactment. Section 4 of the earlier Act begins with the preamble, "And whereas it is expedient to make further provision for the punishment of aggravated assaults," and then proceeds in the words of the present section, with a trifling and unimportant difference in their arrangement.

Infection by the application of an animal poison appears to me to be of a different character from an assault. The administration of poison is dealt with by section 24, which would be superfluous if poisoning were an "infliction of grievous bodily harm either with or without a weapon or instrument." The one act differs from the other in the immediate and necessary connection between a cut or a blow and the wound or harm inflicted, and the uncertain and delayed operation of the act by which infection is communicated. If a man by a grasp of the hand infects another with small-pox, it is impossible to trace out in detail the connection between the act and the disease, and it would, I think, be an unnatural use of language to say that man by such an act, "inflicted small-pox on another." It would be wrong in interpreting an Act of Parliament to lay much stress on etymology, but I may just observe that "inflict" is "derived" from "infligo", for which Facciolati's Lexicon three Italian and three Latin equivalents are given, all meaning "to strike" ...'

Hawkins J (dissenting):

'In my opinion the legislature, in framing the various sections of the statute already and hereafter referred to, used the words "inflict," "cause" and "occasion" as synonymous terms for the following among other reasons. Let me begin by calling attention to the language of the eighteenth section, which runs thus: "whosoever shall unlawfully and maliciously by any means whatsoever wound or *cause* any grievous bodily harm to any person, etc, with intent, etc, shall be guilty of felony." If the prisoner had been indicted under this section, could anybody doubt that upon proof of his intention to cause the grievous bodily harm he in fact occasioned, he would have fallen within not only the spirit but the precise language of the section according to the strictest interpretation which could be applied to it? I next ask myself what was the object of the 20th section? Clearly it was to provide for cases in which the grievous bodily harm mentioned in section 18, though unlawfully and maliciously caused, was unaccompanied by the felonious intent, which is the aggravating feature of the felony created by that section, and accordingly section 20 made such last-mentioned offence a misdemeanour only, by enacting as follows, "whosoever shall unlawfully or maliciously wound or *inflict* any grievous bodily harm upon any person either with or without any weapon or instrument shall be guilty of a misdemeanour." Surely the object of these two sections could only have been to make the doing of grievous bodily harm with intent a felony, without intent, a mere misdemeanour, and to hold that no man could be convicted under section 20 without proof of an assault would practically amount to holding that maliciously to do grievous bodily harm to another without felonious intent is unpunishable, unless such harm is done through the medium of an assault. It is impossible the legislature could have intended this.'

Commentary

See further *R* v *Wilson*, below. On the issue of marital rape see *R* v *R*, below.

R v Cogan and Leak [1976] QB 217

See chapter 9.

R v Court [1988] 2 WLR 1071 House of Lords (Lords Keith, Fraser, Griffiths, Ackner and Goff)

Proof of indecency in indecent assault

Facts

The defendant had accused a 12 year old girl of shoplifting in his store, and had spanked her several times on her buttocks, over her clothing. The girl complained to her parents, and the defendant was interviewed by the police. In explaining why he had done it, he made the statement that he might have been motivated by his 'buttock fetish'. The defendant was convicted of indecent assault contrary to s14 of the Sexual Offences Act 1956, following a trial in which the judge had permitted evidence of the defendant's statement to go before the jury. The defendant appealed on the ground that evidence of his secret indecent intent could not convert an act that was not overtly indecent into an indecent assault. The Court of Appeal dismissed the appeal holding that the evidence of his 'buttock fetish' was correctly admitted, and the defendant appealed further to the House of Lords.

Held (Lord Goff dissenting)

The appeal would be dismissed.

Lord Ackner:

'It also was common ground before your Lordships, as it was in the Court of Appeal, that if the circumstances of the assault are *incapable* of being regarded as indecent, then the undisclosed intention of the accused could not make the assault an indecent one. The validity of this proposition is well illustrated by *R* v *George* [1956] Crim LR 52. The basis of the prosecution's case was that the defendant on a number of occasions removed a shoe from a girl's foot and that he did so, as indeed he admitted, because it gave him a kind of perverted sexual gratification. Counsel for the prosecution submitted that an assault was indecent if it was committed to gratify an indecent motive in the mind of a defendant, even though there was no overt circumstances of indecency. Streatfeild J ruled that an assault became indecent only if it was accompanied by circumstances of indecency towards the person alleged to have been assaulted, and that none of the assaults (the removal or attempted removal of the shoes) could possibly amount to an indecent assault.

Again it was common ground that if, as in this case, the assault involved touching the victim, it was not necessary to prove that she was aware of the circumstances of indecency or apprehended indecency. An indecent assault can clearly be committed by the touching of someone who is asleep or unconscious.

As to the facts of this case, it is important to bear in mind that at the trial, not only did the appellant admit that he was guilty of an assault, but on his behalf his counsel expressly conceded that what had happened *was capable* of amounting to an indecent assault. That concession was repeated in the Court of Appeal and accepted by the court as being a correct concession. Sensibly no attempt was made before your Lordships to withdraw this concession, for the sound reason that the explanation of this unprovoked assault could reveal that the assault was an indecent one, as indeed the girl's father suspected and, as the jury so decided.

The assault which the prosecution seek to establish may be of a kind which is inherently indecent. The defendant removes against her will, a woman's clothing. Such a case, to my mind raises no problem. Those very facts, *devoid of any explanation,* would give rise to the irresistible inference that the defendant intended to assault his victim in a manner which right-minded persons would clearly think was indecent. Whether he did so for his own personal sexual gratification or because, being a misogynist or for some other reason, he wished to embarrass or humiliate his victim, seems to me to be irrelevant. He has failed, ex-hypothesi, to show any lawful justification for his indecent conduct. This, of course, was not such a case. The conduct of the appellant in assaulting the girl by spanking her was only *capable* of being an indecent assault. To decide whether or not right-minded persons might think that assault was indecent, the following factors were clearly relevant - the relationship of the defendant to his victim - were they relatives, friends or virtually complete strangers? How had the defendant come to embark on this conduct and why was he behaving in this way? Aided by such material, a jury would be helped to determine the quality of the act, the true nature of the assault and to answer the vital question - were they sure that the defendant not only intended to commit an assault upon the girl, but an assault which was indecent - was such an inference irresistible? For the defendant to be liable to be convicted of the offence of indecent assault, where the circumstances of the alleged offence can be given an innocent as well as an indecent interpretation, without the prosecution being obliged to establish that the defendant intended to commit both an assault and an indecent one, seems to me quite unacceptable and not what Parliament intended.

Much reliance was placed by counsel for the appellant upon the definition of "indecent assault" in *Beal* v *Kelley* [1951] 2 All ER 763, 764 as approved by Lord Goddard CJ "an assault, accompanied with circumstances of indecency on the part of the prisoner." It was submitted to your Lordships that an indecent motive can only become "a circumstance of indecency" if it is communicated to the victim by means of words or gestures at the time of the assault. If the motive is not communicated it is not such a circumstance. However the definition which Lord Goddard CJ accepted has not the force of a statute. It was wholly appropriate to the facts of that case, where the defendant had indecently exposed himself to a young boy and when the boy refused to handle him indecently, he got hold of the boy's arm and pulled him towards himself. In such a case and in many others cited to us, the assault in itself was not indecent. It was the combination of the assault with circumstances of indecency, that established the constituents of the offence. In the instant case, it is the assault itself - its true nature - an assault for sexual gratification, which was capable of amounting to an indecent assault.

The jury in their question to the judge were concerned with the position of a doctor who carried out an intimate examination on a young girl. Mars-Jones J dealt with their point succinctly by saying:

"In that situation what is vital is whether the examination was necessary or not. If it was not necessary, but indulged in by the medical practitioner, it would be an indecent assault. But if it was necessary, even though he got sexual satisfaction out of it, that would not make it an indecent assault."

I entirely agree. If it could be proved by the doctor's admission that the consent of the parent, or if over 16 the patient, was sought and obtained by the doctor falsely representing that the examination was necessary, then, of course, no true consent to the examination had ever been given. The examination would be an assault and an assault which right-minded persons could well consider was an indecent one. I would not expect that it would make any difference to the jury's decision whether the doctor's false representations were motivated by his desire for the sexual gratification which he might achieve from such an examination, or because he had some other reason, entirely of his own, unconnected with the medical needs or care of the patient, such as private research, which had caused him to act fraudulently. In either case the assault could be, and I expect would be, considered as so offensive to contemporary standards of modesty or privacy as to be indecent. A jury would therefore be entitled to conclude that he in both cases intended to assault the patient and to do so indecently. I can see nothing illogical in such a result. On the contrary, it would indeed be surprising if in such circumstances the only offence that could be properly charged would be that of common assault. No doubt the judge would treat the offence which had been motivated by the indecent motive as the more serious.'

Lord Goff (dissenting):

'In their *Criminal Law*, 5th ed (1983), p424, Professor Smith and Professor Hogan state that: "While an indecent motive cannot convert an objectively decent act into an indecent assault, a decent motive may justify what would otherwise be an indecent act." With that proposition, I respectfully find myself to be broadly in agreement, though I would myself (unaffected by the pressures on space in a text book) express it rather more fully as follows. First, if the prosecution cannot establish that an assault is objectively indecent, they are not allowed to fortify their case by calling evidence of a secret indecent intention on the part of the defendant. Second, if an assault is prima facie indecent, the defendant may seek to show that the circumstances of the assault were not in fact indecent, and for that purpose evidence of this intention would be relevant and admissible.

It was on the basis that evidence of the defendant's secret intention was probative of the true nature of the circumstances accompanying the assault that Mr Carlile submitted that it was admissible in the present case. With this submission, I am unable to agree. For on this basis the prosecution would be seeking, in my opinion illegitimately, to fortify what is assumed to be a doubtful case of an objectively indecent assault by calling evidence of a secret indecent intention on the part of the defendant. In truth, the evidence was admitted on the erroneous basis that an indecent intention is an ingredient of the offence, which, in my opinion, it is not; and the conviction cannot, in my opinion, be salvaged by defending the admissibility of the evidence on some other ground.

I would only add that, on the approach which I favour, it is only in very rare cases that evidence of the defendant's intention will be of any relevance. In the vast majority of cases, as in the present, the jury have simply to consider the evidence of what happened, and ask themselves the common sense questions: did the defendant assault the complainant? And if so, were the circumstances of the assault such as to render it indecent? If a man gives a young woman a good spanking on the backside, the jury will, unless the defendant's case is that there were circumstances by virtue of which the assault was not indecent, have to consider whether the assault was such an affront to her modesty as to amount to an indecent assault. I myself do not think that, in most cases, they would have much difficulty in reaching a conclusion; but, if in the end they are in doubt, they must of course acquit. Likewise, as it seems to me, on the law as it has hitherto been understood, juries and magistrates can, if they think it right to do so, having regard to all the circumstances, hold that an undergraduate "debagging" is no more than a harmless prank, whereas stripping a woman naked in public transcends any such thing and so constitutes an indecent assault, without any inquiry into the secret motive of the assailant.

In my opinion, evidence of the defendant's secret motive was, in the present case, inadmissible. I would accordingly allow the appeal and quash the conviction.'

R v Cunningham [1957] 2 QB 96
See chapter 2.

R v Donovan [1934] 2 KB 498
See chapter 4.

R v Fotheringham [1988] Crim LR 846 Court of Appeal (Criminal Division) (Watkin LJ, McNeill and McCowan JJ)

Rape - mistaken belief in identity of complainant - caused by drunkenness.

Facts

'F and his wife went out for the evening, leaving a 14 year old girl to babysit. F's wife (probably in F's absence) told the girl to sleep in the matrimonial bed with the child if it became late. When F and his wife returned F got into the matrimonial bed and had sexual intercourse with the girl without her consent. His wife appeared and F desisted. At his trial for rape (although not in his statement to the police) F said that because of the amount he had had to drink, he had mistaken the girl for his wife; he admitted that he would not have made this mistake if sober. The judge directed the jury to disregard F's self-induced intoxication in considering whether there were reasonable grounds for his believing that he was having sexual intercourse with a consenting woman *ie* his wife. F was convicted and appealed, submitting that this was misdirection.

Held

The appeal would be dismissed. It had been conceded on F's behalf that self-induced intoxication was not relevant where the issue was consent (Sexual Offences (Amendment) Act 1976, s1(2); *R v Woods* (1982) 74 Cr App R 312, 314 *per* Griffiths LJ); likewise where recklessness was sufficient to constitute *mens rea* (*R v Majewski* [1977] AC 443, 492 *per* Lord Edmund-Davies; *R v Caldwell* (1981) 73 Cr App R 13, 21 *per* Lord Diplock). Moreover mistake induced by self-induced intoxication was not generally a defence. (*R v O'Grady* [1987] 3 WLR 321.) Although there was no direct authority whether such intoxication was relevant in considering mistaken identity in a rape case, in principle it should not be relevant. (*DPP v Morgan* [1976] AC 182 considered.)'

[*Reported by Tom Rees, Barrister.*]

R v George [1956] Crim LR 52

See *R v Court*, above.

R v Gillard (1988) 87 Cr App R 189 Court of Appeal (Criminal Division) (O'Connor LJ, McNiell and Ognal JJ)

Offences Against the Person Act 1861 s24 - meaning of administering.

Facts (as stated by McNeill J)

'On October 14 or 15, 1986, a number of young men, including the appellant and Smith, went to Dieppe. On their return Smith was stopped at Newhaven and was found in possession of a gas pistol, gas cartridge and a gas spray. It was the prosecution case that the others, who were not stopped, brought in CS gas in spray cans and that these had been obtained for a planned attack on the doorman of a public house or wine bar called Drummonds in Richmond.

At about 10.50 pm the attack took place: the doorman was sprayed in the face by what he though to be three aerosols. He was in great discomfort; according to his deposition he felt as if his eyes were on fire, his face, neck and right shoulder were burning and he found extreme difficulty in breathing. He received some first aid and later was taken to hospital for treatment. A witness saw three members of a group produce spray cans which they sprayed in the doorman's face and they also sprayed the general area causing the witness herself to be affected: her eyes and throat were stinging: she too was taken to hospital. Other witnesses described the effects of the spray upon them: eyes watering and throats hurting. Yet another group of witnesses described the group of youths making their way off and the arrival of the police. One police officer had gas from a canister sprayed into his face by Smith who managed to get away but was arrested later. The appellant was arrested then and there: he had no spray can in his possession but one was found thrown over a nearby wall. A stocking said by the prosecution to have been used by him as a mask was found in his possession when taken into custody.

A CS gas canister found in Smith's possession when stopped at Newhaven was examined by a higher scientific officer of the Department of Trade and Industry. It was of the usual type; on depressing the valve of the spray canister an aerosol was emitted. On analysis it was shown to be W-Chloroacetophenone, a riot control agent which is a potent eye, throat and skin irritant.

Each of nine other victims of the effects of the spray on the doorman were found by a doctor to be complaining of itching skin and eyes and had been exposed to CS gas. A forensic scientist described in his statement how CS gas can cause the eyes to sting and stream with tears, severely irritate the nose and throat bringing about a choking effect and it can produce an acute burning sensation on facial skin. Fortunately, the effects are usually short-lived and do not result in lasting harm.

On July 8, 1987, at the Central Criminal Court (Judge Butler QC) the appellant was convicted of conspiracy to cause a noxious thing to be administered with intent contrary to section1(1) of the Criminal Law Act 1977. He was sentenced to $2^1/2$ years' imprisonment. In addition he was sentenced to six months' imprisonment consecutive in respect of a breach of a probation order, imposed for an offence of theft, made on January 6, 1986 for two years.

The basis on which this appeal is brought, by leave of the single judge, in this: that upon the true construction of section 24 of the 1861 Act the word "administer" is not apt in law to encompass the spraying of CS gas from a canister into the face of a victim: that such conduct ought properly and only to be charged as assault, or, where the facts justify it, assault occasioning actual bodily harm.

Held

The appeal would be dismissed.

McNeill J:

'At the conclusion of the evidence for the prosecution before the Crown Court, Mr Boyd submitted to His Honour Judge Butler QC in the absence of the jury that there was no case to answer in terms which he has advanced and developed in this Court. The judge rejected the submissions and after completion of the evidence and final speeches directed the jury as to the law which they were to apply.

His direction is at p27 of the transcript, and reads:

"Here, say the prosecution, CS gas is a noxious thing, and although it is a matter for you, because it is an issue of fact, you may think it perfectly obvious, and no-one has sought to argue the contrary, that that is so. You may also think it obvious that if someone deliberately and intentionally points a canister of CS gas at another person, and causes the CS gas to be discharged from the canister, towards a person's face, by pressing the appropriate button or valve on the canister, then there would be an intent to injure, aggrieve or annoy that unfortunate person. But you also have to ask this: if someone acts in this way, is he causing CS gas to be administered? That is important because as you know, the crime that the prosecution say was here agreed to be carried out was the causing of CS gas to be administered to another person or persons with the intent I have mentioned. Now the word 'administer' although perhaps not used by all of us every day of the week, is an ordinary English word. I would say to you that it is capable of a meaning wider than, for example, putting poison in someone's drink. It may be, although it is a matter for you, that if you were satisfied there was an agreement to use CS gas, as the prosecution say there was, then that would amount, in the particular circumstances of this case, to an agreement to cause a noxious thing to be administered."

Mr Boyd put his argument in this Court in this way. He relied on the use in s24 of the word "administered" in conjunction with the word "taken" as indicating Parliament's intention in this section to make criminal only acts which by physical contact obliged the victim to ingest the noxious thing. Where there was no physical contact and so no battery the act could nevertheless be charged and should be charged as an assault: to spray CS gas into someone's face is, he said, an assault in law.

The *Shorter Oxford English Dictionary* includes among definitions of "administer", "to apply, as medicine, etc. Hence to dispense, give (anything beneficial; also (jocular) a rebuke, a blow, etc)."

The Court does not find the dictionary definitions helpful: too many and too diverse alternatives are offered.

Mr Boyd contended that his construction of "administer" is consistent with and supported by its use in other sections of the Act. Thus, in sections 22 and 29, "administer" is used in conjunction with "apply": where "apply" is not used "administer" is used in conjunction with "take" (as in section 24) and also in the "poison" sections.

In support of this submission, Mr Boyd invited attention to the only reported decision on the construction of "administer" in section 24. In *Dones* [1987] Crim LR 682 Recorder Walsh QC, sitting at the Central Criminal Court, had a case under section 24 where the defendant was charged with spraying a solution of ammonia from a plastic lemon at the victim, some of which struck his eye and caused irritation. This Court has had the advantage of reading a transcript of the recorder's ruling.

The defendant there had first appeared before Mr Recorder Hawkins who accepted that on these facts there was an "administration" for the purposes of section 24; but the point was not argued fully or at all. In the event, however, the jury disagreed and so the case came before Mr Recorder Walsh for re-trial. He was able, therefore, to consider the matter untrammelled by any decision upon it by Mr Recorder Hawkins.

In this Court, Mr Boyd relied on Mr Recorder Walsh's ruling and adopted it as part of his argument. It is necessary to set out the relevant part of his ruling which reads:

"It is worth noting that in all the sections where 'administer' applies on its own, it is in conjunction with poisons, and the word 'taking' or 'causing to be taken by,' and it seems to me that, if one looks at all those sections together, the offences which the draftsmen and Parliament were clearly aiming at were the taking (the 'ingestion,' as it were) of some poisonous or noxious matter by the victim or in the case of the pregnant woman by herself, in what the public commonly understand the ordinary word of 'taking' for consuming food, medicine or so forth. Section 22 (of the Offences against the Person Act 1861) is different because, as I have said before, the word 'apply' is added; the words being; 'apply or administer … chloroform, laudanum or other stupefying drug.' One can see why that is, because stupefying drug can be administered in the same way as I have previously described, but one can also 'apply' chloroform in what I suppose was the time-honoured fashion of many, many years ago of the villain sneaking up on the victim, with a handkerchief, suitably impregnated, pressing it over his or her mouth or nose, and overpowering him or her. That seems to me to cover the 'applying' situation and to distinguish it from the 'administering' situation. One looks further at section 29, which is the section under which the defendant initially was committed for trial and one notices, after the initial lines about 'sending, delivering, causing to be taken or received by any person' - I miss out certain words - 'any other dangerous or noxious thing,' it then continues, 'or whoever shall put or lay at any place or' - and these are the important words - 'cast or *throw at or upon,* or otherwise *apply* to any person any corrosive fluid,' shall be guilty of this offence if they have certain intentions. So it seems to me quite clear that what Parliament and what the draftsmen of this Act had in mind were different sets of circumstances; one of which can be described with the verb 'apply,' another by the verb 'to administer,' and yet another by the verbs 'to cast' or 'to throw'; and when one finds in a statute (and, in particular, in the same parts of a statute) a series of offences where those words are used, either separately or sometimes in conjunction with different sections, it is plain to me that they (the drafters and Parliament) intended them to cover different situations, and in my view they do, and it seems to me that if Parliament had in mind it being an offence to cast or throw upon somebody a noxious thing, as well as a corrosive fluid, the Act would have said so, and it does not. There may have been an error in that, and that the danger then thought the more serious because it was the more prevalent - lemon Jifs not having been invented - was the throwing or casting of corrosive fluid which was likely or intended to maim, disfigure, disable or do serious harm. It may be that that was the mischief to which the Act was intending to apply, but in my judgment 'administer' was not intended to cover a situation such as this."

This Court does not accept that the words or purport of sections other than section 24 is relevant. A well established canon of construction is that if the words of a section are capable on their own of bearing a clear and ascertainable meaning there is no scope for reference over to other sections of the same statute; such recourse may only be had in the event of ambiguity or uncertainty or if that meaning is apparently inconsistent with the general intention of the statute. This is not the case here.

Where, in the view of this Court, the learned recorder was in error was in holding that "administering" and "taking" were to be treated effectively as synonymous or as conjunctive words in the section; on the contrary, the repeated use of the word "or" makes it clear that they are disjunctive. The word "takes" postulates some "ingestion" by the victim; "administer" must have some other meaning and there is no difficulty in including in that meaning such conduct as spraying the victim with noxious fluid or vapour, whether from a device such as a gas canister or, for example, hosing down with effluent. There is no necessity when the word "administer" is used to postulate any form of entry into the victim's body, whether through any orifice or by absorption; a court dealing with such a case should not have to determine questions of pathology such as, for example, the manner in which skin irritation results from exposure to CS gas or the manner in which the eye waters when exposed to irritant. The word "ingest" should be reserved to its natural meaning of intake into the digestive system and not permitted to obscure the statutory words.

In the view of this Court, the proper construction of "administer" in section 24 includes conduct which not being the application of direct force to the victim nevertheless brings the noxious thing into contact with his body.

While such conduct might in law amount to an assault, this court considers that so to charge it would tend to mislead a jury.

The Court has been assisted by the note by Professor J.C. Smith in the report of *Dones* [1987] Crim LR 682. The learned recorder, as the note submits, was correct in treating the question as one of construction and as a matter of law, following *R v Maginnis* (1987) 85 Cr App R 127.

In this respect, Judge Butler was in error in following as he presumably did the approach of the House of Lords in *Brutus* v *Cozens* (1972) 56 Cr App R799, [1973] AC 854 which, in relation to the word "insulting" regarded the meaning of that word as a matter of fact for the jury. This court regards the word "administer" as one to be construed as was the word "supply" in *R v Maginnis* (supra). However, the trial Judge's error - and an understandable error - was, if anything, to the advantage of the defendant, as he then was, and can in no way be regarded as a material irregularity.

As Mr Recorder Walsh correctly said; "It is for the Court to interpret and construe the word here, as having a particular meaning, and for the Court to direct the jury as to what it means." In concluding as follows: "I am satisfied that the word 'administer' does not apply to a situation such as this," that is squirting ammonia from a plastic lemon - he was in error.

Accordingly, this appeal is dismissed.'

R v Hill [1968] Crim LR 815 House of Lords (Lords Bridge, Brandon, Griffiths, Mackay and Ackner)

Specific intent required for s24 Offences Against the Person Act 1861

Facts

'The defendant was charged with two offences of administering a noxious thing with intent to injure, contrary to section 24 of the Offences against the Person Act 1861. The facts were not in dispute. The defendant, a homosexual, had purchased a number of tablets of the drug tenuate dospan on the "black market." The drug is available only on prescription and is used as an aid to slimming. The normal adult dose was one tablet per day. There was no evidence that the defendant knew the prescribed dose. The defendant spent an evening with two boys, aged 12 and 13. During the evening each boy took three tablets the defendant having told them they were "speed" and would make them happy. The 12-year-old then spent the night with the defendant. The boy agreed to do so after he had made it clear that if the defendant laid a hand on him in an indecent way he would tell his mother and the police. At the defendant's flat the boy took a fourth tablet. They both lay naked on the defendant's bed but the defendant made no advances towards the boy. The boy stayed awake all night as a result of the overdose of the drug and both boys suffered from vomiting and diarrhoea during the next two days also as a result of the overdose. At the trial the defence conceded that the tablets were a noxious thing and that the defendant had unlawfully administered them. The only issue for the jury was whether he did so with an intent to injure them. The defendant was convicted and appealed to the Court of Appeal on the ground that the judge had erred in directing the jury that an intention on the defendant's part to keep the victims awake was capable of amounting to an intention to injure. The Court of Appeal (see (1985) 81 Cr App R 206) said that the judge had appeared to direct the jury that an intention to keep the boys awake was by itself sufficient to constitute an intent to injure. They held that to be a misdirection and quashed the conviction. The prosecutor appealed to the House of Lords the certified question being "whether the offence of administering a noxious thing with intent to injure ... is capable of being committed when a noxious thing is administered to a person without lawful excuse with the intention only of keeping that person awake."

Held

Allowing the appeal and restoring the conviction, that their Lordships would decline to answer the certified question as they were unable to accept the Court of Appeal's interpretation of the judge's direction. The judge was not suggesting that an intention to keep awake was *of itself* an intention to cause injury. The jury would not have understood from the summing-up that an intention to keep a child awake *by itself,* say for some benevolent purpose such as enjoying the fireworks, or to greet his father on a late return from work, could amount to an intent to injure. The summing-up read as a whole made it clear that the jury should only convict if they were sure that the defendant intended to injure the boys in the sense of causing them physical harm by the administration of the drugs. That was a correct direction. The jury by their verdict found that the defendant had such an intent and any other verdict would have been astonishing. Here was a man who admitted being sexually attracted to young boys plying them with a drug which he knew would overstimulate and excite them and doing so with a reckless disregard for what might be the safe dosage and, in fact, giving them a gross overdose. The only reasonable inference to draw from such conduct was an intention that the drug should injure the boys in the sense of causing harm to the metabolism of their bodies by overstimulation with the motive of either ingratiating himself with them, or more probably rendering them susceptible to homosexual advances. The defendant caused some physical harm and there was overwhelming evidence that this was his intention.

On the view taken of the summing-up the certified question did not call for an answer. It was, in any event, a question which it was not sensible to attempt to answer without knowing the factual background against which it was asked. If the noxious thing was administered for a purely benevolent purpose such as keeping the pilot of an aircraft awake the answer would almost certainly be no, but if administered for a malevolent purpose such as a prolonged interrogation the answer would almost certainly be yes.'

[*Reported by Maggy Pigott, Barrister.*]

R v **Khan and Others** (1990) 91 Cr App R 29   Court of Appeal (Criminal Division)   (Russell LJ, Rose and Morland JJ)

Facts

The appellants were charged with the attempted rape of a 16-year-old girl. During the course of the trial the judge directed the jury in the following terms: ' ... As in the case of rape, the principles relevant to consent apply in exactly the same way in attempted rape. I do not suppose you need me to go through it again. Apply the same principles as to rape.' Following conviction, the appellants sought to appeal contending that there had been a material misdirection, on the basis that whilst recklessness, as a state of mind on the part of an offender, was relevant to the completed crime of rape, it had no place in the offence of attempted rape.

Held

The appeals would be dismissed.

Russell LJ [Having referred to the wording of section 1(1) of the Criminal Attempts Act 1981]:

'The impact of the words of section 1 of the 1981 Act and in particular the words "with intent to commit an offence" has been the subject matter of much debate amongst distinguished academic writers. We were referred to and we have read and considered an article by Professor Glanville Williams entitled "The Problem of Reckless Attempts" [1983] Crim LR 365. The argument there advanced is that recklessness can exist within the concept of attempt and support is derived from *Pigg* [1982] 2 All ER 591, albeit that authority was concerned with the law prior to the Criminal Attempts Act 1981. This approach also receives approval from Smith and Hogan Criminal Law 6th ed (1988) at pp287 to 289. Contrary views, however, have been expressed by Professor Griew and Mr Richard Buxton QC who have both contended that the words "with intent to commit an offence" involve an intent as to every element constituting the crime. Finally we have had regard to the observations of Mustill LJ giving the judgment of the Court of Appeal Criminal Division in *Millard and Vernon* [1987] Crim LR 393. That was a case involving a charge of attempting to damage property, the Particulars of Offence reading: "Gary Mann Millard and Michael Elliot Vernon, on May 11, 1985, without lawful excuse, attempted to damage a wooden wall at the Leeds Road Football Stand belonging to Huddersfield Town Association Football Club, intending to damage the said wall or being reckless as to whether the said wall would be damaged . "

Mustill LJ said:

"The appellants' case is simple. They submit that in ordinary speech the essence of an attempt is a desire to bring about a particular result, coupled with steps towards that end. The essence of recklessness is either indifference to a known risk or (in some circumstances) failure to advert to an obvious risk. The two states of mind cannot co-exist. Section 1(1) of the Criminal Attempts Act 1981 expressly demands that a person shall have an intent to commit an offence if he is to be guilty of an attempt to commit that offence. The word 'intent' may, it is true, have a specialised meaning in some contexts. But even if this can properly be attributed to the word where it is used in s1(1) there is no warrant for reading it as embracing recklessness, nor for reading into it whatever lesser degree of mens rea will suffice for the particular substantive offence in question. For an attempt nothing but conscious volition will do. Accordingly that part of the particulars of offence which referred to recklessness was meaningless, and the parts of the direction which involved a definition of recklessness, and an implied invitation to convict if the jury found the appellants to have acted recklessly, were misleading. There was thus, so it was contended, a risk that the jury convicted on the wrong basis of the verdict cannot safely be allowed to stand."

At the conclusion of the argument it appeared to us that this argument was logically sound and that it was borne out by the authorities cited to us, especially *Whybrow* (1951) 35 Cr App R 141. *Cunliffe* v *Goodman* [1950] 2 KB 237, 253 and *Mohan* (1975) 60 Cr App R 272, [1976] QB 1, and that it was not inconsistent with anything in *Hyam* v *Director of Public Prosecutions* (1974) 59 Cr App R

91, [1975] AC 55. Our attention had however been drawn to a difference of opinion between commentators about the relationship between the mens rea in an attempt and the ingredients of the substantive offence, and we therefore reserved judgment so as to consider whether the question was not perhaps more difficult than it seemed. In the event we have come to the conclusion that there does exist a problem in this field, and that it is by no means easy to solve; but also that it need not be solved for the purpose of deciding the present appeal. In our judgment two different situations must be distinguished. The first exists where the substantive offence consists simply of the act which constitutes the actus reus (which for present purposes we shall call the "result") coupled with some element of volition, which may or may not amount to a full intent. Here the only question is whether the intent to bring about the result called for by s1(1) is to be watered down to such a degree, if any, as to make it correspond with the mens rea of the substantive offence. The second situation is more complicated. It exists where the substantive offence does not consist of one result and one mens rea, but rather involves not only the underlying intention to produce the result, but another state of mind directed to some circumstance or act which the prosecution must also establish in addition to proving the result. The problem may be illustrated by reference to the offence of attempted rape. As regards the substantive offence the "result" takes the shape of sexual intercourse with a woman. But the offence is not established without proof of an additional circumstance (namely that the woman did not consent), and a state of mind relative to that circumstance (namely that the defendant knew she did not consent, or was reckless as to whether she consented). When one turns to the offence of attempted rape, one thing is obvious, that the result, namely the act of sexual intercourse, must be intended in the full sense. Also obvious is the fact that proof of an intention to have intercourse with a woman, together with an act towards that end, is not enough: the offence must involve proof of something about the woman's consent, and something about the defendant's state of mind in relation to that consent. The problem is to decide precisely what that something is. Must the prosecution prove not only that the defendant intended the act, but also that he intended it to be non-consensual? Or should the jury be directed to consider two different states of mind, intend as to the act and recklessness as to the circumstances? Here the commentators differ: contrast Smith & Hogan, Criminal Law, 5th ed, pp255 et seq., with a note on the Act by Professor Griew in Current Law Statutes 1981.

We must now grapple with the very problem that Mustill LJ identifies in the last paragraph of the passage cited. In our judgment an acceptable analysis of the offence of rape is as follows:

1) The intention of the offender is to have sexual intercourse with a woman.

2) The offence is committed if, but only if, the circumstances are that:

   a) the woman does not consent; and

   b) the defendant knows that she is not consenting or is reckless as to whether she consents.

Precisely the same analysis can be made of the offence of attempted rape:

1) The intention of the offender is to have sexual intercourse with a woman.

2) The offence is committed if, but only if, the circumstances are that:

   a) the woman does not consent; and

   b) the defendant knows that she is not consenting or is reckless as to whether she consents.

The only difference between the two offences is that in rape sexual intercourse takes place whereas in attempted rape it does not, although there has to be some act which is more than preparatory to sexual intercourse. Considered in that way, the intent of the defendant is precisely the same in rape and in attempted rape and the mens rea is identical, namely, an intention to have intercourse plus a knowledge of or recklessness as to the woman's absence of consent. No question of attempting to achieve a reckless state of mind arises; the attempt relates to the physical activity; the mental state of the defendant is the same. A man does not recklessly have sexual intercourse, nor does he recklessly attempt it. Recklessness in rape and attempted rape arises not in relation to the physical act of the accused but only in his state of mind when engaged in the activity of having or attempting to have sexual intercourse. If this is the true analysis, as we believe it is, the attempt does not require any different intention on the part of the accused from that for the full offence of rape. We believe this to be a desirable result which in the instant case did not require the jury to be burdened with different directions as to the accused's state of mind, dependent upon whether the individual achieved or failed to achieve sexual intercourse.

We recognise, of course, that our reasoning cannot apply to all offences and all attempts. Where, for example, as in causing death by reckless driving or reckless arson, no state of mind other than recklessness is involved in the offence, there can be no attempt to commit it. In our judgment, however, the words "with intent to commit an offence" to be found in s1 of the 1981 Act mean, when applied to rape, "with intent to have sexual intercourse with a woman in circumstances where she does not consent and the defendant knows or could not care less about her absence of consent." The only "intent", giving that word its natural and ordinary meaning, of the rapist is to have sexual intercourse. He commits the offence because of the circumstances in which he manifests that intent, ie when the woman is not consenting and he either knows it or could not care less about the absence of consent. Accordingly we take the view that in relation to the four appellants the judge was right to give the directions that he did when inviting the jury to consider the charges of attempted rape.'

Commentary

Note that the current DCCB (Law Com No 177, vol 1, 1989) clause 49(2) provides:

'For the purposes of subsection (1) [attempt to commit an offence], an intention to commit an offence is an intention with respect to all the elements of the offence other than fault elements, except that recklessness with respect to circumstances suffices where it suffices for the offence itself.'

This expresses as a general principle the approach demonstrated by the court in the present case to rape.

R v Miller [1954] 2 QB 282 Hampshire Assizes (Lynskey J)

Meaning of actual bodily harm

Facts

The defendant was charged with raping his wife and assault contrary to s47. Lynskey J directed the jury on the assault charge in the following terms:

'The point has been taken that there is no evidence of bodily harm. The bodily harm alleged is said to be the result of the prisoner's actions, and that is, if the jury accept the evidence, that he threw the wife down three times. There is evidence that afterwards she was in a hysterical and nervous condition, but it is said by counsel that that is not actual bodily harm. Actual bodily harm, according to Archbold, 32nd ed, p959, includes "any hurt or injury calculated to interfere with the health or comfort of the prosecutor." There was a time when shock was not regarded as bodily hurt, but the day has gone by when that could be said. It seems to me now that if a person is caused hurt or injury resulting, not in any physical injury, but in an injury to her state of mind for the time being, that is within the definition of actual bodily harm, and on that point I would leave the case to the jury.'

Held

The defendant was acquitted of rape on the basis of his wife's deemed consent, but was convicted of the assault.

R v Mowatt [1968] 1 QB 421 Court of Appeal (Criminal Division) (Diplock LJ, Brabin and Waller JJ)

Meaning of 'malicious' under s20 Offences Against the Person Act 1861

Facts

The defendant was convicted under s20 of the Offences Against the Person Act 1861 following an attack he had carried out on a police officer, during which he had rained blows on the officer's face and pushed him roughly to the ground. The defendant appealed on the ground that the trial judge had failed to give an adequate direction to the jury as to the meaning of 'maliciously'.

Held

The appeal would be dismissed.

Diplock LJ:

'In the offence under section 20 ... the word "maliciously" does import upon the part of the person who unlawfully inflicts the wound or other grievous bodily harm an awareness that his act may have the consequence of causing some physical harm to some other person. That is what is meant by "the particular kind of harm"; in the citation from Professor Kenny. It is quite unnecessary that the accused should have foreseen that his unlawful act might cause physical harm of the gravity described in the section, ie a wound or serious physical injury. It is enough that he should have foreseen that some physical harm to some person, albeit of a minor character, might result.

In many cases in instructing a jury upon a charge under section 20 ... it may be unnecessary to refer specifically to the word "maliciously".... Where the evidence for the prosecution, if accepted, shows that the physical act of the accused which caused the injury to another person was a direct assault which any ordinary person would be bound to realise was likely to cause some physical harm to the other person (as, for instance, an assault with a weapon or the boot or violence with the hands) and the defence put forward on behalf of the accused is not that the assault was accidental or that he did not realise that it might cause some physical harm to the victim, but is some other defence such as that he did not do the alleged act or that he did it in self-defence, it is unnecessary to deal specifically in the summing-up with what is meant by the word "maliciously" in the section. It can only confuse the jury.'

R v Olugboja (1981) 73 Cr App R 344 (Dunn LJ, Milmo and May JJ)

Rape - consent - direction to the jury

Facts

The appellant was convicted of raping the complainant, J. The point of law raised in the appeal was stated by Dunn LJ as being:

'... whether to constitute the offence of rape it is necessary for the consent of the victim of sexual intercourse to be vitiated by force, the fear of force, or fraud; or whether it is sufficient to prove that in fact the victim did not consent.'

Held

The appeal would be dismissed.

Dunn LJ:

[Having considered the Report of the Heilbron group (Cmnd 6352), and the CLRC Working Paper on Sexual Offences (1980)]

'Although "consent" is [a] common word it covers a wide range of states of mind in the context of intercourse between a man and a woman, ranging from actual desire on the one hand to reluctant acquiescence on the other. We do not think that the issue of consent should be left to a jury without some further direction. What this should be will depend on the circumstances of each case. The jury will have been reminded of the burden and standard of proof required to establish each ingredient, including lack of consent, of the offence. They should be directed that consent, or the absence of it, is to be given its ordinary meaning and if need be, by way of example, that there is a difference between consent and submission; every consent involves a submission, but it by no means follows that a mere submission involves consent (*per* Coleridge J in *Day* (1841) 9 C & P 722, 724).

In the majority of cases, where the allegation is that the intercourse was had by force or the fear of force, such a direction coupled with specific references to and comments on the evidence relevant to the absence of real consent will clearly suffice. In the less common type of case where intercourse takes place after threats not involving violence or the fear of it, as in the examples given by Mrs Trewella [counsel for the appellant] to which we have referred earlier in this judgment, we think that an appropriate direction to a jury will have to be fuller. They should be directed to concentrate on the state of mind of the victim immediately before the act of sexual intercourse, having regard to all the relevant circumstances and in particular the events leading up to the act, and her reaction to them showing their impact on her mind.

Apparent acquiescence after penetration does not necessarily involve consent, which must have occurred before the act takes place. In addition to the general direction about consent which we have outlined, the jury will probably be helped in such cases by being reminded that in this context consent does comprehend the wide spectrum of states of mind to which we earlier referred, and that the dividing line in such circumstances between real consent on the one hand and mere submission on the other may not be easy to draw. Where it is to be drawn in a given case is for the jury to decide, applying their combined good sense, experience and knowledge of human nature and modern behaviour to all the relevant facts of that case.

Looked at in this way we find no misdirection by the judge in this case.'

R v R [1991] 3 WLR 767 House of Lords (Lord Keith, Lord Brandon, Lord Griffiths, Lord Ackner and Lord Lowry)

Whether a husband can be convicted of the rape of his wife

Facts

The defendant married his wife in 1984, but she left him to return to her parents in 1989, indicating that she intended to commence proceedings for divorce. While his wife was staying with her parents, the defendant visited her, and attempted to have sexual intercourse with her. The defendant was, in due course, convicted of the attempted rape of his wife, and appealed unsuccessfully to the Court of Appeal on the ground that the trial judge had made a wrong decision in law in ruling that a husband could be guilty of raping his wife where she has revoked her consent to sexual intercourse. The defendant appealed to the House of Lords.

Held

The appeal would be dismissed.

Lord Keith:

'Sir Matthew Hale, in his *History of the Pleas of the Crown* (1736) vol 1, ch 58, p629, wrote:

"But the husband cannot be guilty of a rape committed by himself upon his lawful wife, for by their mutual matrimonial consent and contract the wife hath given herself up in this kind unto her husband which she cannot retract."

There is no similar statement in the works of any earlier English commentator. In 1803 East, in his *Treatise of the Pleas of the Crown*, vol 1. ch X, p446, wrote: "a husband cannot by law be guilty of ravishing his wife, on account of the matrimonial consent which she cannot retract." In the first (1822) edition of *Archbold's, A Summary of the Law Relative to Pleading and Evidence in Criminal Cases*, at p259 it was stated, after a reference to *Hale*, "A husband also cannot be guilty of a rape upon his wife."

For over 150 years after the publication of Hale's work there appears to have been no reported case in which judicial consideration was given to his proposition. The first such case was *R v Clarence* (1888) 22 QBD 23, to which I shall refer later. It may be taken that the proposition was generally regarded as an accurate statement of the common law of England. The common law is, however, capable of evolving in the light of changing social, economic and cultural developments. Hale's proposition reflected the state of affairs in these respects at the time it was enunciated. Since then the status of women, and particularly of married women, has changed out of all recognition in various ways which are very familiar and upon which it is unnecessary to go into detail. Apart from property matters and the availability of matrimonial remedies, one of the most important changes is that marriage is in modern times regarded as a partnership of equals, and no longer one in which the wife must be the subservient chattel of the husband. Hale's proposition involves that by marriage a wife gives her irrevocable consent to sexual intercourse with her husband under all circumstances and irrespective of the state of her health or how she happens to be feeling at the time. In modern times any reasonable person must regard that conception as quite unacceptable.

In *S v H M Advocate*, 1989 SLT 469 the High Court of Justiciary in Scotland recently considered the supposed martial exemption in rape in that country. In two earlier cases, *H M Advocate v Duffy*, 1983 SLT 7 and *H M Advocate v Paxton*, 1985 SLT 96 it had been held by single judges that the exemption did not apply where the parties to the marriage were not cohabiting. The High Court held that the exemption, if it had ever been part of the law of Scotland, was no longer so. The principal authority for the exemption was to be found in Hume's *Criminal Law of Scotland*, first published in 1797. The same statement appeared in each edition up to the fourth, by Bell, in 1844. At p306 of vol 1 of that edition, dealing with art and part guilt of abduction and rape, it was said:

"This is true without exception even of the husband of the woman, who though he cannot himself commit a rape on his own wife, who has surrendered her person to him in that sort, may, however be accessory to that crime … committed upon her by another."

It seems likely that this pronouncement consciously followed *Hale*.

The Lord Justice-General, Lord Emslie, who delivered the judgment of the court, expressed doubt whether Hume's view accurately represented the law of Scotland even at the time when it was expressed and continued 1989 SLT 459, 473:

"We say no more on this matter which was not the subject of debate before us, because we are satisfied that the Solicitor-General was well founded in his contention that whether or not the reason for the husband's immunity given by Hume was a good one in the eighteenth and early nineteenth centuries, it has since disappeared altogether. Whatever Hume meant to encompass in the concept of a wife's 'surrender of her person' to her husband 'in that sort' the concept is to be understood against the background of the status of women and the position of a married woman at the time when he wrote. Then, no doubt, a married woman could be said to have subjected herself to her husband's dominion in all things. She was required to obey him in all things. Leaving out of account the absence of rights of property, a wife's freedoms were virtually non-existent, and she had in particular no right whatever to interfere in her husband's control over the lives and upbringing of any children of the marriage.

"By the second half of the twentieth century, however, the status of women, and the status of a married woman, in our law have changed quite dramatically. A husband and wife are now for all practical purposes equal partners in marriage and both husband and wife are tutors and curators of their children. A wife is not obliged to obey her husband in all things nor to suffer excessive sexual demands on the part of her husband. She may rely on such demands as evidence of unreasonable behaviour for the purposes of divorce. A live system of law will always have regard to changing circumstances to test the justification for any exception to the application of a general rule. Nowadays it cannot seriously be maintained that by marriage a wife submits herself irrevocably to sexual intercourse in all circumstances. It cannot be affirmed nowadays, whatever the position may have been in earlier centuries, that it is an incident of modern marriage that a wife consents to intercourse in all circumstances, including sexual intercourse obtained only by force. There is no doubt that a wife does not consent to assault upon her person and there is no plausible justification for saying today that she nevertheless is to be taken to consent to intercourse by assault. The modern cases of *H M Advocate* v *Duffy*, 1983 SLT 7 and *H M Advocate* v *Paxton*, 1985 SLT 96 show that any supposed implied consent to intercourse is not irrevocable, that separation may demonstrate that such consent has been withdrawn, and that in these circumstances a relevant charge of rape may lie against a husband. This development of the law since Hume's time immediately prompts the question: is revocation of a wife's implied consent to intercourse, which is revocable, only capable of being established by the act of separation? In our opinion the answer to that question must be no. Revocation of a consent which is revocable must depend on the circumstances. Where there is no separation this may be harder to prove but the critical question in any case must simply be whether or not consent has been withheld. The fiction of implied consent has no useful purpose to serve today in the law of rape in Scotland. The reason given by Hume for the husband's immunity from prosecution upon a charge of rape of his wife, if it ever was a good reason, no longer applies today. There is now, accordingly, no justification for the supposed immunity of a husband. Logically the only question is whether or not as matter of fact the wife consented to the acts complained of, and we affirm the decision of the trial judge that charge 2(b) is a relevant charge against the appellant to go to trial."

I consider the substance of that reasoning to be no less valid in England than in Scotland. On grounds of principle there is now no justification for the marital exception in rape.

It is now necessary to review how the matter stands in English case law. In *R* v *Clarence*, 22 QBD 23 a husband who knew that he suffered from a venereal disease communicated it to his wife through sexual intercourse. He was convicted on charges of unlawfully inflicting grievous bodily harm contrary to s20 of the Offences Against the Person Act 1861 and of assault occasioning actual bodily harm contrary to s47 of the same Act. The convictions were quashed by a court of 13 judges of Crown Cases Reserved, with four dissents. Consideration was given to Hale's proposition, and it appears to have been accepted as sound by a majority of the judges. However, Wills J said, at p33, that he was not prepared to assent to the proposition that rape between married persons was impossible. Field J (in whose judgment Charles J concurred) said, at p57, that he should hesitate before he adopted Hale's proposition, and that he thought there might be many cases in which a wife might lawfully refuse intercourse and in which, if the husband imposed it by violence, he might be held guilty of a crime.

In *Rex* v *Clarke* [1949] 2 All ER 488 a husband was charged with rape upon his wife in circumstances where justices had made an order providing that the wife should no longer be bound to cohabit with the husband. Byrne J refused to quash the charge. He accepted Hale's proposition as generally sound, but said, at p449:

"The position, therefore, was that the wife, by process of law, namely, by marriage, had given consent to the husband to exercise the marital right during such time as the ordinary relations created by the marriage contract subsisted between them, but by a further process of law, namely, the justices' order, her consent to marital intercourse was revoked. Thus, in my opinion, the husband was not entitled to have intercourse with her without her consent."

In *R* v *Miller* [1954] 2 QB 282 the husband was charged with rape of his wife after she had left him and filed a petition for divorce. He was also charged with assault upon her occasioning actual bodily harm. Lynskey J quashed the charge of rape but refused to quash that of assault. He proceeded on the basis that Hale's proposition was correct, and also that *Rex* v *Clarke* had been rightly decided, but took the view, at p290, that there was no evidence which entitled him to say that the wife's implied consent to marital intercourse had been revoked by an act of the parties or by an act of the court. As regards the count of assault, having referred to *R* v *Jackson* [1891] 1 QB 671, where it was held that a husband had no right to confine his wife in order to enforce a decree for restitution of conjugal rights, he said, at pp291–292:

"It seems to me, on the reasoning of that case, that although the husband has a right to marital intercourse, and the wife cannot refuse her consent, and although if he does have intercourse against her actual will, it is not rape, nevertheless he is not entitled to use force or violence in the exercise of that right, and if he does so he may make himself liable to the criminal law, not for the offence of rape, but for whatever other offence the facts of the particular case warrant. If he should wound her he might be charged with wounding or causing actual bodily harm, or he may be liable to be convicted of common assault. The result is that in the present case I am satisfied that the second count is a valid one and must be left to the jury for their decision."

So the case had the strange result that although the use of force to achieve sexual intercourse was criminal the actual achievement of it was not. Logically, it might be thought that if a wife be held to have by marriage given her implied consent to sexual intercourse she is not entitled to refuse her husband's advances, and that if she resists then he is entitled to use reasonable force to overcome that resistance. This indicates the absurdity of the fiction of implied consent. In the law of Scotland, as Lord Emslie observed in *S* v *H M Advocate*, 1989 SLT 469, 473, rape is regarded as an aggravated assault, of which the achievement of sexual intercourse is the worst aggravating feature. It is unrealistic to sort out the sexual intercourse from the other acts involved in the assault and to allow the wife to complain of the minor acts but not of the major and most unpleasant one.

The next case is *R* v *O'Brien (Edward)* [1974] 3 All ER 663, where Park J, held that a decree nisi effectively terminated a marriage and revoked the wife's implied consent to marital intercourse, so that subsequent intercourse by the husband without her consent constituted rape. There was a similar holding by the Criminal Division of the Court of Appeal in *R* v *Steele* (1976) 65 Cr App R 22 as regards a situation where the spouses were living apart and the husband had given an undertaking to the court not to molest his wife. A decision to the like effect was given by the same court in *R* v *Roberts* [1986] Crim LR 188, where the spouses had entered into a formal separation agreement. In *R* v *Sharples* [1990] Crim LR 198, however, it was ruled by Judge Fawcus that a husband could not be convicted of rape upon his wife in circumstances where there was in force a family protection order in her favour and he had had sexual intercourse with her against her will. The order was made under s16 of the Domestic Proceedings and Magistrates Courts Act 1978 in the terms that "the respondent shall not use or threaten to use violence against the person of the applicant." Judge Fawcus took the view that it was not to be inferred that by obtaining an order in these terms the wife had withdrawn her consent to sexual intercourse.

There should be mentioned next a trio of cases which were concerned with the question whether acts done by a husband preliminary to sexual intercourse with an estranged wife against her will could properly be charged as indecent assaults. The cases are *R* v *Caswell* [1984] Crim LR 111, *R* v *Kowalski* (1987) 86 Cr App R 339, and *R* v *H* (unreported), 5 October 1990, Auld J. The effect of these decisions appears to be that in general acts which would ordinarily be indecent but which are preliminary to an act of normal sexual intercourse are deemed to be covered by the wife's implied consent to the latter, but that certain acts, such as fellatio, are not to be so deemed. Those cases illustrate the contortions to which judges have found it necessary to resort in face of the fiction of implied consent to sexual intercourse.

The foregoing represent all the decisions in the field prior to the ruling by Owen J in the present case. In all of them lip service, at least, was paid to Hale's proposition. Since then there have been three further decisions by single judges. The first of them is *R* v *C (Rape: Marital Exemption)*

[1991] 1 All ER 755. There were nine counts in an indictment against a husband and a co-defendant charging various offences of a sexual nature against an estranged wife. One of these was of rape as a principal. Simon Brown J followed the decision in *S v H M Advocate*, 1989 SLT 469 and held that the whole concept of a marital exemption in rape was misconceived. He said, at p758:

"Were it not for the deeply unsatisfactory consequences of reaching any other conclusion on the point, I would shrink, if sadly, from adopting this radical view of the true position in law. But adopt it I do. Logically, I regard it as the only defensible stance, certainly now as the law has developed and arrived in the late twentieth century. In my judgment, the position in law today is, as already declared in Scotland, that there is no marital exemption to the law of rape. That is the ruling I give. Count seven accordingly remains and will be left to the jury without any specific direction founded on the concept of marital exemption."

A different view was taken in the other two cases, by reason principally of the terms in which rape is defined in s1(1) of the Sexual Offences (Amendment) Act 1976, viz:

"For the purposes of s1 of the Sexual Offences Act 1956 (which relates to rape) a man commits rape if - (a) he has unlawful sexual intercourse with a woman who at the time of the intercourse does not consent to it; and (b) at that time he knows that she does not consent to the intercourse or he is reckless as to whether she consents to it; ..."

In *R v J (Rape: Marital Exemption)* [1991] 1 All ER 759 a husband was charged with having raped his wife, from whom he was living apart at the time. Rougier J ruled that the charge was bad, holding that the effect of s1(1)(a) of the Act of 1976 was that the marital exemption embodied in Hale's proposition was preserved, subject to those exceptions established by cases decided before the Act was passed. He took the view that the word "unlawful" in the subsection meant "illicit", ie outside marriage, that being the meaning which in *R v Chapman* [1959] 1 QB 100 it had been held to bear in s19 of the Sexual Offences Act 1956. Then in *R v S* (unreported), 15 January 1991, Swinton-Thomas J followed Rougier J in holding that s1(1) of the Act of 1976 preserved the marital exemption subject to the established common law exceptions. Differing, however, from Rougier J, he took the view that it remained open to judges to define further exceptions. In the case before him the wife had obtained a family protection order in similar terms to that in *R v Sharples* [1900] Crim LR 198. Differing from Judge Fawcus in that case, Swinton-Thomas J held that the existence of the family protection order created an exception to the marital exemption. It is noteworthy that both Rougier J and Swinton-Thomas J expressed themselves as being regretful that s1(1) of the Act of 1976 precluded them from taking the same line as Simon Brown J in *R v C (Rape: Marital Exemption)* [1991] 1 All ER 755.

The position then is that that part of Hale's proposition which asserts that a wife cannot retract the consent to sexual intercourse which she gives on marriage has been departed from in a series of decided cases. On grounds of principle there is no good reason why the whole proposition should not be held inapplicable in modern times. The only question is whether s1(1) of the Act of 1976 presents an insuperable obstacle to that sensible course. The argument is that "unlawful" in the subsection means outside the bond of marriage. That is not the most natural meaning of the word, which normally describes something which is contrary to some law or enactment or is done without lawful justification or excuse. Certainly in modern times sexual intercourse outside marriage would not ordinarily be described as unlawful. If the subsection proceeds on the basis that a woman on marriage gives a general consent to sexual intercourse, there can never be any question of intercourse with her by her husband being without her consent. There would thus be no point in enacting that only intercourse without consent outside marriage is to constitute rape.

R v Chapman [1959] 1 QB 100 is founded on in support of the favoured construction. That was a case under s19 of the Sexual Offences Act 1956, which provides:

"(1) It is an offence, subject to the exception mentioned in this section, for a person to take an unmarried girl under the age of 18 out of the possession of her parent or guardian against his will, if she is so taken with the intention that she shall have unlawful sexual intercourse with men or with a particular man. (2) A person is not guilty of an offence under this section because he takes such a girl out of the possession of her parent or guardian as mentioned above, if he believes her to be of the age of 18 or over and has reasonable cause for the belief."

It was argued for the defendant that "unlawful" in that section connoted either intercourse contrary to some positive enactment or intercourse in a brothel or something of that kind. Donovan J, giving the judgment of the Court of Criminal Appeal, rejected both interpretations and continued, at p105:

"If the two interpretations suggested for the appellant are rejected, as we think they must be, then the word 'unlawful' in s19 is either surplusage or means 'illicit'. We do not think it is surplusage, because otherwise a man who took such a girl out of her parents' possession against their will with the honest and bona fide intention of marrying her might have no defence, even if he carried out that intention. In our view, the word simply means 'illicit,' ie, outside the bond of marriage. In other words, we take the same view as the trial judge. We think this interpretation accords with the common sense of the matter, and with what we think was the obvious intention of Parliament.

It is also reinforced by the alternatives specifically mentioned in ss17 and 18 of the Act, that is, 'with the intent that she shall marry, or have unlawful intercourse …'"

In that case there was a context to the word "unlawful" which by cogent reasoning led the court to the conclusion that it meant outside the bond of marriage. However, even though it is appropriate to read the Act of 1976 alongside that of 1956, so that the provisions of the latter Act form part of the context of the former, there is another important context to s1(1) of the Act of 1976, namely the existence of the exceptions to the marital exemption contained in the decided cases. Sexual intercourse in any of the cases covered by the exceptions still takes place within the bond of marriage. So if "unlawful" in the subsection means "outside the bond of marriage" it follows that sexual intercourse in a case which falls within the exceptions is not covered by the definition of rape, notwithstanding that it is not consented to by the wife. That involves that the exceptions have been impliedly abolished. If the intention of Parliament was to abolish the exceptions it would have been expected to do so expressly, and it is in fact inconceivable that Parliament should have had such an intention. In order that the exceptions might be preserved, it would be necessary to construe "unlawfully" as meaning "outside marriage or within marriage in a situation covered by one of the exceptions to the marital exemption." Some slight support for that construction is perhaps to be gathered from the presence of the words "who at the time of the intercourse does not consent to it," considering that a woman in a case covered by one of the exceptions is treated as having withdrawn the general consent to intercourse given on marriage but may nevertheless have given her consent to it on the particular occasion. However, the gloss which the suggested construction would place on the word "unlawfully" would give it a meaning unique to this particular subsection, and if the mind of the draftsman had been directed to the existence of the exceptions he would surely have dealt with them specifically and not in such an oblique fashion. In *R* v *Chapman* Donovan LJ accepted, at p102, that the word "unlawfully" in relation to carnal knowledge had in many early statutes not been used with any degree of precision, and he referred to a number of enactments making it a felony unlawfully and carnally to know any woman-child under the age of 10. He said, at p103 "one would think that all intercourse with a child under 10 would be unlawful; and on that footing the word would be mere surplusage." The fact is that it is clearly unlawful to have sexual intercourse with any woman without her consent, and that the use of the word in the subsection adds nothing. In my opinion there are no rational grounds for putting the suggested gloss on the word, and it should be treated as being mere surplusage in this enactment, as it clearly fell to be in those referred to by Donovan LJ. That was the view taken of it by this House in *McMonagle* v *Westminster City Council* [1990] 2 AC 716 in relation to paragraph 3A of Schedule 3 to the Local Government (Miscellaneous Provisions) Act 1983.

I am therefore of the opinion that s1(1) of the Act of 1976 presents no obstacle to this House declaring that in modern times the supposed marital exception in rape forms no part of the law of

England. The Court of Appeal (Criminal Division) took a similar view. Towards the end of the judgment of that court Lord Lane CJ said, at p1074:

"The remaining and no less difficult question is whether, despite that view, this is an area where the court should step aside to leave the matter to the Parliamentary process. This is not the creation of a new offence, it is the removal of a common law fiction which has become anachronistic and offensive and we consider that it is our duty having reached that conclusion to act upon it."

I respectfully agree.

My Lords, for these reasons I would dismiss this appeal, and answer the certified question in the affirmative.'

R v Roberts (1971) 56 Cr App R 95 Court of Appeal (Criminal Division) (Stephenson LJ, Thompson and Bridge JJ)

Meaning of 'occasioning' under s47 Offences Against the Person Act 1861

Facts

The defendant had given a lift to the victim, a young woman, and during the journey he made a number of improper suggestions to her, and at one stage touched her breasts over the front of her coat. The victim jumped from the car whilst it was moving (the speed was variously stated as being between 20 and 40 miles per hour), and suffered grazing and concussion in her fall. The defendant was convicted under s47, and appealed on the ground that the victim's action in jumping from the car had broken the chain of causation, thus relieving him of liability for the harm.

Held

The appeal would be dismissed.

Stephenson LJ:

'We have been helpfully referred to a number of reported cases, some well over a century old, of women jumping out of windows, or jumping or throwing themselves into a river, as a consequence of threats of violence or actual violence. The most recent case is the case of *Lewis* [1970] Crim LR 647. An earlier case is that of *Beech* (1912) 7 Cr App R 197, which was a case of a woman jumping out of a window and injuring herself, and a man who had friendly relations with her, whom she knew and might have had reason to be afraid of, being prosecuted for inflicting grievous bodily harm upon her, contrary to section 20 of the Offences against the Person Act. In that case the Court of Criminal Appeal (at p200) approved the direction given by the trial judge in these terms: "Will you say whether the conduct of the prisoner amounted to a threat of causing injury to this young woman, was the act of jumping the natural consequence of the conduct of the prisoner, and was the grievous bodily harm the result of the conduct of the prisoner?" That, said the Court, was a proper direction as far as the law went, and they were satisfied that there was evidence before the jury of the prisoner causing actual bodily harm to the woman. "No-one could say," said Darling J when giving the judgment of the Court, "that if she jumped from the window it was not a natural consequence of the prisoner's conduct. It was a very likely thing for a woman to do as the result of the threats of a man who was conducting himself as this man indisputably was."

This Court thinks that that correctly states the law, and that Mr Carus was wrong in submitting to this Court that the jury must be sure that a defendant, who is charged either with inflicting grievous bodily harm or assault occasioning actual bodily harm, must foresee the actions of the victim which result in the grievous bodily harm, or the actual bodily harm. That, in the view of this Court, is not the test. The test is: Was it the natural result of what the alleged assailant said and did, in the sense that it was something that could reasonably have been foreseen as the consequence of what he was saying or doing? As it was put in one of the old cases, it had got to be shown to be his act, and if of course the victim does something so "daft," in the words of the appellant in this case, or so unexpected, not that this particular assailant did not actually foresee it but that no reasonable man could be expected to foresee it, then it is only in a very remote and unreal sense a consequence of his assault, it is really occasioned by a voluntary act on the part of the victim which could not reasonably be foreseen and which breaks the chain of causation between the assault and the harm or injury.'

R v Savage: R v Parmenter [1991] 3 WLR 914 House of Lords (Lord Keith, Lord Brandon, Lord Ackner, Lord Jauncey and Lord Lowry)

Mens rea for s20: mens rea for s47

R v Savage

Facts

The appellant was charged with unlawful wounding contrary to s20 of the Offences Against the Persons Act 1861. The case for the prosecution was that there had been bad feeling between the appellant and another young woman (Miss Beal) that the appellant had approached this other woman and thrown the contents of an almost full pint glass of beer at her, and that she had let go of the glass which broke, with the result that Miss Beal suffered cuts. The appellant admitted that it had been her intention to throw the beer over Miss Beal but denied any intention to cut her with the glass. The trial judge directed the jury that they were entitled to conclude that the appellant had wounded 'maliciously' if they were sure that her unlawful act in throwing the liquid from the glass caused it to slip from her hand and cut Miss Beal. The appellant's appeal against the conviction under s20 was allowed, but a conviction for assault occasioning actual bodily harm contrary to s47 of the Offences Against the Persons Act 1861 was substituted. The following question was certified for consideration by the House of Lords:

'(1) Whether a verdict of guilty of assault occasioning actual bodily harm is a permissible alternative verdict on a count alleging unlawful wounding contrary to s20 of the Offences against the Persons Act 1861. (2) Whether a verdict of guilty of assault occasioning actual bodily harm can be returned upon proof of an assault and of the fact that actual bodily harm was occasioned by the assault. (3) If it is proved that an assault has been committed and that actual bodily harm has resulted from that assault, whether a verdict of assault occasioning actual bodily harm may be returned in the absence of proof that the defendant intended to cause some actual bodily harm or was reckless as to whether such harm would be caused.'

R v Parmenter

Facts

The appellant was charged with four offences of inflicting grievous bodily harm contrary to s20 of the Offences Against the Persons Act 1861 in respect of injuries caused to his three month old son as a result of rough handling on his part. It was contended for the appellant at his trial that he had not had the intent required for the offence, given his lack of experience with small babies. Expert evidence suggested that the handling of the child would not have been inappropriate in the case of a three to four year old child but that it would have been quite inappropriate as regards a new born baby.

On the issue of intent the trial judge directed the jury, inter alia, that it was unnecessary that the accused should have foreseen that his unlawful act might cause physical harm in the form of grievous bodily harm. The jury were directed that it was sufficient that the appellant should have foreseen that some physical harm to some person, albeit of a minor character, might result from his actions. The appellant appealed successfully against his conviction, and the Crown appealed to the House of Lords. The following question was certified for consideration by the House of Lords:

'(1)(a) Whether in order to establish an offence under s20 of the Offences Against the Person Act 1861 the prosecution must prove that the defendant actually foresaw that his act would cause the particular kind of harm which was in fact caused, or whether it is sufficient to prove that (objectively) he ought so to have foreseen. (b) The like question in relation to s47 of the Act. (2)(a) For the purposes of the answer to question (1)(a), whether the particular kind of harm to be foreseen may be any physical harm, or harm of (i) the nature, or (ii) the degree, or (iii) the nature and the degree of the harm which actually occurred? (b) the like question in relation to s47 of the Act.'

R v Savage

Held

The appeal would be dismissed.

R v Parmenter

Held

The Crown's appeal would be allowed to the extent that a verdict of guilty of assault occasioning actual bodily harm contrary to s47 would be substituted for the conviction under s20.

Lord Ackner:

Given the overlap in the questions certified in both cases, Lord Ackner elected to deal with the issues raised seriatim. His Lordship had observed that in order for the first question certified in the *Savage* appeal to be decided in the appellant's favour, the House would have to depart from its own previous decision in *R v Wilson* [1984] AC 242 extracted later in this chapter. Lord Ackner quoted at length from the speech of Lord Roskill in *R v Wilson* and concluded:

'Having reviewed the relevant authorities Lord Roskill was content to accept that there can be an infliction of grievous bodily harm contrary to s20 without an assault being committed. For example, grievous bodily harm could be inflicted by creating panic. Another example provided to your Lordships in the course of the argument in the current appeals was interfering with the braking mechanism of a car, so as to cause the driver to be involved in an accident and thus suffer injuries. These are somewhat far-fetched examples. The allegation of inflicting grievous bodily harm or for that matter wounding, as was observed by Glidewell LJ, giving the judgment of the court in the *Savage* case [1991] 2 WLR 418, 421, inevitably imports or includes an allegation of assault, unless there are some quite extraordinary facts.

The critical question remained - do the allegations in a s20 charge "include either expressly or by implication" allegations of assault occasioning actual bodily harm. As to this, Lord Roskill concluded [1984] AC 247, 261:

"If 'inflicting' can, as the cases show, include 'inflicting by assault,' then even though such a charge may not necessarily do so, I do not for myself see why on a fair reading of s6(3) these allegations do not at least impliedly *include* 'inflicting by assault.' That is sufficient for present purposes though I also regard it as also a possible view that those former allegations *expressly* include the other allegations."

I respectfully agree with this reasoning and accordingly reject the submission that *R v Wilson* was wrongly decided. I would therefore answer the first of the certified questions in the *Savage* case in the affirmative. A verdict of guilty of assault occasioning actual bodily harm is a permissible alternative verdict on a count alleging unlawful wounding contrary to s20 of the Offences Against the Persons Act 1861.

[2] *Can a verdict of assault occasioning actual bodily harm be returned upon proof of an assault together with proof of the fact that actual bodily harm was occasioned by the assault, or must the prosecution also prove that the defendant intended to cause some actual bodily harm or was reckless as to whether such harm would be caused?*

Your Lordships are concerned with the mental element of a particular kind of assault, an assault "occasioning actual bodily harm." It is common ground that the mental element of assault is an intention to cause the victim to apprehend immediate and unlawful violence or recklessness whether such apprehension be caused: see *R v Venna* [1976] QB 421. It is of course common ground that Mrs Savage committed an assault upon Miss Beal when she threw the contents of her glass of beer over her. It is also common ground that however the glass came to be broken and Miss Beal's wrist thereby cut, it was, on the finding of the jury, Mrs Savage's handling of the glass which caused Miss Beal "actual bodily harm." Was the offence thus established or is there a further mental state that has to be established in relation to the bodily harm element of the offence? Clearly the section, by its terms, expressly imposes no such a requirement. Does it do so by necessary implication? It neither uses the word "intentionally" or "maliciously" The words "occasioning actual bodily harm" are descriptive of the word "assault," by reference to a particular kind of consequence.

In neither *Savage*, nor *Spratt*, nor in *Parmenter*, was the court's attention invited to the decision of the Court of Appeal in *R v Roberts* (1971) 56 Cr App R 95. This is perhaps explicable on the basis that this case is not referred to in the index to the current, edition of *Archbold, Criminal Pleading, Evidence and Practice*, 43rd ed (1988). The relevant text, at para 20-117 states: "The mens rea required [for actual bodily harm] is that required for common assault" without any authority being provided for this proposition.

It is in fact *Roberts'* case which provides authority for this proposition.'

Lord Ackner recited the facts of the case and the reasoning of the Court of Appeal (extracted later in this chapter), and concluded:

'Thus once the assault was established, the only remaining question was whether the victim's conduct was the natural consequence of that assault. The words "occasioning" raised solely a question of causation, an objective question which does not involve inquiring into the accused's state of mind. In *R v Spratt* [1990] 1 WLR 1073 McCowan LJ said, at p1082:

"However, the history of the interpretation of the Act of 1861 shows that, whether or not the word 'maliciously' appears in the section in question, the courts have consistently held that the mens rea of every type of offence against the person covers both actual intent and recklessness, in the sense of taking the risk of harm ensuing with foresight that it might happen."

McCowan LJ then quotes a number of authorities for that proposition. The first is *R v Ward* (1872) LR 1 CCR 356, but that was a case where the prisoner was charged with wounding with intent (s18) and convicted of malicious wounding (s20); next, *R v Bradshaw* (1878) 14 Cox CC 83, but that was a case where the accused was charged with manslaughter, which has nothing to do with a s47 case. Then *R v Cunningham* [1957] 2 QB 396, is quoted, a case under s23 of the Act concerned with unlawfully and maliciously administering, etc, a noxious thing which endangers life. And finally *R v Venna* [1976] QB 421 in which there was no issue as to whether in a s47 case, recklessness had to extend to actual bodily harm. Thus, none of the cases cited were concerned with the mental element required in s47 cases. Nevertheless, the Court of Appeal in *R v Parmenter* [1991] 2 WLR 408, 415, preferred the decision in *R v Spratt* [1990] 1 WLR 1073 to that of *R v Savage (Note)* [1991] 2 WLR 418 because the former was "founded on a line of authority leading directly to the conclusion there expressed."

My Lords, in my respectful view, the Court of Appeal in *Parmenter* were wrong in preferring the decision in *Spratt*'s case. The decision in *Roberts'* case, 56 Cr App R 95 was correct. The verdict of assault occasioning actual bodily harm may be returned upon proof of an assault together with proof of the fact that actual bodily harm was occasioned by the assault. The prosecution are not obliged to prove that the defendant intended to cause some actual bodily harm or was reckless as to whether such harm would be caused.

[3] *In order to establish an offence under s20 of the Act, must the prosecution prove that the defendant actually foresaw that his act would cause harm, or is it sufficient to prove that he ought so to have foreseen?*

Although your Lordships' attention has been invited to a plethora of decided cases, the issue is a narrow one. Is the decision of the Court of Criminal Appeal in *R v Cunningham* [1957] 2 QB 396 still good law, subject only to a gloss placed upon it by the Court of Appeal Criminal Division in *R v Mowatt* [1968] 1 QB 421, or does the later decision of your Lordships' House in *R v Caldwell* [1982] AC 341 provide the answer to this question? These three decisions require detailed consideration.'

Lord Ackner related the salient details of the Court of Appeal's decision in *R v Cunningham* [1957] 2 QB 396, and continued:

'Mr Sedley (counsel for Parmenter) has not invited your Lordships to reconsider the majority decision of your Lordships' House (in *R v Caldwell*). He chose a much less ambitious task. He submits that *R v Cunningham* cannot be bad law, since it is inconceivable that your Lordships' House, in its majority judgement, would have steered such a careful path around it. Your Lordships having power to overrule it, would, so he submits, have felt obliged to do so in order to avoid creating a false double standard of "recklessness." He further submits that it is significant that Lord Diplock, whose speech represented the views of the majority of your Lordships, nowhere suggests that his own judgment in *R v Mowatt* [1968] 1 QB 421 which clarified or modified *Cunningham*, was of doubtful validity.

In the light of these submissions it is necessary to deal in some detail with the *Caldwell* decision [1982] AC 341.'

Lord Ackner then proceeded to detail the facts of the case, and referred at length to the speech of Lord Diplock, and the judgment of Diplock LJ (as he then was in the Court of Appeal in *R v Mowatt* [1968] 1 QB 421. Lord Ackner concluded:

'Mr Sedley submitted that in *Caldwell*'s case your Lordships' House could have followed either of two possible paths to its conclusion as to the meaning of "recklessly" in the Act of 1971. These were: (a) to hold that *Cunningham* (and *Mowatt*) were wrongly decided and to introduce a single test, wherever recklessness was an issue; or (b) to accept that *Cunningham*, (subject to the *Mowatt* "gloss" to which no reference was made), correctly states the law in relation to the Offences Against the Person Act 1861, because the word "maliciously" in that statute was a term of legal art which imported into the concept of recklessness a special restricted meaning, thus distinguishing it from "reckless" or "recklessly" in modern "revising" statutes then before the House, where those words bore their then popular or dictionary meaning.

I agree with Mr Sedley that manifestly it was the latter course which the House followed. Therefore in order to establish an offence under s20 the prosecution must prove either the defendant intended or that he actually foresaw that his act would cause harm.

[4] *In order to establish an offence under s20 is it sufficient to prove that the defendant intended or foresaw the risk of some physical harm or must he intend or foresee either wounding or grievous bodily harm?*

It is convenient to set out once again the relevant part of the judgment of Diplock LJ in *R v Mowatt* [1968] 1 QB 421, 426. Having considered Professor Kenny's statement, which I have quoted above, he then said:

"In the offence under s20 ... for ... which [no] specific intent is required, the word 'maliciously' does import ... an awareness that his act may have the consequence of causing some physical harm to some other person. That is what is meant by 'the particular kind of harm' in the citation from Professor Kenny. It is quite unnecessary that the accused should have foreseen that his unlawful act might cause physical harm of the gravity described in the section, ie, a wound or serious physical injury. *It is enough that he should have foreseen that some physical harm to some person, albeit of a minor character, might result.*" (Emphasis added.)

Mr Sedley submits that this statement of the law is wrong. He contends that properly construed, the section requires foresight of a wounding or grievous bodily harm. He drew your Lordships' attention to criticisms of the *Mowatt* decision made by Professor Glanville-Williams and by Professor JC Smith in their text books and in articles or commentaries. They argue that a person should not be criminally liable for consequences of his conduct unless he foresaw a consequence falling into the same legal category as that set out in the indictment.

Such a general principle runs contrary to the decision in *Roberts'* case, 56 Cr App R 95 which I have already stated to be, in my opinion, correct. The contention is apparently based on the proposition that as the actus reus of a s20 offence is the wounding or the infliction of grievous bodily harm, the mens rea must consist of foreseeing such wounding or grievous bodily harm. But there is no such hard and fast principle. To take but two examples, the actus reus of murder is the killing of the victim, but foresight of grievous bodily harm is sufficient and indeed, such bodily harm, need not be such as to be dangerous to life. Again, in the case of manslaughter, death is frequently the unforeseen consequence of the violence used.

The argument that as s20 and s47 have both the same penalty, this somehow supports the proposition that the foreseen consequences must coincide with the harm actually done, overlooks the oft repeated statement that this is the irrational result of this piecemeal legislation. The Act "is a rag-bag of offences brought together from a wide variety of sources with no attempt, as the draftsman frankly acknowledged, to introduce consistency as to substance or as to form." (Professor Smith in his commentary on *R v Parmenter* [1991] CLR 43.)

If s20 was to be limited to cases where the accused does not desire but does foresee wounding or grievous bodily harm, it would have a very limited scope. The mens rea in a s20 crime is comprised in the word "maliciously." As was pointed out by Lord Lane CJ, giving the judgment of the Court of Appeal in *R v Sullivan* on 27 October 1980 (unreported save in [1981] Crim LR 46) the "particular kind of harm" in the citation from Professor Kenny was directed to "harm to the person" as opposed to "harm to property." Thus it was not concerned with the degree of the harm foreseen. It is accordingly in my judgment wrong to look upon the decision in *Mowatt* [1968] 1 QB 421 as being in any way inconsistent with the decision in *Cunningham* [1957] 2 QB 396.

My Lords, I am satisfied that the decision in *Mowatt* was correct and that it is quite unnecessary that the accused should either have intended or have foreseen that his unlawful act might cause physical harm of the gravity described in s20, ie a wound or serious physical injury. It is enough that he should have foreseen that some physical harm to some person, albeit of a minor character, might result.

In the result I would dismiss the appeal in *Savage's* case, but allow the appeal in *Parmenter's* case, but only to the extent of substituting, in accordance with the provisions of s3(2) of the Criminal Appeal Act 1968, verdicts of guilty of assault occasioning actual bodily harm contrary to s47 of the Act for the four s20 offences of which he was convicted.'

R v Spratt (1990) 91 Cr App R 362 Court of Appeal (Criminal Division) (McCowan LJ, Tudor Evans and Brooke JJ)

Mens rea for s47 assault

Facts

The appellant had fired an air pistol from the window of his dwelling into a courtyard below. He claimed that he had been aiming at a sign. A pellet from the gun struck a child playing in the yard. The appellant denied any knowledge that children were in the vicinity of the sign. The appellant was charged with actual bodily harm contrary to s47 of the Offences Against the Persons Act 1861. Following defence counsel's advice that *Caldwell* recklessness now applied to the offence, the appellant pleaded guilty. He had stated in interview, however, that he would not have fired the gun had he known children were playing close by. The appellant appealed initially against the sentence imposed, but in the course of the appeal sought to challenge the conviction on the basis that he had pleaded guilty following erroneous advice from counsel. He contended that the recklessness applicable to s47 was that expounded in *R* v *Cunningham*, and on that basis he would have pleaded not guilty.

Held

The appeal would be allowed.

McCowan LJ [Having referred to ss20 and 47 of the 1861 Act, and the definition of recklessness relied upon by Byrne J in *R* v *Cunningham* (1957) Cr App R 155 at 159, continued]:

'We turn to consider recklessness under section 47. In *Bradshaw* [1878] 14 Cox CC 83, the accused was charged with manslaughter arising from what he had done to a member of the opposing team in a game of football. In summing up to the jury Bramwell LJ said at pp84-85:

"The question for you to decide is whether the death of the deceased was caused by the unlawful act of the prisoner ... if the prisoner intended to cause serious hurt to the deceased, or if he knew that, in charging as he did, he might produce serious injury and was indifferent and reckless as to whether he would produce serious injury or not, then the act would be unlawful. In either case he would be guilty of a criminal act and you must find him guilty; if you are of a contrary opinion you will acquit him."

"Recklessness" was there defined in a manner consistent with that in the case of *Cunningham* (supra). In *Venna* (1975) 61 Cr App R 310, [1976] QB 421 the charge was one of assault occasioning actual bodily harm. Police officers called to the scene of a street disturbance had sought to arrest the accused. He resisted violently and in the process went to the ground where two officers held him by the arm. He continued to kick and, in so doing, fractured the hand of one of the officers. The trial judge summed up in these terms:

"If he lashed out with his feet, knowing that there are officers about him and knowing that by lashing out he will probably or is likely to kick somebody or hurt his hand by banging his heel down on it, then he is equally guilty of the offence. Venna can therefore be guilty of the offence in count 3 in the indictment if he deliberately brought his foot down on Police Constable Spencer's hand or if he lashed out simply reckless as to who was there, not caring an iota as to whether he kicked somebody or brought his heel down on his hand."

Giving the judgment of the court, James LJ referred to the fact that counsel for Crown had "sought support from the distinction between the offences which assaults and offences which by statute include the element contained in the 'maliciously', eg unlawful and malicious wounding contrary to s20 of the Offences Against the Person Act 1861, in which recklessness will suffice to support the charge: see *Cunningham* (1957) 41 Cr App R 155, [1957] 2 QB 396".

A little later James LJ continued at p314 and pp428-429 respectively:

"*Bradshaw* [1878] 14 Cox CC 83 can be read as supporting the view that unlawful physical force applied recklessly constitutes a criminal assault. In our view the element of mens rea in the offence of battery is satisfied by proof that the defendant intentionally or recklessly applied force to the person of another. If it were otherwise, the strange consequence would be that an offence of unlawful wounding contrary to s20 of the Offences Against the Person Act 1861 could be established by proof that the defendant wounded the victim either intentionally or recklessly but, if the victim's skin was not broken and the offence was therefore laid as an assault occasioning actual bodily harm contrary to s47 of the Act, it would be necessary to prove that the physical force was intentionally applied.

We see no reason in logic or in law why a person who recklessly applies physical force to the person of another should be outside the criminal law of assault. In many cases the dividing line between intention and recklessness is barely distinguishable. This is such a case. In our judgment the direction was right in law and this ground of appeal fails."

As Mr Arlidge concedes, if this case is still good law, the *Cunningham* test lies to both s20 and s23 type cases on the one hand and to s47 type case on the other. He argues that while still applying to s20 and s23, it no longer applies to s47. To adapt the words of James LJ, the strange consequence, if he is right, would be that when directing a jury in a case containing counts both under s47 and s20, the judge would have to try to explain the *Caldwell* test to the jury (a notoriously difficult task) under s47 and then go on to tell the jury that they must apply a completely different test under s20.

Next we must consider *DPP* v *Majewski* (1976) 62 Cr App R 262, [1977] 443. In this case the appellant had been charged with assault occasioning actual bodily harm and assault on a police officer in the execution of his duty. His defence was that when the offences were committed he was suffering from the effect of alcohol and drugs. The trial judge directed the jury that self-induced intoxication by drink and drugs could not be a defence and the House of Lords upheld that direction. The importance of this case in the present context is what the Lord Chancellor, Lord Elwyn-Jones, had to say about the case of *Venna* (supra) at p270 and p474 respectively:

"If a man of his own volition takes a substance which causes him to cast off the restraints of reason and conscience, no wrong is done to him by holding him answerable criminally for any injury he may do while in that condition. His course of conduct in reducing himself by drugs and drink to that condition in my view supplies the evidence of mens rea or guilty mind certainly sufficient for crimes of basic intent. It is a reckless course of conduct and recklessness is enough to constitute the necessary mens rea in assault cases: see *Venna* (1975) 61 Cr App R 310, [1976] QB 421 per James LJ at p314 and p429. Drunkeness is itself an intrinsic, an integral part of the crime, the other part being the evidence of the unlawful use of force against the victim. Together they add up to criminal recklessness. On this I adopt the conclusion of Stroud in [1920] 36 LQR 273 that: '... it would be contrary to all principle and authority to suppose that drunkeness' (and what is true of drunkeness can equally be true of intoxication by drugs) 'can be a defence for crime in general on the ground that "a person cannot be convicted of a crime unless the mens was rea" '. By allowing himself to get drunk, and thereby putting himself in such a condition as to be no longer amenable to the law's commands, a man shows such regardlessness as amounts to mens rea for the purpose of all ordinary crimes."

This approach is in line with the American Model Penal Code (s2 (8(2)):

"When recklessness establishes an element of the offence, if the actor, due to self-induced intoxication is unaware of a risk of which he would have been aware had he been sober, such unawareness is immaterial."

There is no suggestion there or elsewhere in the speeches in the House of criticism of the decision in *Venna* (supra).

That takes us on to *R* v *Caldwell* (1981) 73 Cr App R 13, [1982] AC 341. [His Lordship referred in detail to Lord Diplock's analysis of *Cunningham* recklessness to be found at pp17-20, and 351-354 respectively, and Lord Diplock's analysis, at pp21 and 355 respectively, of the speech of Lord Elwyn-Jones LC in *DPP* v *Majewski* (1976) 62 Cr App R 262.]

It is plain from this passage that *Venna*, far from having been overruled by the House of Lords in *R* v *Majewski* or for that matter in *R* v *Caldwell*, has been approved by it. In *R* v *Lawrence* (1981) 73 Cr App R 1, [1982] AC 510, which was a case under s1 of the Road Traffic Act 1972, as substituted by s50(1) of the Criminal Law Act 1977, which provided that 'a person who causes the death of another person by driving a motor vehicle on a road recklessly shall be guilty of an offence'. The House of Lords held that an appropriate direction to a jury on what was meant by driving recklessly would be that they had to be satisfied (a) that the defendant was in fact driving the vehicle in such a manner as to create an obvious and serious risk of causing physical injury to some other person who might happen to be using the road or of doing substantial damage to property and (b) that in driving in that manner the defendant did so without having given any thought to the possibility of there being any such risk or, having recognised that there was some risk involved, had nonetheless gone on to take it.

Mr Arlidge founds his argument before us on some words in the speech of Lord Roskill with which their Lordships all agreed in *R* v *Seymour* (1983) 77 Cr App R 215, [1983] 2 AC 493. There the defendant was prepared to plead guilty to the offence of causing death by reckless driving contrary to s1 of the Act of 1972, but the prosecution refused to accept that plea, preferring to obtain a jury's verdict upon the only count charged in the indictment, that being manslaughter. The defendant appealed on the ground that the trial judge had misdirected the jury in that where manslaughter was charged, and the charge arose out of the reckless driving of the defendant on the highway, the direction propounded in *R* v *Lawrence* (1981) 73 Cr App R 1, [1982] AC 510, was inadequate and that in such circumstances the jury should be directed that the prosecution must further prove that the defendant recognised that some risk was involved and had nevertheless proceeded to take that risk. The Court of Appeal (Criminal Division) ((1983) 76 Cr App R 211) and the House of Lords (77 Cr App R 215) dismissed the defendant's appeals. The passage relied upon by Mr Arlidge is to be found at p223 and p506 where Lord Roskill said:

"My Lords, I would accept the submision of Mr Hamilton for the Crown that once it is shown that the two offences co-exist it would be quite wrong to give the adjective 'reckless' or the adverb 'recklessly' a different meaning according to whether the statutory or the common law offence is charged. 'Reckless' should today be given the same meaning in relation to all offences which involve 'recklessness' as one of the elements unless Parliament has otherwise ordained."

The words "unless Parliament has otherwise ordained" may well have been intended to refer not only to modern Acts of Parliament which use the word "recklessly" but also to the 1861 Act where the word "maliciously" is used. However, the history of the interpretation of the 1861 Act shows that, whether or not the word "maliciously" appears in the section in question, the courts have consistently held that the mens rea of every type of offence against the person covers both actual intent and recklessness, in the sense of taking the risk of harm ensuing with foresight that it might happen (see *Ward* [1871] 1 CCR 356, *Bradshaw* (supra), *Cunningham* (supra) and *Venna* (supra)). Hence, according to judicial interpretation of the 1861 Act, these are all instances where Parliament "has otherwise ordained".

The sentence: "'Reckless' should today be given the same meaning in relation to all offences which involve 'recklessness' as one of the elements unless Parliament has otherwise ordained" seems to us to be obiter. In any event we cannot believe that by the use of those words their Lordships intended to cast any doubt either upon the decision in *Cunningham* or, more importantly for present purposes, upon the decision in *Venna* which was approved by the House of Lords in both *Majewski* and *Caldwell*.

Finally, Mr Arlidge argues that while *Venna* says that *Cunningham* recklessness will amount to guilt under s47, it does not say that nothing else will do. In other words, it is now possible to add on failure to give thought to the possibility of risk as also qualifying for guilt. We do not accept that interpretation of the decision in *Venna*. Moreover, we are not attracted by what would be the consequence of accepting Mr Arlidge's argument, namely that responsibility for the offence of assault occasioning actual bodily harm (in respect of which Parliament used neither the word "maliciously" nor "recklessly") would be wider than for the offence of unlawful wounding (in respect of which Parliament used the word "maliciously"). Accordingly, we consider ourselves bound by the case of *Venna*. It follows that the basis upon which the appellant pleaded guilty does not amount to an offence in law. His appeal against conviction on count 2 must, therefore, be allowed and his conviction quashed. We should, however, mention the case of *DPP* v *K* (a minor) (1990) 91 Cr App R 23, [1990] 1 All ER 331, in which a boy was charged with assault occasioning actual bodily harm but the justices dismissed the charge. The Divisional Court, applying the *Caldwell* test, allowed the appeal and remitted the case to the magistrates with a direction to convict. However, the point advanced in the present case was never taken before the Divisional Court and they were not referred to the cases of *Cunningham* (supra) or *Venna* (supra). In consequence, that case was, in our judgment, wrongly decided.'

Commentary

Note that the court certified under s33(2) of the Criminal Appeal Act 1968, that the following point of law of general public importance was involved in its decision, viz 'When recklessness is relied upon as the mens rea for the offence of assault occasioning actual bodily harm contrary to s47 of the Offences Against the Person Act 1861, should it be defined by the test of (1) foreseeing that the particular kind of harm might be done and yet going on to take the risk of it, not caring about the possible consequences; and/or (2) failing to give any thought to the possibility of there being any such risk: or by some other test? Leave to appeal to the House of Lords was refused.

See also *R* v *Savage*, above.

R v Venna [1975] QB 421

See chapter 4.

W v Dolbey [1983] Crim LR 681

See chapter 2.

R v Wilson [1983] 3 WLR 686   House of Lords (Lords Fraser, Elwyn-Jones, Edmund Davies, Roskill and Brightman)

Whether 'inflicting' requires proof of an assault.

Facts

The defendant motorist had been involved in an argument with a pedestrian, which culminated in the defendant punching the pedestrian in the face. The defendant was charged under s20 of the 1861 Act, and the jury found him not guilty under this section, but guilty of the lesser offence under s47. The defendant appealed on the ground that it had not been open to the jury, under s6(3) of the Criminal Law Act 1967, to return such a verdict, because s47 was not a lesser included offence within s20 if the defendant's contention, that s20 did not require proof of an assault, was correct. The Court of Appeal quashed his conviction, but certified the following point of law for consideration by the House of Lords:

> 'Whether on a charge of inflicting grievous bodily harm contrary to s20 of the Offences Against the Persons Act 1861 it is open to a jury to return a verdict of not guilty as charged but guilty of assault occasioning actual bodily harm.'

Held

A defendant could be acquitted under s20 and instead be convicted under s47. The s20 charge did not have to 'necessarily' include an allegation of assault for this to be the case. It was sufficient for the purposes of s6(3) of the Criminal Law Act 1967 that the more serious charge against a defendant should expressly, or impliedly, amount to, or include, the lesser offence of which he had actually been convicted.

Lord Roskill:

> 'Stated briefly, the reason [for the Court of Appeal quashing the conviction of Wilson] was that the decision of the Court of Appeal (Criminal Division) in *R* v *Springfield* (1969) 53 Cr App R 608 made it impossible to justify a conviction for assault occasioning actual bodily harm, contrary to section 47 of the Offences Against the Person Act 1861, since the offence charged of "*inflicting* grievous bodily harm" did not, upon the authorities, *necessarily* include the offence of *assault* occasioning actual bodily harm. The emphasis added to these three words is mine.

… In the present case, the issue to my mind is not whether the allegations in the section 20 charge, expressly or impliedly, *amount* to an allegation of a section 47 charge, for they plainly do not. The issue is whether they either expressly or impliedly *include* such an allegation. The answer to that question must depend upon what is expressly or impliedly *included* in a charge of "inflicting any grievous bodily harm" …

What then, are the allegations expressly or impliedly included in a charge of "inflicting grievous bodily harm"? Plainly that allegation must, so far as physical injuries are concerned, at least impliedly if not indeed expressly, include the infliction of "actual harm" because infliction of the more serious injuries must include the infliction of the less serious injuries. But does the allegation of "inflicting" include an allegation of "assault"? The problem arises by reason of the fact that the relevant English case law has proceeded along two different paths. In one group it has, as has already been pointed out, been held that a verdict of assault was a possible alternative verdict of a charge of inflicting grievous bodily harm contrary to section 20. In the other group grievous bodily harm was said to have been inflicted without any assault having taken place, unless of course the offence of assault were to be given a much wider significance than is usually attached to it. This problem has been the subject of recent detailed analysis in the Supreme Court of Victoria in *R* v *Salisbury* [1976] VR 452. In a most valuable judgment – I most gratefully acknowledge the assistance I have derived from that judgment in preparing this speech – the full court drew attention, in relation to comparable legislation in Victoria, to the problems which arose from this divergence in the main stream of English authority. The problem with which your Lordships' House is now faced arose in *Salisbury* in a different way from the present appeals. There, the appellant was convicted of an offence against the Victoria equivalent of section 20. He appealed on the ground that the trial judge had refused to leave to the jury the possibility of convicting him on that single charge of assault occasioning actual bodily harm or of common assault. The full court dismissed the appeal on the ground that at common law these latter offences were not "necessarily included" in the offence of "inflicting grievous bodily harm." The reasoning leading to this conclusion is plain:

"It may be that the somewhat different wording of section 20 of the English Act has played a part in bringing about the existence of the two lines of authority in England, but, be that as it may, we have come to the conclusion that, although the word "inflicts" … does not have as wide a meaning as the word "causes" … the word "inflicts" does have a wider meaning than it would have if it were construed so that inflicting grievous bodily harm always involved assaulting the victim. In our opinion, grievous bodily harm may be inflicted … either where the accused has directly and violently "inflicted" it by assaulting the victim, or where the accused has "inflicted" it by doing something, intentionally, which, although it is not itself a direct application of force to the body of the victim, does directly result in force being applied violently to the body of the victim, so that he suffers grievous bodily harm. Hence, the lesser misdemeanours of assault occasioning actual bodily harm and common assault … are not necessarily included in the misdemeanour of inflicting grievous bodily harm …" (see p461).

This conclusion was reached after careful consideration of English authorities such as *R* v *Taylor*, LR 1 CCR 194; *R* v *Martin* (1881) 8 QBD 54; *R* v *Clarence* (1888) 22 QBD 23 and *R* v *Halliday* (1889) 6 TLR 109. My Lords, it would be idle to pretend that these cases are wholly consistent with each other …

My Lords, I doubt any useful purpose would be served by further detailed analysis of these and other cases, since to do so would only be to repeat less felicitously what has already been done by the full court of Victoria in *Salisbury* [1976] VR 452. I am content to accept, as did the full court, that there can be an infliction of grievous bodily harm contrary to section 20 without an assault being committed. The critical question is, therefore, whether it being accepted that a charge of inflicting grievous bodily harm contrary to section 20 may not necessarily involve an allegation of assault, but may nonetheless do so, and in very many cases will involve such an allegation, the allegations in a section 20 charge "include either expressly or by implication" allegations of assault occasioning actual bodily harm. If "inflicting" can, as the cases show, *include* "inflicting by assault," then even though such a charge may not necessarily do so, I do not for myself see why these allegations do not at least impliedly include "inflicting by assault". That is sufficient for present purposes though I also regard it as a possible view that those former allegations *expressly* include the other allegations.'

6   HOMICIDE I

R v **Armstrong** [1989] Crim LR 149 St Albans Crown Court, (Owen J)

Causation - supply of heroin - whether self-injection by the victim a novus actus.

Facts

'The defendant, a drug addict, supplied to C, who had already consumed a potentially lethal quantity of alcohol, heroin and the means by which to mix and inject the heroin. There was no evidence that D had injected the heroin into C. The case proceeded upon the assumption that C injected himself. Shortly after injecting himself, C died.

D was charged inter alia with manslaughter. At the trial the Crown called a pathologist and a toxicologist; the former opined that death was caused primarily by the deceased's alcohol intake and said that it was "possible" that heroin had been a contributory cause; the latter initially expressed a different view but deferred to the pathologist's opinion.

It was submitted at the close of the Crown's case (1) that there was no or insufficient evidence that heroin had been a substantial cause of death, alternatively (2) that if heroin did cause death, C injecting himself was a novus actus interveniens breaking the chain of causation flowing from D's acts.

Held

Upholding the submissions, (1) that if the experts could not be sure that heroin caused C's death, the jury could not be and (2) that the alternative submission was well-founded. Regard was held to *Cato* 62 Cr App R 41 and *Dalby* 74 Cr App R 348: the facts proved were closest to *Dalby*.'

R v **Blaue** (1975) 61 Cr App Rep 271 Court of Appeal (Criminal Division) (Lawton LJ, Thompson and Shaw JJ)

The 'thin skull' rule

Facts

The defendant stabbed the victim, who was a Jehovah's Witness, 13 times. She was rushed to hospital where doctors diagnosed that she would need an immediate blood transfusion if her life was to be saved. The victim refused the necessary transfusion because it was against her religious beliefs. She died from her wounds shortly after. The defendant appealed against his conviction for manslaughter on the ground that the refusal of treatment had broken the chain of causation.

Held

The appeal would be dismissed.

Lawton LJ:

'... Towards the end of the trial and before the summing up started counsel on both sides made submissions as to how the case should be put to the jury. Counsel then appearing for the defendant invited the judge to direct the jury to acquit the defendant generally on the count of murder. His argument was that her refusal to have a blood transfusion had broken the chain of causation between the stabbing and her death. As an alternative he submitted that the jury should be left to decide whether the chain of causation had been broken. Mr Herrod submitted that the judge should direct the jury to convict, because no facts were in issue and when the law was applied to the facts there was only one possible verdict, namely, manslaughter by reason of diminished responsibility.

When the judge came to direct the jury on this issue he did so by telling them that they should apply their common sense. He then went on to tell them they would get some help from the cases to which counsel had referred in their speeches. He reminded them of what Lord Parker CJ had said in *R v Smith* [1959] 2 QB 35, 42 and what Maule J had said 133 years before in *R v Holland* (1841) 2 Mood. & R 351, 352. He placed particular reliance on what Maule J had said. The jury, he said, might find it "most material and most helpful." He continued:

"This is one of those relatively rare cases, you may think, with very little option open to you but to reach the conclusion that was reached by your predecessors as members of the jury in *R v Holland*, namely, 'yes' to the question of causation that the stab was still, at the time of the girl's death, the operative cause of death – or a substantial cause of death. However, that is a matter for you to determine after you have withdrawn to consider your verdict."

Mr Comyn has criticised that direction on three grounds: first, because *R v Holland* should no longer be considered good law; secondly, because *R v Smith,* when rightly understood, does envisage the possibility of unreasonable conduct on the part of the victim breaking the chain of causation; and thirdly, because the judge in reality directed the jury to find causation proved although he used words which seemed to leave the issue open for them to decide.

In *R v Holland,* 2 Mood. & R 351, the defendant in the course of a violent assault, had injured one of his victim's fingers. A surgeon had advised amputation because of the danger to life through complications developing. The advice was rejected. A fortnight later the victim died of lockjaw. Maule J said at p352: "the real question is, whether in the end the wound inflicted by the prisoner was the cause of death". That distinguished judge left the jury to decide that question as did the judge in this case. They had to decide it as juries always do, by pooling their experience of life and using their common sense. They would not have been handicapped by a lack of training in dialectic or moral theology.

Maule J's direction to the jury reflected the common law's answer to the problem. He who inflicted an injury which resulted in death could not excuse himself by pleading that his victim could have avoided death by taking greater care of himself: see Hale*'s Pleas of the Crown* (1800 ed), pp427-428. The common law in Sir Matthew Hale's time probably was in line with contemporary concepts of ethics. A man who did a wrongful act was deemed morally responsible for the natural and probable consequence of that act. Mr Comyn asked us to remember that since Sir Matthew Hale's day the rigour of the law relating to homicide has been eased in favour of the accused. It has been – but this has come about through the development of the concepts of intent, not by reason of a different view of causation. Well known practitioner's textbooks, such as H*alsbury's Laws of England*, 3rd ed, vol 10 (1955), p706 and *Russell on Crime,* 12th ed (1964), vol 1, p30 continue to reflect the common law approach. Textbooks intended for students or as studies in jurisprudence have queried the common law rule; see Hart and Honoré, C*ausation in Law* (1959), pp320-321 and Smith and Hogan, *Criminal Law*, 3rd ed (1973), p214.

There have been two cases in recent years which have some bearing upon this topic; *R v Jordan* (1956), [below] and *R v Smith*, [below]. The physical cause of death in this case was the bleeding into the pleural cavity arising from the penetration of the lung. This had not been brought about by any decision made by the deceased but by the stab wound.

Mr Comyn tried to overcome this line of reasoning by submitting that the jury should have been directed that if they thought the deceased's decision not to have a blood transfusion was an unreasonable one, then the chain of causation would have been broken. At once the question arises – reasonable by whose standards? Those of Jehovah's Witnesses? Humanists? Roman Catholics? Protestants of Anglo-Saxon descent? The man on the Clapham omnibus? But he might well be an admirer of Eleazar who suffered death rather than eat the flesh of swine (2 Maccabees, ch.6, vv. 18-31) or of Sir Thomas Moore who, unlike nearly all his contemporaries was unwilling to accept Henry VIII as Head of the Church of England. Those brought up in the Hebraic and Christian traditions would probably be reluctant to accept that these martyrs caused their own deaths.

As was pointed out to Mr Comyn in the course of argument, two cases, each raising the same issue of reasonableness because of religious beliefs, could produce different verdicts depending on where the cases were tried. A jury drawn from Preston, sometimes said to be the most Catholic town in England, might have different views about martyrdom to one drawn from the inner suburbs of London. Mr Comyn accepted that this might be so: it was, he said, inherent in trial by jury. It is not inherent in the common law as expounded by Sir Matthew Hale and Maule J. It has long been the policy of the law that those who use violence on other people must take their victims as they find them. This in our judgment means the whole man, not just the physical man. It does not lie in the mouth of the assailant to say that the victim's religious beliefs which inhibited him from accepting certain kinds of treatment were unreasonable. The question for decision is what caused her death. The answer is the stab wound. The fact that the victim refused to stop this end coming about did not break the causal connection between the act and death ...'

R v Cheshire (1991) 93 Cr App R 251 Court of Appeal (Criminal Division) (Beldam LJ, Boreham and Auld JJ)

Homicide - causation - inadequate medical treatment

Facts

The appellant fired two shots at the deceased (Trevor Jeffrey) during an argument at the 'Ozone' fish and chip shop in Greenwich. The deceased received injuries to his leg and abdomen and died two months later in hospital. The appellant was convicted of murder and appealed on the ground that the trial judge had misdirected the jury on the issue of causation. The cause of the victim's death was given as 'cardio-respiratory arrest due to gunshot wounds', but the appellant had introduced expert evidence to the effect that the death had been caused by a rare complication resulting from the medical treatment he had received, and that the chain of causation had been broken by the negligent medical treatment. The trial judge had directed the jury that the medical treatment could not be regarded as a novus actus interveniens unless the doctors had been reckless in their disregard for the patient's health.

Held

The appeal would be dismissed.

Beldam LJ reviewed the factual background to the case and took, as his basis for the law relating to causation, the judgment of Goff LJ in *R* v *Pagett* (1983) 76 Cr App R 279. His Lordship continued:

'Goff LJ went on to express his indebtedness to the work of Professors Hart and Honoré in *Causation in the Law* (2nd ed, 1985). We too are indebted to section IV of Chapter 12 of that work. Under the heading "Doctor's or Victim's Negligence" the authors deal with cases in which an assault or wounding is followed by improper medical treatment or by refusal of treatment by the victim or failure on his part to take proper care of the wound or injury. The authors trace from Hale's *Pleas of the Crown* (PC i, 428) and Stephen's *Digest of the Criminal Law* (art 262) the emergence of a standard set by Stephen of common knowledge or skill which they suggest appears to require proof of something more than ordinary negligence in order that one who inflicts a wound may be relieved of liability for homicide. And they refer to most American authorities as requiring at least gross negligence to negative causal connection. English decisions, however, have not echoed these words. In conclusion at p362 the authors state:

"Our survey of the place of doctor's and victim's negligence in the law of homicide, where differences of policy between civil and criminal law might be expected to make themselves felt, yields a meagre harvest.

(i) On Stephen's view, which has some modern support, there is no difference between civil and criminal law as regards the effect of medical negligence; in each case gross negligence (want of common knowledge or skill) is required to negative responsibility for death ..."

Whatever may be the differences of policy between the approach of the civil and the criminal law to the question of causation, there are we think reasons for a critical approach when importing the language of the one to the other. Since the apportionment of responsibility for damage has become commonplace in the civil law, judges have sought to distinguish the blameworthiness of conduct from its causative effect. Epithets suggestive of degrees of blameworthiness may be of little help in deciding how potent the conduct was in causing the result. A momentary lapse of concentration may lead to more serious consequences than a more glaring neglect of duty. In the criminal law the jury considering the factual question, did the accused's act cause the deceased's death, will we think derive little assistance from figures of speech more appropriate for conveying degrees of fault or blame in questions of apportionment. Unless authority suggests otherwise, we think such figures of speech are to be avoided in giving guidance to a jury on the question of causation. Whilst medical treatment unsuccessfully given to prevent the death of a victim with the care and skill of a competent medical practitioner will not amount to an intervening cause, it does not follow that treatment which falls below that standard of care and skill will amount to such a cause. As Professors Hart and Honoré comment, treatment which falls short of the standard expected of the competent medical practitioner is unfortunately only too frequent in human experience for it to be considered abnormal in the sense of extraordinary. Acts or omissions of a doctor treating the victim for injuries he has received at the heads of an accused may conceivably be so extraordinary as to be capable of being regarded as acts independent of the conduct of the accused but it is most unlikely that they will be.'

His Lordship referred to *Jordan* and *Smith*, extracted in this chapter, and continued:

'Both these cases were considered by this court in the cases of *Malcherek and Steel* (1981) 73 Cr App R 173, [1981] 1 WLR 690, in which it had been argued that the act of a doctor in disconnecting a life support machine had intervened to cause the death of the victim to the exclusion of injuries inflicted by the appellants. In rejecting this submission Lord Lane CJ, after considering *Jordan* (supra) and *Smith* (supra), said at p181 and p696D:

"In the view of this Court, if a choice has to be made between the decision in *Jordan* (supra) and that in *Smith* (supra) which we do not believe it does (*Jordan* being a very exceptional case), then the decision in *Smith* is to be preferred."

Later in the same judgment Lord Lane CJ said (ibid) and p696F):

"There may be occasions, although they will be rare, when the original injury has ceased to operate as a cause at all, but in the ordinary case if the treatment is given bona fide by competent and careful medical practitioners, then evidence will not be admissible to show that the treatment would not have been administered in the same way by other medical practitioners. In other words, the fact that the victim has died, despite or because of medical treatment for the initial injury given by careful and skilled medical practitioners, will not exonerate the original assailant from responsibility for the death."

In those two cases it was not suggested that the actions of the doctors in disconnecting the life support machine were other than competent and careful. The court did not have to consider the effect of medical treatment which fell short of the standard of care to be expected of competent medical practitioners.

A case in which the facts bear a close similarity to the case with which we are concerned is the case of *Evans and Gardiner (No 2)* [1976] VR 523. In that case the deceased was stabbed in the stomach by the two applicants in April 1974. After operation the victim resumed an apparently healthy life but nearly a year later, after suffering abdominal pain and vomiting and undergoing further medical treatment, he died. The cause of death was a stricture of the small bowel, a not uncommon sequel to the operation carried out to deal with the stab wound inflicted by the applicants. It was contended that the doctors treating the victim for the later symptoms ought to have diagnosed the presence of the stricture, that they had been negligent not to do so and that timely operative treatment would have saved the victim's life.

The Supreme Court of Victoria held that the test to be applied in determining whether a felonious act has caused a death which follows, in spite of an intervening act, is whether the felonious act is still an operating and substantial cause of the death.

The summing up to the jury had been based on the passage already quoted from Lord Parker's judgment in *Smith* (supra) and the Supreme Court endorsed a direction in those terms. It commented upon the limitations of the decision of *Jordan* (supra) and made observations on the difference between the failure to diagnose the consequence of the original injury and cases in which medical treatment has been given which has a positive adverse effect on the victim. It concluded at p528:

"But in the long run the difference between a positive act of commission and an omission to do some particular act is for these purposes ultimately a question of degree. As an event intervening between an act alleged to be felonious and to have resulted in death, and the actual death, a positive act of commission or an act of omission will serve to break the chain of causation only if it can be shown that the act or omission accelerated the death, so that it can be said to have caused the death and thus to have prevented the felonious act which would have caused death from actually doing so."

Later in the judgment the court said at p534:

"In these circumstances we agree with the view of the learned trial judge expressed in his report to this court that there was a case to go to the jury. The failure of the medical practitioners to diagnose correctly the victim's condition, however inept or unskillful, was not the cause of death. It was the blockage of the bowel which caused death and the real question for the jury was whether that blockage was due to the stabbing. There was plenty of medical evidence to support such a finding, if the jury chose to accept it."

It seems to us that these two passages demonstrate the difficulties in formulating and explaining a general concept of causation but what we think does emerge from this and the other cases is that when the victim of a criminal attack is treated for wounds or injuries by doctors or other medical staff attempting to repair the harm done, it will only be in the most extraordinary and unusual case that such treatment can be said to be so independent of the acts of the accused that it could be regarded in law as the cause of the victim's death to the exclusion of the accused's acts.

Where the law requires proof of the relationship between an act and its consequences as an element of responsibility, a simple and sufficient explanation of the basis of such relationship has proved notoriously elusive.

In a case in which the jury have to consider whether negligence in the treatment of injuries inflicted by the accused was the cause of death we think it is sufficient for the judge to tell the jury that they must be satisfied that the Crown have proved that the acts of the accused caused the death of the deceased adding that the accused's acts need not be the sole cause or even the main cause of death it being sufficient that his acts contributed significantly to that result. Even though negligence in the treatment of the victim was the immediate cause of his death, the jury should not regard it as excluding the responsibility of the accused unless the negligent treatment was so independent of his acts, and in itself so potent in causing death, that they regard the contribution made by his acts as insignificant.

It is not the function of the jury to evaluate competing causes or to choose which is dominant provided they are satisfied that the accused's acts can fairly be said to have made a significant contribution to the victim's death. We think the word "significant" conveys the necessary substance of a contribution made to the death which is more than negligible. In the present case the passage in the summing up complained of has to be set in the context of the remainder of the direction given by the learned judge on the issue of causation. He directed the jury that they had to decide whether the two bullets fired into the deceased on 10 December caused his death on 15 February following. Or, he said, put in another way, did the injuries caused cease to operate as a cause of death because something else intervened? He told them that the prosecution did not have to prove that the bullets were the only cause of death but they had to prove that they were one operative and substantial cause of death. He was thus following the words used in *Smith* (supra). The judge then gave several examples for the jury to consider before reverting to a paraphrase of the alternative formulation used by Lord Parker CJ in *Smith*. Finally, he reminded the jury of the evidence which they had heard on this issue. We would remark that on several occasions during this evidence the jury had passed notes to the judge asking for clarification of expressions used by the medical witnesses which showed that they were following closely the factual issues they had to consider. If the passage to which exception has been taken had not been included, no possible criticism could have been levelled at the summing up. Although for reasons we have stated we think that the judge erred when he invited the jury to consider the degree of fault in the medical treatment rather than its consequences, we consider that no miscarriage of justice has actually occurred. Even if more experienced doctors than those who attended the deceased would have recognised the rare complication in time to have prevented the deceased's death, that complication was a direct consequence of the appellant's acts which remained a significant cause of his death. We cannot conceive that, on the evidence given, any jury would have found otherwise. Accordingly, we dismissed the appeal.'

R v Coroner for Inner West London, ex parte De Luca [1988] Crim LR 541 Divisional Court (Bingham LJ and Hutchison J)

Year and a day rule

Facts

'The applicant sought to quash a coroner's verdict upon his son that he killed himself whilst the balance of his mind was disturbed. The cause of death was stated to be bronchopneumonia and gunshot wound of the brain. The ground of the application was that the coroner erred in law in that death occurred more than a year and a day after the wound was inflicted and a verdict that the deceased killed himself was thereby precluded.

Held

Allowing the application, and remitting the matter to the coroner, while suicide was a crime the year and a day rule appeared to have applied to it. It still applied to offences under section 4(1) of the Homicide Act 1957 (suicide pact) or section 2(1) of the Suicide Act 1961 (complicity in suicide). So long as that was so, it should be regarded as applying to suicide itself even though suicide was no longer a crime.'

[*Reported by Lynne Knapman, Barrister*]

DPP v Daley and McGhie [1980] AC 237 Privy Council (Lord Diplock, Lord Hailsham, Lord Salmon, Lord Edmund-Davies, and Lord Keith)

Manslaughter - victim's apprehention of assault

Facts

The defendants chased the deceased, Sydney Smith, and threw stones at him. In attempting to escape he tripped and fell and was subsequently found to be dead.

The defendants were charged with murder and convicted of constructive manslaughter following the trial judge's directions to the jury that:

'... where one person causes in the mind of another by violence or the threat of violence a well-founded sense of danger to life or limb as to cause him to suffer or to try to escape and in the endeavour to escape he is killed, the person creating that state of mind is guilty of at least manslaughter.'

The defendants appealed successfully to the Court of Appeal, and the prosecutor appealed to the Judicial Committee of the Privy Council.

Held

The appeal would be allowed and the convictions restored.

Lord Keith:

'The law regarding manslaughter of the species with which this appeal is concerned was considered by the Court of Appeal (Criminal Division) in *Reg* v *Mackie* (1973) 57 Cr App R 453. It is unnecessary to recite the facts of the case or to quote any passages from the judgment of the court delivered by Stephenson LJ. It is sufficient to paraphrase what in their Lordships' view were there held to constitute the essential ingredients of the prosecution's proof of a charge of manslaughter, laid upon the basis that a person has sustained fatal injuries while trying to escape from assault by the defendant. These are: (1) that the victim immediately before he sustained the injuries was in fear of being hurt physically; (2) that his fear was such that it caused him to try to escape; (3) that whilst he was trying to escape, and because he was trying to escape, he met his death; (4) that his fear of being hurt there and then was reasonable and was caused by the conduct of the defendant; (5) that the defendant's conduct which caused the fear was unlawful; and (6) that his conduct was such as any sober and reasonable person would recognise as likely to subject the victim to at least the risk of some harm resulting from it, albeit not serious harm. Their Lordships have to observe that it is unnecessary to prove the defendant's knowledge that his conduct was unlawful. This was made clear by Lord Salmon speaking with general concurrence in a slightly different but nevertheless relevant context in *Director of Public Prosecutions* v *Newbury* [1977] AC 500, 507. It is sufficient to prove that the defendant's act was intentional, and that it was dangerous on an objective test.

Their Lordships are of opinion at upon the evidence in the present case there was material before the jury upon which, if they did not consider the defendant's guilt of murder to be established beyond reasonable doubt, they were entitled to find them guilty of manslaughter upon the basis which has been described. There was evidence that the defendants threw stones at the deceased. The jury by their verdict showed that they accepted that evidence. There was evidence that the deceased was struck by a stone or stones, but the jury were clearly entitled to regard that evidence as not being of sufficient quality to establish the fact beyond reasonable doubt. There could be no doubt that the deceased in the course of running across the yard sustained injuries which caused his death. If those injuries did not result from his being struck by stones thrown by the defendants, they could only have resulted from his tripping over the ramp and sustaining the injuries in his fall. Did he trip and fall because he was fleeing in haste on account of fear inspired by the defendants' conduct, or, as the defendants suggested, in the course of running to get a gun with which to threaten or attack them? Their Lordships are satisfied that upon a fair view of the evidence as a whole any jury would have been entitled to infer that the former was the true explanation of the deceased's fall, and generally to hold that all the ingredients described above as necessary for a verdict of manslaughter had been proved beyond reasonable doubt. Therefore the issue of manslaughter was a proper one to put before the jury.'

Commentary

See *R* v *Williams*, below.

R v Dyson [1908] 2 KB 454   Court of Criminal Appeal

Year and a day rule

Facts

The defendant assaulted his own child causing a fractured skull in November 1906. The child died in March 1908, the medical evidence being that the fractured skull was the main cause of death. The defendant was convicted of manslaughter and appealed.

Held

The conviction would be quashed.

Lord Alverstone CJ:

'[The] Appellant had inflicted injuries on the child in November, 1906, and December, 1907 and had suffered imprisonment for both offences. This was an ordinary indictment for manslaughter on March 5, 1908. The misdirection complained of was that Coleridge J had directed the jury that they might find prisoner guilty if the death was caused by the injuries of November, 1906, though the full effect of those injuries was not seen till later. There were no qualifying words in these passages in the summing-up, or they would have given effect to them. It was admitted by counsel for the Crown that this direction was wrong. The cruelty was so clearly established that a somewhat recondite rule of law had been overlooked, viz, that unless deceased dies within a year and a day of the injury a charge of manslaughter cannot be maintained. That rule was stated by Coke, 3 *Institutes,* 47, 53; by Hawkins, 1 *Pleas of the Crown,* c 31, s 9; by East, 1 *Pleas of the Crown,* c5, s112, pp343, 344 and was still the law of England: 3 *Russell on Crimes* (6th ed), p4, where the authorities are collected. What, then ought the Court to do? If he had not been already convicted of the assaults, he might have been convicted under sect. 1 (3) of the Prevention of Cruelty to Children Act, 1904, so that, as it was, this Court could not proceed under sect. 5 (2) of the Criminal Appeal Act. At the same time, *Morris,* LR 1 CCR 90; 36 LJMC 84 (1867), is a clear authority that these two convictions are no bar to an indictment for manslaughter. Can the Court, then, act under the proviso in sect. 4(1) of the Act that they should dismiss the appeal if there was "no substantial miscarriage of justice"? After most careful thought they had come to the conclusion that they could not. For what question should have been left to the jury? Whether appellant accelerated the death by his injury of December, 1907. With a proper direction, as in *Martin,* 5 C & P 128 (1832), deceased's condition having been deteriorated by previous ill-treatment, the jury might and probably would have found appellant guilty of accelerating the death, and he quite accepted the statement of counsel for the Crown that he did so put the case to them. But the reason that they could not use that power was – and it was so very important that it must be stated clearly – that the Court ought not to substitute itself for the jury. It was much to be regretted that Parliament had not given the Court power to order a new trial: such a power might only be wanted in a few instances, but this is one of them. Here, as they could not substitute themselves for the jury, they could not positively say that there would be no miscarriage of justice; they could not say that the jury mus*t* have come to the conclusion that the death was accelerated by the previous assault – probably they would have done so, but there was some evidence – not, indeed, the bulk of the evidence – that death may have been due to a fall: and there was no sign of external injury, and therefore it was not absolutely certain that the death had been accelerated as suggested. It was too serious in such a case to say that the jury must have come to a verdict of guilty. In *Makin* v *A-G for New South Wales*, 1894 AC at 70, Lord Herschell, C, said: "their Lordships do not think it can properly be said that there has been no substantial wrong or miscarriage of justice, where on a point material to the guilt or innocence of the accused the jury have, notwithstanding objection, been invited by the judge to consider in arriving at their verdict matters which ought not to have been submitted to them." If for "invited … . matters" be read the words "have been told by the judge they might find a verdict of guilty on matters which ought not to have been submitted to them," the cases are very similar.'

R v Hancock and Shankland [1986] AC 455

See chapter 2.

R v Jordan (1956) 40 Cr App R 152 Court of Criminal Appeal (Hallett, Ormrod and Donovan JJ)

Medical treatment as a novus actus interveniens

Facts

The defendant had stabbed the victim, a man named Beaumont, who was admitted to hospital where he died some eight days later. The defendant was convicted of murder, but appealed when new evidence came to light that the victim had been given a drug whilst in hospital to which he was allergic.

Held

The conviction would be quashed.

Hallett J:

'... We are disposed to accept it as the law that death resulting from any normal treatment employed to deal with a felonious injury may be regarded as caused by the felonious injury, but we do not think it necessary to examine the cases in details or to formulate for the assistance of those who have to deal with such matters in the future the correct test which ought to be laid down with regard to what is necessary to be proved in order to establish causal connection between the death and the felonious injury. Not only one feature, but two separate and independent features, of treatment were, in the opinion of the doctors, palpably wrong and these produced the symptoms discovered at the post-mortem examination which were the direct and immediate cause of death, namely, the pneumonia resulting from the conditions of oedema which was found.'

Commentary

See *R* v *Cheshire*, above and *R* v *Malcherek*; *R* v *Steel*, below.

R v Malcherek; R v Steel (1981) 73 Cr App R 173 Court of Appeal (Criminal Division) (Lord Lane CJ, Ormrod LJ and Smith J)

Medical treatment as a novus actus interveniens

Facts

Both defendants had, in separate incidents, attacked women causing injuries that were so severe, their victims had to be placed on life support machines in hospital. In both cases doctors decided to switch off the machines after determining that the victims were 'brain dead' and that there was no prospect of recovery. Both defendants were convicted of murder. The common ground of appeal in each case was that the doctors had broken the chain of causation between the defendants' attacks and the deaths of the victims by deliberately switching off the life support machines.

Held

The appeals would be dismissed.

Lord Lane CJ:

'The question posed for answer to this Court is simply whether the judge in each case was right in withdrawing from the jury the question of causation. Was he right to rule that there was no evidence on which the jury could come to the conclusion that the assailant did not cause the death of the victim?

The way in which the submissions are put by Mr Field-Fisher on the one hand and by Mr Wilfred Steer [counsel for the defendants] on the other is as follows; the doctors, by switching off the ventilator and the life support machine were the cause of death or, to put it more accurately, there was evidence which the jury should have been allowed to consider that the doctors, and not the assailant, in each case may have been the cause of death.

In each case it is clear that the initial assault was the cause of the grave head injuries in the one case and of the massive abdominal haemorrhage in the other. In each case the initial assault was the reason for the medical treatment being necessary. In each case the medical treatment given was normal and conventional. At some stage the doctors must decide if and when treatment has become otiose. This decision was reached, in each of the two cases here, in circumstances which have already been set out in some detail. It is no part of the task of this Court to inquire whether the criteria, the Royal Medical College confirmatory tests, are a satisfactory code of practice. It is not part of the task of this Court to decide whether the doctors were, in either of these two cases, justified in omitting one or more of the so called "confirmatory tests." The doctors are not on trial: the applicant and the appellant respectively were.

There are two comparatively recent cases which are relevant to the consideration of this problem.

[His Lordship considered the first of these, *R* v *Jordan,* above, and continued]

The other decision is that of *Smith* (1959) 43 Cr App R 121; [1959] 2 QB 35. In that case the appellant had stabbed a fellow soldier with a bayonet. One of the wounds had pierced the victim's lung and had caused bleeding. Whilst being carried to the medical hut or reception centre for treatment, the victim was dropped twice and then, when he reached the treatment centre, he was given treatment which was subsequently shown to have been incorrect. Lord Parker CJ, who gave the judgment of the Court, stressed the fact – if it needed stressing – that the case of *Jordan* (supra) was a very particular case depending upon its own exact facts, as indeed Hallett J himself in that case had said.

In *Smith* (*supra*) counsel for the appellant argued that if there was any other cause, whether resulting from negligence or not, operating; if something happened which impeded the chance of the deceased recovering, then the death did not result from that wound.

A very similar submission to that has been made to this Court by counsel in the instant case. The Court in *Smith* (*supra*) was quite unable to accept that contention. What Lord Parker CJ said at p131 and pp42, 43, of the respective reports: "It seems to the Court that if at the time of death the original wound is still an operating cause and a substantial cause, then the death can properly be said to be the result of the wound, albeit that some other cause of death is also operating. Only if it can be said that the original wounding is merely the setting in which another cause operates can it be said that the death does not result from the wound. Putting it in another way, only if the second cause is so overwhelming as to make the original wound merely part of the history can it be said that the death does not flow from the wound."

In the view of this Court, if a choice has to be made between the decision in *Jordan* (supra) and that in *Smith* (supra) which we do not believe it does (*Jordan* (supra) being a very exceptional case), then the decision in *Smith* (supra) is to be preferred.

The only other case to which reference has been made, it having been drawn to our attention by Mr Steer, is the case of *Blaue* (1975) 61 Cr App R 271. That was the case where the victim of a stabbing incident was a Jehovah's Witness who refused to accept a blood transfusion although she had been told that to refuse would mean death for her – a prophecy which was fulfilled. The passage that has been drawn to our attention in that case is at p275, the last paragraph of the judgment of Lawton LJ: "The issue of the cause of death in a trial for either murder or manslaughter is one of fact for the jury to decide. But if, as in this case, there is no conflict of evidence and all the jury has to do is to apply the law to the admitted facts, the judge is entitled to tell the jury what the result of that application will be. In this case the judge would have been entitled to have told the jury that the appellant's stab wound was an operative cause of death. The appeal fails."

There is no evidence in the present case here that at the time of conventional death, after the life support machinery was disconnected, the original wound or injury was other than a continuing, operating and indeed substantial cause of the death of the victim, although it need hardly be added that it need not be substantial to render the assailant guilty. There may be occasions, although they will be rare, when the original injury has ceased to operate as a cause at all, but in the ordinary case if the treatment is given bona fide by competent and careful medical practitioners, then evidence will not be admissible to show that the treatment would not have been administered in the same way by other medical practitioners. In other words, the fact that the victim has died, despite or because of medical treatment for the initial injury given by careful and skilled medical practitioners, will not exonerate the original assailant from responsibility for the death. It follows that so far as the ground of appeal in each of these cases relates to the direction given on causation, that ground fails. It also follows that the evidence which it is sought to adduce now, although we are prepared to assume that it is both credible and was not available properly at the trial – and a reasonable explanation for not calling it at the trial has been given – if received could, under no circumstances, afford any ground for allowing the appeal.

The reason is this. Nothing which any of the two or three medical men whose statements are before us could say would alter the fact that in each case the assailant's actions continued to be an operating cause of the death. Nothing the doctors could say would provide any ground for a jury coming to the conclusion that the assailant in either case might not have caused the death. The furthest to which their proposed evidence goes, as already stated, is to suggest, first, that the criteria or the confirmatory tests are not sufficiently stringent and, secondly, that in the present case they were in certain respects inadequately fulfilled or carried out. It is no part of this Court's function in the present circumstances to pronounce upon this matter, nor was it a function of either of the juries at these trials. Where a medical practitioner adopting methods which are generally accepted comes bona fide and conscientiously to the conclusion that the patient is for practical purposes dead, and that such vital functions as exist – for example, circulation – are being maintained solely by mechanical means, and therefore discontinues treatment, that does not prevent the person who inflicted the initial injury from being responsible for the victim's death. Putting it in another way, the discontinuance of treatment in those circumstances does not break the chain of causation between the initial injury and the death.

Although it is unnecessary to go further than that for the purpose of deciding the present point, we wish to add this thought. Whatever the strict logic of the matter may be, it is perhaps somewhat bizarre to suggest, as counsel have impliedly done, that where a doctor tries his conscientious best to save the life of a patient brought to hospital in extremis, skilfully using sophisticated methods, drugs and machinery to do so, but fails in his attempt and therefore discontinues treatment, he can be said to have caused the death of the patient.'

Commentary

See *R* v *Cheshire*, above.

R v Nedrick [1985] Crim LR 742

See chapter 2.

R v Pagett (1983) 76 Cr App R 279 Court of Appeal (Criminal Division) (Robert Goff LJ, Cantley and Farquharson JJ)

Chain of causation not broken by reasonably foreseeable actions of third parties

Facts

The defendant armed himself with a shotgun and took a pregnant girl (Gail Kinchen) hostage. The police besieged the flat in which the defendant was holding the girl and called on him to come out. He eventually did so, holding the girl in front of him as a human shield. The defendant fired the shotgun at the police officers who returned fire, striking and killing the girl hostage. The defendant was convicted of her manslaughter and appealed on the ground that the judge had misdirected the jury as to causation.

Held

The appeal would be dismissed.

Robert Goff LJ:

'We turn to the first ground of appeal, which is that the learned judge erred in directing the jury that it was for him to decide *as a matter of law* whether by his unlawful and deliberate acts the appellant caused or was a cause of Gail Kinchen's death. It is right to observe that this direction of the learned judge followed upon a discussion with counsel, in the absence of the jury; though the appellant, having dismissed his own counsel, was for this purpose without legal representation. In the course of this discussion, counsel for the prosecution referred the learned judge to a passage in Professor Smith and Professor Hogan's *Criminal Law* (4th ed (1978), p272), which reads as follows: "Causation is a question of both fact and law. D's act cannot be held to be the cause of an event if the event would have occurred without it. The act, that is, must be a sine qua non of the event and whether it is so is a question of fact. But there are many acts which are sine qua non of a homicide and yet are not either in law, or in ordinary parlance, the cause of it. If I invite P to dinner and he is run over and killed on the way, my invitation may be a sine qua non of his death, but no one would say I killed him and I have not caused his death in law. Whether a particular act which is a sine qua non of an alleged actus reus is also a cause of it is a question of law. Where the facts are admitted the judge may direct the jury that a particular act did, or did not, cause a particular result." There follows a reference to *Jordan* (1956) 40 Cr App R 152.

For the appellant, Lord Gifford criticised the statement of the learned authors that "Whether a particular act which is a sine qua non of an alleged actus reus is also a cause of it is a question of law." He submitted that the question had to be answered by the jury as a question of fact. In our view, with all respect, both the passage in Smith and Hogan's *Criminal Law,* and Lord Gifford's criticism of it, are over-simplifications of a complex matter.

We have no intention of embarking in this judgment on a dissertation on the nature of causation, or indeed of considering any matters other than those which are germane to the decision of the issues now before us. Problems of causation have troubled philosophers and lawyers throughout the ages; and it would be rash in the extreme for us to trespass beyond the boundaries of our immediate problem. Our comments should therefore be understood to be confined not merely to the criminal law, but to cases of homicide (and possibly also other crimes of violence to the person); and it must be emphasised that the problem of causation in the present case is specifically concerned with the intervention of another person (here one of the police officers) whose act was the immediate cause of the death of the victim, Gail Kinchen.

In cases of homicide, it is rarely necessary to give the jury any direction on causation as such. Of course, a necessary ingredient of the crimes of murder and manslaughter is that the accused has by his act caused the victim's death. But how the victim came by his death is usually not in dispute. What is in dispute is more likely to be some other matter: for example, the identity of the person who committed the act which indisputably caused the victim's death; or whether the accused had the necessary intent; or whether the accused acted in self-defence, or was provoked. Even where it is necessary to direct the jury's minds to the question of causation, it is usually enough to direct them simply that in law the accused's act need not be the sole cause, or even the main cause, of the victim's death, it being enough that his act contributed significantly to that result. It is right to observe in passing, however, that even this simple direction is a direction of law relating to causation, on the basis of which the jury are bound to act in concluding whether the prosecution has established, as a matter of fact, that the accused's act did in this sense cause the victim's death. Occasionally, however, a specific issue of causation may arise. One such case is where, although an act of the accused constitutes a causa sine qua non of (or necessary condition for) the death of the victim, nevertheless the intervention of a third person may be regarded as the sole cause of the victim's death, thereby relieving the accused of criminal responsibility. Such intervention, if it has such an effect, has often been described by lawyers as a novus actus interveniens. We are aware that this time-honoured Latin term has been the subject of criticism. We are also aware that attempts have been made to translate it into English, though no simple translation has proved satisfactory, really because the Latin term has become a term of art which conveys to lawyers the crucial feature that there has not merely been an intervening act of another person, but that that act was so independent of the act of the accused that it should be regarded in law as the cause of the victim's death, to the exclusion of the act of the accused. At the risk of scholarly criticism, we shall for the purposes of this judgment continue to use the Latin term ...

... There can, we consider, be no doubt that a reasonable act performed for the purpose of self-preservation, being of course itself an act caused by the accused's own act, does not operate as a novus actus interveniens. If authority is needed for this almost self-evident proposition, it is to be found in such cases as *Pitts* (1842) C & M 284, and *Curley* (1909) 2 Cr App R 96. In both these cases, the act performed for the purpose of self-preservation consisted of an act by the victim in attempting to escape from the violence of the accused, which in fact resulted in the victim's death. In each case it was held as a matter of law that, if the victim acted in a reasonable attempt to escape the violence of the accused, the death of the victim was caused by the act of the accused. Now one form of self-preservation is self-defence; for present purposes, we can see no distinction in principle between an attempt to escape the consequences of the accused's act, and a response which takes the form of self-defence. Furthermore, in our judgment, if a reasonable act of self-defence against the act of the accused causes the death of a third party, we can see no reason in principle why the act of self-defence, being an involuntary act caused by the act of the accused, should relieve the accused from criminal responsibility for the death of the third party. Of course, it does not necessarily follow that the accused will be guilty of the murder, or even of the manslaughter, of the third party; though in the majority of cases he is likely to be guilty at least of manslaughter. Whether he is guilty of murder or manslaughter will depend upon the question whether all the ingredients of the relevant offence have been proved; in particular, on a charge of murder, it will be necessary that the accused had the necessary intent, on the principles stated by the House of Lords in *Hyam* v *DPP* (1974) 59 Cr App R 91; [1975] AC 55.

No English authority was cited to us, nor we think to the learned judge, in support of the proposition that an act done in the execution of a legal duty, again of course being an act itself caused by the act of the accused, does not operate as a novus actus interveniens. Before the judge, the cases relied on by the prosecution in support of this proposition were the two Pennsylvanian cases already referred to, *Commonwealth* v *Moyer* (supra) and *Commonwealth* v *Almeida* (supra). However, since the case of *Redline* (supra), neither of these cases can be regarded as authority in the State of Pennsylvania: *Redline* was not cited to the learned judge, we suspect because it is not referred to in Hart and Honoré's *Causation in the Law*, almost certainly because the report of *Redline* was not available to the learned authors when their treatise went to the press. Even so, we agree with the learned judge that the proposition is sound in law, because as a matter of principle such an act cannot be regarded as a voluntary act independent of the wrongful act of the accused. A parallel may be drawn with the so-called "rescue" cases in the law of negligence, where a wrongdoer may be held liable in negligence to a third party who suffers injury in going to the rescue of a person who has been put in danger by the defendant's negligent act. Where, for example, a police officer in the execution of his duty acts to prevent a crime, or to apprehend a person suspected of a crime, the case is surely a fortiori. Of course, it is inherent in the requirement that the police officer, or other person, must be acting in the execution of his duty that his act should be reasonable in all the circumstances: see section 3 of the Criminal Law Act 1967. Furthermore, once again we are only considering the issue of causation. If intervention by a third party in the execution of a legal duty, caused by the act of the accused, results in the death of the victim, the question whether the accused is guilty of the murder or manslaughter of the victim must depend on whether the necessary ingredients of the relevant offence have been proved against the accused, including in particular, in the case of murder, whether the accused had the necessary intent.

The principles which we have stated are principles of law. This is plain from, for example, the case of *Pitts* (1842) C & M 284, to which we have already referred. It follows that where, in any particular case, there is an issue concerned with what we have for convenience called *novus actus interveniens*, it will be appropriate for the judge to direct the jury in accordance with these principles.

It does not however follow that it is accurate to state broadly that causation is a question of law. On the contrary, generally speaking causation is a question of fact for the jury. Thus in, for example, *Towers* (1874) 12 Cox CC 530, the accused struck a woman; she screamed loudly, and a child whom she was then nursing turned black in the face, and from that day until it died suffered from convulsions. The question whether the death of the child was caused by the act of the accused was left by the judge to the jury to decide as a question of fact. But that does not mean that there are no principles of law relating to causation, so that no directions on law are ever to be given to a jury on the question of causation. On the contrary, we have already pointed out one familiar direction which is given on causation, which is that the accused's act need not be the sole, or even the main, cause of the victim's death for his act to be held to have caused the death. Similarly, it was held by this Court in the case of *Blaue* [1975] 1 WLR 1411 that "It has long been the policy of the law that those who use violence on other people must take their victims as they find them. This in our judgment means the whole man, not just the physical man. It does not lie in the mouth of the assailant to say that his victim's religious belief which inhibited her from accepting certain kinds of treatment was unreasonable. The question for decision is what caused her death. The answer is the stab wound. The fact that the victim refused to stop this end coming about did not break the causal connection between the act and death" (see at pp274 and 1415, per Lawton LJ delivering the judgment of the Court). This was plainly a statement of a principle of law. Likewise, in cases where there is an issue whether the act of the victim or of a third party constituted a novus actus interveniens, breaking the causal connection between the act of the accused and the death of the victim, it would be appropriate for the judge to direct the jury, of course in the most simple terms, in accordance with the legal principles which they have to apply. It would then fall to the jury to decide the relevant factual issues which, identified with reference to those legal principles, will lead to the conclusion whether or not the prosecution have established the guilt of the accused of the crime of which he is charged.'

R v Roberts (1971) 56 Cr App R 95

See chapter 5.

R v Williams; R v Davies [1992] 1 WLR 380 Court of Appeal (Criminal Division) (Stuart-Smith LJ, Waterhouse and Morland JJ)

Homicide - causation - victim's escape

Facts

Williams was the driver of a car who had stopped to give a lift to the deceased, a man called Shephard. Five miles further on, Shephard jumped out of the car whilst it was travelling at 30 miles per hour and suffered fatal head injuries. The evidence indicated that Williams had asked Shephard to make a contribution to the cost of petrol. Davis, also a passenger in the car, alleged that Williams had threatened Shephard with violence if he did not hand over the money, with the result that Shephard had jumped from the car whilst it was moving. Williams contended that Shephard had jumped out following threats made by Davis. In Davis's case, the trial judge had dealt with the issue of causation by directing the jury on the basis of *DPP v Daley* (extracted above).

Held

Davis's appeal would be allowed.

Stuart-Smith LJ:

His Lordship referred to the speech of Lord Keith in *DPP v Daley* at p245, and continued:

'Miss Hare [Counsel for the Crown] submits that this direction is sufficient in all cases and is all-embracing. In most cases that is no doubt so, but in some cases, and in our judgment this is one of them, it is necessary to give the jury a direction on causation, and explain the test by which the voluntary act of the deceased may be said to be caused by the defendant's act and is not a novus actus interveniens, breaking the chain of causation between the threat of violence and the death. There must be some proportionality between the gravity of the threat and the action of the deceased in seeking to escape from it. The difficulty in this case was that there was no direct evidence of the nature of the threat …'

His Lordship then recited extracts from *R* v *Roberts* (1971) 56 Cr App R 95, and *R* v *Mackie* (1973) 57 Cr App R 453:

'It is plain that in fatal cases there are two requirements. The first, as in non-fatal cases, relates to the deceased's conduct which would be something that a reasonable and responsible man in the assailant's shoes would have foreseen. The second, which applies only in fatal cases, relates to the quality of the unlawful act which must be such that all sober and reasonable people would inevitably recognise must subject the other person to some harm resulting therefrom, albeit not serious harm. It should be noted that the headnote is inaccurate and tends to confuse these two limbs.

The harm must be physical harm. Where the unlawful act is a battery, there is no difficulty with the second ingredient. Where, however, the unlawful act is merely a threat unaccompanied and not preceded by any actual violence, the position may be more difficult. In the case of a life-threatening assault, such as pointing a gun or knife at the victim, all sober and reasonable people may well anticipate some physical injury through shock to the victim, as for example in *Reg* v *Dawson* (1985) 81 Cr App R 150 where the victim died of a heart attack following a robbery in which two of the appellants had been masked, armed with a replica gun and pickaxe handles. But the nature of the threat is of importance in considering both the foreseeability of harm to the victim from the threat and the question whether the deceased's conduct was proportionate to the threat: that is to say that it was within the ambit of reasonableness and not so daft as to fake it his own voluntary act which amounted to a novus actus interveniens and consequently broke the chain of causation. It should of course be borne in mind that a victim may in the agony of the moment do the wrong thing.

In this case there was an almost total lack of evidence as to the nature of the threat. The prosecution invited the jury to infer the gravity of the threat from the action of the deceased. The judge put it this way:

"what was he frightened of was robbery, that this was going to be taken from him by force, and the measure of the force can be taken from his reaction to it. The prosecution suggests that if he is prepared to get out of a moving car, then it was a very serious threat involving him in the risk of, as he saw it, serious injury."

In our judgment that was a wholly impermissible argument and was simply a case of the prosecution pulling itself up by its own bootstraps.

Moreover in a case of robbery the threat of force is made to persuade the victim to hand over money: if the money is handed over actual violence may not eventuate. The jury should consider two questions: first, whether it was reasonably foreseeable that some harm, albeit not serious harm, was likely to result from the threat itself: and, secondly, whether the deceased's reaction in jumping from the moving car was within the range of responses which might be expected from a victim placed in the situation which he was. The jury should bear in mind any particular characteristic of the victim and the fact that in the agony of the moment he may act without thought and deliberation.

In our judgment the direction in *Director of Public Prosecutions* v *Daley* [1980] AC 237 is not sufficient where there is a real issue as to causation. In that case it could hardly be disputed that a reasonable man should foresee that the victim would flee if he was being stoned and that while fleeing he might slip and fall. In the present case the judge did not include this direction as being part of the necessary ingredients of the offence, replying no doubt on *Director of Public Prosecutions* v *Daley*. He referred to the victim's need for a well founded and not a fanciful fear that was out of all proportion to the threat. But that does not relate to his reaction in jumping out of the car. In the last sentence of the passage quoted he refers to the attempt to get out of the car being out of all proportion to the force used. But even here it is put as an alternative and not as an additional requirement and begs the question of what, if any, force was used.

In our judgment the failure of the judge to give any direction on causation was a misdirection and the conviction on this count just be quashed.'

7 HOMICIDE II: VOLUNTARY MANSLAUGHTER

Bedder v DPP [1954] 2 All ER 801

See *DPP* v *Camplin*, extracted in this chapter.

R v Byrne [1960] 2 QB 396 Court of Criminal Appeal (Lord Parker CJ, Hilbery and Diplock JJ)

Abnormality of the mind for the purposes of diminished responsibility

Facts

The defendant had strangled a young woman. There was evidence that he was a sexual psychopath, and could exercise but little control over his actions. The defence of diminished responsibility was rejected by the trial judge, and the defendant was convicted of murder. He appealed on the basis that the defence should have been put to the jury.

Held

The appeal would be allowed, and a conviction for manslaughter substituted for murder, but the sentence of life imprisonment should remain.

Lord Parker CJ:

'In his summing-up the learned judge, after summarising the medical evidence, gave to the jury a direction of law on the correctness of which this appeal turns. He told the jury if on the evidence they came to the conclusion that the facts could be fairly summarised as follows: "(1) From an early age he has been subject to these perverted violent desires and in some cases has indulged his desires; (2) the impulse or urge of these desires is stronger than the normal impulse or urge of sex to such an extent that the subject finds it very difficult or perhaps impossible in some cases to resist putting the desire into practice; (3) the act of killing this girl was done under such an impulse or urge; and (4) that setting aside these sexual addictions and practices, this man was normal in every other respect," those facts with nothing more would not bring a case within the section and do not constitute such abnormality of mind as substantially to impair a man's mental responsibility for his acts. "In other words," he went on, "mental affliction is one thing. The section is there to protect them. The section is not there to give protection where there is nothing else than what is vicious and depraved." Taken by themselves, these last words are unobjectionable, but it is contended on behalf of the appellant that the direction taken as a whole involves a misconstruction of the section, and had the effect of withdrawing from the jury an issue of fact, which it was peculiarly their province to decide.

[The Lord Chief Justice then considered the pre-1957 situation, and continued:]

It is against that background of the existing law that section 2 (1) of the Homicide Act, 1957, falls to be construed. To satisfy the requirements of the subsection the accused must show: (a) that he was suffering from an abnormality of mind; and (b) that such abnormality of mind: (i) arose from a condition of arrested or retarded development of mind or any inherent causes or was induced by disease or injury; and (ii) was such as substantially impaired his mental responsibility for his acts in doing or being a party to the killing. "Abnormality of mind," which has to be contrasted with the time-honoured expression in the M'Naughten Rules "defect of reason," means a state of mind so different from that of ordinary human beings that the reasonable man would term it abnormal. It appears to us to be wide enough to cover the mind's activities in all its aspects, not only the perception of physical acts and matters, and the ability to form a rational judgment whether an act is right or wrong, but also the ability to exercise will power to control physical acts in accordance with that rational judgment. The expression "mental responsibility for his acts" points to a consideration of the extent to which the accused's mind is answerable for his physical acts, which must include a consideration of the extent of his ability to exercise will power to control his physical acts.

Whether the accused was at the time of the killing suffering from any "abnormality of mind" in the broad sense which we have indicated above is a question for the jury. On this question medical evidence is, no doubt, of importance, but the jury are entitled to take into consideration all the evidence including the acts or statements of the accused and his demeanour. They are not bound to accept the medical evidence, if there is other material before them which, in their good judgment, conflicts with it and outweighs it. The etiology of the abnormality of mind (namely, whether it arose from a condition of arrested or retarded development of mind or any inherent causes or was induced by disease or injury) does, however, seem to be a matter to be determined on expert evidence.

Assuming that the jury are satisfied on the balance of probabilities that the accused was suffering from "abnormality of mind" from one of the causes specified in the parenthesis of the subsection, the crucial question nevertheless arises: was the abnormality such as substantially impaired his mental responsibility for his acts in doing or being a party to the killing? This is a question of degree and essentially one for the jury. Medical evidence is, of course, relevant, but the question involves a decision not merely whether there was some impairment of the mental responsibility of the accused for his acts, but whether such impairment can properly be called "substantial," a matter upon which juries may quite legitimately differ from doctors.

Furthermore, in a case where the abnormality of mind is one which affects the accused's self-control the step between "he did not resist his impulse" is, as the evidence in this case shows, one which is incapable of scientific proof. A fortiori there is no scientific measurement of the degree of difficulty which an abnormal person finds in controlling his impulses. These problems which in the present state of medical knowledge are scientifically insoluble the jury can only approach in a broad, common-sense way. This court has repeatedly approved directions to the jury which have followed directions given in Scots cases where the doctrine of diminished responsibility forms part of the common law. We need not repeat them. They are quoted in *Spriggs* (1958) 42 Cr App R 69; [1958] 1 QB 270. They indicate that such abnormality as "substantially impairs his mental responsibility" involves a mental state which in popular language (not that of the M'Naughten Rules) a jury would regard as amounting to partial insanity or being on the border line of insanity.

It appears to us that the learned judge's direction to the jury that the defence under section 2 of the Act was not available, even though they found the facts set out in numbers 2 and 3 of the learned judge's summary, amounted to a direction that difficulty or even inability of an accused person to exercise will-power to control his physical acts could not amount to such abnormality of mind as substantially impairs his mental responsibility. For the reasons which we have already expressed we think that this construction of the Act is wrong. Inability to exercise will-power to control physical acts, provided that it is due to abnormality of mind from one of the causes specified in the parenthesis in the subsection is, in our view, sufficient to entitle the accused to the benefit of the section; difficulty in controlling his physical acts, depending on the degree of difficulty, may be sufficient. It is for the jury to decide upon the whole of the evidence whether such inability or difficulty has, not as a matter of scientific certainty but on the balance of probabilities, been established and in the case of difficulty whether the difficulty is so great as to amount in their view to a substantial impairment of the accused's mental responsibility for his acts. The direction in the present case thus withdrew from the jury the essential determination of fact which it was their province to decide.

As already indicated, the medical evidence of the appellant's ability to control his physical acts at the time of the killing was all one way. The evidence of the revolting circumstances of the killing and the subsequent mutilations, as of the previous sexual history of the appellant, pointed, we think plainly, to the conclusion that the appellant was what would be described in ordinary language as on the border line of insanity or partially insane. Properly directed, we do not think that the jury could have come to any other conclusion than that the defence under section 2 of the Homicide Act was made out.

The appeal will be allowed and a verdict of manslaughter substituted for the verdict of murder. The only possible sentence, having regard to the tendencies of the appellant, is imprisonment for life. The sentence will, accordingly, not be disturbed.'

DPP v Camplin [1978] AC 705   House of Lords (Lords Diplock, Morris, Simon, Fraser and Scarman)

Reasonable man test for provocation

Facts

The defendant was a 15 year old boy who, having been buggered by the deceased, was then taunted by him. The defendant killed the deceased by hitting him over the head with a chapatti pan. He was convicted of murder following a direction by the trial judge to the jury that they were to judge the defendant by the standard of the reasonable adult, not a reasonable 15 year old boy. The Court of Appeal allowed the appeal on the basis that the more subjective test, which took account of the defendant's age, should have been applied. The Crown appealed to the House of Lords.

Held

The appeal would be dismissed.

Lord Diplock:

'In his address to the jury on the defence of provocation ... counsel for Camplin, had suggested to them that when they addressed their minds to the question whether the provocation relied on was enough to make a reasonable man do as Camplin had done, what they ought to consider was not the reaction of a reasonable adult but the reaction of a reasonable boy of Camplin's age. The judge thought that this was wrong in law. So in his summing-up he took pains to instruct the jury that they must consider whether –

" ... the provocation was sufficient to make a reasonable man in like circumstances act as the defendant did. Not a reasonable boy, as ... (counsel for Camplin) would have it, or a reasonable lad; it is an objective test – a reasonable man."

The jury found Camplin guilty of murder. On appeal the Court of Appeal (Criminal Division) allowed the appeal and substituted a conviction for manslaughter on the ground that the passage I have cited from the summing-up was a misdirection. The court held that –

" ... the proper direction to the jury is to invite the jury to consider whether the provocation was enough to have made a reasonable person of the same age as the appellant in the same circumstances do as he did."

The point of law of general public importance involved in the case has been certified as being:

"Whether, on the prosecution for murder of a boy of 15, where the issue of provocation arises, the jury should be directed to consider the question, under section 3 of the Homicide Act 1957 whether the provocation was enough to make a reasonable man do as he did by reference to a 'reasonable adult' or by reference to a 'reasonable boy of 15' ..."

... [U]ntil the 1957 Act was passed there was a condition precedent which had to be satisfied before any question of applying this dual test could arise. The conduct of the deceased had to be of such a kind as was capable in law of constituting provocation; and whether it was or not was a question for the judge, not for the jury. The House so held in *Mancini v DPP* ([1942] AC 1) where it also laid down a rule of law that the mode of resentment, as for instance the weapon used in the act that caused the death, must bear a reasonable relation to the kind of violence that constituted the provocation.

It is unnecessary for the purposes of the present appeal to spend time on a detailed account of what conduct was or was not capable in law of giving rise to a defence of provocation immediately before the passing of the Act of 1957 ... What, however, is important to note is that this House in *Holmes* v *DPP* ([1946] AC 588) had recently confirmed that words alone, save perhaps in circumstances of a most extreme and exceptional nature, were incapable in law of constituting provocation.

My Lords, this was the state of law when *Bedder* v *DPP* ([1959] 1 WLR 1119) fell to be considered by this House. The accused had killed a prostitute. He was sexually impotent. According to his evidence he had tried to have sexual intercourse with her and failed. She taunted him with his failure and tried to get away from his grasp. In the course of her attempts to do so she slapped him in the face, punched him in the stomach and kicked him in the groin, whereupon he took a knife out of his pocket and stabbed her twice and caused her death. The struggle that led to her death thus started because the deceased taunted the accused with his physical infirmity; but in the state of the law as it then was, taunts unaccompanied by any physical violence did not constitute provocation. The taunts were followed by violence on the part of the deceased in the course of her attempt to get away from the accused, and it may be that this subsequent violence would have a greater effect on the self-control of an impotent man already enraged by the taunts than it would have had upon a person conscious of possessing normal physical attributes. So there might have been some justification for the judge to instruct the jury to ignore the fact that the accused was impotent when they were considering whether the deceased's conduct amounted to such provocation as would cause a reasonable or ordinary person to loose his self control. This indeed appears to have been the ground on which the Court of Criminal Appeal had approved the summing-up when they said at p1121:

"... no distinction is to be made in the case of a person who, though it may not be a matter of temperament is physically impotent, is conscious of the impotence, *and therefore mentally liable to be more excited unduly* if he is 'twitted' or attacked on the subject of that particular infirmity."

This statement, for which I have myself supplied the emphasis, was approved by Lord Simonds LC speaking on behalf of all the members of this House who sat on the appeal; but he also went on to lay down the broader proposition at 1123, that:

"It would be plainly illogical not to recognise an unusually excitable or pugnacious temperament in the accused as a matter to be taken into account but yet to recognise for that purpose some unusual physical characteristic, be it impotence or another."

... My Lords, ... section [3] ... was intended to mitigate in some degree the harshness of the common law of provocation as it had been developed by recent decisions in this House. It recognises and retains the dual test: the provocation must not only have caused the accused to lose his self-control but also be such as might cause a reasonable man to react to it as the accused did. Nevertheless it brings about two important changes in the law. The first is it abolishes all previous rules of law as to what can or cannot amount to provocation and in particular the rule of law that, save in the two exceptional cases I have mentioned, word unaccompanied by violence could not do so. Secondly it makes clear that if there was any evidence that the accused himself at the time of the act which caused the death in fact lost his self-control in consequence of some provocation however slight it might appear to the judge, he was bound to leave to the jury the question, which is one of opinion not of law, whether a reasonable man might have reacted to that provocation as the accused did.

I agree with my noble and learned friend Lord Simon of Glaisdale that since this question is one for the opinion of the jury the evidence of witnesses as to how they think a reasonable man would react to the provocation is not admissible.

The public policy that underlay the adoption of the "reasonable man" test in the common law doctrine of provocation was to reduce the incidence of fatal violence by preventing a person relying on his own exceptional pugnacity or excitability as an excuse for loss of self-control. The rationale of the test may not be easy to reconcile in logic with more universal propositions as to the mental element in crime. Nevertheless it has been preserved by the Act of 1957 but falls to be applied now in the context of a law of provocation that is significantly different from what it was before the Act was passed.

Although it is now for the jury to apply the "reasonable man" test, it still remains for the judge to direct them what, in the new context of the section, is the meaning of this apparently inapt expression, since powers of ratiocination bear no obvious relationships to powers of self-control. Apart from this the judge is entitled, if he thinks it helpful, to suggest considerations which may influence the jury in forming their own opinions as to whether the test is satisfied; but he should make it clear that these are not instructions which they are required to follow: it is for them and no one else to decide what weight, if any, ought to be given to them.

As I have already pointed out, for the purposes of the law of provocation the "reasonable man" has never been confined to the adult male. It means an ordinary person of either sex, not exceptionally excitable or pugnacious, but possessed of such powers of self-control as everyone is entitled to expect that his fellow citizens will exercise in society as it is today. A crucial factor in the defence of provocation from earliest times has been the relationship between the gravity of provocation and the way in which the accused retaliated, both being judged by the social standards of the day. When Hale was writing in the seventeenth century, pulling a man's nose was thought to justify retaliation with a sword: when *Mancini* v *DPP* ... was decided by this House, a blow with a fist would not justify retaliation with a deadly weapon. But so long as words unaccompanied by violence could not in common law amount to provocation the relevant proportionality between provocation and retaliation was primarily one of the degrees of violence. Words spoken to the accused before the violence started were not normally to be included in the proportion sum. But now that the law has been changed so as to permit of words being treated as provocation, even though unaccompanied by any other acts, the gravity of verbal provocation may well depend on the particular characteristics or circumstances of the person to whom a taunt or insult is addressed. To taunt a person because of his race, his physical infirmities or some shameful incident in his past may well be considered by the jury to be more offensive to the person addressed, however equable his temperament, if the facts on which the taunt is founded are true than it would be if they were not. It would stultify much of the mitigation of the previous harshness of the common law in ruling out verbal provocation as capable of reducing murder to manslaughter if the jury could not take into consideration all those factors which in their opinion would affect the gravity of taunts and insults when applied to the person to whom they are addressed. So to this extent at any rate the unqualified proposition accepted by this House in *Bedder* v *DPP*... that for the purposes of the "reasonable man" test any unusual physical characteristics of the accused must be ignored requires revision as a result of the passing of the Act of 1957.

That he was only 15 years of age at the time of the killing is the relevant characteristic of the accused in the instant case. It is a characteristic which may have its effects on temperament as well as physique. If the jury think that the same power of self-control is not be be expected in an ordinary, average or normal boy of 15 as in an older person, are they to treat the lesser powers of self-control possessed by an ordinary, average or normal boy of 15 as the standard of self-control with which the conduct of the accused is to be compared?

It may be conceded that in strict logic there is a transition between treating age as a characteristic that may be taken into account in assessing the gravity of the provocation addressed to the accused and treating it as a characteristic to be taken into account in determining what is the degree of self-control to be expected of the ordinary person with whom the accused's conduct is to be compared. But to require old heads on young shoulders is inconsistent with the law's compassion of human infirmity to which Sir Michael Foster ascribed the doctrine of provocation more than two centuries ago. The distinction as to the purposes for which it is legitimate to take the age of the accused into account involves considerations of too great nicety to warrant a place in deciding a matter of opinion, which is no longer one to be decided by a judge trained in logical reasoning but by a jury drawing on their experience of how ordinary human beings behave in real life.

There is no direct authority prior to the Act of 1957 that expressly states that the age of the accused could not be taken into account in determining the standard of self-control for the purposes of the reasonable man test – unless this is implicit in the reasoning of Lord Simonds LC in *Bedder* ... The Court of Appeal distinguished the instant case from that of *Bedder* on the ground that what it was there said must be ignored was an unusual characteristic that distinguished the accused from ordinary normal persons, whereas nothing could be more ordinary or normal than to be aged 15. The reasoning in *Bedder* would, I think, permit of this distinction between normal and abnormal characteristics, which may affect the powers of self-control of the accused; but for reasons that I have already mentioned the proposition stated in *Bedder* requires qualification as a consequence of changes in the law affected by the Act of 1957. To try to salve what can remain of it without conflict with the Act could in my view only lead to unnecessary and unsatisfactory complexity in a question which has now become a question for the jury alone. In my view *Bedder*, like *Mancini* ... and *Holmes* ... ought no longer to be treated as an authority on the law of provocation.

In my opinion a proper direction to a jury on the question left to their exclusive determination by section 3 of the Act of 1957 would be on the following lines. The judge should state what the question is using the very terms of the section. He should then explain to them that the reasonable man referred to in the question is a person having the power of self-control to be expected of an ordinary person of the sex and age of the accused, but in other respects sharing such of the accused's characteristics as they think would affect the gravity of the provocation to him; and that the question is not merely whether such a person would in like circumstances be provoked to lose his self-control but also whether he would react to the provocation as the accused did.

I accordingly agree with the Court of Appeal that the judge ought not to have instructed the jury to pay no account to the age of the accused even though they themselves might be of opinion that the degree of self-control to be expected in a boy of that age was less than in an adult. So to direct them was to impose a fetter on the right and duty of the jury which the Act accords to them to act on their own opinion on the matter.'

R v Ibrams and Gregory (1981) 74 Cr App R 154   Court of Appeal (Criminal Division)

Cooling time: provocation

Facts

The defendants and a young woman had been terrorised and bullied by the deceased, a man called Monk, over a period of time. Believing that police protection would be ineffective, they devised a plan which involved the woman enticing the deceased to her bed, whereupon the defendants would burst into the room and attack him. The plan was carried out as arranged, resulting in the death of Monk. The defendants were convicted of murder following the trial judge's decision to withdraw the defence of provocation from the jury. The defendants appealed to the Court of Appeal.

Held

The appeal would be dismissed. '

Lawton LJ:

[His Lordship considered the submissions made on behalf of the appellants to the effect that provocation could take effect some time after the provoking event.]

'There are, it seems to us, three answers to that proposition. The first is to be found in the history of the law relating to provocation which was set out in the speech of Lord Diplock in *Director of Public Prosecutions v Camplin* (1978) 67 Cr App R; [1978] AC 705. That history shows that, in the past at any rate, provocation and loss of self-control tended to be regarded by the courts as taking place with a very short interval of time between the provocation and the loss of self-control. But Lord Diplock in the course of his speech went a little further with regard to this matter. At p19 and p716 respectively, having reviewed section 3 of the Homicide Act 1957, he said, referring to the section:

"Secondly it makes it clear that if there was any evidence that the accused himself at the time of the act which caused the death in fact lost his self-control in consequence of some provocation however slight it might appear to the judge, he was bound to leave to the jury the question which is one of opinion not of law: Whether a reasonable man might have reacted to that provocation as the accused did."

In our judgment, Lord Diplock clearly thought that the loss of self-control must occur at or about the time of the act of provocation.

Here the last act of provocation was on Sunday, October 7. It was not in any way suggested that the dead man had provoked anybody on the night of his death [October 14]. In fact, when Gregory and Ibrams went into the bedroom he was asleep. The first blow he received was inflicted on him by Gregory, and it dazed him but did not knock him unconscious. He was able to sit up in bed, and he was then attacked by Ibrams. Nothing happened on the night of the killing which caused Ibrams to lose his self-control. There having been a plan to kill Monk, his evidence that when he saw him all the past came to his mind does not, in our judgment, provide any evidence of loss of self-control.

In our judgment, the matter is really concluded by the summing-up to the jury of Devlin J (as he then was) in *Duffy* [1949] 1 All ER 932n, which was approved by the Court of Criminal Appeal. There is a passage in the summing-up so approved which is referred to time and time again in cases and in the textbooks; but, whether we look at the whole of the summing-up or at those parts of it which were approved by the Court of Criminal Appeal, it appears that there was another passage which is directly relevant to the facts of this case. The part which has been referred to many times with approval, and in particular with the approval of this Court in *Whitfield* (1976) 63 Cr App R 39, 42, is as follows:

"Provocation is some act or series of acts done by the dead man to the accused which would cause in any reasonable person and actually causes in the accused, a sudden and temporary loss of self-control, rendering the accused so subject to passion as to make him for the moment not master of his mind."

That passage refers to "a sudden and temporary loss of self-control," which has to be of such a kind as to make the accused for the moment not master of his mind.

Later in the same summing-up, in another passage which also approved by the Court of Criminal Appeal in *Duffy* (supra), are these words: [1949] 1 All ER at p932H)

"Indeed, circumstances which induce a desire for revenge are inconsistent with provocation, since the conscious formulation of a desire for revenge means that a person has had time to think, to reflect, and that would negative a sudden temporary loss of self-control, which is of the essence of provocation." '

R v Johnson [1989] 1 WLR 740 Court of Appeal (Criminal Division) (Watkins LJ, McCowan and Judge JJ)

Provocation - self induced

Facts

The appellant had made unpleasant comments to the deceased and his female companion. The deceased had retaliated by threatening the appellant with a beer glass. The appellant responded by fatally stabbing the deceased with a flick knife. At his trial the judge, following *Edwards* v *R* [1973] AC 648, refused to leave the defence of provocation to the jury on the basis that it had been self-induced. The appellant was convicted of murder and appealed.

Held

The appeal would be allowed, the conviction for murder would be quashed and a conviction for manslaughter substituted. Section 3 of the Homicide Act 1957 provides that anything can amount to provocation, including actions provoked by the accused. The appellant had been deprived of the opportunity of having his defence considered properly by the jury.

Watkins LJ:

'In the course of the submissions from both counsel for defence and the Crown, the judge raised the matter of "self-induced" provocation. He said: "It is rather difficult to see how a man who excites provocative conduct can in turn rely upon it as provocation in the criminal law."

He was referring there to the unpleasant threatening behaviour by the appellant at the start of the incident. No authority on this point was cited to the judge. The concept of self-induced provocation was not analysed. Counsel for the Crown did not rely on it and, in giving his ruling, the judge did not refer to it. In his conclusion the judge agreed with the submission of the Crown that it would be inappropriate, having regard to the evidence, to leave provocation to the jury. Hence the lack of direction to the jury on this issue.'

His Lordship then referred to s3 of the Homicide Act 1957, *DPP* v *Camplin* [1978] AC 705, and the Privy Council's decision in *Edwards* v *R* [1973] AC 648, and continued:

'On the particular facts of the case Lord Pearson, giving the judgment of the Board, said, at p658:

"On principle it seems reasonable to say that - (1) a blackmailer cannot rely on the predictable results of his own blackmailing conduct as constituting provocation... and the predictable results may include a considerable degree of hostile reaction by the person sought to be blackmailed... (2) but if the hostile reaction by the person sought to be blackmailed goes to extreme lengths it might constitute sufficient provocation even for the blackmailer; (3) there would in many cases be a question of degree to be decided by the jury."

Those words cannot, we think, be understood to mean, as was suggested to us, that provocation which is "self-induced" ceases to be provocation for the purposes of section 3.

The relevant statutory provision being considered by the Privy Council was in similar terms to section 3. In view of the express wording of section 3, as interpreted in *R* v *Camplin* [1978] AC 705 which was decided after *Edwards* v *The Queen* [1973] AC 648, we find it impossible to accept that the mere fact that a defendant caused a reaction in others, which in turn led him to lose his self-control, should result in the issue of provocation being kept outside a jury's consideration. Section 3 clearly provides that the question is whether things done or said or both provoked the defendant to lose his self-control. If there is any evidence that it may have done, the issue must be left to the jury. The jury would then have to consider all the circumstances of the incident, including all the relevant behaviour of the defendant, in deciding (a) whether he was in fact provoked and (b) whether the provocation was enough to make a reasonable man do what the defendant did.

Accordingly, whether or not there were elements in the appellant's conduct which justified the conclusion that he had started the trouble and induced others, including the deceased, to react in the way they did, we are firmly of the view that the defence of provocation should have been left to the jury.

Since it is not possible for us to infer from their verdict that the jury inevitably would have concluded that provocation as well as self-defence had been disproved the verdict of murder will be set aside. A conviction for manslaughter on the basis of provocation will be substituted.'

Commentary

The decision of the Privy Council in *Edwards* v *R*, which is clearly only persuasive, is very difficult to reconcile with the present case. It is submitted that the broader approach of the Court of Appeal represents the more accurate and desirable statement of the law.

R v Newell (1980) 71 Cr App R 331 Court of Appeal (Criminal Division) (Lord Lane CJ, Park and Lincoln JJ)

Reasonable man test for provocation

Facts

The defendant, a chronic alcoholic, had been in a severely depressed state because his girlfriend had left him. The deceased, who had been a friend of the defendant, made some disparaging remarks about the woman, and the defendant responded by hitting him over the head with a heavy ashtray several times, eventually killing him. Four days before the killing the defendant had taken a drug overdose in an attempted suicide, and he was still suffering from the after effects of this at the time of the killing. At his trial, the defendant sought to have his chronic alcoholism, depression and drug taking, introduced as characteristics with which the reasonable man should be endowed in determining whether he had been provoked. The trial judge had directed the jury to ignore the defendant's alcoholism, and they found him guilty of murder. The defendant appealed to the Court of Appeal.

Held

The appeal would be dismissed.

Lord Lane CJ:

'[*R v Mc Gregor* [1962] NZLR 1069] contains the following passage which appears to us to be entirely apt to the situation in the instant case: " ... The offender must be presumed to possess in general the power of self-control of the ordinary man, save in so far as his power of self-control is weakened because of some particular characteristic possessed by him. It is not every trait or disposition of the offender than [sic] can be invoked to modify the concept of the ordinary man. The characteristic must be something definite and of sufficient significance to make the offender a different person from the ordinary run of mankind, and have also a sufficient degree of permanence to warrant its being regarded as something constituting part of the individual's character or personality. A disposition to be unduly suspicious or to lose one's temper readily will not suffice, nor will a temporary or transitory state of mind such as mood or depression, excitability or irascibility. These matters are either not of sufficient significance or not of sufficient permanency to be regarded as 'characteristics' which enable the offender to be distinguished from the ordinary man ... still less can a self-induced transitory state be relied upon, as where it arises from the consumption of liquor. The word 'characteristics' in the context of the section is wide enough to apply not only to physical qualities but also to mental qualities and such more indeterminate attributes as colour, race, creed. It is to be emphasised that of whatever nature the characteristic may be, it must be such that it can fairly be said that the offender is thereby marked off or distinguished from the ordinary man of the community. Moreover *it is to be equally emphasised that there must be some real connection between the nature of the provocation and the particular characteristic of the offender by which it is sought to modify the ordinary man test.* [*] The words or conduct must have been exclusively or particularly provocative to the individual because, and only because, of the characteristic ... such a connection may be seen readily enough where the offender possesses some unusual physical peculiarity. Though he might in all other respects be an ordinary man, provocative words alluding for example to some infirmity or deformity from which he was suffering might well bring about a loss of self-control. So too, if the colour, race or creed of the offender be relied on as constituting a characteristic, it is to be repeated that the provocative words or conduct must be related to the particular characteristic relied upon. Thus, it would not be sufficient, for instance, for the offender to claim merely that he belongs to an excitable race, or that members of his nationality are accustomed to resort readily to some lethal weapon ...

... In our opinion it is not enough to constitute a characteristic that the offender should merely in some general way be mentally deficient."

That passage, and the reasoning therein contained, seems to us to be impeccable. It is not only expressed in plain, easily comprehended language; it represents also, we think, the law of this country as well as that of New Zealand.'[*] (Emphasis added).

R v Raven [1982] Crim LR 51 Central Criminal Court (The Recorder of London)

Reasonable man test in provocation

Facts

'The defendant was charged with murder. The defendant did not give evidence, but in interviews, with the police and to others he complained of sexual attacks on him by the victim. The issue, among others was whether the defendant had been provoked. It was agreed that the defendant had a physical age of 22 years but a mental age of approximately nine years: and had lived in squats for two to three years of his life.

Held

The Learned Recorder in the absence of the jury ruled that, having regard to the test of the reasonable man as enunciated in *Camplin* [1978] 2 WLR 679 in order to attribute to the reasonable man the age and other characteristics of the accused the jury should be directed to consider the reasonable man as having lived the same type of life as the accused for 22 years but with the retarded development and mental age of the accused. The Learned Recorder directed the jury accordingly.'

[*Reported by Jane Bennington, Barrister.*]

R v Sanders (1991) 93 Cr App R 245 Court of Appeal (Criminal Division) (Watkins LJ, Boreham and Tucker JJ)

Diminished responsibility - weigh to be given to medical evidence

Facts

The appellant had lived with the deceased as his common law wife. He suffered from diabetes, as a result of which he was only partially sighted. He became heavily reliant upon the deceased, and when he was no longer able to work started to suffer from depression. The appellant discovered that the deceased had started a relationship with another man, and as a result formed the intention to kill her, and then take his own life. On the day of her death the deceased visited the appellant, and during the course of the visit he attacked her with a hammer, killing her. He then attempted, unsuccessfully, to take his own life. At his trial for murder the appellant put forward evidence of diminished responsibility. The two expert witnesses both agreed that the appellant was suffering from an abnormality of the mind (caused by a reactive depression) that substantially impaired his responsibility for his actions. The Crown accepted that the appellant suffered from an abnormality of the mind, but did not accept that it affected his responsibility for his actions. Following conviction for murder the appellant appealed to the Court of Appeal on the ground that the trial judge had failed to point out to the jury that the expert testimony as to his state of mind was unanimous in finding that the requirements of s2(1) Homicide Act 1957 were satisfied.

Held

The appeal would be dismissed.

Watkins LJ:

In considering the submission (by Mr Gale, counsel for the appellant) that the trial judge's direction was defective in its failure to remind the jury, that in considering whether the requirements of s2(1) were met, they should note that the medical evidence was 'all one way', Watkins LJ stated the following:

'We were referred to the following authorities. *Matheson* [1958] 42 Cr App R 145; [1958] 2 All ER 87, was a five judge court and it was held that where on a charge of murder a defence of diminished responsibility is relied on, and the medical evidence that diminished responsibility exists is uncontradicted and the jury return a verdict of guilty of murder, if there are facts entitling the jury to reject or differ from the opinions of the medical men the Court of Criminal Appeal will not interfere with the verdict unless it can be said that the verdict would amount to a miscarriage of justice. There may be cases where evidence of the conduct of the accused before, at the time of and after the killing may be a relevant consideration for the jury in determining this issue. Where, however, there is unchallenged medical evidence of abnormality of mind and consequent substantial impairments of mental responsibility and no facts or circumstances appear which can displace or throw doubt on that evidence a verdict of guilty of murder is one which cannot be supported having regard to the evidence within the meaning of s4(1) of the Criminal Appeal Act 1907. In the course of the judgment of the Court, which was given by the Lord Goddard CJ, he said at p151 and p89 respectively:

"Here it is said there was evidence of premeditation and undoubtedly there was, but an abnormal mind is as capable of forming an intention and desire to kill as one that is normal; it is just what an abnormal mind might do. A desire to kill is quite common in cases of insanity."

In the holding (42 Cr App R 145) the Court went on:

"Where a defence of diminished responsibility is raised, a plea of guilty to manslaughter on this ground should not be accepted; the issue must be left to the jury, as in the case of a defence of insanity."

It was complained in the perfected grounds in this case if not in the course of submissions to us that the judge had made no reference to premeditation being not necessarily inconsistent with diminished responsibility. That complaint was, we think, quite unjustified for the judge said of it in the green bundle at p4C:

"Even if the killing was premeditated, the doctors say that does not exclude or discount diminished responsibility as a defence, or in any way alter their opinions. Although Dr Holland accepted that if the killing was in fact premeditated that would mean that the defendant had not told him the truth. It is for you to assess that evidence and say what you make of it."

The next case which we were referred to was *Bailey* in 1961; reported in (1978) 66 Cr App R 31 [as a note, following *Walton* v *R*, below]. In that case a 17 year old youth was convicted of murder and sentenced to be detained at Her Majesty's pleasure. The Lord Chief Justice in giving the judgment of the Court said at p32:

"This Court has said on many occasions that of course juries are not bound by what the medical witness say, but at the same time they must act on evidence, and if there is nothing before them, no facts and no circumstances shown before them which throw doubt on the medical evidence, then that is all they are left with, and the jury, in those circumstances, must accept it. That was the effect of the decision of this court, sitting as a court of five judges, in the case of *Matheson* and as we understand it, nothing that this court said in the case of *Byrne* (1960) 44 Cr App R 246 throws any doubt upon what was said in *Matheson's* case."

In *Walton* v *R* (1978) 66 Cr App R 25 [1978] AC 788, a Privy Council case, in the course of giving the opinion of the Board, Lord Keith of Kinkel stated at p30 and p793:

"These cases make clear that upon an issue of diminished responsibility the jury are entitled and indeed bound to consider not only the medical evidence but the evidence upon the whole facts and circumstances of the case. These include the nature of the killing, the conduct of the accused before, at the time of and after it and any history of mental abnormality. It being recognised that the jury on occasion may properly refuse to accept medical evidence, it follows that they must be entitled to consider the quality and weight of that evidence. As was pointed out by Lord Parker CJ in *Byrne* (1960) 44 Cr App R 246, 254 what the jury are essentially seeking to ascertain is whether at the time of the killing the accused was suffering from a state of mind bordering on but not amounting to insanity. That task is to be approached in a broad common sense way."

Finally, we were asked to look at *Kiszko* (1979) 68 Cr App R 62. In that case Bridge LJ, giving the judgment of the Court stated at p69:

"The most recent pronouncement on this subject, in a judgment of the Privy Council in the case of *Walton* v *R* (1978) 66 Cr App R 25 seems to us still to encapsulate the law entirely accurately and not to require any modification in the light of the provisions of s2(1)(a) of the Criminal Appeal Act 1968. After referring to earlier authorities, the judgment delivered by Lord Keith of Kinkel is in these terms at page 30. ..."

He then sets out the passage which I have already read. From these cases, in our opinion, two clear principles emerge where the issue is diminished responsibility. The first is that if there are no other circumstances to consider, unequivocal, uncontradicted medical evidence favourable to a defendant should be accepted by a jury and they should be so directed. The second is that where there are other circumstances to be considered the medical evidence, though it be unequivocal and uncontradicted, must be assessed in the light of the other circumstances. Turning again then to the summing up it is right to say that viewed in isolation the judge did not specifically refer to the medical evidence in the main passage of the summing up upon which Mr Gale concentrated his attention. Having dealt faultlessly, it is conceded, with the first two elements, namely abnormality of mind and whether that arose from inherent causes or disease, the judge went on in the orange bundle at p9E:

"As to the third element, was the abnormality of mind such as substantially impaired the defendant's mental responsibility for his acts? This question is one of degree. It is essentially one for you, the jury. You must approach this question also in a board, common sense way. It means more than some trivial degree of impairment which does not make any appreciable difference to a person's ability to control himself, but it means, equally obviously, something less than total impairment. I can put that in a slightly different way. Substantial does not mean total, that is to say the mental responsibility need not be totally impaired, so to speak, destroyed altogether. It is something in between, and Parliament has left it to you, the jury, to say on the evidence, was the mental responsibility impaired and, if so, was it substantially impaired? The real issue, you may think, remember always that you decide this case, I do not so, is not whether the defendant was suffering from an abnormality of mind arising from inherent causes or induced by disease. The real question, you may think, the real issue is whether that abnormality of mind substantially impaired the defendant's mental responsibility for his acts."

Mr Gale relies heavily on the absence of reference to medical evidence there and in the early stages of the resumed summing up on the final day of the trial. Those passages simply cannot be viewed in isolation. There is, even in the passage relied upon, a reference to the evidence and in the green bundle at p3 the learned judge had this to say:

"As to diminished responsibility, the defendant relies upon two doctors, whose evidence I will remind you of, who say, in a word, that looking at all the defendant's circumstances namely: his diabetes and its very considerable effect on him; his unemployment over two years, his deteriorating medical condition, particularly affecting his sight, his increasing dependency upon Mrs Sadlier; his deep affection for Mrs Sadlier and his realisation that he was losing her to another man; Mrs Sadlier's final rejection of him; the defendant's entirely genuine and very nearly successful suicide attempt; the defendant's depression and increasing preoccupation with Mrs Sadlier, his appetite, concentration and sleep being affected. Looking at all those matters, the doctors say that the defendant, at the time of the killing, was suffering from abnormality of mind arising from reactive depression which substantially impaired his mental responsibility for his acts in killing Mrs Sadlier. If you find that it is more likely than not that the doctors are right, having looked at all those circumstances, then the defendant will have established diminished responsibility and will thus be entitled to a verdict of manslaughter.

Having regard to that entirely correct direction we are satisfied that there is no substance whatever in the complaint that the judge did not direct the jury properly on the third element. That in our view he clearly did. We are also satisfied that the judge was not called upon to go further than he did with regard to the medical evidence, that is to say beyond reminding them, as he did, that it was so to speak all one way, that it was in the purely medical sense but it did not stand alone for the jury's consideration of the appellant's state of mind. It needs to be said anyway that the medical evidence was challenged upon certain of its assumptions by cross-examination. Regardless of that the jury had to bear in mind, among other matters, the manner of the killing, the contents of the will and the letters, when the last letter was written and certain admissions made by the appellant to the police in interview. We conclude that the summing up, without exception, was a model, to use Mr Gale's words, and therefore cannot in any way be complained of.'

R v Seers (1984) 79 Cr App R 261 Court of Appeal (Criminal Division) (Griffiths LJ, Stocker J, and Sir John Thompson)

Diminished responsibility - whether borderline insanity

Facts (as stated by Griffiths J)

'The appellant killed his wife on November 21, 1981, by stabbing her in the chest in the street outside the hostel in which she had been living with their two children after she had left the matrimonial home on October 18. The appellant pleaded guilty to the manslaughter of his wife but raised the defences of provocation and diminished responsibility in answer to the charge of murder.

His defence on the ground of diminished responsibility was supported by the prison medical officer, Dr Rahman, whose evidence was that the appellant was suffering from chronic reactive depression that amounted to a mental illness properly characterised as an abnormality of mind within the meaning of section 2 of the Homicide Act 1957 and that it was of a degree that substantially impaired his mental responsibility at the time of the killing.

The prosecution called a consultant psychiatrist Dr Anton-Stevens who agreed that the appellant was suffering from reactive depression but in his opinion it was not so severe as to amount to an abnormality of mind and did not substantially impair his mental responsibility for killing his wife. Both doctors agreed that a reactive depressive illness could be so severe as to amount to an abnormality of mind and to substantially impair mental responsibility at the time of a killing. The issue between them in this case was the degree of severity of the reactive depression and on which side of the line it fell when applying the test contained in section 2 of the Act.

The prosecution also relied upon the evidence of a number of witnesses who had heard the appellant threaten to kill his wife in the days leading up to the killing which they said indicated a degree of premeditation. The defence, on the other hand, interpreted this evidence as supporting a diagnosis of abnormality of mind on the ground that no normal person intending a murder goes around announcing his intention to commit it.

There was also some lay evidence on which the defence relied indicating a deterioration in the physical appearance and the behaviour of the appellant in the month after his wife left him and before he killed her. The learned judge, no doubt basing himself upon a passage in the judgment of this Court in *Byrne* (1960) 44 Cr App R. 246; [1960] 2 QB 396, directed the jury that the test to be applied to determine whether the appellant was suffering from diminished responsibility was whether he could be described in popular language as partially insane or on the borderline of insanity. This was the only test propounded by the judge and he repeated it in various passages of his summing-up.'

[The appellant was convicted of the murder of his wife. He appealed against his conviction on the ground that the judge misdirected the jury on the issue of diminished responsibility.]

Held

The appeal would be allowed.

Per Griffiths LJ

'When first dealing with the defence of diminished responsibility, which is notoriously difficult to explain to a jury, after reading the words of section 2 of the Homicide Act 1957 the judge said:

"Now, that abnormality does not have to go to the extent that the defendant was what could properly be called insane. That would provide a wholly different and separate defence of its own in law, insanity certifiable as such, and no-one suggests that. This defendant falls within that degree of the diminished responsibility test involving his mental state which, in popular language, or ordinary language, would be described as either partial insanity or being on the borderline of insanity, and juries have often been directed that that is a good test for considering whether a man suffers from diminished responsibility and that test has been approved in higher courts than this, and it is for that reason that those very words were put to Dr Rahman to ask if he agreed that this man was not such as could be described as partially insane or being on the borderline of being insane, and he agreed that that description did not apply. That is a test that you can properly take into account." Later he said: "You must consider to what extent you think his condition at that stage, in the circumstances he was in was particularly abnormal, bearing in mind, no doubt, that in our modern age tens of thousands of marriages break up and tens of thousands of marriages result in broken homes in which one parent is deprived of the loss of having the children to live with him or her. Some of them, a large number of them, undoubtedly cause the greatest possible stress of a broken marriage in which children are separated and people become desperately worried and anxious in such circumstances, and the more so if it is against the background of either a business failure or, at the present time, being out of work, but that does not mean that people can be called, in ordinary language, on the borderline of insanity, does it, and that is the issue that you are looking at here." Finally he said: "The just and fair way of putting this, which I have already referred you to in this case, is to ask yourselves the question whether the mental abnormality in this man's case amounts to such a degree that it could be described in popular language as partial insanity or being on the borderline of insanity. When that was put to Dr Rahman he agreed not only that it did not apply to this defendant but he agreed ... anyway the question was put to him that the defendant came nowhere near it, and that is the view of Dr Anton-Stevens from his assessment too."

It is submitted on behalf of the appellant that this was not a case in which the jury would be assisted to determine either the question of mental abnormality or diminution of mental responsibility by reference to borderline or partial insanity.

Although both doctors agreed that a depressive illness could result in an abnormality of mind which would substantially impair a person's mental responsibility, Mr Taylor [for the appellant] submitted that the layman did not readily assimilate a depressive illness with insanity which was associated in the lay mind with such illnesses as schizophrenia or paranoia. Furthermore, says Mr Taylor, the judge virtually withdrew the defence of diminished responsibility from the jury by pointing out to them that both doctors agreed that the appellant was not on the borderline of insanity. It is submitted that the judge should have given a direction in accordance with the substance of the direction in *Byrne* (supra) and in particular should have directed the jury to consider whether the appellant's ability to control his hostility towards his wife had been substantially impaired by a depressive illness, and that this was not an appropriate case to introduce the concept of partial insanity, and still less to give that as the sole test.

The appellant relies upon the decision of the Privy Council in *Rose* v *The Queen* (1961) 45 Cr App R 102, 106; [1961] AC 496, 507, 508 in which Lord Tucker after citing the judgment of Lord Parker CJ in *Byrne* (1960) 44 Cr App R 246, 252; [1960] 2 QB 396, 403, had this to say of the test of partial insanity: "Their Lordships respectfully accept this interpretation of the words 'abnormality of mind' and 'mental responsibility' as authoritative and correct. They would not, however, consider that the Court of Criminal Appeal was intending to lay down that in every case the jury must necessarily be directed that the test is always to be the borderline of insanity. There may be cases in which the abnormality of mind relied upon cannot readily be related to any of the generally recognised types of 'insanity'. If, however, insanity is to be taken into consideration, as undoubtedly will usually be the case, the word must be used in its broad popular sense. It cannot too often be emphasised that there is no formula that can safely be used in every case – the direction to the jury must always be related to the particular evidence that has been given and there may be cases where the words 'borderline' and 'insanity' might not be helpful."

We respectfully agree with that passage. It is to be remembered that in *Byrne* (supra) all the doctors agreed that Byrne could be described as partially insane; he was a sexual psychopath who had hideously mutilated a young woman he had killed. In such a case the evidence justifies inviting a jury to determine the defence of impairment of mental responsibility by a test of partial insanity. But it is not a legitimate method of construing an Act of Parliament to substitute for the words of the Act an entirely different phrase and to say that it is to apply in all circumstances. We are sure that this was not the intention of the Court in *Byrne* (supra), and the phrase was, used as one way of assisting the jury to determine the degree of impairment of mental responsibility in an appropriate case, and no doubt to point out that Parliament by the use of the word "substantial" was indicating a serious degree of impairment of mental responsibility. However, we do not think that in a case such as this dealing with a depressive illness it is appropriate to direct a jury solely in terms of partial or borderline insanity. Indeed, we doubt if it is a helpful test at all in such a case. It is interesting to see how Dr Rahman dealt in his evidence with such a test in relation to a reactive depression. "(Q) There are, of course, certain recognised forms of mental illness like schizophrenia? (A) That is insanity. (Q) So far as reactive depression is concerned, how is that termed by the psychiatrist? (A) It is not described as insanity. (Q) Insanity, how is it described? (A) It is a mental state, a psychosis."

We think a jury would be likely to view the matter in the same way, and however seriously depressed they might have thought this appellant, with whatever effect that might have had on his mental state, they would not consider him to be partially insane or on the borderline of insanity. This being so they were bound on the judge's direction to find that the appellant had not made out the defence of diminished responsibility. There was in the view of this Court evidence in this case that would have justified a jury in returning a verdict of manslaughter on grounds of diminished responsibility if directed in accordance with *Byrne* (supra) but leaving out what we consider on the evidence in this case to be the inappropriate test of partial or borderline insanity. For the reasons we have given we are satisfied that the summing-up contained a material misdirection on the issue of diminished responsibility....'

R v Tandy (1988) 87 Cr App R 46 Court of Appeal (Criminal Division) 45 (Watkins LJ, Rose J, and Roch J)

Diminished responsibility - relationship with alcoholism

Facts

The defendant, an alcoholic, admitted killing her daughter by strangulation whilst intoxicated. She was convicted following the trial judge's direction to the jury that, as she had chosen to start drinking on the day of the killing, she could not plead that she was suffering from diminished responsibility brought on by the 'disease' of alcoholism. The defendant appealed on the ground that this had been a mis-direction.

Held

The appeal would be dismissed

Watkins LJ:

'The second issue raised at the trial was the defence of diminished responsibility under section 2(1) of the Homicide Act 1957.

It was raised in this way: the appellant was at all material times an alcoholic. According to her first husband she had by 1980 been in that condition. Her own evidence was that she had been drinking heavily for a number of years, her drinking being due to loneliness and two unhappy marriages. She told the doctors who examined her, and the jury, that she normally drank either Barley Wine or Cinzano, but that on Monday, March 3, she had purchased a bottle of vodka. She had not opened this until the morning of the Wednesday, but having opened and started the bottle of vodka, she had consumed 9/10ths of it during the course of that day. She had had her last drink at about 6.30 p.m. She had not previously drunk vodka. Vodka contains more alcohol than Cinzano which the appellant said she had drunk on Monday, March 3. She could not recall whether or not she had had a drink on the Tuesday.

Forensic evidence showed that her blood alcohol level at midnight on Wednesday, March 5, when a sample of blood was taken from her by Dr Stoker, was 240 mgs of alcohol per 100 mls of blood. The opinion of Dr Wood, a Consultant Forensic Psychiatrist called by the defence, was that at the time of the act of strangulation the level of alcohol in the appellant's blood would have been not less than 330 mgs of alcohol per 100 mls of blood and could have been anything up to 400 mgs of alcohol per 100 mls of blood. Dr Lawson, who gave evidence for the Crown, said that in his view the appellant's blood at the time of the strangulation would have contained approximately 300 mgs of alcohol per 100 mls of blood. The medical evidence indicated that this level of alcohol would be a lethal intake of intoxicants for a normal person, but that alcoholics, because of their persistent abuse of alcohol, become able to tolerate such levels of alcohol in their blood streams and to dissipate alcohol from their blood streams more quickly than non-alcoholics are able to do. Indeed in this case the evidence of Dr Stoker, who examined the appellant when at midnight he obtained the sample of blood from her, was that her movements were co-ordinated, her speech was all right and the appellant displayed no clinical evidence of intoxication. Dr Stoker had observed her walking up two flights of stairs. There were three principal areas of conflict between the medical witnesses called at the trial on behalf of the appellant and the medical witness called by the Crown. The first was as to whether alcoholism is or is not a disease. Dr Wood and Dr Milne (a Consultant Psychiatrist) both expressed the view that alcohol dependence syndrome, or alcoholism in the severity manifested in the appellant's case, constituted a disease. Dr Lawson, who accepted that the appellant was an alcoholic, expressed the opinion that alcoholism, even chronic alcoholism, is not a disease. In summing up the judge told the jury with regard to that (page 36E):

"... it is totally unnecessary for you to involve yourselves in that medical controversy about labelling. You have to apply the words of the Act of Parliament in a common sense way and those words are reflected in the wording on that sheet before you." (Here the judge was referring to a document headed, "Questions for the jury" which he had prepared and provided to the jury.)

"If you find that a woman is suffering from an abnormality of mind in the form of grossly impaired judgment and emotional responses and if you find that she is so suffering as a direct result of a condition over which she has – and I emphasise the words – no immediate control, then you can say that the second element in this defence is proved because her abnormality of mind is induced by disease or injury."

The judge was there telling the jury that the issue they had to decide was not whether alcoholism is or is not a disease, but whether the appellant was suffering from an abnormality of mind, in the form of grossly impaired judgment and emotional responses, as a direct result of her alcoholism, or whether, as the Crown on the evidence of Dr Lawson contended, her abnormal state of mind at the moment of the act of strangulation was due to the fact that she was drunk on vodka. The second area of conflict between the doctors was whether the appellant's drinking on the Wednesday was voluntary or involuntary.

Dr Wood said of this that he thought it would have been very difficult for her to resist the temptation of drink on that day. She was under some pressure to continue drinking to stave off the shakiness and other symptoms of withdrawal affecting her. He also said he would argue that drinking to that extent (that is to say most of a bottle of vodka) was an inherent part of the disease. He considered that compulsion was certainly partly causative of her drinking as she did on that day in that the choice to do so was not a free choice. Compulsion stemmed from her being an alcoholic and her experience that to deny herself drink would lead her to being severely uncomfortable, if not ill. When asked if the appellant in his view at that time had control over her drinking habits, he replied, "No none whatsoever." Dr Milne said that he believed the appellant drank involuntarily, because she was an alcoholic.

Dr Lawson agreed that a person who is an alcoholic has a craving for alcohol and a compulsion to drink. His view was that the appellant had control over whether she had the first drink of the day, but once she had had the first drink she was no longer in control. The third area of conflict in the medical evidence was on the question whether if the appellant had not taken drink that day, she would have strangled her daughter. Dr Lawson put his view in one short answer: "I could not see her killing the child if she were sober." Dr Milne, when asked whether he went as far as to say that if the appellant had not consumed any drink that day she would have still committed this offence, answered "No." Dr Wood agreed that an alcoholic may do something which he or she would not otherwise do but for the intake of alcohol. When asked whether, if the appellant had not consumed any drink that day, she would have still done what she did to her daughter, he said, "I do not know. I think had she not consumed drink on that day she would have been quite seriously ill in another fashion by 8 o'clock that evening." He amplified that answer by saying that the appellant's problem on March 5, was serious alcoholism and until she had withdrawn from alcohol, whether or not she was intoxicated, she would have suffered from seriously disturbed judgment and emotional control. He thought that her judgment and emotional control would have continued to be severely disturbed on the Wednesday, even had she not drunk the vodka which she drank that day.

The ground of appeal is that there was material misdirection of the jury in regard to the defence of diminished responsibility. The relevant passages in the summing up are where the judge said (page 38E): "The choice [of the appellant whether to drink or not to drink on Wednesday March 5 1986] may not have been easy but ... if it was there at all it is fatal to this defence, because the law simply will not allow a drug user, whether the drug be alcohol or any other, to shelter behind the toxic effects of the drug which he or she need not have used."

And where he stated earlier (page 37A):

"If she had taken no drink on March 5, 1986, or if you were satisfied that Dr Wood is right in saying that judgment and emotional response would have been grossly impaired even if no drink had been taken, then the answer would be easy, but clearly she did take drink on March 5, and if she did that as a matter of choice, she cannot say in law or in common sense that the abnormality of mind which resulted was induced by disease."

Mr Stewart, the appellant's counsel, submits that these are misdirections, because: (1) The medical evidence had been unanimous that there might be compulsion to drink at least after the first drink of the day; that it was the cumulative effect of the consumption of 9/10ths of the bottle of vodka which caused her to be in the state of intoxication she was in at the time of the killing. By his directions the judge removed the question of compulsion after the taking of the first drink from the jury's consideration. (2) The directions removed from the jury's consideration Dr Wood's evidence that the alcoholism alone produced an abnormal state of mind which substantially impaired her mental responsibility for her acts. (3) The directions removed from the jury the issue which this Court in *Fenton* (1975) 61 Cr App R 261, 263 recognised could arise when an accused person proves such a craving for drink as to produce in itself an abnormality of mind. Lord Widgery CJ's actual words were: "... cases may arise hereafter where the accused proves such a craving for drink or drugs as to produce in itself an abnormality of mind; but that is not proved in this case. The appellant did not give evidence and we do not see how self-induced intoxication can of itself produce an abnormality of mind due to inherent causes." (The jury had been rightly told to ignore the effect of alcohol.) Section 2(1) of the Homicide Act 1957 provides: "Where a person kills ... he shall not be convicted of murder if he was suffering from such abnormality of mind (whether arising from a condition of arrested or retarded development of mind or any inherent causes or induced by disease or injury) as substantially impaired his mental responsibility for his acts and omissions in doing or being a party to the killing." The authority of *Byrne* (1960) 44 Cr App R 246, 252 [1960] 2 QB, 396, 403 established that the phrase "abnormality of mind" was wide enough to cover the mind's activities in all its aspects, including the ability to exercise will power to control physical acts in accordance with rational judgment. But "abnormality of mind" means a state of mind so different from that of ordinary human beings that a reasonable man would term it abnormal. The defence of diminished responsibility was derived from the law of Scotland, in which one of the colloquial names for the defence was "partial insanity." Normal human beings frequently drink to excess and when drunk do not suffer from abnormality of mind, within the meaning of that phrase in section 2(1) of the Act of 1957. Whether an accused person was at the time of the act which results in the victim's death suffering from any abnormality of mind is a question for the jury; and as this Court stated in *Byrne* (supra), although medical evidence is important on this question, the jury are not bound to accept medical evidence if there is other material before them from which in their judgment a different conclusion may be drawn. The Court of Appeal in *Gittens* (1984) 79 Cr App R 272 said that it was a misdirection to invite the jury to decide whether it was inherent causes on the one hand or drink and pills on the other hand which were the main factor in causing the appellant in that case to act as he did. The correct direction in that case was to tell the jury that they had to decide whether the abnormality arising from the inherent causes substantially impaired the appellant's responsibility for his actions .... At p4A of the summing up and in the document headed "Questions for the Jury," the judge set out the three matters which the defence had to establish on the balance of probability for the defence of diminished responsibility to succeed. No criticism of that part of the summing up or that part of the "Questions for the Jury" has been made nor could it have been. So in this case it was for the appellant to show: (1) that she was suffering from an abnormality of mind at the time of the act of strangulation; (2) that that abnormality of mind was induced by disease, namely the disease of alcoholism; and (3) that the abnormality of mind induced by the disease of alcoholism was such as substantially impaired her mental responsibility for her act of strangling her daughter. The principles involved in seeking answers to these questions are, in our view, as follows. The appellant would not establish the second element of the defence unless the evidence showed that the abnormality of mind at the time of the killing was due to the fact that she was a chronic alcoholic. If the alcoholism had reached the level at which her brain had been injured by the repeated insult from intoxicants so that there was gross impairment of her judgment and emotional responses then the defence of diminished responsibility was available to her, provided that she satisfied the jury that the third element of the defence existed. Further, if the appellant were able to establish that the alcoholism had reached the level where although the brain had not been damaged to the extent just stated, the appellant's drinking had become involuntary, that is to say she was no longer able to resist the impulse to drink, then the defence of diminished responsibility would be available to her, subject to her establishing the first and third elements, because if her drinking was involuntary, then her abnormality of mind at the time of the act of strangulation was induced by her condition of alcoholism. On the other hand, if the appellant had simply not resisted an impulse to drink and it was the drink taken on the Wednesday which brought about the impairment of judgment and emotional response, then the defence of diminished responsibility was not available to the defendant. In our judgment the direction which the judge gave the jury accurately reflected these principles. There was evidence on which the jury, directed as they were, could reach their verdict. The appellant had chosen to drink vodka on the Wednesday rather than her customary drink of Cinzano. Her evidence was that she might not have had a drink at all on the Tuesday. She certainly did not tell the jury that she must have taken drink on the Tuesday or Wednesday because she could not help herself. She had been able to stop drinking at 6.30 pm on the Wednesday evening although her supply of Vodka was not exhausted. Thus her own evidence indicated that she was able to exercise some control even after she had taken the first drink, evidence indicated that she was able to exercise some control even after she had taken the first drink, contrary to the view of the doctors. There was the evidence of Dr Lawson that the appellant would have had the ability on that Wednesday to abstain from taking the first drink of the day. Mr Smith, who appeared for the Crown, pointed out in his submissions that the abnormality of mind described by Dr Wood and Dr Milne was of grossly impaired judgment and emotional responses and it did not include an irresistible craving for alcohol. The three matters on which the appellant relies in the perfected grounds of appeal for saying that there was a misdirection can be dealt with shortly. As to the first, in our judgment the judge was correct in telling the jury that if the taking of the first drink was not involuntary, then the whole of the drinking on the Wednesday was not involuntary. Further, as we have pointed out, the appellant's own evidence indicated that she still had control over her drinking on that Wednesday after she had taken the first drink. As to the second, the jury were told correctly that the abnormality of mind with which they were concerned was the abnormality of mind at the time of act of strangulation and as a matter of fact by that time on that Wednesday the appellant had drunk 9/10ths of a bottle of vodka. On the third point we conclude that for a craving for drinks or drugs in itself to produce an abnormality of mind within the meaning of section 2(1) of 1957 Act, the craving must be such as to render the accused's use of drink or drugs involuntary. Therefore in our judgment the judge correctly defined how great the craving for drink had to be before it could in itself produce an abnormality of mind. In any event, it was not the evidence of the doctors called, on behalf of the appellant, that her abnormality of mind included, let alone consisted solely, of a craving for alcohol. For those reasons we find that there was no material misdirection of the jury and we dismiss this appeal.'

8 HOMICIDE III: INVOLUNTARY MANSLAUGHTER

R v Arobieke [1988] Crim LR 314 Court of Appeal (Criminal Division) (Glidewell LJ, Hodgson and Waite JJ)

Need for an unlawful act in constructive manslaughter

Facts

'There was animosity between the appellant and the deceased (K). On June 15, 1986, K and some friends came out of the swimming baths in New Brighton and saw the appellant sitting outside. On seeing him, K became apprehensive and walked on alone to the station where he was electrocuted trying to cross the lines. The appellant was charged with manslaughter on the basis that K's attempt to cross the tracks was caused by his imminent fear of unlawful injury being inflicted by the appellant. A prosecution witness, D, said that K had walked onto the platform, and looked about nervously before getting onto a train. Then, the appellant had walked along the opposite platform, looking into the train, before going back to the ticket barrier. K had then run in the same direction and suddenly crouched down close to where he had subsequently descended on to the tracks. Another witness saw someone whom he thought to be K climbing over a gate at the station in a way which would have avoided him passing the ticket barrier and which route, had it been taken by him, would have brought him onto the line at the point where he was electrocuted. When K's body was found, he had no railway ticket.

Counsel for the Crown had submitted, in effect, that the appellant's mere presence at the station, given the antecedent history of unlawful acts and threats, was sufficient for manslaughter because it recklessly caused in K an apprehension of immediate and unlawful violence. Rejecting a submission of "no case" by counsel for the appellant, the judge had formulated eight facts which he directed the jury they should find before they could convict the appellant of manslaughter. Three of these were: (4) that the appellant was on the platform whilst K was on the train and had looked for K, intending to physically hurt or threaten him with violence; (5) that K saw the appellant behaving in that manner and reasonably apprehended that he was in imminent danger of physical attack; (8) that the appellant's conduct in relation to K was such that any reasonable person would recognise it as being likely to subject K to at least the risk of some, albeit not serious, harm. The appellant was convicted and appealed by the trial judge's certificate, the relevant ground being: "In the light of the criticism by the judge in his summing-up of the evidence of [D], the only witness upon whom a number of crucial findings of fact could be founded, no reasonable jury could be satisfied that such facts were proved and consequently the verdict … was wholly unsafe and unsatisfactory."

Held

Allowing the appeal and quashing the conviction, D's evidence could not amount to evidence of an assault by the appellant against K. Merely to look at the train, without knowing if K was on it, could not amount to an unlawful act (*Fagan* v *MPC* [1969] 1 QB 439). Thus, the jury could not have concluded proposition (4) against the appellant. Nor could the objective tests formulated in propositions (5) and (8) have been so concluded.

Even if their Lordships were wrong in those conclusions, they had substantially more than a lurking doubt as to the safety and satisfactory nature of the conviction, and that was sufficient under section 2(1) Criminal Appeal Act 1968. In answer to the submission for the Crown that the Court ought not to substitute its own view of the adequacy or otherwise of D's evidence for that of the jury: as had been made clear in *R v Galbraith* (1981) 73 Cr App R 124, the test applied by their Lordships was different to that applied by the trial judge on a submission of "no case". The supervision of the Court of Appeal extended beyond and operated at a later stage than the discretion or the decision of the trial judge at the end of the prosecution case.'

[*Reported by Veronica Cowan, Barrister.*]

R v Cato [1976] 1 WLR 110 Court of Appeal (Criminal Division) (Lord Widgery CJ, O'Conner and Jupp JJ)

Nature of unlawful act in constructive manslaughter

Facts

The defendant and the deceased (Farmer), agreed to inject each other with heroin. The deceased had consented to a number of such injections during the course of an evening. The following morning he was found to have died from the effects of the drug taking. The defendant was convicted of maliciously administering a noxious substance contrary to s23 of the Offences Against the Person Act 1861, and of manslaughter, either on the basis that his unlawful act had caused death, or on the basis that he had recklessly caused Farmer's death. The defendant appealed against his convictions on the grounds, inter alia, that there had been no unlawful act since the deceased had consented to the injection of heroin, and that the consent should have been taken into account in determining whether or not the defendant had acted recklessly.

Held

The appeal would be dismissed.

Lord Widgery CJ:

'The next matter, I think, is the unlawful act. Of course, on the first approach to manslaughter in this case it was necessary for the prosecution to prove that Farmer had been killed in the course of an unlawful act. Strangely enough, or it may seem strange to most of us, although the possession or supply of heroin is an offence, it is not an offence to take it, and although supplying it is an offence, it is not an offence to administer it. At least it is not made to be an offence, and so Mr Blom-Cooper [counsel for the defendant] says there was no unlawful act here. That which Cato did - taking Farmer's syringe already charged and injecting the mixture into Farmer as directed - is not an unlawful act, says Mr Blom-Cooper, because there is nothing there which is an offence against the Misuse of Drugs Act 1971, and when he shows us the terms of the section it seems that that is absolutely right.

Of course if the conviction on count 2 remains (that is the charge under section 23 of administering a noxious thing), then that in itself would be an unlawful act. The prohibition in that statute would be enough in itself, and it is probably right to say that, as we are going to uphold the conviction on count 2, as will appear presently, that really answers the problem and destroys the basis of Mr Blom-Cooper's argument.

But since he went to such trouble with the argument, and in respect for it, we think we ought to say that had it not been possible to rely on the charge under section 23 of the Offences against the Person Act 1861, we think there would have been an unlawful act here, and we think the unlawful act would be described as injecting the deceased Farmer with a mixture of heroin and water which at the time of the injection and for the purposes of the injection the accused had unlawfully taken into his possession.'

R v Church [1966] 1 QB 59 Court of Criminal Appeal (Edmund-Davies, Marshall and Widgery JJ)

Nature of the dangerous unlawful act in constructive manslaughter

Facts

The defendant had gone to his van with the deceased, Mrs Nott, for sexual purposes. She had mocked his impotence and he had attacked her, knocking her out. The defendant panicked, and wrongly thinking he had killed her, threw her unconscious body into a river, where she drowned. The defendant appealed against his conviction for manslaughter.

Held

The appeal would be dismissed.

Edmund-Davies LJ:

'In the judgment of this court [the trial judge's direction on unlawful manslaughter] ... was a misdirection. It amounted to telling the jury that, whenever any unlawful act is committed in relation to a human being which resulted in death there must be, at least, a conviction for manslaughter. This might at one time have been regarded as good law: ... But it appears to this court that the passage of years has achieved a transformation in this branch of the law and, even in relation to manslaughter, a degree of mens rea has become recognised as essential ... [T]he conclusion of this court is that an unlawful act causing the death of another cannot, simply because it is an unlawful act, render a manslaughter verdict inevitable. For such a verdict inexorably to follow, the unlawful act must be such as all sober and reasonable people would inevitably recognise must subject the other person to, at least, the risk of some harm resulting therefrom, albeit not serious harm ...'

Commentary

See *R v Dawson*, below.

R v Dalby [1982] 1 WLR 425 Court of Appeal (Criminal Division) (Waller LJ, Jupp and Waterhouse JJ)

Nature of the unlawful act in constructive manslaughter

Facts

The defendant had been in lawful possession of a controlled drug. He had supplied a quantity of the drug to the deceased (a man named O'Such). The deceased had consumed a large quantity of the drug in one session, and subsequently injected himself with other substances. The following morning the deceased was found to have died of a drug overdose. The defendant was convicted of unlawful act manslaughter, based on his unlawful supply of the controlled drug, and he appealed on the basis that his supply of the drug was not a dangerous act which had operated as the direct cause of death. He contended that the death was due to the deceased's act in consuming such a large dose of the drug in such a short space of time.

Held

The conviction would be quashed.

Waller LJ:

'The difficulty in the present case is that the act of supplying a scheduled drug was not an act which caused direct harm. It was an act which made it possible, or even likely, that harm would occur subsequently, particularly if the drug was supplied to somebody who was on drugs. In all the reported cases, the physical act has been one which inevitably would subject the other person to the risk of some harm from the act itself. In this case, the supply of drugs would itself have caused no harm unless the deceased had subsequently used the drugs in a form and quantity which was dangerous ...

In the judgment of this Court, the unlawful act of supplying drugs was not an act directed against the person of O'Such and the supply did not cause any direct injury to him. The kind of harm envisaged in all the reported cases of involuntary manslaughter was physical injury of some kind as an immediate and inevitable result of the unlawful act, eg, a blow on the chin which knocks the victim against a wall causing a fractured skull and death, or threatening him with a loaded gun which accidentally fires, or dropping a large stone on a train (*DPP* v *Newbury*) or threatening another with an open razor and stumbling with death resulting (*Larkin*).

In the judgment of this Court, where the charge of manslaughter is based on an unlawful and dangerous act, it must be directed at the victim and likely to cause immediate injury, however slight.'

Commentary

See *R* v *Goodfellow*, below.

R v Dawson (1985) 81 Cr App R 150 Court of Appeal (Criminal Division) (Watkins LJ, Wood J, Sir John Thompson)

Constructive manslaughter - nature of unlawful act causing death.

Facts

Dawson, accompanied by two other men, Nolan and Walmsley, carried out an attempted robbery at a petrol station. The cashier at the petrol station (Mr Black) was a 60 year old man who, unknown to the appellants, suffered from a heart disease. Dawson had pointed a replica hand gun at the cashier, and Walmsley had banged a pick axe handle on the counter. Money was demanded, but the cashier pressed the alarm button and the appellants fled empty handed. Shortly afterwards the cashier collapsed and died from a heart attack. Following conviction, the appellants sought to appeal on the grounds that the jury had been mis-directed as regards the law relating to the 'dangerous unlawful act' in manslaughter.

Held

[As regards the convictions for manslaughter] the appeals would be allowed.

Watkins LJ:

His Lordship recited the six perfected grounds of appeal, of which, the second and sixth are of relevance here. The second stated that the judge, wrongly in law, 'directed the jury that putting a person in such terror that he may suffer such emotional or physical disturbance as would be detrimental could for the relevant purpose constitute harm. It is argued that it is not open to a jury to convict if they find merely that an emotional disturbance that was detrimental was suffered by a deceased.'

The sixth stated that the judge, wrongly in law, 'directed the jury that the sane and reasonable people referred to in the test for the creation of the risk of some harm to the person must connote people who know all the facts, including, it is to be inferred, that the deceased suffered from chronic heart disease. There was no evidence that the appellants were aware of that condition. Whilst Walmsley did not include this in his perfected grounds, we shall assume that he seeks to rely on it nevertheless.'

'Counts 2 and 6, which can be taken together, have caused us much concern. It has, in our experience, been generally understood that the harm referred to in the second element of the offence of manslaughter, namely, the unlawful act, must be one that all sober and reasonable people would realise was likely to cause some, albeit not serious, harm, means physical harm ... there seems to us to be no sensible reason why shock produced by fright should not come within the definition of harm in this context. From time to time one hears the expression "frightened to death" without thinking that the possibility of such event occurring would be an affront to reason or medical knowledge. Shock can produce devastating and lasting effects, for instance upon the nervous system. That is surely harm, ie injury to the person. Why not harm in this context?

In another context, s1 of the Prevention of Crime Act 1953, this Court in *Rapier* (1980) 70 Cr App R 17, seems to have no difficulty in comprehending that one effect of shock can be to produce injury to the person. At p19 Park J said:

"The judgment of the Court in that case [ie *Edmonds* (1963) 47 CR App R 114; [1963] 2 QB 142] was delivered by Winn J (as he then was). Towards the end of the judgment, at p121 and pp150, 151 of the respective reports, he said: 'The justification, the court assumes, which the learned commissioner had in mind for the adoption of his own phraseology including reference to intent to frighten is to be found in a decision of the Divisional Court reported in the name of *Woodward* v *Koessler* [1958] 3 All ER 557; [1958] 1 WLR 1255. That was a case where upon the facts it was plain that a sheath knife had been so brandished with such accompanying threatening behaviour that injury might very well be conclusively assumed to have been done as a result of the shock thereby caused. Whether that case must stand upon its own facts, it seems to the court that it is, to put it at its lowest, unsafe and undesirable that directions to juries based upon s1(4) [of the Prevention of Crime Act 1953] should include any reference to intent to frighten unless it be made clear in the passage in which such reference is made that the frightening must be of a kind for which the term 'intimidation' is far more appropriate and of a sort which is capable of producing injury through the operation of shock ...' This Court in the instant case wishes to emphasise that passage in the judgment of Winn J. In our view, in directing a jury in respect of an offence under this section the use of the word 'intimidate' should be avoided unless the evidence discloses that the intention of the person having with him the article alleged to be an offensive weapon was to cause injury by shock and hence injury to the person; it would seem that circumstances giving rise to that situation must be exceedingly rare."

We shall assume without deciding the point, although we incline to favour the proposition, that harm in the context of manslaughter includes injury to the person through the operation of shock emanating from fright and examine how the judge dealt with this in the second element of the offence. He said:

"But the second question is, would all reasonable people realise it must inevitably create the risk of some harm to Mr Black? That is to say, all reasonable people who knew the facts that you know, including the fact that the gun was a replica and could not fire and thus knew that actually Mr Black could not be injured by a bullet, in other words, but also knowing that Mr Black did not know that; that he might very well think he was being threatened by a real firearm. He did not know it was not loaded with live ammunition. He did not know that at any minute the trigger might not be pulled. All of them have accepted that they intended to secure the money by putting Mr Black in fright. So fear was both to be expected and was intended. I direct you that if an act puts a person in such terror that he or she may suffer emotional or physical disturbance which is detrimental then that disturbance is harm within the meaning of what you have to consider. If, therefore, you conclude that all sober and reasonable people, which means you, because it is your standards that have got to be applied, could only come to the conclusion that the result of the threats with the pickaxe handle and the firearm in the middle of the night was likely to be that inevitably there was a risk that Mr Black would be put in such terror that he would suffer some such disturbance which would be bad for him, then that can be harm and the second element that you have to find is made out."

These directions have been roundly attacked as being wholly erroneous. It was argued that, contrary to an indication given by him to counsel, the judge in that passage directed the jury that a definition of harm was "emotional disturbance which is detrimental produced by terror". He had, as we have seen from a transcript of discussion between him and counsel, intended to direct the jury that a definition of harm for present purposes was emotional *and* physical disturbance produced by terror. We think it was unfortunate that the judge, probably through inadvertence, used the disjunctive "or". As it was, the jury were left with a choice. Which they chose and acted upon we cannot tell. If they acted upon the basis that emotional disturbance was enough to consititute harm then, in our judgment, they would have done so upon a misdirection. Emotional disturbance does not occur to us as sensibly descriptive of injury or harm to the person through the operation of shock produced by terror or fright; moreover, we do not think the word "detrimental" assists to clarify whatever the expression "emotional disturbance" is meant to convey. The further phrase used, namely, "some such disturbance which would be bad for him" is likewise not helpful.

In his endeavours to give the jury appropriate guidance upon the meaning of harm within the facts of this case the judge was sailing uncharted seas. We have every sympathy with him. Unfortunately we think that what he said, other than the use of the phrase "physical disturbance which is detrimental" (this was, we think, by itself, though easier to understand, inadequate) could have led the jury to contemplate merely a disturbance of the emotions as harm sufficient for the purpose of the second element when clearly, in our view, it is not.

In our judgment, a proper direction would have been that the requisite harm is caused if the unlawful act so shocks the victim as to cause him physical injury.

We look finally at the direction, "That is to say all reasonable people who knew the facts that you know." What the jury knew included, of course, the undisputed fact that the deceased had a very bad heart which at any moment could have ceased to function. It may be the judge did not intend that this fact should be included in the phrase "the facts that you know". If that was so, it is regrettable that he did not make it clear. By saying as he did, it is argued "including the fact that the gun was a replica" and so on, the jury must have taken him to be telling them that all facts known to them, including the heart condition, should be taken into account in performing that is undoubtedly an objective test. We think there was a grave danger of that.

This test can only be undertaken upon the basis of the knowledge gained by a sober and reasonable man as though he were present at the scene of and watched the unlawful act being performed and who knows that, as in the present case, an unloaded replica gun was in use, but that the victim may have thought it was a loaded gun in working order. In other words, he has the same knowledge as the man attempting to rob and no more. It was never suggested that any of these appellants knew that their victim had a bad heart. They knew nothing about him.

A jury must be informed by the judge when trying the offence of manslaughter what facts they may and those which they may not use for the purpose of performing the test in the second element of this offence. The judge's direction here, unlike the bulk of an admirable summing-up, lacked that necessary precision and in the form it was given may, in our view, have given the jury an erroneous impression of what knowledge they could ascribe to the sober and reasonable man.

For these reasons we see no alternative to quashing the convictions for manslaughter as unsafe and unsatisfactory. The appeal against the convictions for manslaughter is therefore allowed.'

Commentary

See *R* v *Watson*, below.

DPP v Newbury and Jones [1976] AC 500 House of Lords (Lords Diplock, Simon, Kilbrandon, Salmon, and Edmund-Davies)

Mens rea for unlawful act manslaughter

Facts

The defendants, both teenage boys, had thrown a piece of paving stone from a railway bridge onto a train which had been passing beneath them. The missile struck and killed the guard who had been sitting in the driver's compartment. The defendants were convicted of manslaughter, and appealed on the ground that they had not foreseen that their actions might cause harm to any other person.

Held

The appeals would be dismissed.

Lord Salmon:

'In *R* v *Larkin*, Humphreys J said:

"Where the act which a person is engaged in performing is unlawful, then if at the same time it is a dangerous act, that is, an act which is likely to injure another person, and quite inadvertently the doer of the act causes the death of that other person by that act, then he is guilty of manslaughter."

I agree entirely ... that that is an admirably clear statement of the law which has been applied many times. It makes it plain (a) that an accused is guilty of manslaughter if it is proved that he intentionally did an act which was unlawful and dangerous and that that act inadvertently caused death and (b) that it is unnecessary to prove that the accused knew that the act was unlawful or dangerous. This is one of the reasons why cases of manslaughter vary so infinitely in their gravity. They may amount to little more than pure inadvertence and sometimes to little less than murder ..."

The test is still the objective test. In judging whether the act was dangerous the test is not did the accused recognise that it was dangerous but would all sober and reasonable people recognise its danger? ...'

Lord Edmund-Davies:

[After expressing his agreement with Lord Salmon, and having referred to *R* v *Church*, his Lordship continued:]

'I believe that *R* v *Church* accurately applied the law as it then existed. I believe, further, that, since it was decided, nothing has happened to change the law in relation to the constituents of involuntary manslaughter caused by an unlawful act. The Criminal Justice Act 1967 has certainly effected no such change, for, as I sought to show in *R* v *Majewski* [1977] AC 443, section 8 thereof has nothing to do with *when* intent or foresight or any other mental state has to be established, but simply *how* it is to be determined where such determination is called for.

That is not to say that a change in the law may not be opportune. If I may be permitted to introduce a personal note into a judgment, I have the best reason to know that the forthcoming working paper of the Criminal Law Revision Committee on offences against the person will afford those concerned in such important matters an opportunity to assess the cogency of the argument for a drastic change in the law applicable to such cases as the present. But, unless and until such argument prevails and so leads on to legislation, the existing law has to be applied. I hold that the direction of the learned trial judge, Watkins J, was in strict accordance with the settled law and that these appeals should therefore be refused.'

R v Goodfellow (1986) 83 Cr App R 23 Court of Appeal (Criminal Division) (Lord Lane CJ, Boreham and Taylor JJ)

Nature of the unlawful act in constructive manslaughter

Facts

As related in the judgment of the Lord Chief Justice:

'On August 14, 1984 in the early hours of the morning, the appellant set light to the council house he occupied at 24 Cossock Terrace, Pallion. He poured petrol over the sideboard, chair and walls of the downstairs living room, and then set the house on fire by igniting the petrol. In the ensuing blaze three people died: his wife Sarah aged 22, another young woman named Jillian Stuart with whom the appellant was having a liaison, who was in the house that night, and the appellant's two year old son Darren.

The background to these events was as follows. The appellant had been having difficulties with two men in the locality. One of them had been fined for damaging the front door of No. 24. Hence the appellant wanted to move. He had no chance of exchanging his council house for another because he was some "£300 in arrears with his rent." He therefore conceived the idea of setting No. 24 on fire and making it look as though the fire had been caused by a petrol bomb thrown through the window by one of the men. This story was what he initially told the police when they started to make inquiries.

In fact he had obtained the petrol from the motorbike of a friend of his called Dalzell. Part of it, according to him, he used as an experiment in the garden, when the flames simply ignited in one place. The remainder he used as already described.

According to Dalzell, he, Dalzell, told the appellant it was a stupid idea, and Jillian, who was present at the time, disapproved of the plan saying that she was not going to risk her life and the lives of the bairns for him (the appellant). The appellant however told the jury that the fire was Jillian's own idea and that she talked him into carrying it into effect. Jillian had (wisely) arranged for her three children to sleep elsewhere.

The appellant's three children remained in the house because, as he said, it would have been suspicious if they had not been there. The idea was that once the fire started the adults would take the children from the house and all would therefore escape. However the fire spread very rapidly. The appellant fetched a ladder from a neighbour's house, put it against a bedroom window and took to safety two of his children handed out to him by his wife. The fire by then was too intense for anyone else to be saved. Jillian was asphyxiated inside the house. Sarah and Darren died in hospital from their burns.

The grounds of appeal are that the judge failed to direct the jury on the law of manslaughter in relation to the facts of the case, and in particular directed them on the basis of a passage in *Archbold*, 41st ed, which was the subject of adverse criticism by their Lordships in the Privy Council in *Kong Cheuk Kwan* v *The Queen* (1985) 82 Cr App R 18.'

Held

The appeal would be dismissed.

Lord Lane CJ:

'We are told that there was some discussion between counsel and the judge during the course of the trial as to whether the jury should be directed on the "*Lawrence*" or the "unlawful acts" basis, and that the judge appeared to favour the former. Whether that is so or not, we have to decide whether the direction he in fact gave was correct.

It seems to us that this was a case which was capable of falling within either or both types of manslaughter. On the *Lawrence* aspect, the jury might well have been satisfied that the appellant was acting in such a manner as to create an obvious and serious risk of causing physical injury to some person, and secondly that he, having recognised that there was some risk involved, had nevertheless gone on to take it.

This was equally, in our view, a case for the "unlawful and dangerous act" direction. Where the defendant does an unlawful act of such a kind as all sober and reasonable people would inevitably recognise must subject another person to, at least, the risk of some harm resulting therefrom, albeit not serious harm and causes death thereby, he is guilty of manslaughter: *Church* (1965) 49 Cr App R 206, [1966] 1 QB 59.

Lord Salmon in *Director of Public Prosecutions* v *Newbury* (1976) 62 Cr App R 291; [1976] 2 All ER 365 approved a dictum of Humphreys J in *Larkin* [1943] 1 All ER 217, 219: "Where the act which a person is engaged in performing is unlawful, then if at the same time it is a dangerous act, that is, an act which is likely to injure another person, and quite inadvertently he causes the death of that other person by that act, then he is guilty of manslaughter." Their Lordships in that case (*Newbury*) expressly disapproved of a passage in the judgment of Lord Denning MR in the civil case of *Gray* v *Barr* [1971] 2 All ER 949, 956, in which he asserted that the unlawful act must be done by the defendant with the intention of frightening or harming someone or with the realisation that it is likely to frighten or harm someone. That decision of the House of Lords is, of course, binding upon us.

It is submitted by Mr Stewart on behalf of the appellant that this was not a case of "unlawful act" manslaughter, because the actions of the appellant were not directed at the victim. The authority for that proposition is said to be *Dalby* (1982) 74 Cr App R 348.

In that case the appellant, a drug addict, supplied a class A drug which he had lawfully obtained to a friend, also an addict. Each injected himself intravenously. After the appellant had left, the friend administered to himself two further injections, the nature of which was unknown. When the appellant returned he was unable to wake up his friend. When medical help eventually arrived, the friend was found to be dead. The appellant was convicted of manslaughter either on the unlawful and dangerous act basis, or alternatively on the basis that he was grossly negligent in not calling an ambulance at an earlier stage.

It was held that since the act of supplying the scheduled drug was not an act which caused direct harm and since the unlawful act of supply of the dangerous drug by Dalby per se did not constitute the actus reus of the offence of manslaughter, the conviction had to be quashed. Waller LJ, at page 352, said: "... where the charge of manslaughter is based on an unlawful and dangerous act, it must be an act directed at the victim and likely to cause immediate injury, however slight."

However we do not think that he was suggesting that there must be an intention on the part of the defendant to harm or frighten or a realisation that his acts were likely to harm or frighten. Indeed it would have been contrary to the dicta of Lord Salmon in *DPP* v *Newbury* (supra) if he was. What he was, we believe, intending to say was that there must be no fresh intervening cause between the act and the death. Indeed at p351 he said this: "... the supply of drugs would itself have caused no harm unless the deceased had subsequently used the drugs in a form and quantity which was dangerous."

If we may say so respectfully, we doubt the assertion in Smith and Hogan, *Criminal Law*, 5th ed, p315, that because the Appellate Committee refused the [prosecutor] leave to appeal, *Dalby* (supra) must then be taken to represent the law.

Mr Bethel for the Crown drew our attention to two further cases, namely, *Pagett* (1983) 76 Cr App R 279 and *Mitchell* (1983) 76 Cr App R 293, both of which seem to support our interpretation of *Dalby* (supra).

The questions which the jury have to decide on the charge of manslaughter of this nature are: (1) Was the act intentional? (2) Was it unlawful? (3) Was it an act which any reasonable person would realise was bound to subject some other human being to the risk of physical harm, albeit not necessarily serious harm? (4) Was that act the cause of death?

Whatever indications the judge may have given earlier as to his intentions, he did in fact direct the jury on this type of manslaughter in the passage which we have already quoted. It is true that he went further and added observations which were more appropriate to the *Lawrence* type of manslaughter. If anything, those passages resulted in a direction which was more favourable to the appellant than if they had been omitted.

We do not consider that the jury may have been confused as Mr Stewart contends. The convictions on counts 1 to 3 were neither unsafe nor unsatisfactory.

Finally, as to count 5, Mr Stewart submits that the judge failed to direct the jury specifically that they must be satisfied that the appellant was reckless as to whether the lives of the people upstairs were in danger.

What he said on this point was as follows: "And recklessness, please note as I have already told you, in fact applies equally to the fifth count in the indictment. Indeed it is the only issue in the fifth count in the indictment. So I repeat in relation to count 5 the recklessness, that Goodfellow would have acted recklessly if the prosecution have proved either that first, when he set fire to the house he gave no thought at all to the possibility that the inmates might be injured in circumstances where, if he had given any thought to the matter, it would have been obvious that there was some risk. Or secondly, that he appreciated the risk of injury but nonetheless went on to take it."

We consider that in the circumstances of this case if there was risk of injury at all to the people upstairs then it must follow that there was risk of death. Even had that not been the case we would have applied the proviso. If the judge, instead of using the words "might be injured" had used the words "might be killed," the result would inevitably have been the same. Accordingly this appeal is dismissed.'

Kong Cheuk Kwan v R (1985) 82 Cr App R 18 Privy Council (Lords Fraser, Roskill, Bridge, and Brandon, and Sir Owen Woodhouse)

Mens rea for reckless manslaughter

Facts

In perfect weather conditions at about 9.25 am one morning in July, two hydrofoils, said to be travelling at a combined speed of some 64 mph, collided with resultant loss of life. The appellant was the captain of one of the vessels and he and his first mate and the captain and deck officer of the other vessel were all charged with manslaughter. At their trial none of the four gave evidence. There was much anecdotal evidence but little direct oral evidence of the respective relevant position of the two hydrofoils and what precisely was seen and done as a result of observations made in the minutes and seconds before the collision. The judge withdrew the case against the appellant's first mate, the captain and deck officer of the other vessel were both acquitted and only the appellant was convicted. He appealed on the ground that the jury had been misdirected on the question of manslaughter by negligence, the judge having directed them that the relevant risk they had to consider was the risk "of causing some injury albeit not necessarily serious but not so slight that an ordinarily prudent individual would feel justified in treating it as negligible" (adopting a passage in Archbold, 41st ed, para 20-49, 2nd Supp.)

Held

That the model direction suggested by the House of Lords in *Lawrence* (1981) 73 Cr App R 1 applied in the present case - the jury should have been directed to consider whether the appellant's act of navigation created an obvious and serious risk of causing physical damage to some other ship and thus to other persons who might have been travelling in the area of the collision at the relevant time. Where such a risk was created, the jury should have considered whether the appellant had navigated without giving any thought to the possibility of that risk or whether he had recognised that risk existed, but had nevertheless gone on to take it. Thus, there had been a fundamental misdirection and as the case was not one for the operation of the proviso to section 2(1) of the Criminal Appeal Act 1968, the appeal would be allowed and the conviction quashed.

Lord Roskill:

[Having considered *Caldwell* v *MPC*; *R* v *Lawrence*; and *R* v *Seymour*, his Lordship continued]

'It is plain that, as often happens in English criminal and civil law, the law applicable to involuntary manslaughter has developed on a case by case basis and indeed has developed rapidly in recent years since the offence of causing death by reckless driving appeared in section 50 of the Criminal Law Act 1977.

Their Lordships are of the view that the present state of the relevant law in England and Wales and thus in Hong Kong is clear. The model direction suggested in *Lawrence* (supra) and held in *Seymour* (supra) equally applicable to cases of motor manslaughter requires first, proof that the vehicle was in fact being driven in such a manner as to create an obvious and serious risk of causing physical injury to another and second, that the defendant so drove either without having given any thought to the possibility of there being such a risk or having recognised that there was such a risk nevertheless took it. Once that direction is given, it is for the jury to (decide whether or not on their view of the evidence the relevant charge has been proved.)

In principle their Lordships see no reason why a comparable direction should not have been given in the present case as regards that part of the case which concerned the alleged navigation of the *Flying Goldfinch* by Kong and indeed as regards the alleged navigation of the *Flying Flamingo* by the other two defendants. (Did their respective acts of navigation create an obvious and serious risk of causing physical damage to some other ship and thus to other persons who might have been travelling in the area of the collision at the material time? If so did any of the defendants by their respective acts of navigation so navigate either without having given any thought to the possibility of that risk or, while recognising that the risk existed, take that risk?)

Unfortunately this direction was not given. The direction given and its source in *Archbold*, 41st ed, Second Supplement, in the passage which reads "his conduct was capable of causing some injury albeit not necessarily serious to the deceased ... and that the risk was not so slight that an ordinary prudent individual would feel justified in treating it as negligible" has been taken from Lord Diplock's negative proposition. This has then been turned round and the proposition treated as an affirmative statement of the relevant risk. With all respect, that cannot be justified and in their Lordships' view vitiates the direction. The first part of the second limb purports to repeat in part the model direction in *Lawrence* (supra) but unhappily that direction is vitiated by the reference back to the statement of the nature of this risk to which their Lordships have already referred. The second part of the second limb appears to be a throwback to *Bateman* [1925] 19 Cr App R 8. Though Lord Atkin in his speech in *Andrews v Director of Public Prosecutions* (1937) 26 Cr App R 34; [1937] AC 576 did not disapprove of what was there said, he clearly thought, (at p47 and p583), that it was better to use the word "reckless" rather than to add to the word "negligence" various possible vituperative epithets. Their Lordships respectfully agree. Indeed they further respectfully agree with the comment made by Watkins LJ in delivering the judgment of the Court of Appeal (Criminal Division) in *Seymour* (1983) 76 Cr App R 211, 216:

"We have to say that the law as it stands compels us to reject Mr Connell's persuasive submissions and to hold that the judge's directions were correct, although we are of the view that it is no longer necessary or helpful to make reference to compensation and negligence. The *Lawrence* direction on recklessness is comprehensive and of general application to all offences, including manslaughter involving the driving of motor vehicles recklessly and should be given to juries without in any way being diluted. Whether a driver at the material time was conscious of the risk he was running or gave no thought to its existence, is a matter which affects punishment for which purposes the judge will have to decide, if he can, giving the benefit of the doubt to the convicted person, in which state of mind that person had driven at the material time."

Learned counsel for the Crown pressed their Lordships to apply the proviso to section 2(1) of the Criminal Appeal Act 1968 even though their Lordships felt obliged to hold that there had been the misdirection already mentioned. Their Lordships find themselves unable to take this course. They regard the misdirection as so fundamental (especially as it was in writing and given to the jury on retirement) that it is impossible to assert that a properly directed jury must inevitably have reached a verdict of guilty against Kong. There was in connection with this part of the submission on behalf of the Crown much discussion regarding the facts, with a view to showing that on a proper direction a conviction was inevitable. Their Lordships did not find it necessary to hear counsel for Kong on this issue and it would not be right for them to offer any detailed comments upon the facts beyond observing that the summing-up does not seem to have distinguished between an obvious risk created by those navigating each hydrofoil by their own navigation and the response by those on board one hydrofoil to any obvious risk created by the navigation of the other.

Their Lordships thus do not find it necessary to discuss the evidence afforded by the written statements of those involved or their evidential status. This last matter is now concluded by the decision of the Board in *Leung Kam-Kwok* v *R* (1985) 81 Cr App R 83, judgment in which was given after the hearing in the Court of Appeal in the present case.

It was for these reasons that their Lordships, in respectful disagreement with the Court of Appeal regarding the misdirection by the learned judge, felt constrained humbly to advise her Majesty that this appeal must be allowed and Kong's conviction quashed. The Crown must pay Kong's costs at the trial in the Court of Appeal and before the Board.'

R v Lawrence [1982] AC 510

See chapter 2.

R v Mitchell [1983] 2 WLR 938 Court of Appeal (Criminal Division) (Purchas LJ, Talbot and Staughton JJ)

Constructive manslaughter: whether unlawful act must be the direct cause of death

Facts

The defendant had become involved in an altercation whilst queuing in a busy post office. He pushed an elderly man, causing him to fall accidentally onto the deceased, an elderly woman. She was admitted to hospital where she later died from a pulmonary embolism caused by thrombosis of the veins in her injured leg. The defendant was convicted of manslaughter, and appealed on the grounds that his unlawful act had not been directed at the victim, and that the trial judge had not directed the jury adequately on the mens rea required for the offence.

Held

The appeal would be dismissed.

Staughton J:

'Both counsel were agreed that there are four elements in this class of manslaughter, as follows: first, there must be an act which is unlawful; secondly, it must be a dangerous act, in the sense that a sober and reasonable person would inevitably recognise that it carried some risk of harm, albeit not serious harm (that being an objective test); thirdly, the act must be a substantial cause of death; fourthly, the act itself must be intentional. No question relating to any other class of manslaughter (such as manslaughter by gross negligence) arose in this case.

The main question argued was whether the person at whom the act is aimed must also be the person whose death is caused. On that question, it was suggested, there is no authority directly in point. Counsel for Mitchell also argued that the act must have been directed at the victim in the sense, as we understand the point, that it must have had some immediate impact upon the victim. For that proposition the case of *Dalby* (1982) 74 Cr App R 348; [1982] 1 WLR 425, was said to be authority.

There are cases which apparently support the first part of this argument. Thus in *Larkin* (1942) 29 Cr App R 18, Humphreys J, at p23 referred to - "an act which is likely to injure another person, and quite inadvertently the doer of the act causes the death of *that* other person." Similarly in *Church* (1965) 49 Cr App R 206, 213; [1966] 1 QB 59, 70, Edmund Davies J said: "... the unlawful act must be such as all sober and reasonable people would inevitably recognise must subject *the* other person to, at least, the risk of some harm resulting therefrom, albeit not serious harm." (Emphasis supplied in both cases).

However, in neither case was there any question raised of an act, which carried the risk of harm to A, in fact causing the death of B. We cannot treat either case as authority upon that question. It is possible that such a question could have been raised in *Larkin* (supra), but it was not.

Nor does any such question appear to have been raised in the leading case of *Director of Public Prosecutions* v *Newbury and Jones* (1976) 62 Cr App R 291; [1977] AC 500, although it might have been. There two youths aged 15 were on a railway bridge. One of them pushed part of a paving-stone over the bridge parapet towards an oncoming train. It fell on the driver's cab, killing the guard, who was sitting next to the driver. Both were convicted of manslaughter of the guard. Their convictions were upheld by the House of Lords.

Presumably it could have been said that the act of the two youths was aimed at the driver, if at anyone, or perhaps at the passengers, if there were any; it may be that the guard was the least likely to be injured, unless it were known that he was travelling in the front of the train. However, no argument on those lines appears to have been advanced. The whole contest was as to mens rea. It was argued that the youths themselves had to be proved to have foreseen that they might cause harm to someone. That argument was rejected. Lord Salmon, at pp296 and 506 respectively said: "The learned trial judge did not direct the jury that they should acquit the appellants unless they were satisfied beyond a reasonable doubt that the appellants had foreseen that they might cause harm to someone by pushing the piece of paving stone off the parapet into the path of the approaching train. In my view the learned trial judge was quite right not to give such a direction to the jury. The direction which he gave is completely in accordance with established law, which, possibly with one exception to which I shall presently refer, has never been challenged. In *Larkin* (1942) 29 Cr App R 18, Humphreys J said at p23, "Where the act which a person is engaged in performing is unlawful, then if at the same time it is a dangerous act, that is, an act which is likely to injure another person, and quite inadvertently the doer of the act causes the death of that other person by that act, then he is guilty of manslaughter." I agree entirely with Lawton LJ that that is an admirably clear statement of the law which has been applied many times. It makes it plain (a) that an accused is guilty of manslaughter if it is proved that he intentionally did an act which was unlawful and dangerous and that that act inadvertently caused death and (b) that it is unnecessary to prove that the accused knew that the act was unlawful or dangerous. This is one of the reasons why cases of manslaughter vary so infinitely in their gravity. They may amount to little more than pure inadvertence and sometimes to little less than murder. I am sure that in *Church* (1965) 49 Cr App R 206; [1966] 1 QB 59, Edmund Davies J (as he then was), in giving the judgment of the Court, did not intend to differ from or qualify anything which had been said in *Larkin* (*supra*). Indeed he was restating the principle laid down in that case by illustrating the sense in which the word "dangerous" should be understood. Edmund Davies J said "For such a verdict" (guilty of manslaughter) "inexorably to follow, the unlawful act must be such as all sober and reasonable people would inevitably recognise must subject the other person to, at least, the risk of some harm resulting therefrom, albeit not serious harm." The test is still the objective test. In judging whether the act was dangerous the test is not did the accused recognise that it was dangerous but would all sober and reasonable people recognise its danger?

He went on to say that juries should continue to be directed in accordance with the law as laid down in *Larkin* (supra) and *Church* (supra).

We do not read Lord Salmon as saying that the unlawful and dangerous act must necessarily be aimed at the same other person whose death is caused. No such limitation was contended for in the House of Lords. If it had been, it was at least open to question, as we have suggested, whether the act of the youths was aimed at the guard; and therefore it would have had to be considered whether on that different ground their convictions should be quashed.

Then there is the case of *Dalby* (1982) 74 Cr App R 348; [1982] 1 WLR 425. [His Lordship considered this authority and continued:] For the present it is enough to say that this case too was not concerned with an act aimed at A which in fact causes the death of B. The Court was there concerned with the quality of the act rather than the identity of the person at whom it was aimed. Again we do not read Waller LJ as saying that the unlawful and dangerous act must be aimed at that very person whose death is caused. If, however, that was what the Court was saying, then we would, with the greatest respect, hold that it was not part of the ratio decidendi of the case.

The only authority (if such it be) which we have found to be directly in point is *Russell on Crime* 12th ed (1964) Vol 1, p588, citing the 1839 HM Commissioners on Criminal Law: "Involuntary homicide, which is not by misadventure, includes all cases where, without intention to kill or do great bodily harm, or wilfully to endanger life, death occurs in any of the following instances: Where death results from any unlawful act or omission done or omitted with intent to hurt the person of another, whether the mischief light on the person intended, or on any other person; where death results from any wrong wilfully occasioned to the person of another; where death results from any unlawful act or unlawful omission, attended with risk of hurt to the person of another; where death results from want of due caution either in doing an act, or neglecting to prevent mischief, which the offender is bound by law to prevent."

We can see no reason of policy for holding that an act calculated to harm A cannot be manslaughter if it in fact kills B. The criminality of the doer of the act is precisely the same whether it is A or B who dies. A person who throws a stone at A is just as guilty if, instead of hitting and killing A, it hits and kills B. Parliament evidently held the same view in relation to the allied offence of unlawful and malicious wounding contrary to section 20 of the Offences Against the Person Act 1861: see *Latimer* (1886) 17 QBD 359. We accordingly reject the argument of counsel for Mitchell that, because Mitchell's acts were aimed at Mr Smith, it cannot have been manslaughter when they caused the death of Mrs Crafts.

The second limb of the argument was based wholly on *Dalby* (1982) 74 Cr App R 348; [1982] 1 WLR 425. It was argued that for manslaughter to be established the act of the defendant must be shown to have caused direct harm to the victim. On that ground, although it would be manslaughter to throw a stone at A which hits and kills B, it was submitted that there was no manslaughter in the present case, because there was no physical contact between Mitchell and Mrs Crafts.

The passage which we have already read from *Dalby* was relied on in support of that argument. In particular, there is this sentence in the judgment of the Court (at pp351 and 429 respectively): "The kind of harm envisaged in all the reported cases of involuntary manslaughter was physical injury of some kind as an immediate and inevitable result of the unlawful act, eg a blow on the chin which knocks the victim against a wall causing a fractured skull and death, or threatening with a loaded gun which accidentally fires, or dropping a large stone on a train or threatening another with an open razor and stumbling with death resulting."

We can well understand, if we may say so, why the Court held that there was no sufficient link between Dalby's wrongful act (supplying the drug) and his friend's death. As Waller LJ said: "the supply of drugs would itself have caused no harm unless the deceased had subsequently used the drugs in a form and quantity which was dangerous ... the supply did not cause any direct injury to him."

Here however the facts were very different. Although there was no direct contact between Mitchell and Mrs Crafts, she was injured as a direct and immediate result of his act. Thereafter her death occurred. The only question was one of causation: whether her death was caused by Mitchell's act. It was open to the jury to conclude that it was so caused; and they evidently reached that conclusion.

Since the conclusion of the argument we have seen a transcript of the judgment of this Court in *Pagett* [see chapter 6]. This supports the views we have expressed in two respects. At p291 Robert Goff LJ, delivering the judgment of the Court, said: "If, as the jury must have found to have occurred in the present case, the appellant used Gail Kinchen by force and against her will as a shield to protect him from any shots fired by the police, the effect is that he committed not one but two unlawful acts, both of which were dangerous - the act of firing at the police, and the act of holding Gail Kinchen as a shield in front of him when the police might well fire shots in his direction in self-defence. Either act could, in our judgment ... constitute the actus reus of the manslaughter."

In the case of the first act mentioned - firing at the police - it could scarcely be said to have been *aimed* at the ultimate victim, Gail Kinchen; nor could it be said by itself to have caused harm to the victim by direct physical contact. We agree that neither requirement exists for manslaughter.

Granted an unlawful and dangerous act, the test is one of causation. That is clear from p287 ante where Robert Goff LJ said: "The question whether an accused person can be guilty of homicide, either murder or manslaughter, of a victim the immediate cause of whose death is the act of another person must be determined on the ordinary principles of causation ... "

As to ground (iii), it was argued that the learned judge failed to direct the jury that Mitchell's act had to be a deliberate act, in the sense that he intended to do it. The direction was as follows: "You have been told, and told perfectly accurately, what this offence of manslaughter is: it is where an act a person is engaged in is unlawful and if, at the same time, it is a dangerous act and another person is injured, and is injured even through inadvertence, and as result of an injury death is caused to that other person, then the offence is one of manslaughter. Even if that act is one which is likely to injure another person and it is done quite inadvertently, the offence is one of manslaughter. Again, you have been told, and told quite properly, that it does not matter whether the accused person knows that the act is an unlawful one, or indeed a dangerous one. It does not depend upon what he believes to be unlawful or dangerous. If you came to a conclusion in this case that what this young man, Mitchell, was doing was unlawful, inasmuch as it constituted an assault upon Mr Smith, then your consideration would have to be on whether or not it was dangerous at the same time. In judging whether the act is a dangerous act, the test which you apply is not whether the accused recognises that it was a dangerous act, but whether all sober and reasonable people would have recognised it to be dangerous in the circumstances which attain in this particular case: in other words, whether you consider it was dangerous in the circumstances of this case."

The learned judge there used the words "inadvertence" and "inadvertently". He was perfectly right to do so, in dealing with the connection between the act and the injury or death. There need not be any intention to injure or kill, or any foresight that injury or death would be caused, provided that all sober and reasonable people would have recognised the act to be dangerous. That is the sense in which Humphreys J used the word "inadvertently" in *Larkin* (supra).

But it is said that the judge may have conveyed to the jury that the act need not itself have been a deliberate act. Whether he did or not is, in the context of this case, wholly immaterial. All of Mitchell's actions, whether hitting, pushing, grabbing or throwing, were obviously and admittedly deliberate actions. There was no suggestion of inadvertence, or even automation, in any part of his conduct. The issues before the jury, on this aspect of the case, were firstly self-defence, and secondly whether he did all the things he was said to have done or only some of them. As we have already observed, there is no appeal against the conviction of assault occasioning actual bodily harm. In many if not most cases the judge should direct the jury that the act relied on for an offence of manslaughter must have been a deliberate or intentional act. Here it was quite unnecessary.'

R v Seymour [1983] 2 AC 493 House of Lords (Lords Diplock, Fraser, Roskill, Bridge, and Templeman)

Reckless manslaughter

Facts

During an argument with the deceased, his common law wife, the defendant drove his truck towards her car, intending to push it out of the way. In fact he hit the deceased, jamming her between his truck and her car, as a result of which she sustained severe injuries from which she subsequently died. Although the defendant could have been charged with causing death by reckless driving contrary to the Road Traffic Act 1972, the prosecution brought a charge of common law manslaughter (which gave the judge a discretion to impose a higher sentence upon conviction), and the defendant was convicted. The trial judge had directed the jury that they should convict if they were satisfied that the defendant had caused death, and had been reckless in so doing, recklessness here having the meaning attributed to it by the House of Lords in *R v Lawrence* [1982] AC 510. The defendant appealed on the ground that proof of common law manslaughter required evidence that he had been aware of the risk of harm to the victim.

Held

The appeal would be dismissed.

Lord Roskill:

'The appellant was charged only with manslaughter, no doubt because of the view which the prosecuting authorities took of the gravity of the case ...

After the close of the evidence, Mr Michael Connell, for the appellant, invited the learned judge not to give the jury what I will call for brevity the *"Lawrence* direction" simpliciter, arguing that that direction was applicable only where the statutory offence was charged. He submitted that where the common law offence of manslaughter was charged, the jury should be directed that the Crown must further prove that the appellant recognised that some risk was involved and had nonetheless proceeded to take that risk.

The learned judge rejected the submission and gave the *"Lawrence* direction" subject only to the omission of any reference to the "obvious and serious risk ... of doing substantial damage to property": see *Reg* v *Lawrence (Stephen)* [1982] AC 510, 526. In my view, he was entirely right not to refer to damage to property, a reference to which was irrelevant in this case and might well have confused the jury. His admirably clear direction not only properly reflected the decision of this House in *Lawrence* but also Lord Atkin's speech in *Andrews* [1937] AC 576 ...

In his able submissions on behalf of the appellant, Mr Connell accepted, as he was indeed bound to accept, that the common law and statutory offences co-existed but he challenged that it necessarily followed that the same direction was appropriate in both cases. He founded upon the phrase "aggravating circumstances" - a phrase used by Mr Littman, counsel for the respondent in *Jennings* [1983] AC 624 and adopted in the last paragraph but two of my speech.

Mr Connell urged that the reference to "aggravating circumstances" showed that there might be different degrees of recklessness in the different cases. He also urged that what I had said regarding the ingredients of the two offences being identical was obiter and should not be followed, especially as there had been no argument that knowledge of the risk involved was a prerequisite to conviction for manslaughter though not for the statutory offence ...

My Lords, I have carefully considered these criticisms but I am unable to accept any of them as valid ...

Since for the reasons given the two offences co-existed and the ingredients were thus the same, there was no room for Mr Littman's argument on "aggravating circumstances." ...

Mr Connell also submitted that if the *"Lawrence* direction" were given in manslaughter cases and a conviction followed, the trial judge when considering sentence would not know whether the jury took the view that the defendant had deliberately taken a risk of which he was aware or not. My Lords' juries do not and should not be asked to explain their verdicts. It is by no means unusual for a guilty verdict to be properly founded for a number of reasons and it is for the judge, who is the person best placed to assess the degree of turpitude involved in the light of the evidence and the jury's verdict, to pass such sentence as he thinks right in all the circumstances. That sentence is of course always open to review if necessary.

My Lords, I would accept the submission of Mr Hamilton for the Crown that once it is shown that the two offences co-exist it would be quite wrong to give the adjective "reckless" or the adverb "recklessly" a different meaning according to whether the statutory or the common law offence is charged. "Reckless" should today be given the same meaning in relation to all offences which involve "recklessness" as one of the elements unless Parliament has otherwise ordained ...

That simple and single meaning should be the ordinary meaning of those words as stated in this House in *Caldwell* ... and in *Lawrence*.

Parliament must however be taken to have intended that "motor manslaughter" should be a more grave offence than the statutory offence. While the former still carries a maximum penalty of imprisonment for life, Parliament had thought fit to limit the maximum penalty for the statutory offence to five years' imprisonment, the sentence in fact passed by the learned trial judge upon the appellant upon his conviction for manslaughter. This difference recognises that there are degrees of turpitude which will vary according to the gravity of the risk created by the manner of a defendant's driving. In these circumstances your Lordships may think that in future it will only be very rarely that it will be appropriate to charge "motor manslaughter": that is where, as in the instant case, the risk of death from a defendant's driving was very high.

My Lords, there was some debate before your Lordships whether in England and Wales it should, since the decision in *Jennings* [1983] 1 AC 624, be permissible to join in the same indictment one count alleging manslaughter and another alleging the statutory offence, it now being clear that these offences co-existed and their ingredients were identical in point of law.

I know of nothing in the Indictments Act 1915 or the Indictments Rules 1971 to preclude such joinder but in my view there are considerable practical difficulties in permitting it arising from the fact that, as I have just endeavoured to explain, though the legal ingredients of the two offences are the same, the degrees of turpitude may vary greatly between one case and another. Under the practice in England and Wales the assessment of differing degrees of turpitude between one case and another is not a matter relevant to the determination by jury of a defendant's guilt or innocence of the particular offence charged. It is a matter relevant to the determination by the judge of the appropriate penalty to be inflicted upon a defendant found guilty of the offence with which he has been charged. Yet a jury if required to make a choice between convicting a defendant of motor manslaughter at common law and convicting him of the less grave statutory offence, would have to be told what criteria they should apply in determining on which side of the boundary line between the two offences the case against the defendant falls. The only criterion that Parliament has laid down is that the statutory offence does not merit a punishment exceeding five years' imprisonment while the common law offence of motor manslaughter may. To tell the jury this ... would make it difficult to avoid leaving them with the impression that only if they think that what the defendant did deserved to be punished by more than five years' imprisonment should they find him guilty of motor manslaughter. If the judge were then to sentence him to five years (as in the present case) or less, as well he might, the jury would be left with a very poor impression of the trial process.

In England and Wales it is for the prosecution and not for the court to decide what charge or charges should be made against a particular defendant. The prosecution is entitled to consider all the circumstances of the case before so deciding. In the instant case the prosecution properly charged manslaughter and manslaughter alone ...

In future in any case in England and Wales any such joinder should occur I think it must behove the trial judge to require the prosecution to elect upon which of the two counts in the indictment they wish to proceed and not to allow the trial to proceed upon both counts ...

I would therefore answer the certified question as follows: "Where manslaughter is charged and the circumstances are that the victim was killed as a result of the reckless driving of the defendant on a public highway, the trial judge should give the jury the direction suggested in *Reg v Lawrence* but it is appropriate also to point out that in order to constitute the offence of manslaughter the risk of death being caused by the manner of the defendant's driving must be very high."

I would dismiss this appeal.'

R v Stone and Dobinson [1977] QB 345

See chapter 2.

R v Watson [1989] 1 WLR 684 Court of Appeal (Criminal Division) (Lord Lane CJ, Farquharson and Potts JJ)

Constructive manslaughter - dangerous act

Facts

The appellant had burgled a house occupied by an 87 year old man, Mr Moyler, who suffered from a heart condition. The occupant disturbed the appellant, who abused him verbally, but the appellant made off without stealing anything. The police were called shortly afterwards, and a local council workman arrived to repair the windows broken by the appellant in gaining entry. An hour and a half after the burglary Mr Moyler had a heart attack and died. The appellant was convicted of manslaughter and appealed.

Held

The conviction for manslaughter would be quashed on the ground that the appellant's counsel had been denied a sufficient opportunity to address the jury on the issue of whether the excitement caused by the arrival of the police and the council workman could have taken over as the operating and substantial cause of death.

Lord Lane CJ:

His Lordship considered the nature of the unlawful act required as the basis for constructive manslaughter:

'It is accepted that the judge correctly defined the offence of manslaughter as it applied to the circumstances as follows:

"Manslaughter is the offence committed when one person causes the death of another by an act which is unlawful and which is also dangerous, dangerous in the sense that it is an act which all sober and reasonable people would inevitably realise must subject the victim to the risk of some harm resulting whether the defendant realised that or not."

The first point taken on behalf of the appellant is this. When one is deciding whether the sober and reasonable person (the bystander) would realise the risk of some harm resulting to the victim, how much knowledge of the circumstances does one attribute to the bystander? The appellant contends that the unlawful act here was the burglary as charged in the indictment.

The charge was laid under s9(1)(a) of the Theft Act 1968, the allegation being that the appellant had entered the building as a trespasser with intent to commit theft. Since that offence is committed at the first moment of entry, the bystander's knowledge is confined to that of the defendant at that moment. In the instant case there was no evidence that the appellant, at the moment of entry, knew the age or physical condition of Mr Moyler or even that he lived there alone.

The judge clearly took the view that the jury were entitled to ascribe to the bystander the knowledge which the appellant gained during the whole of his stay in the house and so directed them. Was this a misdirection? In our judgment it was not. The unlawful act in the present circumstances comprised the whole of the burglarious intrusion and did not come to an end upon the appellant's foot crossing the threshold or windowsill. That being so, the appellant (and therefore the bystander) during the course of the unlawful act must have become aware of Mr Moyler's frailty and approximate age, and the judge's directions were accordingly correct. We are supported in this view by the fact that no one at the trial seems to have thought otherwise.'

9   PARTICIPATION

R v Anderson and Morris [1966] 2 QB 110 (Court of Criminal Appeal) (Lord Parker CJ, Edmund Davies, Marshall, Roskill and James JJ)

Deliberate departure from the common design

Facts

Anderson and Morris agreed to beat up a man named Welch. Unknown to Morris, Anderson took a knife with him, and during the attack, he deliberately stabbed the victim to death. Anderson was convicted of murder, and Morris was convicted of manslaughter on the basis that, although he had not contemplated death or serious bodily harm, he had contemplated an attack on Welch. Morris appealed.

Held

Morris' conviction as an accomplice to manslaughter would be quashed.

Lord Parker CJ:

'What is complained of is a passage of the summing-up. It is unnecessary to read the direction on law in full. The material direction is:

"If you think there was a common design to attack Welch but it is not proved, in the case of Morris, that he had any intention to kill or cause grievous bodily harm, but that Anderson, without the knowledge of Morris, had a knife, took it from the flat and at some time formed the intention to kill or cause grievous bodily harm to Welch and did kill him - an act outside the common design to which Morris is proved to have been a party - then you would or could on the evidence find it proved that Anderson committed murder and Morris would be liable to be convicted of manslaughter provided you are satisfied that he took part in the attack or fight with Welch."

Mr Lane [counsel for the appellant] submits that that was a clear misdirection. He would put the principle of law to be invoked in this form: that where two persons embark on a joint enterprise, each is liable for the acts done in pursuance of that joint enterprise, that that includes liability for unusual consequences if they arise from the execution of the agreed joint enterprise but (and this is the crux of the matter) that, if one of the adventurers goes beyond what has been tacitly agreed as part of the common enterprise, his co-adventurer is not liable for the consequences of that unauthorised act. Finally he says it is for the jury in every case to decide whether what was done was part of the joint enterprise, or went beyond it and was in fact an act unauthorised by that joint enterprise.

In support of that, he refers to a number of authorities to which this court finds it unnecessary to refer in detail, which in the opinion of this court shows that at any rate for the last 130 or 140 years that has been the true position ... In *R v Smith* (*Wesley*) ([1963] 1 WLR 1200) the co-adventurer who in fact killed was known by the defendant to have a knife, and it was clear on the facts of that case that the common design involved an attack on a man, in that case a barman, in which the use of a knife would not be outside the scope of the concerted action. Reference was there made to the fact that the case might have been different if in fact the man using the knife had used a revolver, a weapon which he had, unknown to Smith ...

Mr Caulfield [counsel for the Crown], on the other hand, while recognising that he cannot go beyond this long string of decided cases, has said really that they are all part and parcel of a much wider principle which he would put in this form, that if two or more persons engaged in an unlawful act and one suddenly develops an intention to kill whereby death results, not only he is guilty of murder, but all those who have engaged in the unlawful act are guilty of manslaughter. He recognises that the present trend of authority is against that proposition, but he goes back to *Salisbury's* case (1

Plow. 100) in 1553. In that case a master had laid in wait to attack a man, and his servants, who had no idea of what his, the master's, idea was, joined in the attack, whereby the man was killed. It was held there that those servants were themselves guilty of manslaughter.

The court is by no means clear on the facts as reported that *Salisbury's* case is really on all fours, but it is in the opinion of the court quite clear that the principle is wholly out of touch with the position today. It seems to this court that to say that adventurers are guilty of manslaughter when one of them has departed completely from the concerted action of the common design and has suddenly formed an intent to kill and has used a weapon and acted in a way which no party to that common design could suspect is something which would revolt the conscience of people today.

Mr Caulfield, in his attractive argument, points to the fact that it would seem to be illogical that, if two people had formed a common design to do an unlawful act and death resulted by an unforeseen consequence, they should be held, as they would undoubtedly be held, guilty of manslaughter; whereas if one of them in those circumstances had in a moment of passion decided to kill, they would be acquitted altogether. The law, of course, is not completely logical, but there is nothing really illogical in such a result, in that it could well be said as a matter of common sense that in the latter circumstances the death resulted or was caused by the sudden action of the adventurer who decided to kill and killed. Considered as a matter of causation there may well be an overwhelming supervening event which is of such a character that it will relegate into history matters which would otherwise be looked upon as causative factors. Looked at in that way, there is really nothing illogical in the result to which Mr Caulfield points.'

Attorney-General's Reference (No 1 of 1975) (1975) 61 Cr App R 118 Court of Appeal (Criminal Division) (Lord Widgery CJ, Bristow and May JJ)

Facts

The accused had surreptitiously laced a friend's drinks with double measures of alcohol knowing the friend would shortly afterwards be driving home. The friend was convicted of drunken driving. The accused was charged as an accomplice to this offence, but was acquitted following a successful submission of no case. The trial judge took the view that there had to be evidence of some agreement between the accomplice and the principal. The following question was referred to the court:

'Whether an accused who surreptitiously laced a friend's drinks with double measures of spirits when he knew that his friend would shortly be driving his car home, and in consequence his friend drove with an excess quantity of alcohol in his body and was convicted of the offence under the Road Traffic Act 1972 s 6 (1) is entitled to a ruling of no case to answer on being later charged as an aider and abettor, counsellor and procurer, on the ground that there was no shared intention between the two that the accused did not by accompanying him or otherwise positively encourage the friend to drive, or on any other ground.'

Held

The question posed should be answered in the negative.

Lord Widgery CJ:

'The language in the section which determines whether a "secondary party", as he is sometimes called, is guilty of a criminal offence committed by another embraces the four words "aid, abet, counsel or procure". The origin of those words is to be found in s 8 of the Accessories and Abettors Act 1861 which provides:

"Whosoever shall aid, abet, counsel, or procure the commission of any misdemeanour, whether the same be a misdemeanour at common law or by virtue of any Act passed or to be passed, shall be liable to be tried, indicted, and punished as a principal offender."

Thus, in the past, when the distinction was still drawn between felony and misdemeanour, it was sufficient to make a person guilty of a misdemeanour if he aided, abetted, counselled or procured the offence of another. When the difference between felonies and misdemeanours was abolished in 1967, s1 of the Criminal Law Act 1967 in effect provided that the same test should apply to make a secondary party guilty either of treason or felony.

Of course it is the fact that in the great majority of instances where a secondary party is sought to be convicted of an offence there has been a contact between the principal offender and the secondary party. Aiding and abetting almost inevitably involves a situation in which the secondary party and the main offender are together at some stage discussing the plans which they may be making in respect of the alleged offence, and are in contact so that each knows what is passing through the mind of the other.

In the same way it seems to us that a person who counsels the commission of a crime by another, almost inevitably comes to a moment when he is in contact with that other, when he is discussing the offence with that other and when, to use the words of the statute, he counsels the other to commit the offence.

The fact that so often the relationship between the secondary party and the principal will be such that there is a meeting of minds between them caused the trial judge in the case from which this reference is derived to think that this was really an essential feature of proving or establishing the guilt of the secondary party and, as we understand his judgment, he took the view that in the absence of some sort of meeting of minds, some sort of mental link between the secondary party and the principal, there could be no aiding, abetting or counselling of the offence within the meaning of the section.

So far as aiding, abetting and counselling is concerned we would go a long way with that conclusion. It may very well be, as I said a moment ago, difficult to think of a case of aiding, abetting or counselling when the parties have not met and have not discussed in some respects the terms of the offence which they have in mind. But we do not see why a similar principle should apply to procuring. We approach s 8 of the 1861 Act on the basis also that if four words are employed here, "aid, abet, counsel or procure", the probability is that there is a difference between each of those four words and the other three, because, if there were no such difference, then Parliament would be wasting time in using four words where two or three would do. Thus, in deciding whether that which is assumed to be done under our reference was a criminal offence we approach the section on the footing that each word must be given its ordinary meaning.

To procure means to produce by endeavour. You procure a thing by setting out to see that it happens and taking the appropriate steps to produce that happening. We think that there are plenty of instances in which a person may be said to procure the commission of a crime by another even though there is no sort of conspiracy between the two, even thought there is no attempt at agreement or discussion as to the form which the offence should take. In our judgment the offence described in this reference is such a case.

If one looks back at the facts of the reference: the accused surreptitiously laced his friend's drink. This is an important element and, although we are not going to decide today anything other than the problem posed to us, it may well be that in similar cases where the lacing of the drink or the introduction of the extra alcohol is known to the driver quite different considerations may apply. We say that because where the driver has no knowledge of what is happening, in most instances he would have no means of preventing the offence from being committed. If the driver is unaware of what has happened, he will not be taking precautions. He will get into his car seat, switch on the ignition and drive home and, consequently, the conception of another procuring the commission of the offence by the driver is very much stronger where the driver is innocent of all knowledge of what is happening, as in the present case where the lacing of the drink was surreptitious.

The second thing which is important in the facts set out in our reference is that following and in consequence of the introduction of the extra alcohol, the friend drove with an excess quantity of alcohol in his blood. Causation here is important. You cannot procure an offence unless there is a causal link between what you do and the commission of the offence, and here we are told that in consequence of the addition of this alcohol the driver, when he drove home, drove with an excess quantity of alcohol in his body.

Giving the words their ordinary meaning in English, and asking oneself whether in those circumstances the offence has been procured, we are in no doubt that the answer is that it has. It has been procured because, unknown to the driver and without his collaboration, he has been put in a position in which in fact he has committed an offence which he never would have committed otherwise. We think that there was a case to answer and that the trial judge should have directed the jury that an offence is committed if it is shown beyond reasonable doubt that the accused knew that his friend was going to drive, and also knew that the ordinary and natural result of the additional alcohol added to the friend's drink would be to bring him above the recognised limit of 80 milligrammes per 100 millilitres of blood.

It was suggested to us that, if we held that there may be a procuring on the facts of the present case, it would be but a short step to a similar finding for the generous host, with somewhat bibulous friends, when at the end of the day his friends leave him to go to their own homes in circumstances in which they are not fit to drive and in circumstances in which an offence under the Road Traffic Act 1972 is committed. The suggestion has been made that the host may in those circumstances be guilty with his guests on the basis that he has either aided, abetted, counselled or procured the offence.

The first point to notice in regard to the generous host is that that is not a case in which the alcohol is being put surreptitiously into the glass of the driver. That is a case in which the driver knows perfectly well how much he has to drink and where to a large extent it is perfectly right and proper to leave him to make his own decision.

Furthermore, we would say that if such a case arises, the basis on which the case will be put against the host is, we think, bound to be on the footing that he has supplied the tool with which the offence is committed. This of course is a reference back to such cases as those where oxyacetylene equipment was bought by a man knowing it was to be used by another for a criminal offence. There is ample and clear authority as to the extent to which supplying the tools for the commission of an offence may amount to aiding and abetting for present purposes.

Accordingly, so far as the generous host type of case is concerned we are not concerned at the possibility that difficulties will be created, as long as it is borne in mind that in those circumstances the matter must be approached in accordance with well-known authority governing the provision of the tools for the commission of an offence, and never forgetting that the introduction of the alcohol is not there surreptitious, and that consequently the case for saying that the offence was procured by the supplier of the alcohol is very much more difficult.'

R v Bainbridge [1959] 3 WLR 356 Court of Criminal Appeal (Lord Parker CJ, Byrne and Winn JJ)

Mens rea required of accomplices

Facts

The defendant had obtained and supplied some cutting equipment which was subsequently used to break into the Midland Bank in Stoke Newington, London. When charged with being an accessory before the fact, the defendant contended that he had known that something illegal was going to be done with the equipment, for example breaking up stolen goods, but that he had not known that it was going to be used to break into a bank. The jury convicted him after being directed by the trial judge that it was sufficient for the prosecution to prove that the defendant had known what 'type' of crime the principals were going to commit. The defendant appealed.

Held

The appeal would be dismissed.

Lord Parker CJ:

'The complaint here is that Judge Aarvold, who tried the case, gave the jury a wrong direction in regard to what it was necessary for them to be satisfied of in order to hold the appellant guilty of being an accessory before the fact. The passages in question are these:

"To prove that, the prosecution have to prove these matters; first of all, they have to prove that the felony itself was committed. Of that there is no doubt. That is not contested. Secondly, they have to prove that the [appellant] knew that a felony of that kind was intended and was going to be committed, and with that knowledge he did something to help the felons commit the crime. The knowledge that is required to be proved in the mind of the [appellant] is not the knowledge of the precise crime. In other words, it need not be proved that he knew that the Midland Bank, Stoke Newington branch, was going to be broken and entered, and money stolen from that particular bank, but he must know the type of crime that was in fact committed. In this case it is a breaking and entering of premises and the stealing of property from those premises. It must be proved that he knew that that sort of crime was intended and was going to be committed. It is not enough to show that he either suspected or knew that some crime was going to be committed, some crime which might have been a breaking and entering or might have been disposing of stolen property or anything of that kind. That is not enough. It must be proved that he knew that the type of crime which was in fact committed was intended."

There are other passages to the same effect; in particular when the jury returned for further directions before they came to their verdict, the learned judge said this:

"If in fact, before it has happened, [the appellant], knowing what is going to happen, with full knowledge that a felony of that kind is going to take place, deliberately and wilfully helps it on its way, he is an accessory ... If he was not present he would not be guilty as a principal, but then you would have to decide whether he helped in purchasing this equipment for Shakeshaft knowing full well the type of offence for which it was going to be used, and, with that knowledge, buying it and helping in that way."

Counsel for the appellant, who argued this case very well, contended that that direction was wrong. As he put it, in order that a person should be convicted of being accessory before the fact, it must be shown that, at the time when he bought the equipment in a case such as this, he knew that a particular crime was going to be committed; and by "a particular crime" counsel meant that the premises in this case which were going to be broken into were known to the appellant and contemplated by him, and not only the premises in question but the date when the crime was going to occur; in other words, that he must have known that on a particular date the Stoke Newington branch of the Midland Bank was intended to be broken into.

The court fully appreciates that it is not enough that it should be shown that a person knew that some illegal venture was intended. To take this case, it would not be enough if the appellant knew - he says that he only suspected - that the equipment was going to be used to dispose of stolen property. That would not be enough. Equally, this court is quite satisfied that it is unnecessary that knowledge of the intention to commit the particular crime which was in fact committed should be shown, and by "particular crime" I am using the words in the same way as that in which counsel for the appellant used them, namely, on a particular date and particular premises.

It is not altogether easy to lay down a precise form of words which will cover every case that can be contemplated. But, having considered the cases and the law, this court is quite clear that the direction of Judge Aarvold in this case cannot be criticised. Indeed, it might well have been made with the passage in Foster's *Crown Cases* (3rd edn) (1792) at p369, in mind, because there the learned author says:

"If the principal totally and substantially varieth, if being solicited to commit a felony of one kind he *wilfully and knowingly* committeth a felony of another, *he* will stand single in that offence, and the person soliciting will not be involved in his guilt. For on *his* part it was no more than a fruitless ineffectual temptation."

The converse of course is that, if the principal does not totally and substantially vary the advice or the help and does not wilfully and knowingly commit a different form of felony altogether, the man who has advised or helped, aided or abetted, will be guilty as an accessory before the fact.

Judge Aarvold in this case, in the passages to which I have referred, makes it clear that there must be not merely suspicion but knowledge that a crime of the type in question was intended, and that the equipment was bought with that in view. In his reference to the felony of the type intended it was, as he states, the felony of breaking and entering premises and the stealing of property from those premises. The court can see nothing wrong in that direction.'

R v Baldessare (1930) 22 Cr App R 70 (Court of Criminal Appeal) (The Lord Chief Justice, Talbot and MacNaghten JJ)

Accomplice's liability for accidental departures from the common design

Facts

The defendant was a passenger in a car that had been taken for the purposes of 'joyriding'. The driver (a man named Chapman) killed another road user and was convicted of manslaughter. The defendant was convicted as an accomplice to the manslaughter, as it was an unforeseen consequence of the common design being carried out. He appealed against conviction.

Held

Appeal dismissed.

The Lord Chief Justice:

'The appellant appeals on two grounds - first, that there was no evidence on which the jury could properly convict him of manslaughter, and secondly, as he alleges, that there was misdirection in the summing-up of the learned judge. With reference to a considerable part of the case, there was no real dispute. [After stating the facts, His Lordship continued:] It is undoubtedly a cardinal fact in the case that the jury thought fit to acquit both the appellant and Chapman on the charge of stealing the car. The question, therefore, was whether, nevertheless, the two men were associated together in the driving of the car so that, when death resulted from the collision, each was guilty of manslaughter. With regard to the summing-up, we are all of opinion that this was an excellent summing-up; it stated the law clearly and fairly, and if there was any error in it, the error was in favour of the appellant. After that perfectly fair summing-up, the jury came to the conclusion that the appellant was guilty of manslaughter; in other words, they came to the conclusion that the appellant and Chapman were acting together and joined in responsibility, not merely for the taking away of the car from the owner's possession, but also for the driving of it in the way in which it was in fact driven.

The only question for this Court is whether there was any evidence on which the jury could properly find that community of purpose and action. The matter was very carefully argued before us, and we have very carefully considered it, and our conclusion is that we are not prepared to say that there was not evidence on which the jury were entitled to arrive at their verdict. Here was a clandestine ride - commonly called a "joy-ride" - on a dark night in February, without proper lights, and the two men had taken the car for a purpose, which the jury have found was not felonious, but which had as its object a "joy-ride" without the knowledge and assent of the owner. Looking at these facts, and at the actual speed of the car and its movements before and after the collision, we think that the jury were entitled to find that both the appellant and Chapman were responsible for the way in which the car was being driven at the moment of collision.'

Commentary

See *R* v *Betts and Ridley*, below.

R v Becerra and Cooper (1975) 62 Cr App R 212 Court of Appeal (Criminal Division) (Roskill and Bridge LJJ and Kilner Brown J)

Withdrawal from the common design

Facts

Becerra and Cooper agreed to burgle a house, Becerra giving Cooper a knife to use in case there was any trouble. When they were disturbed by the householder, Becerra jumped out of a window and ran off, shouting 'Let's go'. Cooper remained behind and murdered the householder. Becerra was convicted as an accomplice to the murder despite his contention that he had withdrawn from the enterprise. He appealed against his conviction.

Held

The appeal would be dismissed.

Roskill LJ:

'It was argued in the alternative on behalf of Becerra, ... [that he] ... had open to him a second line of defence, namely that ... - whatever Cooper did immediately before and at the time of the killing of Lewis, Becerra had by then withdrawn from that common design and so should not be convicted of the murder of Lewis, even though the common design had previously been that which I have stated.

Mr Owen [counsel for the appellant] says ... the learned judge in effect, though perhaps not in so many words, withdrew the defence of "withdrawal" from the jury, because the learned judge was saying to the jury that the only evidence of Becerra's suggested "withdrawal" was the remark, if it were made, "come on let's go," coupled with the fact of course that Becerra then went out through the window and ran away and that that could not in those circumstances amount to "withdrawal" and therefore was not available as a defence, even if they decided the issue of common design against Becerra. It is upon that passage in the summing-up that Mr Owen has principally focused his criticism.

It is necessary, before dealing with that argument in more detail, to say a word or two about the relevant law. [Roskill LJ then cited a decision of the Court of Appeal of British Columbia in *Whitehouse* (*alias Savage*) (1941) 1 WWR 112, at pp115 and 116]. "Can it be said on the facts of this case that a mere change of mental intention and a quitting of the scene of the crime just immediately prior to the striking of the fatal blow will absolve those who participate in the commission of the crime by overt acts up to that moment from all the consequences of its accomplishment by the one who strikes in ignorance of his companion's change of heart? I think not. After a crime has been committed and before a prior abandonment of the common enterprise may be found by a jury there must be, in my view, in the absence of exceptional circumstances, something more than a mere mental change of intention and physical change of place by those associates who wish to dissociate themselves from the consequences attendant upon their willing assistance up to the moment of the actual commission of that crime. I would not attempt to define too closely what must be done in criminal matters involving participation in a common unlawful purpose to break the chain of causation and responsibility. That must depend upon the circumstances of each case but it seems to me that one essential element ought to be established in a case of this kind. Where practicable and reasonable there must be timely communication of the intention to abandon the common purpose from those who wish to dissociate themselves from the contemplated crime to those who desire to continue in it. What is "timely communication" must be determined by the facts of each case but where practicable and reasonable it ought to be such communication, verbal or otherwise, that will serve unequivocal notice upon the other party to the common unlawful cause that if he proceeds upon it he does so without the further aid and assistance of those who withdraw. The unlawful purpose of him who continues alone is then his own and not one in common with those who are no longer parties to it nor liable to its full and final consequences." ...

In the view of each member of this Court, that passage, if we may respectfully say so, could not be improved upon and we venture to adopt it in its entirety as a correct statement of the law which is to be applied in this case ...

We therefore turn back to consider the direction which the learned judge gave in the present case to the jury and what was the suggested evidence that Becerra had withdrawn from the common agreement. The suggested evidence is the use by Becerra of the words "Come on let's go," coupled, as I said a few moments ago, with his act in going out through the window. The evidence, as the judge pointed out, was that Cooper never heard that nor did the third man. But let it be supposed that that was said and the jury took the view that it was said.

On the facts of this case, in the circumstances then prevailing, the knife having already been used and being contemplated for further use when it was handed over by Becerra to Cooper for the purpose of avoiding (if necessary) by violent means the hazards of identification, if Becerra wanted to withdraw at that stage, he would have to "countermand," to use the word that is used in some of the cases or "repent" to use another word so used, in some manner vastly different and vastly more effective than merely to say "Come on, let's go" and go out through the window.

It is not necessary, on this application, to decide whether the point of time had arrived at which the only way in which he could effectively withdraw, so as to free himself from joint responsibility for any act Cooper thereafter did in furtherance of the common design, would be physically to intervene so as to stop Cooper attacking Lewis, as the judge suggested, by interposing his own body between them or somehow getting in between them or whether some other action might suffice. That does not arise for decision here. Nor is it necessary to decide whether or not the learned judge was right or wrong, on the facts of this case, in that passage which appears at the bottom of p206, which Mr Owen criticised: "and at least take all reasonable steps to prevent the commission of the crime which he had agreed the others should commit." It is enough for the purposes of deciding this application to say that under the law of this country as it stands, and on the facts (taking them at their highest in favour of Becerra), that which was urged as amounting to withdrawal from the common design was not capable of amounting to such withdrawal. Accordingly Becerra remains responsible in the eyes of the law, for everything that Cooper did and continued to do after Becerra's disappearance through the window as much as if he had done them himself.'

R v Betts and Ridley (1930) 22 Cr App R 148 (Court of Criminal Appeal) (Avory, Swift, and Charles JJ)

Accomplice's liability for accidental departures from the common design

Facts

The defendants agreed that Betts would rob a victim by hitting him to the ground and snatching his property, and that Ridley would wait around the corner at the wheel of the 'getaway' car. The plan was carried out, but Betts struck the victim with such force that the victim died from the blow. They were both convicted of murder and appealed.

Held

The appeals would be dismissed. With regard to Ridley's appeal, the common design was carried out, but with an unforeseen consequence, the death of the victim. Where the principal did not deliberately exceed the common design in causing such a result, the accomplice would be jointly responsible for it.

Avory J:

'Now with regard to the case of Ridley, Mr Marshall [counsel for the appellant] has, in a very able address to the Court, attempted to satisfy us that a distinction ought to have been drawn by the jury in the case of Ridley, and that the learned Commissioner ought in his direction to them, to have told them that, even though they found Betts guilty of murder, they yet might find Ridley guilty only of manslaughter. No suggestion is made that Ridley was guilty of anything less than manslaughter, or that he could properly be acquitted altogether. The only question in his case is, whether there was any misdirection of the jury in regard to his case, and whether on the facts of this case, he ought to have been convicted only of manslaughter.

Now bearing in mind that by his own confession he was a party to the agreement that this deceased man should be robbed, and that by his own admission in his own statement he anticipated that he would, at least, be pushed down, it is necessary to see whether upon the authorities there was any ground for distinguishing his case from that of Betts.

First of all, it is clear that in the circumstances he was a principal in the second degree to the robbery with violence, which in fact took place. It is clear law that it is not necessary that the party, to constitute him a principal in the second degree, should be actually present, an eye-witness or ear-witness, of the transaction. He is, in construction of law, present aiding and abetting if with the intention of giving assistance, he is near enough to afford it, should occasion arise. Thus, if he be outside the house, watching to prevent surprise, whilst his companions are in the house committing a felony, such constructive presence is sufficient to make him a principal in the second degree. It is clear that Ridley was present in that sense, so as to make him a principal in the second degree to this crime of robbery with violence; and although it might be true to say that he had not agreed beforehand that Andrews should be struck on the head in a way likely to cause his death, it is clear upon the authorities that if he was a party to this felonious act of robbery with violence - some violence - and that the other person, the principal in the first degree, in the course of carrying out that common design does an act which causes the death, then the principal in the second degree is equally responsible in law. As was said in East's Pleas of the Crown, at page 256, dealing for the moment again with Betts: "He who voluntarily, knowingly and unlawfully intends hurt to the person of another, though he intend not death, yet if death ensue, is guilty of murder or manslaughter according to the circumstances. As if A intending to beat B happen to kill him, if done from preconceived malice" - if done from preconceived intention to rob with violence, it would be the same thing as if done with malice - "it will be no alleviation that he did not intend all the mischief that followed."

That being the position of Betts, what is the position of the principal in the second degree. He is at least, if not more, responsible than an accessory before the fact, and in Foster's Crown Cases, at page 369, dealing with an accessory before the fact, it is said: "Much has been said by writers who have gone before me, upon cases where a person supposed to commit a felony at the instigation of another hath gone beyond the terms of such instigation, or hath, in the execution varied from them. If the principal totally and substantially varieth, if being solicited to commit a felony of one kind he wilfully and knowingly committeth a felony of another, he will stand single in that offence, and the person soliciting will not be involved in his guilt ... but if the principal in substance complieth with the temptation, varying only in circumstance of time or place, or in the manner of execution, in these cases the person soliciting to the offence will, if absent, be an accessory before the fact, if present a principal." It appears to the Court in this case that the case of Ridley comes precisely within this description. Even if Betts did vary in the manner of execution of this agreed plan to rob, and obviously it must have been a plan to rob with some degree of violence, Ridley being present as a principal in the second degree is equally responsible. Therefore, in any view, if the learned Commissioner had made the distinction which is suggested between the two cases, it is obvious that upon a correct view of the law, Ridley in fact in this case was a principal in the second degree to this crime of murder. As the direction stands, and as it was given to the jury, they must, in finding Ridley guilty of murder, be presumed to have found that he was actually a party and privy to an act which was calculated in the judgment of ordinary people to cause death; and having so found, it is impossible that this Court, upon such evidence as this, can interfere with their verdict.'

Blakely, Sutton v DPP [1991] Crim LR 763 Queen's Bench Division (Bingham LJ and McCullough J)

Whether recklessness sufficient for procuring

Facts

'T was an associate of B's. On the nights when he intended to stay with B, he would leave his car at the meeting place, but if he intended to go home, he would drink no more than two pints, thereafter drinking tonic water. On the night in question, he told B that he intended to go home to his wife. She discussed this with S, who suggested that if T had alcohol he might be unwilling to drive. Unknown to T, they added vodka to his tonic water. B intended to tell him later believing that he would not be prepared to drive. However, at closing time, T left before B had told him. He was arrested, and charged with a drink-driving offence. He advanced special reasons for not being disqualified B and S testified with the result that T was given an absolute discharge. They were charged with "aiding, abetting, counselling, procuring and commanding" T to drive when his blood-alcohol level exceeded that prescribed. It was contended that they did not intend T to drive; contrariwise, they intended that he should not drive. Following dismissal of their appeal to the Crown Court, they appealed by case stated, the questions being (i) whether the offence of procuring could be committed by someone who brought it about, not intending that the offence should be committed but reckless as to whether it be committed or not; (ii) if so, whether the meaning of recklessness in such a case was that given to it by Lord Diplock in *Lawrence* [1981] 2 WLR 524, 535.

Held

Allowing the appeal, recklessness had two limbs: (a) pursing a course of conduct and giving no thought to the possibility that it involved a risk when there was an obvious risk (inadvertent); (b) recognising that the conduct involved a risk but going on nevertheless to run it (advertent). Although the charge was framed compendiously only procuring was alleged, so only the *mens rea* of procuring the commission of an offence by another need be considered. The relevant issue was what must be proved to have been the state of the accused's mind in relation to the offence which the principal offender went on to commit? Counsel for the appellants submitted that the accused must not only have done his own act intentionally but must also have intended thereby to bring about the principal offence. Alternatively, he must have been aware that his intentional act might bring about the principal offence and have been prepared to do it nevertheless. Counsel for the DPP contended that an accused might be convicted of procuring an offence of strict liability if he intentionally did an act, or brought about a state of affairs, without which the offence would not have been committed and, at the time, he either intended that offence to occur or was reckless, in either of the *Caldwell* and *Lawrence* senses, as to whether the other essential acts or states constituting that offence would occur.

In *Carter v Richardson* [1974] RTR 314, the supervising driver was charged with aiding and abetting the learner driver's drink-driving offence. There was only one reference (317H) to recklessness which was not part of the *ratio*. Elsewhere in his judgment, Lord Widgery referred to the supervisor's knowledge or awareness, and there was nothing to suppose that, in approving the justices' opinion containing the word "reckless," he was thinking of anything other than advertent recklessness. In *Attorney-General's Reference (No 1)* [1975] 2 All ER 684, Lord Widgery said that to procure meant "to produce by endeavour. You procure a thing by setting out to see that it happens and taking the appropriate steps to produce that happening." That strongly suggested that the procurer must be shown to have intended to bring about the commission of the principal offence, and that mere awareness that it might result would not suffice. The language throughout the judgment was of knowledge of the offence the driver went on to commit; there was no hint that recklessness, let alone inadvertent recklessness, might suffice to convict the procurer.

There was no warrant for the suggestion that an accessory before the fact, whether aider and abettor, counsellor, commander or procurer, might be convicted on what might be called a less strict *mens rea* than would suffice to convict a principal in the second degree. Indeed, in *Ferguson* v *Weaving* [1851] 1 KB 814, it was suggested that something more might be required to convict one who "counsels and procures." That case would also appear to negate the submission for the DPP that it might be the case that the *mens rea* for procuring an absolute offence was less strict than that required of a person accused of procuring an offence which itself required *mens rea* (see also *Thomas* v *Lindop* [1950] 1 All ER 966). The conclusions on the question of the *mens rea* of an accessory before the fact were as follows. While it might now be the law that advertent recklessness to the consequences of his deliberate act of assistance might suffice to convict some, if not all, of those accused of being an accessory before the fact, it was clear that inadvertent recklessness did not. It must, at least, be shown that the accused contemplated that his act would or might bring about or assist the commission of the principal offence: he must have been prepared nevertheless to do his own act, and he must have done that act intentionally. Those requirements matched those needed to convict principals in the second degree, and they fitted well with the liability of the parties to a joint enterprise. In relation to those accused only of procuring and perhaps also those accused only of counselling and commanding, it might be, as Lord Goddard's judgment in *Ferguson* v *Weaving* would permit and as Lord Widgery's judgment in *Attorney-General's Reference (No 1 of 1975)* strongly suggested, that it was necessary to prove that the accused intended to bring about the principal offence. The present case did not require that to be decided. The stated question would be answered: (1) the use of the word "recklessness" was best avoided when considering the *mens rea* of a person accused of procuring the commission of a substantive offence; (ii) in so far as the correct approach to that *mens rea* accorded with the concept of "recklessness." "No.'"

[*Reported by Veronica Cowan, Barrister.*]

R v Bourne (1952) 36 Cr App R 125 (Court of Criminal Appeal) (Lord Goddard CJ, Hilbery and Slade JJ)

Accomplice's liability where principal has a complete defence

Facts

The defendant was convicted of aiding and abetting the offence of buggery by his wife on an alsatian dog. His wife was acquitted on the basis that she could rely on the defence of duress because the defendant had forced her to commit the offence. The defendant contended, inter alia, that given the wife's defence, there was no crime for him to aid and abet.

Held

The appeal would be dismissed.

Lord Goddard CJ:

'The case against the appellant was that he was a principal in the second degree to the crime of buggery which was committed by his wife, because if a woman has connection with a dog, or allows a dog to have connection with her, that is the full offence of buggery. She may be able to show that she was forced to commit the offence. I will assume that the plea of duress could have been set up by her on the evidence, and in fact we have allowed Mr Green to argue this case on the footing that the wife would have been entitled to be acquitted on the ground of duress. The learned judge left no question to the jury on duress, but the jury have found that she did not consent. Assuming that she could have set up duress, what does that mean? It means that she admits that she has committed the crime but prays to be excused from punishment for the consequences of the crime by reason of the duress, and no doubt in those circumstances the law would allow a verdict of Not Guilty to be entered. I have only to read a passage from Blackstone's Commentaries (Vol 4, p27) to show that that is the true position: "The same principle which excuses those who have no mental will in the perpetration of an offence protects from the punishment of the law those who commit crimes in subjection to the power of others, and not as the result of an uncontrolled free action proceeding from themselves. Thus, if A by force takes the hand of B in which is a weapon, and therewith kills C, A is guilty of murder, but B is excused; but if a merely moral force is used, as threats, duress of imprisonment, or even an assault to the peril of his life, in order to compel him to kill C, it is no legal excuse." See also 1 Hale's Pleas of the Crown, pp44, 51. That means that duress is not a legal excuse for murder. There may be certain doctrines with regard to murder which do not apply to other cases, but I am willing to assume for the purpose of this case, and I think my brethren are too, that if this woman had been charged herself with committing the offence, she could have set up the plea of duress, not as showing that no offence had been committed, but as showing that she had no mens rea because her will was overborne by threats of imprisonment or violence so that she would be excused from punishment. But the offence of buggery whether with man or beast does not depend upon consent; it depends on the act, and if an act of buggery is committed, the felony is committed.

A point is raised here that the appellant was charged with being not merely an accessory before the fact but with being an aider and abettor. So he was, because the charge is: "you being present aided and abetted, counselled and procured." The only questions that were left to the jury by the learned judge, and he was not asked to leave any more, were these: (1) "Did the prisoner on a day in or about the month of September 1949, in the County of Stafford cause his wife Adelaide Bourne to have carnal knowledge of a dog?" and the jury have found that he did. (2) "Are you satisfied that she did not consent to having such carnal knowledge?" The answer of the jury was: "Yes, we are satisfied she did not consent." Then the same two questions were asked with regard to the other day on which an offence was alleged to have been committed.

In the opinion of the court, there is no doubt that the appellant was properly indicted for being a principal in the second degree to the commission of the crime of buggery. That is all that it is necessary to show. The evidence was, and the jury by their verdict have shown they accepted it, that he caused his wife to have connection with a dog, and if he caused his wife to have connection with a dog he is guilty, whether you call him an aider and abettor or an accessory, as a principal in the second degree. For that reason, this appeals fails and is dismissed.'

R v Calhaem [1985] QB 808 Court of Appeal (Criminal Division) (Parker LJ, Tudor Evans J and Sir John Thompson)

Whether principal's actions a departure from the common design

Facts

The defendant had hired a man named Zajac to kill a woman named Shirley Rendell, who was a rival for the affections of Mr Pigot, with whom the defendant was infatuated. Zajac was paid £5,000 by the defendant to carry out the killing. At his trial for the murder of Mrs Rendell, Zajac testified that after being paid the money by the defendant he had resolved not to carry out the killing, but instead to visit Mrs Rendell's house, carrying an unloaded shotgun and a hammer, to act out a charade that would give the appearance that he had tried to kill her. He claimed that when he had stepped inside the front door of the victim's house, she had screamed and he panicked, hitting her several times with the hammer. On the basis of this evidence, the defendant had contended that she could not be guilty of counselling the victim's murder as the killing had been a direct result of Zajac's panic, not her instructions, which he had in any event decided not to follow.

Held

The appeal would be dismissed.

Parker LJ:

[His Lordship referred to Lord Widgery CJ's judgment in *Attorney-General's Reference (No 1 of 1975)*, extracted in chapter 9, and continued]

'We must therefore approach the question raised on the basis that we should give the word "counsel" its ordinary meaning, which is, as the judge said, "advise," "solicit," or something of that sort. There is no implication in the word itself that there should be any causal connection between the offence of incitement at common law, the actual offence must have been committed, and committed by the person counselled. To this extent there must clearly be, first, contact between the parties, and, secondly, a connection between the counselling and the murder. Equally, the act done must, we think, be done within the scope of the authority or advice, and not, for example, accidentally when the mind of the final murderer did not go with his actions. For example, if the principal offender happened to be involved in a football riot in the course of which he laid about him with a weapon of some sort and killed someone who, unknown to him, was the person whom he had been counselled to kill, he would not, in our view, have been acting within the scope of his authority; he would have been acting entirely outside it, albeit what he had done was what he had been counselled to do.

We see, however, no need to import anything further into the meaning of the word, unless authority drives us to do so. It is of course possible, and both counsel took this course, to take examples of cases which appear to be anomalous, whichever construction is put upon the wording. Such anomalies do not, in our view, assist. There will always be cases in which difficulties are raised and they are disposed of in the ordinary way by sensible action on the part of the prosecuting authority. So far as the authorities are concerned, there are in them, we accept, phrases which may appear, at any rate at first sight, to assist the view put forward by Mr Carman. We do not propose to go through all the authorities, but some of them must be mentioned.

[His Lordship considered these, and continued:]

'... The natural meaning of the word does not imply the commission of the offence. So long as there is counselling - and there was ample evidence in this case of that fact - so long as the principal offence is committed by the one counselled, and so long as the one counselled is acting within the scope of his authority, and not in the accidental way or some such similar way as I have suggested with regard to an incident in a football riot, we are of the view that the offence is made out.

Accordingly, we reject Mr Carman's first submission and hold that the direction by the judge was correct. We would add on this matter however that had we accepted his submission we should have felt unable to apply the proviso, because of the possibility that the jury might have accepted the view that there was no substantial cause and come to the conclusion that it was merely authority which enabled them to convict.

Mr Carman's other points were that (a) the judge erred in his treatment of Zajac's evidence, (b) the judge should have directed the jury that without Zajac's evidence there was no evidence, and (c) the judge failed to give directions as to the importance of two notes which Zajac had written to a fellow-prisoner, one Gillard. As to these, having considered the passages complained of and also the omissions complained of, in the context of the whole of the summing up we need say very little. As to (a), in our view the judge gave the jury the clearest warnings possible with regard to the unreliability of Zajac, which was common ground, and of the need for corroboration of his evidence. He told them that it was open to them, if they wished to do so, to reject his account of his state of mind immediately preceding and at the time of the murder, whilst at the same time to accept the corroborated parts of his evidence. We see nothing wrong in what the judge did and consider that he gave perfectly adequate directions with regard to Zajac.

With respect to the second point, that the judge should have directed the jury that without Zajac's evidence there was no evidence, in our view such a submission is wholly untenable. If there is evidence to go to the jury it is not for the judge to say. "If you reject this bit or that bit of the evidence there is nothing left." Were it to be so the judge would have the task, as we see it, of eliminating piece by piece each bit of evidence until he came down to nothing. If he were to take such a course he would be usurping the function of the jury. Accordingly, we reject that submission.'

Chan Wing Siu v R [1985] AC 168 Privy Council (Lords Keith, Bridge, Brandon, and Templeman, and Sir Robin Cooke)

(Mens rea required for accomplices to murder)

Facts

The appellants were members of a gang who had gone to the deceased's house to commit a robbery, arming themselves with knives. During the robbery the deceased was stabbed to death by a member of the gang. The appellants were convicted as accomplices to the murder and appealed against their convictions on the ground that the trial judge had misdirected the jury as to the mens rea required.

Held

The appeals would be dismissed. For an accomplice to be guilty of murder it was sufficient for the prosecution to establish that he foresaw death or grievous bodily harm as a possible incident of the common design being carried out.

Sir Robin Cooke:

[After referring to a number of Commonwealth authorities on the mens rea required for the conviction of accomplices]

'What public policy requires was rightly identified in the submissions of the Crown. Where a man lends himself to a criminal enterprise knowing that potentially murderous weapons are to be carried, and in the event they are in fact used by his partner with an intent sufficient for murder, he should not escape the consequences by reliance on a nuance of prior assessment, only too likely to have been optimistic.

On the other hand, if it was not even contemplated by the particular accused that serious bodily harm would be intentionally inflicted, he is not a party to murder.

[Reference was then made to *Davies v DPP* [1954] AC 378, and his Lordship continued:]

The test of mens rea here is subjective. It is what the individual accused in fact contemplated that matters. As in other cases where the state of a person's mind has to be ascertained, this may be inferred from his conduct and any other evidence throwing light on what he foresaw at the material time, including of course any explanation that he gives in evidence or in a statement put in evidence by the prosecution. It is no less elementary that all questions of weight are for the jury. The prosecution must prove the necessary contemplation beyond reasonable doubt, although that may be done by inference as just mentioned. If, at the end of the day and whether as a result of hearing evidence from the accused or for some other reason, the jury conclude that there is a reasonable possibility that the accused did not even contemplate the risk, he is in this type of case not guilty of murder or wounding with intent to cause serious bodily harm.

In some cases in this field it is enough to direct the jury by adapting to the circumstances the simple formula common in a number of jurisdictions. For instance, did the particular accused contemplate that in carrying out a common unlawful purpose one of his partners in the enterprise might use a knife or a loaded gun with the intention of causing really serious bodily harm? ...

In cases where an issue of remoteness does arise it is for the jury (or other tribunal of fact) to decide whether the risk *as recognised by the accused* was sufficient to make him a party to the crime committed by the principal. Various formulae have been suggested, including a substantial risk, a real risk, a risk that something might well happen. No one formula is exclusively preferable; indeed it may be advantageous in a summing up to use more than one. For the question is not one of semantics. What has to be brought home to the jury is that occasionally a risk may have occurred to an accused's mind, fleetingly or even causing him some deliberation, but may genuinely have been dismissed by him as altogether negligible. If they think there is a reasonable possibility that the case is in that class, taking the risk should not make that accused a party to such a crime of intention as murder or wounding with intent to cause grievous bodily harm. The judge is entitled to warn the jury to be cautious before reaching that conclusion; but the law can do no more by way of definition; it can only be for the jury to determine any issue of that kind on the facts of the particular case.

The present case not being in that class, their Lordships agree with the Court of Appeal that the attack on the summing up fails and will humbly advise Her Majesty that the appeals should be dismissed.'

R v Clarkson [1971] 1 WLR 1402 Courts-Martial Appeal Court (Megaw LJ, Geoffrey Lane and Kilner Brown JJ)

Inactivity at the scene of a crime: whether sufficient for liability

Facts

Two soldiers (the defendants) had entered a room following the noise from a disturbance therein. They found some other soldiers raping a woman, and remained on the scene to watch what was happening. They were convicted of abetting the rapes and appealed on the basis that their mere presence alone could not have been sufficient for liability.

Held

The appeals would be allowed.

Megaw LJ:

'*Coney* [(1882) 8 QBD 534] decided that non-accidental presence at the scene of the crime is not conclusive of aiding and abetting. The jury has to be told by the judge, or as in this case the court-martial has to be told by the judge-advocate, in clear terms what it is that has to be proved before they can convict of aiding and abetting; what it is of which the jury or the court-martial, as the case may be, must be sure as matters of inference before they can convict of aiding and abetting in such a case where the evidence adduced by the prosecution is limited to non-accidental presence ... It is not enough, then, that the presence of the accused has, in fact, given encouragement. It must be proved that he *wilfully* encouraged. In such a case as the present, more than in many other cases where aiding and abetting is alleged, it was essential that that element should be stressed; for there was here at least the possibility that a drunken man with his self-discipline loosened by drink, being aware that a woman was being raped, might be attracted to the scene and might stay on the scene in the capacity of what is known as a voyeur; and, while his presence and the presence of others might in fact encourage the rapers or discourage the victim, he himself, enjoying the scene or at least standing by assenting, might not intend that his presence should offer encouragement to rapers and would-be rapers or discouragement to the victim; he might not realise that he was giving encouragement; so that, while encouragement there might be, it would not be a case in which ... the accused person wilfully encouraged ... it follows that mere intention is not in itself enough. There must be an intention to encourage; and there must also be encouragement in fact, in cases such as the present case.'

R v Cogan and Leak (1976) 61 Cr App R 217 Court of Appeal (Criminal Division) (Lawton, James LJJ, and Bristow J)

Accomplice's liability where principal lacks mens rea

Facts

Leak persuaded Cogan to have sexual intercourse with Mrs Leak, telling him that she liked being forced to have sex against her will. Cogan was convicted of rape, but appealed successfully on the ground that he had honestly thought she was consenting. Leak now appealed against his conviction for aiding and abetting the rape, on the ground that he could not be liable where the principal offender was acquitted.

Held

The appeal would be dismissed.

Lawton LJ:

'Leak's appeal against conviction was based on the proposition that he could not be found guilty of aiding and abetting Cogan to rape his wife if Cogan was acquitted of that offence as he was deemed in law to have been when his conviction was quashed ... Counsel for Leak conceded, however, that his proposition had some limitations. The law on this topic lacks clarity as a perusal of some of the textbooks shows: ... We do not consider it appropriate to review the law generally because as was said by this court in *R v Quick* [1973] QB 910, 923 when considering this kind of problem:

"The facts of each case ... have to be considered and in particular what is alleged to have been done by way of aiding and abetting."

The only case which counsel for Leak submitted had a direct bearing on the problem of Leak's guilt was *Walters v Lunt* [1951] 2 All ER 645. In that case the respondents had been charged under the Larceny Act 1916, s33(1), with receiving from a child aged seven years, certain articles knowing them to have been stolen. In 1951 a child under eight years was deemed in law to be incapable of committing a crime: it followed that at the time of receipt by the respondents the articles had not been stolen and that the charges had not been proved. That case is very different from this because here one fact is clear - the wife had been raped.

Cogan had had sexual intercourse with her without her consent. The fact that Cogan was innocent of rape because he believed that she was consenting does not affect the position that she was raped.

Her ravishment had come about because Leak had wanted it to happen and had taken action to see that it did by persuading Cogan to use his body as the instrument for the necessary physical act. In the language of the law the act of sexual intercourse without the wife's consent was the actus reus; it had been procured by Leak who had the appropriate mens rea, namely his intention that Cogan should have sexual intercourse with her without her consent. In our judgment it is irrelevant that the man whom Leak had procured to do the physical act himself did not intend to have sexual intercourse with the wife without her consent. Leak was using him as a means to procure a criminal purpose.

Before 1861 a case such as this, pleaded as it was in the indictment, might have presented a court with problems arising from the old distinctions between principals and accessories in felony. Most of the old law was swept away by s8 of the Accessories and Abettors Act 1861 and what remained, by s1 of the Criminal Law Act 1967. The modern law allowed Leak to be tried and punished as a principal offender. In our judgment he could have been indicted as a principal offender. It would have been no defence for him to submit that if Cogan was an "innocent" agent, he was necessarily in the old terminology of the law a principal in the first degree, which was a legal impossibility as a man cannot rape his own wife during co-habitation. The law no longer concerns itself with niceties of degrees in participation of crime; but even if it did, Leak would still be guilty. The reason a man cannot by his own physical act rape his wife during co-habitation is because the law presumes consent from the marriage ceremony: see *Hale, Pleas of the Crown*, (1778) vol. 1, p.629. There is no such presumption when a man procures a drunken friend to do the physical act for him. Hale CJ put this case in one sentence; at p629:

"tho in marriage she hath given up her body to her husband, she is not to be by him prostituted to another."

Had Leak been indicted as a principal offender, the case against him would have been clear beyond argument. Should he be allowed to go free because he was charged with "being aider and abettor to the same offence"? If we are right in our opinion that the wife had been raped (and no one outside a court of law would say that she had not been), then the particulars of offence accurately stated what Leak had done, namely he had procured Cogan to commit the offence. This would suffice to uphold the conviction. We would prefer, however, to uphold it on a wider basis. In our judgment convictions should not be upset because of mere technicalities of pleading in an indictment. Leak knew what the case against him was and the facts in support of that case were proved. But for the fact that the jury thought that Cogan in his intoxicated condition might have mistaken the wife's sobs and distress for expressions of her consent, no question of any kind would have arisen about the form of pleading. By his written statement Leak virtually admitted what he had done. As Judge Chapman said in *R* v *Humphreys* [1965] 3 All ER 689, 692:

"It would be anomalous if a person who admitted to a substantial part in the perpetration of a misdemeanour as aider and abettor could not be convicted on his own admission merely because the person alleged to have been aided and abetted was not or could not be convicted."

In the circumstances of this case it would be more than anomalous: it would be an affront to justice and to the common sense of ordinary folk. It was for these reasons that we dismissed the appeal against conviction.

The sentence passed on Leak for his part in the rape was severe; but the circumstances were horrible. We can see nothing wrong with that sentence. The assault on the wife the previous day had been brutal. The doctor found no less than 13 bruises in the middle and lower region on the left hand side of her spine. There were other bruises on her back and multiple bruises on her left hip. These bruises were consistent with punching and kicking. Men who use violence of this kind on their wives must expect severe sentences. The sentence of three years was not too severe.'

DPP for Northern Ireland v Maxwell (1978) 68 Cr App R 128 House of Lords (Viscount Dilhorne, Lords Hailsham, Edmund-Davies, Fraser, and Scarman)

Accomplice's liability where he contemplates the principal committing any one of a large number of offences

Facts

The appellant drove some members of the Ulster Volunteer Force to the Crosskeys Inn where a pipe bomb was planted, and was convicted as an accomplice to these unlawful acts. He appealed against his conviction on the ground that, although he had contemplated a number of offences being committed during the visit to the Inn, he had not known exactly what offences the principals were going to commit.

Held

The appeal would be dismissed.

Lord Scarman:

[His Lordship referred to Lowry LCJ's statement in the court below, that:

'The relevant crime must be within the contemplation of the accomplice and only exceptionally would evidence be found to support the allegation that the accomplice had given the principal a completely blank cheque.'

and continued:]

'The principle thus formulated has great merit. It directs attention to the state of mind of the accused: not what he ought to have in contemplation, but what he did have. It avoids definition and classification, while ensuring that a man will not be convicted of aiding and abetting any offence his principal may commit, but only one which is within his contemplation. He may have in contemplation only one offence, or several; and the several which he contemplates he may see as alternatives. An accessory who leaves it to his principal to choose is liable, provided always the choice is made from the range of offences from which the accessory contemplates the choice will be made. Although the court's formulation of the principle goes further than the earlier cases, it is a sound development of the law and in no way inconsistent with them. I accept it as good judge-made law in a field where there is no statute to offer guidance.'

R v Dunbar [1988] Crim LR 693 Court of Appeal (Criminal Division) (Russell LJ, Hodgson and Turner JJ.

Manslaughter - acts beyond the scope of the common design.

Facts

'The appellant was convicted of manslaughter. Her co-defendants were convicted of murder. It was the prosecution case that the appellant had incited her co-defendants to murder her former lover. The victim died after being hit on the head with a metal bar; the cause of death was asphyxiation when the metal bar was used to garotte her with such force that her voice box was shattered. The appellant denied inciting murder; she admitted that she may have expressed a wish to see the victim dead but claimed that was rambling associated with drink and drugs. She had suspected that the co-defendants planned to burgle the victim's flat and that in the course of the burglary some violence might be done to her former lover. The appellant appealed against conviction on the ground that the verdict of manslaughter was not open to the jury.

Held

Allowing the appeal and quashing the conviction, [the court held that] the jury's verdict must have been reached upon the basis that while the appellant contemplated the use of some unlawful violence, short of the infliction of grievous bodily harm, one or other or both of her co-defendants must have gone beyond the scope of that design and used the extreme violence which was intended to cause grievous bodily harm or death. The judge's direction in the appellant's case did not deal with that situation and the appropriate verdict of not guilty should the jury find that the second and/or third defendant went beyond what was contemplated by the appellant. On the facts of the case there were only two verdicts open to the jury, guilty or not guilty of murder. If, as the Crown contended, she was a party to an agreement to kill, she was guilty of murder. If she was a party to an agreement to inflict some harm, short of grievous bodily harm, then she was guilty of neither murder nor manslaughter. The victim's killing and the manner of the killing could not be within the ambit of the agreement to which the appellant was a party, if the ambit was confined on her part to an intention that only some harm should befall the deceased, albeit not death or really serious injury. The issues involved could not be distinguished from those adumbrated by Widgery LJ in *Lovesey and Peterson* (1969) 54 Cr App R 461. The judge failed to remind the jury of the law as laid down in *Anderson and Morris* (1966) 50 Cr App R 216 and followed in *Lovesey and Peterson* (1969) 53 Cr App R 461. The result of that non-direction was that the jury returned a verdict which was not open to them.'

[*Reported by Lynne Knapman, Barrister.*]

R v Dunnington [1984] QB 472 Court of Appeal (Criminal Division) (Ackner LJ, Beldam J, and Sir John Thompson)

Aiding and abetting an attempt

Facts

The defendant had agreed with two other men, Ryan and Peterson, that they should carry out a robbery on a shop. The defendant stole a car for use in the offence, and waited outside the shop whilst Peterson and Ryan went in and ordered the shopkeeper to hand over money. The shopkeeper resisted, and the defendants fled empty handed. The defendant was convicted of attempted robbery as an accomplice and appealed on the ground that such liability had been abolished by s1(4)(b) of the Criminal Attempts Act 1981.

Held

The appeal would be dismissed.

Beldam J:

'It was conceded by the Crown before the learned judge, as it was before us, that the part played by the appellant was solely that of aider and abettor of the offence of attempted robbery. He had been charged as a principal, pursuant to the provisions of section 8 of the Accessories and Abettors Act 1861, as amended by Schedule 12 to the Criminal Law Act 1977.

[His Lordship referred to ss1(1) and 1(4) of the Criminal Attempts Act 1981, as to which see chapter 12, and continued:]

For the appeal it was argued that section 1, when read with subsection (4) must mean, "If, with intent to commit any offence other than aiding, abetting, counselling, procuring or suborning the commission of an offence, a person does an act which is more than merely preparatory to the commission of the offence, he is guilty of attempting to commit the offence." Although the appellant's acts were more than merely preparatory to the commission of the offence of aiding and abetting, they were done with intent to aid and abet the commission of an offence and so were excluded from the operation of subsection (1) of section 1.

The learned judge ruled against the appellant's submission in these words: "I think that this means the section does not apply to an attempt to aid and abet, and I think, when one looks at it carefully and puts all the words together, that is the clear meaning of it. You cannot attempt to conspire and you cannot attempt to aid and abet, but here the evidence is, which is accepted on the face of it, that the aiding and abetting was completed. He did all that was required for the aiding and abetting. It was the offence that he was aiding and abetting that, fortunately, was not completed, so I think that the Criminal Attempts Act 1981, section 1, does apply."

Before us the arguments for the parties were expanded. For the appellant it was accepted that the Criminal Attempts Act 1981 was based upon the Criminal Attempts Bill, a draft of which was contained in the report of the Law Commission No. 102 and that the intention of the Law Commission was that, whilst it should remain an offence to aid and abet an attempt to commit a crime, it should be made clear that an attempt to aid and abet a crime was not a criminal offence. Nevertheless, on the true construction of the language used in the Act, because Parliament had chosen to exclude attempts to aid and abet by the particular form of language used in the Act and by reference to the intention of the offender, aiding and abetting an attempt was in fact excluded from the operation of section 1(1) of the Act. Finally, it was urged that a person in the position of the appellant could nevertheless be charged with conspiring to commit robbery.

For the prosecution it was argued that the appellant was not charged with attempting to aid and abet, but with aiding and abetting the attempted robbery. He was in fact an aider and abettor and only charged as a principal for procedural reasons. He had, in fact, completed all the acts necessary for the offence of aiding and abetting Peterson and Ryan in their attempt to rob Mr Boagey. Notwithstanding the language of subsection (4) of section 1 of the Criminal Attempts Act 1981, the appellant could still be charged as a principal under the provisions of the Accessories and Abettors Act 1861. The exception did not apply to acts of aiding and abetting which were completed and this was borne out by the use in subsection (4) of the words, "… which, if it were completed, would be triable …"

The Criminal Attempts Act 1981, closely follows the wording of the draft Bill contained in the Report of the Law Commission No. 102.

Whilst recourse can be had to that Report, in approaching the interpretation of the section for the background of the law as it was and for the legislative intention, it is not proper or desirable that we should use it as a direct statement of what the proposed Bill was to mean or to take the meaning of the section from its commentary of recommendations. We cannot, therefore, take the meaning of the section from the clear indications in part 2G, paragraph 2.123 in the commentary, or from the recommendation No. 5, 1(9), of the Law Commission Paper.

It is to be observed at the outset that if the construction contended for by the appellant is correct, then section 1 of the Act, which was intended to clarify and define the offence of attempting to commit a crime, has relieved of criminal responsibility all accessories or secondary parties in the commission of crimes which are thwarted, because attempts to commit crime at common law are abolished by section 6(2) of the Act. Thus, for example, persons who participate in an unsuccessful crime, by keeping watch for the perpetrators or driving a getaway car (as in the instant case) would be relieved of criminal liability. It can, therefore, be confidently stated that such a result was not the intention of Parliament and we would only give effect to such a construction if the words permitted of no other sensible meaning. We bear in mind, of course, that this is a penal Statute and that conduct exempted from its operation must be given a wide rather than a narrow construction where both are equally compatible with the language used.

Approaching the construction of the section in this way we begin by reminding ourselves that since section 8 of the Accessories and Abettors Act 1861 became law, any person who aided and abetted, counselled or procured the commission of an offence has been liable to be indicted, tried and punished as a principal offender. Accordingly, any person who actually takes part in the commission of an offence by aiding and abetting another to commit it, is liable in law as a principal. It has been a moot question whether in a case in which no person actually participates in the commission of an offence, an accused person can be guilty of the separate offence of attempting to aid and abet the commission of that offence.

For over 120 years those whose proximate acts are done with the intention of aiding and abetting actual participators in crime have been tried and indicted as principals rather than as secondary participants. In excepting from the application of section 1(1) the offences referred to in section 1(4), the draftsman of the section clearly treated aiding, abetting, counselling, procuring or suborning the commission of an offence as if it were a separate offence.

Therefore, returning to section 1(1), it is clear that the words "the offence," where they appear in the phrase, "he is guilty of attempting to commit the offence," must be taken to refer to the same offence as is referred to in the phrase earlier in section 1(1), "with intent to commit an offence." Thus, rephrasing section 1(1), for the purposes of this case, it would, but for the exception, read: "If, with intent to commit the offence of aiding and abetting an offence, a person does an act which is more than merely preparatory to the offence of aiding and abetting an offence he is guilty of attempting to commit the offence of aiding and abetting an offence."

However, so to provide would have created a new offence. Accordingly, to avoid this situation, section 1(4) provided, inter alia, that the provisions of section 1 should not apply to aiding, abetting, counselling, procuring or suborning the commission of an offence. Thus, the Act prevented the creation of the separate offence of attempting to aid and abet the commission of a crime. It did not remove from criminal responsibility the offence of aiding and abetting an attempt to commit a crime.

We therefore conclude that the submission made on behalf of the appellant was rightly rejected by the learned judge and this appeal is, accordingly, dismissed.'

R v Howe [1987] AC 417

[For the facts see chapter 13. The following extracts from the speeches in the House of Lords concern the legality of charging an accomplice with a greater offence than that charged against the principal.

The second of the three questions certified for the House of Lords was:

'Can one who incites or procures by duress another to kill or to be a party to a killing be convicted of murder if that other is acquitted by reason of duress?']

Lord Mackay:

'I turn now to the second certified question. In the view that I take on question one the second does not properly arise. However, I am of opinion that the Court of Appeal reached the correct conclusion upon it as a matter of principle.

Giving the judgment of the Court of Appeal Lord Lane CJ said [1986] QB 626, 641-642:

"The judge based himself on a decision of this court in *R v Richards* [1974] QB 776. The facts in that case were that Mrs Richards paid two men to inflict injuries on her husband which she intended should 'put him in hospital for a month.' The two men wounded the husband but not seriously. They were acquitted of wounding with intent but convicted of unlawful wounding. Mrs Richards herself was convicted of wounding with intent, the jury plainly, and not surprisingly, believing that she had the necessary intent, though the two men had not. She appealed against her conviction on the ground that she could not properly be convicted as accessory before the fact to a crime more serious than that committed by the principals in the first degree. The appeal was allowed and the conviction for unlawful wounding was substituted. The court followed a passage from *Hawkins' Pleas of the Crown*, vol. 2. c. 29, para. 15: 'I take it to be an uncontroverted rule that [the offence of the accessory can never rise higher than that of the principal]; it seeming incongruous and absurd that he who is punished only as a partaker of the guilt of another, should be adjudged guilty of a higher crime than the other.'

James LJ delivering the judgment in *R v Richards* [1974] QB 776 said, at p780: 'If there is only one offence committed, and that is the offence of unlawful wounding, then the person who has requested that offence to be committed, or advised that that offence be committed, cannot be guilty of a graver offence than that in fact which was committed.' The decision in *R v Richards* has been the subject of some criticism - see for example *Smith & Hogan, Criminal Law*, 5th ed (1983), p140. Counsel before us posed the situation where A hands a gun to D informing him that it is loaded with blank ammunition only and telling him to go and scare X by discharging it. The ammunition is in fact live, as A knows, and X is killed. D is convicted only of manslaughter, as he might be on those facts. It would seem absurd that A should thereby escape conviction for murder. We take the view that *R v Richards* [1974] QB 776 was incorrectly decided, but it seems to us that it cannot properly be distinguished from the instant case."

I consider that the reasoning of Lord Lane CJ is entirely correct and I would affirm his view that where a person has been killed and that result is the result intended by another participant, the mere fact that the actual killer may be convicted only of the reduced charge of manslaughter for some reason special to himself does not, in my opinion in any way, result in a compulsory reduction for the other participant.'

R v Hyde [1990] 3 WLR 1115 Court of Appeal (Criminal Division) Lord Lane CJ, Rose and Tucker JJ

Murder - joint enterprise - correct direction on mens rea of accomplices

Facts

(As stated by Lord Lane CJ)

'The incident resulting in the death of Gallagher took place outside the Merlin public house, Andover, at about 10.25 pm on 3 June 1988. There was no dispute that Gallagher sustained a violent blow to the forehead, consistent with a heavy kick from a shod foot, which crushed the front of his skull. He died

73 days later, having never regained consciousness. The prosecution case was that the three appellants carried out a joint attack on the victim and were all equally responsible for his death, even though it was not possible to say who had actually struck the fatal blow or blows; furthermore, that their intention had been to cause serious injury; or that each knew that such was the intention of the others when he took part. By 10.00 pm that evening all three, who were regular customers at the Merlin public house, had probably had too much to drink. Sussex and Collins were both overheard making unspecific threatening remarks. When Gallagher left he was closely followed by Hyde and Sussex, and then Collins. Other customers, in the belief that serious trouble was about to break out, gathered on the balcony to watch events unfold. Gallagher was accompanied by a man called Burkwood, who related how Hyde had said to Gallagher, "Hey, feller, you've got a problem." When Gallagher asked "Why?" he was felled by a blow.

Collins told Burkwood, "Get out if you know what's good for you." Burkwood was then knocked against a car, and when he recovered his breath he saw all three appellants round Gallagher (who was already on the ground) kicking him. Other witnesses saw Hyde kicking Gallagher's legs from under him; Sussex punching Gallagher's head; Hyde kicking him between the legs … and Collins running back for five yards as they left and kicking Gallagher on the head … .

Each of the three men was questioned by the police. Hyde agreed that he had hit Gallagher, asserting that no one else was involved. He said that he had had a bad day and Gallagher kept picking on him in the public house. He was asked if Gallagher had remained conscious, to which he replied, "Don't think so, not the way I hit him." He was then asked how he had hit him, and replied "With my fist on his face, square on his face with all my bloody weight behind it." Sussex said he had been drunk and had punched Gallagher a few times. Collins said that there was a fight between Hyde and Gallagher with Sussex present. He, Collins, did not hit Gallagher and accompanied the other two after the incident back to the public house.

All three gave evidence before the jury denying that there was any joint enterprise or any intent to do serious harm to Gallagher. Hyde and Sussex said each had acted on his own with no intention beyond a simple assault. Collins, according to them, was responsible for the fatal blow. His actions and intention were nothing to do with them, nor did they foresee what he might intend to do. Collins for his part maintained that there was no joint attack or, if there was, it involved only Hyde and Sussex. The jury, it was submitted, could not be sure whose act caused the death, and that therefore no one should be convicted as the killer.

As to joint enterprise, the trial judge had directed the jury in the followng terms:

> "As I say, ordinarily speaking, if he does something which is beyond the scope of the agreement, that is as you might say the end of the agreement. But, what if the others anticipated that he might do some such thing – and here we have to apply common sense. Fights do get out of hand and escalate. A man who starts by punching may get excited and decide to kick. If there was a tacit agreement to punch and kick, a man who is kicking may decide to give a kick like that which was allegedly given by Collins and which has been described as a place-kick or a penalty kick, a description which if the basic facts are right is not a bad description of the kick. If either of the other two, and you have to consider the case of each of them separately, foresaw and contemplated a real possibility that one of his fellows might in the excitement of the moment go beyond the actual plan and intend to do and do grievous bodily harm, then you have to consider whether that man, the one who had the foresight, did not in truth intend that result himself."

Having explained to the jury that they should distinguish between intention and foresight, the trial judge concluded:

"We may summarise it shortly by saying that if all three intended to do grievous bodily harm, then that is that, they are all guilty of murder. If they did not, but one of them decided to do it, then if either of the others can be shown to have had the same intention, inasmuch as he foresaw the real possibility that

that might be the result of the fight which he was putting in train, then he too shares in the responsibility as in commonsense he must."

The defendants were each convicted of murder, and appealed on the grounds that:

1) The judge, in the circumstances of the case, erred in directing the jury upon foreseeability, such a direction being unnecessary and confusing.

2) Alternatively, the judge erred in directing the jury that the defendant's foresight of the state of mind of another defendant was a relevant consideration in determining whether the defendant having that foresight had the intention to do grievous bodily harm.

3) Alternatively, the judge's direction on foreseeability did not sufficiently distinguish between foreseeability and intention and/or did not sufficiently underline the necessity for the prosecution to prove the specific intent required for the offence of murder.'

Held

The appeals would be dismissed. The mental element of an accomplice to murder was established by proof that he foresaw death or serious harm as a consequence that might result from the action of the principal offender.

Lord Lane CJ:

'The judgment of this court in *R* v *Slack* [1989] QB 775 was not delivered until some four months after the conclusion of the hearing of the instant case. Consequently the judge here did not have before him the distinction which we endeavoured to draw in *Slack's* case between the mental element required to be proved vis a vis the secondary party (hereinafter called "B") and that required in the case of the principal party, the actual killer (hereinafter called "A"). In the passages we have cited from the summing up of which complaint is made, the judge was endeavouring to apply the principles which were, prior to *Slack's* case, thought to apply to cases of joint enterprise. The question is whether the directions in the present case were sufficient to comply with the law as it now stands.

There are, broadly speaking, two main types of joint enterprise cases where death results to the victim. The first is where the primary object of the participants is to do some kind of physical injury to the victim. The second is where the primary object is not to cause physical injury to any victim but, for example, to commit burglary. The victim is assaulted and killed as a possibly unwelcome incident of the burglary. The latter type of case may pose more complicated questions than the former, but the principle in each is the same. A must be proved to have intended to kill or to do serious bodily harm at the time he killed as was pointed out in *R* v *Slack* [1989] QB 775 at 781. B, to be guilty, must be proved to have lent himself to a criminal enterprise involving the infliction of serious harm or death, or to have had an express or tacit understanding with A that such harm or death should, if necessary, be inflicted.

We were there endeavouring, respectfully, to follow the principles enunciated by Sir Robin Cooke in *Chan Wing Sui* v *The Queen* [1985] AC 168, at 175:

"The case must depend rather on the wider principle whereby a secondary party is criminally liable for acts by the primary offender of a type which the former foresees but does not necessarily intend. That there is such a principle is not in doubt. It turns on contemplation or, putting the same idea in other words, authorisation, which may be expressed but is more usually implied. It meets the case of a crime foreseen as a possible incident of the common unlawful enterprise. The criminal culpability lies in participating in the venture with that foresight."

It has been pointed out by Professor J C Smith, in his commentary on *R* v *Wakely* [1990] Crim LR 119, 120-121, that in the judgments of *R* v *Slack* ... and also in *R* v *Wakely* ... to both of which I was a party, insufficient attention was paid by the court to the distinction between on the one hand tacit agreement by B that A should use violence, and on the other hand a realisation by B that A, the principal party, may use violence despite B's refusal to authorise or agree to its use. Indeed in *R* v *Wakely* we went so far as to say:

"The suggestion that a mere foresight of the real or definite possibility of violence being used is sufficient to constitute the mental element of murder is prima facie, academically speaking at least, not sufficient."

On reconsideration, that passage is not in accordance with the principles set out by Sir Robin Cooke which we were endeavouring to follow and was wrong, or at least misleading. If B realises (without agreeing to such conduct being used) that A may kill or intentionally inflict serious injury, but nevertheless continues to participate with A in the venture, that will amount to a sufficient mental element for B to be guilty of murder if A, with the requisite intent, kills in the course of the venture. As Professor Smith points out, B has in those circumstances lent himself to the enterprise and by so doing he has given assistance and encouragement to A in carrying out an enterprise which B realises may involve murder.'

Johnson v Youden [1950] 1 KB 544 Divisional Court (Lord Goddard CJ, Humphreys and Lynskey JJ)

Mens rea needed by accomplices to strict liability offences

Facts

The principal offender, a builder, was granted a licence by a local authority permitting him to build a house. The licence was granted subject to a condition limiting the maximum price at which it could be sold to £1,025. It was an offence of strict liability, contrary to s7(1) of the Building Materials and Housing Act 1945 to sell the house in excess of any such condition. The builder induced another to buy it from him for £1,275. The defendants in the present case were the partners in the firm of solicitors who had dealt with the sale of the house, and who had been acquitted of aiding and abetting the builder in committing an offence under the 1945 Act. The prosecution appealed.

Held

The appeal would be dismissed in respect of the two partners who had not known that the house was being sold at a price above the maximum permitted by the licence, but would be allowed in respect of the third partner who had known of the higher price that was being paid.

Lord Goddard CJ:

'In regard to the respondents, the justices found that, until 6 April 1949, none of them knew anything about the extra £250 which the builder was receiving, and that the first two respondents, Mr Henry Wallace Youden and Mr George Henry Youden, did not know about it at any time, as the builder deliberately concealed the fact and even refused to give the purchaser a receipt for that £250. The justices, therefore, were right, in our opinion, in dismissing the information against the first two respondents on the ground that they could not be guilty of aiding and abetting the commission of the offence as they did not know of the matter which constituted the offence. If they had known that the builder was receiving the extra £250 and had continued to ask the purchaser to complete, they would have committed an offence by continuing to assist the builder to offer the property for sale, contrary to the provisions of s 7 (1) of the Act of 1945, and, as ignorance of the law is no defence, they would have been guilty of the offence even if they had not realised that they were committing an offence, but a person cannot be convicted of aiding and abetting the commission of an offence if he does not know of the essential matters which would constitute the offence.

In regard to their partner, Mr Brydone, the third respondent, the facts are different. Until 6 or 7 April 1949, he was as ignorant as were his partners that the builder had insisted on receiving £250 beyond what he was entitled to charge, but on 6 April he received a letter from the purchaser's solicitor saying:

"I duly received your letter of 26 March informing me that you are ready to settle at any time and that the amount payable on completion is £925."

The sum was £925, because the controlled price was £1,025, and £100 had been paid as deposit. The letter continued:

"I think I ought to let you know the reason why I have not as yet proceeded to completion. It is that I have felt compelled to report to the town clerk what I consider to be a breach by your client of provisions of s 7 of the Building Materials and Housing Act 1945."

This letter naturally put the third respondent, who was dealing with the matter, on inquiry, and he thereupon read the relevant provisions of the Act of 1945 and also spoke to the builder who told him a story which, even if it were true, was on the face of it obviously a colourable evasion of the Act. The builder's story was that he had placed the extra £250 in a separate deposit account and that it was to be spent on payment for work as and when he (the builder) would be lawfully able to execute it in the future on the house on behalf of the purchaser.

It seems impossible to imagine that anyone could believe such a story. Who has ever heard of a purchaser, when buying a house from a builder, putting money into the builder's hands because he may want some work done thereafter? I think that the third respondent could not have read s 7 (5) of the Act as carefully as he should have done, because I cannot believe that any solicitor, or even a layman, would not understand that the bargain which the builder described was just the kind of transaction which the Act prohibits. Section 7 (5) provides:

"In determining for the purposes of this section the consideration for which a house has been sold or let, the court shall have regard to any transaction with which the sale or letting is associated ..."

If the third respondent had read and appreciated those words he would have seen at once that the extra £250 which the builder was getting was in regard to a transaction with which the sale was associated, and was, therefore, an unlawful payment. Unfortunately, however, he did not realise it, but either misread the Act or did not read it carefully, and on the following day he called on the purchaser to complete. He was, therefore, clearly aiding and abetting the builder in the offence which the builder was committing. The result is that, so far as the first two respondents are concerned, the appeal fails and must be dismissed, but, so far as the third respondent is concerned, the case must go back to the justices with an intimation that an offence has been committed, and there must be a conviction.'

R v Leahy [1985] Crim LR 99 (Leeds Crown Court) (Mr Assistant Recorder M Carr)

Transferred malice and accomplices

Facts

'Philip Horsman pleaded guilty to section 18 wounding on Andrew Gallagher and Mark Leahy pleaded not guilty to aiding and abetting, counselling and procuring the same offence. PH did not give evidence for the Crown. The facts were that PH had a fight with John Pearson. PH had lost. When he returned to the public house and met the defendant ML, the prosecution case was that ML had encouraged PH to retaliate against JP by saying: "If he'd done that to me I'd have glassed him," and "Glass him."

PH having heard these words left ML, and broke a glass on the side of the neck of AG The defence submitted that there was no case for ML to answer on the basis that the prosecution must prove as regards the intention of the aider and abettor, either the intention on the part of PH that he commit the specific offence, ie to wound AG with intent or that the doctrine of transferred malice applied, ie that PH had intended to hit JP but had missed and hit AG; or that PH had thought he was hitting JP when in fact he had struck AG What the prosecution had failed to disprove was the possibility that having been encouraged to hit JP, PH had changed his mind and decided to hit AG, in which case ML could not be convicted of the offence charged. The prosecution submitted that *Thambiah v R* [1966] AC 37 demonstrated that a person can be an aider and abettor of a crime without it being a specific crime.

Held

Allowing the submission of no case, that the only way the evidence could be interpreted was that ML was encouraging PH to hit JP Where there was specific evidence to the effect that ML encouraged PH to strike JP with a glass and the evidence is in fact PH, for some reason not fully understood, struck AG with a glass - not by mistake or accident - the offence carried out was not the offence ML sought to encourage and ML cannot be guilty of aiding and abetting. *Thambiah* distinguished, because here there was not a general contemplation of crime but evidence of a specific crime against a particular person. *Archbold*, para. 29-24 "If however, the principal deliberately committed the crime which had been counselled and procured against B, instead of A, Hale's view is that the Counsellor and Procurer would not be liable. 1 Hale 617." If the indictment had alleged incitement to wound that would have covered the present facts but it was now too late to amend.'

R v Saunders and Archer (1573) 2 Plowd. 473 (Warwick Assizes)

Transferred malice and accomplices

Facts

John Saunders wanted to kill his wife so that he could marry his mistress. Alexander Archer provided him with poison in the form of a roasted apple containing arsenic and roseacre. Saunders gave the poisoned apple to his wife, and stood by as she, finding it not to her taste, passed it on to their three year old daughter Eleanor who died as a result. Saunders was found guilty of the murder on the basis of transferred malice. Archer was found not to be a party to the murder because the principal had wilfully exceeded the common design in allowing the child to eat the apple.

Lord Dyer CJ:

'But the most difficult point in this case ... was, whether or no Archer should be adjudged accessory to the murder. For the offence which Archer committed was the aid and advice which he gave to Saunders, and that was only to kill his wife, and no other, for there was no parol communication between them concerning the daughter, and although by the consequences which followed from the giving of the poison by Saunders the principal, it so happened that the daughter was killed, yet Archer did not precisely procure her death, nor advise him to kill her, and therefore whether or not he should be accessory to this murder which happened by a thing consequential to the first act, seemed to them to be doubtful. For which reason they thought proper to advise and consider of it until the next gaol delivery, and in the meantime to consult with the justices in the term ... [It was agreed] that they ought not to give judgment against the said Alexander Archer, because they took the law to be that he could not be adjudged accessory to the said offence of murder, for that he did not assent that the daughter should be poisoned, but only that the wife should be poisoned, which assent cannot be drawn further than he gave it, for the poisoning of the daughter is a distinct thing from that to which he was privy, and therefore he shall not be adjudged accessory to it; and so they were resolved before this time.'

R v Smith [1988] Crim LR 616 Court of Appeal (Criminal Division) (Russell LJ, Leonard and Pill JJ)

Section 18 grievous bodily harm - mens rea of accomplice

Facts

'The appellant was convicted of causing grievous bodily harm with intent. The victim and his friend were attacked because the appellant and his co-defendants believed them to be rival football club supporters. The defendants attacked the victim and his friend twice. During the second attack they were kicked as they lay on the ground; the victim died after the appellant's trial. The appellant admitted to the police that he had kicked a man lying on the ground; his description of that man matched the victim. At the trial the prosecution relied upon the appellant's involvement in a joint enterprise with his co-defendants rather than upon direct evidence of physical violence by the appellant. The judge directed the jury that if two persons agree to do some harm but it was no part of the agreement to do really serious bodily harm, the second person is guilty of causing grievous bodily harm with intent even though he did not himself intend that his partner should cause the victim really serious bodily harm, if he could and did foresee that in the course of the agreed attack there was a real risk that his partner might attack one of the victims viciously with the intention of causing him really serious bodily harm. The appellant appealed against conviction on the ground that the judge's directions erred in that (1) it was left open to the jury to convict even if the co-defendant acted outside the scope of the agreement; (2) the concept of foresight was equated with the concept of intent; (3) the jury could have convicted even though there was no intent demonstrated on the part of the appellant; (4) the case was regarded as one which could be equated with the Privy Council decision in *Chan Wing-Siu and others* [1984] All ER 877.

Held

Allowing the appeal and quashing the conviction, the Court bore in mind the decisions in *Anderson* v *Morris* [1966] 50 Cr App R 216; *Moloney* [1985] 81 Cr App R 93 and *Hancock and Shankland* [1986] 82 Cr App R 264. The present case concerned a specific intent and it was incumbent upon the judge to direct in the plainest terms that the appellant could only be convicted if the jury were sure that he had the requisite intent to cause grievous bodily harm and that the foresight the judge referred to was not of itself to be regarded as an intent, though it could properly be regarded as evidence supporting the existence of the intent necessary to establish the offence. The Court agreed that the present case was not to be equated with *Chan Wing Siu and others* (supra). The Court regarded it as impossible to substitute a verdict on the lesser count of inflicting grievous bodily harm because of the judge's direction that the appellant could be convicted of that offence even though he did not personally intend that the victim should suffer any physical injury whatsoever, provided that he foresaw a real risk of the co-defendant causing some physical harm in the course of carrying out their agreement to attack the victim.'

[*Reported by Lynne Knapman, Barrister.*]

R v Wakely, R v Symonds, R v Holly [1990] Crim LR 119 Court of Appeal (Criminal Division) (Lord Lane CJ, Leonard and Rose JJ)

Murder in course of aggravated burglary - joint enterprise - foresight of the possibility of violence - adequacy of direction to jury

Facts

'W, S and H were all charged with murder and aggravated burglary. It was alleged that they went to the house of an elderly man, killed him by repeated blows to the head with a pickaxe handle and stole a small quantity of money from his meter. The prosecution case was that H had inflicted the blows and that the other two were party to the attack on the basis of joint enterprise. When interviewed H denied murder and declined to answer further questions. W first invented an alibi which he later admitted was false and then admitted burglary. S likewise admitted burglary and said that he saw H repeatedly hitting the deceased with the pickaxe handle. At trial W and S both admitted burglary but not aggravated burglary or murder, while H maintained that he took no part. At the trial W gave evidence that, while the burglary was being planned H brought along the pickaxe handle which he said he would use if anyone turned up; W and S would not agree to that, so H took away the handle and it was agreed that the burglary would proceed without it. At the scene, however, H to W's surprise produced and used the pickaxe handle. S gave evidence that H had brought along the pickaxe handle not to use on anyone but to break open the meter (for which it could not satisfactorily be used). He first denied having it in his possession but after his fingerprints were found on it said that he had taken it along to stop H from using it and left it outside; H had brought it in without S's knowledge and used it on the deceased. H in evidence continued to deny being involved at the burglary at all. The judge directed the jury inter alia that even if it had not been agreed expressly that violence would or might be used all three would be responsible for the violence if they had foreseen a real possibility of it arising if they were disturbed, and had nevertheless continued with the burglary; and that if any defendant might have genuinely dismissed from his mind the possibility of violence being used by anyone he should be acquitted of the violence which ensued. The jury convicted all three who appealed, alleging that in the light of *Slack* [1989] 3 WLR 513 the judge had misdirected the jury.

Held

Dismissing the appeals, it could be said that the judge at one point in the summing-up misdirected the jury by concentrating on foreseeability rather than tacit agreement or understanding, the test laid down in *Slack* (above). However, in the present case foreseeability that the pickaxe handle might be used as a weapon of violence was practically indistinguishable from tacit agreement that the weapon should be used for that purpose; and the jury convicted on ample evidence. Insofar as there was a misdirection, the proviso to s1 of the Criminal Appeal 1968 would be applied.'

[*Reported by Tom Rees, Barrister.*]

R v Whitefield (1984) 79 Cr App Rep 36 Court of Appeal (Criminal Division) (Dunn LJ, Bristow J, and Sir John Thompson)

Aiding and abetting - withdrawal from common enterprise

Facts

A quantity of goods were taken from a flat in south London when the occupier was away. Following the arrest and charging of two persons in connection with this offence (Anthony Gallagher and Helen Coffey), the police interviewed the appellant. In the course of the interview the appellant denied taking any part in the burglary, but admitted telling Gallagher that the flat (which was next door to the appellant's) would be empty at the time the offence was committed. He also admitted that he had agreed to carry out the burglary with Gallagher, but that he had later changed his mind. The appellant was present in his flat the night the burglary was committed. He heard the flat being broken into but did nothing to prevent the offence. At his trial for burglary, the appellant unsuccessfully submitted that there was no case to answer as he had withdrawn from the common enterprise to burgle the adjoining flat.

He appealed against his conviction on the ground that the issue of withdrawal should have been left to the jury.

Held

The appeal would be allowed.

Dunn LJ:

'In this Court two grounds of appeal were advanced on his behalf. (1) The judge was wrong to reject the submission of no case because the only evidence before the jury was contained in the record of the interview, and the only proper inference from that record was that the appellant had withdrawn from participation in the burglary by informing Gallagher that he did not wish to take part in it, and by refusing to allow him access to his flat and balcony for the purpose of effecting entry to his neighbour's flat. Alternatively (2) it should have been left to the jury as a matter of fact and degree whether, on a proper interpretation of the police evidence of the interview, the appellant had withdrawn from the burglary, and that by his ruling the judge had effectively indicated that he would withdraw that issue from the jury, and direct them as a matter of law that the record of the police interview did not disclose sufficient evidence of withdrawal to afford a defence to the count of burglary. So far as the first ground of appeal is concerned, the record of the interview contained certain incriminating statements viz that the appellant had set up the burglary with Gallagher, had offered him the facility of his flat to effect entry, and had agreed on a division of the proceeds; and it also contained a certain self-serving statement ... that the appellant had eventually withdrawn from the joint venture. It is now established since *Duncan* (1981) 73 Cr App R 359, that both parts of such a "mixed" statement are evidence of the facts they state, though they are not to be regarded as having equal weight. In that situation questions of weight are usually a matter for the jury, although there may be cases in which the judge is able to decide that the weight to be given to the exculpatory part so far exceeds the weight to be given to the incriminatory part, that he is justified in withdrawing the case from the jury. But in this case we cannot say that the judge was wrong as a matter of discretion in rejecting the submission of no case, provided that he left the question of withdrawal or not properly to the jury, with a suitable direction on the lines suggested by this Court in *Duncan* (supra). If the defendant did not give evidence this is a matter to which the judge would have been entitled to refer, with a suitable warning, in directing the jury as to the weight to be given to the self-exculpatory part of the statement. The question on the second and alternative ground of appeal however is whether the judge did properly leave the issue of withdrawal to the jury. Mr Reekers submitted that the judge's ruling, read in the context of the previous discussion with counsel, amounted to no more than his reasons for rejecting the submission of no case, though he recognised that the language used by the judge made that a difficult submission for him to sustain. In our judgment, the judge's ruling, read as a whole, amounted to a forecast of the way in which he proposed to direct the jury as to the law relating to withdrawal. Although it may be that the judge did not intend that result, it seems to us to be the only fair inference to be drawn from the way in which he expressed himself, and certainly it was so taken by counsel for the appellant and resulted in the change of plea. The law upon withdrawal is stated in *Becerra and Cooper* (1976) 62 Cr App R 212 and *Grundy* [1977] Crim LR 543. So far as material to the facts of this case, the law may be shortly stated as follows. If a person has counselled another to commit a crime, he may escape liability by withdrawal before the crime is committed, but it is not sufficient that he should merely repent or change his mind. If his participation is confined to advice or encouragement, he must at least communicate his change of mind to the other, and the communication must be such as will serve "unequivocal notice upon the other party to the common unlawful cause that if he proceeds upon it he does so without the aid and assistance of those who withdraw." (See the Canadian case of *Whitehouse* [1941] 1 WWR 112, 116, per Sloane JA, approved in *Becerra and Cooper* (supra) and *Grundy* (supra). In this case there was, if the jury accepted it, evidence in the answers given by the appellant to the police that he had served unequivocal notice on Gallagher that if he proceeded with the burglary he would do so without the aid or assistance of the appellant. In his ruling the judge stated that such notice was not enough, and that in failing to communicate with the police or take any other steps to prevent the burglary he remained "liable in law for what happened, for everything that was done that night."

In the judgment of this court, in making that statement the judge fell into an error of law. The direct result of it was that the appellant changed his plea to one of guilty. A change of plea founded upon an error of law by the judge cannot stand, and the conviction must be quashed....'

10 INCHOATE OFFENCES I

R v Anderson [1986] AC 27 (House of Lords) (Lords Scarman, Diplock, Keith, Bridge, and Brightman)

Mens rea of statutory conspiracy

Facts

The defendant, whilst sharing a prison cell with another man named Andaloussi, agreed that he would help effect Andaloussi's escape from prison once he himself was released, and that he would received £20,000 in return for his efforts. The defendant was released from prison shortly afterwards and received £2,000 from Andaloussi's brothers as an initial payment for his help. The defendant was then injured in a road accident and took no further part in executing the planned escape. When charged with conspiring to effect the release of Andaloussi from prison, the defendant contended that he had lacked the mens rea for conspiracy because, although he had intended to acquire some diamond cutting wire that could be used to cut through prison bars, he had never intended the escape plan to be carried into effect and had not believed that it could actually succeed. The trial judge ruled that, as a matter of law, there was still evidence that the defendant had mens rea, as a result of which he changed his plea to one of guilty, and appealed unsuccessfully to the Court of Appeal. The defendant renewed his appeal before the House of Lords.

Held

The appeal would be dismissed.

Lord Bridge:

[His Lordship considered s1(1)(A) of the Criminal Law Act 1977 and continued:]

'The Act of 1977, subject to exceptions not presently material, abolished the offence of conspiracy at common law. It follows that the elements of the new statutory offence of conspiracy must be ascertained purely by interpretation of the language of section 1(1) of the Act of 1977. For purposes of analysis it is perhaps convenient to isolate the three clauses each of which must be taken as indicating an essential ingredient of the offence as follows: (1) "if a person agrees with any other person or persons that a course of conduct shall be pursued" (2) "which will necessarily amount to or involve the commission of any offence or offences by one or more of the parties to the agreement" (3) "if the agreement is carried out in accordance with their intentions."

Clause (1) presents, as it seems to me, no difficulty. It means exactly what it says and what it says is crystal clear. To be convicted, the party charged must have agreed with one or more others that "a course of conduct shall be pursued." What is important is to resist the temptation to introduce into this simple concept ideas derived from the civil law of contract. Any number of persons may agree that a course of conduct shall be pursued without undertaking any contractual liability. The agreed course of conduct may be a simple or an elaborate one and may involve the participation of two or any larger number of persons who may have agreed to play a variety of roles in the course of conduct agreed.

Again, clause (2) could hardly use simpler language. Here what is important to note is that it is not necessary that more than one of the participants in the agreed course of conduct shall commit a substantive offence. It is, of course, necessary that any party to the agreement shall have assented to play his part in the agreed course of conduct, however innocent in itself, knowing that the part to be played by one or more of the others will amount to or involve the commission of an offence.

It is only clause (3) which presents any possible ambiguity. The heart of the submission for the appellant is that in order to be convicted of conspiracy to commit a given offence the language of clause (3) requires that the party charged should not only have agreed that a course of conduct shall be pursued which will necessarily amount to or involve the commission of that offence by himself or one or more other parties to the agreement, but must also be proved himself to have intended that that offence should be committed. Thus, it is submitted here that the appellant's case that he never intended that Andaloussi should be enabled to escape from prison raised an issue to be left to the jury, who should have been directed to convict him only if satisfied that he did so intend. I do not find it altogether easy to understand why the draftsman of this provision chose to use the phrase "in accordance with their intentions." But I suspect the answer may be that this seemed a desirable alternative to the phrase "in accordance with its terms" or any similar expression, because it is a matter of common experience in the criminal courts that the "terms" of a criminal conspiracy are hardly ever susceptible of proof. The evidence from which a jury may infer a criminal conspiracy is almost invariably to be found in the conduct of the parties. This was so at common law and remains so under the statute. If the evidence in a given case justifies the inference of an agreement that a course of conduct should be pursued, it is a not inappropriate formulation of the test of the criminality of the inferred agreement to ask whether the further inference can be drawn that a crime would necessarily have been committed if the agreed course of conduct had been pursued in accordance with the several intentions of the parties. Whether that is an accurate analysis or not, I am clearly driven by consideration of the diversity of roles which parties may agree to play in criminal conspiracies to reject any construction of the statutory language which would require the prosecution to prove an intention on the part of each conspirator that the criminal offence or offences which will necessarily be committed by one or more of the conspirators if the agreed course of conduct is fully carried out should in fact be committed. A simple example will illustrate the absurdity to which this construction would lead. The proprietor of a car hire firm agrees for a substantial payment to make available a hire car to a gang for use in a robbery and to make false entries in his books relating to the hiring to which he can point if the number of the car is traced back to him in connection with the robbery. Being fully aware of the circumstances of the robbery in which the car is proposed to be used he is plainly a party to the conspiracy to rob. Making his car available for use in the robbery is as much a part of the relevant agreed course of conduct as the robbery itself. Yet, once he has been paid, it will be a matter of complete indifference to him whether the robbery is in fact committed or not. In these days of highly organised crime the most serious statutory conspiracies will frequently involve an elaborate and complex agreed course of conduct in which many will consent to play necessary but subordinate roles, not involving them in any direct participation in the commission of the offence or offences at the centre of the conspiracy. Parliament cannot have intended that such parties should escape conviction of conspiracy on the basis that it cannot be proved against them that they intended that the relevant offence or offences should be committed.

There remains the important question whether a person who has agreed that a course of conduct will be pursued which, if pursued as agreed, will necessarily amount to or involve the commission of an offence is guilty of statutory conspiracy irrespective of his intention, and, if not, what is the mens rea of the offence. I have no hesitation in answering the first part of the question in the negative. There may be many situations in which perfectly respectable citizens, more particularly those concerned with law enforcement, may enter into agreements that a course of conduct shall be pursued which will involve commission of a crime without the least intention of playing any part in furtherance of the ostensibly agreed criminal objective, but rather with the purpose of exposing and frustrating the criminal purpose of the other parties to the agreement. To say this is in no way to encourage schemes by which police act, directly or through the agency of informers, as agents provocateurs for the purpose of entrapment. That is conduct of which the courts have always strongly disapproved. But it may sometimes happen, as most of us with experience in criminal trials well know, that a criminal enterprise is well advanced in the course of preparation when it comes to the notice either of the police or of some honest citizen in such circumstances that the only prospect of exposing and frustrating the criminals is that some innocent person should play the part of an intending collaborator in the course of criminal conduct proposed to be pursued. The mens rea implicit in the offence of statutory conspiracy must clearly be such as to recognise the innocence of such a person, notwithstanding that he will, in literal terms, be obliged to agree that a course of conduct be pursued involving the commission of an offence.

I have said already, but I repeat to emphasise its importance, that an essential ingredient in the crime of conspiring to commit a specific offence or offences under section 1(1) of the Act of 1977 is that the accused should agree that a course of conduct be pursued which he knows must involve the commission by one or more of the parties to the agreement of that offence or those offences. But, beyond the mere fact of agreement, the necessary mens rea of the crime is, in my opinion, established if, and only if, it is shown that the accused, when he entered into the agreement, intended to play some part in the agreed course of conduct in furtherance of the criminal purpose which the agreed course of conduct was intended to achieve. Nothing less will suffice; nothing more is required.

Applying this test to the facts which, for the purposes of the appeal, we must assume, the appellant, in agreeing that a course of conduct be pursued that would, if successful, necessarily involve the offence of effecting Andaloussi's escape from lawful custody, clearly intended, by providing diamond wire to be smuggled into the prison, to play a part in the agreed course of conduct in furtherance of that criminal objective. Neither the fact that he intended to play no further part in attempting to effect the escape, nor that he believed the escape to be impossible, would, if the jury had supposed they might be true, have afforded him any defence.'

NB: See *R* v *Siracusa* below.

R v Curr [1968] 2 QB 944 (Court of Appeal (Criminal Division)) (Lord Parker CJ, Salmon LJ and Fenton Atkinson J)

Actus reus of incitement

Facts

The defendant ran a loan business whereby he would lend money to women with children in return for their handing over their signed Family Allowance books. The defendant would then use other women to cash the Family Allowance vouchers. He was charged with inciting an offence under s9(b) of the Family Allowance Act 1945, which made it an offence for any person to receive any sum by way of Family Allowance knowing it was not properly payable. The defendant appealed.

Held

The appeal would be allowed and conviction quashed.

Fenton Atkinson J:

'Count 3 was of soliciting the commission of a summary offence contrary to section 9 (*b*) of the Act of 1945, the particulars being that on a day unknown the defendant unlawfully "solicited a woman unknown to obtain on his behalf from HM's Postmaster-General the sum of £2 18s as on account of an allowance knowing that it was not properly receivable by her." Mr Kershaw [counsel for the defendant] took a preliminary point on that count that incitement to commit a summary offence is not in fact an idictable offence, and he referred to some old authorities which might lend some countenance to that view. But it appears to this court that Parliament in the Magistrates' Courts Act 1952, in paragraph 20 of Schedule 1, has in fact recognised incitement of this kind as an indictable offence, and it is not necessary, therefore, to go further into that matter, all the more because Mr Kershaw's main point is this, that the offence the commission of which the defendant is said to have solicited is not an absolute statutory offence, but it is one requiring knowledge on the part of the female agent that she is doing something unlawful in receiving the allowance.

Section 9 is headed "Penalty for obtaining or receiving payment wrongfully," and provides:

"If any person - ... (b) obtains or receives any such sum as on account of an allowance, either as in that person's own right or as on behalf of another, knowing that it was not properly payable, or not properly receivable by him or her; that person shall be liable on summary conviction to imprisonment for a term not exceeding three months or to a fine not exceeding fifty pounds or to both such imprisonment and such fine."

Mr Kershaw's argument was that if the woman agent in fact has no guilty knowledge, knowing perhaps nothing of the assignment, or supposing that the defendant was merely collecting for the use and benefit of the woman concerned, then she would be an innocent agent, and by using her services in that way the defendant would be committing the summary offence himself, but would not be inciting her to receive money knowing that it was not receivable by her. He contends that it was essential to prove to support this charge, that the woman agent in question in this transaction affecting a Mrs Currie knew that the allowances were not properly receivable by her. Mr Hugill's [counsel for the Crown] answer to that submission was that the woman agent must be presumed to know the law, and if she knew the law, she must have known, he contends, that the allowance was not receivable by her. He refers to section 4 (2) of the Act of 1945, to which reference has already been made, and to the Family Allowances (Making of Claims and Payments) Regulations 1946, reg. 8, which provides:

"Sums on account of an allowance shall become receivable at the times hereinafter prescribed and shall be paid either - (1) by means of allowance orders payable in respect of every week to a person by whom such sums are receivable" that is to say, the wife or husband under section 4 (2) of the Act of 1945 - "or (2) in such other special manner as the Minister may in any particular case and for any particular period determine."

Provision is made also by regulation 12 that, where any person entitled to an allowance becomes unable to act for the time being, the minister may appoint some person to act on their behalf. Provision is made by administrative direction in the case of sickness by the book holder, and there is an instruction No. 12 on a coloured page at the end of the book:

"Payment during illness: If you are ill for a short time and cannot go to the Post Office to draw the money and, where there is a second payee, he also cannot go, someone else may cash the orders for you if you fill up and sign" a certain form at the back of the voucher.

The argument is that in no other circumstances may an agent lawfully collect for the use and benefit of the book holder, and Mr Hugill was ready to contend, for example, that if a mother with, say, eight children to look after at home asks a neighbour to go and collect her allowance for her, and the neighbour does so, the neighbour would be committing an offence under section 9 (b) of the Act of 1945, and the mother would be guilty of the offence of soliciting. We are by no means satisfied that any agent who collects with the full authority of the book holder and for her use and benefit would commit an offence under that subsection. There appears to be no express prohibition, certainly we were referred to no express prohibition, in the Family Allowances Act, 1945, or any orders making such collection unlawful. On the evidence, the Post Office in practice appear to allow this to be done in certain cases; in our view there can be situations, or may be situations, in which an agent, however well she may know the statute and regulations, could properly suppose that her action in receiving an allowance of this kind was lawful.

In our view the prosecution argument here gives no effect to the word "knowing" in section 9 (b), and in our view the defendant could only be guilty on count 3 if the woman solicited, that is, the woman agent sent to collect the allowance, knew that the action she was asked to carry out amounted to an offence. As has already been said, the defendant himself clearly knew that his conduct in the matter was illegal and contrary to section 9 (b), but it was essential in our view for the jury to consider the knowledge, if any, of the woman agent. The assistant recorder dealt with this count by referring to soliciting as follows: "Solicited means encouraged or incited another person to go and draw that money which should have been paid, you may think, to Mrs Currie." He later dealt with ignorance of the law being no excuse. He went on to deal with statutory offences, section 4 of the Family Allowances Act, 1945, telling the jury in effect that, apart from the case of sickness, nobody else could legally receive these allowances, and then went on to consider the position of the defendant, asking the rhetorical question whether he could be heard to say with his knowledge of this matter and his trafficking in these books that it was not known to be wrong to employ an agent to go and collect the family allowances. But the assistant recorder never followed that with the question of the knowledge of the women agents, and in the whole of the summing-up dealing with this matter he proceeded on the assumption that either guilty knowledge in the woman agent was irrelevant, or, alternatively, that any woman agent must be taken to have known that she was committing an offence under section 9 (*b*).

If the matter had been left on a proper direction for the jury's consideration, they might well have thought that the women agents, other than Mrs Nicholson, whom they acquitted, must have known very well that they were doing something wrong; some of them were apparently collecting as many as 10 of these weekly payments. But the matter was never left to them for their consideration, and here again, so it seems to this court, there was a vital matter where the defence was not left to the jury at all and there was no sufficient direction; it would be quite impossible to say that on a proper direction the jury must have convicted on this count.'

DPP v Nock [1978] AC 979 (House of Lords) (Lords Diplock, Edmund-Davies, Russell, Keith, and Scarman)

Impossibility as a defence to common law conspiracy

Facts

The defendants were convicted of conspiring to produce cocaine, contrary to s4(2) of the Misuse of Drugs Act 1971. Unknown to the defendants, the chemicals they had agreed to use would not have produced cocaine, and they appealed to the Court of Appeal on the ground that they should have been permitted the defence of impossibility. The appeal was dismissed, on the ground that the conspiracy was committed as soon as the agreement was made, regardless of whether it was capable of execution. The defendants renewed their appeal before the House of Lords.

Held

The appeal would be allowed.

Lord Scarman:

'Upon these facts the appellants submit that the evidence reveals no "conspiracy at large," by which they mean an agreement in general terms to produce cocaine if and when they could find a suitable raw material, but only the limited agreement, to which I have referred. Counsel for the appellants concedes that, if two or more persons decide to go into business as cocaine producers, or, to take another example, as assassins for hire (eg "Murder Incorporated"), the mere fact that in the course of performing their agreement they attempt to produce cocaine from a raw material which could not possibly yield it or (in the second example), stab a corpse, believing it to be the body of a living man, would not avail them as a defence: for the performance of their general agreement would not be rendered impossible by such transient frustrations. But performance of the limited agreement proved in this case could not in any circumstances have involved the commission of the offence created by the statute.

The answer sought to be made by the Crown (and accepted by the Court of Appeal) is that the offence of conspiracy is committed when an agreement to commit, or to try to commit, a crime is reached, whether or not anything is, or can be, done to perform it. It is wrong, upon their view, to treat conspiracy as a "preliminary" or "inchoate" crime: for its criminality depends in no way upon its being a step towards the commission of the substantive offence (or, at common law, the unlawful

CRIMINAL LAW

act). Upon this view of the law the scope of agreement is irrelevant: all that is needed to constitute the crime is the intention to commit the substantive offence and the agreement to try to do so.

If the Court of Appeal is right, *R v Smith* [1975] AC 476 can have no application in cases of conspiracy. But neither history nor principle supports this view of the law. In *Board of Trade* v *Owen* [1957] AC 602, 623-625 Lord Tucker, quoting with approval some observations from R S Wright J's little classic, *The Law of Criminal Conspiracies and Agreements* (1873) and some passages from Sir William Holdsworth's (somewhat larger) work, *The History of English Law*, accepted that the historical basis of the crime of conspiring to commit a crime (the case with which we are now concerned) was that it developed as an "auxiliary" (R S Wright's word) to the law which creates the crime agreed to be committed. Lord Tucker accepted Holdsworth's comment (at p625) that "It was inevitable therefore, as Stephen has said, that conspiracy should come to be regarded as a form of attempt to commit a wrong." Lord Tucker concluded his survey with these words at p626:

"Accepting the above as the historical basis of the crime of conspiracy, it seems to me that the whole object of making such agreements punishable is to prevent the commission of the substantive offence before it has even reached the stage of an attempt, ... "

Lord Tucker, in whose opinion the other noble and learned Lords sitting with him concurred, by stressing the "auxiliary" nature of the crime of conspiracy and by explaining its justification as being to prevent the commission of substantive offences, has placed the crime firmly in the same class and category as attempts to commit a crime. Both are criminal because they are steps towards the commission of a substantive offence. The distinction between the two is that, whereas a "proximate" act is that which constitutes the crime of attempt, agreement is the necessary ingredient in conspiracy. The importance of the distinction is that agreement may, and usually will, occur well before the first step which can be said to be an attempt. The law of conspiracy thus makes possible an earlier intervention by the law to prevent the commission of the substantive offence. But the distinction has no relevance in determining whether the impossibility of committing the substantive offence should be a defence. Indeed upon the view of the law authoritatively explained and accepted in *Owen's* case [1957] AC 602, logic and justice would seem to require that the question as to the effect of the impossibility of the substantive offence should be answered in the same way, whether the crime charged be conspiracy or attempt.

It is necessary, therefore, to analyse the decision in *R v Smith* [1975] AC 476 in order to determine whether it can reasonably be applied to cases of conspiracy. The Court of Appeal thought that there were difficulties. But I do not agree.

It was - somewhat half-heartedly - suggested by the Crown that the House might reconsider the decision, which we were told is causing difficulties in some respects. It is, however, a very recent decision; and a unanimous one reached after full argument which brought to the attention of this House the relevant case law and exposed the difficulties. More importantly, the decision is, in my respectful opinion, correct in principle. I would not question the decision, though its proper limits may have to be considered. The House decided the case upon two grounds, either of which would have sufficed, standing alone, to support the decision, but both of which commended themselves to the House. They may be described as the statutory (and narrower) ground and the common law principle.

The statutory ground was provided by sections 22 and 24 (3) of the Theft Act 1968. The offence being considered by the House was one of attempting to handle stolen goods. At the time of the attempted handling, the goods had been (this was conceded) restored to lawful custody. The House ruled that, in the case of a statutory offence:

"The only possible attempt would be to do what Parliament has forbidden. But Parliament has not forbidden that which the accused did, ie, handling goods which have ceased to be stolen goods ... Here the mens rea was proved but there was no actus reus so the case is not within the scope of the section," per Lord Reid at p498c.

With all respect to the Court of Appeal, there is no difficulty in applying this line of reasoning to a case in which the allegation is not an attempt but a conspiracy to commit a statutory offence. First, there is no logical difficulty in applying a rule that an agreement is a conspiracy to commit a statutory offence only if it is an agreement to do that which Parliament has forbidden. It is no more than the application of the principle that an actus reus as well as mens rea must be established. And in the present case there was no actus reus, because there was no agreement upon a course of conduct forbidden by the statute. Secondly, the application of such a rule is consistent with principle. Unless the law requires the actus reus as well as mens rea to be proved, men, whether they be accused of conspiracy or attempt, will be punished for their guilty intentions alone. I conclude the consideration of this ground of decision with a further quotation from Lord Reid's speech, at p500: "But such a radical change in the principles of our law should not be introduced in this way even if it were desirable."

The second ground of decision - the common law principle - can be summarised in words which commended themselves to all the noble and learned Lords concerned with the case. In *R v Percy Dalton (London) Ltd* Birkett J, giving the judgment of the Court of Criminal Appeal said (1949) 33 Cr App R 102, 110:

"Steps on the way to the commission of what would be a crime, if the acts were completed, may amount to attempts to commit that crime, to which, unless interrupted, they would have led; but steps on the way to the doing of something, which is thereafter done, and which is no crime, cannot be regarded as attempts to commit a crime."

In his speech Lord Hailsham of St Marylebone LC added the rider (a logical one) to the effect "that equally steps on the way to do something which is thereafter *not* completed, but which if done would not constitute a crime, cannot be indicted as attempts to commit that crime," [1975] AC 476, 496C. As in the case of the statutory ground, there is no logical difficulty in the way of applying this principle to the law relating to conspiracy provided it is recognised that conspiracy is a "preliminary" or "auxiliary" crime. And again, as with the statutory ground, common sense and justice combine to require of the law that no man should be punished criminally for the intention with which he enters an agreement unless it can also be shown that what he has agreed to do is unlawful.

The Crown's argument, as developed before your Lordships, rests, in my judgment, upon a misconception of the nature of the agreement proved. This is a case not of an agreement to commit a crime capable of being committed in the way agreed upon, but frustrated by a supervening event making its completion impossible, which was the Crown's submission, but of an agreement upon a course of conduct which could not in any circumstances result in the statutory offence alleged, ie the offence of producing the controlled drug, cocaine.

I conclude therefore that the two parallel lines of reasoning upon which this House decided *R v Smith* [1975] AC 476 apply equally to criminal conspiracy as they do to attempted crime. We were referred to a recent case in the Court of Appeal, *R v Green (Harry)* [1976] QB 985, in which the contrary view was expressed, but not developed at any length. The court in that case, as also the Court of Appeal in this case, attached importance to some observations of Lord Hailsham of St Marylebone LC in *R v Smith* [1975] AC 476, where the indictment undoubtedly included, as the second count, a charge of conspiracy with persons unknown to handle stolen goods. The Lord Chancellor (p489F) remarked that he was unable to understand why the prosecution did not proceed with this charge. He reverted to the point at p497D, and there is an echo of it in Viscount Dilhorne's speech at p503E. In *Green's* case [1976] QB 985, 993 Ormrod LJ treated these remarks as an indication that *R v Smith* [1975] AC 476 is not applicable in cases of conspiracy. The Court of Appeal in the instant case took the same view. But I do not think that either the Lord Chancellor or Viscount Dilhorne was saying anything of the sort. The conspiracy charged in the second count must have ante-dated the police seizure of the van and the return of the goods to lawful custody. Smith must have agreed to help in the disposal of the goods at a time when they were stolen goods and the agreement could be performed. It was an agreement to commit an offence which, but for the police interruption, would have been committed. There is nothing in *R* v *Smith* which would prevent such an agreement in such circumstances from being treated as a criminal conspiracy.

Our attention was also drawn to two cases, upon which it may be helpful to comment very briefly. In *R* v *McDonough* (1962) 47 Cr App R 37 the Court of Criminal Appeal held that an incitement to receive stolen goods was complete on the making of the incitement even though there were no stolen goods - perhaps even, no goods at all. In *Haggard* v *Mason* [1976] 1 WLR 187 the Divisional Court held that the offence of offering to supply a controlled drug was committed, even though the drug in fact supplied was not a controlled drug. Neither of these cases infringes the principle of *R* v *Smith*: for in each, as Lord Widgery CJ pointed out in *Haggard* v *Mason* (p189), the offence was complete. In *McDonough*, 47 Cr App R 37 the actus reus was the making of the incitement and in *Haggard's* case it was the making of the offer.

For these reasons I would allow the appeal.'

R v Evans [1986] Crim LR 470 (Court of Appeal (Criminal Division)) (Lord Lane CJ, Mann J, Sir Roger Ormrod)

Inciting incitement

Facts

'The appellant was charged, inter alia, with incitement to solicit to murder, the particulars being that she unlawfully incited B to solicit, encourage, persuade, endeavour to persuade and propose to a person or persons unknown, to murder E. The appellant had visited B, a clairvoyant and practitioner in the art of tarot cards. B also had a local reputation as a witch. The appellant told B her husband (E) had put a black magic curse on her. She said to B "In your business I am sure you can see someone who can put a contract out on him ... I want him dead." The appellant offered B £1,000 and gave a description of her husband and his habits and movements. B said she would contact someone but instead went to the police. Later B gave the appellant the telephone number of another astrologer. The appellant telephoned him and they agreed to meet. At that meeting two police officers turned up instead pretending to be "hit men." The appellant again gave details and said they could make it appear an accident. The appellant denied the accounts given by B and the officers. She was convicted of incitement to solicit to murder and of soliciting to murder. She appealed against the conviction for incitement on the ground that the Criminal Law Act 1977, s5(7) had abolished incitement to conspire and, it was submitted, to incite to solicit murder was in the circumstances the same as to incite to conspire to commit murder. The offence was an attempt to avoid the provisions of section 5(7) and an offence not known to the law.

Held

Dismissing the appeal, that the validity of that argument depended on whether inciting X to solicit murder was necessarily the same as inciting X to conspire with someone to murder. Was there any distinction between inciting to murder and conspiracy to commit murder? Prima facie there was a distinction between incitement and conspiracy. A person could incite another by threats or pressure as well as by persuasion. And if, as suggested, practically every incitement was a conspiracy to commit the offence incited, there would be no need to have an offence for incitement at all. In the present case the facts of the appellant's incitement of B were not actually to enter into an agreement with X or anyone for the commission of a crime. B was being urged to procure an assassin and was not being urged to enter into a conspiracy with anyone, although a conspiracy might have resulted. If this was an incitement to conspire rather than an incitement to incite then almost every incitement, as indicated, amounted to a conspiracy with all that that would entail. Indeed section 4 of the Offences Against the Person Act (soliciting to murder) should in those circumstances be construed as a potential allegation of conspiracy. So far as the present case was concerned the charge had been properly laid and the appeal would be dismissed.' (The Court considered *Sirat*, [1986] Crim LR 245.)

[Reported by Maggy Pigott, Barrister.]

R v Fitzmaurice [1983] 2 WLR 227 Court of Appeal (Criminal Division) (Lord Justice O'Connor, Neill and Taylor JJ)

Inciting the impossible

Facts

The defendant, acting on false information given to him by his father, arranged for three men to carry out a wages snatch on a woman delivering money to a bank at Bow in East London. The three men were arrested in a van parked outside the bank by the police who had been tipped off by the defendant's father, whose only motive in all this had been to receive some reward money. As there was, in reality, no woman carrying wages to be robbed, the three men arrested outside the bank were acquitted of attempted robbery on the ground of impossibility (note these events took place before the Criminal Attempts Act 1981 came into effect). The defendant was convicted of inciting the robbery, and he now appealed on the basis that he could not be guilty of inciting the impossible.

Held

The appeal would be dismissed.

Neill J:

'Mr Cocks' [Counsel for the appellant] second submission, however, is at first sight more formidable. Incitement is one of the three inchoate offences - incitement, conspiracy and attempt. Mr Cocks argued that there was no logical basis for treating the three offences differently when considering their application in circumstances where the complete offence would be impossible to commit, and that therefore the court should apply the principles laid down by the House of Lords in the case of attempts in *Haughton* v *Smith* (1973) 58 Cr App R 198; [1975] AC 476 and in the case of conspiracy in *Director of Public Prosecutions* v *Nock* [1978] AC 979; (1978) 67 Cr App R 116.

Mr Cocks pointed to the fact that though the law as laid down by the House of Lords in those two cases had been altered by statute by section 1 (2) and section 5 (1) of the Criminal Attempts Act 1981, there had been no change in the law relating to the offence of incitement. Accordingly, he said, the common law rule as to impossibility should be applied.

It is to be observed that the omission of the crime of incitement from the Criminal Attempts Act 1981 followed the recommendations of the Law Commission in their Report No. 102 and was in accordance with the draft bill set out in Appendix A to that report. The Law Commission explained the omission of incitement from the Draft Bill on the basis that in their view the House of Lords in *DPP* v *Nock* (supra) was prepared to distinguish the law relating to incitement from that relating to attempts: see paragraphs 4.2 to 4.4. We have had to give careful attention to these paragraphs in the Law Commission's Report.

We have also had to consider with care the passage in the speech of Lord Scarman in *DPP* v *Nock* (supra) which appears to have formed the basis for the decision by the Law Commission to exclude incitement from their recommendations for change and from their draft bill.

In *DPP* v *Nock* (1978) 67 Cr App R 116; [1978] AC 979, Lord Scarman at p129 and p999 of the respective reports made reference to two cases which had been cited to their Lordships. He said this: "Our attention was also drawn to two cases, upon which it may be helpful to comment very briefly. In *McDonough* (1962) 47 Cr App R 37, the Court of Criminal Appeal held that an incitement to receive stolen goods was complete on the making of the incitement even though there were no stolen goods - perhaps even, no goods at all. In *Haggard* v *Mason* [1976] 1 WLR 187, the Divisional Court held that the offence of offering to supply a controlled drug was committed, even though the drug in fact supplied was not a controlled drug. Neither of these cases infringes the principle in *Haughton* v *Smith* (supra) for, in each, as Lord Widgery CJ pointed out in *Haggard* v *Mason* (supra, p189), the offence was complete. In *McDonough* (supra) the *actus reus* was the making of the incitement; and in *Haggard* v *Mason* (supra) it was the making of the offer."

We have come to the conclusion that, on analysis, this passage in Lord Scarman's speech does not support the proposition that cases of incitement are to be treated quite differently at common law from cases of attempt or conspiracy.

The decision in *Haggard* v *Mason* (supra) related to the statutory offence of offering to supply a controlled drug and, as Lord Scarman pointed out, the actus reus which the prosecution had to prove was the making of the offer.

The explanation of *McDonough's* case, (supra) as it seems to us, is that though there may have been no stolen goods or no goods at all which were available to be received at the time of the incitement, the offence of incitement to receive stolen goods could nevertheless be proved because it was not impossible that at the relevant time in the future the necessary goods would be there.

In our view, therefore, the right approach in a case of incitement is the same as that which was underlined by Lord Scarman in *DPP* v *Nock* (supra) when he considered the offence of conspiracy. In every case it is necessary to analyse the evidence with care to decide the precise offence which the defendant is alleged to have incited.

In *DPP* v *Nock* (1978) 67 Cr App R 116; [1978] AC 979, Lord Scarman said this at p125 and p995 respectively: "The indictment makes plain that the Crown is alleging in this case a conspiracy to commit a crime: and no one has suggested that the particulars fail to disclose an offence known to the law. But the appellants submit, and it is not disputed by the Crown, that the agreement as proved was narrower in scope than the conspiracy charged. When the case was before the Court of Appeal, counsel on both sides agreed that the evidence went to prove that the appellants agreed together to obtain cocaine by separating it from the other substance or substances contained in a powder which they had obtained from one of their co-defendants, a Mr Mitchell. They believed that the powder was a mixture of cocaine and lignocaine, and that they would be able to produce cocaine from it. In fact the powder was lignocaine hydrochloride, an anaesthetic used in dentistry, which contains no cocaine at all. It is impossible to produce by separation or otherwise, cocaine from lignocaine ... The trial judge in his direction to the jury, and the Court of Appeal in their judgment dismissing the two appeals, treated this impossibility as an irrelevance. In their view the agreement was what mattered: and there was plain evidence of an agreement to produce cocaine, even though unknown to the two conspirators it could not be done. Neither the trial judge nor the Court of Appeal thought it necessary to carry their analysis of the agreement further. The trial judge described it simply as an agreement to produce cocaine. The Court of Appeal thought it enough that the prosecution had proved 'an agreement to do an act which was forbidden by section 4 of the Misuse of Drugs Act 1971.' Both descriptions are accurate, as far as they go. But neither contains any reference to the limited nature of the agreement proved: it was an agreement upon a specific course of conduct with the object of producing cocaine, and limited to that course of conduct. Since it could not result in the production of cocaine, the two appellants by pursuing it could not commit the statutory offence of producing a controlled drug."

In our view these words suggest the correct approach at common law to any inchoate offence. It is necessary in every case to decide on the evidence what was the course of conduct which was (as the case may be) incited or agreed or attempted. In some cases the evidence may establish that the persuasion by the inciter was in quite general terms whereas the subsequent agreement of the conspirators was directed to a specific crime and specific target. In such cases where the committal of the specific offence is shown to be impossible it may be quite logical for the inciter to be convicted even though the alleged conspirators (if not caught by section 5 of the Criminal Attempts Act 1981) may be acquitted. On the other hand, if B and C agree to kill D, and A, standing beside B and C, though not intending to take any active part whatever in the crime, encourages them to do so, we can see no satisfactory reason, if it turns out later that D was already dead, why A should be convicted of incitement to murder whereas B and C at common law would be entitled to an acquittal on a charge of conspiracy. The crucial question is to establish on the evidence the course of conduct which the alleged inciter was encouraging.

We return to the facts of the instant case. Mr Cocks submitted that the "crime" which Bonham and the two Browns were being encouraged to commit was a mere charade. The appellant's father was not planning a real robbery at all and therefore the appellant could not be found guilty of inciting the three men to commit it. In our judgment, however, the answer to Mr Cocks' argument is to be found in the facts which the prosecution proved against the appellant. As was made clear by Mr Purnell on behalf of the Crown, the case against the appellant was based on the steps he took to recruit Bonham. At that stage the appellant believed that there was to be a wage snatch and he was encouraging Bonham to take part in it. As Mr Purnell put it, "The appellant thought he was recruiting for a robbery not for a charade." It is to be remembered that the particulars of offence in the indictment included the words "by robbing a woman at Bow." By no stretch of the imagination was that an impossible offence to carry out and it was that offence which the appellant was inciting Bonham to commit.'

R v Hollinshead [1985] AC 978 House of Lords (Lords Fraser, Diplock, Roskill, Bridge, and Brandon)

Scope of common law conspiracy to defraud

Facts

The defendants agreed to supply 'black boxes' (devices which caused electricity meters to under-record the amount of electricity used by a consumer), to a 'middle man' who would then sell them on to customers of various Electricity Boards. The defendants were charged on two counts; count one alleging a statutory conspiracy to aid, abet, counsel or procure an offence under s2(1)(b) of the Theft Act 1978, and count two which alleged a common law conspiracy to defraud. The defendants were convicted on the second count, and appealed successfully to the Court of Appeal on the ground that there could be no conspiracy to defraud where the dishonest conduct contemplated was to be carried out by a third party (the 'middle man') not the conspirators. The Crown now appealed to the House of Lords.

The two questions certified for consideration by their Lordships were:

'1. If parties agree (a) to manufacture devices whose only use is fraudulently to alter electricity meters and (b) to sell those devices to a person who intends merely to re-sell them and not himself to use them, does that agreement constitute a common law conspiracy to defraud?

2. Alternatively, is such an agreement properly charged as a statutory conspiracy to aid, abet, counsel or procure persons unknown to commit offences under section 2 of the Theft Act 1978?'

Held

The appeal would be allowed and the convictions of the defendants on count two [conspiracy to defraud] would be restored.

Lord Roskill:

[His Lordship referred to ss1(1) and 5(1) of the Criminal Law Act 1977, and the speech of Lord Bridge in *R v Ayres* extracted above, and continued]

'My Lords, junior counsel for the prosecution told your Lordships that when settling the indictment he had thought it right to put in the forefront of the prosecution case the charge of conspiracy to defraud in count 2. But, having regard to what the House had said in *R v Ayres* [1984] AC 447, he had also thought it right, lest his own view were not accepted as correct, to add a charge of statutory conspiracy in the terms of count 1. For my part I think he was entirely right to approach the matter in this way. Indeed the very difficulty he encountered in evolving a satisfactory formulation of a charge of statutory conspiracy, of which I shall say more later, reinforces the correctness of his approach.

I therefore turn to consider whether it was necessary for the prosecution in order to secure a conviction on count 2 to aver and prove a dishonest agreement actually to use the black boxes so as to defraud the intended victims, various electricity boards. It was said, and the Court of Appeal (Criminal Division) accepted, that it was not enough that the agreement charged was only dishonestly to manufacture and sell those boxes in order to defraud the intended victims.

Mr Spokes QC, for the respondents, put in the forefront of his submissions a pleading point, namely, that count 2 was in any event bad because it did not aver an agreement to use but only an agreement to manufacture and sell. In my view it is now much too late to take a point of this kind. It should have been taken, if at all, at the trial when if necessary the count could have been amended. But in any event, the point is without substance as well as without merit. It is obvious from the formulation of count 2 that the fraud upon the intended victims could not be successfully practised without use of the black boxes, and that the manufacture and sale was for the dishonest purpose of enabling those black boxes to be used by persons other than the respondents to the detriment of the intended victim.

The real question, as already stated, is whether in order to secure conviction on count 2 it was necessary to aver and prove a dishonest agreement by the respondents actually to use the black boxes, the submission being that it was not enough to show only an intention that such a dishonest use should follow their dishonest manufacture and sale.

My Lords, in my view, with all respect to those who have taken a different view, this submission is contrary to authority. I start with the decision of this House in *R v Scott* [1975] AC 819. It is to be observed that this case was decided before the passing of the Act of 1977. Scott was charged with two offences. First, he was charged with conspiracy to defraud and secondly, with conspiracy to infringe section 21(1)(*a*) of the Copyright Act 1956. He ultimately pleaded guilty to both and was sentenced on both counts: see p822. In this connection I have the permission of my noble and learned friend, Lord Bridge of Harwich, to say that he was in error in saying in *R v Ayres* [1984] AC 447, 454 that the conspiracy under consideration in *R v Scott* [1975] AC 819 did not involve the commission of any identifiable offence. But the House was not there concerned with what would now be called a statutory conspiracy. Indeed since *R v Ayres* the two counts would be mutually exclusive and Scott could not have been convicted on both. That is, however, of no importance in the present case. The importance of the decision in *R v Scott* lies in the conclusion summarised in the headnote:

"(3) That the common law offence of conspiracy to defraud was not limited to an agreement between two or more persons to deceive the intended victim and by such deceit to defraud him; and accordingly, as deceit was not an essential ingredient of the offence, the count was not bad in law and the appellant had been rightly convicted."

Viscount Dilhorne said, at p839: "One must not confuse the object of a conspiracy with the means by which it is intended to be carried out." My noble and learned friend Lord Diplock said, at p841:

"(2) Where the intended victim of a 'conspiracy to defraud' is a private individual the purpose of the conspirators must be to cause the victim economic loss by depriving him of some property or right, corporeal or incorporeal, to which he is or would or might become entitled. The intended means by which the purpose is to be achieved must be dishonest. They need not involve fraudulent misrepresentation such as is needed to constitute the civil tort of deceit. Dishonesty of any kind is enough."

In *Attorney-General's Reference (No. 1 of 1982)* [1983] QB 751, (the whisky label case), the Court of Appeal (Criminal Division) (Lord Lane CJ and Taylor and McCowan JJ) were primarily concerned with the question of jurisdiction to try persons for conspiracy which had been entered into in England but which was to be carried out abroad though that conspiracy would cause economic damage to persons in England. The court held that there was no such jurisdiction. But it is apparent from a passage in the judgment of that court delivered by Lord Lane CJ, at p757, that, but for the question of jurisdiction, the former defendants would have been guilty of conspiracy to defraud. Lord Lane CJ said:

"In each case to determine the object of the conspiracy, the court must see what the defendants actually agreed to do. Had it not been for the jurisdictional problem, we have no doubt the charge against these conspirators would have been conspiracy to defraud potential purchasers of the whisky, for that was the true object of the agreement."

The dishonest agreement there under consideration was to produce, label and distribute bottles of whisky so as to represent them as containing whisky of a well-known brand which in fact they did not contain. The object as the Lord Chief Justice said was to defraud potential purchasers of the whisky outside this country.

In my view the respondents were liable to be convicted of conspiracy to defraud because they agreed to manufacture and sell and thus put into circulation dishonest devices, the sole purpose of which was to cause loss just as the former defendants in the case just referred to would, apart from the jurisdictional problem, have been liable to be convicted of conspiracy to defraud because they agreed dishonestly to produce, label and distribute bottles of whisky, the sole purpose of the sale of which was to defraud potential purchasers of those bottles.

For these reasons, I think, with great respect, the decision of the Court of Appeal (Criminal Division) cannot be supported and that the trial judge's ruling was correct. The convictions on count 2 should therefore be restored.

I wish to make plain that in inviting your Lordships' House to agree with this conclusion I am not suggesting that the principles applicable to common law conspiracy to defraud should in any way be expanded or extended. On the contrary in my view the present cases fall well within existing principles and authorities. I do not arrive at this conclusion with any regret. On the contrary I am sure that the Court of Appeal (Criminal Division) arrived at their conclusion only because they thought that they were compelled to do so. I think commonsense suggests that what the respondents agreed to do plainly constituted a conspiracy to defraud and that no-one save perhaps the most enthusiastic lawyer would willingly hold otherwise.

I can deal with the question raised in connection with count 1 more briefly. As was pointed out in *R v Ayres* [1984] AC 447, 455, in the passage to which I have already referred, offences of statutory conspiracy and of common law conspiracy to defraud are mutually exclusive. It follows that if your Lordships agree with me that the respondents were properly convicted on count 2 of the conspiracy to defraud, this conclusion presupposes that the respondents could not properly have been convicted on count 1 of the statutory conspiracy there charged. The Court of Appeal (Criminal Division) were of the opinion that they could not have been so convicted for the reason that section 1(1) of the Act of 1977 did not upon its true construction make a charge of conspiracy to aid, abet, counsel or procure possible in law. The foundation for this view is a passage in *Smith and Hogan, Criminal Law*, 5th ed (1983), pp234-235, which is quoted in full in the judgment delivered by Hodgson J and with which the Court of Appeal (Criminal Division) expressed complete agreement.

My Lords, I do not find it necessary to consider whether or not this view is correct for this reason. Even if such a charge of conspiracy to aid, abet, counsel or procure were possible in law, I can see no evidence whatever that the respondents ever agreed so to aid, abet, counsel or procure or indeed did aid, abet, counsel or procure those who as the ultimate purchasers or possessors of the black boxes were destined to be the actual perpetrators of the intended frauds upon electricity boards. It follows that on no view could the respondents have been convicted on count 1 even if that count were sustainable in law. The last question is obviously one of some difficulty and a case in which that question arose for direct decision is likely to be a rarity. I suggest that in any future case in which that question does arise it should be treated as open for consideration de novo, as much may depend on the particular facts of the case in question.

In the result I would allow the appeals, answer certified question 1 "Yes" and certified question 2 "No." I would restore the convictions of the respondents on count 2.'

R v McDonough (1962) 47 Cr App R 37

See *DPP* v *Nock*, and *R* v *Fitzmaurice*, both above.

R v Reed [1982] Crim LR 819 Court of Appeal (Criminal Division) (Donaldson LJ, McNeill and Taylor JJ)

Conspiracy - whether agreement would 'necessarily' result in the commission of an offence

Facts

'At the Central Criminal Court, before Lawson J, applicant R was convicted on two counts of conspiring with L to aid and abet suicide and of two substantive offences of aiding and abetting suicide. L was convicted at the same trial on the counts of conspiracy and five substantive counts of aiding and abetting suicide.

Application was made for leave to appeal against conviction and sentence. Leave was granted for appeal against sentence and sentence reduced to 18 months' imprisonment concurrent on all counts. Application for leave to appeal against conviction was refused.

R made five principal submissions of which the third and fourth are reported here.

The third submission concerned the judge's direction on the elements of the substantive offence. It was argued that the crucial question in this case was whether or not R could be said to have "counselled or procured: the act of suicide. The jury should have been directed that some act of encouragement by R had to be proved (cf Stephen's *Digest* (9th ed), Art 18; Kenny's *Outlines* (19th ed), para 69). Instead the judge directed that R should be convicted if he put L in touch with a potential suicide "knowing and intending that L should help suicide if circumstances permitted."

Held

The Court held that the definition of "procure" remained that given by Lord Widgery CJ in *Att-Gen's Reference (No 1) of 1975*: "To procure is to produce by endeavour. You procure a thing by setting out to see that it happens and taking the appropriate steps to produce that happening." The issue in this case was therefore simply that of determining what was the result intended by the applicant, and the direction was wholly appropriate.

The fourth submission was that the summing up had not adequately conveyed the requirements of the Criminal Law Act 1977, s1(1). These, it was said, clearly indicate that a course of conduct agreed upon must necessarily amount to or involve the commission of an offence if the agreement is carried out in accordance with the parties' intentions. The agreement on the relevant course of conduct must therefore not be capable of a successful conclusion without a crime being committed (cf Smith and Hogan, *Criminal Law* (4th ed), pp 226-227). It was argued that the most that could be inferred about the nature of the agreement between L and R was that L would visit individuals and either give them faith healing, consolation and comfort while discouraging suicide or he would actively help them to commit suicide, depending on his assessment of the appropriate course of action. Such an agreement was capable of execution without the law being broken, and therefore should not have attracted the charge of conspiracy. It was argued that the jury should have at least been made aware of such a possible defence in the directions given.

The Court held against the applicant on this point. Donaldson LJ considered two examples: "In the first, A and B agree to drive from London to Edinburgh in a time which can be achieved without exceeding the speed limits, but only if the traffic which they encounter is exceptionally light. Their agreement will not necessarily involve the commission of any offence, even if it is carried out in accordance with their intentions, and they do arrive from London to Edinburgh within the agreed time. Accordingly the agreement does not constitute the offence of statutory conspiracy or indeed of any offence. In the second example, A and B agree to rob a bank, if when they arrive at the bank it seems safe to do so. Their agreement will necessarily involve the commission of the offence of robbery if it is carried out in accordance with their intentions. Accordingly, they are guilty of the statutory offence of conspiracy. The instant case is an example of the latter type of agreement. If circumstances had permitted and the agreement of R and L had been carried out in accordance with their intentions L would have aided, abetted, counselled, and procured a suicide ..." '

[Reported by Sheldon L Leader, Barrister.]

R v Siracusa (1990) 90 Cr App R 340   Court of Appeal (Criminal Division) (O'Connor LJ, Boreham J, Ian Kennedy J)

Statutory conspiracy - mens rea

Facts [as stated by O'Connor LJ]

'On December 13, 1984, a consignment of 52 packing cases of furniture from India consigned to Elongate Ltd arrived at Felixstowe. Customs officers found in some articles of furniture cannabis with a street value of £0.5 million in England and £3 million in Canada. They repacked and waited and watched. The consignment was cleared by shipping agents and delivered to a warehouse, Unit 5, Batsworth Road, Mitcham. The customs moved in on December 18, 1984, seized the consignment and arrested Siracusa and a man named Gaultieri. Unit 5 is a spacious warehouse. There was nothing in it except the 52 cases of furniture and a fork-lift truck. The work in hand was the painting out of the Indian shipping marks with black paint.

On May 28, 1985, a consignment of 84 packing cases of furniture from Thailand consigned to Ital Provisions Ltd arrived at Southampton. Customs officers found in some articles of furniture heroin with a street value of £15 million in England and £75 million in Canada. They repacked some of the heroin and waited and watched. The consignment was not delivered in this country, but trans-shipped and left for Canada on June 8, 1985. After delivery in Canada on June 21, 1985, enforcement officers moved in, seized the consignment and arrested three men. It was found that they had gone unerringly to the cases containing the pieces in which heroin was concealed. In England, Monteleone, Luciani and Di Carlo were arrested on June 21, 1985. The importation of controlled drugs into this country is prohibited by section 3(1)(a) of the Misuse of Drugs Act 1971. That section does not create any offence. The offence is created by section 170(2)(b) of the Customs and Excise Management Act 1979 which provides:

> "(2) . . if any person is, in relation to any goods, in any way knowingly concerned in any fraudulent evasion or attempt at evasion: ... (b) of any prohibition or restriction for the time being in force with respect to the goods under or by virtue of any enactment ... he shall be guilty of an offence.... "

At the relevant time, the effect of section 170(4) and Schedule 1 of the Act was that importation of drugs of Class A or Class B was punishable with up to 14 years' imprisonment.

In cases where controlled drugs are imported into this country and a substantive offence is charged as a contravention of section 170(2)(b), the particulars of the offence identify the drug and the class to which it belongs so that the appropriate penalty is not in doubt. Case law has established that although separate offences are created as a result of the different penalties authorised, the mens rea is the same. The prosecution must prove that the defendant knew that the goods were prohibited goods. They do not have to prove that he knew what the goods in fact were. Thus it is no defence for a man charged with importing a Class A drug to say he believed he was bringing in a Class C drug or indeed any other prohibited goods: *Hussain* (1969) 53 Cr App R448; *Shivpuri* (1986) 83 Cr App R 178; *Ellis* (1987).

The appellants contend that where conspiracy to contravene section 170(2)(b) is charged, the position is different so that in this case the prosecution had to prove against each defendant that he knew that the Kashmir operation involved cannabis and that the Thailand operation involved heroin. If this submission is well-founded, then it is said that the learned judge's direction on conspiracy is flawed and strength is added to the contentions of those appellants who submit that in respect of one, other or both counts, there was no case to go to the jury at the end of the prosecution case.'

Held

The appeals would be dismissed.

O'Connor LJ:

[His Lordship referred to the facts of *R* v *Anderson*, and the passages from Lord Bridge's speech, extracted elswhere in this chapter, that end with Lord Bridge's comment:]

"I have said already, but I repeat to emphasise its importance, that an essential ingredient in the crime of conspiring to commit a specific offence or offences under section 1(1) of the Act of 1977 is that the accused should agree that a course of conduct be pursued which he knows must involve the commission by one or more of the parties to the agreement of that offence or those offences. But, beyond the mere fact of agreement, the necessary mens rea of the crime is, in my opinion, established if, and only if, it is shown that the accused, when he entered into the agreement, intended to play some part in the agreed course of conduct in furtherance of the criminal purpose which the agreed course of conduct was intended to achieve. Nothing less will suffice; nothing more is required."

O'Connor LJ then continued:

'The last paragraph above cited must be read in the context of that case. We think it obvious that Lord Bridge cannot have been intending that the organiser of a crime who recruited others to carry it out would not himself be guilty of conspiracy unless it could be proved that he intended to play some active part himself thereafter. Lord Bridge had pointed out ... that in these days of highly organised crime the most serious statutory conspiracies will frequently involve an elaborate and complex agreed course of conduct in which many will consent to play necessary but subordinate roles, not involving them in any direct participation in the commission of the offence or offences at the centre of the conspiracy.

The present case is a classic example of such a conspiracy. It is the hallmark of such crimes that the organisers try to remain in the background and more often than not are not apprehended.

Secondly, the origins of all conspiracies are concealed and it is usually quite impossible to establish when or where the initial agreement was made, or when or where other conspirators were recruited. The very existence of the agreement can only be inferred from overt acts. Participation in a conspiracy is infinitely variable: it can be active or passive. If the majority shareholder and director of a company consents to the company being used for drug smuggling carried out in the company's name by a fellow director and minority shareholder, he is guilty of conspiracy. Consent, that is the agreement or adherence to the agreement, can be inferred if it is proved that he knew what was going on and the intention to participate in the furtherance of the criminal purpose is also established by his failure to stop the unlawful activity. Lord Bridge's dictum does not require anything more.

We return to the first sentence of this paragraph in Lord Bridge's speech. He starts by saying: " I have said already, but I repeat to emphasise its importance.... ". We have cited what he had already said when dealing with his clause 2. It is clear that he was not intending to say anything different. So when he goes on to say:

" ... an essential ingredient in the crime of conspiring to commit a specific offence or offences under section 1(1) of the Act of 1977 is that the accused should agree that a course of conduct be pursued which he knows must involve the commission by one or more of the parties to the agreement of that offence or those offences,..." he plainly does not mean that the prosecution have to prove that persons who agree to import prohibited drugs into this country know that the offence which will be committed will be a contravention of section 170(2) of the Customs and Excise Act.

He is not to be taken as saying that the prosecution must prove that the accused knew the name of the crime. We are satisfied that Lord Bridge was doing no more than applying the words of section 1 of the Criminal Law Act 1977, namely, that when the accused agreed to the course of conduct, he knew that it involved the commission of an offence. The mens rea sufficient to support the commission of a substantive offence will not necessarily be sufficient to support a charge of conspiracy to commit that offence. An intent to cause grievous bodily harm is sufficient to support the charge of murder, but is not sufficient to support a charge of conspiracy to murder or of attempt to murder.

We have come to the conclusion that if the prosecution charge a conspiracy to contravene section 170(2) of the Customs and Excise Management Act by the importation of heroin, then the prosecution must prove that the agreed course of conduct was the importation of heroin. This is because the essence of the crime of conspiracy is the agreement and in simple terms, you do not prove an agreement to import heroin by proving an agreement to import cannabis.

We are confident that in coming to this conclusion, we are not making the enforcement of the anti-drug laws more difficult. If the facts suggest that the agreement was to import prohibited drugs of more than one class, that can be appropriately laid because section 1(1) of the Criminal Law Act expressly provides for the agreed course of conduct to involve the commission of more than one offence.

We are in no doubt that the learned judge made it quite clear to the jury that count 1 required proof of an agreement to import cannabis and count 2, heroin. The learned judge's main direction to the jury on conspiracy is found at p47 of the summing-up. It is sufficient to cite the following passages:

"Now, members of the jury, would you please take in your hands your copies of the indictment. You will see that each of the two counts charges a conspiracy to contravene a section of the Customs and Excise Management Act of 1979. In those counts all these defendants are charged, but there are different named conspirators in addition to the defendants in the counts. So, the first thing you will have to consider is: What is a conspiracy?

Now, a conspiracy is an agreement between two or more persons to do an unlawful act – in this case to commit a crime. You will see the crime which is set out. You will appreciate, of course, more than one person would have to be involved, you may think, in the commission of the sort of offences you are dealing with here. The question for you is whether it has been proved that each of the defendants is party to such an agreement.

When you look to see what it is that they are alleged to have agreed to have done, you will see that the offence concerned in count 1 is being knowingly concerned, and I stress the word "knowingly," in the fraudulent evasion of the prohibition on the importation of Class B drugs, namely, cannabis resin. Now, you will realise at once that if you are innocently involved, if you have been duped by others, as the first two defendants claim, then of course you are not committing this offence, because you are not being knowingly concerned in the fraudulent evasion of the prohibition on the importation of drugs. Now, 'knowingly concerned' means that you have to know that the goods are subject to prohibition, and there is no suggestion by any of these defendants that they would not know that, and that what they were concerned in was an agreement to effect, in an operation, the evasion of the prohibition fraudulently. 'Fraudulently' means by dishonest conduct, deliberately intended to evade the prohibition on the importation of controlled drugs. Of course, 'importation' means bringing them into this country. Members of the jury, if you turn to count 2, you will see that a similar offence, the ingredients of which I have just explained to you and are the same, is laid, but in this case in relation to the prohibition on the importation of what are called class A drugs, namely, Diamorphine Hydrocholonde, which is heroin.

Now, members of the jury, so far as conspiracy is concerned, if a defendant agrees with any other defendant or named conspirator that a course of conduct should be pursued which, if carried out in accordance with their intentions, would necessarily amount to the offence of being concerned in the fraudulent evasion of the prohibition either on the importation of cannabis in count 1 or heroin in count 2 by one or more parties to the agreement, then he is guilty of conspiracy."

Thereafter the learned judge frequently used the word "drugs", but in circumstances where the jury must have appreciated that for count 1, drugs meant cannabis and for count 2, heroin. For example, at p13, after reminding the jury that Luciani had resigned his directorship in November 1984 and Siracusa had been arrested in December 1984, that is some six months before the heroin shipment arrived, he said that it did not matter:

"if you are satisfied from the whole of the evidence that they were parties to the agreement of those importations of drugs and that is something you can only decide from everything that happened before and what their participation in it was, they do not have to be on the scene taking an active part when the drugs actually arrive."

There are numerous other similar examples in the summing-up, but as we have said they cannot in any way have confused the jury.'

R v Sirat [1986] Crim LR 245 Court of Appeal (Criminal Division) (Parker LJ, French and Mann JJ)

Inciting incitement

Facts

(As stated in the judgment of Parker LJ)

'The facts may be shortly stated. Between Thursday, August 16, 1984, and Monday, August 20, both dates inclusive, the appellant had four meetings with Mr Bashir, the last of which was recorded by the police, to whom Mr Bashir had reported after the first two had taken place. It is unnecessary to set out the details of the conversations. It is sufficient to say that they plainly showed that the appellant desired the death of his wife or, if not that, her serious injury, and that he was urging Bashir to (i) either kill or injure her himself, or (ii) pay a man who was in fact non-existent to do so, or (iii) procure the result, whether by doing the deed himself or by paying someone else, not necessarily the non-existent man, to do so.

At the close of the prosecution case a submission, inter alia, that there was no such offence in law as inciting a person to counsel or abet a third person to commit an offence was overruled by the trial judge, who directed the jury that if the appellant urged B to incite a third man to cause grievous bodily harm to the appellant's wife he was guilty of incitement to cause grievous bodily harm. The appellant was convicted and appealed.'

Held

The appeal would be allowed.

Parker LJ:

'At the close of the prosecution case it was submitted on behalf of the appellant that (i) there was no such offence in law as inciting a person to counsel or abet a third person to commit an offence, and (ii) there was not sufficient evidence to go to the jury that the appellant had incited Bashir himself to murder or cause grievous bodily harm to the appellant's wife. The judge rightly rejected the second of those two submissions and no complaint is made as to that.

We are now only indirectly concerned with the ruling on the first submission; for what now matters is not the ruling itself but the subsequent direction to the jury which was based on it. Of this complaint is made. In the only ground of appeal which was pursued it is contended that the learned judge erred in law "in directing the jury that if the defendant urged the witness Bashir to incite a third man to cause grievous bodily harm to the defendant's wife the defendant was guilty of the offence charged in count 2 of the indictment and in rejecting a submission by defence counsel that there was no such offence in law as inciting a person to counsel or abet a third person to commit an offence."

There is no doubt that at common law incitement to commit a crime is an offence. This being so, it follows logically that if A incites B to incite C to commit a crime, eg to wound D, A is guilty of incitement to commit a crime, namely, incitement. This however is subject to the qualification that if C is non-existent, being either dead or fictional, A would not be guilty, because he would be inciting the commission of an impossible crime. B cannot incite C, because C does not exist. On the basis of *Fitzmaurice* (1983) 76 Cr App R 17; [1983] QB 1083, the judge rightly so directed the jury. Hence, since the jury convicted on count 2, it follows that they must have concluded that the appellant had not urged Bashir to get the fictional man and no other to do the deed.

With regard to the remaining possibilities, the essence of the learned judge's directions appears from the following passages in his summing-up:

"If a man wants a murder to be committed and he tries to persuade somebody else to commit it or he tries to persuade that second person to get a third person to commit it, then the first man is guilty of the crime of incitement ... incitement to murder."

"If you are sure that in reality the effect of what he was saying to Bashir was this, 'I want you to get her seriously injured, do it yourself or get the white man from Leeds to do it,' then what Sirat was proposing was a possibility because the white man from Leeds was only one way in which he was making his proposal. Another, on the basis that I am putting it to you, was that Bashir might do it himself and that was obviously possible, so in that event he would be guilty of count 2 and, equally, if the effect of what he was saying was this, 'I want you to get her seriously injured, get the white man from Leeds to do it if you like, get somebody else to do it if you like, so long as you get somebody,' if that is the effect of what he was saying, then once again the serious injury which he wanted brought about would be a possibility and he would then be guilty of count 2."

"Similarly with count 2, you have to be sure before you can convict him that he desired his wife to be seriously injured and that he tried to persuade Bashir to bring about her serious injury in a way which was, in fact, possible."

In principle there is nothing wrong with these directions, but complication is introduced by the provisions of the Criminal Law Act 1977. Section 1 of that Act created the statutory offence of conspiracy and section 5(1), subject to exceptions which do not matter, abolished the offence of conspiracy at common law. Section 5(7) then provided: "Incitement and attempt to commit the offence of conspiracy (whether the conspiracy incited or attempted would be an offence at common law or under section 1 above or any other enactment) shall cease to be offences." If, therefore, A incites B to agree with C that C will wound D, A's incitement of B is by statute not an offence.

There is, in our view, no doubt that one possible view of the evidence was that the appellant was inciting Bashir to agree, with either the non-existent man or anyone else who would do it at the right price, that such person should cause grievous bodily harm to the appellant's wife. It is therefore clearly possible that the jury may have convicted him of something which by statute is no longer an offence. Moreover, as was accepted by the prosecution, they may have convicted him of an offence with which he was not charged, namely, incitement to incite to cause grievous bodily harm, whereas the prosecution charged incitement to cause grievous bodily harm.

This being so, we allowed the appeal on two grounds: (a) that the appellant may have been convicted of an offence of which he was not charged, and (b) that he may have been convicted of an offence which does not exist.

Lest there be any doubt, we do not intend to indicate that the common law offence of inciting to incite no longer exists. Where however the facts are that the accused's incitement of B is actually to enter into an agreement with C for the commission of a crime, it would in our judgment be impossible to hold that the accused can be guilty of incitement, on the ground that B must of necessity propose the crime to C on the way to making the agreement. Whether other forms of incitement to incite survive will fall for decision when the question arises. It may appear to be absurd that, where a person is inciting actual agreement to be made for the commission of a crime, he should be guilty of no offence, but that where he does not seek actual agreement but mere encouragement he should be guilty. This however is not necessarily absurd, for there may well be circumstances where there is no question of an agreement being sought but where the particular form of incitement is more effective than any attempt to secure agreement.'

Wai Yu-Tsang v R [1991] 3 WLR 1006 Privy Council (Lord Bridge, Lord Griffiths, Lord Goff, Lord Jauncey and Lord Lowry)

Mens rea of conspiracy to defraud

Facts

The defendant was convicted of conspiring to defraud the Hang Lung Bank ('the bank'), of which he was the chief accountant, of US$124M. The allegation had been that he had conspired with the managing director, the general manager and others to dishonestly conceal the dishonouring of certain cheques by not recording them in the bank's account. The defendant contended that he was not guilty as he had been acting on the instructions of the managing director, and had acted in good faith to prevent a run on the bank. The trial judge had directed the jury that for conspiracy to defraud, no desire to cause loss on the part of the defendant need be shown. It was sufficient that he had imperilled the economic or proprietary interests of another party. The defendant appealed unsuccessfully to the Court of Appeal Hong Kong, and now appealed to the Privy Council.

Held

The trial judge's direction on the mens rea of conspiracy to defraud had been correct and the appeal would be dismissed.

Lord Goff:

Having reviewed the complex factual background, Lord Goff considered the authorities:

'Before the Court of Appeal (of Hong Kong) a number of issues were raised by the defendant founded upon criticisms of the summing up of the judge. All of those criticisms were rejected by the Court of Appeal. Before their Lordships, however, the defendant's case was directed solely on the judge's direction on the mental element required for a conspiracy to defraud. The judge explained to the jury that the defendant must have been party to an agreement with one or more of the other named conspirators which had a common intention to defraud one or more of the persons or categories of persons named in the indictment. He explained that such an intention must involve dishonesty on the part of the conspirators, and continued:

"It is fraud if it is proved that there was the dishonest taking of a risk which there was no right to take which - to [the defendant's] knowledge at least - would cause detriment or prejudice to another, detriment or prejudice to the economic or proprietary rights of another. That detriment or prejudice to somebody else is very often incidental to the purpose of the fraudsman himself. The prime objective of fraudsmen is usually to gain some advantage for themselves, any detriment or prejudice to somebody else is often secondary to that objective but nonetheless is a contemplated or predictable outcome of what they do. If the interests of some other person - the economic or proprietary interests of some other person are imperilled, that is sufficient to constitute fraud even though no loss is actually suffered and even though the fraudsman himself did not desire to bring about any loss."

It is plain that that direction was founded upon the judgment of the Court of Appeal in *R v Allsop* (1976) 64 Cr App R 29. It was the contention of the defendant that the direction was erroneous in so far as it stated that, for this purpose, the imperilling of an economic interest or the threat of financial prejudice was sufficient to establish fraud, whatever the motive of the accused may have been; and that in so far as *R* v *Allsop* so decided, it was wrong and should not be followed.

In the course of argument, their Lordships were referred to a number of authorities as well as to *R* v *Allsop* itself. They do not however find it necessary for the present purposes to refer to more than a few of these authorities. The first is *Welham* v *Director of Public Prosecutions* [1961] AC 103. That case was in fact concerned with forgery, and in particular with the meaning of the words "intent to defraud" in s4(1) of the Forgery Act 1913. The case has however since been referred to as providing guidance in cases of conspiracy to defraud: see *R* v *Scott* [1975] AC 819, 838, per Viscount Dilhorne, a proposition with which their Lordships are respectfully in agreement. In *Welham* v *Director of Public Prosecutions* [1961] AC 103, the appellant had witnessed forged hire purchase agreements, on the basis of which finance companies advanced large sums of money. His defence was that he had no intention of depriving the finance companies by deceit of any economic advantage, his belief being that the only function of the agreements was to enable the companies to circumvent certain credit restrictions. His only purpose was to mislead the authority which might inspect the records and whose duty was to prevent contravention of the credit restrictions. The House of Lords held that there was no warrant for confining the words "intent to defraud" to an intent to deprive a person by deceit of an economic advantage or to inflict upon him an economic loss, and further that such an intent could exist where there was no other intention than to deceive a person responsible for a public duty into doing something, or failing to do something, which he would not have done, or failed to have done, but for the deceit. Lord Denning, who delivered the leading speech, rejected the argument that an intention to defraud involves an intention to cause economic loss. He referred to opinions of academic lawyers to that effect, and said, at p131:

"I cannot agree with them on this. If a drug addict forges a doctor's prescription so as to enable him to get drugs from a chemist, he has, I should have thought, an intent to defraud, even though he intends to pay the chemist the full price and no one is a penny the worse off."

Later, at pp132-133, Lord Denning referred to a passage in *East's Please of the Crown* (1803 ed) vol 2, p852, to the effect that forgery at common law denotes a false making - "a making malo animo" - of any written instrument for the purpose of fraud and deceit. He then said, at p133:

"That was written in 1803, but it has been always accepted as authoritative. It seems to me to provide the key to the cases decided since it was written, as well as those before. The important thing about this definition is that it is not limited to the idea of economic loss, nor to the idea of depriving someone of something of value. It extends generally to *the purpose of fraud and deceit*. Put shortly, 'with intent to defraud' means 'with intent to practice a fraud' on someone or other. It need not be anyone in particular. Someone in general will suffice. If anyone may be prejudiced in any way by the fraud, that is enough."

Lord Radcliffe agreed with the speech of Lord Denning, but went on to express in his own words his view of the meaning of the words "intent to defraud" in s4(1) of the Act of 1913. He rejected the proposition that in ordinary speech "to defraud" is confined to the idea of depriving a man by deceit of some economic advantage or inflicting upon him some economic loss and continued, at p124:

"Has the law ever so confined it? In my opinion there is no warrant for saying that it has. What it has looked for in considering the effect of cheating upon another person and so in defining the criminal intent is the prejudice of that person: what Blackstone (*Commentaries*, 18th ed, vol 4, at p247) called 'to the prejudice of another man's right.' *East, Pleas of the Crown* (1803), vol 2, at pp852, 854, makes the same point in the chapter on Forgery: 'in all cases of forgery, properly so called, it is immaterial whether any person be actually injured or not, provided any may be prejudiced by it.'"

He went on to say that the special line of cases where the person deceived is a public authority or a person holding public office, and there is no intention on the part of the deceiver to inflict upon him any pecuniary or economic harm, shows that such an intention is not necessary to convict a man of an intention to defraud. The remainder of the Appellate Committee agreed with both Lord Radcliffe and Lord Denning.

This authority establishes that the expression "intent to defraud" is not to be given a narrow meaning, involving an intention to cause economic loss to another. In broad terms, it means simply an intention to practise a fraud on another, or an intention to act to the prejudice of another man's right.

Their Lordships turn next to *R* v *Scott* [1975] AC 819. That case was concerned with a conspiracy temporarily to abstract films from a cinema to enable the appellant to make and distribute copies of the films on a commercial scale, the operation being carried on without the consent of the owners of the copyright or distribution rights in the films. The appellant's argument was to the effect that he could not be guilty of any conspiracy, because the facts did not disclose an agreement to deceive the persons alleged to have been the object of the conspiracy. This argument was rejected by the House of Lords. The leading speech was delivered by Viscount Dilhorne, with whom the remainder of the Appellate Committee agreed. He reviewed the authorities, including *Welham* v *Director of Public Prosecutions* [1961] AC 103, and said [1975] AC 819, 839:

"I have not the temerity to attempt an exhaustive definition of the meaning of 'defraud.' As I have said, words take colour from the context in which they are used, but the words 'fraudulently' and 'defraud' must ordinarily have a very similar meaning. If, as I think, and as the Criminal Law Revision Committee appears to have thought, 'fraudulently' means 'dishonestly', then 'to defraud' ordinarily means, in my opinion, to deprive a person dishonestly of something which is his or of something to which he is or would or might but for the perpetration of the fraud be entitled. In *Welham* v *Director of Public Prosecutions* [1961] AC 103, 124, Lord Radcliffe referred to a special line of cases where the person deceived is a person holding public office or a public authority and where the person deceived was not caused any pecuniary or economic loss. Forgery whereby the deceit has been accomplished, had, he pointed out, been in a number of cases treated as having been done with intent to defraud despite the absence of pecuniary or economic loss. In this case it is not necessary to decide that a conspiracy to defraud may exist even though its object was not to secure a financial advantage by inflicting an economic loss on the person at whom the conspiracy was directed. But for myself I see no reason why what was said by Lord Radcliffe in relation to forgery should not equally apply in relation to conspiracy to defraud."

In a brief speech Lord Diplock (although he, like the remainder of the Appellate Committee, agreed with the speech of Viscount Dilhorne) was more specific. He said, at p841:

"(2) Where the intended victim of a 'conspiracy to defraud' is a private individual the purpose of the conspirators must be to cause the victim economic loss by depriving him of some property or right, corporeal or incorporeal, to which he is or would or might become entitled. ... (3) Where the intended victim of a 'conspiracy to defraud' is a person performing public duties as distinct from a private individual it is sufficient if the purpose is to cause him to act contrary to his public duty ..."

With the greatest respect to Lord Diplock, their Lordships consider this categorisation to be too narrow. In their opinion, in agreement with the approach of Lord Radcliffe in *Welham* v *Director of Public Prosecutions* [1961] AC 103, the cases concerned with persons performing public duties are not to be regarded as a special category in the manner described by Lord Diplock, but rather as exemplifying the general principle that conspiracies to defraud are not restricted to cases of intention to cause the victim economic loss. On the contrary, they are to be understood in the broad sense described by Lord Radcliffe and Lord Denning in *Welham* v *Director of Public Prosecutions* - the view which Viscount Dilhorne favoured in *R* v *Scott* [1975] AC 819, as apparently did the other members of the Appellate Committee who agreed with him in that case (apart, it seems, from Lord Diplock).

With these principles in mind, their Lordships turn to *R* v *Allsop*, 64 Cr App R 29 itself. In that case the defendant was a sub-broker for a hire-purchase company. Acting in collusion with others, he entered false particulars in forms submitted to the company, to induce it to accept applications for hire-purchase facilities which it might otherwise have rejected, although the defendant both expected and believed that the transactions in question would be completed satisfactorily and that the company would achieve its contemplated profit, as it appears in fact to have done. Examples of the false particulars were that the price of the car concerned would be inflated so as to allow an illusory deposit to be shown as having been paid by the intending hire-purchaser; or the value of the car taken in part exchange would be stated at more than the true figure; or a car dealer would be named as the seller when the transaction was a private one and no established car dealer played any part in it. What the defendant sought to achieve was an increase in the company's business, and therefore of his own commission. The defendant was charged with conspiracy to defraud. The judge directed the jury that they must be sure that the conspirators knew that they were inducing the company to act in circumstances in which they might cause or create the likelihood of economic loss or prejudice. The jury convicted the defendant. He appealed on the ground that the judge's direction was too wide; he should, it was submitted, have directed the jury that they must be sure that the defendant intended to cause economic loss to the company. The Court of Appeal dismissed the appeal. The judgment of the court was delivered by Shaw LJ. The central passage in the judgment reads, at p31:

"It seemed to this court that Mr Heald's argument traversed the shadowy region between intent and motive. Generally the primary objective of fraudsmen is to advantage themselves. The detriment that results to their victims is secondary to that purpose, and incidental. It is 'intended' only in the sense that it is a contemplated outcome of the fraud that is perpetrated. If the deceit which is employed imperils the economic interest of the person deceived, this is sufficient to constitute fraud even though in the event no actual loss is suffered and notwithstanding that the deceiver did not desire to bring about an actual loss."

In reaching this conclusion, the Court of Appeal found it necessary to reconcile it with the narrow definition of conspiracy to defraud expressed in the speech of Lord Diplock in *R* v *Scott* [1975] AC 819, 841, to which their Lordships have already referred. This they did on the basis that "economic loss" may be "ephemeral and not lasting, or potential and not actual; but even a threat of financial prejudice while it exists may be measured in terms of money." They continued, at p32:

"In the present case, the part of the history which is common ground reveals that in this sense [the company] did suffer actual loss for they paid too much for cars worth less than their pretended value; and they relied upon the creditworthiness of hire-purchasers as measured by the deposit stated to have been paid when none had been paid. It matters not that in the end the hire-purchasers concerned paid to [the company] what was due to them ..."

They concluded by praying in aid a passage from the speech of Lord Diplock in *R* v *Hyam* [1975] AC 55, 86, - a case concerned with the mental element in the crime of murder.

In the context of conspiracy to defraud, it is necessary to bear in mind that such a conspiracy is an agreement to practise a fraud on somebody (cf *Welham* v *Director of Public Prosecutions* [1961] AC 103, 133, per Lord Denning). In *R* v *Allsop*, 64 Cr App R 29 what the defendant agreed to do was to present the company with false particulars, in reliance upon which, as he knew, the company would decide whether to enter into hire purchase transactions. It is then necessary to consider whether that could constitute a conspiracy to defraud, notwithstanding that the defendant's underlying purpose or motive was not to damage any economic interest of the company but to ensure that the transaction went through so that he would earn his commission. Their Lordships can see no reason why such an agreement should not be a conspiracy to defraud the company, substantially for the reasons given by the Court of Appeal. The defendant was, for his own purposes, dishonestly supplying the company with false information which persuaded it to accept risks which it would or might not have accepted if it had known the true facts. Their Lordships cannot see why this was not an agreement to practise a fraud on the company because, as Shaw LJ said, it was a dishonest agreement to employ a deceit which imperilled the economic interests of the company.

The attention of their Lordships was drawn to a critique of *R* v *Allsop* in *Smith & Hogan, Criminal Law*, 6th ed (1988), p273, to which they have given careful consideration. The authors first criticise the reference by the Court of Appeal to *R* v *Hyam* [1975] AC 55. With this criticism, their Lordships are inclined to agree, doubting whether an authority on the mental element in the crime of murder throws much light on the nature of a conspiracy to defraud. However, the Court of Appeal only felt it necessary to pray in aid Lord Diplock's speech in *R* v *Hyam* in order to circumnavigate the dictum of Lord Diplock in *R* v *Scott* [1975] AC 819, an exercise which their Lordships do not need to embark upon since they consider that dictum to be, for the reasons they have explained, too narrowly expressed. Next, the authors suggest that *R* v *Allsop* can be explained on the basis that there was an intention on the part of the defendant to defraud the company, since he intended the company to pay, as indeed it did pay, money for cars which it would not have paid, even though in the outcome it suffered no loss. There is force in this suggestion, as was recognised by the Court of Appeal itself: 64 Cr App R 29, 31. But the Court of Appeal was concerned with the question whether the conviction could stand on the basis of the summing up of the trial judge; and their Lordships are now concerned with the correctness of the reasoning of the Court of Appeal on that question, at p31.

Lastly it is suggested that, on the rationalisation which the authors prefer, the case was not about recklessness, and did not decide that anything less than intention in the strict sense would suffice for conspiracy to defraud. Their Lordships are however reluctant to allow this part of the law to become enmeshed in a distinction, sometimes artificially drawn, between intention and recklessness. The question whether particular facts reveal a conspiracy to defraud depends upon what the conspirators have dishonestly agreed to do, and in particular whether they have agreed to practise a fraud on somebody. for this purpose it is enough for example that, as in *R* v *Allsop* and in the present case, the conspirators have dishonestly agreed to bring about a state of affairs which they realise will or may deceive the victim into so acting, or failing to act, that he will suffer economic loss or his economic interests will be put at risk. It is however important in such a case, as the Court of Appeal stressed in *R* v *Allsop*, to distinguish a conspirator's intention (or immediate purpose) dishonestly to bring about such a state of affairs from his motive (or underlying purpose). The latter may be benign to the extent that he does not wish the victim or potential victim to suffer harm; but the mere fact that it is benign will not of itself prevent the agreement from constituting a conspiracy to defraud. Of course, if the conspirators were not acting dishonestly, there will have been no conspiracy to defraud; and in any event their benign purpose (if it be such) is a matter which, if they prove to be guilty, can be taken into account at the stage of sentence.

In forming this view of the matter, their Lordships draw comfort from the fact that *R* v *Allsop* has been accepted as good authority by the Supreme Court of Canada in *R* v *Olan, Hudson and Hartnett* (1978) 41 CCC (2d) 145, 150, per Dickson J delivering the judgment of the court, in a passage subsequently followed by the Supreme Court of Canada in *Vézina* v *The Queen* (1986) 25 DLR (4th) 82, 96, per Lamer J likewise delivering the judgment of the court.

For these reasons their Lordships, like the Court of Appeal, are satisfied that there was no misdirection by the judge in the present case. Their Lordships will humbly advise Her Majesty that this appeal should be dismissed.'

11 INCHOATE OFFENCES II

Anderton v Ryan [1985] AC 560

See *R* v *Shivpuri*, below.

R v Campbell (1991) 93 Cr App R 350 Court of Appeal (Criminal Division) (Watkins LJ, Hirst and Popplewell JJ)

Actus reus of attempt - proper direction to the jury

Facts

The appellant was observed by the police who, acting on information received, suspected that he was planning to rob a sub-post office. He was seen loitering in the vicinity of the sub-post office on a number of occasions, wearing dark glasses, and carrying what appeared to be a heavy object. On being arrested outside the sub-post office, the appellant was found to be in possession of an imitation firearm, and a threatening note. He claimed that he originally had intended to carry out the robbery, but had changed his mind before he was arrested. At his trial for attempted robbery his submission of no case was rejected. The trial judge, in directing the jury as regards the actus reus of attempt, referred approvingly to the common law authorities that prevailed before the enactment of the Criminal Attempts Act 1981. On appeal against conviction:

Held

The appeal would be allowed.

Watkins LJ:

Having referred to *DPP* v *Stonehouse* (1977) 65 Cr App R 192, and *R* v *Gulleffer* (Note) (1990) 91 Cr App R 356, stated:

'In *Jones* (1990) 91 Cr App R 351, [1990] 1 WLR 1057 Taylor LJ giving the judgment of the Court stated that - and these are my words - it was infinitely preferable that a judge, when giving directions to the jury upon what involved an attempt to commit a crime, should stick to the definition of an attempt in the Act itself and with that we respectfully and entirely agree.

The judge in the present case properly and accurately directed the jury upon what is contained in s1(1) of the Criminal Attempts Act 1981. But he also regaled them with references to the law which obtained before that Act was passed. We believe that to be wholly unnecessary as we have already indicated.

It is sufficient for a judge, when directing a jury upon the law of attempt, to say, before you, the jury, can convict the defendant you must be satisfied so as to feel sure of two things; first, that he intended to commit a robbery, for instance, and, secondly, that with that intent he did an act which was more than an act of preparation to commit that offence. It is for you to decide whether the act relied upon by the prosecution was more than merely preparatory.

To embark discursively upon what the law was previously and to provide a jury with elaborate instances of what can and what cannot constituted an attempt may serve to confuse the jury especially seeing that the law contained in the Act itself is clear. ... Looking at the circumstances here it was beyond dispute that the appellant, at the material time, was carrying an imitation firearm which he made no attempt to remove from his clothing. He was not, as he had done previously that day, wearing, as a form of disguise, sun-glasses. It was not suggested that he had, in the course of making his way down the road past the post-box, turned and, so to speak, moved towards the door of the post office so as to indicate that he intended to enter that place.

In order to effect the robbery it is equally beyond dispute it would have been quite impossible unless obviously he had entered the post office, gone to the counter and made some kind of hostile act - directed, of course, at whoever was behind the counter and in a position to hand him money. A number of acts remained undone and the series of acts which he had already performed - namely, making his way from his home or other place where he commenced to ride his motor cycle on a journey to a place near a post office, dismounting from the cycle and walking towards the post office door - were clearly acts which were, in the judgment of this court, indicative of mere preparation, even if he was still of a mind to rob the post office, of the commission that is of the offence of robbery. If a person, in circumstances such as this, has not even gained the place where he could be in a position to carry out the offence, it is extremely unlikely that it could ever be said that he had performed an act which could be properly said to be an attempt.

It would be unwise of a court to lay down hard and fast rules as to when, in varying circumstances, an attempt has begun. The matter has to be decided on a case by case basis as the issue arises. Always remembering that it is for the judge, as has already been said as a matter of judgment, to come to the conclusion whether or not the Crown, at the end of its case, had brought before the court evidence which properly and safely can be left to the jury to consider upon the vital issue.

In our judgment in this case, the judge was in error in coming to the conclusion that on the evidence - which was, as I have already said, undisputed - the jury could properly conclude that an attempt had been made. He should have stopped the trial as he was invited to by learned defence counsel. That being so, and for all the reasons previously stated, including the state of the law, in our view, this appeal must be allowed and the conviction quashed.'

R v Gullefer (1990) 91 Cr App R 356 (The Lord Chief Justice, Mr Justice Kennedy and Mr Justice Owen)

Actus reus of attempt

Facts (as taken from the judgment of Lord Lane CJ)

'On March 5, 1988, the appellant attended the Greyhound Racing Stadium at Romford. During the last race, as the dogs rounded the final bend, he climbed the fence on to the track in front of the dogs, waving his arms and attempting to distract them. His efforts were only marginally successful and the stewards decided that it was unnecessary to declare "no race". Had they made such a declaration, by the rules the bookmakers would have been obliged to repay the amount of his stake to any punter, but would not have been liable to pay any winnings to those punters who would have been successful if the race had been valid.

When interviewed by the police the appellant said the reasons for his behaviour were partly that a year earlier he had lost a large bet at the stadium by reason of one of the stadium's staff leaning over the rails and distracting the dog on which he had gambled. He also admitted that he had attempted to stop the race because the dog on which he had staked £18 was losing. He hoped that by his actions the dogs would be distracted, that the stewards would declare "no race" and that he would therefore recover his stake from the bookmaker.

The perfected grounds of appeal contained four grounds. First, that the property which was the subject of the alleged attempted theft was not "property belonging to another" within the meaning of the Theft Act 1968. Secondly, that even if the appellant had successfully completed his plan and had recovered the £18 from the bookmaker, that would not have amounted to an "appropriation of property belonging to another". Those two grounds of appeal were abandoned by Mr Copeman at the outset of his submissions to this court. In the light of our decision on the third ground of appeal, it is unnecessary for us to inquire whether that abandonment was proper. The main burden of counsel's submission to us has been the third ground of appeal, namely, that the acts proved to have been carried out by the appellant were not sufficiently proximate to the completed offence of theft to be capable of comprising an attempt to commit theft.'

Held

The appeal would be allowed.

Lord Lane CJ:

'We have been referred to a number of decisions, many of them of respectable antiquity, which show, if nothing else, the difficulties which abound in this branch of the criminal law. The present law is, however, now enshrined in the words of the Criminal Attempts Act 1981. Section 1(1) provides: "If, with intent to commit an offence to which this section applies, a person does an act which is more than merely preparatory to the commission of the offence, he is guilty of attempting to commit the offence."

Section 4(3) provides:

"Where, in proceedings against a person for an offence under section 1 above, there is evidence sufficient in law to support a finding that he did an act falling within subsection (1) of that section, the question whether or not his act fell within that subsection is a question of fact."

Thus the judge's task is to decide whether there is evidence upon which a jury could reasonably come to the conclusion that the appellant had gone beyond the realm of mere preparation and had embarked upon the actual commission of the offence. If not, he must withdraw the case from the jury. If there is such evidence, it is then for the jury to decide whether the defendant did in fact go beyond mere preparation. That is the way in which the judge approached this case. He ruled that there was sufficient evidence. Mr Copeman (counsel for the appellant) submits that he was wrong in so ruling.

The first task of the court is to apply the words of the Act of 1981 to the facts of the case. Was the appellant still in the stage of preparation to commit the substantive offence, or was there a basis of fact which would entitle the jury to say that he had embarked on the theft itself? Might it properly be said that when he jumped on to the track he was trying to steal £18 from the bookmaker?

Our view is that it could not properly be said that at that stage he was in the process of committing theft. What he was doing was jumping on to the track in an effort to distract the dogs, which in its turn, he hoped, would have the effect of forcing the stewards to declare "no race", which would in its turn give him the opportunity to go back to the bookmaker and demand the £18 he had staked. In our view there was insufficient evidence for it to be said that he had, when he jumped on to the track, gone beyond mere preparation.

So far at least as the present case is concerned, we do not think that it is necessary to examine the authorities which preceded the Act of 1981, save to say that the sections we have already quoted in this judgment seem to be a blend of various decisions, some of which were not easy to reconcile with others.

However, in deference to the arguments of counsel, we venture to make the following observations. Since the passing of the Act of 1981, a division of this court in *Ilyas* (1984) 78 Cr App R 17, has helpfully collated the authorities. As appears from the judgment in that case, there seem to have been two lines of authority. The first was exemplified by the decision in *Eagleton* (1855) Dears CC 515. That was a case where the defendant was alleged to have attempted to obtain money from the guardians of a parish by falsely pretending to the relieving officer that he had delivered loaves of bread of the proper weight to the outdoor poor, when in fact the loaves were deficient in weight.

Parke B, delivering the judgment of the court of nine judges, said, at p538:

"Acts remotely leading towards the commission of the offence are not to be considered as attempts to commit it, but acts immediately connected with it are; and if, in this case, after the credit with the relieving officer for the fraudulent overcharge, any further step on the part of the defendant had been necessary to obtain payment, as the making out a further account or producing the vouchers to the Board, we should have thought that the obtaining credit in account with the relieving officer would not have been sufficiently proximate to obtaining the money. But, on the statement in this case, no other act on the part of the defendant would have been required. It was the last act, depending on himself, towards the payment of the money, and therefore it ought to be considered as an attempt."

Lord Diplock in *DPP* v *Stonehouse* (1977) 65 Cr App R 192, 208, [1978] AC 55, 68, having cited part of that passage from *Eagleton*, added: "In other words the offender must have crossed the Rubicon and burnt his boats."

The other line of authority is based on a passage in Stephen's Digest of the Criminal Law, 5th ed (1894) art 50: "An attempt to commit a crime is an act done with intent to commit that crime, and forming part of a series of acts which would constitute its actual commission if it were not interrupted." As Lord Edmund-Davies points out in *DPP* v *Stonehouse* at p224 and p85, that definition has been repeatedly cited with judicial approval: see Byrne J in *Hope* v *Brown* [1954] 1 WLR 250, 253 and Lord Parker CJ in *Davey* v *Lee* (1967) 51 Cr App R 303, [1968] 1 QB 366. However, as Lord Parker CJ in the latter case points out, at p370G, Stephen's definition falls short of defining the exact point of time at which the series of acts can be said to begin.

It seems to us that the words of the Act of 1981 seek to steer a midway course.

They do not provide, as they might have done, that the *Eagleton* test is to be followed, or that, as Lord Diplock suggested, the defendant must have reached a point from which it was impossible for him to retreat before the actus reus of an attempt is proved. On the other hand the words give perhaps as clear a guidance as is possible in the circumstances on the point of time at which Stephen's "series of acts" begin. It begins when the merely preparatory acts come to an end and the defendant embarks upon the crime proper. When that is will depend, of course, upon the facts in any particular case.

Mr Copeman advanced certain other arguments before us on the basis that the judge had been guilty of misdirections in his summing up to the jury. In the light of our decision upon the main ground of appeal it is unnecessary for us to consider whether those complaints are justified or not. The appeal against conviction is allowed and the conviction quashed.'

R v Shivpuri [1986] 2 WLR 988 House of Lords (Lords Hailsham, Elwyn-Jones, Scarman, Bridge, and Mackay)

Impossibility as a defence to attempt

Facts

The defendant, whilst in India, was paid £1,000 to act as a drugs courier. He was required to collect a package containing a consignment of drugs which would be delivered to him in England, and distribute its contents according to instructions which would be given to him. On collecting the package, the defendant was arrested by police officers, and he confessed to them that he believed its contents to be either heroin or cannabis. On further analysis by the police the package was found to contain only a harmless vegetable substance. The defendant was convicted of attempting to be knowingly concerned in dealing with and harbouring a controlled drug, namely heroin, and he appealed unsuccessfully to the Court of Appeal. The defendant renewed his appeal before the House of Lords.

Held

The appeal would be dismissed.

Lord Bridge:

'The certified question depends on the true construction of the Criminal Attempts Act 1981. That

Act marked an important new departure since, by section 6, it abolished the offence of attempt at common law and substituted a new statutory code governing attempts to commit criminal offences. It was considered by your Lordships' House last year in *Anderton v Ryan* [1985] AC 560 after the decision in the Court of Appeal which is the subject of the present appeal. That might seem an appropriate starting point from which to examine the issues arising in this appeal. But your Lordships have been invited to exercise the power under the *Practice Statement (Judicial Precedent)* [1966] 1 WLR 1234 to depart from the reasoning in that decision if it proves necessary to do so in order to affirm the convictions appealed against in the instant case. I was not only a party to the decision in *Anderton v Ryan*, I was also the author of one of the two opinions approved by the majority which must be taken to express the House's ratio. That seems to me to afford a sound reason why, on being invited to re-examine the language of the statute in its application to the facts of this appeal, I should initially seek to put out of mind what I said in *Anderton v Ryan*. Accordingly I propose to approach the issue in the first place as an exercise in statutory construction, applying the language of the Act to the facts of the case, as if the matter were res integra. If this leads me to the conclusion that the appellant was not guilty of any attempt to commit a relevant offence, that will be the end of the matter. But if this initial exercise inclines me to reach a contrary conclusion, it will then be necessary to consider whether the precedent set by *Anderton v Ryan* bars that conclusion or whether it can be surmounted either on the ground that the earlier decision is distinguishable or that it would be appropriate to depart from it under the *Practice Statement*.

[His Lordship then related section 1 of the Criminal Attempts Act 1981 and continued]

Applying this language to the facts of the case, the first question to be asked is whether the appellant intended to commit the offence of being knowingly concerned in dealing with and harbouring drugs of Class A or Class B with intent to evade the prohibition on their importation. Translated into more homely language the question may be rephrased, without in any way altering its legal significance, in the following terms: did the appellant intend to receive and store (harbour) and in due course pass on to third parties (deal with) packages of heroin or cannabis which he knew had been smuggled into England from India? The answer is plainly yes, he did. Next, did he in relation to each offence, do an act which was more than merely preparatory to the commission of the offence? The act relied on in relation to harbouring was the receipt and retention of the packages found in the lining of the suitcase. The act relied on in relation to dealing was the meeting at Southall station with the intended recipient of one of the packages. In each case the act was clearly more than preparatory to the commission of the *intended* offence; it was not and could not be more than merely preparatory to the commission of the *actual* offence, because the facts were such that the commission of the actual offence was impossible. Here then is the nub of the matter. Does the "act which is more than merely preparatory to the commission of the offence" in section 1(1) of the Act of 1981 (the actus reus of the statutory offence of attempt) require any more than an act which is more than merely preparatory to the commission of the offence which the defendant intended to commit? Section 1(2) must surely indicate a negative answer; if it were otherwise, whenever the facts were such that the commission of the actual offence was impossible, it would be impossible to prove an act more than merely preparatory to the commission of that offence and subsections (1) and (2) would contradict each other.

This very simple, perhaps over simple, analysis leads me to the provisional conclusion that the appellant was rightly convicted of the two offences of attempt with which he was charged. But can this conclusion stand with *Anderton v Ryan*? The appellant in that case was charged with an attempt to handle stolen goods. She bought a video recorder believing it to be stolen. On the facts as they were to be assumed it was not stolen. By a majority the House decided that she was entitled to be acquitted. I have re-examined the case with care. If I could extract from the speech of Lord Roskill or from my own speech a clear and coherent principle distinguishing those cases of attempting the impossible which amount to offences under that statute from those which do not, I should have to consider carefully on which side of the line the instant case fell. But I have to confess that I can find no such principle.

Running through Lord Roskill's speech and my own in *Anderton* v *Ryan* [1985] AC 560 is the concept of "objectively innocent" acts which, in my speech certainly, are contrasted with "guilty acts." A few citations will make this clear. Lord Roskill said, at p580:

"My Lords, it has been strenuously and ably argued for the respondent that these provisions involve that a defendant is liable to conviction for an attempt even where his actions are innocent but he erroneously believes facts which, if true, would make those actions criminal, and further, that he is liable to such conviction whether or not in the event his intended course of action is completed."

He proceeded to reject the argument. At p582 I referred to the appellant's purchase of the video recorder and said: "Objectively considered, therefore, her purchase of the recorder was a perfectly proper commercial transaction." A further passage from my speech proceeded, at pp582-583:

"The question may be stated in abstract terms as follows. Does section 1 of the Act of 1981 create a new offence of attempt where a person embarks on and completes a course of conduct which is objectively innocent, solely on the ground that the person mistakenly believes facts which, if true, would make that course of conduct a complete crime? If the question must be answered affirmatively it requires convictions in a number of surprising cases: the classic case, put by Bramwell B. in *R* v *Collins* (1864) 9 Cox CC 497, of the man who takes away his own umbrella from a stand, believing it not to be his own and with intent to steal it; the case of the man who has consensual intercourse with a girl over 16 believing her to be under that age; the case of the art dealer who sells a picture which he represents to be and which is in fact a genuine Picasso, but which the dealer mistakenly believes to be a fake. The common feature of all these cases, including that under appeal, is that the mind alone is guilty, the act is innocent."

I then contrasted the case of the man who attempts to pick the empty pocket, saying:

"Putting the hand in the pocket is the guilty act, the intent to steal is the guilty mind, the offence is appropriately dealt with as an attempt, and the impossibility of committing the full offence for want of anything in the pocket to steal is declared by [subsection (2)] to be no obstacle to conviction."

If we fell into error, it is clear that our concern was to avoid convictions in situations which most people, as a matter of common sense, would not regard as involving criminality. In this connection it is to be regretted that we did not take due note of paragraph 2.97 of the Law Commission's report (Criminal Law: Attempt, and Impossibility in Relation to Attempt, Conspiracy and Incitement (1980) (Law Commission No. 102)) which preceded the enactment of the Act of 1981, which reads:

"If it is right in principle that an attempt should be chargeable even though the crime which it is sought to commit could not possibly be committed, we do not think that we should be deterred by the consideration that such a change in our law would also cover some extreme and exceptional cases in which a prosecution would be theoretically possible. An example would be where a person is offered goods at such a low price that he believes that they are stolen, when in fact they are not; if he actually purchases them, upon the principles which we have discussed he would be liable for an attempt to handle stolen goods. Another case which has been much debated is that raised in argument by Bramwell B. in *R* v *Collins* (1864) 9 Cox CC 497. If A takes his own umbrella, mistaking it for one belonging to B and intending to steal B's umbrella, is he guilty of attempted theft? Again, on the principles which we have discussed he would in theory be guilty, but in neither case would it be realistic to suppose that a complaint would be made or that a prosecution would ensue."

The prosecution in *Anderton* v *Ryan* itself falsified the Commission's prognosis in one of the "extreme and exceptional cases." It nevertheless probably holds good for other such cases, particularly that of the young man having sexual intercourse with a girl over 16, mistakenly believing her to be under that age, by which both Lord Roskill and I were much troubled.

However that may be, the distinction between acts which are "objectively innocent" and those which are not is an essential element in the reasoning in *Anderton* v *Ryan* and the decision, unless it can be supported on some other ground, must stand or fall by the validity of this distinction. I am satisfied on further consideration that the concept of "objective innocence" is incapable of sensible application in relation to the law of criminal attempts. The reason for this is that any attempt to commit an offence which involves "an act which is more than merely preparatory to the commission of the offence" but for any reason fails, so that in the event no offence is committed, must ex hypothesi, from the point of view of the criminal law, be "objectively innocent." What turns what would otherwise, from the point of view of the criminal law, be an innocent act into a crime is the intent of the actor to commit an offence. I say "from the point of view of the criminal law" because the law of tort must surely here be quite irrelevant. A puts his hand into B's pocket. Whether or not there is anything in the pocket capable of being stolen, if A intends to steal, his act is a criminal attempt; if he does not so intend, his act is innocent. A plunges a knife into a bolster in a bed. To avoid the complication of an offence of criminal damage, assume it to be A's bolster. If A believes the bolster to be his enemy B and intends to kill him, his act is an attempt to murder B; if he knows the bolster is only a bolster, his act is innocent. These considerations lead me to the conclusion that the distinction sought to be drawn in *Anderton* v *Ryan* between innocent and guilty acts considered "objectively" and independently of the state of mind of the actor cannot be sensibly maintained.

Another conceivable ground of distinction which was to some extent canvassed in argument, both in *Anderton* v *Ryan* and in the instant case, though no trace of it appears in the speeches in *Anderton* v *Ryan*, is a distinction which would make guilt or innocence of the crime of attempt in a case of mistaken belief dependent on what, for want of a better phrase, I will call the defendant's dominant intention. According to the theory necessary to sustain this distinction, the appellant's dominant intention in *Anderton* v *Ryan* was to buy a cheap video recorder; her belief that it was stolen was merely incidental. Likewise in the hypothetical case of attempted unlawful sexual intercourse, the young man's dominant intention was to have intercourse with the particular girl; his mistaken belief that she was under 16 was merely incidental. By contrast, in the instant case the appellant's dominant intention was to receive and distribute illegally imported heroin or cannabis.

Whilst I see the superficial attraction of this suggested ground of distinction, I also see formidable practical difficulties in its application. By what test is a jury to be told that a defendant's dominant intention is to be recognised and distinguished from his incidental but mistaken belief? But there is perhaps a more formidable theoretical difficulty. If this ground of distinction is relied on to support the acquittal of the appellant in *Anderton* v *Ryan*, it can only do so on the basis that her mistaken belief that the video recorder was stolen played no significant part in her decision to buy it and therefore she may be acquitted of the intent to handle stolen goods. But this line of reasoning runs into head-on collision with section 1(3) of the Act of 1981. The theory produces a situation where, apart from the subsection, her intention would not be regarded as having amounted to any intent to commit an offence. Section 1(3)(*b*) then requires one to ask whether, if the video recorder had in fact been stolen, her intention would have been regarded as an intent to handle stolen goods. The answer must clearly be yes, it would. If she had bought the video recorder knowing it to be stolen, when in fact it was, it would have availed her nothing to say that her dominant intention was to buy a video recorder because it was cheap and that her knowledge that it was stolen was merely incidental. This seems to me fatal to the dominant intention theory.

I am thus led to the conclusion that there is no valid ground on which *Anderton* v *Ryan* can be distinguished. I have made clear my own conviction, which as a party to the decision (and craving the indulgence of my noble and learned friends who agreed in it) I am the readier to express, that the decision was wrong. What then is to be done? If the case is indistinguishable, the application of the strict doctrine of precedent would require that the present appeal be allowed. Is it permissible to depart from precedent under the *Practice Statement (Judicial Precedent)* [1966] 1 WLR 1234 notwithstanding the especial need for certainty in the criminal law? The following considerations lead me to answer that question affirmatively. First, I am undeterred by the consideration that the decision in *Anderton* v *Ryan* was so recent. The *Practice Statement* is an effective abandonment of our pretention to infallibility. If a serious error embodied in a decision of this House has distorted the law, the sooner it is corrected the better. Secondly, I cannot see how, in the very nature of the case, anyone could have acted in reliance on the law as propounded in *Anderton* v *Ryan* in the belief that he was acting innocently and now find that, after all, he is to be held to have committed a criminal offence. Thirdly, to hold the House bound to follow *Anderton* v *Ryan* because it cannot be distinguished and to allow the appeal in this case would, it seems to me, be tantamount to a declaration that the Act of 1981 left the law of criminal attempts unchanged following the decision *R* v *Smith* [1975] AC 476. Finally, if, contrary to my present view, there is a valid ground on which it would be proper to distinguish cases similar to that considered in *Anderton* v *Ryan*, my present opinion on that point would not foreclose the option of making such a distinction in some future case.

I cannot conclude this opinion without disclosing that I have had the advantage, since the conclusion of the argument in this appeal, of reading an article by Professor Glanville Williams entitled "The Lords and Impossible Attempts, or Quis Custodiet Ipsos Custodes?" [1986] CLJ 33. The language in which he criticises the decision in *Anderton* v *Ryan* is not conspicuous for its moderation, but it would be foolish, on that account, not to recognise the force of the criticism and churlish not to acknowledge the assistance I have derived from it.

I would answer the certified question in the affirmative and dismiss the appeal.'

R v Walker & Hayles (1990) 90 Cr App R 226 Court of Appeal (Criminal Division) (Lloyd LJ, Gatehouse and Pill JJ)

Attempted murder - mens rea

Facts

The appellants carried out a violent attack upon a man named Royston John, which involved dropping him from a third floor balcony to the ground. The appellants were charged with attempted murder. The jury were directed that they could convict if they were sure that the appellants intended to kill the victim, in the sense that they were sure that the appellants knew that there was a 'very high degree of probability' that the victim would be killed. Following conviction, the appellants appealed on the basis that the trial judge had misdirected the jury as to the mental element required on a charge of attempted murder.

Held

The appeal would be dismissed.

Lloyd LJ:

'We turn to the main ground of appeal, namely the direction on intention. Since the charge was attempted murder, the prosecution had to prove an intention to kill. Intention to cause really serious harm would not have been enough. We were told that this is the first case in which this Court has had to consider the correct direction in a case of attempted murder since *R* v *Moloney* (1985) 81 Cr App R 93, [1985] AC 905, *R* v *Hancock and Shankland* (1986) 82 Cr App R 264, [1986] AC 55, and *Nedrick* (1986) 83 Cr App R 267, [1986] 3 All ER 1.

We have already said that there could be no criticism of the initial direction at the start of the summing-up, and repeated at the conclusion. The recorder was right to keep it short. "Trying to kill" was the expression he used as a paraphrase. That was easy for the jury to understand, and could not on any view of the law be regarded as too favourable to the prosecution. "Trying to kill" is synonymous with purpose. It has never been suggested that a man does not intend what he is trying to achieve. The difficulty only arises when he brings about a result which he is not trying to achieve.

But when the jury returned, the recorder, as we have seen, went further. The first question we have had to consider is whether he was right to go further, or whether he should simply have repeated what he had already said, perhaps adding that the jury should consider all the circumstances and use their commonsense. One of the recorder's difficulties - as it has been a difficulty for us - is that the question is not strictly grammatical. But we think that what the jury probably wanted to know could be paraphrased as follows:

"If we are satisfied that the appellants threw him over, are we bound to go on to consider the question of intention, ie whether they intended to kill or whether it was done in the heat of the moment without any intent? Or is the fact that they threw him over enough?"

If that was indeed the meaning of the question, then it would have been sufficient for the recorder to repeat the direction he had already given. The constant theme of *Moloney* (supra), *Hancock* (supra) and *Nedrick* (supra) is that it is only in rare and exceptional cases that the judge needs to elaborate. Mr Bevan, on behalf of the prosecution, submitted that this was one of those rare and exceptional cases where the recorder was required to elaborate, since the jury were in terms asking for a foresight direction. We do not accept that submission. If our understanding of the question is correct, the jury would have been content with a repetition of the direction which they had already received. We can, however, understand why the recorder went further, since he had only just given a direction in simple terms, which was as clear as could be. Moreover the position is not quite the same in a case of attempted murder as it is in murder. In the great majority of murder cases, as the Court pointed out in *Nedrick* (supra), the defendant's desire goes hand in hand with his intention. If he desires serious harm, and death results from his action, he is guilty of murder. A simple direction suffices in such cases. The rare and exceptional case is where the defendant does not desire serious harm, or indeed any harm at all. But where a defendant is charged with attempted murder, he may well have desired serious harm, without desiring death. So the desire of serious harm does not provide the answer. It does not go hand in hand with the relevant intention, as it does in the great majority of murder cases, since in attempted murder the relevant intention must be an intention to kill.

Considerations such as these may have led the recorder to give the expanded direction in terms of foresight. But, as we have said, it would have been better if he had not done so. The mere fact that a jury calls for a further direction on intention does not of itself make it a rare and exceptional case requiring a foresight direction. In most cases they will only need to be reminded of the simple direction which they will already have been given, namely that the relevant intention is an intention to kill, and that nothing less will suffice.

But the mere fact that the recorder gave a foresight direction in this case, when he need not have done, does not afford any ground of appeal. And so we turn to the direction itself. The main criticism of the direction is that the recorder should have answered the second half of the question with a resounding "No."

Instead he may have confused the jury. He may have led them to equate the probability of death and the foresight of death with an intention to kill. That was the very error exposed in *R v Moloney* (supra) and *Nedrick* (1986) 83 Cr App R 267.

We do not regard this criticism as justified. It ignores the third question which the recorder suggested that the jury should ask themselves. Looking at the further direction as a whole, and not piecemeal, the recorder was following the guidelines in *Nedrick*. We quote from page 270:

"In *R v Hancock* (1986) 82 Cr App R 264, [1986] AC 455, the House decided that the *Moloney* guidelines require a reference to probability. Lord Scarman said at p276 and p473: 'They also require an explanation that the greater the probability of a consequence the more likely it is that the consequence was foreseen and that if that consequence was foreseen the greater the probability is that that consequence was also intended.'"

When determining whether the defendant had the necessary intent, it may therefore be helpful for a jury to ask themselves two questions:

(1) How probable was the consequence which resulted from the defendant's voluntary act? (2) Did he foresee that consequence? If he did not appreciate that death or really serious harm was likely to

result from his act, he cannot have intended to bring it about. If he did, but thought that the risk to which he was exposing the person killed was only slight, then it may be easy for the jury to conclude that he did not intend to bring about that result. On the other hand, if the jury are satisfied that at the material time the defendant recognised that death or serious harm would be virtually certain (barring some unforeseen intervention) to result from his voluntary act, then that is a fact from which they may find it easy to infer that he intended to kill or do serious bodily harm, even though he may not have had any desire to achieve that result."

Questions (1) and (2) in the recorder's further direction correspond precisely with questions (1) and (2) in *Nedrick*. If the answers to (1) and (2) had been no, then no further question would have arisen. But if the answers were to be yes, and the jury were to be sure of it, then the third question would arise. I will read it again:

"If you are sure of that, the last question is this one: you are entitled to draw the inference that when he joined in chucking John over that balcony wall, he was actually trying to kill him if he could, knowing quite well there was a very high degree of possibility that he would be killed when he hit the ground."

It may be that that could have been better expressed. Few summings-up are perfect. But the message is clear enough. What the recorder was saying was:

"If you are sure of (1) and (2), you would be entitled to draw the inference that they were intending or trying to kill the victim."

It is important to note that the recorder said that the jury would be entitled to draw the inference: he was not saying that they must draw the inference. By the use of the word "entitled," he was making it sufficiently clear to the jury that the question whether they drew the inference or not was a question for them. This is borne out by the passage which immediately followed in which the recorder said that the jury would be entitled to bear in mind the speed of events on the one hand and the speed at which a man can make up his mind on the other.

So we reject the submission that the recorder was equating foresight with intent, or that he may have given that impression to the jury. He was perfectly properly saying that foresight was something from which the jury could infer intent. He was treating the question as part of the law of evidence, not as part of the substantive law of attempted murder.

The second criticism advanced by both appellants is directed to the use of the expression "very high degree of possibility." We were at once struck by the curious use of the word "possibility" when the recorder had twice referred to "high degree of probability." It occurred to us that "possibility" might be a mistranscription, more especially as degrees of possibility are not easy to understand. A thing is either possible, or it is not. Our view was confirmed when counsel for one of the appellants told us that according to his note of the direction, the recorder did indeed refer to "very high degree of probability," not "possibility." We are greatly obliged to counsel for the very proper assistance thus afforded to the court.

But it does not end there. It was argued that even "very high degree of probability" is a misdirection. The recorder should have used the words "virtual certainty." Counsel relied on the concluding passage from the judgment in *Nedrick* (1986) 83 Cr App R 267, 271, [1986] 3 All ER 1, 4.

"As Lord Bridge said in *Moloney* (p106 and p925): ' … the probability of the consequence taken to have been foreseen must be little short of overwhelming before it will suffice to establish the necessary intent.' At p926 he uses the expression 'moral certainty'; at p929 he said, ' … will lead to a certain consequence unless something unexpected supervenes to prevent it.'

Where the charge is murder and in the rare cases where the simple direction is not enough, the jury should be directed that they are not entitled to infer the necessary intention, unless they feel sure that death or serious bodily harm was a virtual certainty (barring some unforeseen intervention) as a result of the defendant's actions and that the defendant appreciated that such was the case. Where a man realises that it is for all practical purposes inevitable that his actions will result in death or serious harm, the inference may be irresistible that he intended that result, however little he may have desired or wished it to happen. The decision is one for the jury to be reached upon a consideration of all the evidence."

Counsel submitted that virtual certainty is the correct test in all cases where the simple direction is not enough, and that to substitute high degree of probability is to water down that test. We agree with counsel this far, that in the rare cases where an expanded direction is required it is better that the judge should continue to use the term "virtual certainty," which has the authority of this Court in *Nedrick*. We also agree that there is no difference in this respect between the kind of case considered in *Nedrick*, where the question was whether serious harm was intended, even though it was not desired, and the present case, where serious harm was clearly desired and the only question is whether death was intended. In the rare cases where a foresight direction is required, the same language should be used.

But we do not accept that the reference to "very high degree of probability" was a misdirection. The truth is, as Messrs Smith and Hogan point out in Criminal Law 6th ed, at p59, that once one departs from absolute certainty, there is bound to be a question of degree. We do not regard the difference of degree, if there is one, between very high degree of probability on the one hand and virtual certainty on the other as being sufficient to render what the recorder said a misdirection. We note that in Lord Bridge's view no reasonable jury could have acquitted the defendant in *Hyam* v *DPP* (1974) 59 Cr App R 91, (1975) AC 55 if they had been given the correct direction; yet we would venture to wonder whether serious injury in that case would have been regarded by the jury as more than very highly probable. Whatever the direction we suspect that in practice juries will continue to use their commonsense.

We also note that in the Court of Appeal in *Hancock* (1986) 82 Cr App R 264, this Court chose "highly likely" as the test. Although the House of Lords (ibid [1986] AC 455) did not approve the guideline directions suggested by the Court of Appeal, that was on the ground that juries "are not chosen for their understanding of a logical and phased process leading by question and answer to a conclusion but are expected to exercise practical common sense" (a quotation from Lord Scarman's speech), not because of the use of the term "highly likely." Reading Lord Scarman's speech in *Hancock* at p276 and p473, and the first of the two passages which we have quoted from *Nedrick*, we are not persuaded that it is only when death is a virtual certainty that the jury can infer intention to kill. Providing the dividing line between intention and recklessness is never blurred, and provided it is made clear, as it was here, that it is a question for the jury to infer from the degree of probability in the particular case whether the defendant intended to kill, we would not regard the use of the words "very high degree of probability" as a misdirection. To avoid any misunderstanding, we repeat that in the great majority of cases of attempted murder, as in murder, the simple direction will suffice, without any reference to foresight. In the rare case where an expanded direction is required in terms of foresight, courts should continue to use virtual certainty as the test, rather than high probability.'

R v Widdowson (1986) 82 Cr App R 314 Court of Appeal (Criminal Division) (Ackner LJ, Drake and Saville JJ)

Actus reus of attempt

Facts

The defendant had completed a form on which he was applying for credit facilities with which he wished to purchase a vehicle. Because of his poor credit record he signed the form using the name of a neighbour, Steven Pitman, and was subsequently convicted of attempting to obtain services by deception. The defendant appealed, contending that the credit facilities would not constitute a service within s1 of the Theft Act 1978.

Held

The appeal would be allowed.

Saville J:

[On the question of whether the defendant had progressed far enough for a charge of attempt to succeed]

'There remains the question of attempt. In our judgment there was no evidence of an attempt to commit the crime alleged within the meaning of section 1(1) of the Criminal Attempts Act 1981. It seems to us that at most all the appellant had actually done was to attempt to ascertain whether or not Steven Pitman was creditworthy, in the sense of being acceptable to the finance company as a prospective hire purchaser. It was not suggested that a favourable reply from the finance company could have constituted the obtaining of services within the meaning of the Theft Act 1978, if only because there was no question of payment being made for such a reply. Thus the question is whether this appellant's act in giving the false particulars on the form can reasonably be said to have been more than merely preparatory to the obtaining of hire purchase facilities. In our view this cannot be said. Assuming that the finance company had responded favourably to the proposal, it still remained for the appellant to seek a hire purchase deal from them. To our minds it is that step which would constitute an attempt to obtain the services relied upon in this case. If one asks whether this appellant had carried out every step which it was necessary for him to perform to achieve the consequences alleged to have been attempted, the answer must be that he did not.

Equally, it seems to us, this appellant's acts cannot be described as immediately rather than merely remotely connected with the specific offence alleged to have been attempted. Thus whichever of the tests described in *Ilyas* (1984) 78 Cr App R 17 is applied, what the appellant did cannot reasonably be described as more than merely preparatory.

In the passage we have cited from his ruling in the court below, it would appear that the learned judge was influenced by the suggested inevitability of the transaction going ahead, ie that the appellant's intentions would have remained the same. That, with great respect, ignores the fact that dishonest intentions alone do not constitute criminal attempts and that in addition it is necessary to establish, to use the words of Lord Diplock, that the offender has crossed the Rubicon and burned his boats. He had not done so (as the learned judge himself held) in the sense of attempting to obtain the vehicle. In our judgment, he equally had not done so in attempting to obtain the hire purchase of the vehicle.'

Commentary

See chapter 21 for extracts dealing with other aspects of the offence under s1 of the 1978 Act.

12 DEFENCES I

R v Allen [1988] Crim LR 698 Court of Appeal (Criminal Division) (Stocker LJ, Tudor Evans and Potts JJ

Ignorance as to strength of alcoholic drink - whether intoxication involuntary

Facts

'The appellant was convicted of buggery and indecent assault. It was the appellant's alternative line of defence that if, contrary to his basic assertion that he was not the attacker, he was so drunk at the time that he was not responsible for his actions and was in effect acting in a state of automatism; and that that drunken condition was due to his involuntarily having imbibed a quantity of alcohol which he was not responsible for consuming. The appellant gave evidence that he had consumed some drink in a public house and had later been given wine by a friend. He had not realised that the wine had a high alcohol content. The second line of defence was not left to the jury by the judge. The appellant appealed against conviction on the ground that the judge erred in ruling that involuntary drunkenness could not be a defence to a crime of non-specific intent.

Held

Dismissing the appeal, the judge was correct in ruling that there was no evidence before him that the drinking was other than voluntary. Further, where an accused knows that he is drinking alcohol, such drinking does not become involuntary for the reason alone that he may not know the precise nature or strength of the alcohol that he is consuming.'

[*Reported by Lynne Knapman, Barrister.*]

Attorney-General for Northern Ireland v Gallagher [1963] AC 349 House of Lords (Lords Reid, Goddard, Tucker, Denning, and Morris)

Premeditated intoxication

Facts

The defendant, who may have been a psychopath, decided to kill his wife. After drinking nearly half a bottle of whisky, he stabbed her to death with a knife. One of the matters for consideration by the House of Lords was whether the defence of intoxication was open to the defendant.

Held

Lord Denning:

'My Lords, this case differs from all others in the books in that the accused man, whilst sane and sober, before he took to the drink, had already made up his mind to kill his wife. This seems to me to be far the worse - and far more deserving of condemnation - than the case of a man who, before getting drunk, has no intention to kill, but afterwards in his cups, whilst drunk, kills another by an act which he would not dream of doing when sober. Yet by the law of England in this latter case his drunkenness is no defence even though it has distorted his reason and his will-power. So why should it be a defence in the present case? And is it made any better by saying that the man is a psychopath?

The answer to the question is, I think, that the case falls to be decided by the general principle of English law that, subject to very limited exceptions, drunkenness is no defence to a criminal charge, nor is a defect of reason produced by drunkenness. This principle was stated by Sir Matthew Hale in his Pleas of the Crown, I, p32, in words which I would repeat here:

"This vice (drunkenness) doth deprive men of the use of reason, and puts many men into a perfect, but temporary phrenzy ... By the laws of England such a person shall have no privilege by this voluntary contracted madness, but shall have the same judgment as if he were in his right senses".

This general principle can be illustrated by looking at the various ways in which drunkenness may produce a defect of reason:

(a) It may impair a man's powers of perception so that he may not be able to foresee or measure the consequences of his actions as he would if he were sober. Nevertheless he is not allowed to set up his self-induced want of perception as a defence. Even if he did not himself appreciate that what he was doing was dangerous, nevertheless if a reasonable man in his place, who was not befuddled with drink, would have appreciated it, he is guilty: see *R* v *Meade*, [1909] 1 KB 895; 25 TLR 359; 2 Cr App R 54, CCA, as explained in *Director of Public Prosecutions* v *Beard*, [1920] AC 479, 502-504.

(b) It may impair a man's power to judge, between right or wrong, so that he may do a thing when drunk which he would not dream of doing while sober. He does not realise he is doing wrong. Nevertheless he is not allowed to set up his self-induced want of moral sense as a defence. In *Beard's* case Lord Birkenhead LC distinctly ruled that it was not a defence for a drunken man to say he did not know he was doing wrong.

(c) It may impair a man's power of self-control so that he may more readily give way to provocation than if he were sober. Nevertheless he is not allowed to set up his self-induced want of control as a defence. The acts of provocation are to be assessed, not according to their effect on him personally, but according to the effect they would have on a reasonable man in his place. The law on this point was previously in doubt (see the cases considered in *Beard's* case), but it has since been resolved by *R* v *McCarthy*, [1954] 2 QB 105; [1954] 2 WLR 1044; [1954] 2 All ER 262; 38 Cr App R 74, CCA, *Bedder* v *Director of Public Prosecutions* [1954] 1 WLR 1119; [1954] 2 All ER 801; 38 Cr App R 133, HL; and section 3 of the Homicide Act, 1957.

The general principle which I have enunciated is subject to two exceptions:

1. If a man is charged with an offence in which a specific intention is essential (as in murder, though not in manslaughter), then evidence of drunkenness, which renders him incapable of forming that intention, is an answer: see *Beard's* case. This degree of drunkenness is reached when the man is rendered so stupid by drink that he does not know what he is doing (see *R* v *Moore* (1852) 3 Car. & Kir. 319), as where, at a christening, a drunken nurse put the baby behind a large fire, taking it for a log of wood (Gentleman's Magazine, 1748, p570); and where a drunken man thought his friend (lying in his bed) was a theatrical dummy placed there and stabbed him to death (The Times, January 13, 1951). In each of those cases it would not be murder. But it would be manslaughter.

2. If a man by drinking brings on a distinct disease of the mind such as delirium tremens, so that he is temporarily insane within the M'Naughten Rules, that is to say, he does not at the time know what he is doing or that it is wrong, then he has a defence on the ground of insanity: see *R* v *Davis* (1881) 14 Cox CC 563 and *Beard's* case.

Does the present case come within the general principle or the exceptions to it? It certainly does not come within the first exception. This man was not incapable of forming an intent to kill. Quite the contrary. He knew full well what he was doing. He formed an intent to kill, he carried out his intention and he remembered afterwards what he had done. And the jury, properly directed on the point, have found as much, for they found him guilty of murder. Then does the case come within the second exception? It does not, to my mind, for the simple reason that he was not suffering from a disease of the mind brought on by drink. He was suffering from a different disease altogether. As the Lord Chief Justice observed in his summing up: "If this man was suffering from a disease of the mind, it wasn't a kind that is produced by drink."

So we have here a case of the first impression. The man is a psychopath. That is he has a disease of the mind which is not produced by drink. But it is quiescent. And whilst it is quiescent he forms an intention to kill his wife. He knows it is wrong but still he means to kill her. Then he gets himself so drunk that he has an explosive outburst and kills his wife. At that moment he knows what he is doing but does not know it is wrong. So in that respect - in not knowing it is wrong - he has a defect of reason at the moment of killing. If that defect of reason is due to the drink, it is no defence in law. But if it is due to the disease of the mind, it gives rise to a defence of insanity. No one can say, however, whether it is due to the drink or to the disease. It may well be due to both in combination. What guidance does the law give in this difficulty? That is, as I see it, the question of general public importance which is involved in this case.

My Lords, I think the law on this point should take a clear stand. If a man, whilst sane and sober, forms an intention to kill and makes preparation for it, knowing it is a wrong thing to do, and then gets himself drunk so as to give himself Dutch courage to do the killing, and whilst drunk carries out his intention, he cannot rely on this self-induced drunkenness as a defence to a charge of murder, nor even as reducing it to manslaughter. He cannot say that he got himself into such a stupid state that he was incapable of an intent to kill. So also when he is a psychopath, he cannot by drinking rely on his self-induced defect of reason as a defence of insanity. The wickedness of his mind before he got drunk is enough to condemn him, coupled with the act which he intended to do and did do. A psychopath who goes out intending to kill, knowing it is wrong, and does kill, cannot escape the consequences by making himself drunk before doing it. That is, I believe, the direction which the Lord Chief Justice gave to the jury and which the Court of Criminal Appeal found to be wrong. I think it was right and for this reason I would allow the appeal.

I would agree, of course, that if before the killing he had discarded his intention to kill or reversed it - and then got drunk - it would be a different matter. But when he forms the intention to kill and without interruption proceeds to get drunk and carry out his intention, then his drunkenness is no defence and nonetheless so because it is dressed up as a defence of insanity.'

R v Bailey (1983) 77 Cr App R 76 Court of Appeal (Criminal Division) (Griffiths LJ, Pain and Stuart - Smith JJ)

Self-induced automatism

Facts

The defendant was diabetic. His girlfriend had left him to live with a man named Harrison. The defendant visited Harrison to discuss the situation, and whilst there felt unwell. He took a mixture of sugar and water, but ate nothing. Ten minutes later the defendant struck Harrison on the head with an iron bar. The defendant later claimed to have been unable to control his actions because he had been in a hypoglycaemic state. He was charged, inter alia, under s18 of the Offences Against the Person Act 1861. The trial judge directed the jury that the defence of automatism was not available to the defendant because his automatism had been 'self-induced'. The defendant was convicted under s18, and appealed.

Held

Applying the proviso, the appeal would be dismissed.

Griffiths LJ:

[His Lordship reviewed the facts of the case, and continued]

'It was therefore the appellant's case that the attack had taken place during a period of loss of consciousness occurring due to hypoglycaemia caused by his failure to take sufficient food following his last dose of insulin. Accordingly, it was submitted that he had neither the specific intent to cause grievous bodily harm for the purpose of section 18, nor the appropriate mens rea or basic intent for the purpose of the section 20 offence.

But the learned recorder, in effect, told the jury that this defence was not available to the appellant. He said: "One thing is equally clear, members of the jury, that if that state of malfunctioning was induced by any agency or self-induced incapacity, then the defence of automatism does not apply." It is clear from the rest of the summing-up that "self-induced" in this context meant or included the appellant's failure to take sufficient food after his dose of insulin. The recorder appears to have derived this proposition, which he applied to both counts of the indictment, from *Quick* and *Paddison* (1973) 57 Cr App R 722; [1973] QB 910. In that case the appellant, a nurse in a mental hospital, had attacked a patient. Quick was a diabetic and his defence was that he was in a state of automatism at the time due to hypoglycaemia. The trial judge had ruled that, if established, this amounted to a disease of the mind and could only be relied upon in support of a defence of insanity. Following this ruling, Quick pleaded guilty to assault occasioning actual bodily harm.

The Court of Appeal held that this ruling was wrong and that the malfunctioning caused by the hypoglycaemia was not a disease of the mind and that the appellant was entitled to have his defence considered by the jury. At pp735 and 922 of the respective reports Lawton LJ said: "Such malfunctioning, unlike that caused by a defect of reason from disease of the mind, will always relieve an accused from criminal responsibility. A self-induced incapacity will not excuse (see *Lipman* (1969) 53 Cr App R 600; [1970] 1 QB 152) nor will one which could have been reasonably foreseen as a result of either doing, or omitting to do something, as, for example, taking alcohol against medical advice after using certain prescribed drugs, or failing to have regular meals whilst taking insulin. From time to time difficult border line cases are likely to arise. When they do, the test suggested by the New Zealand Court of Appeal in *Cottle* [1958] NZLR 999, 1011, is likely to give the correct result, viz, can this mental condition be fairly regarded as amounting to or producing a defect of reason from disease of mind?"

But in that case, the offence, assault occasioning actual bodily harm was an offence of basic intent. No specific intent was required. It is now quite clear that even if the incapacity of mind is self-induced by the voluntary taking of drugs or alcohol, the specific intent to kill or cause grievous bodily harm may be negatived. See *Director of Public Prosecution* v *Majewski* (1976) 62 Cr App R 262; [1977] AC 443. This being so, as it is conceded on behalf of the Crown, the direction to which we have referred cannot be correct so far as the offence under section 18 is concerned.

But it is also submitted that the direction is wrong or at least in too broad and general terms, so far as the section 20 offence is concerned. If the passage quoted above from *Quick* (supra) correctly represents the law, then the direction given by the recorder was correct so far as the second count was concerned, even though the appellant may have had no appreciation of the consequences of his failure to take food and even though such failure may not have been due to deliberate abstention, but because of his generally distressed condition. In our judgment, the passage from Lawton LJ's judgment was obiter and we are free to re-examine it.

Automatism resulting from intoxication as a result of a voluntary ingestion of alcohol or dangerous drugs does not negative the mens rea necessary for crimes of basic intent, because the conduct of the accused is reckless and recklessness is enough to constitute the necessary mens rea in assault cases where no specific intents forms part of the charge. See *DPP* v *Majewski* (supra) at pp270 and 474 in the speech of Lord Elwyn Jones LC and at pp287 and 496 respectively in the speech of Lord Edmund-Davies where he said: "The law therefore establishes a conclusive presumption against the admission of proof of intoxication for the purpose of disproving mens rea in ordinary crimes. Where this presumption applies, it does not make 'drunkenness' itself a crime, but the drunkenness is itself an integral part of the crime, as forming, together with the other unlawful conduct charged against the defendant, a complex act of criminal recklessness."

The same considerations apply where the state of automatism is induced by the voluntary taking of dangerous drugs. See *Lipman* (1969) 53 Cr App R 600; [1970] 1 QB 152 where a conviction for manslaughter was upheld, the appellant having taken LSD and killed his mistress in the course of an hallucinatory trip. It was submitted on behalf of the Crown that a similar rule should be applied as a matter of public policy to all cases of self-induced automatism. But it seems to us that there may be material distinctions between a man who consumes alcohol or takes dangerous drugs and one who fails to take sufficient food after insulin to avert hypoglycaemia.

It is common knowledge that those who take alcohol to excess or certain sorts of drugs may become aggressive or do dangerous or unpredictable things; they may be able to foresee the risks of causing harm to others, but nevertheless persist in their conduct. But the same cannot be said without more of a man who fails to take food after an insulin injection. If he does appreciate the risk that such a failure may lead to aggressive, unpredictable and uncontrollable conduct and he nevertheless deliberately runs the risk or otherwise disregards it, this will amount to recklessness. But we certainly do not think that it is common knowledge, even among diabetics, that such is a consequence of a failure to take food; and there is no evidence that it was known to this appellant. Doubtless he knew that if he failed to take his insulin or proper food after it, he might lose consciousness, but as such he would only be a danger to himself unless he put himself in charge of some machine such as a motor car, which required his continued conscious control.

In our judgment, self-induced automatism, other than due to intoxication from alcohol or drugs, may provide a defence to crimes of basic intent. The question in each case will be whether the prosecution have proved the necessary element of recklessness. In cases of assault, if the accused knows that his actions or inaction are likely to make him aggressive, unpredictable or uncontrolled with the result that he may cause some injury to others, and he persists in the action or takes no remedial action when he knows it is required, it will be open to the jury to find that he was reckless.

Turning again to *Quick's* case (supra) and the passage we have quoted, we think that notwithstanding the unqualified terms in which the proposition is stated, it is possible that the Court may not have intended to lay down such an absolute rule. In the following paragraph Lawton LJ considers a number of questions, which are not necessarily exhaustive, which the jury might have wanted to consider if the issue had been left to them. One such question was whether the accused knew that he was getting into a hypoglycaemia episode and if so, why he did not use the antidote of taking sugar which he had been advised to do. These questions suggest that even if the hypoglycaemia was induced by some action or inaction by the accused his defence will not necessarily fail.

In the present case the recorder never invited the jury to consider what the appellant's knowledge or appreciation was of what would happen if he failed to take food after his insulin or whether he realised that he might become aggressive. Nor were they asked to consider why the appellant had omitted to take food in time. They were given no direction on the elements of recklessness. Accordingly, in our judgment, there was also a misdirection in relation to the second count in the indictment of unlawful wounding.

But we have to consider whether, notwithstanding these misdirections, there has been any miscarriage of justice and whether the jury properly directed could have failed to come to the same conclusion. As Lawton LJ said in *Quick's* case (1973) 57 Cr App R 722; [1973] QB 910 at pp734 and 922 respectively, referring to the defence of automatism, it is a "quagmire of law, seldom entered nowadays save by those in desperate need of some kind of defence." This case is no exception. We think it very doubtful whether the appellant laid a sufficient basis for the defence to be considered by the jury at all. But even if he did, we are in no doubt that the jury properly directed must have rejected it. Although an episode of sudden transient loss of consciousness or awareness was theoretically possible, it was quite inconsistent with the graphic description that the appellant gave to the police both orally and in his written statement. There was abundant evidence that he had armed himself with the iron bar and gone to Harrison's house for the purpose of attacking him, because he wanted to teach him a lesson and because he was in the way.

Moreover, the doctor's evidence to which we have referred showed it was extremely unlikely that such an episode could follow some five minutes after taking sugar and water. For these reasons we are satisfied that no miscarriage of justice occurred and the appeal will be dismissed.'

Commentary

DPP v *Majewski* appears below.

R v Bell [1984] Crim LR 685   Court of Appeal (Criminal Division) (Robert Goff LJ, Caulfield J, and Sir John Thompson)

Insanity: defendant believing himself to be instructed by God

Facts

'The applicant was charged with reckless driving. On March 1, 1982 the applicant suffered a schizophrenic attack. He had suffered a similar attack some six years previously but had apparently made a complete recovery. On that day he smashed up his own MG sports car which he had spent over a year restoring. He felt as if he was driven on by an outside force which he thought was God. He drove off in a white Volkswagen van and used that van as a weapon to attack various targets which he regarded as evil. He first drove at speed through the closed gates of Butlins Holiday Camp near Filey, ripping the gate off its hinges. He drove straight out through the other locked gates, subsequently telling the police, "It was like a Secret Society there, I wanted to do my bit against it." He drove on to Bridlington where he knocked down No Entry signs and was involved in a number of collisions with separate cars. His animosity was directed towards cars and not to the people inside them. He drove through a police road block and then deliberately collided with the rear of a police car and was eventually diverted into a field by police who took him from the van. He appeared to the police officers to be deranged and incoherent. At his trial at York Crown Court he pleaded Not Guilty and gave evidence that he felt himself possessed. Medical evidence was given to the effect that he was suffering a schizophrenic illness at the time of the incident. The applicant's case was that he either gave no thought to the possibility of any risk of damage or injury following from his driving or that he recognised there was a risk but felt that he was able to cope with it because he was driven on by God. At the conclusion of all the evidence the judge was asked to rule that it was open to the jury to return a simple verdict of Not Guilty on the ground that, by reason of his state of mind, he lacked the mens rea necessary for the offence. The judge rejected the submission ruling that if the jury were satisfied that, for whatever reason, the applicant did not give any thought to the risk but nevertheless persisted in his act of driving then he was guilty of reckless driving. In the light of the judge's ruling the applicant changed his plea to one of Guilty. The applicant sought leave to appeal on the ground that the judge was wrong in law in ruling that medical evidence could not be relevant to the state of mind of the defendant, namely whether he had failed to give any thought to the possibility of there being a risk of causing injury or damage by his driving.

Held

Dismissing the application, that where a driver seeks to excuse his driving because for example he had been attacked by a swarm of bees or a malevolent passenger or because he had been affected by a sudden blinding pain or because of some mechanical failure of his vehicle such as a blow-out or through the brakes failing that would constitute involuntary conduct of a kind which would not constitute reckless driving. But here the applicant was plainly in physical control of his actions and following Lawrence (1981) 73 Cr App R 1, the applicant did not give any thought to the possibility of there being a risk of the relevant kind by his driving and his explanation that he was driven on by God could not displace any inference to that effect; it would merely explain how it came about that he was in fact in one of the states of mind necessary to constitute the offence.'

[*Reported by Paul Worsley, Barrister*]

R v Bingham [1991] Crim LR 43 Court of Appeal (Criminal Division) (Lord Lane CJ, Henry and Hidden JJ)

Automatism - hypoglycaemia

Facts

'Following arrest for shop-lifting, B, a diabetic, was charged with theft of a can of "coke" and sandwiches, worth £1.16, at a time when he had £90 in his pocket. He had paid for one can of coke, and was stopped on leaving the store, following which he replied to questions with "no comment." His defence was automatism based on the claim that, at the time, he was suffering from hypoglycaemia and was unaware of his actions. The judge refused to leave that defence to the jury. [B appealed.]

Held

Allowing the appeal, the arguments put to the judge failed to distinguish between hyperglycaemia and hypoglycaemia, the former being too much sugar in the blood, and the latter too little. Hyperglycaemia might raise difficult problems about the *M'Naghten* rules and verdicts of not guilty by reason of insanity. Hypoglycaemia was not caused by the initial disease of diabetes, but by the treatment in the form of too much insulin, or by insufficient quality or quantity of food to counterbalance the insulin. Generally speaking, that would not give rise to a verdict of not guilty by reason of insanity but would, if it was established and showed that the necessary intent was or might be lacking, provide a satisfactory defence to an alleged crime such as theft, due to lack of *mens rea*. Those simple facts would be plain to anyone who troubled to read *Quick* (1973) 57 Cr App R and *Hennessy* [1989] 1 WLR 287. In the present case, the problem was hypoglycaemia and the judge had to decide whether, on the evidence, there was a prima facie case for the jury to decide whether B was suffering from its effects and, if so, whether the Crown had shown that he had the necessary intent under the Theft Act. It was not doubted that B was a diabetic and the evidence that he might have been suffering from the effects of a low blood sugar level at the relevant time was (1) a lady had observed that his eyes were not behaving normally, which she had attributed to the fact that he was shop-lifting and shop-lifters tended to look around before stealing. (2) His behaviour in answering "no comment" was strange. Further, when it was suggested to him that if he gave his name and address the police would not be called and he, presumably, would escape with a caution, he did not take advantage of the offer which, in a perfectly intelligent man, seemed a very strange thing. As against that was his failure to tell the police doctor that he was suffering from a hypoglycaemia attack, which he explained at trial on the basis that he feared it would prolong his arrest. There was therefore some evidence to support his defence, although the jury might well have dismissed it as insufficient. It was not for their Lordships to decide whether the jury would have thought the evidence to be impressive. It should have been left to them and the failure so to do was a material irregularity.'

[*Reported by Veronica Cowan, Barrister.*]

Bratty v Attorney-General for Northern Ireland [1963] AC 386 House of Lords (Viscount Kilmuir LC, Lords Tucker, Denning, Morris, and Hodson)

Automatism and insanity distinguished

Facts

The defendant had killed a girl and was charged with her murder. At his trial, evidence was put forward that he may have been suffering from psychomoter epilepsy at the time of the offence. The trial judge directed the jury on the defence of insanity but ruled that the defence of automatism was not available to the defendant. The jury rejected the defence of insanity, and the defendant appealed unsuccessfully to the Court of Criminal Appeal in Northern Ireland. The defendant appealed further to the House of Lords.

Held

The appeal would be dismissed.

Lord Denning:

'My Lords, in the case of *Woolmington* v *Director of Public Prosecutions* [1935] AC 462, 482. Viscount Sankey LC said that "when dealing with a murder case the Crown must prove (a) death as a result of a voluntary act of the accused and (b) malice of the accused."

The requirement that it should be a voluntary act is essential, not only in a murder case, but also in every criminal case. No act is punishable if it is done involuntarily: and an involuntary act in this context – some people nowadays prefer to speak of it as "automatism" – means an act which is done by the muscles without any control by the mind, such as a spasm, a reflex action or a convulsion; or an act done by a person who is not conscious of what he is doing, such as an act done whilst suffering from concussion or whilst sleep-walking. The point was well put by Stephen J in 1889:

"Can anyone doubt that a man who, though he might be perfectly sane, committed what would otherwise be a crime in a state of somnambulism, would be entitled to be acquitted? And why is this? Simply because he would not know what he was doing,"

See *R* v *Tolson* (1889) 23 QBD 168, 187. The term "involuntary act" is, however, capable of wider connotations: and to prevent confusion it is to be observed that in the criminal law an act is not to be regarded as an involuntary act simply because the doer does not remember it. When a man is charged with dangerous driving, it is no defence to him to say "I don't know what happened. I cannot remember a thing," see *Hill* v*Baxter* [1958] 1 QB 277. Loss of memory afterwards is never a defence in itself, so long as he was conscious at the time, see *Russell* v *H M Advocate* [1946] SC(J) 37; *R* v *Podola* [1960] 1 QB 325; [1959] 3 WLR 718; [1959] 3 All ER 418; 43 Cr App R 220, CCA. Nor is an act to be regarded as an involuntary act simply because the doer could not control his impulse to do it. When a man is charged with murder, and it appears that he knew what he was doing, but he could not resist it, see *Attorney-General for South Australia* v *Brown* [1960] AC 432; [1960] 2 WLR 588; [1960] 1 All ER 734, PC: though it may go towards a defence of diminished responsibility, in places where that defence is available, see *R* v *Byrne* [1960] 2 QB 396; [1960] 3 WLR 440; [1960] 3 All ER 1; 44 Cr App R 246, CCA: but it does not render his act involuntary, so as to entitle him to an unqualified acquittal. Nor is an act to be regarded as an involuntary act simply because it is unintentional or its consequences are unforeseen. When a man is charged with dangerous driving, it is no defence for him to say, however truly, "I did not mean to drive dangerously." There is said to be an absolute prohibition against that offence,whether he had a guilty mind or not, see *Hill* v *Baxter* [1958] 1 QB 277, 282 by Lord Goddard CJ But even though it is absolutely prohibited, nevertheless he has a defence if he can show that it was an involuntary act in the sense that he was unconscious at the time and did not know what he was doing, see *H M Advocate* v *Ritchie*, 1926 SC (J) 45. *R* v *Minor* (1955) 15 WWR (NS) 433 and *Cooper* v *McKenna*, *Ex parte Cooper* [1960] Qd LR 406.

… [A]gain, if the involuntary act proceeds from a disease of the mind, it gives rise to a defence of insanity, but not to a defence of automatism. Suppose a crime is committed by a man in a state of automatism or clouded consciousness due to a recurrent disease of the mind. Such an act is no doubt involuntary, but it does not give rise to an unqualified acquittal, for that would mean that he would be let at large to do it again. The only proper verdict is one which ensures that the person who suffers from the disease is kept secure in a hospital so as not to be a danger to himself or others. That is, a verdict of guilty but insane.

[His Lordship then referred to *R* v *Charlson* [1955] 1 WLR 317, and Devlin J's ruling in *R* v *Kemp* (see below), and continued]

Upon the other point discussed by Devlin J, namely, what is a "disease of the mind" within the M'Naughten Rules, I would agree with him that this is a question for the judge. The major mental diseases, which the doctors call psychoses, such as schizophrenia, are clearly diseases of the mind.

But in *Charlson's* case, Barry J seems to have assumed that other diseases such as epilepsy or cerebral tumour are not diseases of the mind, even when they are such as to manifest themselves in violence. I do not agree with this. It seems to me that any mental disorder which has manifested itself in violence and is prone to recur is a disease of the mind. At any rate it is the sort of disease for which a person should be detained in hospital rather than be given an unqualified acquittal.

It is to be noticed that in *Charlson's* case and *Kemp's* case the defence raised only automatism, not insanity. In the present case the defence raised both automatism and insanity. And herein lies the difficulty because of the burden of proof. If the accused says he did not know what he was doing, then, so far as the defence of automatism is concerned, the Crown must prove that the act was a voluntary act, see *Woolmington's* case. But so far as the defence of insanity is concerned, the defence must prove that the act was an involuntary act due to disease of the mind, see *M'Naughten's* case. This apparent incongruity was noticed by Sir Owen Dixon, the Chief Justice of Australia, in an address which is to be found in 31 Australian Law Journal, p255, and it needs to be resolved. The defence here say: Even though we have not proved that the act was involuntary, yet the Crown have not proved that it was a voluntary act: and that point at least should have been put to the jury.

My Lords, I think that the difficulty is to be resolved by remembering that, whilst the *ultimate* burden rests on the Crown of proving every element in the crime, nevertheless in order to prove that the act was a voluntary act, the Crown is entitled to rely on the *presumption* that every man has sufficient mental capacity to be responsible for his crimes: and that if the defence wish to displace that presumption they must give some evidence from which the contrary may reasonably be inferred. Thus a drunken man is presumed to have the capacity to form the specific intent necessary to constitute the crime, unless evidence is given from which it can reasonably be inferred that he was incapable of forming it, see the valuable judgment of the Court of Justiciary in *Kennedy v H M Advocate* 1944 SC(J) 171, 177 which was delivered by Lord Normand. So also it seems to me that a man's act is presumed to be a voluntary act unless there is evidence from which it can reasonably be inferred that it was involuntary. To use the words of Devlin J, the defence of automatism "ought not to be considered at all until the defence has produced at least prima facie evidence," see *Hill v Baxter* [1958] 1 QB 277, 285; and the words of North J in New Zealand "unless a proper foundation is laid," see *R v Cottle* [1958] NZLR 999, 1025. The necessity of laying down the proper foundation is on the defence: and if it is not so laid, the defence of automatism need not be left to the jury, any more than the defence of drunkenness (*Kennedy v H M Advocate* 1944 SC(J) 171), provocation (*R v Gauthier* (1943) 29 Cr App R 113, CCA) or self-defence (*R v Lobell* [1957] 1 QB 547; [1957] 2 WLR 524; [1957] 1 All ER 734; 41 Cr App R 100, CCA) need be.

What, then, is a proper foundation? The presumption of mental capacity of which I have spoken is a provisional presumption only. It does not put the legal burden on the defence in the same way as the presumption of sanity does. It leaves the legal burden on the prosecution, but nevertheless, until it is displaced, it enables the prosecution to discharge the ultimate burden of proving that the act was voluntary. Not because the presumption is evidence itself, but because it takes the place of evidence. In order to displace the presumption of mental capacity, the defence must give sufficient evidence from which it may reasonably be inferred that the act was involuntary. The evidence of the man himself will rarely be sufficient unless it is supported by medical evidence which points to the cause of the mental incapacity. It is not sufficient for a man to say "I had a black-out": for "black-out" as Stable J said in *Cooper v McKenna, Ex parte Cooper* [1960] Qd LR 406 at 419,"is one of the first refuges of a guilty conscience and a popular excuse." The words of Devlin J in *Hill v Baxter* should be remembered: "I do not doubt that there are genuine cases of automatism and the like, but I do not see how the layman can safely attempt without the help of some medical or scientific evidence to distinguish the genuine from the fraudulent."

When the only cause that is assigned for an involuntary act is drunkenness, then it is only necessary to leave drunkenness to the jury, with the consequential directions, and not to leave automatism at all. When the only cause that is assigned for it is a disease of the mind, then it is only necessary to leave insanity to the jury, and not automatism. When the cause assigned is concussion or sleep-walking, there should be some evidence from which it can reasonably be inferred before it should be left to the jury. If it is said to be due to concussion, there should be evidence of a severe blow shortly beforehand. If it is said to be sleep-walking, there should be some credible support for it. His mere assertion that he was asleep will not suffice.

Once a proper foundation is thus laid for automatism, the matter becomes at large and must be left to the jury. As the case proceeds, the evidence may weigh first to one side and then to the other: and so the burden may appear to shift to and fro. But at the end of the day the legal burden comes into play and requires that the jury should be satisfied beyond reasonable doubt that the act was a voluntary act.'

R v Burgess (1991) 93 Cr App R 41 Court of Appeal (Criminal Division) (Lord Lane CJ, Roch and Morland JJ)

Sleep-walking - whether automatism or insanity

Facts

The appellant lived alone but was friendly with the woman, who lived in the flat below his, a Ms Katrina Curtis. On the evening in question he visited her flat to watch a video. During the course of the evening she fell asleep on the sofa. She was awoken by the appellant smashing a bottle over her head. Before she could stop him he had picked up the video recorder and brought it down on her head causing cuts and bruises. The appellant was charged on two counts alleging wounding and wounding with intent. At his trial the appellant adduced expert medical evidence to the effect that he had been sleep-walking at the time of the attack and that the defence of automatism should be put before the jury. The trial judge ruled that the only defence the evidence revealed was that of insanity, and the jury in due course found him not guilty by reason of insanity. The appellant's contention was that the defence of automatism should have been left to the jury.

Held

The appeal would be dismissed.

Lord Lane CJ:

After considering the facts of the case, and the meaning given to the concept 'disease of the mind' by Devlin J in *R* v *Kemp* [1957] 1 QB 399, Lord Lane CJ continued:

'The appellant (Burgess) plainly suffered from a defect of reason from some sort of failure (for lack of a better term) of the mind causing him to act as he did without conscious motivation. His mind was to some extent controlling his actions which were purposive rather than the result simply of muscular spasm, but without his being consciously aware of what he was doing. Can it be said that that "failure" was a *disease* of the mind rather than a defect or failure of the mind not due to disease? That is the distinction, by no means always easy to draw, upon which this case depends, as others have depended in the past.

One can perhaps narrow the field of inquiry still further by eliminating what are sometimes called the "external factors" such as concussion caused by a blow on the head. There were no such factors here. Whatever the cause may have been, it was an "internal" cause. The possible disappointment or frustration caused by unrequited love is not to be equated with something such as concussion. On this aspect of the case, we respectfully adopt what was said by Martin J and approved by a majority in the Supreme Court of Canada in *Rabey* v *The Queen* [1980] 2 SCR 513, 519, 520 (where the facts bore a similarity to those in the instant case although the diagnosis was different):

"Any malfunctioning of the mind or mental disorder having its source primarily in some subjective condition or weakness internal to the accused (whether fully understood or not) may be a 'disease of the mind' if it prevents the accused from knowing what he is doing, but transient disturbances of consciousness due to certain specific external factors do not fall within the concept of disease of the mind ... In my view, the ordinary stresses and disappointments of life which are the common lot of mankind do not constitute an external cause constituting an explanation for a malfunctioning of the mind which takes it out of the category of a 'disease of the mind.' To hold otherwise would deprive the concept of an external factor of any real meaning."'

Lord Lane CJ then referred to the speeches of Lord Diplock in *R* v *Sullivan* [1984] AC 156 (at p172), and Lord Denning in *Bratty* v *Attorney-General for Northern Ireland* [1963] AC 386 (at p412) and continued:

'It seems to us that if there is a danger of recurrence that may be an added reason for categorising the condition as a disease of the mind. On the other hand, the absence of the danger of recurrence is not a reason for saying that it cannot be a disease of the mind. Subject to that possible qualification, we respectfully adopt Lord Denning's suggested definition.

There have been several occasions when during the course of judgments in the Court of Appeal and the House of Lords observations have been made, obiter, about the criminal responsibility of sleep walkers, where sleep walking has been used as a self-evident illustration of non-insane automatism. For example in the speech of Lord Denning, from which we have already cited an extract, appears this passage, at p409:

"No act is punishable if it is done involuntarily: and an involuntary act in this context - some people nowadays prefer to speak of it as 'automatism' - means an act which is done by the muscles without any control by the mind, such as a spasm, a reflex action or a convulsion; or an act done by a person who is not conscious of what he is doing, such as an act done whilst suffering from concussion or whilst sleep-walking. The point was well put by Stephen J in 18889: 'Can anyone doubt that a man who, though he might be perfectly sane, committed what would otherwise be a crime in a state of somnambulism, would be entitled to be acquitted? And why is this? Simply because he would not know what he was doing.'"

We have also been referred to a Canadian decision, *R* v *Parks* (1990) 56 CCC (3d) 449. In that case the defendant was charged with murder. The undisputed facts were that he had, whilst according to him he was asleep, at night driven his motor car some 23 kilometres to the house of his wife's parents where he had stabbed and beaten both his mother-in-law and his father-in-law. His mother-in-law died as a result and his father-in-law sustained serious injuries. A number of defence witnesses, including experts in sleep disorders, gave evidence to the effect that sleep-walking is not regarded as a disease of the mind, mental illness or mental disorder, and the trial judge directed the jury that if the accused was in a state of somnambulism at the time of the killing, then he was entitled to be acquitted on the basis of non-insane automatism. The defendant was acquitted of the murder of his mother-in-law and subsequently acquitted of the attempted murder of his father-in-law.

The Crown appealed from the accused's acquittal and it was held by the Ontario Court of Appeal that the appeal should be dismissed. The court concluded that sleep is a normal condition and "the impairment of the respondent's faculties of reason, memory and understanding was caused not by any disorder or abnormal condition but by a natural, normal condition - sleep:" pp465-466.

We accept of course that sleep is a normal condition, but the evidence in the instant case indicates that sleep-walking, and particularly violence in sleep, is not normal. We were told that *R* v *Parks* is to be taken to the Supreme Court of Canada. That case apart, in none of the other cases where sleep-walking has been mentioned, so far as we can discover, has the court had the advantage of the sort of expert medical evidence which was available to the judge here.

One turns then to examine the evidence upon which the judge had to base his decision and for this purpose the two medical experts called by the defence are the obvious principal sources. Dr d'Orban in examination-in-chief said:

"On the evidence available to me, and subject to the results of the tests when they became available, I came to the same conclusion as Dr Nicholas and Dr Eames whose reports I had read, and that was that Mr Burgess's actions had occurred during the course of a sleep disorder."

He was asked, "Assuming this is a sleep associated automatism, is it an internal or external factor?" Answer: "In this particular case, I think that one would have to see it as an internal factor."

Then in cross-examination: Questions: "Would you go so far as to say that it was liable to recur?" Answer: "Is is possible for it to recur, yes." Finally, in answer to a question from the judge, namely, "Is this a case of automatism associated with a pathological condition or not?" Answer: "I think the answer would have to be yes, because it is an abnormality of the brain function, so it would be regarded as a pathological condition."

Dr Eames in cross-examination agreed with Dr d'Orban as to the internal rather than the external factor. He accepted that there is a liability to recurrence of sleep-walking. He could not go so far as to say that there is no liability of recurrence of serious violence but he agreed with the other medical witnesses that there is no recorded case of violence of this sort recurring.

The prosecution, as already indicated, called Dr Fenwick, whose opinion was that this was not a sleep-walking episode at all. If it was a case where the appellant was unconscious of what he was doing, the most likely explanation was that he was in what is described as an hysterical dissociative state. That is a state in which, for psychological reasons, such as being overwhelmed by his emotions, the person's brain works in a different way. He carries out acts of which he has no knowledge and for which he has no memory. It is quite different from sleep-walking. He then went on to describe features of sleep-walking. This is what he said:

"Firstly, violent acts in sleep-walking are very common. In just an exposure of one day to a sleep-walking clinic, you will hear of how people are kicked in bed, hit in bed, partially strangled - it is usually just arms around the neck, in bed, which is very common. Serious violence fortunately is rare. Serious violence does recur, or certainly the propensity for it to recur is there, although there are very few cases in the literature - in fact I know of none - in which somebody has come to court twice for a sleep-walking offence. This does not mean that sleep-walking violence does not recur; what it does mean is that those who are associated with the sleeper take the necessary precautions. Finally, should a person be detained in hospital? The answer to this is: Yes, because sleep-walking is treatable. Violent night terrors are treatable. There is a lot which can be done for the sleep-walker, so sending them to hospital after a violent act to have their sleep-walking sorted out, makes good sense."

Dr Fenwick was also of the view that in certain circumstances hysterical dissociative states are also subject to treatment.

It seems to us that on this evidence the judge was right to conclude that this was an abnormality or disorder, albeit transitory, due to an internal factor, whether functional or organic, which had manifested itself in violence. It was a disorder or abnormality which might recur, though the possibility of it recurring in the form of serious violence was unlikely. Therefore since this was a legal problem to be decided on legal principles, it seems to us that on those principles the answer was as the judge found it to be. It does however go further than that. Dr d'Orban, as already described, stated it as his view that the condition would be regarded as pathological. Pathology is the science of diseases. It seems therefore that in this respect at least there is some similarity between the law and medicine.'

Commissioner of the Metropolitan Police v Caldwell [1982] AC 341

For the facts see chapter 2. The following extracts deal with the availability of the defence of self-induced intoxication.

Lord Diplock:

'As respects the charge under section 1 (2) the prosecution did not rely upon an actual intent of the respondent to endanger the lives of the residents but relied upon his having been reckless whether the lives of any of them would be endangered. His act of setting fire to it was one which the jury were entitled to think created an obvious risk that the lives of the residents would be endangered; and the only defence with which your Lordships are concerned is that the respondent had made himself so drunk as to render him oblivious of that risk. If the only mental state capable of constituting the necessary mens rea for an offence under section 1 (2) were that expressed in the words "intending by the destruction or damage to endanger the life of another," it would have been necessary to consider whether the offence was to be classified as one of "specific" intent for the purposes of the rule of law which this House affirmed and applied in *R* v *Majewski* [1977] AC 443; and this it plainly is. But this is not, in my view, a relevant inquiry where "being reckless as to whether the life of another would be thereby endangered" is an alternative mental state that is capable of constituting the necessary mens rea of the offence with which he is charged.

The speech of Lord Elwyn-Jones LC in *R* v *Majewski* [1977] AC 443, 475, with which Lord Simon of Glaisdale, Lord Kilbrandon and I agreed, is authority that self-induced intoxication is no defence to a crime in which recklessness is enough to constitute the necessary mens rea. The charge in *Majewski* was of assault occasioning actual bodily harm and it was held by the majority of the House, approving *R* v *Venna* [1976] QB 421, 428, that recklessness in the use of force was sufficient to satisfy the mental element in the offence of assault. Reducing oneself by drink or drugs to a condition in which the restraints of reason and conscience are cast off was held to be a reckless course of conduct and an integral part of the crime. The Lord Chancellor accepted at p475 as correctly stating English law the provision in section 2.08 (2) of the American Model Penal Code:

"When recklessness establishes an element of the offence, if the actor due to self-induced intoxication, is unaware of a risk of which he would have been aware had he been sober, such awareness is immaterial."

So, in the instant case, the fact that the respondent was unaware of the risk of endangering lives of residents in the hotel owing to his self-induced intoxication, would be no defence if that risk would have been obvious to him had he been sober.

My Lords, the Court of Appeal in the instant case regarded the case as turning upon whether the offence under section 1 (2) was one of "specific" intent or "basic" intent. Following a recent decision of the Court of Appeal by which they were bound, *R* v *Orpin* [1980] 1 WLR 1050, they held that the offence under section 1 (2) was one of "specific" intent in contrast to the offence under section 1 (1) which was of basic intent. This would be right if the only mens rea capable of constituting the offence were an actual intention to endanger the life of another. For the reasons I have given, however, classification into offences of "specific" and "basic" intent is irrelevant where being reckless as to whether a particular harmful consequence will result from one's act is a sufficient alternative mens rea.

My Lords, the learned recorder's summing up was not a model of clarity. Contrary to the view of the Court of Appeal she was right in telling the jury that in deciding whether the respondent was reckless as to whether the lives of residents in the hotel would be endangered, the fact that, because of his drunkenness, he failed to give any thought to that risk was irrelevant; but there were other criticisms of the summing up made by the Court of Appeal which your Lordships very properly have not been invited to consider, since it makes no practical difference to the respondent whether the appeal is allowed or not. Since it is not worth while spending time on going into these criticisms, I would dismiss the appeal.

I would give the following answers to the certified question: (a) If the charge of an offence under section 1 (2) of the Criminal Damage Act 1971 is framed so as to charge the defendant only with "*intending* by the destruction or damage [of the property] to endanger the life of another," evidence of self-induced intoxication can be relevant to his defence. (b) If the charge is, or includes, a reference to his "being reckless as to whether the life of another would thereby be endangered," evidence of self-induced intoxication is not relevant.'

Lord Edmund-Davies [dissenting]

'... the second error [on the part of the trial judge] lay in directing the jury without qualification that (a) all arson is an offence of basic intent and, consequently, that (b) since *R* v *Majewski* [1977] AC 443 it matters not if, by reasons of the defendant's self-intoxication, he may not have foreseen the possibility that his admittedly unlawful actions endangered life.

Something more must be said about (b), having regard to the view expressed by my noble and learned friend, Lord Diplock, ante, p355 D-E, that the speech of Lord Elwyn-Jones LC in *R* v *Majewski* "is authority that self-induced intoxication is no defence to a crime in which recklessness is enough to constitute the necessary mens rea." It is a view which, with respect, I do not share. In common with all the noble and learned Lords hearing that appeal, Lord Elwyn-Jones LC adopted the well-established (though not universally favoured) distinction between basic and specific intents. *R* v *Majewski* [1977] 443 related solely to charges of assault, undoubtedly an offence of basic intent, and the Lord Chancellor made it clear that his observations were confined to offences of that nature; see pp473B-C and G-H, 474H-475E, and 476A-D. My respectful view is that *Majewski* accordingly supplies no support for the proposition that, in relation to crimes of specific intent (such as section 1 (2) (b) of the Act of 1971) incapacity to appreciate the degree and nature of the risk created by his action which is attributable to the defendant's self-intoxication is an irrelevance. The Lord Chancellor was dealing simply with crimes of basic intent, and in my judgment it was strictly within that framework that he adopted the view expressed in the American Penal Code quoted at p475D, and recklessness as an element in crimes of specific intent was, I am convinced, never within his contemplation.

For the foregoing reasons, the Court of Appeal were in my judgment right in quashing the conviction under section 1 (2) (b) and substituting a finding of guilty of arson contrary to section 1 (1) and (3) of the Act of 1971. It follows, therefore, that I agree with learned counsel for the respondent that the certified point of law should be answered in the following manner:

Yes, evidence of self-induced intoxication can be relevant both to (a) whether the defendant intended to endanger the life of another, and to (b) whether the defendant was *reckless* as to whether the life of another would be endangered, within the meaning of section 1 (2) (b) of the Criminal Damage Act 1971.

My Lords, it was recently predicted that,"There can hardly be any doubt that all crimes of recklessness except murder will now be held to be crimes of basic intent within *Majewski*": see *Glanville Williams, Textbook of Criminal Law*, p431. That prophecy has been promptly fulfilled by the majority of your Lordships, for, with the progressive displacement of "maliciously" by "intentionally" or "recklessly" in statutory crimes, that will surely be the effect of the majority decision in this appeal. That I regret, for the consequence is that, however grave the crime charged, if recklessness can constitute its mens rea the fact that it was committed in drink can afford no defence. It is a very long time since we had so harsh a law in this country. Having revealed in *R* v *Majewski* [1977] AC 443, 495B-497C my personal conviction that, on grounds of public policy, a plea of drunkenness cannot exculpate crimes of basic intent and so exercise unlimited sway in the criminal law, I am nevertheless unable to occur that your Lordships' decision should now become the law of the land. For, as Eveleigh LJ said in *R* v *Orpin* [1980] 1 WLR 1050, 1054:

"There is nothing inconsistent in treating intoxication as irrelevant when considering the liability of a person who has willed himself to do that which the law forbids (for example, to do something which wounds another), and yet to make it relevant when a further mental state is postulated as an aggravating circumstance making the offence even more serious."

By way of a postscript I would add that the majority view demonstrates yet again the folly of totally ignoring the recommendations of the Butler Committee (Report of the Committee on Mentally Abnormal Offenders (1975) (Cmnd 6244), paras 18, 53-58).

My Lords, I would dismiss the appeal.'

DPP v Beard [1920] AC 479

See references made to this authority in the extracts from speeches in *DPP* v *Majewski* (below).

DPP v Majewski [1977] AC 142   House of Lords (Lords Elwyn-Jones, Diplock, Simon, Kilbrandon, Salmon, Edmund-Davies and Russell)

Self-induced intoxication as a defence to crimes of basic intent

Facts

The defendant had been convicted on various counts alleging actual bodily harm, and assaults upon police officers. The offences had occurred after the defendant had consumed large quantities of alcohol and drugs, but at the trial Judge Petre had directed the jury that self-induced intoxication was not available as a defence to these basic intent crimes. The defendant appealed unsuccessfully to the Court of Appeal, and now appealed to the House of Lords.

Held

The appeal would be dismissed.

Lord Elwyn-Jones LC:

'Self-induced alcoholic intoxication has been a factor in crimes of violence, like assault, throughout the history of crime in this country. But voluntary drug taking with the potential and actual dangers to others it may cause has added a new dimension to the old problem with which the courts have had to deal in their endeavour to maintain order and to keep public and private violence under control. To achieve this is the prime purpose of the criminal law. I have said "the courts," for most of the relevant law has been made by the judges. A good deal of the argument in the hearing of the appeal turned on that judicial history, for the crux of the case for the Crown was that, illogical as the outcome may be said to be, the judges have evolved for the purpose of protecting the community a substantive rule of law that, in crimes of basic intent as distinct from crimes of specific intent, self-induced intoxication provides no defence and is irrelevant to offences of basic intent, such as assault.

Mr Tucker's case for the appellant was that there was no such substantive rule of law and that if there was, it did violence to logic and ethics and to fundamental principles of the criminal law which had been evolved to determine when and where criminal responsibility should arise.

[His Lordship then referred to counsel for the appellant's main propositions on the need for mens rea to be proved before criminal liability would be imposed and continued]

A great deal of the argument in the hearing of the appeal turned on the application to the established facts of what Cave J in *R* v *Tolson* (1889) 23 QBD 168, 181 called "the somewhat uncouth maxim 'actus non facit reum, nisi mens sit rea'." The judgment of Stephen J in that case has long been accepted as authoritative. He said, at p185:

"Though this phrase is in common use, I think it most unfortunate, and not only likely to mislead, but actually misleading, on the following grounds. It mutually suggests that, apart from all particular definitions of crimes, such a thing exists as a 'mens rea,' or 'guilty mind,' which is always expressly or by implication involved in every definition. This is obviously not the case, for the mental elements of different crimes differ widely. 'Mens rea' means in the case of murder, malice aforethought; in the case of theft, an intention to steal; in the case of rape, an intention to have forcible connection with a woman without her consent; and in the case of receiving stolen goods, knowledge that the goods were stolen. In some cases it denotes mere inattention. For instance, in the case of manslaughter by negligence it may mean forgetting to notice a signal. It appears confusing to call so many dissimilar states of mind by one name."

Stephen J concluded, at p187:

"the principle involved appears to me, when fully considered, to amount to no more than this. The full definition of every crime contains expressly or by implication a proposition as to a state of mind. Therefore, if the mental element of any conduct alleged to be a crime is proved to have been absent in any given case, the crime so defined is not committed; or, again, if a crime is fully defined, nothing amounts to that crime which does not satisfy that definition."

When then is the mental element required in our law to be established in assault? This question has been most helpfully answered in the speech of Lord Simon of Glaisdale in *R* v *Morgan* [1976] AC 182, 216:

"By 'crimes of basic intent' I mean those crimes whose definition expresses (or, more often, applies) a mens rea which does not go beyond the actus reus. The actus reas generally consists of an act and some consequence. The consequence may be closely connected with the act or remotely connected with it: but with a crime of basic intent the mens rea does not extend beyond the act and its consequence, however, remote, as defined in the actus reus. I take assault as an example of a crime of basic intent where the consequence is very closely connected with the act. The actus reus of assault is an act which causes another person to apprehend immediate and unlawful violence. The mens rea corresponds exactly. The prosecution must prove that the accused foresaw that his act would probably cause another person to have apprehension of immediate and unlawful violence, or would possibly have that consequence, such being the purpose of the act, or that he was reckless as to whether or not his act caused such apprehension. This foresight (the term of art is 'intention') or recklessness is the mens rea in assault. For an example of a crime of basic intent where the consequence of the act involved in the actus reus as defined in the crime is less immediate, I take the crime of unlawful wounding. The act is say, the squeezing of a trigger. A number of consequences (mechanical, chemical, ballistic and physiological) intervene before the final consequence involved in the defined actus reus – namely, the wounding of another person in circumstances unjustified by law. But again here the mens rea corresponds closely to the actus reus. The prosecution must prove that the accused foresaw that some physical harm would ensure to another person in circumstances unjustified by law as a probable (or possible and desired) consequence of his act, or that he was reckless as to whether or not such consequence ensued."

How does the fact of self-induced intoxication fit into that analysis? If a man consciously and deliberately takes alcohol and drugs not on medical prescription, but in order to escape from reality, to go "on a trip," to become hallucinated, whatever the description may be and thereby disables himself from taking the care he might otherwise take and as a result by his subsequent actions causing injury to another – does our criminal law enable him to say that because he did not know what he was doing he lacked both intention and recklessness and accordingly is entitled to an acquittal?

Originally the common law would not and did not recognise self-induced intoxication as an excuse. Lawton LJ spoke of the "merciful relaxation" to that rule which was introduced by the judges during the 19th century, and he added, at p411:

"Although there was much reforming zeal and activity in the 19th century, Parliament never once considered whether self-induced intoxication should be a defence generally to a criminal charge. It would have been a strange result if the merciful relaxation of a strict rule of law had ended, without any Parliamentary intervention, by whittling it away to such an extent that the more drunk a man became, provided he stopped short of making himself insane, the better chance he had of an acquittal ... The common law rule still applied but there were exceptions to it which Lord Birkenhead LC, tried to define by reference to specific intent."

There are, however, decisions of eminent judges in a number of Commonwealth cases in Australia and New Zealand, (but generally not in Canada nor in the United States) as well as impressive academic comment in this country, to which we have been referred, supporting the view that it is illogical and inconsistent with legal principle to treat a person who of his own choice and volition has taken drugs and drink, even though he thereby creates a state in which he is not conscious of what he is doing, any differently from a person suffering from the various medical conditions like epilepsy or diabetic coma and who is regarded by the law as free from fault. However our courts have for a very long time regarded in quite another light the state of self-induced intoxication. The authority which for the last half century has been relied upon in this context has been the speech of the Earl of Birkenhead LC in *Director of Public Prosecutions* v *Beard* [1920] AC 479, who stated, at p494:

"Under the law of England as it prevailed until early in the 19th century voluntary drunkenness was never an excuse for criminal misconduct; and indeed the classic authorities broadly assert that voluntary drunkenness must be considered rather an aggravation than a defence. This view was in terms based upon the principle that a man who by his own voluntary act debauches and destroys his will power shall be no better situated in regard to criminal acts than a sober man."

Lord Birkenhead LC made an historical survey of the way the common law from the 16th century on dealt with the effect of self-induced intoxication upon criminal responsibility. This indicates how, from 1819 on, the judges began to mitigate the severity of the attitude of the common law in such cases as murder and serious violent crime when the penalties of death or transportation applied or where there was likely to be sympathy for the accused, as in attempted suicide. Lord Birkenhead LC concluded, at p499, that (except in cases where the insanity is pleaded) the decisions he cited

"establish that where a specific intent is an essential element in the offence, evidence of a state of drunkenness rendering the accused incapable of forming such an intent should be taken into consideration in order to determine whether he had in fact formed the intent necessary to constitute the particular crime. If he was so drunk that he was incapable of forming the intent required he could not be convicted of a crime which was committed only if the intent was proved ... In a charge of murder based upon intention to kill or to do grievous bodily harm, if the jury are satisfied that the accused was, by reason of his drunken condition, incapable of forming the intent to kill or to do grievous bodily harm ... he cannot be convicted of murder. But nevertheless unlawful homicide has been committed by the accused, and consequently he is guilty of unlawful homicide without malice aforethought, and that is manslaughter: *per* Stephen J, in *R* v *Doherty* (1887) 16 Cox CC 306, 307."

He concludes the passage:

"the law is plain beyond all question that in cases falling short of insanity a condition of drunkenness at the time of committing an offence causing death can only, when it is available at all, have the effect of reducing the crime from murder to manslaughter."

From this it seemed clear – and this is the interpretation which the judges have placed upon the decision during the ensuing half century – that it is only in the limited class of cases requiring proof of specific intent that drunkenness can exculpate. Otherwise in no case can it exempt completely from criminal liability.

Unhappily what Lord Birkenhead LC described on p500 as "plain beyond all question" becomes less plain in the passage in his speech on p504 upon which Mr Tucker not unnaturally placed great emphasis. It reads

"I do not think that the proposition of law deduced from these earlier cases is an exceptional rule applicable only to cases in which it is necessary to prove a specific intent in order to constitute the graver crime eg, wounding with intent to do grievous bodily harm or with intent to kill. It is true that in such cases the specific intent must be proved to constitute the particular crime, but this is, on ultimate analysis, only in accordance with the ordinary law applicable to crime, for, speaking generally (and apart from certain special offences), a person cannot be convicted of a crime unless the mens was rea. Drunkenness, rendering a person incapable of the intent, would be an answer, as it is for example in a charge of attempted suicide."

Why then would it not be an answer in a charge of manslaughter, contrary to the earlier pronouncement at p499? In my view these passages are not easy to reconcile, but I do not dissent from the reconciliation suggested by my noble and learned friend Lord Russell of Killowen. Commenting on the passage on p504 in 1920 shortly after it was delivered, however, Stroud wrote (36 LQR 270):

"The whole of these observations ... suggest an extension of the defence of drunkenness far beyond the limits which have hitherto been assigned to it. The suggestion, put shortly, is that drunkenness may be available as a defence, upon any criminal charge, whenever it can be shown to have affected mens rea. Not only is there no authority for the suggestion: there is abundant authority, both ancient and modern, to the contrary."

It has to be said that it is on the latter footing that the judges have applied the law before and since *Beard's* case and have taken the view that self-induced intoxication, however gross and even if it has produced a condition akin to automatism, cannot excuse crimes of basic intent such as the charges of assault which have given rise to the present appeal.

[His Lordship then referred to *Attorney-General for Northern Ireland* v *Gallagher* (above), and *Bratty* v *Attorney-General for Northern Ireland* (above), and continued]

In no case has the general principle of English law as described by Lord Denning in *Gallagher's* case [1963] AC 349 and exposed again in *Bratty's* case [1963] AC 386 been overruled in this House and the question now to be determined is whether it should be.

I do not for my part regard that general principle as either unethical or contrary to the principles of natural justice. If a man of his own volition takes a substance which causes him to cast off the restraints of reason and conscience, no wrong is done to him by holding him answerable criminally for any injury he may do while in that condition. His course of conduct in reducing himself by drugs and drink to that condition in my view supplies the evidence of mens rea, of guilty mind certainly sufficient for crimes of basic intent. It is a reckless course of conduct and recklessness is enough to constitute the necessary mens rea in assault cases: see *R* v *Venna* [1976] QB 421, per James LJ at p429. The drunkenness is itself an intrinsic, an integral part of the crime, the other part being the evidence of the unlawful use of force against the victim. Together they add up to criminal recklessness. On this I adopt the conclusion of Stroud in 1920, 36 LQR 273 that:

"... it would be contrary to all principle and authority to suppose that drunkenness" (and what is true of drunkenness is equally true of intoxication by drugs) "can be a defence for crime in general on the ground that a 'person cannot be convicted of a crime unless the mens was rea'. By allowing himself to get drunk, and thereby putting himself in such a condition as to be no longer amenable to the law's commands, a man shows such regardlessness as amounts to mens rea for the purpose of all ordinary crimes."

This approach is in line with the American Model Penal Code (S. 2.08 (2)):

"When recklessness establishes an element of the offence, if the actor, due to self-induced intoxication, is unaware of a risk of which he would have been aware had he been sober, such unawareness is immaterial."

Acceptance generally of intoxication as a defence (as distinct from the exceptional cases where some additional mental element above that of ordinary mens rea has to be proved) would in my view undermine the criminal law and I do not think that it is enough to say, as did Mr Tucker, that we can rely on the good sense of the jury or of magistrates to ensure that the guilty are convicted. It may well be that Parliament will at some future time consider, as I think it should, the recommendation in the Butler Committee Report on Mentally Abnormal Offenders (Cmnd 6244, 1975) that a new offence of "dangerous intoxication" should be created. But in the meantime it would be irresponsible to abandon the common law rule, as "mercifully relaxed," which the courts have followed for a century and a half.

How the court of trial should deal with an offender in the circumstances we are considering is not a problem which arises on this appeal. It would no doubt take full account of the relevant medical evidence and of all mitigating factors and give careful consideration to the various alternatives, custodial and non-custodial, punitive and curative, now available to the courts. There is no minimum punishment for the class of assaults with which this appeal is concerned and the court's discretion as to how to deal with the offender is wide.

The final question that arises is whether section 8 of the Act of 1967 has had the result of abrogating or qualifying the common law rule. That section emanated from the consideration the Law Commission gave to the decision of the House in *Director of Public Prosecutions* v *Smith* [1961] AC 290. Its purpose and effect was to alter the law of evidence about the presumption of intention to produce the reasonable and probable consequences of one's acts. It was not intended to change the common law rule.

In referring to "all the evidence" it mean to all the *relevant* evidence. But if there is a substantive rule of law that in crimes of basic intent, the factor of intoxication is irrelevant (and such I hold to be the substantive law), evidence with regard to it is quite irrelevant. Section 8 does not abrogate the substantive rule and it cannot properly be said that the continued application of that rule contravenes the section. For these reasons, my conclusion it that the certified question should be answered "Yes," that there was no misdirection in this case and that the appeal should be dismissed.

My noble and learned friends and I think it may be helpful if we give the following indication of the general lines on which in our view the jury should be directed as to the effects upon the criminal responsibility of the accused of drink and drugs or both, whenever death or physical injury to another person results from something done by the accused for which there is no legal justification and the offence with which the accused is charged is manslaughter or assault at common law or the statutory offence of unlawful wounding under section 20, or of assault occasioning actual bodily harm under section 47 of the Offences against the Person Act 1861.

In the cases of these offences it is no excuse in law that, because of drink or drugs which the accused himself had taken knowingly and willingly, he had deprived himself of the ability to exercise self-control, to realise the possible consequences of what he was doing, or even to be conscious that he was doing it. As in the instant case, the jury may be properly instructed that they "can ignore the subject of drink or drugs as being in any way a defence" to charges of this character.'

R v Hardie (1985) 80 Cr App R 157 Court of Appeal (Criminal Division) (Parker LJ, McCowan and Stuart-Smith J)

Non-reckless self-induced intoxication

Facts

The defendant had voluntarily consumed up to seven valium tablets (a non-controlled drug having a sedative effect). Whilst under the influence of the drug he had started a fire in the flat in which he had been living, but claimed to have been unable to remember anything about it. The defendant was convicted of causing criminal damage being reckless as to whether life would be endangered, following the trial judge's direction to the jury that self-induced intoxication was not available by way of defence to a basic intent crime. The defendant appealed.

Held

The appeal would be allowed.

Parker LJ:

'We deal first with the second of Mr Slowe's [Counsel for the appellant] two contentions. Mr Slowe appreciated that the argument was difficult to sustain in the light of *Caldwell* [above] but distinguished that case on the ground that, there, the accused had pleaded guilty to a charge under section 1(1) of the Act and had himself given evidence that his actual intention was to damage the property in question. The distinction is valid but in our view of no assistance. The argument advanced really stems from Lord Diplock's speech at page 20 and pages 354 and 355 of the respective reports where he says: "Where the charge is under section 1(2) the question of the state of mind of the accused must be approached in stages, corresponding to paragraphs (a) and (b). The jury must be satisfied that what the accused did amounted to an offence under section 1(1), either because he actually intended to destroy or damage the property or because he was reckless (in the sense that I have described) as to whether it might be destroyed or damaged. Only if they are so satisfied must the jury go on to consider whether the accused also either actually intended that the destruction or damage of the property should endanger someone's life or was reckless (in a similar sense) as to whether a human life might be endangered."

For the convenience of the jury in their deliberations it is no doubt necessary that they approach the question of the accused's state of mind by stages. They are, however, concerned with the state of mind at one stage only, namely when he does the relevant act. If, when doing that act, he creates an obvious risk both that property will be destroyed and that the life of another will be endangered and gives no thought to the possibility of there being either risk, the requirements of the subsection are in our judgment clearly satisfied. If, for example, a person drops a lighted match at a petrol station into a bin containing oily rag by a pump in use by the attendant to fill a car and he thereby creates an obvious risk both that property will be damaged and that the life of the attendant will be endangered, but has given no thought to either matter, it would be farcical to say that the elements of the offence in subsection (1) had been fulfilled but those of subsection (2) had not. We reject the contention on the second point.

We now revert to the first point. It is clear from *Caldwell* [above] that self-induced intoxication can be a defence where the charge is only one of specific intention. It is equally clear that it cannot be a defence where, as here, the charge included recklessness. Hence, if there was self-intoxication in this case the judge's direction was correct. The problem is whether, assuming that the effect of the valium was to deprive the appellant of any appreciation of what he was doing it, should properly be regarded as self-induced intoxication and thus no answer.

In *DPP* v *Majewski* [above] the Lord Chancellor said at pp 268 and 471 of the respective reports: "If a man consciously and deliberately takes alcohol and drugs not on medical prescription, but in order to escape from reality, to go 'on a trip,' to become hallucinated, whatever the description may be and thereby disables himself from taking the care he might otherwise take and as a result by his subsequent actions causes injury to another - does our criminal law enable him to say that because he did not know what he was doing he lacked both intention and recklessness and accordingly is entitled to an acquittal?"

Later at pp 270 and 474-476 respectively, he said "If a man of his own volition takes a substance which causes him to cast off the restraints of reason and conscience, no wrong is done to him by holding him answerable criminally for any injury he may do while in that condition. His course of conduct in reducing himself by drugs and drink to that condition in my view supplies the evidence of mens rea, of guilty mind certainly sufficient for crimes of basic intent. It is a reckless course of conduct and recklessness is enough to constitute the necessary mens rea in assault cases: see *Venna* (1975) 61 Cr App R 310; (1976) QB 421, per James LJ at page 314 and page 429 respectively. The drunkenness is itself an intrinsic, and integral part of the crime, the other part being the evidence of the unlawful use of force against the victim. Together they add up to criminal recklessness. On this I adopt the conclusion of Stroud in (1920) 36 LQR 273 that: '... it would be contrary to all principle and authority to suppose that drunkenness' (and what is true of drunkenness is equally true of intoxication by drugs) 'can be a defence for crime in general on the ground that "a person cannot be convicted of a crime unless the mens was rea."' By allowing himself to get drunk, and thereby putting himself in such a condition as to be no longer amenable to the law's commands, a man shows such regardlessness as amounts to mens rea for the purpose of all ordinary crimes."

Later at pp 271 and 476 he said: "In the case of these offences it is no excuse in law that, because of drink or drugs which the accused himself had taken knowingly and willingly, he had deprived himself of the ability to exercise self-control, to realise the possible consequences of what he was doing, or even to be conscious that he was doing it." *DPP* v *Majewski* [above] was a case of drunkenness resulting from alcoholic consumption by the accused whilst under the influence of non-medically prescribed drugs. *Caldwell* [above] was a case of plain drunkenness. There can be no doubt that the same rule applies both to self-intoxication by alcohol and intoxication by hallucinatory drugs, but this is because the effects of both are well known and there is therefore an element of recklessness in the self administration of the drug. *Lipman* (1969) 53 Cr App R 600; [1970] 1 QB 152 is an example of such a case.

"Intoxication" or similar symptoms may, however, arise in other circumstances. In *Bailey* (1983) 77 Cr App R 76; [1983] 2 All ER 503 this Court had to consider a case where a diabetic had failed to take sufficient food after taking a normal dose of insulin and struck the victim over the head with an iron bar. The judge directed the jury that the defence of automatism, ie that the mind did not go with the act, was not available because the incapacity was self-induced. It was held that this was wrong on two grounds (a) because on the basis of *DPP* v *Majewski* [above] it was clearly available to the offence embodying specific intent and (b) because although self-induced by the omission to take food it was also available to negative the other offence which was of basic intent only.

Having referred to *DPP* v *Majewski* [above] and *Lipman* [below] Griffiths LJ, giving the considered judgment of the Court, said at page 80 and page 507 respectively: "It was submitted on behalf of the Crown that a similar rule should be applied as a matter of public policy to all cases of self-induced automatism. But it seems to us that there may be material distinctions between a man who consumes alcohol or takes dangerous drugs and one who fails to take sufficient food after insulin to avert hypoglycaemia. It is common knowledge that those who take alcohol to excess or certain sorts of drugs may become aggressive or do dangerous or unpredictable things; they may be able to foresee the risks of causing harm to others, but nevertheless persist in their conduct. But the same cannot be said, without more, of a man who fails to take food after an insulin injection. If he does appreciate the risk that such a failure may lead to aggressive, unpredictable and uncontrollable conduct and he nevertheless deliberately runs the risk or otherwise disregards it, this will amount to recklessness. But we certainly do not think that it is common knowledge, even among diabetics, that such is a consequence of a failure to take food; and there is no evidence that it was known to this appellant. Doubtless he knew that if he failed to take his insulin or proper food after it he might lose consciousness but as such he would only be a danger to himself unless he put himself in charge of some machine such as a motor car, which required his continued conscious control. In our judgment, self-induced automatism, other than that due to intoxication from alcohol or drugs, may provide a defence to crimes of basic intent. The question in each case will be whether the prosecution has proved the necessary element of recklessness. In cases of assault, if the accused knows that his actions or inaction are likely to make him aggressive, unpredictable or uncontrolled with the result that he may cause some injury to others and he persists in the action or takes no remedial action when he knows it is required, it will be open to the jury to find that he was reckless."

In the present instance the defence was that the valium was taken for the purpose of calming the nerves only, that it was old stock and that the appellant was told it would do him no harm. There was no evidence that it was known to the appellant or even generally known that the taking of valium in the quantity taken would be liable to render a person aggressive or incapable of appreciating risks to others or have other side effects such that its self-administration would itself have an element of recklessness. It is true that valium is a drug and it is true that it was taken deliberately and not taken on medical prescription, but the drug is, in our view, wholly different in kind from drugs which are liable to cause unpredictability or aggressiveness. It may well be that the taking of a sedative or soporific drug will, in certain circumstances, be no answer, for example in a case of reckless driving, but if the effect of a drug is merely soporific or sedative the taking of it, even in some excessive quantity, cannot in the ordinary way raise a *conclusive* presumption against the admission of proof of intoxication for the purpose of disproving mens rea in ordinary crimes, such as would be the case with alcoholic intoxication or incapacity or automatism resulting from the self-administration of dangerous drugs.

In the present case the jury should not, in our judgment, have been directed to disregard any incapacity which resulted or might have resulted from the taking of valium. They should have been directed that if they came to the conclusion that, as a result of the valium, the appellant was, as the time, unable to appreciate the risks to property and persons from his actions they should then consider whether the taking of valium was itself reckless. We are unable to say what would have been the appropriate direction with regard to the elements of recklessness in this case for we have not seen all the relevant evidence, nor are we able to suggest a model direction, for circumstances will vary infinitely and model directions can sometimes lead to more rather than less confusion. It is sufficient to say that the direction that the effects of valium were necessarily irrelevant was wrong.

In *Bailey* (supra) the Court upheld the conviction notwithstanding the misdirection, being satisfied that there had been no miscarriage of justice and that the jury properly directed could not have failed to come to the same conclusion. That is not so in the present case. Properly directed the jury might well have come to the same conclusion. There was, for example, evidence that the valium really did not materially effect the appellant at all at the relevant time, but we are quite unable to say that they must have come to the same conclusion.'

R v Hennessy [1989] 1 WLR 287 Court of Appeal (Criminal Division) (Lord Lane CJ, Rose and Pill JJ)

Nature of automatism and insanity

Facts

The appellant was a diabetic who needed a twice daily insulin injection in order to stabilise his metabolism. For several days the appellant had not eaten or taken insulin. He was stopped by police officers whilst driving a stolen car. In evidence to the police the appellant stated that he could not remember taking the car, and there was medical evidence to suggest that the appellant had been in a state of hyperglycaemia (high blood sugar level) at the time the car was taken. The appellant was charged, inter alia, with taking a conveyance contrary to s12 Theft Act 1968. He sought to rely on the defence of automatism, but the trial judge indicated that he would only be prepared to direct the jury on the defence of insanity, as defined by the M'Naghten Rules (1843), whereupon the appellant changed his plea to one of guilty, and now appealed to the Court of Appeal.

Held

The appeal would be dismissed. Since the appellant had put his state of mind in issue at the trial, the judge had been quite entitled to raise the issue of insanity. In the present case, the appellant's loss of awareness had not resulted from the operation of external factors upon his body, such as the injection of insulin (see *R* v *Quick* [1973] QB 910 - injection of insulin causing hypoglycaemia, or low blood sugar levels), but instead had resulted from an inherent physical defect, ie diabetes. The hyperglycaemia suffered by diabetics, which was not corrected by insulin, was to be regarded as a disease of the body which affected the mind for the purposes of the M'Naghten rules.

Lord Lane CJ (Having considered the facts his Lordship continued):

'The defence to these charges accordingly was that the appellant had failed to take his proper twice a day dose of insulin for two or three days and at the time the events in question took place he was in a state of automatism and did not know what he was doing. Therefore it is submitted that the guilty mind, which is necessary to be proved by the prosecution, was not proved, and accordingly that he was entitled to be acquitted.

The judge took the view, rightly in our view, that the appellant, having put his state of mind in issue, the preliminary question which he had to decide was whether this was truly a case of automatism or whether it was a case of legal "insanity" within the M'Naghten Rules - *M'Naghten's Case* (1843) 10 Cl & Fin 200. He concluded that it was the latter, and he so ruled, whereupon the appellant changed his plea to guilty and was sentenced to the terms of imprisonment suspended which we have already mentioned. The judge then certified the case fit for appeal in the terms which I have already described.

The M'Naghten Rules in the earlier part of the last century have in many ways lost their importance; they certainly have lost the importance they once had, but they are still relevant in so far as they may affect the defence of automatism. Although the rules deal with what they describe as insanity, it is insanity in the legal sense and not in the medical or psychological sense. The rules were, as is well known, embodied in replies given by the judges of that day to certain abstract questions which were placed before them. The historical reasons for the questions being posed it is not necessary for us to describe, interesting though they are.

The answer to the questions were these: first that

"every man is presumed to be sane, and to possess a sufficient degree of reason to be responsible for his crimes, until the contrary be proved to the satisfaction of the jury."

The second rule is:

"to establish a defence on the ground of insanity, it must be clearly proved that, at the time of the committing of the act, the party accused was labouring under such a defect of reason, from disease of the mind, as not to know the nature and quality of the act he was doing, or, if he did know it, that he did not know what he was doing was wrong."

The importance of the rules in the present context, namely, the context of automatism, is this. If the defendant did not know the nature and quality of his act because of something which *did not* amount to defect of reason from disease of the mind, then he will probably be entitled to be acquitted on the basis that the necessary criminal intent which the prosecution has to prove is not proved. But if, on the other hand, his failure to realise the nature and quality of his act was due to a defect of reason from disease of the mind, then in the eyes of the law he is suffering from insanity, albeit M'Naghten insanity.

It should perhaps be added, in order to complete the picture, though it is not relevant to the present situation, that where a defendant's failure to appreciate what he was doing was wrong, (that is, the second part of rule 2 of the M'Naghten Rules) where the failure is due to some reason other than a defect of reason from disease of the mind, he will generally have no valid defence at all.

If one wants any confirmation, it is to be found, if we may respectfully say so, in *Smith and Hogan, Criminal Law,* 6th ed (1988), p186, where these matters are very helpfully and clearly set out. If we may just cite the passage from that page, it runs as follows:

"When a defendant puts his state of mind in issue, the question whether he has raised the defence of insanity is one of law for the judge. Whether D, or indeed his medical witnesses, would call the condition on which he relies 'insanity,' is immaterial. The expert witnesses may testify as to the factual nature of the condition but it is for the judge to say whether that is evidence of 'a defect of reason, from disease of the mind,' because, as will appear, these are legal, not medical, concepts."

Then section 2 of the Trial of Lunatics Act 1883, as amended, by section 1 of the Criminal Procedure (Insanity) Act 1964 provides:

"(1) Where in any indictment or information any act or omission is charged against any person as an offence, and it is given in evidence on the trial of such person for that offence that he was insane, so as not to be responsible, according to law, for his actions at the time when the act was done or omission made, then, if it appears to the jury before whom such person is tried that he did the act or made the omission charged, but was insane as aforesaid at the time when he did or made the same, the jury shall return a special verdict that the accused is not guilty by reason of insanity."

In the present case therefore what had to be decided was whether the defendant's condition was properly described as a disease of the mind. That does not mean any disease of the brain. It means a disease which affects the proper functioning of the mind. There have been a series of authorities on that particular subject. One such instance is *Reg* v *Kemp* [1957] 1 QB 399 and the judgment of Devlin J therein.

The question in many cases, and this is one such case, is whether the function of the mind was disturbed on the one hand by disease or on the other hand by some external factor.'

[His Lordship then considered the views of Lord Diplock expressed in *R* v *Sullivan* [1984] AC 156, at p172, and the comments of Lawton LJ in *R* v *Quick* [1973] QB 910, at pp 922-923, and continued]

'Thus in *Quick's* case the fact that his condition was, or may have been due to the injections of insulin, meant that the malfunction was due to an external factor and not to the disease. The drug it was that caused the hypoglycaemia, the low blood sugar. As suggested in another passage of the judgment of Lawton LJ (at p922G-H), hyperglycaemia, high blood sugar, caused by an inherent defect, and not corrected by insulin is a disease, and if, as the defendant was asserting here, it does cause a malfunction of the mind, then the case may fall within M'Naghten Rules.

The burden of Mr Owen's argument to us is this. It is that the appellant's depression and marital troubles were a sufficiently potent external factor in his condition to override, so to speak, the effect of the diabetic shortage of insulin upon him. He refers us not only to the passage which I have already cited in *R* v *Quick* [1973] QB 910, 922 but also to a further passage in *Hill* v *Baxter* [1958] 1 QB 277, 285-286, which is part of the judgment of Devlin J, sitting with Lord Goddard CJ and Pearson J, in the Divisional Court:

"I have drawn attention to the fact that the accused did not set up a defence of insanity. For the purposes of the criminal law there are two categories of mental irresponsibility, one where the disorder is due to disease and the other where it is not. The distinction is not an arbitrary one. If disease is not the cause, if there is some temporary loss of consciousness arising accidentally, it is reasonable to hope that it will not be repeated and that it is safe to let an acquitted man go entirely free. But if disease is present, the same thing may happen again, and therefore, since 1800, the law has provided that persons acquitted on this ground should be subject to restraint."

That is the submission made by Mr Owen as a basis for saying the judge's decision was wrong and that this was a matter which should have been decided by the jury.

In our judgment, stress, anxiety and depression can no doubt be the result of the operation of external factors, but they are not, it seems to us, in themselves separately or together external factors of the kind capable in law of causing or contributing to a state of automatism. They constitute a state of mind which is prone to recur. They lack the feature of novelty or accident, which is the basis of the distinction drawn by Lord Diplock in *R* v *Sullivan* [1984] AC 156, 172. It is contrary to the observations of Devlin J, to which we have just referred in *Hill* v *Baxter* [1958] 1 QB 277, 285. It does not, in our judgment, come within the scope of the exception of some external physical factor such as a blow on the head or the administration of an anaesthetic.

For those reasons we reject the arguments, able though they were, of Mr Owen. It is not in those circumstance necessary for us to consider the further arguments which he addressed to us based upon the decision *R* v *Bailey* [1983] 1 WLR 760.

In our judgment the reasoning and judgment of the circuit judge were correct. Accordingly this appeal must be dismissed.'

Commentary

See *R* v *Bingham*, above.

R v Kemp [1957] 1 QB 399 Bristol Assizes (Devlin J)

Disease of the mind for the purposes of insanity

Facts

The defendant had attacked his wife with a hammer. The evidence put forward at his trial showed that he had not appreciated the nature and quality of his action because of arteriosclerosis, which caused a congestion of blood in the brain, and manifested itself in the defendant's irrational behaviour. The defence had submitted that the defendant was not insane within the M'Naghten Rules, and Devlin J considered the matter:

Held

The jury returned a verdict of guilty, but insane.

Devlin J:

[Referred to the fact that the only aspect of the M'Naghten Rules in issue here was whether the defendant had been suffering from a disease of the mind, and continued]

'The law is not concerned with the brain but with the mind, in the sense that "mind" is ordinarily used, the mental faculties of reason, memory and understanding. If one read for "disease of the mind" "disease of the brain", it would follow that in many cases the plea of insanity would not be established because it could not be proved that the brain had been affected in any way, either by degeneration of the cells or in any other way. In my judgment the condition of the brain is irrelevant and so is the question of whether the condition of the mind is curable or incurable, transitory or permanent. There is no warranty for introducing those considerations into the definition in the M'Naghten Rules. Temporary insanity is sufficient to satisfy them. It does not matter whether it is incurable and permanent or not.

I think that the approach of Mr Lee [Counsel for the Crown] to the definition in the Rules is the right one. He points out the order of the words "a defect of reason, from disease of the mind." The primary thing that has to be looked for is the defect of reason. "Disease of the mind" is there for some purpose, obviously, but the prime thing is to determine what is admitted here, namely, whether or not there is a defect of reason. In my judgment, the words "from disease of the mind" are not to be construed as if they were put in for the purpose of distinguishing between diseases which have a mental origin and diseases which have a physical origin, a distinction which in 1843 was probably little considered. They were put in for the purpose of limiting the effect of the words "defect of reason." A defect of reason is by itself enough to make the act irrational and therefore normally to exclude responsibility in law. But the Rule was not intended to apply to defects reason caused simply by brutish stupidity without rational power. It was not intended that the defence should plead "although with a healthy mind he nevertheless had been brought up in such a way that he had never learned to exercise his reason, and therefore he is suffering from a defect of reason." The words ensure that unless the defect is due to a diseased mind and not simply to an untrained one there is insanity within the meaning of the Rules.

Hardening of the arteries is a disease which is shown on the evidence to be capable of affecting the mind in such a way as to cause a defect, temporarily or permanently, of its reasoning, understanding and so on, and so is in my judgment a disease of the mind which comes within the meaning of the Rules.'

R v Lipman [1970] 1 QB 152 Court of Appeal (Criminal Division) (Widgery and Fenton Atkinson LJJ, and James J)

Intoxication as a defence to basic intent crimes

Facts

The defendant, having voluntarily consumed a quantity of an hallucenogenic drug, killed a woman whilst under the delusion that he was fighting snakes in the centre of the earth. His defence of intoxication was rejected at his trial. He was convicted of manslaughter, and appealed.

Held

The appeal would be dismissed.

Widgery LJ:

'As to manslaughter, the jury were directed that it would suffice for the Crown to prove that "he must have realised before he got himself into the condition he did by taking the drugs that acts such as those he subsequently performed and which resulted in the death were dangerous." In this court Mr Eastham contends that this was a misdirection, and that the jury should have been directed further that it was necessary for the Crown to prove that the defendant intended to do acts likely to result in harm, or foresaw that harm would result from what he was doing.

For the purposes of criminal responsibility we see no reason to distinguish between the effect of drugs voluntarily taken and drunkenness voluntarily induced. As to the latter there is a great deal of authority.

[After referring, inter alia, to *DPP v Beard* [1920] AC 479, *Bratty v Attorney-General for Northern Ireland*, above, and *Attorney-General for Northern Ireland v Gallagher*, above, his Lordship continued]

We can dispose of the present application by reiterating that when the killing results from an unlawful act of the prisoner no specific intent has to be proved to convict of manslaughter, and self-induced intoxication is accordingly no defence. Since in the present case the acts complained of were obviously likely to cause harm to the victim (and did, in fact, kill her) no acquittal was possible and the verdict of manslaughter, at the least, was inevitable.

If and so far as this matter raises a point of law on which the defendant was entitled to appeal without leave, such appeal is dismissed.'

R v Quick [1973] QB 910 Court of Appeal (Criminal Division) (Lawton LJ, Mocatta and Milmo JJ)

Automatism and insanity distinguished

Facts

The defendant, a diabetic, was employed as a nurse in a psychiatric hospital. He was charged with assaulting a patient, but had contended that this had occurred whilst he had been in a hypoglycaemia state (low blood sugar level due to an excess of insulin). Following the trial judge's direction that the evidence did not disclose the defence of automatism, the defendant changed his plea to one of guilty, and appealed.

Held

The appeal would be allowed.

Lawton LJ:

[His Lordship referred, inter alia, to *Bratty v Attorney-General for Northern Ireland* (above) and *R v Kemp* (above) and continued]

'Applied without qualification of any kind, Devlin J's statement of the law [in *R v Kemp*] would have some surprising consequences. Take the not uncommon case of the rugby player who gets a kick on the head early in the game and plays on to the end in a state of automatism. If, whilst he was in that state, he assaulted the referee, it is difficult to envisage any court adjudging that he was not guilty by reason of insanity. Another type of case which could occur is that of the dental patient who kicks out whilst coming round from an anaesthetic. The law would be in a defective state if a patient accused of assaulting a dental nurse by kicking her whilst regaining consciousness could only excuse himself by raising the defence of insanity.

In *Hill* v *Baxter* [1958] 1 QB 277, the problem before the Divisional Court was whether the accused had put forward sufficient evidence on a charge of dangerous driving to justify the justices adjudging that he should be acquitted, there having been no dispute that at the time when his car collided with another one he was at the driving wheel. At the trial the accused had contended that he became unconscious as a result of being overcome by an unidentified illness. The court (Lord Goddard CJ, Devlin and Pearson JJ) allowed an appeal by the prosecution against the verdict of acquittal. In the course of examining the evidence which had been put forward by the accused the judges made some comments of a general nature. Lord Goddard CJ referred to some observations of Humphreys J in *Kay* v *Butterworth* (1945) 173 LT 191 which seemed to indicate that a man who became unconscious whilst driving due to the onset of a sudden illness should not be made liable at criminal law and went on as follows, at 282,

"I agree that there may be cases when the circumstances are such that the accused could not really be said to be driving at all. Suppose he had a stroke or an epileptic fit, both instances of what may properly be called Acts of God; he might well be in the driver's seat even with his hands on the wheel but in such a state of unconsciousness that he could not be said to be driving ... In this case, however, I am content to say that the evidence falls far short of what would justify a court holding that this man was in some automatous state."

Lord Goddard CJ did not equate unconsciousness due to a sudden illness, which must entail the malfunctioning of the mental process of the sufferer, with disease of the mind, and in our judgment no one outside the court of law would. Devlin J in his judgment at 285 accepted that some temporary loss of consciousness arising *accidentally* (the italics are ours) did not call for a verdict based on insanity. It is not clear what he meant by "accidentally". The context suggests that he may have meant "unexpectedly" as can happen with some kind of virus infections. He went on as follows:

"If, however, disease is present the same thing may happen again and therefore since 1800 the law has provided that persons acquitted on this ground should be subject to restraint."

If this be right anyone suffering from a tooth abscess who knows from past experience that he reacts violently to anaesthetics because of some constitutional bodily disorder which can be attributed to disease might have to go on suffering or take the risk of being found insane unless he could find a dentist who would be prepared to take the risk of being kicked by a recovering patient. It seems to us that the law should not give the words "defect of reason from disease of the mind" a meaning which would be regarded with incredulity outside the court.

The last of the English authorities is *Watmore* v *Jenkins* [1962] 2 QB 572 ... In the course of the argument in that case counsel for the accused is reported as having submitted, on the basis of how Lord Murray had directed the jury in *H M Advocate* v *Ritchie* 1926 JC 45:

"Automatism is a defence to a charge of dangerous driving provided that a person takes reasonable steps to prevent himself from acting involuntarily in a manner dangerous to the public. It must be caused by some factor which he could not reasonably foresee and not by a self-induced incapacity ... "

Subject to the problem of whether the conduct said to have been in a state of automatism was caused by a disease of the mind, we agree with this submission. In this case, had the jury been left to decide whether the appellant Quick at the material time was insane, or in a state of automatism or just drunk, they probably would not have had any difficulty in making up their minds.

[Having referred to a number of Commonwealth authorities, his Lordship continued]

In this quagmire of law seldom entered nowadays save by those in desperate need of some kind of defence, *Bratty* v *Attorney-General for Northern Ireland,* (supra), provides the only firm ground. Is there any discernible path? We think there is - judges should follow in a common sense way their sense of fairness. This seems to have been the approach of the New Zealand Court of Appeal in *R* v *Cottle* [1958] NZLR 999, and of Sholl J in *R* v *Carter* [1959] VR 105. In our judgment no help can be obtained by speculating (because that is what we would have to do) as to what the judges who answered the House of Lords' questions in 1843 meant by disease of the mind, still less what Sir Matthew Hale meant in the second half of the 17th century [(1682) Vol J, Ch IV.] A quick backward look at the state of medicine in 1843 will suffice to show how unreal it would be to apply the concepts of that age to the present time. Dr Simpson had not yet started his experiments with chloroform, the future Lord Lister was only 16 and laudanum was used and prescribed like aspirins are today. Our task has been to decide what the law means now by the words "disease of the mind". In our judgment the fundamental concept is of a malfunctioning of the mind caused by disease. A malfunctioning of the mind of transitory effect caused by the application to the body of some external factor such as violence, drugs, including anaesthetics, alcohol and hypnotic influences, cannot fairly be said to be due to disease. Such malfunctioning, unlike that caused by a defect of reason from disease of the mind, will not always relieve an accused from criminal responsibility. A self-induced incapacity will not excuse [see *R* v *Lipman,* [1970] 1 QB 152] nor will one which could have been reasonably foreseen as a result of either doing, or omitting to do something, as, for example, taking alcohol against medical advice after using certain prescribed drugs, or failing to have regular meals whilst taking insulin. From time to time difficult borderline cases are likely to arise. When they do, the test suggested by the New Zealand Court of Appeal in *R* v *Cottle* [1958] NZLR 999 is likely to give the correct result, viz. can this mental condition be fairly regarded as amounting to or producing a defect of reason from disease of the mind?

In this case Quick's alleged mental condition, if it ever existed,was not caused by his diabetes but by his use of the insulin prescribed by his doctor. Such malfunctioning of the mind as there was, was caused by an external factor and not a bodily disorder in the nature of a disease which disturbed the working of his mind. It follows in our judgment that Quick was entitled to have his defence of automatism left to the jury and that Bridge J's ruling as to the effect of the medical evidence called by him was wrong. Had the defence of automatism been left to the jury, a number of questions of fact would have had to be answered. If he was in a confused mental condition, was it due to a hypoglycaemic episode or to too much alcohol? If the former, to what extent had he brought about his condition by not following his doctor's instructions about taking regular meals? Did he know that he was getting into a hypoglycaemic episode? If Yes, why did he not use the antidote of eating a lump of sugar as he had been advised to do? On the evidence which was before the jury Quick might have had difficulty in answering these questions in a manner which would have relieved him of responsibility for this acts. We cannot say, however, with the requisite degree of confidence, that the jury would have convicted him. It follows that this conviction must be quashed on the ground that the verdict was unsatisfactory.'

R v Sullivan [1984] AC 156 House of Lords (Lords Diplock, Scarman, Lowry, Bridge and Brandon)

Automatism and insanity distinguished

Facts

The defendant, whilst suffering from a minor epileptic fit, had kicked another man about the head and body. He was charged under s20 of the Offences Against the Person Act 1861, and sought to rely on the defence of automatism. The trial judge ruled that he would be willing to direct the jury on the defence of insanity, but not automatism, whereupon the defendant changed his plea to one of guilty, and appealed unsuccessfully to the Court of Appeal. On appeal to the House of Lords;

Held

The appeal would be dismissed.

Lord Diplock:

'The evidence as to pathology of a seizure due to psychomotor epilepsy can be sufficiently stated for the purposes of this appeal by saying that after the first stage, the prodram, which precedes the fit itself, there is a second stage, the ictus, lasting a few seconds, during which there are electrical charges into the temporal lobes of the brain of the sufferer. The effect of these discharges is to cause him in the post-ictal stage to make movements which he is not conscious that he is making, including, and this was a characteristic of previous seizures which the appellant had suffered, automatic movements of resistance to anyone trying to come to his aid. These movements of resistance might, though in practice they very rarely would, involve violence.

At the conclusion of the evidence, the judge, in the absence of the jury, was asked to rule whether the jury should be directed that if they accepted this evidence it would not be open to them to bring in a verdict of "not guilty," but they would be bound in law to return a special verdict of "not guilty by reason of insanity." The judge ruled that the jury should be so directed.

After this ruling, the appellant, on the advice of his counsel and with the consent of the prosecution and the judge, changed his plea to guilty of assault occasioning actual bodily harm. The jury, on the direction of the judge, brought in a verdict of guilty of that offence, for which the judge sentenced him to three years' probation subject to the condition that during that period he submitted to treatment under the direction of Dr Fenwick at the Maudsley Hospital.

My Lords, neither the legality nor the propriety of the procedure adopted after the judge's ruling has been canvassed in this House; nor was it canvassed in the Court of Appeal to which an appeal was brought upon the ground that the judge ought to have left to the jury the defence of non-insane automatism which, if accepted by them, would have entitled the appellant to a verdict of "not guilty." In these circumstances the present case does not appear to be one in which it would be appropriate of this House to enter into a consideration of the procedure following in the Central Criminal Court after the judge's ruling; more particularly, as it raises some questions that will shortly come before your Lordships for argument in another appeal.

The Court of Appeal held that Judge Lymbery's ruling had been correct. It dismissed the appeal and certified that a point of law of general public importance was involved in the decision, namely: "Whether a person who is proved to have occasioned, contrary to section 47 of the Offences against the Person Act 1861, actual bodily harm to another, whilst recovering from a seizure due to psychomotor epilepsy and who did not know what he was doing when he caused such harm and has no memory of what he did should be found not guilty by reason of insanity."

My Lords, for centuries up to 1843, the common law relating to the concept of mental disorder as negativing responsibility for crimes was in the course of evolution, but I do not think it necessary for your Lordships to embark upon an examination of the pre-1843 position. In that year, following upon the acquittal of one Daniel McNaghten, for shooting Sir Robert Peel's secretary, in what today would probably be termed a state of paranoia, the question of insanity and criminal responsibility was the subject of debate in the legislative chamber of the House of Lords, the relevant statute then in force being the Criminal Lunatics Act 1800 (39 & 40 Geo 3, c 94) "for the safe custody of Insane Persons charged with Offences," which referred to persons who were "insane" at the time of the commission of the offence, but contained no definition of insanity. The House invited the judges of the courts of common law to answer five abstract questions on the subject of insanity as a defence to criminal charges. The answer to the second and third of these questions combined was given to Tindal CJ on behalf of all the judges, except Maule J, and constituted what became known as the McNaghten Rules. The judge's answer is in the following well-known terms (see *McNaghten's Case* (1843) 10 Cl & Fin 200, 210): "the jurors ought to be told in all cases that every man is to be presumed to be sane, and to possess a sufficient degree of reason to be responsible for his crimes, until the contrary be proved to their satisfaction; and that to establish a defence on the ground of insanity, it must be clearly proved that, at the time of the committing of the act, the party accused was labouring under a defect of reason, from disease of the mind, as not to know the nature and quality of the act he was doing; or, if he did know it, that he did not know he was doing what was wrong."

Although the questions put to the judges by the House of Lords referred to the insane delusions of various kinds, the answer to the second and third question (the McNaghten Rules) is perfectly general in its terms. It is stated to be applicable "in all cases" in which it is sought to "establish a defence on the ground of insanity."

This answer was intended to provide a comprehensive definition of the various matters which had to be proved (on balance of probabilities, as it has since been held) in order to establish that he accused was insane within the meaning of the statute of 1800 which, like its successors of 1883 and 1964, make it incumbent upon a jury, if they find the accused to have been "insane" at the time that he committed the acts with which he is charged, to bring in a verdict neither of "guilty" nor of "not guilty" but a special verdict the terms of which have varied under the three successive statutes, but are currently "not guilty by reason of insanity."

The McNaghten Rules have been used as a comprehensive definition for this purpose by the courts for the past 140 years. Most importantly, they were so used by this House in *Bratty v Att-Gen For Northern Ireland* [above]. That case was in some respects the converse of the instant case. Bratty was charged with murdering a girl by strangulation. He claimed to have been unconscious of what he was doing at the time he strangled the girl and he sought to run as alternative defences non-insane automatism and insanity. The only evidential foundation that he laid for either of these pleas was medical evidence that he might have been suffering from psychomotor epilepsy which, if he were, would account for his having been unconscious of what he was doing. No other pathological explanation of his actions having been carried out in a state of automatism was supported by evidence. The trial judge first put the defence of insanity to the jury. The jury rejected it; they declined to bring in the special verdict. Thereupon, the judge refused to put to the jury the alternative defence of automatism. His refusal was upheld by the Court of Criminal Appeal of Northern Ireland and subsequently by this House.

The question before this House was whether, the jury having rejected the plea of insanity, there was any evidence of non-insane automatism fit to be left to the jury. The ratio decidendi of its dismissal of the appeal was that the jury having negatived the explanation that Bratty might have been acting unconsciously in the course of an attack of psychomotor epilepsy, there was no evidential foundation for the suggestion that he was acting unconsciously from any other cause.

In the instant case, as in *Bratty* (supra), the only evidential foundation that was laid for any finding by the jury that the appellant was acting unconsciously and involuntarily when he was kicking Mr Payne, was that when he did so he was in the post-ictal stage of a seizure of psychomotor epilepsy. The evidential foundation in the case of *Bratty*, that he was suffering from psychomotor epilepsy at the time he did the act with which he was charged, was very weak and was rejected by the jury; the evidence in the appellant's case, that he was so suffering when he was kicking Mr Payne, was very strong and would almost inevitably be accepted by a properly directed jury. It would be the duty of the judge to direct the jury that if they did accept the evidence the law required them to bring in a special verdict and none other. The governing statutory provision is to be found in section 2 of the Trial of Lunatics Act 1883. This says "the jury *shall* return a special verdict."

My Lords, I can deal briefly with the various grounds on which it has been submitted that he instant case can be distinguished from what constituted the ratio decidendi in *Bratty*, and that it falls outside the ambit of the McNaghten Rules.

First, it is submitted the medical evidence in the instant case shows that psychomotor epilepsy is not a disease of the mind, whereas in *Bratty* it was accepted by all the doctors that is was. The only evidential basis for this submission is that Dr Fenwick said that in medical terms to constitute a "disease of the mind" or "mental illness," which he appeared to regard as interchangeable descriptions, a disorder of brain functions (which undoubtedly occurs during a seizure in psychomotor epilepsy) must be prolonged for a period of time, usually more than a day; while Dr Taylor would have it that the disorder must continue for a minimum of a month to qualify for the description "disease of the mind."

The nomenclature adopted by the medical profession may change from time to time; Bratty was tried in 1961. But the meaning of the expression "disease of the mind" as the cause of "defect of reason" remains unchanged for the purposes of the application of the McNaghten Rules. I agree with what was said by Devlin J in *Kemp* (1956) 40 Cr App R 121, 128; [1957] 1 QB 399, 407, that "mind" in the McNaghten Rules is used in the ordinary sense of the mental faculties of reason, memory and understanding. If the effect of a disease is to impair these facilities so severely as to have either of the consequences referred to in the later part of the Rules, it matters not whether the aetiology of the impairment is organic, as in epilepsy, or functional, or whether the impairment itself is permanent or is transient and intermittent, provided that it subsisted at the time of the commission of the act. The purpose of the legislation relating to the defence of insanity, ever since its origin in 1800, has been to protect society against recurrence of the dangerous conduct. The duration of a temporary suspension of the mental faculties of reason, memory and understanding, particularly if, as in the appellant's case, it is recurrent, cannot on any rational ground be relevant to the application by the Courts of the McNaghten Rules, though it may be relevant to the course adopted by the Secretary of State, to whom the responsibility for how the defendant is to be dealt with passes after the return of the special verdict of "not guilty by reason of insanity."

To avoid misunderstanding I ought perhaps to add that in expressing my agreement with what was said by Devlin J in *Kemp* (supra) where the disease that caused the temporary and intermittent impairment of the mental faculties was arteriosclerosis, I do not regard that learned judge as excluding the possibility of non-insane automatism (for which the proper verdict would be a verdict of "not guilty") in cases where temporary impairment (not being self-induced by consuming drink or drugs) results from some external physical factor such as a blow on the head causing concussion or the administration of an anaesthetic for therapeutic purposes. I mention this because in *Quick and Paddison* (1973) 57 Cr App R 722, Lawton LJ appears to have regarded the ruling in *Kemp* as going so far as this. If it had done, it would have been inconsistent with the speeches in this House in *Bratty*, where *Kemp* was alluded to without disapproval by Viscount Kilmuir and received the express approval of Lord Denning. The instant case, however, does not in my view afford an appropriate occasion for exploring possible causes of non-insane automatism.

The only other submission in support of the appellant's appeal which I think it necessary to mention is that, because the expert evidence was to the effect that the appellant's acts in kicking Mr Payne were unconscious and thus "involuntary" in the legal sense of that term, his state of mind was not one dealt with by the McNaghten Rules at all, since it was not covered by the phrase "as not to know the nature and quality of the act he was doing." Quite apart from being contrary to all three speeches in this House in *Bratty* (supra) this submission appears to me, with all respect to counsel, to be quite unarguable. Dr Fenwick himself accepted it as an accurate description of the appellant's mental state in the post-ictal stage of a seizure. The audience to whom the phrase in the McNaghten Rules was addressed consisted of peers of the realm in the 1840s when a certain orotundity of diction had not yet fallen out of fashion. Addressed to an audience of jurors in the 1980s it might more aptly be expressed as "He did not know what he was doing."

My Lords, it is natural to feel reluctant to attach the label of insanity to a sufferer from psychomotor epilepsy of the kind to which the appellant was subject, even though the expression in the context of a special verdict of "not guilty by reason of insanity" is a technical one which includes a purely temporary and intermittent suspension of the mental faculties of reason, memory and understanding resulting from the occurrence of an epileptic fit. But the label is contained in the current statute, it has appeared in this statute's predecessors ever since 1800. It does not lie within the power of the courts to alter it. Only Parliament can do that. It has done so twice; it could do so once again.

Sympathise though I do with the appellant, I see no other course open to your Lordships than to dismiss this appeal.'

R v T [1990] Crim LR 256 Snaresbrook Crown Court (Southan J)

Post-traumatic stress disorder and dissociative state - defence of non-insane automatism or 'insanity'?

Facts

'T, a young French woman aged 23 and two others (R and B) were arrested and charged with robbery (two cases) and T was further charged with ABH. The Crown alleged a joint enterprise by all three to rob two females whilst armed with a Stanley knife (not recovered) and a pen knife, of their handbags, as the two victims were returning to a car late at night. When first seen, T was leaning on the victims' car and said "I'm ill, I'm ill". The three accused then surrounded one of the girls and there was a scuffle. Her bag opened and the contents spilled out, whereupon the two victims ran away. A few minutes later, they met another young woman, dressed in a dark coloured jogging suit, who offered to accompany them to the local police station. On route to the car, T saw the two victims and (allegedly) misidentified the third person as a male. T then followed the three women to the motor vehicle and she was followed by R and B. Near the car, the contents of the first victim's handbag were recovered and she got behind the wheel of the car. The second victim sat in the rear nearside passenger seat and the third woman was standing by the open front nearside passenger's door when they were approached by the three defendants. R went to the driver's side and held a Stanley-type knife to the face of the first victim and demanded her bag, which he was given. T approached the open passenger's door where the third woman was standing. When asked what she was doing and why, T stabbed the third woman in the stomach causing a small puncture wound (no medical treatment required other than a dressing). T then pushed past the third woman, leant into the car and demanded the second victim's handbag, which was given to her. All three defendants remained in the vicinity for about one minute. The third woman realised she had been stabbed and started to scream, whereupon the three defendants decamped. The three victims drove away and pointed out T, R and B to a police officer whereupon R and B decamped. R was seen to discard a pen knife in a rubbish bin and discard the first victim's handbag, both of which were recovered. After a short chase R was arrested and brought back to where the victims were, and the officer also detained T who was standing at the side of the road. On being arrested, T was described as being passive and indifferent to what was happening.

During a subsequent interview, T could only recollect some of the events. B was arrested the following day and all three were charged. Seven days later, T was examined by a doctor at HM Prison Holloway when it was found that her hymen was ruptured and was bleeding, and that there were injuries posterior to the hymen. T complained that she had been raped three days prior to her arrest but had not told anyone about it. T was later examined on a number of occasions by a psychiatrist who diagnosed that after the rape she was suffering from Post Traumatic Stress Disorder and at the time of the offence she had entered a dissociative state and the offences had been committed during a psychogenic fugue and she was not acting with a conscious mind or will. The defence submitted that the "defence" of "non-insane automatism" was open to T on the grounds that the categories of non-insane automatism are not limited to a blow causing concussion, an injection of insulin or anaesthetic or sleep walking (per Lord Diplock in *Sullivan* [1983] 3 WLR 123); that rape is the application of an "external force" (per Lawton LJ in *Quick* [1973] 3 WLR 26 at p35); that the rape was such an extraordinary external event that might be presumed to affect the average normal person and it contained features of novelty of accident (per Lord Lane CJ in *Hennessy* [1989] 1 WLR 287 at p294 and Martin J in *Rabey*, 79 Dominion Law Reports 435 (Ontario Court of Appeal)), that a proper foundation has been laid for leaving the defence to the jury (per Lord Denning in *Bratty v Att-Gen for Northern Ireland* [1963] AC 368 at p413. The Crown argued that the evidence showed the defendant had some recollection of what happened. Further that the opening of the blade of the pen knife required a controlled and positive action by the defendant, therefore this was a case where there was "partial control" (per *Broom v Perkins* (1987) 85, Crim App R 321 and *Issit*

[1977] RTR 211) and the only "defence" open to T was 'insane automatism' under the M'Naghton Rules.

Held

That there had been no previous case in which an incident of rape had been held to be "an external factor" causing a malfunctioning of the mind within the definition laid down in *Quick*; that, if what the defendant says about the rape is true, such an incident could have an appalling effect on any young woman, however well balanced normally, and that could satisfy the requirement; that a condition of post traumatic stress involving a normal person in an act of violence is not itself a disease of the mind, even if there is a delay before a period of dissociation manifests itself; that if the medical evidence is correct this case is distinguishable from *Broom* and *Issit* where there was only a partial loss of control whereas in this case T was acting as though in a "dream"; that the categories of automatism are not closed and that, on the evidence before the court, a proper foundation had been laid for the matter to go before the jury.'

[*Reported by Brian Riley, Barrister.*]

R v Windle [1952] 2 QB 826 Court of Criminal Appeal (Lord Goddard CJ, Jones and Parker JJ)

Insanity: defendant's ignorance of illegality

Facts

The defendant had killed his wife by administering an overdose of aspirins to her. When interviewed by the police he indicated that he thought he would be hanged for murder. At his trial the judge had refused to allow the defence of insanity to go to the jury on the ground, inter alia, that he had known his actions were unlawful. The defendant appealed.

Held

The appeal would be dismissed.

Lord Goddard CJ:

'The point we have to decide can be put into a very small compass. We are asked to review – I am not sure we are not asked to make new law – what are known as the M'Naghten Rules which in 1843 the judges agreed were the proper tests to be applied in considering the defence of insanity. All the judges, except Maule J, who differed on small points, gave, through the mouth of Tindall CJ, these answers to questions put by the House of Lords ((1843) 10 Cl & F 200, at p210; 4 St Tr (NS) 847, at p931):

"That the jury ought to be told in all cases that every man is presumed to be sane, and to possess a sufficient degree of reason to be responsible for his crimes, until the contrary be proved to their satisfaction; and that, to establish a defence on the ground of insanity, it must be clearly proved that, at the time of the committing of the act, the party accused was labouring under such a defect of reason, from disease of the mind, as not to know the nature and quality of the act he was doing, or, if he did know it, that he did not know he was doing what was wrong."

The argument in this appeal really has been concerned with what is meant by the word "wrong." The evidence that was given on the issue of insanity was that of the doctor called by the appellant and that of the prison doctor who was called by the prosecution. Both doctors expressed without hesitation the view that when the appellant was administering this poison to his wife he knew that he was doing an act which the law forbade. I need not put it higher than that. It may well be that, in the misery in which he had been living with his nagging and tiresome wife who constantly expressed the desire to commit suicide, he thought she was better out of the world than in it. He may have thought it was a kindly act to put her out of her sufferings or imagined sufferings, but the law does not permit such an act as that. There was some exceedingly vague evidence that the appellant was suffering from a defect of reason owing to this communicated insanity, and if the only question in the case had been whether the appellant was suffering from a disease of the mind, that question must have been left to the jury because there was some evidence of it, but that was not the question. The question, as I endeavoured to point out in giving judgment in *Rivett* (1950) 34 Cr App R 87, in all these cases is one of responsibility. A man may be suffering from a defect of reason, but, if he knows that what he is doing is wrong – and by "wrong" is meant contrary to law – he is responsible. Counsel for the appellant, in his very careful argument, suggested that the word "wrong" as it is used in the McNaghten Rules did not mean contrary to law, but had some qualified meaning, that is to say, morally wrong, and that, if a person was in a state of mind through a defect of reason that he thought that what he was doing, although he knew it was wrong in law, was really beneficial, or kind, or praiseworthy, that would excuse him.

Courts of law, however, can only distinguish between that which is in accordance with law and that which is contrary to law. There are many acts which we all know, to use an expression to be found in some of the old cases, are contrary to the law of God and man. In the Decalogue, are the commandments "Thou shalt not kill" and "Thou shalt not steal." Such acts are contrary to the law of man and they are contrary to the law of God. In regard to the Seventh Commandment, "Thou shalt not commit adultery" it will be found that, so far as the criminal law is concerned, though that act is contrary to the law of God, it is not contrary to the law of man. That does not mean that the law encourages adultery: I only say it is not a criminal offence.

The test must be whether an act is contrary to law. In *Rivett* (supra) I referred to the Trial of Lunatics Act, 1883, section 2 (1) of which provides:

"Where in any indictment or information any act or omission is charged against any person as an offence, and it is given in evidence on the trial of such person for that offence that he was insane, so as not to be responsible, according to law, for his actions at the time when the act was done or omission made, then, if it appears to the jury before whom such person is tried that he did the act or made the omission charged, but was insane as aforesaid at the time when he did or made the same, the jury shall return a special verdict... "

I emphasise again that the test is responsibility "according to law."

I am reminded by Parker J that counsel for the appellant argued that the M'Naghten Rules only applied to delusions. This court cannot agree with that. It is true that when the judges were summoned by their Lordships the occasion had special reference to *McNaghten's case* (supra) but the M'Naghten Rules have ever since that date been generally applied to all cases of insanity, whatever the nature of the insanity or disease of the mind from which the offender is suffering.

In the opinion of the court, there is no doubt that the word "wrong" in the M'Naghten Rules means contrary to law and does not have some vague meaning which may vary according to the opinion of different persons whether a particular act might not be justified. There seems to have been no doubt in this case that it could not be challenged that the appellant knew that what he was doing was contrary to law. In those circumstances what evidence was there that could be left to the jury to suggest that he was entitled to a verdict of Guilty but insane – ie, insane at the time of the act complained of?

Devlin J was right to withdraw the case from the jury. This appeal fails.'

13 DEFENCES II

Abbott v R [1977] AC 755

See reference to this authority in extracts from the speeches in *R* v *Howe*, below.

Beckford v R [1987] 3 WLR 611

See chapter 14.

R v Bourne [1939] 1 KB 687

See chapter 5.

R v Dudley and Stephens (1884) 14 QBD 273 Queen's Bench Division (Lord Coleridge CJ, Grove and Denman JJ, Pollock and Huddlestone BB)

Availability of the defence of necessity

Facts

The two defendants, a third man and a cabin boy, were cast adrift in a boat following a shipwreck. They were 1600 miles from land, and had endured seven days without food and water, when the defendants decided to kill the cabin boy, who was in any case close to death, so that they might eat his flesh and drink his blood, in the hope that they might then survive long enough to be rescued. Four days after the killing, the three survivors were picked up by a passing vessel. On returning to England the defendants were charged with the boy's murder. The jury returned a special verdict whereby they found that, although the defendants would probably not have survived had they not killed the boy, and that he was likely to have died first anyway, there was no greater necessity for killing the boy than any of the other survivors. The jury's finding was referred to the judges of the Queen's Bench Division.

Held

The defendants could not raise the defence of necessity to a charge of murder.

Lord Coleridge CJ:

'Now, except for the purpose of testing how far the conservation of a man's own life is in all cases and under all circumstances, an absolute, unqualified, and paramount duty, we exclude from our consideration all the incidents of war. We are dealing with a case of private homicide, not one imposed upon men in the service of their Sovereign and in the defence of their country. Now it is admitted that the deliberate killing of this unoffending and unresisting boy was clearly murder, unless the killing can be justified by some well-recognised excuse admitted by the law. It is further admitted that there was in this case no such excuse, unless the killing was justified by what has been called "necessity." But the temptation to the act which existed here was not what the law has ever called necessity. Nor is this to be regretted. Though law and morality are not the same, and many things may be immoral which are not necessarily illegal, yet the absolute divorce of law from morality would be of fatal consequence; and such divorce would follow if the temptation to murder in this case were to he held by law an absolute defence of it. It is not so. To preserve one's life is generally speaking a duty, but it may be the plainest and the highest duty to sacrifice it. War is full of instances in which it is a man's duty not to live, but to die. The duty, in case of shipwreck, of a

259

captain to his crew, of the crew to the passengers, of soldiers to women and children, as in the noble case of the *Birkenhead*; these duties impose on men the moral necessity, not of the preservation, but of the sacrifice of their lives for others, from which in no country, least of all, it is to be hoped, in England, will men ever shrink, as indeed, they have not shrunk. It is not correct, therefore, to say that there is any absolute or unqualified necessity to preserve one's life. "Necesse est ut eam, non ut vivam," is a saying of a Roman officer quoted by Lord Bacon himself with high eulogy in the very chapter on necessity to which so much reference has been made. It would be a very easy and cheap display of commonplace learning to quote from Greek and Latin authors, from Horace, from Juvenal, from Cicero, from Euripides, passage after passage, in which the duty of dying for others has been laid down in glowing and emphatic language as resulting from the principles of heathen ethics; it is enough in a Christian country to remind ourselves of the Great Example whom we profess to follow. It is not needful to point out the awful danger of admitting the principle which has been contended for. Who is to be the judge of this sort of necessity? By what measure is the comparative value of lives to be measured? Is it to be strength, or intellect, or what? It is plain that the principle leaves to him who is to profit by it to determine the necessity which will justify him in deliberately taking another's life to save his own. In this case the weakest, the youngest, the most unresisting, was chosen. Was it more necessary to kill him than one of the grown men? The answer must be "No" –

> "So spake the Friend, and with necessity,
> The tyrant's plea, excused his devilish deeds."

It is not suggested that in this particular case the deeds were "devilish" but it is quite plain that such a principle once admitted might be made the legal cloak for unbridled passion and atrocious crime. There is no safe path for judges to tread but to ascertain the law to the best of their ability and to declare it according to their judgment; and if in any case the law appears to be too severe on individuals, to leave it to the Sovereign to exercise that prerogative of mercy which the Constitution has intrusted to the hands fittest to dispense it.

It must not be supposed that in refusing to admit temptation to be an excuse for crime it is forgotten how terrible the temptation was; how awful the suffering; how hard in such trials to keep the judgment straight and the conduct pure. We are often compelled to set up standards we cannot reach ourselves, and to lay down rules which we could not ourselves satisfy. But a man has no right to declare temptation to be an excuse, though he might himself have yielded to it, nor allow compassion for the criminal to change or weaken in any manner the legal definition of the crime. It is therefore our duty to declare that the prisoners' act in this case was wilful murder, that the facts as stated in the verdict are no legal justification of the homicide; and to say that in our unanimous opinion the prisoners are upon this special verdict guilty of murder.'

R v Fitzpatrick [1977] NI 20 Court of Criminal Appeal in Northern Ireland (Lowry LCJ and Jones LJ)

Denial of duress to defendants voluntarily joining criminal associations

Facts

The defendant had voluntarily joined the IRA. He was subsequently forced, by other IRA members, to take part in serious offences, involving robbery and murder. At his trial the defendant had sought to rely on the defence of duress, but the trial judge had ruled that it was not available to a defendant who voluntarily joined a violent criminal association, and subsequently found himself forced by other gang members to commit offences. The defendant appealed against his convictions for murder and robbery.

Held

The appeal would be dismissed.

Lowry LCJ:

[The appeal proceeded on three grounds, inter alia, 1(a), that the trial judge had wrongfully directed himself in deciding that duress was not available to a defendant who voluntarily joined a criminal organisation; and 1(b) if the first ground of appeal should fail, that the trial judge had been wrong in directing himself that the defendant's attempts to dissociate himself from the IRA were of no avail.]

'As to ground 1(a), we consider that the learned trial judge properly directed himself and that he correctly applied the legal principles to the facts.

Counsel on both sides have informed us that the point is devoid of judicial authority and we have not found anything to suggest the contrary. Therefore we have to decide, in the absence of judicial decisions, what is the common law. Assistance may be sought from the opinions of text-writers, judicial dicta and the reports of Commissions and legal committees, and from analogies with legal systems which share our common law heritage, with a view to considering matters of general principle and arriving at the answer.

[His Lordship referred to a number of foreign and Commonwealth penal codes, and the House of Lords' decision in R v *Lynch* (considered in *R v Howe*, below) and continued:]

We recognise that the issue which we have to decide was not before the House in R v *Lynch* and that we cannot seek to extract a binding rule from the passages we have cited, but we believe that their lordships' observations collectively tend towards a rejection of the present appellant's argument.

Lord Edmund-Davies' reference to Lord Diplock's observations in *Hyam's* case helpfully reminds us of the common law approach to a problem when, as here, there is a lack of judicial authority. We are not here dealing with the doctrine of precedent or custom, for none has been established, but with the use of analogy and the observance of what Sir Frederick Pollock in his essay on Judicial Caution and Valour called "the duty of the Court to keep the rules of law in harmony with the enlightened common sense of the nation." This is not a subject which is governed by any doctrines that can be recognised as "rules of the common law," and therefore we must resort to what we believe, within a framework of fairness and justice to the individual, to represent expediency, reasonableness and widely accepted notions of morality. The codes and draft codes to which we have referred and the signs of what is accepted as the common law in the United States furnish, in our opinion, strong indications of the answer to which these criteria should lead us in relation to the questions we have to decide. As Cardozo J pointed out when considering the Nature of the Judicial Process, "The final cause of law is the welfare of society." So far as we may derive assistance from analogy, we have been referred to the law on voluntary drunkenness as affecting criminal responsibility and to the ineffectiveness of pleading the orders of a superior when answering to a criminal charge: *R v Axtell* (1660) Kel 13, where this plea was, not surprisingly, of little avail to one of the regicides. One might also perhaps have regard to the *volenti* principle in relation to tortious liability.

In the Law Commission's Working Paper No. 55 it is stated (correctly, as we respectfully consider) that the defence of duress may be regarded as a concession to human infirmity in the face of an overwhelming evil threatened by another (para 3). In this respect it differs from the doctrine of duress in contract, where the principle is to restore the innocent victim of duress to his rightful position vis-a-vis the other party to the contract who has coerced him into an unfair bargain. Again, returning to the criminal sphere, the defence of duress differs from those of self-defence and provocation, since self-defence exculpates the perpetrator who defends himself against a wrongful attacker and the defence of provocation, which is also concerned with the wrongful behaviour of the victim towards the perpetrator, may mitigate the punishment and can reduce murder to manslaughter. In criminal law, therefore, the defence of duress does not derive from the wrongful conduct of the other party to a contract or of a victim who has himself provoked the criminal act of the accused, but enures for the benefit of a person who has been compelled by the coercion of a third party to commit a crime against society and against an *innocent* victim. Accordingly, it is reasonable to expect that the accused, if he is to benefit from this defence, should himself be morally innocent.

The defence of duress is based on a balance of moral factors. It abandons what may be called the higher morality which adopts the view that death is preferable to dishonour and that man has a paramount duty, at whatever cost to himself, not to inflict unjustified harm on his fellow man. In relation to first degree murder at least, an analogous principle apparently still holds (*R* v *Abbott* [above]) but it is applied more pragmatically than ethically, since a first degree murderer whose only intention was to inflict serious personal injury is morally less culpable than an accomplice in a planned murder, or indeed than a person who attempts to murder. Generally speaking, however, the defence of duress looks to a practical morality. Crime deliberately committed is excusable if the coercive threat to the perpetrator is more than he can be expected to resist. Thus moral excusability erases the criminality of the guilty act and the guilty mind, because the crime was committed, and the conscious intention to commit it was formed, under a compulsion so strong that it is said that the perpetrator ought not to be expected to resist it. Putting the matter thus one can appreciate an argument for saying that duress if proved should merely be reflected in the severity of the punishment and not in exculpation of the crime, but it is now too late to pretend that this approach would reflect the common law. And yet the authorities show that the availability of duress as a defence is quite strictly, and in a sense arbitrarily, limited by reference to the nature of the threats which may be relied on by the accused as constituting duress, even though other kinds of threats might be still more oppressive and effective. This limitation is, incidentally, maintained in the codes and draft codes to which we have referred.

If a person behaves immorally by, for example, committing himself to an unlawful conspiracy, he ought not to be able to take advantage of the pressure exercised on him by his fellow criminals in order to put on when it suits him the breastplate of righteousness. An even more rigorous view which, as we have seen, prevails in the United States, but does not arise for consideration in this case, is that, if a person is culpably negligent or reckless in exposing himself to the risk of being subjected to coercive pressure, he too loses the right to call himself innocent by reason of his succumbing to that pressure.

A practical consideration is that, if some such limit on the defendant's duress does not exist, it would be only too easy for every member of an unlawful conspiracy and for every member of a gang except the leader to obtain an immunity denied to ordinary citizens. Indeed, the better organised the conspiracy and the more brutal its internal discipline, the surer would be the defence of duress for its members. It can hardly be supposed that the common law tolerates such an absurdity.

In making this last observation we are not saying that the ease with which a defence can be put up is a reason for not allowing that defence and impartially considering it when made. Still less do we subscribe to any doctrine that, when society is threatened, the ordinary protection of the common law can, except by statute, be withheld even from those who are alleged to have conspired against it: "Amid the clash of arms the laws are not silent." On the other hand what we are contemplating here is the possibility that any band of criminals could so organise their affairs in advance as to confer mutual immunity in respect of any crime to which duress provides a defence ...

We are continually reminded that the method of the common law is not to draw lines or to attempt exhaustive definitions. It is often enough to say that one knows on which side of the line a case falls without drawing the line itself: *Hobbs* v *L & S W Rly* (1875) LR 10 QB 111, 121, per Blackburn J, *Mayor of Southport* v *Morriss* [1893] 1 QB 359, 361, *per* Lord Coleridge CJ. It may be tempting to go further and try to draw up a system, but it is not always wise. This court is satisfied that there are circumstances in which persons who associate with violent criminals and voluntarily expose themselves to the risk of compulsion to commit criminal acts cannot according to the common law avail themselves of the defence of duress. We are further satisfied that, wherever the line should be drawn, this appellant falls on the side of it where that defence is not available to him.

... [W]e guard ourselves against the use of any expression which might tend to confine the application of that principle to illegal, in the narrow sense of proscribed, organisations. A person may become associated with a sinister group of men with criminal objectives and coercive methods of ensuring that their lawless enterprises are carried out and thereby voluntarily expose himself to illegal compulsion, whether or not the group is or becomes a proscribed organisation.

Nor indeed, so far as the facts are concerned, do we consider that the evidence of the nature and activities of the relevant organisations has necessarily to be the same formal and precise character as it apparently was in this case.

As to ground 1 (b), which we have set out above but which did not seem to be pressed in this court, here again we agree with the trial judge. To say that the appellant could revive for his own benefit the defence of duress by trying to leave the organisation is no more cogent an argument than saying that he tried unavailingly to resist the order to carry out a robbery. In each case the answer is the same: if a person voluntarily exposes and submits himself, as the appellant did, to illegal compulsion, he cannot rely on the duress to which he has voluntarily exposed himself as an excuse either in respect of the crimes he commits against his will or in respect of his continued but unwilling association with those capable of exercising upon him the duress which he calls in aid.'

R v Graham [1982] 1 WLR 294   Court of Appeal (Criminal Division)   (Lord Lane CJ, Taylor and McCullough JJ)

Model direction to the jury on the defence of duress

Facts

The defendant, a homosexual, lived with another man named King, with whom he was having a sexual relationship. King was jealous of the defendant's wife and, having tricked her into visiting the defendant, he strangled her to death with an electrical flex. The defendant had been ordered to help King carry out this killing by pulling on one end of the flex. There was evidence that the defendant, who had been drinking and taking valium, was terrified of King, and at his trial for murder he sought to rely on the defence of duress. The jury rejected the defence and convicted the defendant, following the trial judge's direction, detailed in the extract from Lord Lane CJ's judgment (see below). The defendant appealed.

Held

The appeal would be dismissed.

Lord Lane CJ:

'As a matter of public policy, it seems to us essential to limit the defence of duress by means of an objective criterion formulated in terms of reasonableness. Consistency of approach in defences to criminal liability is obviously desirable. Provocation and duress are analogous. In provocation the words or actions of one person break the self-control of another. In duress the words or actions of one person break the will of another. The law requires a defendant to have the self-control reasonably to be expected of the ordinary citizen in his situation. It should likewise require him to have the steadfastness reasonably to be expected of the ordinary citizen in his situation. So too with self-defence, in which the law permits the use of no more force than is reasonable in the circumstances. And in general, if a mistake is to excuse what would otherwise be criminal, the mistake must be a reasonable one.

It follows that we accept Mr Sherrard's [counsel for the Crown] submission that the direction in this case was too favourable to the appellant. The Crown having conceded that the issue of duress was open to the appellant and was raised on the evidence, the correct approach on the facts of this case would have been as follows. (1) Was the defendant, or may he have been, impelled to act as he did because, as a result of what he reasonably believed King had said or done, he had good cause to fear that if he did not so act King would kill him or (if this is to be added) cause him serious physical injury? (2) If so, have the prosecution made the jury sure that a sober person of reasonable firmness, sharing the characteristics of the defendant, would not have responded to whatever he reasonably believed King said or did by taking part in the killing? The fact that a defendant's will to resist has been eroded by the voluntary consumption of drink or drugs or both is not relevant to this test.'

R v Howe [1987] 2 WLR 568 House of Lords (Lords Hailsham LC, Bridge, Brandon, Griffiths and Mackay)

Duress as a defence to murder

Facts

The House of Lords had before it two appeals, that of Howe and Bannister, and that of Burke and Clarkson. The points of law certified for consideration by the Law Lords were:

'(1) Is duress available as a defence to a person charged with murder as a principal in the first degree (the actual killer)? (2) Can one who incites or procures by duress another to kill or to be a party to a killing be convicted of murder if that other is acquitted by reason of duress? (3) Does the defence of duress fail if the prosecution prove that a person of reasonable firmness sharing the characteristics of the defendant would not have given way to the threats as did the defendant?'

Held

The certified questions would be answered respectively (1) No; (2) Yes; (3) Yes. The defendants' appeals would be dismissed.

For extracts dealing with the second certified question, see chapter 10.

Lord Hailsham LC:

[On the first certified question]

'In my opinion, this must be decided on principle and authority, and the answer must in the end demand a reconsideration of the two authorities of *Director of Public Prosecutions for Northern Ireland* v *Lynch* [1975] AC 653 and *Abbott* v *The Queen* [1977] AC 755. Having been myself a party to *Abbott*, I feel I owe it to the two noble and learned friends then with me in the majority to say that we were very conscious of the fact that our decision would only be of persuasive authority in the English jurisdiction whilst the decision in *Lynch*, though a Northern Irish case, which distinguished for the purposes of duress between principals in the first degree on the one hand, and principals in the second degree and aiders and abettors on the other, being a decision of the House of Lords would be likely to be treated as binding throughout England and Wales as well as Northern Ireland. We did, however, say, at p763:

"Whilst their Lordships feel bound to accept the decision of the House of Lords in *Lynch's* case they find themselves constrained to say that had they considered (which they do not) that the decision is an authority which requires the extension of the doctrine to cover cases like the present they would not have accepted it."

Speaking only for myself, it was precisely because the three noble and learned Lords in the majority in *Lynch* had expressly left open the availability of duress as a defence to the actual participant in a murder that I found it possible to accept the decision in *Lynch* without criticism, and then only because the *Abbott* appeal was solely concerned with the question so expressly left open. One only needs to read the facts in *Abbott* to be aware of exactly what the Board was being asked to do if it extended *Lynch* and allowed the appeal.

The present case, in my opinion, affords an ideal and never to be repeated opportunity to consider as we were invited expressly to do by the respondent, the whole question afresh, if necessary, by applying the *Practice Statement (Judicial Precedent)* [1966] 1 WLR 1234 to the decision in *Lynch*.

I therefore consider the matter first from the point of view of authority. On this I can only say that at the time when *Lynch* was decided the balance of weight in an unbroken tradition of authority dating back to Hale and Blackstone seems to have been accepted to have been that duress was not available to a defendant accused of murder. I quote only from Hale and Blackstone. Thus *Hale's Pleas of the Crown,* (1736) vol 1, p51:

"if a man be desperately assaulted, and in peril of death, and cannot otherwise escape, unless to satisfy his assailant's fury he will kill an innocent person then present, the fear and actual force will not acquit him of the crime and punishment of murder, if he commit the fact; for he ought rather to die himself, than kill an innocent: ..."

Blackstone's Commentaries on the Laws of England, (1857 ed) vol 4, p28 was to the same effect. He wrote that a man under duress: "ought rather to die himself than escape by the murder of an innocent."

I forbear to quote the eloquent and agonised passage in the dissenting speech of Lord Simon of Glaisdale in *Lynch* [1975] AC 653, 695, or the more restrained exposition of Lord Kilbrandon, at p702, on the law as expressed in *R* v *Dudley and Stephens* (1884) 14 QBD 273. These quotations are unnecessary since it seems to have been accepted both by the majority in *Lynch* and the minority in *Abbott*, that, to say the least, prior to *Lynch* there was a heavy preponderance of authority against the availability of the defence of duress in cases of murder.

I would only add that article 8 of the Charter of the International Military Tribunal, Treaty Series No. 27 of 1946 at Nuremberg (Cmd 6903), which was, at the time, universally accepted, save for its reference to mitigation, as an accurate statement of the common law both in England and the United States of America that:

"The fact that the defendant acted pursuant to the order of his government or of a superior shall not free him from responsibility, but may be considered in mitigation of punishment if the tribunal determines that justice so requires."

"Superior orders" is not identical with "duress," but, in the circumstances of the Nazi regime, the difference must often have been negligible. I should point out that under article 6, the expression "war crimes" expressly included that of murder; which, of course, does not include the killing of combatants engaged in combat.

What then is said on the other side? I accept, of course, that duress for almost all other crimes had been held to be a completed defence. I need not cite cases. They are carefully reviewed in *Lynch* and establish I believe that the defence is of venerable antiquity and wide extent. I pause only to say that although duress has, in my view, never been defined with adequate precision, two views of its nature can no longer be viewed as correct in the light of reported authority. The first is that of Stephen in his *History of the Criminal Law of England* (1883), of vol 2, p108 who first promulgated the opinion that duress was not a defence at all but, as in the Nuremberg statute, only a matter of mitigation. The fact is that, where it is applicable at all, in a long line of cases duress has been treated as a matter of defence entitling an accused to a complete acquittal. But in almost every instance where duress is so treated a cautionary note has been sounded excluding murder in terms sometimes more, and sometimes less emphatic, from the number of crimes where it can be put forward.

The second unacceptable view is that, possibly owing to a misunderstanding which has been read into some judgments, duress as a defence affects only the existence or absence of mens rea. The true view is stated by Lord Kilbrandon (of the minority) in *Lynch* [1975] AC 653 and by Lord Edmund-Davies (of the majority) in his analysis, at p709.

Lord Kilbrandon said, at p703:

"the decision of the threatened man whose constancy is overborne so that he yields to the threat, is a *calculated decision to do what he knows to be wrong,* and is therefore that of a man with, perhaps to some exceptionally limited extent, a 'guilty mind.' But he is at the same time a man whose mind is less guilty than is his who acts as he does but under no such constraint." [emphasis mine.]

In coming to the same conclusion Lord Edmund-Davies, at pp709-710 quoted from Professor Glanville Williams' well known treatise Criminal Law, 2nd ed (1961), p751, para 242:

"True duress is not inconsistent with act and will as a matter of legal definition, the maxim being coactus volui. Fear of violence does not differ in kind from fear of economic ills, fear of displeasing others, or any other determinant of choice, it would be inconvenient to regard a particular type of motive as negativing of will."

After approving a paragraph from Lowry CJ, Lord Edmund-Davies went on to say that two quotations from Lord Goddard CJ in the disgusting case of *Reg v Bourne* (1952) 36 Cr App R 125 were subject to criticism on this score: see *Lynch* [1975] AC 653, 710.

Before I leave the question of reported authority I must refer to two other cases. The first is *R v Kray (Ronald)* (1969) 53 Cr App R 569 which was, to some extent, relied on by the majority in *Lynch*, on the score of an obiter dictum of Widgery LJ at p578. I do not myself regard this passage as authoritative. It depends on a concession by the Crown regarding a party who was not before the Court of Appeal as his case had been disposed of at first instance in order to found a submission by the appellants. The dictum is also open to the criticism that Widgery LJ appeared to treat duress as making a person otherwise than an "independent actor" which is contrary to the analysis which I have accepted above.

The other reported authority is the famous and important case of *R v Dudley and Stephens* (1884) 14 QBD 273. That is generally and, in my view correctly, regarded as an authority on the availability of the supposed defence of necessity rather than duress. But I must say frankly that, if we were to allow this appeal, we should, I think, also have to say that *Dudley and Stephens* was bad law. There is, of course, an obvious distinction between duress and necessity as potential defences; duress arises from the wrongful threats or violence of another human being and necessity arises from any other objective dangers threatening the accused. This, however, is, in my view a distinction without a relevant difference, since on this view duress is only that species of the genus of necessity which is caused by wrongful threats. I cannot see that there is any way in which a person of ordinary fortitude can be excused from the one type of pressure on his will rather than the other.

I shall revert to *Dudley and Stephens* when I come to consider some of the issues of principle involved in our response to the first certified question. But at this stage I feel that I should say that in *Abbott* I would have been prepared to accept a distinction between *Abbott* [1977] AC 755 and *Lynch* [1975] AC 653 on the basis of the argument which appeared to attract Lord Morris of Borth-y-Gest at pp671-672 of *Lynch*. I would not myself have immersed myself in the somewhat arcane terminology of accessory, principal in the second degree, and aiding and abetting. But it did seem to me then, and it seems to me now, that there is a valid distinction to be drawn in ordinary language between a man who actually participates in the irrevocable act of murder to save his own skin or that of his nearest and dearest and a man who simply participates before or after the event in the necessary preparation for it or the escape of the actual offender. It is as well to remember that, in *Abbott* the facts were that Abbott had dug a pit, thrown the victim into it, subjected her in co-operation with others to murderous blows and stab wounds and then buried her alive. It seems to me that those academics who see no difference between that case and the comparatively modest part alleged (falsely as is now known) in *Lynch* to have been played by the defendant under duress have parted company with a full sense of reality. Nevertheless and in spite of this, and in the face of the somewhat intemperate criticism to which this type of distinction has sometimes been subjected since *Abbott* I am somewhat relieved to know that the views of my noble and learned friends on the main issue permit me to escape from such niceties and simply to say that I do not think that the decision in Lynch can be justified on authority and that, exercising to the extent necessary, the freedom given to us by the *Practice Statement (Judicial Precedent)* [1966] 1 WLR 1234 which counsel for the respondent urged us to apply, I consider that the right course in the instant appeal is to restore the law to the condition in which it was almost universally thought to be prior to *Lynch*. It may well be that that law was to a certain extent unclear and to some extent gave rise to anomaly. But these anomalies I believe to be due to a number of factors extraneous to the present appeal and to the intrinsic nature of duress. The first is the mandatory nature of the sentence in murder. The second resides in the fact that murder being a "result" crime, only being complete if the victim dies within the traditional period of a year and a day and that, in consequence, a different crime may be charged according to whether or not the victim actually succumbs during the prescribed period. The third lies in the fact (fully discussed amongst many other authorities in *R v Hyam* [1975] AC 55) that, as matters stand, the mens rea in murder consists not simply in an intention to kill, but may include an intent to commit grievous bodily harm. It has always been possible for Parliament to clear up this branch of the law (or indeed to define more closely the nature and extent of the availability of duress as a defence). But Parliament has conspicuously, and perhaps deliberately, declined to do so. In the meantime, I must say that the attempt made in *Lynch* to clear up this situation by judicial legislation has proved to be an excessive and perhaps improvident use of the undoubted power of the courts to create new law by creating precedents in individual cases.

This brings me back to the question of principle. I begin by affirming that, while there can never be a direct correspondence between law and morality, an attempt to divorce the two entirely is and has always proved to be doomed to failure, and, in the present case, the overriding objects of the criminal law must be to protect innocent lives and to set a standard of conduct which ordinary men and women are expected to observe if they are to avoid criminal responsibility

… In general, I must say that I do not at all accept in relation to the defence of murder it is either good morals, good policy or good law to suggest, as did the majority in *Lynch* and the minority in *Abbott* that the ordinary man of reasonable fortitude is not to be supposed to be capable of heroism if he is asked to take an innocent life rather than sacrifice his own. Doubtless in actual practice many will succumb to temptation, as they did in *Dudley and Stephens*. But many will not, and I do not believe that as a "concession to human frailty" the former should be exempt from liability to criminal sanctions if they do. I have known in my own lifetime of too many acts of heroism by ordinary human beings of no more than ordinary fortitude to regard a law as either "just or humane" which withdraws the protection of the criminal law from the innocent victim and casts the cloak of its protection upon the coward and the poltroon in the name of a "concession to human frailty."

I must not, however, underestimate the force of the arguments on the other side, advanced as they have been with such force and such persuasiveness by some of the most eminent legal minds, judicial and academic, in the country.

First, amongst these is, perhaps, the argument from logic and consistency. A long line of cases, it is said, carefully researched and closely analysed, establish duress as an available defence in a wide range of crimes, some at least, like wounding with intent to commit grievous bodily harm, carrying the heaviest penalties commensurate with their gravity. To cap this, it is pointed out that at least in theory, a defendant accused of this crime under section 18 of the Offences against the Person Act 1861, but acquitted on the grounds of duress, will still be liable to a charge of murder if the victim dies within the traditional period of one year and a day. I am not, perhaps, persuaded of this last point as much as I should. It is not simply an anomaly based on the defence of duress. It is a product of the peculiar mens rea allowed on a charge of murder which is not confined to an intent to kill. More persuasive, perhaps, is the point based on the availability of the defence of duress on a charge of attempted murder, where the actual intent to kill is an essential prerequisite. It may be that we must meet this casus omissus in your Lordships' House when we come to it. It may require reconsideration of the availability of the defence in that case too.

I would, however, prefer to meet the case of alleged inconsistency head on. Consistency and logic, though inherently desirable, are not always prime characteristics of a penal code based like the common law on custom and precedent. Law so based is not an exact science. All the same, I feel I am required to give some answer to the question posed. If duress is available as a defence to some crimes of the most grave why, it may legitimately be asked, stop at murder, whether as accessory or principal and whether in the second or the first degree? But surely I am entitled, as in the view of the Common Serjeant in the instant case of Clarkson and Burke, to believe that some degree of proportionality between the threat and the offence must, at least to some extent, be a prerequisite of the defence under existing law. Few would resist threats to the life of a loved one if the alternative were driving across the red lights or in excess of 70 mph. on the motorway. But, to use the Common Serjeant's analogy, it would take rather more than the threat of a slap on the wrist or even moderate pain or injury to discharge the evidential burden even in the case of a fairly serious assault. In such a case the "concession to human frailty" is no more than to say that in such circumstances a reasonable man of average courage is entitled to embrace as a matter of choice the alternative which a reasonable man could regard as the lesser of two evils. Other considerations necessarily arise where the choice is between the threat of death or a fortiori of serious injury and deliberately taking an innocent life. In such a case a reasonable man might reflect that one innocent human life is at least as valuable as his own or that of his loved one. In such a case a man cannot claim that he is choosing the lesser of two evils. Instead he is embracing the cognate but morally disreputable principle that the end justifies the means.

I am not so shocked as some of the judicial opinions have been at the need, if this be the conclusion, to invoke the availability of administrative as distinct from purely judicial remedies for the hardships which might otherwise occur in the most agonising cases. Even in *Dudley and Stephens* in 1884 when the death penalty was mandatory and frequently inflicted, the prerogative was used to reduce a sentence of death by hanging to one of 18 months in prison. In murder cases the available mechanisms are today both more flexible and more sophisticated. The trial judge may make no minimum recommendation. He will always report to the Home Secretary, as he did in the present case of Clarkson and Burke. The Parole Board will always consider a case of this kind with a High Court judge brought into consultation. In the background is always the prerogative and, it may not unreasonably be suggested, that is exactly what the prerogative is for. If the law seems to bear harshly in its operation in the case of a mandatory sentence on any particular offender there has never been a period of time when there were more effective means of mitigating its effect than at the present day. It may well be thought that the loss of a clear right to a defence justifying or excusing the deliberate taking of an innocent life in order to emphasise to all the sanctity of a human life is not an excessive price to pay in the light of these mechanisms. Murder, as every practitioner of the law knows, though often described as one of the utmost heinousness, is not in fact necessarily so, but consists in a whole bundle of offences of vastly differing degrees of culpability, ranging from brutal, cynical and repeated offences like the so called Moors murders to the almost venial, if objectively immoral, "mercy killing" of a beloved partner.

Far less convincing than the argument based on consistency is the belief which appears in some of the judgments that the law must "move with the times" in order to keep pace with the immense political and social changes since what are alleged to have been the bad old days of Blackstone and Hale. I have already dealt with this argument in my respectful criticism of the dissent in *R* v *Hyam* [1975] AC 55. The argument is based on the false assumption that violence to innocent victims is now less prevalent than in the days of Hale or Blackstone. But I doubt whether this is so. We live in the age of the holocaust of the Jews, of international terrorism on the scale of massacre, of the explosion of aircraft in mid air, and murder sometimes at least as obscene as anything experienced in Blackstone's day. Indeed one of the present appeals may provide an example. I have already mentioned the so-called Moors murders. But within weeks of hearing this appeal a man was convicted at the Central Criminal Court, *R* v *Hindawi* [(unreported), 24 October 1986; see The Times, 25 October 1986], of sending his pregnant mistress on board an international aircraft at Heathrow, with her suitcase packed with a bomb and with the deliberate intention of sending the 250 occupants, crew, passengers, mistress and all to a horrible death in mid air. I cannot forbear to say that if *Abbott* [1977] AC 755 was wrongly decided, and had the attempt succeeded, the miscreant who did this would have been free to escape scot free had he been in a position to discharge the evidential burden on duress and had the prosecution, on the normal *Woolmington* principles (*Woolmington* v *Director of Public Prosecutions* [1935] AC 462, 482), been unable to exclude beyond reasonable doubt the possibility of his uncorroborated word being true. I must also point out in this context that known terrorists are more and not less vulnerable to threats than the ordinary man and that a plea of duress in such a case may be all the more plausible on that account. To say this is not to cast doubt on the reliability and steadfastness of juries. Counsel for the appellants was able to say with perfect truth that, where duress in fact has been put forward in cases where it was available, juries have been commendably robust as they were in the instant cases in rejecting it where appropriate. The question is not one of the reliability of juries. It is one of principle. Should the offence of duress be available in principle in such a case as that of *R* v *Hindawi* where, of course, it was not put forward? The point which I am at the moment concerned to make is that it is not clear to me that the observations of Blackstone and Hale, and almost every respectable authority, academic or judicial, prior to *Lynch* are necessarily to be regarded in this present age as obsolescent or inhumane or unjust owing to some supposed improvement in the respect for innocent human life since their time which unfortunately I am too blind to be able for myself to perceive. Still less am I able to see that a law which denies such a defence in such a case must be condemned as lacking in justice or humanity rather than as respectable in its concern for the sanctity of innocent lives. I must add that, at least in my view, if *Abbott* were wrongly decided some hundreds who suffered the death penalty at Nuremberg for murders were surely the victims of judicial murder at the hands of their conquerors owing to the operation of article 8. Social change is not always for the better and it ill becomes those of us who have participated in the cruel events of the 20th century to condemn as out of date those who wrote in defence of innocent lives in the 18th century.

During the course of argument it was suggested that there was available to the House some sort of half way house between allowing these appeals and dismissing them. The argument ran that we might treat duress in murder as analogous to provocation, or perhaps diminished responsibility, and say that, in indictments for murder, duress might reduce the crime to one of manslaughter. I find myself quite unable to accept this. The cases show that duress, if available and made out, entitles the accused to a clean acquittal, without, it has been said, the "stigma" of a conviction. Whatever other merits it may have, at least the suggestion makes nonsense of any pretence of logic or consistency in the criminal law. It is also contrary to principle. Unlike the doctrine of provocation, which is based on emotional loss of control, the defence of duress, as I have already shown, is put forward as a "concession to human frailty" whereby a conscious decision, it may be coolly undertaken, to sacrifice an innocent human life is made as an evil lesser than a wrong which might otherwise be suffered by the accused or his loved ones at the hands of a wrong doer. The defence of diminished responsibility (which might well, had it then been available to *Dudley and Stephens,* have prevailed there) is statutory in England though customary in Scotland, the land of its origin. But in England at least it has a conceptual basis defined in the Homicide Act 1957 which is totally distinct from that of duress if duress be properly analysed and understood. Provocation (unique to murder and not extending even to "section 18" offences) is a concession to human frailty due to the extent that even a reasonable man may, under sufficient provocation, temporarily lose his self control towards the person who has provoked him enough. Duress, as I have already pointed out, is a concession to human frailty in that it allows a reasonable man to make a conscious choice between the reality of the immediate threat and what he may reasonably regard as the lesser of two evils. Diminished responsibility as defined in the Homicide Act 1957 depends on abnormality of mind impairing mental responsibility. It may overlap duress or even necessity. But it is not what we are discussing in the instant appeal.

I must add that, had I taken a different view, in the cases of Bannister and Howe and, for rather different reasons, in the case of Burke, I would have gone on to consider the questions whether in any of these appeals the appellants had discharged the evidential burden in duress, or whether, if they had, on the facts described in the judgment of Lord Lane CJ, the proviso should not have been applied in every case. The case of Clarkson is surely beyond dispute on the assumption that the second certified question is not answered in his favour. But whatever may be the characteristics of duress, even on the existing law the ingredients of immediacy and absence of voluntary association: see *R* v *Fitzpatrick* [1977] NI 20, must be essential components of the evidential burden more or less on the lines of the draft bill annexed to the Law Commission Report No. 83, to which I have referred above. Even apart from this and on the assumption that the matter should properly have been left to the jury, I am rather more than doubtful whether any properly instructed jury could have acquitted on the murder charges in either of the instant cases or on the facts of *Abbott*. It is not necessary to express a concluded opinion on this since, for the reasons I have adumbrated above, I consider that these appeals should be dismissed and the certified questions answered respectively (1) no, (2) yes, (3) yes. If so, the questions relating to the proviso and evidential burden do not arise. So far as I have indicated, the decision of this House in *Lynch* [1975] AC 653 should be regarded as unsatisfactory and the law left as it was before *Lynch* came up for decision. The decision in *Abbott* [1977] AC 755 should be followed.'

R v Hudson and Taylor [1971] 2 QB 202   Court of Appeal (Criminal Division) (Lord Parker CJ, Widgery LJ and Cooke J)

Immediacy of threat in duress

Facts

The defendants were two young women who had given evidence against a man named Wright at his trial on a charge of wounding. Wright was subsequently acquitted, and it emerged that the defendants had given perjured evidence, having been threatened with serious physical harm if they told the truth at Wright's trial. At their trial for perjury the defendants sought to rely on the defence of duress, but the trial judge directed the jury that the defence of duress was not available because the threat was not sufficiently immediate. The defendants were convicted and appealed.

Held

Appeals allowed.

Per Lord Widgery LJ:

'This appeal raises two main questions: first, as to the nature of the necessary threat and, in particular, whether it must be "present and immediate"; secondly, as to the extent to which a right to plead duress may be lost if the accused has failed to take steps to remove the threat as, for example, by seeking police protection.

It is essential to the defence of duress that the threat shall be effective at the moment when the crime is committed. The threat must be a "present" threat in the sense that it is effective to neutralise the will of the accused at that time. Hence an accused who joins a rebellion under the compulsion of threats cannot plead duress if he remains with the rebels after the threats have lost their effect and his own will has had a chance to re-assert itself (*McCrowther's Case* (1746) Fost. 13; and *A-G v Whelan* [1934] IR 518). Similarly a threat of future violence may be so remote as to be insufficient to overpower the will at the moment when the offence was committed, or the accused may have elected to commit the offence in order to rid himself of a threat hanging over him and not because he was driven to act by immediate and unavoidable pressure. In none of these cases is the defence of duress available because a person cannot justify the commission of a crime merely to secure his own peace of mind.

When, however, there is no opportunity for delaying tactics, and the person threatened must make up his mind whether he is to commit the criminal act or not, the existence at that moment of threats sufficient to destroy his will ought to provide him with a defence even though the threatened injury may not follow instantly, but after an interval. This principle is illustrated by *Subramaniam* v *Public Prosecutor* [1956] 1 WLR 965, when the appellant was charged in Malaya with unlawful possession of ammunition and was held by the Privy Council to have a defence of duress, fit to go to the jury, on his plea that he had been compelled by terrorists to accept the ammunition and feared for his safety if the terrorists returned.

In the present case the threats of Farrell were likely to be no less compelling, because their execution could not be effected in the court room, if they could be carried out in the streets of Salford the same night. Insofar, therefore, as the recorder ruled as a matter of law that the threats were not sufficiently present and immediate to support the defence of duress we think that he was in error. He should have left the jury to decide whether the threats had overborne the will of the appellants at the time when they gave the false evidence.

Counsel for the Crown, however, contends that the recorder's ruling can be supported on another ground, namely, that the appellants should have taken steps to neutralise the threats by seeking police protection either when they came to court to give evidence, or beforehand. He submits on grounds of public policy that an accused should not be able to plead duress if he had the opportunity to ask for protection from the police before committing the offence and failed to do so. The argument does not distinguish cases in which the police would be able to provide effective protection, from those when they would not, and it would, in effect, restrict the defence of duress to cases where the person threatened had been kept in custody by the maker of the threats, or where the time interval between the making of the threats and the commission of the offence had made recourse to the police impossible. We recognise the need to keep the defence of duress within reasonable bounds but cannot accept so severe a restriction on it. The duty, of the person threatened, to take steps to remove the threat does not seem to have arisen in an English case but in a full review of the defence of duress in the Supreme Court of Victoria (*R* v *Hurley*, *R* v *Murray* [1967] VR 525), a condition of raising the defence was said to be that the accused "had no means, with safety to himself, of preventing the execution of the threat."

In the opinion of this court it is always open to the Crown to prove that the accused failed to avail himself of some opportunity which was reasonably open to him to render the threat ineffective, and that on this being established the threat in question can no longer be relied on by the defence. In deciding whether such an opportunity was reasonably open to the accused the jury should have regard to his age and circumstances, and to any risks to him which may be involved in the course of action relied on.

In our judgment the defence of duress should have been left to the jury in the present case, as should any issue raised by the Crown and arising out of the appellants' failure to seek police protection. The appeals will, therefore, be allowed and the convictions quashed.'

R v McInnes (1971) 55 Cr App R 551 Court of Appeal (Criminal Division) (Edmund-Davies LJ, Lawton and Forbes JJ)

The nature of self-defence

Facts

The defendant was convicted of stabbing another man, and appealed on the basis that the trial judge had not dealt adequately in his summing-up with the defence of self-defence.

Held

The appeal would be dismissed.

Edmund-Davies LJ:

'The first criticism of the learned judge's treatment of self-defence is that he misdirected the jury in relation to the question of whether an attacked person must do all he reasonably can to retreat before he turns upon his attacker. The direction given was in these terms: "In our law if two men fight and one of them after a while endeavours to avoid any further struggle and retreats as far as he can, and then when he can go no further turns and kills his assailant to avoid being killed himself, that homicide is excusable, but notice that to show that homicide arising from a fight was committed in self-defence it must be shown that the party killing had retreated as far as he could, or as far as the fierceness of the assault would permit him."

One does not have to seek far for the source of this direction. It was clearly quoted from paragraph 2496 of *Archbold's Criminal Pleading, etc* (37th (1969) edition), which is in turn based upon a passage in 1 *Hale's Pleas of the Crown*, 479. In our judgment, the direction was expressed in too inflexible terms and might, in certain circumstances, be regarded as significantly misleading. We prefer the view expressed by the Full Court of Australia that a failure to retreat is only an *element* in the considerations upon which the reasonableness of an accused's conduct is to be judged (see *Palmer v R* (1971) 55 Cr App R 233; [1971] 2 WLR 840), or as it is put in Smith and Hogan, *Criminal Law* (2nd (1969) edition, p231), "... simply a factor to be taken into account in deciding whether it was necessary to use force, and whether the force used was reasonable."

The modern law on the topic was, in our respectful view, accurately set out in *Julien* (1969) 53 Cr App R 407; [1969] 1 WLR 839, by Widgery LJ, as he then was, in the following terms at pp411 and 843 of the respective reports: "It is not, as we understand it, the law that a person threatened must take to his heels and run in the dramatic way suggested by Mr McHale; but what is necessary is that he should demonstrate by his actions that he does not want to fight. He must demonstrate that he is prepared to temporise and disengage and perhaps to make some physical withdrawal; and that that is necessary as a feature of the justification of self-defence is true, in our opinion, whether the charge is a homicide charge or something less serious."

In the light of the foregoing, how stands the direction given in the present case? Viewed in isolation, that is to say, without regard to the evidence adduced, it was expressed in too rigid terms. But the opportunity to retreat remains, as the trial judge said, "an important consideration," and, when regard is had to the evidence as to the circumstances which prevailed, in our view it emerges with clarity that the appellant could have avoided this fatal incident with ease by simply walking or running away – as, indeed, he promptly did as soon as Reilly had been stabbed. It is submitted by the defence that the appellant had manifested an unwillingness to fight, but, in our judgment, the evidence is strongly to the opposite effect. In these circumstances, had the jury been directed on the lines indicated in *Julien* (supra), we cannot think that they would have come to a different conclusion in relation to the plea of self-defence than that which their verdict demonstrates. Accordingly, no miscarriage of justice occurred as a result of the direction given, and, had it been necessary to do so, we should unhesitatingly have applied the proviso to section 2 (1) of the Criminal Appeal Act 1968.'

R v Martin (1989) 88 Cr App R 343 Court of Appeal (Criminal Division) (Lord Lane LCJ, Simon Brown and Roch JJ)

Necessity as a defence to driving whilst disqualified

Facts

The appellant's wife had suicidal tendencies and had in the past attempted to take her own life on a number of occasions. On the day in question, the appellant's son had overslept and was likely to lose his job if he arrived late for work. The appellant's wife became extremely distraught and threatened to kill herself if the appellant did not get the son to work on time. The appellant, who had been disqualified from driving, drove his son to work, in the course of which he was apprehended by the police. The appellant was convicted of driving whilst disqualified following the trial judge's ruling that the defence of necessity was not open to him, and he now appealed against that conviction.

Held

The appeal would be allowed.

Simon Brown J:

'Sceptically though one may regard that defence on the facts - and there were, we would observe, striking difficulties about the detailed evidence when it came finally to be given before the judge in mitigation - the sole question before this court is whether those facts, had the jury accepted that they were or might be true, amounted in law to a defence. If they did, then the appellant was entitled to a trial of the issue before the jury. The jury would of course have had to be directed properly upon the precise scope and nature of the defence, but the decision on the facts would have been for them. As it was, such a defence was pre-empted by the ruling. Should it have been?

In our judgment the answer is plainly not. The authorities are now clear. Their effect is perhaps most conveniently to be found in the judgment of this court in *Conway* (1988) 88 Cr App R 159, [1988] 3 All ER 1025. The decision reviews earlier relevant authorities.

The principles may be summarised thus. First, English law does in extreme circumstances, recognise a defence of necessity. Most commonly this defence arises as duress, that is, pressure upon the accused's will from the wrongful threats or violence of another. Equally, however, it can arise from other objective dangers threatening the accused or others. Arising thus it is conveniently called "duress of circumstances".

Secondly, the defence is available only if, from an objective standpoint, the accused can be said to be acting reasonably and proportionately in order to avoid a threat of death or serious injury.

Thirdly, assuming the defence to be open to the accused on his account of the facts, the issue should be left to the jury, who should be directed to determine these two questions: first, was the accused, or may he have been, impelled to act as he did because as a result of what he reasonably believed to be the situation he had good cause to fear that otherwise death or serious physical injury would result? Secondly, if so, may a sober person of reasonable firmness, sharing the characteristics of the accused, have responded to that situation by acting as the accused acted? If the answer to both those questions was yes, then the jury would acquit: the defence of necessity would have been established.

That the defence is available in cases of reckless driving is established by *Conway (supra)* itself and indeed by an earlier decision of the court in *Willer* (1986) 83 Cr App R 225. *Conway* is authority also for the proposition that the scope of the defence is no wider for reckless driving than for other serious offences. As was pointed out in the judgment, (1988) 88 Cr App R at 164, [1988] 3 All ER at 1029h: "reckless driving can kill".

We see no material distinction between offences of reckless driving and driving whilst disqualified so far as the application of the scope of this defence is concerned. Equally we can see no distinction in principle between various threats of death: it matters not whether the risk of death is by murder or by suicide or, indeed, by accident. One can illustrate the matter by considering a disqualified driver being driven by his wife, she suffering a heart attack in remote countryside and he needing instantly to get her to hospital.

It follows from this that the judge quite clearly did come to a wrong decision on the question of law, and the appellant should have been permitted to raise this defence for what it was worth before the jury.

It is in our judgment a great pity that that course was not taken. It is difficult to believe that any jury would in fact have swallowed the improbably story which this defendant desired to advance. There was, it emerged when evidence was given in mitigation, in the house at the time a brother of the boy who was late for work, who was licensed to drive, and available to do so; the suggestion was that he would not take his brother because of "a lot of aggravation in the house between them". It is a further striking fact that when apprehended by the police the appellant was wholly silent as to why on this occasion he had felt constrained to drive. But those considerations, in our judgment were essentially for the jury, and we have concluded, although not without hesitation that it would be inappropriate here to apply the proviso.'

Palmer v R [1971] AC 814 Privy Council (Lord Morris, Lords Donovan and Avonside)

Self-defence

Facts

The defendant appealed against his conviction for murder, contending that where there was evidence that he had acted by way of self-defence, but that the victim's death had been caused by the defendant's use of excessive force, the jury should be directed to return a verdict of manslaughter not murder.

Held

The appeal would be dismissed.

Lord Morris:

'If the jury are satisfied by the prosecution beyond doubt that an accused did not act in self-defence, then it may be that in some cases (of homicide) they will have to consider whether the accused acted under the stress of provocation. (See for example *Mancini* v *Director of Public Prosecutions* (1941) 28 Cr App R 65; [1942] AC 1 and *Bullard* (1957) 42 Cr App R 1; [1957] AC 635.) If the jury are satisfied by the prosecution that the accused did not act in self-defence and was not provoked, then the jury will have to decide whether the accused had the intent that is necessary if the crime of murder is to be proved. If on the evidence in a case the view is possible that though all questions of self-defence and of provocation are rejected by the jury it would be open to them to conclude that, though the accused acted unjustifiably, he had no intent to kill or to cause serious bodily injury, then manslaughter should be left to the jury. But it is not every fanciful hypothesis that need be presented for their consideration.

On behalf of the appellant it was contended that, if where self-defence is an issue in a case of homicide a jury came to the conclusion that an accused person was intending to defend himself, then an intention to kill or to cause grievous bodily harm would be negatived: so it was contended that, if in such a case the jury came to the conclusion that excessive force had been used, the correct verdict would be one of manslaughter: hence it was argued that in every case where self-defence is left to a jury they must be directed that there are the three possible verdicts, viz Guilty of murder, Guilty of manslaughter, and Not Guilty. But in many cases where someone is intending to defend himself he will have had an intention to cause serious bodily injury or even to kill and, if the prosecution satisfy the jury that he had one of these intentions in circumstances in which or at a time when there was no justification or excuse for having it, then the prosecution will have shown that the question of self-defence is eliminated. All other issues which on the facts may arise will be unaffected.

An issue of self-defence may of course arise in a range and variety of cases and circumstances where no death has resulted. The test as to its rejection or its validity will be just the same as in a case where death has resulted. In its simplest form the question that arises is the question: Was the defendant acting in necessary self-defence? If the prosecution satisfy the jury that he was not, then all other possible issues remain ...

... In their Lordships' view, the defence of self-defence is one which can be and will be readily understood by any jury. It is a straightforward conception. It involves no abstruse legal thought. It requires no set words by way of explanation. No formula need be employed in reference to it. Only common sense is needed for its understanding. It is both good law and good sense that a man who is attacked may defend himself. It is both good law and good sense that he may do, but may only do, what is reasonably necessary. But everything will depend upon the particular facts and circumstances. Of these a jury can decide. It may in some cases be only sensible and clearly possible to take some simple avoiding action. Some attacks may be serious and dangerous. Others may not be. If there is some relatively minor attack, it would not be common sense to permit some action of retaliation which was wholly out of proportion to the necessities of the situation. If an attack is serious so that it puts someone in immediate peril, then immediate defensive action may be necessary. If the moment is one of crisis for someone in imminent danger, he may have to avert the danger by some instant reaction. If the attack is all over and no sort of peril remains, then the employment of force may be by way of revenge or punishment or by way of paying off an old score or may be pure aggression. There may no longer be any link with a necessity of defence. Of all these matters the good sense of a jury will be the arbiter. There are no prescribed words which must be employed in or adopted in a summing-up. All that is needed is a clear exposition, in relation to the particular facts of the case, of the conception of necessary self-defence. If there has been no attack, then clearly there will have been no need for defence. If there has been attack so that defence is reasonably necessary, it will be recognised that a person defending himself cannot weigh to a nicety the exact measure of his necessary defensive action. If a jury thought that in a moment of unexpected anguish a person attacked had only done what he honestly and instinctively thought was necessary, that would be most potent evidence that only reasonable defensive action had been taken. A jury will be told that the defence of self-defence, where the evidence makes its raising possible, will fail only if the prosecution show beyond doubt that what the accused did was not by way of self-defence. But their Lordships consider, in agreement with the approach in the *De Freitas* case [[1960] 2 WIR 523], that if the prosecution have shown that what was done was not done in self-defence, then that issue is eliminated from the case. If the jury consider that an accused acted in self-defence or if the jury are in doubt as to this, then they will acquit. The defence of self-defence either succeeds so as to result in an acquittal or it is disproved, in which case as a defence it is rejected. In a homicide case the circumstances may be such that it will become an issue as to whether there was provocation so that the verdict might be one of manslaughter. Any other possible issues will remain. If in any case the view is possible that the intent necessary to constitute the crime of murder was lacking, then that matter would be left to the jury.'

R v Shepherd (1988) 86 Cr App R 47   Court of Appeal (Criminal Division) (Mustill LJ, Gatehouse J and Rougier J)

Duress - availability to one who voluntarily joins a criminal enterprise

Facts [As stated by Mustill LJ]

'Martin Brian Shepherd, who now appeals by leave of the single judge, was convicted at the Crown Court in Southampton of five counts alleging burglary. Several other offences were taken into consideration when concurrent sentences of nine months' imprisonment were imposed. The offences were all of a similar character. The appellant, in the company of a varying number of other men, would enter retail premises. Some would distract the shopkeeper, whilst others would carry away boxes of goods, usually cigarettes. In this simple way the thieves were able to make off with goods of very considerable value. Ultimately some of them, including the appellant, were caught. In the last of a series of interviews the appellant admitted what he had done, and pointed out to the police the premises concerned. There was reason to believe that another man, whom we shall call P, was also involved in some of the offences, but he was not charged with any of them. P is a man with many convictions for offences of dishonesty and violence. On these facts it would seem that the appellant had no choice but to plead guilty to all the charges. In the event however he sought to raise a defence on the following lines. He had originally been recruited to the joint enterprise by P. The very first of the offences took place during April 1986, and the appellant played a willing part. It was a stroke of great good fortune for the appellant that this offence was on the list of those taken into consideration, and was not the subject of a plea of guilty. But he was unnerved by the experience and wanted to give up. He was however threatened by P with violence to himself and his family and was compelled to carry on with the thefts, and did so until he was caught some weeks later. The story, which was not mentioned in the police records of his interviews, receives some colour from the undoubted fact that P was subsequently sent to prison for an assault on the appellant committed within the precincts of the court whilst the case was awaiting trial, and there was evidence of another assault on him at much the same time. On the appellant's pleas of not guilty the matter came for trial in the Crown Court on January 5, 1987. We mention this date because it was some three months before another division of this Court gave judgment in *Sharp* (1987) 85 Cr App R 207, [1987] 3 WLR 1. If the order of events had been different, and the guidance given in that judgment had been available to counsel and the learned assistant recorder, it may well be that a different course would have been adopted. At all events what happened was this. Counsel for the appellant very properly informed the prosecution that the defence of duress was to be raised, and of the basis for it. Counsel for the prosecution intimated that he would contend that on the authorities the defence was unsound, even if the appellant's story was true, since his original participation in the joint venture had been voluntary. Since the validity of this argument would affect the scope of the evidence and cross-examination, it was thought proper to raise the question of the law at the outset in order to save a possible waste of time and cost. The learned assistant recorder agreed to this proposal, and after argument he ruled in favour of the prosecution. In spite of this the appellant maintained his pleas, and gave evidence on his own behalf. For reasons which we do not follow, he was permitted to give his story of duress, even though the assistant recorder had already ruled that it was immaterial as indeed he was to direct the jury when he reminded them of what the appellant had said. The story was not however tested in any way. The jury retired for only ten minutes before returning verdicts of guilty, having really been left no choice in the matter. The appellant now appeals, contending that the issue of duress should not have been withdrawn from the jury.'

Held

The appeal would be allowed.

Mustill LJ:

'The basis for [the appellant's contention], as it was developed in the course of the appeal, was substantially different from the argument presented at the trial. It was (and still is) accepted on behalf of the prosecution that duress may in appropriate circumstances be available as a defence to a person charged with offences such as the present. It was (and still is) accepted on behalf of the appellant that this defence is not available when the defendant has, to put the matter neutrally, voluntarily brought himself into the situation from which the duress has arisen. The problem concerns the breadth of this exception. At the trial no recourse was had to authority beyond a very compressed account in *Archbold, Criminal Pleading, Evidence and Practice* (42nd ed) paragraph 17-58, of the judgment delivered by the Lord Chief Justice of Northern Ireland in *Fitzpatrick* [1977] NILR 20. This was relied on by counsel for the appellant in support of a submission that the accused forfeits the right to rely on duress only where he has joined an "organisation" possessing some kind of formal, although illicit, structure such as has existed in Northern Ireland and elsewhere. The judge rejected this contention. Any doubts about whether he was right to do so have been laid to rest by *Sharp* (supra), and we need say no more about this point. The exclusion from the defence of duress is undoubtedly capable of operating where the persons with whom the defendant involves himself are simply co-conspirators banded together for a single offence or a group of offences. This was not however the only question of principle which arose on the facts which we have summarised. Does a voluntary participation in any joint criminal act entail that any act of duress thereafter committed by another participant is to be excluded from consideration when the defence is raised? Or is the exception to be more narrowly understood?

The learned assistant recorder did not have the benefit of argument on this point, but evidently understood the passage cited from *Archbold* as supporting the former opinion, for he ruled as follows:

"I read the Lord Chief Justice of Northern Ireland to be saying that those who play with fire cannot complain if they are thereafter burnt. Those who voluntarily associate with others or even only with one other in anticipation of their being led into crime cannot thereafter complain if matters get out of hand and go beyond their contemplation. I see no reason at all to read the judgment as applying only to political organisations or to violent organisation or to large organisations. If it be the case that Mr Shepherd, the defendant in this case, voluntarily went along with the first of those escapades he cannot rely upon threats which arose thereafter to avoid responsibility for his participation in the later escapades."

This ruling, which was in any event debatable, was put seriously in question by the subsequent decision in *Sharp* (supra), and the issue was argued in full before us, with citation from *Hurley and*

Murray [1967] VR 526, *Lynch* (1975 61 Cr App R 6, *Fitzpatrick* (supra), *R* v *Howe* [1987] AC 417 and *Sharp* itself.

At the conclusion of the argument we had arrived at the following opinion:

(1) Although it is not easy to rationalise the existence of duress as a defence rather than a ground of mitigation, it must in some way be founded on concession to human frailty in cases where the defendant has been faced with choice between two evils.

(2) The exception which exists where the defendant has voluntarily allied himself with the person who exercises the duress must be founded on the assumption that, just as he cannot complain if he had the opportunity to escape the duress and failed to take it, equally no concession to frailty is required if the risk of duress is freely undertaken.

(3) Thus, in some instances it will follow inevitably that the defendant has an excuse: for example, if he has joined a group of people dedicated to violence a political end, or one which is overtly ready to use violence for other criminal ends. Members of so called paramilitary illegal groups, or gangs of armed robbers, must be taken to anticipate what may happen to them if their nerve fails, and cannot be heard to complain if violence is indeed threatened.

(4) Other cases will be difficult. There is no need for recourse to extravagant examples. Common sense must recognise that there are certain kinds of criminal enterprises the joining of which, in the absence of any knowledge of propensity to violence on the part of one member, would not lead another to suspect that a decision to think better of the whole affair might lead him into serious trouble. The logic which would appear to underlie the law of duress would suggest that if trouble did unexpectedly materialise, and if it put the defendant into a dilemma in which a reasonable man might have chosen to act as he did, the concession to human frailty should not be denied to him.

Having arrived at these conclusions on the argument addressed to us, it appeared to us plain there had been a question which should properly have been put to the jury and that the appeal must accordingly be allowed. We intimated that this would be so, whilst taking the opportunity to put our reasons in writing.

Naturally a proper scepticism would have been in order when the defence came to be examined at the trial, for there were many aspects on which the appellant could have been pressed. In particular, his prior knowledge of P would require investigation. At the same time the trial would not have been a foregone conclusion since the concerted shoplifting enterprise did not involve violence to the victim either in anticipation or in the way it was actually put into effect. The members of the jury have had to ask themselves whether the appellant could be said to have taken the risk of P's violence simply by joining a shoplifting gang of which he was a member. Of course even if they were prepared to give the appellant the benefit of the doubt in this respect, an acquittal would be far from inevitable. The jury would have then to consider the nature and timing of the threats, and the nature and persistence of the offences, in order to decide whether the defendant was entitled to be exonerated. It may well be that, in the light of the evidence as it emerged, convictions would have followed. But the question was never put to the test. The issues were never investigated. The jury were left with no choice but to convict. In these circumstances we saw no alternative but to hold that the convictions could not stand. The sentences necessarily fell away, leaving the fortunate appellant with no penalty attached to the first offence of which he was undeniably guilty, but which was not the subject of any charge. That was the position at the conclusion of the argument. Since then we have been able to study a transcript of the ruling of the trial judge in *Sharp* (Kenneth Jones J), a ruling which was approved on appeal (see (1987) 85 Cr App R at 212, [1987] AC at 7F). It is sufficiently important in the present context to justify quotation at length:

"In my judgment there is no authority binding upon me on this point, but there are the strongest and most powerful pointers to what is the correct answer. In my judgment the law does not go so far as to embody that which was submitted by the Crown in the Court of Criminal Appeal in Northern Ireland in *Lynch's* case [1975] NI 35, namely that the defence of duress is not available to an accused who voluntarily joins in a criminal enterprise and is afterwards subjected to threats of violence, but in my judgment the defence of duress is not available to an accused who voluntarily exposes and submits himself to illegal compulsion.

It is not merely a matter of joining in a criminal enterprise; it is a matter of joining in a criminal enterprise of such a nature that the defendant appreciated the nature of the enterprise itself and the attitudes of those in charge of it, so that when he was in fact subjected to compulsion he could fairly be said by a jury to have voluntarily exposed himself and submitted himself to such compulsion. Therefore on the facts advanced by or which are about to be advanced by Mr Mylne, I hold that duress is not available as a defence to Sharp to the charge of murder, or indeed of manslaughter.

Of course it follows that it would be a question of fact for the jury as to whether Sharp had voluntarily exposed and submitted himself to this illegal compulsion. The facts, as Mr Mylne proposes to advance them, do not necessarily dispose of that matter. It is still a matter for the jury to decide – though as I am sure he will concede, the evidence lies very heavily against him in view of his client's admitted complicity in this offence, and indeed his client's view of the man who was in charge of it, namely Hussey. If the jury can find it possible to say that he, although joining in this criminal enterprise did not voluntarily expose or submit himself to the possibility of coercion, compulsion by Hussey, then the jury would be putting him then in the position of the innocent bystander, and duress would be available to him as a defence. If the jury took the view on the totality of the evidence it has to be fairly and justly said that he voluntarily disposed and submitted himself to illegal compulsion, then the defence of duress is not open to him. So much for the defence of duress."

This ruling, if we may say so, corresponds exactly with the view which we had independently formed. In the interests of accuracy it must be acknowledged that it was the ruling itself, rather than the whole of the passage in which it was expressed, which was the subject of the approval on appeal. Nevertheless the terms of the judgment delivered by the Lord Chief Justice were such as to make it clear, to our mind, that the approach of the trial judge was correct. In the context of that case, given the facts, such a conclusion was fatal to the appeal. Here, by contrast, it demonstrates that the issue ought to have been left to the jury. In conclusion we should add that we have also examined the provisions of various penal statutes and codes emanating from other common law countries: for example, the Crime Act 1961, section 24 of New Zealand; the Model Penal Code, section 2.09(2) of the United States; and codes of Canada and various states in Australia. These are not identical in their terms, but they are all consistent with the view which we have expressed, as are the opinions set out in Law Commission Working Paper No 83, paragraphs 2.35 to 2.38, and in articles including those by P J Rowe "Duress and Criminal Organisations" (1979), 42 MLR 102, and R S O'Reagan, "Duress and Criminal Conspiracies" [1971 Crim LR 35.

For these reasons therefore we consider that the conviction should be quashed.

R v Valderrama-Vega [1985] Crim LR 220 Court of Appeal (Criminal Division) (Lord Lane CJ, Russell and Kennedy JJ)

Threat sufficient for duress

Facts

'The appellant, who landed at Gatwick airport from Colombia with some two kilogrammes of cocaine, was charged with being knowingly concerned in the fraudulent evasion of the prohibition on importation of a controlled drug. His defence was, inter alia, duress in that in Colombia there was a Mafia-type organisation which would not stop at inflicting injury or death on persons and their families who attempted to thwart the organisation's activities in smuggling, that he and his wife and family had been so threatened, and he had been under severe financial pressure, owing his bank a great deal of money, and had been further threatened with disclosure of his homosexual inclinations. The jury were directed that duress was a defence when the defendant acted "solely as the result of threats of death or serious injury to himself or members of his family operating on his mind at the time of his act and of such gravity, ie the threats, that they might well have caused a reasonable man placed in the same situation to act as he did." The appellant was convicted. He appealed on the ground of misdirection.

Held

Dismissing the appeal, that the only discovered basis of the use of "solely" in the direction was a passage in Archbold, *Criminal Pleading Evidence & Practice* (41st ed, 1982), p1036 para 17-54 under the heading *(a) Principle* (ii). The only clue to its origin was the use of the word "only" in *Director of Public Prosecutions for Northern Ireland* v *Lynch* [1975] AC 653, 669, 671 672 per Lord Morris of Borth y Gest. In that case and the majority of cases concerned with the defence of duress only one single type of threat was involved, namely, of death or bodily injury, and only one single type of inducement to the defendant to act as he did. In the present case other factors possibly acted on the appellant's mind. Taken literally the use of the word "solely" might have led the jury to convict even though they believed that the appellant would not have acted as he did in the absence of threats to his life, if there were other motives or reasons for his actions, such as for example the need to obtain money or fear of disclosure of his homosexuality. The jury might have thought that, if any other matters operated on the appellant's mind duress did not have to be considered because it applied only if there was one operating factor, namely, the threat of death and so on. However, in the circumstances of the context of the direction looked at as a whole, the jury could have been under no misapprehension about what they had to consider. Even if the passage including the use of the word "solely" had amounted to a material misdirection, the proviso would have been applied unhesitatingly.'

[*Reported by L. Norman Williams, Barrister.*]

R v Williams (Gladstone) (1983) 78 Cr App R 276

See chapter 15.

14 DEFENCES III

Beckford v R [1987] 3 WLR 611 Privy Council (Lords Keith, Elwyn-Jones, Templeman, Griffiths and Oliver)

Mistake as to self-defence

Facts

The defendant was a police officer sent to a house where, so he was told, a man with a gun was terrorising the occupants. On arrival at the house he saw the suspect run out of the back door. The defendant fired at the suspect, killing him. He was charged with murder, and raised the defence of self-defence based on his honest belief that the suspect was armed and that therefore his own life was in imminent danger. The trial judge directed the jury that such a belief had to be reasonably held. The defendant was convicted, and appealed to the Privy Council.

Held

The appeal would be allowed.

Lord Griffiths:

'It is accepted by the prosecution that there is no difference on the law of self-defence between the law of Jamaica and the English common law and it therefore falls to be decided whether it was correctly decided by the Court of Appeal in *R v Williams (Gladstone)* (1983) 78 Cr App R 276 that the defence of self-defence depends upon what the accused "honestly" believed the circumstances to be and not upon the reasonableness of that belief – what the Court of Appeal in Jamaica referred to as the "honest belief" and "reasonable belief" schools of thought.

There can be no doubt that prior to the decision of the House of Lords in *R v Morgan* [1976] AC 182 the whole weight of authority supported the view that it was an essential element of self-defence not only that the accused believed that he was being attacked or in imminent danger of being attacked but also that such belief was based on reasonable grounds. No elaborate citation of authority is necessary but counsel for the Crown rightly drew attention to such 19th century authorities as *Foster's Case* (1825) 1 Lew 187; *R v Weston* (1879) 14 Cox CC 346 and *R v Rose* (1884) 15 Cox CC 540 in which the judges charged the jury that self-defence provided a defence to a charge of murder if the accused honestly and on reasonable grounds believed that his or another's life was in peril. It is however to be remembered that it was not until 1898 that an accused was able to give evidence in his own defence and it is natural that the judges in the absence of any direct statement of his belief from the accused should have focused attention upon the inference that could be drawn from the surrounding circumstances. Nevertheless, even after 1898 the law of self-defence continued to be stated as propounded by the judges in the 19th century; see *R v Chisam* (1963) 47 Cr App R 130 in which Lord Parker CJ, at p133, approved the following statement of the law in *Halsbury's Laws of England*, 3rd ed, vol 10 (1955) (Criminal Law), p723, para. 1382:

"Where a forcible and violent felony is attempted upon the person of another, the party assaulted, or his servant, or any other person present, is entitled to repel force by force, and, if necessary, to kill the aggressor. There must be a reasonable necessity for the killing, or at least an honest belief based upon reasonable grounds that there is such a necessity."

In *R v Fennell* [1971] 1 QB 428, 431, Widgery LJ, who was soon to succeed Lord Parker CJ as Lord Chief of Justice, said:

"Where a person honestly and reasonably believes that he or his child is in imminent danger of injury it would be unjust if he were deprived of the right to use reasonable force by way of defence merely because he had made some genuine mistake of fact."

The question then is whether the present Lord Chief Justice, Lord Lane, in *R v Williams (Gladstone)*, 78 Cr App R 276 was right to depart from the law as declared by his predecessors in the light of the decision of the House of Lords in *R v Morgan* [1976] AC 182. *R v Morgan* was a case of rape and counsel for the Crown had submitted that the decision of the majority turned solely upon their view of the specific intention required for the commission of that crime and accordingly had no relevance to the law of self-defence. It was further submitted that the question now before their Lordships was settled by an earlier decision of the Privy Council in *Palmer* v *The Queen* [1971] AC 814. This submission is founded upon the fact that Lord Morris of Borth-y-Gest in giving the judgment of the Board set out a very lengthy passage from the summing up of the judge and commented, at p824:

"Their Lordships conclude that there is no room for criticism of the summing up or of the conduct of the trial unless there is a rule that in every case where the issue of self-defence is left to the jury they must be directed that if they consider that excessive force was used in defence then they should return a verdict of guilt of manslaughter. For the reasons which they will set out their Lordships consider there is no such rule."

The only question raised for the determination of the Board was that stated by Lord Morris of Borth-y-Gest. It is true that, in the passage quoted from the summing up the judge had stated the ingredients of self-defence in the then conventional form of reasonable belief; but it was not this part of his summing up that was under attack nor did it receive any particular consideration by the Board. Their Lordships are unable to attach greater weight to the approval of the summing up than as indicating that it was in conformity with the practice of directing juries that the accused must have reasonable grounds for believing that self-defence was necessary.

In *R v Morgan* [1976] AC 182 each member of the House of Lords held that the mens rea required to commit rape is the knowledge that the woman is not consenting or recklessness as to whether she is consenting or not. From this premise the majority held that unless the prosecution proved that the man did not believe the woman was consenting or was at least reckless as to the consent they had failed to prove the necessary mens rea which is an essential ingredient of the crime. Lord Edmund-Davies in his dissent, at pp221-235, referred to the large body of distinguished academic support for the view that it is morally indefensible to convict a person of a crime when owing to a genuine mistake as to the facts he believes that he is acting lawfully and has no intention to commit the crime and therefore has no guilty mind. He expressed his preference for this moral approach but felt constrained by the weight of authority, including the cases on self-defence, to hold that the law required the accused's belief should not only be genuine but also based upon reasonable grounds.

In *R v Kimber* [1983] 1 WLR 1118 the Court of Appeal applied the decision in *R v Morgan* to a case of indecent assault and held that a failure to direct the jury that the prosecution had to make them sure that the accused had never believed that the woman was consenting was a misdirection. Lawton LJ in the course of his judgment rejected the submission that the decision in *R v Morgan* was confined to rape and clearly regarded it as of far wider significance. Commenting upon an obiter dictum in *R v Phekoo* [1981] 1 WLR 1117, 1127, he said, at p1123:

"the court went on, after referring to *R v Morgan*, to say, clearly obiter, per Hollings J at p1127H: 'It seems to us clear that this decision was confined and intended to be confined to the offence of rape.' We do not accept that this was the intention of their Lordships in *Morgan's* case. Lord Hailsham of St Marylebone started his speech by saying that the issue as to belief was a question of great academic importance in the theory of English criminal law."

[His Lordship then considered *R v Williams (Gladstone)* (below) at some length, and continued:]

Looking back, *R v Morgan* [1976] AC 182 can now be seen as a landmark decision in the development of the common law returning the law to the path upon which it might have developed but for the inability of an accused to give evidence on his own behalf. Their Lordships note that not only has this development the approval of such distinguished criminal lawyers as Professor Glanville Williams and Professor Smith: see *Textbook of Criminal Law*, 2nd ed (1963), pp137-138, and *Smith and Hogan, Criminal Law*, 5th ed (1983), pp329-330; but it also has the support of the Criminal Law Revision Committee: see Fourteenth Report on Offences against the Person (1980) Cmnd 7844) and of the Law Commission: see A Report to the Law Commission on Codification of the Criminal Law (1985) (Law Com No. 143).

There may be a fear that the abandonment of the objective standard demanded by the existence of reasonable grounds for belief will result in the success of too many spurious claims of self-defence. The English experience has not shown this to be the case. The Judicial Studies Board with the approval of the Lord Chief Justice has produced a model direction on self-defence which is now widely used by judges when summing up to juries. The direction contains the following guidance:

"Whether the plea is self-defence or defence of another, if the defendant may have been labouring under a mistake as to the facts, he must be judged according to his mistaken belief of the facts: that is so whether the mistake was, on an objective view, a reasonable mistake or not."

Their Lordships have heard no suggestion that this form of summing up has resulted in a disquieting number of acquittals. This is hardly surprising for no jury is going to accept a man's assertion that he believed that he was about to be attacked without testing it against all the surrounding circumstances. In assisting the jury to determine whether or not the accused had a genuine belief the judge will of course direct their attention to those features of the evidence that make such a belief more or less probable. Where there are no reasonable grounds to hold a belief it will surely only be in exceptional circumstances that a jury will conclude that such a belief was or might have been held.'

DPP v Morgan [1976] AC 182 House of Lords (Lords Cross, Hailsham, Simon, Edmund-Davies and Fraser)

Honest mistake sufficient to negative mens rea

Facts

The defendants were convicted of rape, and appealed on the ground, inter alia, that they had honestly believed the woman to have been consenting. Their appeals were dismissed by the Court of Appeal. On appeal to the House of Lords:

Held

(Applying the proviso to s2(1) Criminal Appeals Act 1968) the appeals would be dismissed.

Lord Hailsham:

His Lordship recited the terms of the trial judge's summing up to the jury, which were:

"'First of all, let me deal with the crime of rape. What are its ingredients? What have the prosecution to prove to your satisfaction before you can find a defendant guilty of rape? The crime of rape consists in having unlawful sexual intercourse with a woman without her consent and by force. By force. Those words mean exactly what they say. It does not mean there has to be a fight or blows have to be inflicted. It means that there has to be some violence used against the woman to overbear her will or that there has to be a threat of violence as a result of which her will is overborne. You will bear in mind that force or the threat of force carries greater weight when there are four men involved than where there is one man involved. In other words, measure the force in deciding whether force is used. One of the elements to which you will have regard is the number of men involved in the incident.

Further, the prosecution have to prove that each defendant intended to have sexual intercourse with this woman without her consent, not merely that he intended to have intercourse with her but that he intended to have intercourse without her consent. Therefore if the defendant believed or may have believed that Mrs Morgan consented to him having sexual intercourse with her, then there would be no such intent in his mind and he would not be guilt of the offence of rape, but such a belief must be honestly held by the defendant in the first place. He must really believe that. And, secondly, his belief must be a reasonable belief; such a belief as a reasonable man would entertain if he applied his mind and thought about the matter. It is not enough for a defendant to rely upon a belief, even though he honestly held it, if it was completely fanciful; contrary to every indication which could be given which would carry some weight with a reasonable man. And, of course, the belief must be not a belief that the woman would consent at some time in the future, but a belief that at the time when intercourse was taking place or when it began that she was then consenting to it."

No complaint was made of the first paragraph where the learned judge is describing what, to use the common and convenient solecism, is meant by the actus reus in rape. Nor is there any complaint by the appellants of the judge's first proposition describing the mental element.

It is upon the second proposition about the mental element that the appellants concentrate their criticism. An honest belief in consent, they contend, is enough. It matters not whether it be also reasonable. No doubt a defendant will wish to raise argument or lead evidence to show that his belief was reasonable, since this will support its honesty. No doubt the prosecution will seek to cross examine or raise arguments or adduce evidence to undermine the contention that the belief is reasonable, because, in the nature of the case, the fact that a belief cannot reasonably be held is a strong ground for saying that it was not in fact held honestly at all. Nonetheless, the appellants contend, the crux of the matter, the factum probandum, or rather the fact to be refuted by the prosecution, is honesty and not honesty plus reasonableness. In making reasonableness as well as honesty an ingredient in this "defence" the judge, say the appellants, was guilty of a misdirection.

My first comment upon this direction is that the propositions described "in the first place" and "secondly" in the above direction as to the mental ingredient in rape are wholly irreconcileable. In practice this was accepted by both counsel for the appellants and for the respondent, counsel for the appellants embracing that described as "in the first place" and counsel for the respondent embracing the "secondly", and each rejecting the other as not being a correct statement of the law. In this, in my view, they had no alternative.

If it be true, as the learned judge says "in the first place," that the prosecution have to prove that

"each defendant intended to have sexual intercourse without her consent, not merely that he intended to have intercourse with her but that he intended to have intercourse without her consent,"

the defendant must be entitled to an acquittal if the prosecution fail to prove just that. The necessary mental ingredient will be lacking and the only possible verdict is "not guilty." If, on the other hand, as is asserted in the passage beginning "secondly," it is necessary for any belief in the woman's consent to be "a reasonable belief" before the defendant is entitled to an acquittal, it must either be because the mental ingredient in rape is not "to have intercourse and to have it without her consent" but simply "to have intercourse" subject to a special defence of "honest and reasonable belief," or alternatively to have intercourse without a reasonable belief in her consent. Counsel for the Crown argued for each of these alternatives, but in my view each is open to insuperable objections of principle. No doubt it would be possible, by statute, to devise a law by which intercourse, voluntarily entered into, was an absolute offence, subject to a "defence" or belief whether honest or honest and reasonable, of which the "evidential" burden is primarily on the defence and the "probative" burden on the prosecution. But in my opinion such is not the crime of rape as it has hitherto been understood. The prohibited act in rape is to have intercourse without the victim's consent. The minimum mens rea or guilty mind in most common law offences, including rape, is the intention to do the prohibited act, and that is correctly stated in the proposition stated "in the first place" of the judge's direction. In murder the situation is different, because the murder is only complete when the victim dies, and an intention to do really serious bodily harm has been held to be enough if such be the case.

The only qualification I would make to the direction of the learned judge's "in the first place" is the refinement for which, as I shall show, there is both Australian and English authority, that if the intention of the accused is to have intercourse nolens volens, that is recklessly and not caring whether the victim be a consenting party or not, that is equivalent on ordinary principles to an intent to do the prohibited act without the consent of the victim.

The alternative version of the learned judge's direction would read that the accused must do the prohibited act with the intention of doing it without an honest and reasonable belief in the victim's consent. This in effect is the version which took up most of the time in argument, and although I find the Court of Appeal's judgment difficult to understand, I think it the version which ultimately commended itself to that court. At all events I think it the more plausible way in which to state the learned judge's "secondly." In principle, however, I find it unacceptable. I believe that "mens rea" means "guilty or criminal mind", and if it be the case, as seems to be accepted here, that mental element in rape is not knowledge but intent, to insist that a belief must be reasonable to excuse is to insist that either the accused is to be found guilty of intending to do that which in truth he did not intend to do, or that his state of mind, though innocent of evil intent, can convict him if it be honest but not rational ...

I believe the law on this point to have been correctly stated by Lord Goddard CJ in *R* v *Steane* [1947] KB 997, 1004, when he said:

"... if on the totality of the evidence there is room for more than one view as to the intent of the prisoner, the jury should be directed that it is for the prosecution to prove the intent to the jury's satisfaction, and if, on a review of the whole evidence, they either think that the intent did not exist or they are left in doubt as to the intent, the prisoner is entitled to be acquitted."

That was indeed, a case which involved a count where a specific, or, as Professor Smith has called it, an ulterior, intent was, and was required to be, charged in the indictment. But, once it be accepted that an intent of whatever description is an ingredient essential to the guilt of the accused I cannot myself see that any other direction can be logically acceptable. Otherwise a jury would in effect be told to find an intent where none existed or where none was proved to have existed. I cannot myself reconcile it with my conscience to sanction as part of the English law what I regard as logical impossibility, and, if there were any authority which, if accepted would compel me to do so, I would feel constrained to declare that it was not to be followed. However for reasons which I will give, I do not see any need in the instant case for such desperate remedies.

The beginning of wisdom in all the "mens rea" cases to which our attention was called is, as was pointed out by Stephen J in *R* v *Tolson*, 23 QBD 168, 185, that "mens rea" means a number of quite different things in relation to different crimes. Sometimes it means an intention, eg, in murder, "to kill or to inflict really serious injury." Sometimes it means a state of mind or knowledge, eg in receiving or handling goods "knowing them to be stolen." Sometimes it means both an intention and a state of mind, eg "dishonestly and without a claim of right made in good faith with intent permanently to deprive the owner thereof." Sometimes it forms part of the essential ingredients of the crime without proof of which the prosecution, as it were, withers on the bough. Sometimes it is a matter, of which, though the "probative" burden may be on the Crown, normally the "evidential" burden may usually (though not always) rest on the defence, eg, "self-defence" and "provocation" in murder, though it must be noted that if there is material making the issue a live one, the matter must be left to the jury even if the defence do not raise it. Moreover, of course, a statute can, and often does, create an absolute offence without any degree of mens rea at all. It follows from this, surely, that it is logically impermissible, as the Crown sought to do in this case, to draw a necessary inference from decisions in relation to offences where mens rea means one thing, and cases where it means another, and in particular from decisions on the construction of statutes, whether these be related to bigamy, abduction or the possession of drugs, and decisions in relation to common law offences ...

... Once one has accepted, what seems to be abundantly clear, that the prohibited act in rape is non-consensual sexual intercourse, and that the guilty state of mind is an intention to commit it, it seems to me to follow as a matter of inexorable logic that there is no room either for a "defence" of honest belief or mistake, or of a defence of honest and reasonable belief or mistake. Either the prosecution proves that the accused had the requisite intent, or it does not. In the former case it succeeds, and in the latter it fails. Since honest belief clearly negatives intent, the reasonableness or other wise of that belief can only be evidence for or against the view that the belief and therefore the intent was actually held, and it matters not whether, to quote Bridge J in the passage cited above, "the definition of a crime includes no specific element beyond the prohibited act." If the mental element be primarily an intention and not a state of belief it comes within his second proposition and not his third. Any other view, as for insertion of the word "reasonable" can only have the effect of saying that a man intends something which he does not.

By contrast, the appellants invited us to overrule the bigamy cases from *R* v *Tolson* ... onwards and perhaps also *R* v *Prince* ... (the abduction case) as wrongly decided at least in so far as they purport to insist that a mistaken belief must be reasonable. The arguments for this view are assembled, and enthusiastically argued, by Professor Glanville Williams in his treatise on *Criminal Law*, ... and by Smith and Hogan.

Although it is undoubtedly open to this House to reconsider *R* v *Tolson* and the bigamy cases, and perhaps *R* v *Prince* which may stand or fall with them, I must respectfully decline to do so in the present case. Nor is it necessary that I should. I am not prepared to assume that the statutory offences of bigamy or abduction are necessarily on all fours with rape, and before I was prepared to undermine a whole line of cases which have been accepted as law for so long, I would need argument in the context of a case expressly relating to the relevant offences. I am content to rest my view of the instant case on the crime of rape by saying that it is my opinion that the prohibited act is and always has been intercourse without consent of the victim and the mental element is and always has been the intention to commit that act, or the equivalent intention of having intercourse willy-nilly not caring whether the victim consents or no. A failure to prove this involves an acquittal because the intent, an essential ingredient, is lacking. It matters not why it is lacking if only it is not there, and in particular it matters not that the intention is lacking only because of a belief not based on reasonable grounds. I should add that I myself am inclined to view *R* v *Tolson* as a narrow decision based on the construction of a statute, which prima facie seemed to make an absolute statutory offence, with a proviso, related to the seven year period of absence, which created a statutory defence. The judges in *R* v *Tolson* decided that this was not reasonable, and, on general jurisprudential principles, imported into the statutory offence words which created a special "defence" of honest and reasonable belief of which the "evidential" but not the probative burden lay on the defence. I do not think it is necessary to decide this conclusively in the present case. But if this is the true view there is a complete distinction between *Tolson* and the other cases based in statute and the present.'

R v Gorrie (1918) 83 JP 136

See *JM* v *Runeckles*, below.

R v Gould [1968] 2 QB 65

See chapter 25.

JM v Runeckles (1984) 79 Cr App R 255 Court of Appeal (Goff LJ and Mann J)

Infancy - mischievous discretion

Facts

The defendant, a 13 year old girl, was convicted of causing actual bodily harm by stabbing another girl with a broken milk bottle. She appealed against the conviction on the ground that the justices had erred in finding the presumption of doli incapax rebutted.

Held

Appeal dismissed.

Mann J:

'The question which the justices posed for the decision of this Court is whether or not there was evidence on which they could come to the conclusion that the defendant had (what in the old language is called) a mischievous discretion.

The court has been referred to the direction of Salter J in *Gorrie* (1919) 83 JP 136, where he said:

"The boy was under 14, and the law presumed that he was not responsible criminally; and if the prosecution sought to show that he was responsible although under 14, they must give them (that is, the jury) very clear and complete evidence of what was called mischievous discretion; that meant that they must satisfy the jury that when the boy did this he knew that he was doing what was wrong - not merely what was wrong, but what was gravely wrong, seriously wrong."

I would respectfully adopt the learned judge's use of the phrase "seriously wrong". I regard an act which a child knew to be morally wrong as being but one type of those acts which a child can appreciate to be seriously wrong. I think it is unnecessary to show that the child appreciated that his or her action was morally wrong. It is sufficient that the child appreciated the action was seriously wrong. A court has to look for something beyond mere naughtiness or childish mischief.

In this case the justices had before them the actions of the defendant; that is, a blow with a milk bottle and a stab with a remnant part of that bottle. They had before them her immediate running away. They had before them her hiding when the police were observed. They also had the defendant's statement under caution, a statement which was coherent in content and which contained the caption written in the defendant's handwriting.

In my judgment, taking the matters together, the justices were justified in finding that they were satisfied so as to be sure that the presumption had been rebutted, and that this 13 year old girl (who from her statement seemed of normal intelligence) appreciated that what she did to her victim was a seriously wrong thing to do. For those reasons, I would answer the question in the case by saying there was evidence on which the justices could conclude that the defendant had mischievous discretion.'

Robert Goff LJ:

'I agree, and I wish only to add a few words in regard to Mr Speller's argument, which was that in cases of this kind the prosecution has, in order to rebut the presumption, to show that the child in question realised that what he or she was doing was morally wrong. On this basis, Mr Speller argued that the evidence that the defendant ran away and hid behind a hedge when she saw two policemen coming was irrelevant because it showed no more than that she realised that what she had done was against the law, but not that she knew that what she had done was morally wrong. I do not however feel able to accept the submission that the criterion in cases of this kind is one of morality. As we can see from the direction to the jury by Salter J in *Gorrie* (1919) 83 JP 136, to which Mann J has just referred, the prosecution has to prove that the child knew that what he or she was doing was seriously wrong. The point is that it is not enough that the child realised that what he or she was doing was naughty or mischievous. It must go beyond childish things of that kind. That, as I understand it, is the real point underlying the presumption that a child under the age of 14 has not yet reached the age of discretion, because children under that age may think what they are doing is nothing more than mischievous. It would not be right for a child under that age to be convicted of a crime, even if they had committed the relevant actus reus and had the relevant mens rea specified in the statute, unless they appreciated that what they were doing was seriously wrong and so went beyond childish activity of that kind.

It follows that, on the facts found in the case by justices, there was, in my judgment, ample evidence on which they could conclude that in the present case the prosecution had rebutted the presumption.

For those reasons, I would agree with the order proposed by Mann J.'

Jaggard v Dickinson [1981] 2 WLR 118

See chapter 3.

R v O'Grady [1987] 3 WLR 321 Court of Appeal (Criminal Division) (Lord Lane CJ, Boreham and McGowan JJ)

Mistake as to self-defence induced by intoxication

Facts

The defendant had spent a day drinking with the deceased, at the end of which they went to the defendant's flat where they fell asleep. The defendant was awoken by blows to his head being administered by the deceased, and retaliated with what he thought were a few mild blows, after which he fell asleep again. When the defendant woke up some time later he found the body of the deceased who had died from blows to the head. The defendant was charged with murder, and claimed at his trial that he was mistaken as to the amount of force that he had needed to use to defend himself because he had been drinking. The trial judge directed the jury that the defendant was entitled to rely on the defence of self-defence, and was to be judged on the facts as he believed them to be, but he was not entitled to go beyond what was reasonable by way of self-defence, and the fact that he might have mistakenly done so due to the effect of drink did not afford him a defence. The defendant appealed against his conviction for manslaughter.

Held

The appeal would be dismissed.

Lord Lane CJ:

'The grounds of appeal advanced by Mr Wadsworth [counsel for the appellant] are as follows. (1) Whilst the judge was correct to refer to mistake induced by drink in connection with self-defence, he was wrong to limit the reference to mistake as to the existence of an attack; he should have included the possibility of mistake as to the severity of an attack which was the most likely possibility on the facts. (2) By leaving the matter to the jury as he did, the judge in effect divorced the reasonableness of the appellant's reaction from the appellant's state of mind at the time. (3) The judge failed when giving his further direction to the jury to remind them that a defendant is never required to judge to a nicety the amount of force which is necessary and that they should give great weight to the view formed by the appellant at the time, even though that view might have been affected by alcohol.

As to the first two grounds, these require an examination of the law as to intoxication in relation to mistake. Counsel have referred us to a number of authorities. It is not necessary for us to refer to all of these. In three of them the jury were invited to take the defendant's drunkenness into account when deciding whether he genuinely apprehended an assault upon himself: *R v Gamlen* (1858) 1 F & F 90; *Marshall's Case* (1830) 1 Lew 76; and *R v Wardrope* [1960] Crim LR 770. However the reports of those cases leave a great deal to be desired and as far as we can discover there is no case directly in point which is binding upon us.

As McCullough J, when granting leave, pointed out helpfully in his observations for the benefit of the court;

"Given that a man who *mistakenly* believes he is under attack is entitled to use reasonable force to defend himself, it would seem to follow that, if he *is* under attack and mistakenly believes the attack to be more serious than it is, he is entitled to use reasonable force to defend himself against an attack of the severity he believed it to have. If one allows a mistaken belief induced by drink to bring this principle into operation, an act of gross negligence (viewed objectively) may become lawful even though it results in the death of the innocent victim. The drunken man would be guilty of neither murder nor manslaughter."

How should the jury be invited to approach the problem? One starts with the decision of this court in *R v Williams (Gladstone)* (1983) 78 Cr App R 276, namely, that where the defendant might have been labouring under a mistake as to the facts he must be judged according to that mistaken view, whether the mistake was reasonable or not. It is then for the jury to decide whether the defendant's reaction to the threat, real or imaginary, was a reasonable one. The court was not in that case considering what the situation might be where the mistake was due to voluntary intoxication by alcohol or some other drug.

We have come to the conclusion that where the jury are satisfied that the defendant was mistaken in his belief that any force or the force which he in fact used was necessary to defend himself and are further satisfied that the mistake was caused by voluntarily induced intoxication, the defence must fail. We do not consider that any distinction should be drawn on this aspect of the matter between offences involving what is called specific intent, such as murder, and offences of so called basic intent, such as manslaughter. Quite apart from the problem of directing a jury in a case such as the present where manslaughter is an alternative verdict to murder, the question of mistake can and ought to be considered separately from the question of intent. A sober man who mistakenly believes he is in danger of immediate death at the hands of an attacker is entitled to be acquitted of both murder and manslaughter if his reaction in killing his supposed assailant was a reasonable one. What his intent may have been seems to us to be irrelevant to the problem of self-defence or no. Secondly, we respectfully adopt the reasoning of McCullough J already set out.

This brings us to the question of public order. There are two competing interests. On the one hand the interest of the defendant who has only acted according to what he believed to be necessary to protect himself, and on the other hand that of the public in general and the victim in particular who, probably through no fault of his own, has been injured or perhaps killed because of the defendant's drunken mistake. Reason recoils from the conclusion that in such circumstances a defendant is entitled to leave the Court without a stain on his character.

We find support for that view in the decision of the House of Lords in *R v Majewski* [1977] AC 443, and in particular in the speeches of Lord Simon of Glaisdale and Lord Edmund-Davies. We cite a passage from the speech of Lord Simon of Glaisdale, at p476:

"(1) One of the prime purposes of the criminal law, with its penal sanctions, is the protection from certain proscribed conduct of persons who are pursuing their lawful lives. Unprovoked violence has, from time immemorial, been a significant part of such proscribed conduct. To accede to the argument on behalf of the appellant would leave the citizen legally unprotected from unprovoked violence where such violence was the consequence of drink or drugs having obliterated the capacity of the perpetrator to know what he was doing or what were its consequences. (2) Though the problem of violent conduct by intoxicated persons is not new to society, it has been rendered more acute and menacing by the more widespread use of hallucinatory drugs. For example, in *R v Lipman* [1970] 1 QB 152, the accused committed his act of mortal violence under the hallucination (induced by drugs) that he was wrestling with serpents. He was convicted of manslaughter. But, on the logic of the appellant's argument, he was innocent of any crime."

Lord Edmund-Davies said, at p492:

"The criticism by the academics of the law presently administered in this country is of a two-fold nature: (1) It is illogical and therefore inconsistent with legal principle to treat a person who of his own volition has taken drink or drugs any differently from a man suffering from some bodily or mental disorder of the kind earlier mentioned or whose beverage had, without his connivance, been 'laced' with intoxicants; (2) it is unethical to convict a man of a crime requiring a guilty state of mind when ex hypothesi, he lacked it."

Lord Edmund-Davies then demonstrated the fallacy of those criticisms.

Finally we draw attention to the decision of this court in *R v Lipman* [1970] 1 QB 152 itself. The defence in that case was put on the grounds that the defendant, because of the hallucinatory drug which he had taken, had not formed the necessary intent to found a conviction for murder, thus resulting in his conviction for manslaughter. If the appellant's contentions here are correct, Lipman could successfully have escaped conviction altogether by raising the issue that he believed he was defending himself legitimately from an attack by serpents. It is significant that no one seems to have considered that possibility.'

R v Smith [1974] QB 354

See chapter 3.

R v Tolson (1889) 23 QBD 168   Court for Crown Cases Reserved   (Lord Coleridge CJ, Denman, Field, Manisty, Hawkins, Stephen, Cave, Day, A L Smith, Wills, Grantham and Charles JJ, Pollock and Huddleston BB)

Mistake as a defence to crimes of strict liability

Facts

The defendant was deserted by her husband in 1881. She was subsequently told by her brother-in-law that he had drowned at sea. In 1887, honestly (although mistakenly) believing herself to be a widow, the defendant remarried. In December 1887 the defendant's husband returned from America, and she was convicted of bigamy contrary to s58 of the Offences Against the Person Act 1861. Her appeal was considered by the Court for Crown Cases Reserved.

Held

(By a majority of nine to five) The conviction would be quashed.

Stephen J:

'My view of the subject is based upon a particular application of the doctrine usually, though I think not happily, described by the phrase "non est reus, nisi mens set rea." ... The principle involved appears to me, when fully considered, to amount to no more than this. The full definition of every crime contains expressly or by implication a proposition as to a state of mind. Therefore, if the mental element of any conduct alleged to be a crime is proved to have been absent in any given case, the crime so defined is not committed; or, again if a crime is fully defined, nothing amounts to that crime which does not satisfy that definition. Crimes are in the present day much more accurately defined by statute or otherwise than they formerly were. The mental element of most crimes is marked by one of the words "maliciously," "fraudulently," "negligently," or "knowingly," but it is the general – I might, I think, say – the invariable – practice of the legislature to leave unexpressed some of the mental elements of crime. In all cases whatever, competent age, sanity and some degree of freedom from some kinds of coercion are assumed to be essential to criminality, but I do not believe they are ever introduced into any statute by which any particular crime is defined.

The meaning of the words "malice," "negligence" and "fraud" in relation to particular crimes has been ascertained by numerous cases. Malice means one thing in relation to murder, another in relation to the Malicious Mischief Act, and a third in relation to libel, and so of fraud and negligence.

With regard to knowledge of fact, the law, perhaps, is not quite so clear, but it may, I think, be maintained that in every case knowledge of fact is to some extent an element of criminality as much as competent age and sanity. To take an extreme illustration, can anyone doubt that a man who, though he might be perfectly sane, committed what would otherwise be a crime in a state of somnambulism, would be entitled to be acquitted? And why is this? Simply because he would not know what he was doing. A multitude of illustrations of the same sort might be given. I will mention one or two glaring ones. *Levett's Case*, (1638) Cro Car 538, decides that a man who, making a thrust with a sword at a place where, upon reasonable grounds, he supposed a burglar to be, killed a person who was not a burglar, was held not to be a felon, though he might be (it was not decided that he was) guilty of killing per infortuniam, or possibly, se defendendo, which then involved certain forfeitures. In other words, he was in the same situation as far as regarded the homicide as if he had killed a burglar. In the decision of the judges in *McNaghten's Case*, ... it is stated that if under an insane delusion one man killed another, and if the delusion was such that it would, if true, justify or excuse the killing, the homicide would be justified or excused. This could hardly be if the same were not law as to a sane mistake ...

It is said, first, that the words of 24 & 25 Vict c 100, s57, are absolute, and that the exceptions which that section contains are the only ones which are intended to be admitted, and this it is said is confirmed by the express proviso in the section – an indication which is thought to negative any tacit exception. It is also supposed that the case of *R v Prince* (1875) LR 2 CCR 154, decided on section 55, confirms this view. I will begin by saying how far I agree with these views. First, I agree that the case turns exclusively upon the construction of section 57 of 24 & 25 Vict c 100. Much was said to us in argument on the old statute, 1 Jac 1, c 11. I cannot see what this has to do with the matter. Of course, it would be competent to the legislature to define a crime in such a way as to make the existence of any state of mind immaterial. The question is solely whether it has actually done so in this case.

In the first place I will observe upon the absolute character of the section. It appears to me to resemble most of the enactments contained in the Consolidation Acts of 1861, in passing over the general mental elements of crime which are presupposed in every case. Age, sanity and more or less freedom from compulsion, are always presumed, and I think it would be impossible to quote any statute which in any case specifies these elements of criminality in the definition of any crime. It will be found that either by using the words wilfully and maliciously, or by specifying some special intent as an element of particular crimes, knowledge of fact is implicitly made part of the statutory definition of most modern definitions of crime, but there are some cases in which this cannot be said. Such are section 55, on which *R v Prince* was decided, section 56, which punishes the stealing of "any child under the age of fourteen years," section 49, as to procuring the defilement of any "woman or girl under the age of twenty-one," in each of which the same question might arise as in *R v Prince*; to these I may add some of the provisions of the Criminal Law Amendment Act of 1885. Reasonable belief that a girl is sixteen or upwards is a defence to the charge of an offence under sections 5, 6 and 7, but this is not provided for as to an offence against section 4, which is meant to protect girls under thirteen.

It seems to me that as to the construction of all these sections the case of *R v Prince* is a direct authority. It was the case of a man who abducted a girl under sixteen, believing, on good grounds, that she was above that age. Lord Esher, then Brett J, was against the conviction. His judgment establishes at much length, and, as it appears to me, unanswerably, the principle above explained, which he states as follows: "That a mistake of facts on reasonable grounds, to the extent that, if the facts were as believed, the acts of the prisoner would make him guilty of no offence at all, is an excuse, and that such an excuse is implied in every criminal charge and every criminal enactment in England."

Lord Blackburn, with whom nine other judges agreed, and Lord Bramwell, with whom seven others agreed, do not appear to me to have dissented from this principle, speaking generally; but they held that it did not apply fully to each part of every section to which I have referred. Some of the prohibited acts they thought the legislature intended to be done at the peril of the person who did them, but not all.

The judgment delivered by Lord Blackburn proceeds upon the principle that the intention of the legislature in section 55 was "to punish the abduction unless the girl was of such an age as to make her consent an excuse."

Lord Bramwell's judgment proceeds upon this principle: "The legislature has enacted that if anyone does this wrong act he does it at the risk of her turning out to be under sixteen. This opinion gives full scope to the doctrine of the mens rea. If the taker believed he had her father's consent, though wrongly, he would have no mens rea; so if he did not know she was in anyone's possession nor in the care or charge of anyone. In those cases he would not know he was doing the act forbidden by statute."

All judges, therefore, in *R v Prince* agreed on the general principle, though they all, except Lord Esher, considered that, the object of the legislature being to prevent a scandalous and wicked invasion of parental rights (whether it was to be regarded as illegal apart from the statute or not), it was to be supposed that they intended that the wrongdoer should act at his peril. As another illustration of the same principle, I may refer to *R v Bishop* (1880) 5 QBD 259. The defendant in that case was tried before me for receiving more than two lunatics into a house not duly licensed, upon an indictment on 8 & 9 Vict c 100, s44. It was proved that the defendant did receive more than two persons, whom the jury found to be lunatics, into her house, believing honestly, and on reasonable grounds, that they were not lunatics. I held that this was immaterial, having regard to the scope of the Act, and the object for which it was apparently passed, and this court upheld that ruling.

The application of this to the present case appears to me to be as follows. The general principle is clearly in favour of the prisoner, but how does the intention of the legislature appear to have been against them? It could not be the object of Parliament to treat the marriage of widows as an act to be if possible prevented as presumably immoral. The conduct of the [woman] convicted was not in the smallest degree immoral, it was perfectly natural and legitimate. Assuming the facts to be as [she] supposed, the infliction of more than a nominal punishment on [her] would have been a scandal. Why, then, should the legislature he held to have wished to subject [her] to punishment at all ...?

It is argued that the proviso that a remarriage after seven years' separation shall not be punishable, operates as a tacit exclusion of all other exceptions to the penal part of the section. It appears to me that it only supplies a rule of evidence which is useful in many cases, in the absence of explicit proof of death. But it seems to me to show not that belief in the death of one married person excuses the marriage of the other only after seven years' separation, but that mere separation for that period had the effect which reasonable belief of death caused by other evidence would have at any time. It would to my mind be monstrous to say that seven years' separation should have a greater effect in excusing a bigamous marriage than positive evidence of death, sufficient for the purpose of recovering a policy of assurance or obtaining probate of a will, would have ...'

R v Williams (1984) 78 Cr App R 276   Court of Appeal (Criminal Division)   (Lord Lane CJ, Skinner and McGowan JJ)

Mistake as to a defence

Facts

A man named Mason saw a youth trying to rob a woman in the street. He chased the youth and knocked him to the ground. The defendant, who had not witnessed the robbery, then came on the scene. Mason told the defendant that he was a police officer (which was untrue). When Mason proved unable to verify this by producing a warrant card, a struggle ensued, which resulted in the defendant being charged with causing bodily harm. At his trial the defendant raised the defence that he had mistakenly believed Mason to be unlawfully assaulting the youth and had intervened to prevent any further harm. The defendant was convicted following a direction to the jury from the trial judge to the effect that the defendant's mistake had to be both honest and reasonable. The defendant appealed.

Held

The appeal would be allowed.

Lord Lane CJ:

'One starts off with the meaning of the word "assault." "Assault" in the context of this case, that is to say using the word as a convenient abbreviation for assault and battery, is an act by which the defendant, intentionally or recklessly, applies unlawful force to the complainant. There are circumstances in which force may be applied to another lawfully. Taking a few examples: first, where the victim consents, as in lawful sports, the application of force to another will, generally speaking, not be unlawful. Secondly, where the defendant is acting in self-defence: the exercise of any necessary and reasonable force to protect himself from unlawful violence is not unlawful. Thirdly, by virtue of section 3 of the Criminal Law Act 1967, a person may use such force as is reasonable in the circumstances in the prevention of crime or in effecting or assisting in the lawful arrest of an offender or suspected offender or persons unlawfully at large. In each of those cases the defendant will be guilty if the jury are sure that first of all he applied force to the person of another, and secondly that he had the necessary mental element to constitute guilt.

The mental element necessary to constitute guilt is the intent to apply unlawful force to the victim. We do not believe that the mental element can be substantiated by simply showing an intent to apply force and no more.

What then is the situation if the defendant is labouring under a mistake of fact as to the circumstances? What if he believes, but believes mistakenly, that the victim is consenting, or that it is necessary to defend himself, or that a crime is being committed which he intends to prevent? He must then be judged against the mistaken facts as he believes them to be. If judged against those facts or circumstances the prosecution fail to establish his guilt, then he is entitled to be acquitted.

The next question is, does it make any difference if the mistake of the defendant was one which, viewed objectively by a reasonable onlooker, was an unreasonable mistake? In other words should the jury be directed as follows: "Even if the defendant may have genuinely believed that what he was doing to the victim was either with the victim's consent or in reasonable self-defence or to prevent the commission of crime, as the case may be, nevertheless if you, the jury, come to the conclusion that the mistaken belief was unreasonable, that is to say that the defendant as a reasonable man should have realised his mistake, then you should convict him."

It is upon this point that the large volume of historical precedent with which Mr Howard threatened us at an earlier stage is concerned. But in our judgment the answer is provided by the judgment of this Court in *Kimber* (1983) 77 Cr App R 255; [1983] 1 WLR 1118, by which, as already stated, we are bound. There is no need for me to rehearse the facts, save to say that that was a case of an alleged indecent assault upon a woman. Lawton LJ deals first of all with the case of *Albert* v *Lavin* (1981) 72 Cr App R 178; [1982] AC 546; then at p229 and p1122 of the respective reports: "The application of the *Morgan* principle ((1975) 61 Cr App R 136; [1976] AC 182) to offences other than indecent assault on a woman will have to be considered when such offences come before the courts. We do, however, think it necessary to consider two of them because of what was said in the judgment. The first is a decision of the Divisional Court in *Albert* v *Lavin* (1981) 72 Cr App R

178; [1982] AC 546. The offence charged was assaulting a police officer in the execution of his duty, contrary to section 51 of the Police Act 1964. The defendant in his defence contended, inter alia, that he had not believed the police officer to be such and in consequence had resisted arrest. His counsel analysed the offence in the same way as we have done and referred to the reasoning in *Director of Public Prosecutions* v *Morgan.* Hodgson J delivering the leading judgment, rejected this argument and in doing so said, at p190 and p561 of the respective reports: 'In my judgment Mr Walker's ingenious argument fails at an earlier stage. It does not seem to me that the element of unlawfulness can properly be regarded as part of the definitional elements of the offence. In defining a criminal offence the word "unlawful" is surely tautologous and can add nothing to its essential ingredients ... And no matter how strange it may seem that a defendant charged with assault can escape conviction if he shows that he mistakenly but unreasonably thought his victim was consenting but not if he was in the same state of mind as to whether his victim had a right to detain him, that in my judgment is the law.' We have found difficulty in agreeing with this reasoning" – and I interpolate, so have we – "even though the judge seems to be accepting that belief in consent does entitle a defendant to an acquittal on a charge of assault. We cannot accept that the word 'unlawful' when used in a definition of an offence is to be regarded as 'tautologous.' In our judgment the word 'unlawful' does import an essential element into the offence. If it were not there social life would be unbearable, because every touching would amount to a battery unless there was an evidential basis for a defence. This case was considered by the House of Lords. The appeal was dismissed, but their Lordships declined to deal with the issue of belief."

That is the end of the citation from *Kimber* (supra) in so far as it is necessary for the second point. I read a further passage from p230 and p1123 respectively which sets out the proper direction to the jury, and is relevant to the first leg of the appellant's argument in this case. It reads as follows: "In our judgment the learned recorder should have directed the jury that the prosecution had to make them sure that the appellant never had believed that Betty was consenting. As he did not do so, the jury never considered an important aspect of his defence."

We respectfully agree with what Lawton LJ said there with regard both to the way in which the defence should have been put and also with regard to his remarks as to the nature of the defence. The reasonableness or unreasonableness of the defendant's belief is material to the question of whether the belief was held by the defendant at all. If the belief was in fact held, its unreasonableness, so far as guilt or innocence is concerned, is neither here nor there. It is irrelevant. Were it otherwise, the defendant would be convicted because he was negligent in failing to recognise that the victim was not consenting or that a crime was not being committed and so on. In other words the jury should be directed first of all that the prosecution have the burden or duty of proving the unlawfulness of the defendant's actions; secondly, if the defendant may have been labouring under a mistake as to the facts, he must be judged according to his mistaken view of the facts; thirdly, that is so whether the mistake was, on an objective view, a reasonable mistake or not.

In a case of self-defence, where self-defence or the prevention of crime is concerned, if the jury came to the conclusion that the defendant believed, or may have believed, that he was being attacked or that a crime was being committed, and that force was necessary to protect himself or to prevent the crime, then the prosecution have not proved their case. If however the defendant's alleged belief was mistaken and if the mistake was an unreasonable one, that may be a powerful reason for coming to the conclusion that the belief was not honestly held and should be rejected.

Even if the jury come to the conclusion that the mistake was an unreasonable one, if the defendant may genuinely have been labouring under it, he is entitled to rely upon it.

We have read the recommendations of the Criminal Law Revision Committee, Part IX, paragraph 72(a), in which the following passage appears: "The common law defence of self-defence should be replaced by a statutory defence providing that a person may use such force as is reasonable in the circumstances as he believes them to be in the defence of himself or any other person." In the view of this Court that represents the law as expressed in *DPP* v *Morgan* (supra) and in *Kimber* (supra) and we do not think that the decision of the Divisional Court in *Albert* v *Lavin* (supra) from which we have cited can be supported.

For those reasons this appeal must be allowed and the conviction quashed.'

R v Woods (1981) 74 Cr App R 312 Court of Appeal (Criminal Division) (Griffiths LJ, May and Hollings JJ)

Rape - intoxicated mistake as to victim's consent

Facts [As stated by Griffiths LJ]

'On July 18, 1980, in the Crown Court at Preston the appellant was convicted of rape and sentenced to three years' imprisonment. He now appeals against that conviction by leave of the single judge. He was indicted, together with three other young men, of a collective rape of one girl. Steven Lyon, one of his co-accused, pleaded guilty and was sentenced to 18 months' imprisonment; another man was acquitted; and the third, John Slater, was also convicted and sentenced to four years' imprisonment.

It arose out of a disgraceful incident on Saturday, September 29, 1979. The victim, who was aged only 19, had been drinking at a club in Blackburn. I can summarise the facts by saying that after she left the club it was alleged that these young men had raped her one after the other.

The appellant made admissions of his part in it to the police. He said he had felt sick ever since it happened and he was disgusted with himself and asked if the girl was all right. When charged with rape he said that he was glad that he had been caught and he admitted that he had been attempting to have intercourse with the girl. He said, and no doubt this is true, it would never have happened if he had not been so drunk. Forensic evidence showed that he had seminal staining on his underpants and there were fragments of grass on the outside of his jacket and a small amount of soil, all consistent with taking part in this rape in the car park.

At his trial he went back on those admissions and said in effect that he had so much to drink that he was not sure what had happened. He did not know whether he had raped her or not and did not realise that she was not consenting to anything that went on. The sole ground of this appeal is that the learned judge wrongly directed the jury that the appellant's self-induced intoxication afforded him no defence to the allegation that he was reckless as to whether the complainant consented to sexual intercourse.'

Held

The appeal would be dismissed.

Griffiths LJ:

'Mr. Bennett [for the appellant] ... founded his submission upon the wording of section 1 of the Sexual Offences (Amendment) Act 1976. Subsection (1) provides: "For the purposes of section 1 of the Sexual Offences Act 1956 (which relates to rape) a man commits rape if (a) he has unlawful sexual intercourse with a woman who at the time of the intercourse does not consent to it; and (b) at the time he knows that she does not consent to the intercourse or he is reckless as to whether she consents to it; and references to rape in other enactments (including the following provisions of this Act) shall be construed accordingly."

Mr Bennett concedes that if the section ended there he could not pursue this appeal in the face of the decision of the House of Lords in *Director of Public Prosecutions* v *Majewski* (1976) 62 Cr App R 262; [1977] AC 443, and in the very recent case of *Caldwell* (1981) 73 Cr App R 13; [1981] 1 All ER 961. To show that he is correct to make his concession at that stage it is only necessary to read a short passage from the speech of Lord Diplock in *Caldwell*. Lord Diplock said, at p21 and p 967g of the respective reports: "The speech of the Lord Chancellor, Lord Elwyn-Jones, in *DPP* v *Majewski* (1976) 62 Cr App R 262, 270; [1977] AC 443, 474, 475, with which Lord Simon, Lord Kilbrandon and I agree, is authority that self-induced intoxication is no defence to a crime in which recklessness is enough to constitute the necessary mens rea. The charge in *DPP* v *Majewski* was of assault occasioning actual bodily harm and it was held by the majority of the House, approving *Venna* (1975) 61 Cr App R 310, 314; [1976] QB 421, 428, that recklessness in the use of force was sufficient to satisfy the mental element in the offence of assault. Reducing oneself by drink or drugs to a condition in which the restraints of reason and conscience are cast off was held to be a reckless course of conduct and an integral part of the crime. The Lord Chancellor accepted as correctly stating English law the provision in paragraph 2.08 (2) of the American Model Penal Code: "When recklessness establishes an element of the offence, if the actor, due to self-induced intoxication, is unaware of a risk of which he would have been aware had he been sober, such awareness is material." "So, in the instant case, the fact that the respondent was unaware of the risk of endangering the lives of residents in the hotel owing to his self-induced intoxication would be no defence if that risk would have been obvious to him had he been sober."

Mr Bennett, however, relies upon the wording of subsection (2) which provides: "It is hereby declared that if at a trial for a rape offence the jury has to consider whether a man believed that a woman was consenting to sexual intercourse, the presence or absence of reasonable grounds for such a belief is a matter to which the jury is to have regard, in conjunction with any other relevant matters in considering whether he so believed."

He submits that the language of this subsection is directing the jury to take into account a defendant's drunken state as a possible reasonable ground for his belief that a woman is consenting to intercourse.

As the law stood immediately before the passing of this Act self-induced intoxication was no defence to a crime of rape (see *DPP* v *Majewski* (supra)). If Parliament had intended to provide in future that a man whose lust was so inflamed by drink that he ravished a woman, should nevertheless be able to pray in aid his drunken state to avoid the consequences we would have expected them to have used the clearest words to excess such a surprising result which we believe would be utterly repugnant to the great majority of people. We are satisfied that Parliament had no such intention and that this is clear from the use of the word "relevant" in the sub-section. Relevant means, in this context, legally relevant. The law, as a matter of social policy, has declared that self-induced intoxication is not a legally relevant matter to be taken into account in deciding as to whether or not a woman consents to intercourse.

Accordingly, the appellant's drunkeness was not a matter that the jury were entitled to take into consideration in deciding whether or not reasonable grounds existed for the appellant's belief that the woman consented to intercourse. The learned judge rightly directed the jury on this issue. In fact we believe that the object of subsection (2) is the very reverse of that contended by the appellant. It was not intended to make it easier for a man who rapes a woman to escape punishment by saying, in spite of the other evidence, that he thought she consented. The subsection directs the jury to look carefully at all the other relevant evidence before making up their minds on this issue. Mr Bennett cited the Divisional Court decision in *Jaggard* v *Dickinson* (1980) 72 Cr App R 33; [1980] 3 All ER 716, in support of his construction of subsection (2). That was a decision upon the wording of a different statute. We do not find it assists us in the resolution of the construction of this statute and we found it unnecessary to express any view upon whether or not we regard it as correctly decided. For these reasons this appeal is dismissed.'

15 INTRODUCTION TO THEFT – THE ACTUS REUS OF THEFT

Attorney-General's Reference (No 1 of 1983) (1984) 79 Cr App R 288   Court of Appeal (Criminal Division) (Lord Lane CJ, Davies and Kennedy JJ)

Property belonging to another - s5(4) Theft Act 1968

Facts

The defendant, a woman police officer, received payment for a day's overtime that she had not in fact worked. The money was credited to her bank account as a result of an error on the part of her employer. Although she received no demand for repayment of the money, there was evidence that she knew it had been paid into her account and intended to allow it to remain there. At her trial for theft of the sum overpaid, the trial judge, at the close of the prosecution case, directed the jury to acquit. The question of whether a charge of theft was possible in such a situation was referred to the Court of Appeal.

Held

Provided there was sufficient evidence of mens rea, a charge of theft could succeed in such a situation.

Lord Lane CJ:

'The question comes up to this court on the Attorney-General's Reference in the following form: "Whether a person who receives overpayment of a debt due to him or her by way of a credit to his or her bank account through the 'direct debit' system operated by the banks and who knowing of that overpayment intentionally fails to repay the amount of the overpayment may be" – which is an amendment Mr Worsley has asked us to make to the reference – "guilty of theft of the credit to the amount of the overpayment."

In our opinion the question posed in that form does not arise from the wording of the charge as laid in the indictment, which I have just read. It does not seem to us that on any view the respondent stole the sum of £74.74. It seems to us that if she stole anything she stole the chose in action, that is to say, the debt which was owed to her by the bank at which she held her account. However, it has emerged in the course of argument this morning that no one was under any illusion at the trial as to what the true issues were before the court, and no one was under any illusion as to what was sought to be proved by the prosecution. We are, therefore, content to proceed with this opinion as though the indictment was in order and was not – as Mr Worsley concedes – infelicitously worded.

First of all, what is the legal position with regard to the payment of money by one bank to another for the credit of a customer's account? The position was described in clear language by Lord Goddard in *Davenport* (1954) 39 Cr App R 37, 41; [1954] 1 All ER 602, 603, where he says "although one talks about a person having money in a bank . . . the only person who has money in a bank is the banker. If I pay money into my bank, either by paying cash or a cheque, that money at once becomes the money of the banker. The relationship between banker and customer is that of debtor and creditor. He does not hold my money as an agent or trustee; the leading case of *Hill* v *Foley* (1848) 2 HL Cas 28 exploded that idea. Directly the money is paid into the bank, it becomes the banker's money, and the contract between the bank and the customer is that the bank receives a loan of money from the customer as against his promise to honour the customer's cheque on demand. When the banker is paying out, whether in cash over the counter or by crediting the bank account of somebody else, he is paying out his own money, not the customer's money, but he is debiting the customer in account. The customer has a chose in action, that is to say, he has a right to expect that the banker will honour his cheque, but the banker does it out of his own money."

From that exposition of the true relationship between bank and client, it follows that what the respondent in the present case got was simply the debt due to her from her own bank. That is so unless her account was overdrawn or overdrawn beyond any overdraft limit, in which case she did not even get that right to money. That point is made in a decision of this Court in *Kohn* (1979) 69 Cr App R 395. There was no evidence in the present case as to whether the respondent's bank balance was in credit, overdrawn or anything about overdraft limits imposed by the manager of the bank. It was assumed on all hands that the account was in credit.

That brings us to the question of the basic definition of theft, which is to be found in section 1 of the Theft Act 1968, which provides: "(1) A person is guilty of theft if he dishonestly appropriates property belonging to another with the intention of permanently depriving the other of it; and 'thief' and 'steal' shall be construed accordingly."

The property in the present case was the debt owed by the bank to the respondent and in order to show that that can be property one turns to section 4(1) of the 1968 Act which reads: "Property includes money and all other property, real or personal, including things in action and other intangible property." The debt here was a thing in action, therefore the property was capable of being stolen.

It will be apparent that, at first blush, that debt did not belong to anyone except the respondent herself. She was the only person who had the right to go to her bank and demand the handing over of that £74.74. Had there been no statutory provision which altered that particular situation that would have been the end of the case, but if one turns to section 5(4) of the Act, one finds these words: "Where a person gets property by another's mistake, and is under an obligation to make restoration (in whole or in part) of the property or its proceeds or of the value thereof, then to the extent of that obligation the property or proceeds shall be regarded (as against him) as belonging to the person entitled to restoration, and an intention not to make restoration shall be regarded accordingly as an intention to deprive that person of the property or proceeds."

In order to determine the effect of that subsection upon this case one has to take it piece by piece to see what the result is read against the circumstances of this particular prosecution. First of all: "Did the respondent get property?" The word "get" is about as wide a word as could possibly have been adopted by the draftsman of the Act. The answer is "yes." The respondent in this case did get her chose in action, that is, her right to sue the bank for the debt which they owed her – money which they held in their hands to which she was entitled by virtue of the contract between bank and customer.

Secondly: "Did she get it by another's mistake?" the answer to that is plainly "yes." The Receiver of the Metropolitan Police made the mistake of thinking she was entitled to £74.74 when she was not entitled to that at all.

"Was she under the obligation to make restoration of either the property or its proceeds or its value?" We take each of those in turn. "Was she under an obligation to make restoration of the property?" – the chose in action. The answer to that is "no." It was something which could not be restored in the ordinary meaning of the word. "Was she under an obligation to make restoration of its proceeds?" The answer to that is "no." There were no proceeds of the chose in action to restore. "Was she under an obligation to make restoration of the value thereof?" – the value of the chose in action. The answer to that seems to us to be "yes."

I should say here, in parenthesis, that a question was raised during the argument this morning as to whether "restoration" is the same as "making restitution." We think that on the wording of section 5(4) as a whole, the answer to that question is "yes." One therefore turns to see whether, under the general principles of restitution, this respondent was obliged to restore or pay for the benefit which she received. Generally speaking the respondent, in these circumstances, is obliged to pay for a benefit received when the benefit has been given under a mistake on the part of the giver as to a material fact. The mistake must be as to a fundamental or essential fact and the payment must have been due to that fundamental or essential fact. The mistake here was that this police officer had been working on a day when she had been at home and not working at all. The authority for that proposition is to be found in *Norwich Union Fire Insurance Society Ltd* v *Wm H Price Limited* [1934] AC 455. That sets out the principles we have in precis form endeavoured to describe.

In the present case – applying that principle to the facts of this case – the value of the chose in action (the property) was £74.74 and there was a legal obligation upon the respondent to restore that value to the Receiver when she found that the mistake had been made. One continues to examine the contents of section 5(4). It follows from what has already been said that the extent of that obligation – the chose in action – has to be regarded as belonging to the person entitled to restoration, that is, the Receiver of the Metropolitan Police.

As a result of the provisions of section 5(4) the debt of £74.74 due from the respondent's bank to the respondent notionally belonged to the Receiver of the Metropolitan Police, therefore the prosecution, up to this point, have succeeded in proving – remarkable though it may seem – that the "property" in this case belonged to another within the meaning of section 1 in the Theft Act from the moment when the respondent because aware that this mistake had been made and that her account had been credited with the £74.74 and she consequently became obliged to restore the value. Furthermore, by the final words of section 5(4) once the prosecution succeed in proving that the respondent intended not to make restoration that is notionally to be regarded as an intention to deprive the Receiver of that property which notionally belongs to him.

That would leave two further matters upon which the prosecution would have to satisfy the jury. First, that there was an appropriation under the wording of section 1, if that is not already established by virtue of the application to the facts of section 3(1) which reads: "Any assumption by a person of the rights of an owner amounts to an appropriation, and this includes, where he has come by the property (innocently or not) without stealing it, any later assumption of a right to it by keeping or dealing with it as owner."

The second matter upon which the prosecution would have to satisfy the jury is that the respondent had acted dishonestly. Whether they would have succeeded in proving either of those two matters we do not pause to enquire.

Before parting with the case we would like to say that it should often be possible to resolve this type of situation without resorting to the criminal law. We do, however, accept that there may be occasions – of which this may have been one – where a prosecution is necessary. We do not feel it possible to answer the question posed to us in any more specific form that the form in which this opinion has been delivered and that is our answer to the question posed to us.'

R v Brewster (1979) 69 Cr App R 375 Court of Appeal (Criminal Division) (Shaw LJ, Purchas and Sheldon JJ)

Property belonging to another - s 5(3) Theft Act 1968

Facts

The defendant, an insurance broker, collected premiums from policy holders as an agent for a number of insurance companies. In each agreement between the defendant and the insurance companies was a clause to the effect that any monies received by the defendant were to be held by him as an agent of the companies, and ownership would rest in them at all times. The defendant used monies received as premiums to finance his own business ventures. When these failed to prosper, he was charged with theft of the sums due to the insurance companies. He appealed on the ground that s 5(3) of the Theft Act 1968 did not operate to make the premiums 'property belonging to another' for the purposes of theft.

Held

The appeal would be dismissed.

Shaw LJ:

'... it was submitted by counsel for the appellant that section 5 (3) did not operate to invest the insurance companies concerned with a title to the actual moneys comprised in premiums received by the appellant. It followed, so the argument went, that his use of those moneys did not violate any title vested in the principals since they had surrendered it and therefore the appellant could not be guilty of theft of those moneys.

The argument is a plausible one but a fallacy lies at its root. The terms of the respective contracts (of which an illustration has been cited) clearly assert the principals' title to the actual moneys received as premiums. Whether by their course of dealing with the appellant they had altered or modified any such contract so as to divest themselves of the title which it sets up is a question involving an issue of intention which the jury would have to consider and to decide under the learned judge's direction as to the legal considerations involved.

If the practice relied upon by the appellant amounted only to an indulgence which the principals were prepared to accord so long as the breach of contract and the resultant technical infraction of their strict title did not give rise to a dishonest conversion, then when any appropriation of what were strictly the moneys of the principal *was* tainted by dishonesty the prior indulgence would be ineffective to support the proposition that the principals had no title to the specific premiums. Which was the actual outcome of the practice in a given history which came before a criminal court would be a matter for the jury to decide. Counsel for the appellant accepted that, by his plea of guilty, the element of dishonesty was admitted and there could be no argument as to the existence of that element of the offence of theft.

The question whether the respective insurance companies had or had not so acted as to abandon (not merely to disregard) their strict contractual titled involved an issue of fact for the jury. The learned judge's ruling was right and the appeal fails and is dismissed.'

Davidge v Bunnett [1984] Crim LR 297 Divisional Court (Ackner LJ and Taylor J)

Property belonging to another - s5(3) Theft Act 1968

Facts

'In July 1982 D shared a flat with two other young women, C and McF. In September 1982 they were joined by H. There was an oral agreement to share the costs of gas, electricity and telephone. The gas account was in C's name. In October 1982 C received a gas bill for £159.75. D, C and McF each agreed to pay £50, and H the balance of £9.75. D did not have a bank account. The others all did, and gave D cheques in the appropriate sums, made payable to P, D's employer. They thought that D would either encash the cheques with P, add her own £50 and pay the gas bill, or that P would write out a cheque for the Gas Board on receipt of funds totalling £159.75. They did not expect D to apply any actual banknotes received from P to the discharge of the bill. On November 18, 1982, £59.75 was paid to the Gas Board. The balance of £100 was carried over to the next account in December. In January 1983 C received a final demand. C asked D to look into the matter, to which D agreed. D then left the flat without giving notice or leaving a forwarding address. C and McF later discovered that their cheques for £50 had been cashed on November 1, 1982. When interviewed by the police, D admitted "I spent the £100 on Christmas presents but intended to pay it back." The magistrates convicted D of theft, finding that D was under a legal obligation to apply the proceeds of C and McF's cheques to the payment of the gas bill. They also found that the proceeds of the cheques were property belonging to another within the meaning of the Theft Act 1968, and that there was evidence of an appropriation of two sums of £50, notwithstanding the payment of £59.75.

Held

Dismissing the appeal, that the position was simple. D was under an obligation to use the cheques or their proceeds in whatever way she saw fit so long as they were applied pro tanto to the discharge of the gas bill. This could have been achieved by one cheque from her employer, or a banker's draft, or her own cheque had she opened her own bank account, or by endorsing the other cheques. Hence the magistrates' finding that she was not obliged to use the actual banknotes. Using the proceeds of the cheques on presents amounted to a very negation of her obligation to discharge the bill. She was under an obligation to deal with the proceeds in a particular way. As against D, the proceeds of the cheques were property belonging to another within section 5 (3) of the Act.'

[*Reported by Nicholas Wikeley, Barrister.*]

R v Davis [1988] Crim LR 762 Court of Appeal (Criminal Division) (Mustill LJ, Farquharson and Tucker JJ)

Section 5(4) property obtained by mistake - theft of proceeds

Facts

'The appellant was convicted of six counts of theft. The counts charged theft of specified amounts of money belonging to the London Borough of Richmond. The appellant was eligible for housing benefit from the local authority. By mistake the authority's computer generated duplicate issues of a number of payments, sending the appellant two cheques. When he ceased to be eligible for the benefit only one of the computer entries was deleted and the remaining entry continued to generate cheques. The appellant admitted to police that he had "cashed" the cheques he had received. The evidence before the jury was that he had either endorsed the cheque over to a shopkeeper in return for cash or had endorsed it to his landlord for accommodation etc. He denied receiving some cheques and was acquitted of counts relating to those cheques. The appellant appealed against conviction.

Held

Allowing the appeal in part and quashing two of the convictions, [the court held that] there was not sufficient evidence in relation to the cheques endorsed to the landlord that the appellant had received cash in exchange for the cheques. As to the remaining counts, the language of the first part of s5(4) of the Theft Act 1968 was framed to cater for the ordinary tangible article and to recognise that by the time the defendant comes to commit his dishonest appropriation, the article may be in one of three conditions; it may still exist, so that it can and should be returned; it may have been exchanged for money or goods, in which case the defendant may be under an obligation to account for the fruits of the exchange, at least if they are traceable; and it may have ceased to exist altogether or to have gone out of reach of recovery, in which event the defendant may be obliged to "restore" the value. In those cases where the defendant is indeed under a duty to "make restoration" the second part of the subsection will put him in peril of conviction for stealing the article or its proceeds, although not its value, since there is no reference to value in this part of the subsection. The deceptively plain words of section 5(4) give rise to problems, eg when is the defendant obliged to "make restoration"; where the property received by the defendant by mistake is exchanged for something else? The Court did not need to answer those questions in the circumstances of the present cases. It was plain that if an article is sold for cash, the sum represents the "proceeds" of the article; there is no reason why this should be any the less so where the transaction involves not simply the piece of paper but also the rights which it conveys. On the assumption that the appellant was paid cash for the cheque, the offences were made out subject to the proof of dishonesty.

In relation to the count concerning a duplicate cheque, counsel for the appellant had submitted that the prosecution had failed to show which cheque had been received by mistake. The court considered that argument to be unsound, it assumed that where the mistake takes the shape of causing the defendant to "get" more "property" than the owner really intends, the prosecution is always obliged to filter what the defendant has got into portions identifiable as right or wrong and then to conduct the case by reference exclusively to the portion which is wrong. Further it gave no weight to the words "in whole or in part" in s5(4). The property which the defendant has mistakenly got, within the meaning of the Act, may include property which he is not obliged to return and he may be guilty of stealing a part, even though the remainder was deliberately sent and properly retained. The task of reconstructing exactly what was the subject-matter of the mistake and how it was dealt with by the defendant need not be attempted. It was not material that the appellant had received two cheques; there was no true difference between an overpayment effected by an excessive number of coins inserted in the same pay packet and an excessive number of cheques transferred separately. When the "property" was turned into "proceeds", in circumstances where these proceeds formed an undifferentiated whole, it is in accordance with the words as well as the spirit of the statute to regard the surplus as the subject matter of the theft, without engaging on the task of ascertaining the exact source of that surplus. This approach may not be effective, if the proceeds of the property take more than one form and if the prosecution is forced to identify which form is the one to have been stolen. Difficulties may also arise in relation to the proof of dishonesty in relation to the acts said to have constituted the appropriation of the surplus. In the present case, there was no difficulty in regarding the surplus cash, from whichever cheque derived, as a proper subject matter for the charge of theft, since the proceeds as a whole represented a pool of cash which, in part, was dishonestly retained and disbursed.'

[*Reported by Lynne Knapman, Barrister.*]

R v Gilks (1972) 56 Cr App R 734 Court of Appeal (Criminal Division) (Cairns and Stephenson LJJ and Willis J)

Property belonging to another - s5(4) Theft Act 1968

Facts

The defendant entered a betting shop and placed a bet on a horse named 'Fighting Scot'. The horse was not successful, the race in which it had run being won by a horse named 'Fighting Taffy'. Due to a cashier's mistake, however, the defendant was paid £106 winnings. The defendant was subsequently convicted of theft of the money, and appealed.

Held

The appeal would be dismissed.

Cairns LJ:

'The gap in the law which section 5 (4) was designated to fill was, as the Deputy Chairman rightly held, that which is illustrated by the case of *Moynes* v *Coopper* (1956) 40 Cr App R 20; [1956] 1 KB 439. There a workman received a paypacket containing £7 more than was due to him, but did not become aware of the overpayment till he opened the envelope some time later. He then kept the £7. This was held not to be theft because there was no animus furandi at the moment of taking, and *Middleton* (supra) was distinguished on that ground. It was observed at pp23 and 445 of the respective reports that the law as laid down in *Middleton* (supra) was reproduced and enacted in section 1 (2) (i) of the Larceny Act 1916. It would be strange indeed if subsection 5 (4) of the 1968 Act, which was designed to bring within the net of theft a type of dishonest behaviour which escaped before, were to be held to have created a loophole for another type of dishonest behaviour which was always within the net.

An alternative ground on which the Deputy Chairman held that the money should be regarded as belonging to Ladbrokes was that "obligation" in section 5 (4) meant an obligation whether a legal one or not. In the opinion of this Court, that was an incorrect ruling. In a criminal statute, where a person's criminal liability is made dependent on his having an obligation, it would be quite wrong to construe that word so as to cover a moral or social obligation as distinct from a legal one. As, however, we consider that the Deputy Chairman was right in ruling that the prosecution did not need to rely on section 5 (4) his ruling on this alternative point does not affect the result.

The other main branch of the appellant's case is the contention that the Deputy Chairman misdirected the jury on the meaning of "dishonestly" in section 1 (1) of the Theft Act. The relevant part of the appellant's evidence is set out in the summing-up in a passage of which no complaint is made: "Now, what this man says is that he did not act dishonestly. He says, in his view, bookmakers and punters are a race apart and that when you are dealing with your bookmaker different rules apply. He agreed it would be dishonest, if his grocer gave him too much change and he knew it and kept the change; he agreed it would be dishonest, but he says bookmakers are different and, if your bookmaker makes a mistake and pays you too much, is nothing dishonest about keeping it."

The Deputy Chairman, having referred to this evidence, and to evidence that the defendant had not hurried away from the betting shop after receiving this large sum, said, "Well, it is a matter for you to consider, members of the jury, but try to place yourselves in that man's position at that time and answer the question whether in your view he thought he was acting honestly or dishonestly." In our view, that was in the circumstances of this case a proper and sufficient direction on the matter of dishonesty. On the face of it the appellant's conduct was dishonest: the only possible basis on which the jury could find that the prosecution had not established dishonesty would be if they thought it possible that the appellant did have the belief which he claimed to have. (There is no complaint about the direction as to onus: the Deputy Chairman expressly said: "The prosecution have to satisfy you that he did appropriate the money dishonestly.")

Mr Galpin [counsel for the defendant] thought that the jury should be specifically reminded of the terms of section 2 (1) (a) of the Act and suggested this to the Deputy Chairman. The Deputy Chairman then summarised the subsection, gave a somewhat irrelevant illustration of a case where it might apply, and then added: "Nor would somebody be guilty of theft if he believed, even if he was wrong, but nevertheless believed he had some right in law to take the property, and that, you see, is the reason why Mr Galpin puts the case on behalf of the defendant that this defendant believed that when dealing with your bookmaker, if he makes a mistake, you can take the money and keep it and there is nothing dishonest about it." The complaint is centred on the word "and." It is contended that the jury may have understood this direction to mean that the appellant would be acting dishonestly unless (a) be believed he had the right to take the money and keep it and (b) he believed there was nothing dishonest about that conduct. It is said that the jury may have thought that the appellant's state of mind was "I believe that in law I am entitled to take from my bookmaker anything he is foolish enough to pay me, though of course I know that it would be dishonest to do so," and he pointed out that under the subsection this would entitle him to be acquitted whereas the direction might be taken to mean that he would be guilty.

In our opinion, this is too refined an argument. We think it is clear that in the context the word "and" meant "and therefore" or "and so" and the jury would understand it in that way. A few minutes earlier the Deputy Chairman had accurately stated the effect of the subsection in words that could not be clearer. The appellant in his evidence had drawn no distinction between what he believed he was in law entitled to do and what he believed it was honest to do. His own words were "there is nothing dishonest about keeping it," not "I think you are entitled in law to keep it." If the two expressions are taken to have different meanings, the appellant had not made out any case under section 2 (1) (a); if they are taken to have the same meaning, then no complaint can be made of the way in which the Deputy Chairman dealt with the matter.

For these reasons this Court is of the opinion that all the grounds of appeal fail and that the appeal must be dismissed.'

R v Hall (1972) 56 Cr App R 547   Court of Appeal (Criminal Division)   (Edmund-Davies and Stephenson LJJ and Boreham J)

Property belonging to another - s5(3) Theft Act 1968

Facts

The defendant, a travel agent, had received sums of money from clients as deposits on airline tickets. He was convicted of theft of the money when the tickets failed to materialise. The defendant claimed that the sums received were deposited in the company's trading account and spent on overheads. The defendant appealed to the Court of Appeal.

Held

The appeal would be allowed.

Edmund-Davies LJ:

[Having referred to the terms of s5(3) of the Theft Act 1968, his Lordship continued]

'Mr Jolly [counsel for the appellant] submitted that in the circumstances arising in these seven cases there arose no such "obligation" upon the accused. He referred us to a passage in the Eighth Report of the Criminal Law Revision Committee (Cmnd 2977), at p127, which reads as follows: "Subsection (3) provides for the special case where property is transferred to a person to retain and deal with for a particular purpose and he misapplies it or its proceeds. An example would be the treasurer of a holiday fund. The person in question is in law the owner of the property; but the subsection treats the property, as against him, as belonging to the persons to whom he owes the duty to retain and deal with the property as agreed. He will therefore be guilty of stealing from them if he misapplies the property or its proceeds."

Mr Jolly submitted that the example there given is, for all practical purposes, identical with the actual facts in *Pulham* [(1971) 15 June unreported] where, incidentally, section 5 (3) was not discussed, the convictions there being quashed, as we already indicated, owing to the lack of a proper direction as to the accused's state of mind at the time when he appropriated. But he submits that the position of a treasurer of a solitary fund is quite different from that of a person like the appellant, who was in general (and genuine) business as a travel agent, and to whom people pay money in order to achieve a certain object - in the present cases, to obtain charter flights to America. It is true, he concedes, that thereby the travel agent undertakes a contractual obligation in relation to arranging flights and at the proper time paying the airline and any other expenses. Indeed, the appellant throughout acknowledged that this was so, though contending that in some of the seven cases it was the other party who was in breach. But what Mr Jolly resists is that in such circumstances the travel agent "is under an obligation" to the client "to retain and deal with ... in a particular way" sums paid to him in such circumstances.

What cannot of itself be decisive of the matter is the fact that the appellant paid the money into the firm's general trading account. As Widgery J (as he then was) said in *Yule* (1963) 47 Cr App R 229, at p234; [1964] 1 QB 5, at p10, decided under section 20 (1) (iv) of the Larceny Act 1916: "The fact that a particular sum is paid into a particular banking account ... does not affect the right of persons interested in that sum or any duty of the solicitor either towards his client or towards third parties with regard to disposal of that sum." Nevertheless, when a client goes to a firm carrying on the business of travel agents and pays them money, he expects that in return he will, in due course, receive the tickets and other documents necessary for him to accomplish the trip for which he is paying, and the firm are "under an obligation" to perform their part to fulfil his expectation and are liable to pay him damages if they do not. But, in our judgment, what was not here established was that these clients expected them to "retain and deal with that property or its proceeds in a particular way," and that an "obligation" to do so was undertaken by the appellant.

We must make clear, however, that each case turns on its own facts. Cases could, we suppose, conceivably arise where by some special arrangement (preferably evidenced by documents), the client could impose upon the travel agent an "obligation" falling within section 5 (3). But no such special arrangement was made in any of the seven cases here being considered. It is true that in some of them documents were signed by the parties; thus, in respect of counts 1 and 3 incidents there was a clause to the effect that the "People to People" organisation [the business operated by the defendant] did not guarantee to refund deposits if withdrawals were made later than a certain date; and in respect of counts 6, 7 and 8 the appellant wrote promising "a full refund" after the flights paid for failed to materialise. But neither in those nor in the remaining two cases (in relation to which there was no documentary evidence of any kind) was there, in our judgment, such a special arrangement as would give rise to an "obligation" within section 5 (3).

It follows from this that, despite what on any view must be condemned as scandalous conduct by the appellant, in our judgment, upon this ground alone this appeal must be allowed and the convictions quashed. But as, to the best of our knowledge, this is one of the earliest cases involving section 5 (3), we venture to add some observations:

(a) Although in *Pulham* (supra), section 5 (3) was not referred to and the case turned on section 2 (1) *(b)* of the Act, it is equally essential for the purposes of the former provision that dishonesty should be present at the time of appropriation. We are alive to the fact that to establish this could present great (and may be insuperable) difficulties when sums are on different dates drawn from a general account. Nevertheless, they must be overcome if the Crown is to succeed.

(b) Where the case turns, wholly or in part, on section 5 (3) a careful exposition of the subsection is called for. Although it was canvassed by counsel in the present case, it was nowhere quoted or even paraphrased by the learned Commissioner in his summing-up. Instead he unfortunately ignored it and proceeded upon the assumption that, as the accused acknowledged the purpose for which clients had paid him money, ipso facto there arose an "obligation . . . to retain and deal with" it for that purpose. He therefore told the jury: "The sole issue to be determined in each count is this: Has it been proved that the money was stolen in the sense I have described, dishonestly appropriated by him for purposes other than the purpose for which the monies were handed over? Bear in mind that this is not a civil claim to recover money that has been lost." We have to say respectfully that this will not do, as cases under section 20 (1) (iv) of the Larceny Act 1916 illustrate. Thus in *Sheaf* (1927) 19 Cr App 46, it was held that whether money had been "entrusted" to the defendant for and on account of other persons was a question of fact for the jury and must therefore be the subject of an express direction, Avory J saying at p48: "It is not sufficient to say that if the question had been left they might have determined it against the appellant. When we once arrive at the conclusion that a vital question of fact has not been left to the jury, the only ground on which we can affirm a conviction is that there has been no miscarriage of justice." The same point was made in *Bryce* (1956) 40 Cr App R 62.

(c) Whether in a particular case the Crown has succeeded in establishing an "obligation" of the kind coming within section 5 (3) of the new Act may be a difficult question. Happily, we are not called upon to anticipate or solve for the purposes of the present case the sort of difficulties that can arise. But, to illustrate what we have in mind, mixed questions of law and fact may call for consideration. For example, if the transaction between the parties is wholly in writing, is it for the judge to direct the jury that, as a matter of law, the defendant had thereby undertaken an "obligation" within section 5 (3)? On the other hand, if it is wholly (or partly) oral, it would appear that it is for the judge to direct them that, if they find certain facts proved, it would be open to them to find that an "obligation" within section 5 (3) had been undertaken – but presumably not that they must so find, for so to direct them would be to invade their territory. In effect, however, the learned Commissioner unhappily did something closely resembling that in the present case by his above-quoted direction that the only issue for their consideration was whether the accused was proved to have been actuated by dishonesty.

We have only to add that Mr Jalland [counsel for the Crown] submitted that, even if the Commissioner's failure to deal with section 5 (3) amounted to a misdirection, this is a fitting case in which to apply the proviso. But point (1), successfully taken by defence counsel, is clearly of such a nature as to render that course impossible. We are only too aware that, in the result, there will be many clients of the appellant who, regarding themselves as cheated out of their money by him, will think little of a law which permits him to go unpunished. But such we believe it to be, and it is for this Court to apply it.'

DPP v Huskinson [1988] Crim LR 620 Divisional Court (Stuart-Smith LJ and Farquharson J)

Theft Act s5(3) - housing benefit spent for other purposes - whether theft

Facts

'The respondent was charged with theft of £279 from the Housing Services Department. He was a tenant of a bed-sitting room who fell into arrears with his rent. He applied for housing benefit and the Housing Services Department averred that he was entitled to £59 per week. He was sent a cheque for £479. He cashed the cheque but only gave his landlord £200 even though his rent arrears had by then amounted to £800. He spent the remaining £279 on himself. The justices dismissed the charges and the prosecutor appealed by way of case stated.

Held

Dismissing the appeal, that the case could not be brought within the Theft Act 1968. The decision turned on section 5(3) of that Act and whether the respondent was under an obligation to the Housing Services Department to deal with the cheque or its proceeds in a particular way. *R v Gilks* (1972) 56 Cr App R 734 held that the obligation referred to in section 5(4) was a legal, not a moral or social, obligation. It was clear the same considerations applied to subsection (3). Any such obligation would have to be found in the statutory provisions which gave rise to the payment of housing benefit. The Court had examined the relevant statute and regulations (ie the Social Security and Housing Benefit Act 1982, s28 and regulations made thereunder which had since been replaced by the Social Security Act, s26 and regulations in force since April 1, 1988). It was quite clear that the regulations did not impose an express obligation on the tenant to pay the sum received directly to the landlord and it was impossible to imply any such obligation. Housing benefit provided a fund from which the tenant was expected to pay his rent. He had a legal obligation to the landlord to pay the rent. However there was no obligation to apply the cheque or proceeds directly in satisfaction of any rent. For example, if the tenant obtained the money from some other source before he received the housing benefit he would be quite entitled to use the cheque or its proceeds for his own purposes. The justices had been right to dismiss the charges.'

[Reported by Maggy Pigott, Barrister.]

Lewis v Lethbridge [1987] Crim LR 59 Divisional Court (Woolf LJ and MacPherson of Cluny J)

Property belonging to another - s5(3) Theft Act 1968

Facts

'The appellant was convicted of theft from a charity. He obtained sponsorship for a colleague who had entered the London Marathon. He also completed sponsorship forms in false names. He received £54 which he did not hand over to the charity. The justices found that although there was no rule of the charity requiring the appellant to hand over the notes and coins actually collected so long as a sum equal to the amount collected was handed over, the appellant had dishonestly appropriated the proceeds of the money received. The appellant appealed by way of case stated.

Held

Allowing the appeal and quashing the conviction, the justices erred in finding that the debt owed by the appellant could be described as proceeds of the property received. In any event he could not be said to have appropriated a debt which he himself owed simply by not paying it. Davidge v Bunnett [1974] Crim LR 297 dist. The Court approved of the summary set out by Professor J. C. Smith in The Law of Theft (5th ed): "the obligation is to deal with that property or its proceeds in a particular way." The words "or its proceeds" make it clear that D need not be under an obligation to retain particular monies. It is sufficient that he is under an obligation to keep in existence a fund equivalent to that which he has received. If the arrangement permits D to do what he likes with the money, his only obligation being to account in due course for an equivalent sum, section 5(3) does not apply.'

[*Reported by Lynne Knapman, Barrister.*]

R v Meech [1974] QB 549 Court of Appeal (Criminal Division) (Roskill LJ, Thompson and Stocker JJ)

Nature of appropriation - whether cheque proceeds property belonging to another

Facts

As stated by Roskill LJ:

'A man named McCord had obtained a cheque for £1,450 from a hire purchase finance company by means of a forged instrument. The cheque itself was a perfectly valid document. McCord, who was an undischarged bankrupt, feared that were he to cash this cheque himself, his crime would be more likely to be discovered than if he persuaded a friend to cash it for him. McCord, therefore, asked Meech (to whom McCord owed £40) to cash the cheque for him and Meech agreed so to do. At the time Meech agreed so to do Meech was wholly unaware of the dishonest means whereby McCord had become possessed of the cheque. Meech paid the cheque into his own account at a branch of Lloyds Bank at High Wycombe on 11th September 1972. The bank was seemingly unwilling to allow him to cash the cheque until it had been cleared. On 13th September Meech drew his own cheque for £1,410 on his own account at that branch and that cheque was duly cashed by the bank on that day. The difference between the two sums was represented by McCord's £40 debt to Meech. By the time this cheque was cashed, the original cheque had been cleared. Between the paying in of the original cheque on 11th September and the obtaining of the cash on 13th September, Meech became aware that McCord had acquired the original cheque dishonestly.

We were told by counsel that Meech, following legal argument at the end of the evidence, was allowed by the judge to be recalled. Meech then told the jury that not only did he find out about McCord's dishonesty but that he then honestly believed that if he cashed the cheque he would commit an offence. In the view of the direction given by the judge to which we refer later, we think it clear that the jury must be taken to have rejected this story of honest belief on Meech's part.

Before the cheque was cashed but after Meech discovered its dishonest origin, Meech agreed with Parslow and Jolliffe that after the cheque was cashed Meech would take the money to a prearranged destination. The two other men were to join him there. A fake robbery with Meech as the victim was to be staged and indeed was staged, the purpose clearly being to provide some explanation to McCord of Meech's inability to hand over the money to McCord.

This was done. Parslow and Jolliffe between them removed the money after leaving Meech as the apparent victim. The bogus robbery was reported to the police, who, being less credulous than the three men imagined McCord might be, investigated the matter and soon became convinced that the robbery story was bogus as indeed it was soon shown to be. It is clear that Meech was influenced by the thought that even if the bogus nature of the robbery were suspected by McCord, McCord would never dare to go to the police and complain for that would involve revealing his own dishonesty.

All the appellants alleged in evidence that the "robbery" was honest in its purpose in that it was designed to enable the money to be returned to the hire purchase finance company whom McCord had defrauded.'

The defendants were convicted of theft and appealed on the ground that the trial judge had misdirected the jury in stating that the proceeds of the cheque were property belonging to another within s5(3) of the

Theft Act 1968, because there had been no legal obligation owed to McCord to deal with the proceeds in any particular way.

Held

Roskill LJ:

[On the nature of the 'obligation' referred to in s5(3)]

'Counsel for all the defendants relied strongly on the series of recent decisions that "obligation" means "legal obligation". The judge so directed the jury. In giving this direction he no doubt had in mind the successive decisions of this court in *R v Hall* [above], *R v Gilks* [above] and *R v Pearce* [1973] Crim LR 321. Reliance was also placed on a passage in Professor Smith's book on The Law of Theft [2nd ed] – a passage written just before the decisions referred to.

Since the judge so directed the jury, we do not find it necessary further to consider those decisions beyond observing that the facts of those cases were vastly different from those of the present case.

Starting from this premise – that "obligation" means "legal obligation" – it was argued that even at the time when Meech was ignorant of the dishonest origin of the cheque, as he was at the time when he agreed to cash the cheque and hand the proceeds less the £40 to McCord, McCord could never have enforced that obligation because McCord had acquired the cheque illegally. In our view this submission is unsound in principle. The question has to be looked at from Meech's point of view not McCord's. Meech plainly assumed an "obligation" to McCord which on the facts then known to him he remained obliged to fulfil and on the facts as found he must be taken at that time honestly to have intended to fulfil. The fact that on the true facts if known McCord might not and indeed would not subsequently have been permitted to enforce that obligation in a civil court does not prevent that "obligation" on Meech having arisen. The argument confuses the creation of the obligation with the subsequent discharge of that obligation either by performance or otherwise. That the obligation might have become impossible of performance by Meech or of enforcement by McCord on grounds of illegality or for reasons of public policy is irrelevant. The opening words of s5(3) clearly look to the time of the creation of or the acceptance of the obligation by the bailee and not to the time of performance by him of the obligation so created and accepted by him.

It is further to be observed in this connection that s5(3) deems property (including the proceeds of property) which does not belong to the bailor to belong to the bailor so as to render a bailee who has accepted an obligation to deal with the property or to account for it in a particular way but then dishonestly fails to fulfil that obligation, liable to be convicted of theft whereas previously he would have been liable to have been convicted of fraudulent conversion though not of larceny. It was not seriously disputed in argument that before 1968 Meech would have had no defence to a charge of fraudulent conversion.

The first branch of the argument therefore clearly fails. The second argument (as already indicated) was that even if Meech initially became under an obligation to McCord, that obligation ceased to bind Meech once Meech discovered McCord had acquired the cheque by fraud. It was argued that once Meech possessed this knowledge, performance of his pre-existing obligation would have involved him in performing an "obligation" which he knew to be illegal. Thus, it was said, he was discharged from performance and at the time of his dishonest misappropriation had ceased to be bound by his obligation so that he could not properly be convicted of theft by virtue of s5(3)

This submission was advanced at considerable length before the trial judge. It is not necessary to relate those arguments more fully. They will be found set out in the transcript which this court has read. The judge rejected the arguments and he directed the jury in the following terms so far as relevant. After saying that there were three considerations which Meech said affected his mind and led him not to carry out his agreement with McCord, the judge dealt correctly with the first two of the three matters. He continued as follows:

"Thirdly, he says that he was worried about being involved in the offence of obtaining money by fraud; that he knew this to be, as he described it, a 'dodgy' cheque – knew not at the time that he was handed it, but knew before he drew the cash; that he alleges that from enquiries made on 11th and 12th September he discovered what was seemingly common knowledge among some motor dealers of High Wycombe, that McCord was involved in a dishonest transaction. His knowledge of this was limited and inaccurate, since he thought that there was a name Harris involved. He is not entitled in law to repudiate his agreement merely on the basis of suspicions about McCord. The only basis on which he was entitled to refuse payment was that he refused because if he had honoured the agreement he, Meech, would have committed a criminal offence, or that was his belief. Only if that was the basis – or if you thought on the evidence that may have been the basis – was there no obligation to pay. Otherwise, although you may well think many people had a better right than McCord, so far as Meech was concerned it was for his obligation to deal with the proceeds of the cheque in the way that he had agreed with McCord that he would."

The judge thus emphasised that the obligation to McCord remained but that Meech would be excused performance if performance would have involved commission of a criminal offence or if Meech genuinely believed that such performance would involve commission of a criminal offence. Of course if Meech acted as he did honestly and had an honest reason for not performing his obligation and for claiming relief from performance of that obligation, this would clearly be the end of any criminal charge against him. But the jury, as already pointed out, clearly negatived any such honest intention or belief on Meech's part. The argument before this court was that even though he was found to have acted dishonestly, he still could not be convicted of theft.

There was considerable discussion whether if he were not guilty of theft, he could have been convicted of any other offence, for example, of conspiracy or of dishonest handling of the proceeds of the cheque which he knew to have been obtained dishonestly. That is not the question. The question is whether he was guilty of theft and not whether if he is not guilty of theft he might have been properly charged with and convicted of some other offence.

The answer to the main contention is that Meech being under the initial obligation already mentioned, the proceeds of the cheque continued as between him and McCord to be deemed to be McCord's property so that if Meech dishonestly misappropriated those proceeds he was by reason of s5(3) guilty of theft even though McCord could not have enforced performance of that obligation against Meech in a civil action. Some reliance was placed on a passage in Professor Smith's book:

"Thus there is no redress in civil or criminal law against a client who is accidentally overpaid by a bookmaker. The same principle no doubt governs other cases where the transaction is void or illegal by statute or at common law. If this is a defect in the law, the fault lies with the civil law and not with the Theft Act. If the civil law says that the defendant is the exclusive owner of the money and under no obligation to repay even an equivalent sum, it would be incongruous for the criminal law to say he had stolen it."

It must be observed that that passage was written with reference to s5(4) of the Theft Act 1968 and not with reference to s5(3) of that Act. It immediately follows a discussion of the Gaming Act cases. We do not think the learned author had a case such as the present in mind. On no view could it be said in the present case that the common law would regard Meech as the "exclusive owner" of the original cheque or of its proceeds. The true owner of the proceeds was the hire purchase finance company. They could have sued Meech to judgment for the full value of the original cheque. But Meech having received the original cheque from McCord under the obligation we have mentioned, the criminal law provides that as between him and McCord the cheque and its proceeds are to be deemed to be McCord's property so that a subsequent dishonest misappropriation of the cheque or its proceeds makes Meech liable to be convicted of theft. We are therefore clearly of the view that Meech was properly convicted of theft just as under the old law he would have been liable to have been convicted of fraudulent conversion. We therefore think that the judge was quite right in leaving this case to the jury and that the direction which he gave was correct. If it be open to criticism at all, the criticism might be that the direction was arguably too favourable to the appellants.'

(For extracts dealing with the nature of appropriation see chapter 16.)

R v Meredith [1973] Crim LR 253 Manchester Crown Court (John Da Cunha J)

Property belonging to another - s5(1) Theft Act 1968

Facts

'The defendant, who owned a car, left it in a road while he attended a football match. The car was removed to a police station yard under regulation 4 of the Removal and Disposal of Vehicles Regulations 1968. After the match the defendant went to the police station adjacent to the yard; it was crowded and he went to the yard not having paid any sum to the police. He found his car with a police Krooklok on the steering wheel and, without consent or authority from the police he drove the car away. Two days later he was seen by the police, to whom he handed the Krooklok, and he was arrested and charged with its theft contrary to section 1 and 7 of the Theft Act 1968. While he was at the police station an entry relating to his car in the found property book was signed by him as his having received his car, the column relating to a £4 charge [under regulation 17 (1) *(a)* (ii)] being marked "not paid" by a police officer. Later he was charged also with theft of the car, the property of the police, contrary to sections 1 and 7 of the 1968 Act, and with taking the vehicle without consent of the owner or other lawful authority, contrary to section 12 of the 1968 Act, and he was committed for trial on the three charges. Subsequently he received a demand from the police for £4, the cost of impounding his car. At his trial no evidence was offered on the count under section 12. At the close of the prosecution's evidence he submitted that he had no case to answer.

Held

Upholding the submission, that the reality of the situation was that the police were removing the car to another situation for the owner to collect it subsequently. An owner was liable to pay the statutory charge only if the car originally caused an obstruction, and he had three choices on going to the police station: to pay the £4, admitting that his car caused an obstruction; to refuse to pay, whereupon inevitably he would face a prosecution for having caused an obstruction; or to agree to pay, and then, no doubt, receive a bill. In all three eventualities he would be allowed to take the car away, for the police had no right, as against the owner, to retain it. Consequently, a charge of theft against the defendant was improper. As to the count of theft of the Krooklok, not merely was it a (comparatively) minor offence, but so short was the time elapsing between its being taken and the defendant's admission that he had it, that he should no longer be in jeopardy of conviction for dishonesty. Accordingly, the jury would be directed to find the defendant not guilty on all three counts.'

[*Reported by L. Norman Williams, Barrister.*]

Moynes v Cooper [1956] 1 QB 439 Divisional Court (Lord Goddard LJ, Hilbery and Stable JJ)

Property belonging to another - s5(4) Theft Act 1968

Facts

The defendant received an overpayment of £6 19s 6d in his wage packet. He was unaware of the overpayment until later he opened the wage packet at home later that day. The defendant spent the money that had been paid to him in error and was charged with stealing it under the Larceny Act 1916.

Held

The defendant was not guilty of stealing the overpayment.

Lord Goddard CJ:

'The problem as to dishonest appropriation in cases where money has been paid under a mistake has been the subject of many cases and much difference of judicial opinion. The appeal committee were of opinion that this case was indistinguishable from *R* v *Prince* (1868) LR 1 CCR 150, decided in 1868. In that case the cashier of a bank, who had authority to pay cheques, was deceived by the presentation of a forged cheque by the prisoner. He paid the amount of the cheque and the prisoner was indicted for stealing the proceeds. It was held that this did not amount to larceny. Blackburn J, lamenting, as we also may, that this was the law, said: "If the owner intended the property to pass, though he would not so have intended had he known the real facts, that is sufficient to prevent the offence of obtaining another's property from amounting to larceny." It was held in that case that the prisoner's offence amounted to obtaining the money by a false pretence, but in the present case no question of false pretences arises as the defendant made no representation of any sort.

The next case which bears on the subject is *R* v *Middleton* (1873) LR 2 CCR 38, and in 1885 there came the much discussed case of *R* v *Ashwell* (1885) 16 QBD 190; 2 TLR 151, in which unfortunately the court was equally divided. We do not propose to discuss these or any subsequent cases on the subject in detail because in our opinion the matter is now concluded by section 1 (2) of the Larceny Act, 1916. It will be remembered that there have been in the last 90 years two codifications of the law of larceny. The first was the Larceny Act of 1861, the long title of which is: "An Act to consolidate and amend the statute law of England and Ireland relating to larceny and other similar offences." While that Act in section 1 defined a considerable number of terms, such as "document of title to goods" and "valuable security" among others, it did not contain a definition of larceny or any of the necessary constituents of that crime. The Larceny Act of 1916, which is now the governing statute, is entitled: "An Act to consolidate and simplify the law relating to larceny triable on indictment and kindred offences," and does contain an elaborate definition of larceny. This Act was not intended to alter the law and, as has often been said, it has not done so; but while the Act of 1861 consolidated, and to some extent amended, the statute law, the later Act consolidates and simplifies the whole law, which includes the common law as expounded by judicial decision. What amounts to a "taking" sufficient to amount to larceny was much discussed in *R* v *Middleton*, and in our opinion it is the effect of that decision which is reproduced and enacted as the law. Section 1 (2) (i) of the Act of 1916 provides: "the expression 'takes' includes obtaining the possession . . . (c) under a mistake on the part of the owner with knowledge on the part of the taker that possession has been so obtained." This, in our opinion, is affirming the common law that the taker must have animus furandi at the same time when he takes the property. In *Middleton's* case the wrong amount of money was paid by the post office clerk before the prisoner, who picked it up knowing of the clerk's mistake and so took it animo furandi. In the present case it is found that the defendant did not know of the mistake when he took the money, so the taking was not animo furandi. We prefer to base our decision on this ground, namely, that there was no taking here within the section. The decision in *R* v *Prince* depended on the fact that the bank, acting thorough its authorised clerk, did intend to pass the property in the money though it was induced to do so not by its own or his mistake but by fraud. Where a transfer of property is obtained by fraud, there is no doubt but that the property does pass, subject, however, to the right of the defrauded party on discovering the fraud to disaffirm the transaction and resume his property. In the present case the action would be for money had and received to the company's use as paid under a mistake of fact.'

(see *R* v *Gilles*, above)

Oxford v Moss (1978) 68 Cr App R 183 Divisional Court (Lord Widgery CJ, Wien and Smith JJ)

Information - whether property under s4(1) Theft Act 1968

Facts

The defendant was an undergraduate at Liverpool University who obtained an unauthorised advance copy of an examination paper. He was charged with theft, but the justices at first instance dismissed the case against him as there was no evidence that he intended to permanently deprive the University of the piece of paper, and the information contained in the paper was not intangible property within s4(1) of the Theft Act 1968. The prosecutor appealed.

Held

The appeal would be dismissed.

Smith J:

'The question for this Court is whether confidential information of this sort falls within that definition contained in section 4 (1). We have been referred to a number of authorities emanating from the area of trade secrets and matrimonial secrets. In particular, we were referred to *Peter Pan Manufacturing Corporation* v *Corsets Silhouette Ltd* [1963] 3 All ER 402, to *Seager* v *Copydex Ltd* [1967] 2 All ER 415, to the case of *Argyll* v *Argyll* [1965] 2 WLR 790, and *Fraser* v *Evans* [1968] 3 WLR 1172.

Those are the cases concerned with what is described as the duty to be of good faith. They are clear illustrations of the proposition that, if a person obtains information which is given to him in confidence and then sets out to take an unfair advantage of it, the courts will restrain him by way of an order of injunction or will condemn him in damages if an injunction is found to be inappropriate. It seems to me, speaking for my part, that they are of little assistance in the present situation in which we have to consider whether there is property in the information which is capable of being the subject of a charge of theft. In my judgment, it is clear that the answer to that question must be no. Accordingly, I would dismiss the appeal.'

R v Shadrokh-Cigari [1988] Crim LR 465 Court of Appeal (Criminal Division) (Wool LJ, McCullough and Saville JJ)

Theft Act 1968 s5(4) - property got by another's mistake - whether theft

Facts

'The appellant was convicted of four counts of theft. He acted as guardian to his nephew whose father in Iran arranged for money to be paid to the child's bank account from the USA.. Through an error by the United States bank $286,000 was credited to the account instead of $286. At the appellant's suggestion the child signed an authority for the issue of four banker's drafts drawn in favour of the appellant for sums of £51,300, £64,000, £53,000 and £29,000. The appellant paid two into his own bank account and used the others to open other accounts to his name. By the time of his arrest some three weeks later only £21,000 remained. He appealed against conviction on the ground that the judge should have directed the jury that they had to be satisfied that the drafts belonged to the Bank and that had he done so the jury would have been bound to have concluded that the drafts did not belong to the bank but were the property of the appellant and so there was no question of him appropriating property belonging to another.

Held

Dismissing the appeal, [the court held that] the submissions erred in assuming that the entire proprietary interest in the drafts existed and vested in the appellant leaving the bank with no rights at all. The mistake of the United States bank totally undermined the basic assumption upon which the English bank issued the drafts, namely that the funds which had been received could properly be dealt with as directed by the account holder. As between the English bank and the appellant, the transaction fell fairly and squarely within the principles of the law relating to the mistake - *Kelly* v *Solari* [1941] (9) M & W 547. The mistake must be fundamental or basic, one in respect of the underlying assumption of the contract or transaction - *Norwich Union* v *Price* [1934] 455. That was so here. If the mistake must be one of fact rather than law, that condition was satisfied in the present case. Thus the appellant was under an obligation to make restoration of the instruments on the basis that the English bank retained an equitable proprietary interest in the drafts as a result of the mistake. The fact that the choses in action created by the drafts could not be owned by the bank, since they were debts due from the bank was irrelevant. The bank created the drafts and before delivery they owned them, although as promissory notes they were inchoate and incomplete. Upon delivery under the mistake, the bank retained an equitable interest in those instruments. Such an equitable interest amounted to property within section 5(1) of the Theft Act 1968. That conclusion was not only supported by section 5(4) of the 1968 Act, but could be reached by another route through the application of that sub-section. Even if it could not be said that the property belonged to another in the sense of that other having proprietary rights over the property itself, nevertheless (other things being equal) the property was to be regarded for the purposes of theft as belonging to that other even if the person getting it was only under an obligation to restore the proceeds of the property or its value as opposed to the property itself. The appellant was obliged to restore the proceeds or value of the instruments. The Court did not consider that knowledge on the part of the recipient was not a necessary precondition to a civil obligation to restore the property, its proceeds or value. In any event the judge had left that question to the jury and the jury must have decided that such knowledge existed.

It was not necessary, save in the most exceptional circumstance, that the jury should be concerned with matters of legal reasoning such as the Court had had to consider. What was required for the jury was a statement of relevant rules of law, the legal requirements of the offence in question and not the legal reasoning behind those rules.'

[Reported by Lynne Knapman, Barrister.]

R v Turner (No 2) (1971) 55 Cr App R 336 Court of Appeal (Criminal Division) (Lord Parker CJ, Widgery LJ and Bridge J)

Property belonging to another – s5(1) Theft Act 1968

Facts

The defendant took his car to be repaired at a garage operated by a man named Arthur Brown. Once the repairs were completed, Brown parked the car in the road outside his garage as he was short of space. The defendant, who had retained a spare key, drove the car away that night. Later, when questioned by police, he denied that he had ever put the car in to be repaired at Brown's garage. He appealed against his conviction for theft on the ground that the car could not be regarded as 'property belonging to another' within s5(1) of the Theft Act 1968.

Held

Appeal dismissed.

Lord Parker CJ:

'The trial lasted, we are told, six days, in the course of which every conceivable point seems to have been taken and argued. In the result, however, when it comes to this Court two points, and two only, are taken. It is said in the first instance that while Brown may have had possession or control in fact, that is not enough, and that it must be shown, before it can be said that the property "belonged to" Brown, those being the words used in section 1 (1) of the Theft Act, that that possession was, as it is said, a right superior to that in anyone else. It is argued from that in default of proof of a lien – and the judge in his summing-up directed the jury that they were not concerned with the question of whether there was a lien – Brown was merely a bailee at will and accordingly had no sufficient possession.

The words "belonging to another" are specifically defined in section 5 of the Act. By subsection (1) it is provided that: "Property shall be regarded as belonging to any person having possession or control of it, or having in it any proprietary right or interest." The judge directed the jury that they were not concerned in any way with lien and the sole question was whether Brown had possession or control.

This Court is quite satisfied that there is no ground whatever for qualifying the words "possession or control" in any way. It is sufficient if it is found that the person from whom the property is taken, or to use the words of the Act, appropriated, was at the time in fact in possession or control. At the trial there was a long argument as to whether that possession or control must be lawful, it being said that, by reason of the fact that this car was subject to a hire-purchase agreement, Brown could never even as against the appellant obtain lawful possession or control. This Court is quite satisfied that the judge was quite correct in telling the jury they need not bother about lien, and that they need not bother about hire-purchase agreements. The only question was: was Brown in fact in possession or control?'

R v Wills (1991) 92 Cr App R 297 Court of Appeal (Criminal Division) Farquharson LJ, Garland and Ognall JJ

Theft - s5(3) - whether knowledge of 'obligation' needed

Facts

The appellant ran a financial consultancy business (Goshen Finance) with the help of two assistants. The assistants each received money from two separate clients (Tasker, and Walker). In each case the monies were for investment in particular investment schemes. In each case the cheques were made out to Goshen Finance. The cheques were cashed and the proceeds utilised to cover the operation of Goshen Finance. In neither case was money invested for the client as instructed. The appellant was not present when the monies were paid over by the clients. The appellant and his assistants were charged, inter alia, with theft of the monies. The appellant contended that he could not be convicted by virtue of s5(3) Theft Act 1968 since he had been unaware of the obligation that existed when the monies were paid over. The trial judge rejected this submission, and the appellant was convicted.

Held

The appeal would be allowed.

Farquharson LJ:

'At the end of the Crown case there was an unsuccessful submission made with regard to these counts by counsel then defending the appellant, as well as on many of the other counts. In fact at the conclusion of the submissions these were the only two counts which were left to the jury. However that may be, the submission was, with regard to those counts, that there was no prima facie case in the sense of there being sufficient evidence supporting the counts to be left to the jury. The basis of the submission was that the prosecution could successfully rely on s5(3) against the appellant they had to prove not only the existence of the obligation, and indeed the nature of it, but that the appellant was also, prima facie, aware of that obligation and the extent of it. In other words, there must be evidence that he knew that the money paid by those cheques had to be paid into investment or exchange bonds and not on the other hand to be applied to the ordinary expenses of his business.

As I have indicated, there can be no doubt in this case that such an obligation had been attached to the monies by the two customers Tasker and Walker, but was there any evidence on the basis of a prima facie case that the appellant knew of the existence of this obligation, knew of its nature and with that knowledge had failed to apply the money accordingly? As I have indicated, there is no doubt that the money was not so applied. But what was the evidence of the appellant's knowledge of the obligation placing on him the responsibility of applying the funds in a particular way? At that stage of the trial there was no evidence of what happened to the cheques after they had been handed to the agents. Were they directly paid into the firm's general account by either of the two agents? Had they been handed to the appellant or banked by some other member of staff? There was no evidence of that at all.

In a number of submissions made by Mr Thomas for sustaining these convictions it was contended that the breach of the obligation to deal with the cheques or their proceeds in a particular way had been proved by the evidence that the cheques had not been dealt with in accordance with the customer's instructions. The answer to that is contained in the terms of the subsection itself. Whether a person is under an obligation to deal with property in a particular way can only be established by providing that he had knowledge of that obligation. Proof that the property was not dealt with in conformity with the obligation is not sufficient in itself. Secondly, it was submitted that where there was knowledge by the agent of the extent of the obligation imposed on the disposal of the property such knowledge was to be imputed to the principal, in this case the appellant. Whatever may be the position in civil law of knowledge by an agent being imputed to the principal, for the purposes of the criminal law it is necessary for the prosecution to prove that the principal had knowledge of the nature and extent of the obligation to deal with property in a particular way before s5(3) of the 1968 Act can apply.

Finally, it is submitted by the prosecution that there was knowledge in the appellant just by the general running of the business and in particular the firm's bank account. It was open to the jury to infer that the appellant had the necessary knowledge.

For my part I have great difficulty with that submission because the cheques had been drawn in favour of Goshen Finance, the appellant's business. One would assume that the cheques would normally be paid into that bank account so that some additional evidence had to be available to show how the monies were to be specifically applied. The fact the monies were being paid into the Goshen Finance account does not assist the prosecution at all in my judgment. The position at the close of the prosecution case, so far as this court is concerned, is that the two counts of theft laid against the appellant were not sufficiently proved. For that reason this appeal must be allowed and the conviction quashed.'

16 APPROPRIATION

Chan Man-Sin v R [1988] 1 WLR 196 Privy Council (Lords Brandon, Ackner and Oliver, Sir John Stephenson and Sir Edward Eveleigh)

Appropriation of funds in bank accounts

Facts

As stated by Lord Oliver:

'The defendant was at all material times an accountant for two companies, Hunter Corporation Ltd ("Hunter") and Merit Investment Co Inc ("Merit") which maintained bank accounts in Hong Kong with the Standard Chartered Bank Ltd. Between 26 July 1983, by means of five forged cheques drawn on Merit's account, he withdrew sums totalling HK$2,750,647 and caused them to be deposited in his personal account with the Overseas Trust Bank Ltd. As a result, Merit's account became overdrawn but it had arranged a facility with the bank up to HK$3,000,000 and this limit was not exceeded. Between 31 December 1983 and 30 March 1984, by means of five further forged cheques, the defendant withdrew from Hunter's account sums totalling HK$2,022,392.30 which he caused to be deposited to the credit of the account of a business of which he was the sole proprietor. Hunter had likewise arranged a facility with the bank up to a limit of HK$4,000,000 and these withdrawals, although the account was overdrawn, did not cause the limit to be exceeded. Between 11 April 1984 and 12 May 1984 the defendant, again by the use of forged cheques, caused five further sums amounting in all the HK$2,690,608 to be withdrawn from Hunter's account. This time, however, the authorised overdraft limit of HK$4,000,000 was exceeded on each occasion.

The defendant's defalcations came to light in July 1984 and he was duly charged in the District Court of Hong Kong at Victoria with five charges of theft of choses in action, namely debts owed by the bank to Merit (charges 1 to 5) and 10 charges of theft of choses in action, namely debts owed by the bank to Hunter, charges 11 to 15 being those relating to the last-mentioned series of forgeries. On 9 December 1985 he was convicted of charges 1 to 10 and sentenced to imprisonment for three years concurrent in respect of each conviction. He was acquitted of charges 11 to 15 on the technical ground that, since there was in respect of the sums of the subject matter of those charges neither a debt due from the bank to Hunter nor any subsisting arrangement under which Hunter was entitled to draw from the bank, there was no chose in action of Hunter capable of being stolen. The defendant sought leave to appeal from the Court of Appeal of Hong Kong against his convictions but that application was dismissed on 30 May 1986. On 5 November 1986 special leave was granted by Order in Council to appeal to their Lordships' Board against the judgment of the Court of Appeal.'

Held

The appeal would be dismissed.

Lord Oliver:

'The argument for the defendant is a simple one and is founded upon the proposition that a bank is not entitled in law, as against its customer, to debit the customer's account with the amount of any cheque which the bank has not, in fact, any authority from the customer to honour. Thus, it is said, if the bank honours a forged cheque and debits the customer's account accordingly, the transaction is, quite simply, a nullity as a matter of law so far as the customer is concerned and the customer, on discovering the unauthorised debit to his account, is entitled to insist upon its being reversed. For this proposition reliance is, quite rightly, placed upon the decision of their Lordships' Board in *Tai Hing Cotton Mill Ltd* v *Liu Chong Hing Bank Ltd* [1986] AC 80. Starting out from this foundation, the defendant argues that the presentation of the 10 forged cheques in respect of which the defendant was convicted produced, as a matter of legal reality, no diminution at all of the respective credit balances of the companies. The bank simply made unauthorised debits to their accounts which they were entitled to have reversed upon demand. Thus, it is argued, although the defendant was no doubt guilty of offences of forgery and obtaining a pecuniary advantage by deception with which he was not charged, he could not have been guilty of the offences with which he was charged, namely, theft of Merit's or Hunter's choses in action.

The Theft Ordinance of Hong Kong follows, in all respects material to the instant case, the provisions of the English Theft Act 1968. Section 2 provides: "(1) A person commits theft if he dishonestly appropriates property belonging to another with the intention of permanently depriving the other of it;" and section 5 includes "things in action and other intangible property" within the statutory definition of "property." It is not disputed that the debt due to the customer from his banker is a chose in action capable of being stolen and this equally applies to the sum which a customer is entitled to overdraw under contractual arrangements which he has made with the bank (see *R* v *Kohn* (1979) 69 Cr App R 395), though strictly in the latter case the chose in action is the benefit of the contractual arrangement with the bank. What is argued, however, is that, since as between the customer and the bank an unauthorised debit entry in the customer's account is a mere nullity, the customer is deprived of nothing and therefore there has been no appropriation. Equally, it is said that, since the customer whose property is alleged to have been stolen has not in fact been deprived of anything, there cannot have been an intention permanently to deprive him of the property. Thus, it is argued, there were lacking two essential ingredients of the offences with which the defendant was charged and he was entitled to an acquittal.

Their Lordships can deal very briefly with the second submission. The defendant did not elect to give evidence and if there was, as the prosecution contended, an appropriation of the companies' property, there was ample evidence from which the intention permanently to deprive them of it could be inferred. Even if it were possible to infer or assume that the defendant contemplated that the fraud would be discovered and appreciated also that his employers would or might challenge the bank's entitlement to payment of the sums debited, he would fall within the provisions of section 7 of the Ordinance. That section provides:

"(1) A person appropriating property belonging to another without meaning the other permanently to lose the thing itself is nevertheless to be regarded as having the intention of permanently depriving the other of it if his intention is to treat the thing as his own to dispose of regardless of the other's rights; ..."

Quite clearly here the defendant was purporting to deal with the companies' property without regard to their rights.

Reverting to the defendant's principal ground of appeal, this has an appealing simplicity. The defendant's difficulty, however, is that it entirely ignores the artificial definition of appropriation which is contained in section 4(1) of the Ordinance and reproduces section 3(1) of the Act of 1968 ...

The owner of the chose in action consisting of a credit with his bank or a contractual right to draw on an account has, clearly, the right as owner to draw by means of a properly completed negotiable instrument or order to pay and it is, in their Lordships' view, beyond argument that one who draws, presents and negotiates a cheque on a particular bank account is assuming the rights of the owner of the credit in the account or (as the case may be) of the pre-negotiated right to draw on the account up to the agreed figure. Ownership, of course, consists of a bundle of rights and it may well be that there are other rights which an owner could exert over the chose in action in question which are not trespassed upon by the particular dealing which the thief chooses to assume. In *R* v *Morris (David)* [1984] AC 320, however, the House of Lords decisively rejected a submission that it was necessary, in order to constitute an appropriation as defined by section 3(1) of the Act of 1968, to demonstrate an assumption by the accused of all the rights of an owner.

Their Lordships are, accordingly, entirely satisfied that the transactions initiated and carried through by the defendant constituted an assumption of the rights of the owner and, consequently, an appropriation. It is unnecessary, for present purposes, to determine whether that occurred on presentation of the forged cheques or when the transactions were completed by the making of consequential entries in the bank accounts of the companies and the defendant or his business respectively. It is, in their Lordships' view, entirely immaterial that the end result of the transaction may be a legal nullity for it is not possible to read into section 4(1) of the Ordinance any requirement that the assumption of rights there envisaged should have a legally efficacious result. Their Lordships are fortified in the view which they have formed by the recent decision of the English Court of Appeal (Criminal Division) in *R* v *Wille* (unreported), 26 January 1987, of which they have been provided with a transcript and in which the court reached the same conclusion in circumstances not materially dissimilar to those in the instant case. It seems probable that if that decision had been reported at the time when special leave was applied for it would not have been granted. Their Lordships will accordingly humbly advise Her Majesty that the appeal should be dismissed.'

(See *R* v *Kohn*, chapter 15.)

Dobson v General Accident plc [1989] 3 WLR 1066 Court of Appeal (Civil Division) (Parker and Bingham LJJ)

Theft - whether absence of consent needs to be proved

Facts [As stated by Parker LJ]

'The contents of the plaintiff's house were insured by the defendant under Part B of their Maxplan Home Insurance Policy against, among other things, "loss or damage caused by theft." On 19 November 1987 the plaintiff advertised for sale his gold Rolex Oyster wristwatch and a diamond ring, at a total price of £5,950. On 2 November he received a telephone call from a person whose identity he did not then and does not now know. I shall refer to him as "the rogue." He expressed interest in purchasing the two articles at the advertised price. It was provisionally agreed between them that payment would be by a building society cheque, ie a cheque drawn by a building society in favour of the plaintiff. This the plaintiff believed would be as good as a banker's draft.

On 21 November the rogue came to the plaintiff's premises and the plaintiff handed over the watch and ring, receiving in return what purported to be a Birmingham and Midland Building Society cheque in the agreed amount of £5,950, for which he gave a receipt. The transaction took place at the weekend. On the Monday he paid the cheque into his bank. A few days later he was informed that the cheque had been stolen and was worthless.

It is common ground between the parties that "theft" in the police means theft within the meaning of the Theft Act 1968. On the plaintiff presenting a claim under the policy the defendant denied liability on the ground that the circumstances in which the plaintiff lost his watch and ring did not amount to a theft under the Act.

The plaintiff commenced proceedings in the Sheffield County Court on 17 March 1988 to recover the value of the watch and ring. On 21 September 1988 in the Sheffield County Court Mr J W M Bullimore sitting as a recorder, held that the plaintiff's loss was caused by theft and gave judgment for the plaintiff for a total of £5,199.30 inclusive of interest.

The issue for determination on the appeal is whether the circumstances constituted theft of the watch and ring by the rogue. If so, the appeal fails. If not, the appeal succeeds.'

Held : The appeal would be dismissed.

Parker LJ. [Having set out the terms of section 1(1) and 3(1) of the Theft Act 1968, continued]

'The Act of 1968 as Viscount Dilhorne said in *Reg* v *Lawrence (Alan)* [1972] AC 626, 631, "made radical changes in and greatly simplified the law relating to theft." Prior to that Act the Larceny Act 1916 had provided the definition of theft, then called larceny, in an immensely complex set of provisions. Section 1(1), so far as immediately relevant, provided: " A person steals who, without the consent of the owner ... takes and carries away anything capable of being stolen." In *Reg v Lawrence (Alan)* [1972] AC 626 it was submitted that although the words "without the consent of the owner" were not included in section 1(1) of the Theft Act 1968, that subsection should be read as if they appeared after the word "appropriates." As to this Viscount Dilhorne said, at pp 631-632:

"I see no ground for concluding that the omission of the words 'without the consent of the owner' was inadvertent and not deliberate, and to read the subsection as if they were included is, in my opinion, wholly unwarranted. Parliament by the omission of these words has relieved the prosecution of the burden of establishing that the taking was without the owner's consent. That is no longer an ingredient of the offence."

Then a little later, at p632:

"Belief or the absence of belief that the owner had ... consented to the appropriation is relevant to the issue of dishonesty, not to the question whether or not there has been an appropriation. That may occur even though the owner has permitted or consented to the property being taken."

This must be read with Lord Dilhorne's agreement, at p632B, with the statement of Megaw LJ when delivering the judgment of the Court of Appeal [1971] 1 QB 373, 376 in the same case, that the offence involved four elements: "(i) a dishonest (ii) appropriation (iii) of property belonging to another (iv) with the intention of permanently depriving the owner of it." It must also be read with the answers given by the House of Lords to the two questions certified by the Court of Appeal. These were: (1) Whether section 1(1) of the Theft Act 1968 is to be construed as though it contained the words "without the consent of the owner" or words to that effect. (2) Whether the provisions of section 15(1) and section 1(1) of the Theft Act 1968 are mutually exclusive in that if the facts proved would justify a conviction under section 15(1) there cannot lawfully be a conviction under section 1(1). Both questions were answered in the negative.

Although on this appeal we are concerned directly with the first question only, the second is indirectly also of importance for in the present case the facts proved would clearly justify a conviction under section 15(1). This, however, as a result of the answer given to the second question, may be disregarded.

On the basis of *Reg v Lawrence (Alan)* [1972] AC 626 the facts of the present case appear to establish that the rogue assumed all the rights of an owner when he took or received the watch and ring from the plaintiff. That he did so dishonestly and with the intention of permanently depriving the plaintiff of it are matters beyond doubt. It was however submitted that the final element was not satisfied because, at the time of appropriation, if there was one, the watch and ring were not property belonging to another. The property had, it was submitted, already passed to the rogue at the time the articles were delivered to him.

This argument is put in two ways. First it is said that there was an agreement of sale over the telephone and accordingly the property passed to the rogue on 20 November 1987. Alternatively it is said that an agreement of sale took place on 21 November 1987 prior to the rogue receiving the articles in exchange for the cheque, and accordingly the property again passed to him, before delivery and receipt of the articles.

The argument is founded upon sections 17 and 18 of the Sale of Goods Act 1979. Section 17 provides:

"(1) Where there is a contract for the sale of specific or ascertained goods the property in them is transferred to the buyer at such time as the parties to the contract intend it to be transferred. (2) For the purpose of ascertaining the intention of the parties regard shall be had to the terms of the contract, the conduct of the parties and the circumstances of the case."

Section 18, so far as relevant, provides:

"Unless a different intention appears, the following are rules for ascertaining the intention of the parties as to the time at which the property in the goods is to pass to the buyer. *Rule 1.* – Where there is an unconditional contract for the sale of specific goods in a deliverable state the property in the goods passes to the buyer when the contract is made, and it is immaterial whether the time of payment or the time of delivery, or both, be postponed."

Having regard to the terms of the contract, the conduct of the parties and the circumstances of the case, I have no doubt that the property was not intended to pass in this case on contract but only in exchange for a valid building society cheque, but even if it may be regarded as intended to pass in exchange for a false, but believed genuine, building society cheque it will not in my view avail the insurers. A somewhat similar point was taken in *Reg* v *Lawrence (Alan)* [1972] AC 626 and was dealt with by Viscount Dilhorne where he said, at p632:

"I now turn to the third element 'property belonging to another.' Mr Back QC, for the appellant, contended that if Mr Occhi consented to the appellant taking the £6, he consented to the property in the money passing from him to the appellant and that the appellant had not, therefore, appropriated property belonging to another. He argued that the old distinction between the offence of false pretences and larceny had been preserved. I am unable to agree with this. The new offence of obtaining property by deception created by section 15(1) of the Theft Act [1968] also contains the words 'belonging to another.' 'A person who by any deception dishonestly obtains property belonging to another, with the intention of permanently depriving the other of it' commits that offence. 'Belonging to another' in section 1(1) and in section 15(1) in my view signifies no more than that, at the time of the appropriation or the obtaining, the property belonged to another, with the words 'belonging to another' having the extended meaning given by section 5. The short answer to this contention on behalf of the appellant is that the money in the wallet which he appropriated belonged to another, to Mr Occhi."

Furthermore, this passage would in my view dispose of the argument that the articles ceased to belong to the plaintiff because the property passed on contract and that this preceded appropriation. If it were right, then the result would merely be that the making of the contract constituted the appropriation. It was by that act that the rogue assumed the rights of an owner and at that time the property did belong to the plaintiff.

It was further submitted on the part of the insurers that, notwithstanding the emphatic statement of the House of Lords that absence of consent on the part of the owner was not an ingredient of the offence and was not relevant to the question whether there had been an appropriation, the later decision of the House in *Reg* v *Morris (David)* 1984] AC 320, 332D, that appropriation "involves not an act expressly or impliedly authorised by the owner but an act by way of adverse interference with or usurpation of those rights" must lead in the present case to the conclusion that there had been no theft.

The difficulties caused by the apparent conflict between the decisions in *Reg* v *Lawrence (Alan)* [1972] AC 626 and *Reg* v *Morris (David)* [1984] AC 320 have provided, not surprisingly, a basis for much discussion by textbook writers and contributors of articles to law journals. It is, however, clear that their Lordships in *Reg* v *Morris* did not regard anything said in that case as conflicting with *Reg* v *Lawrence* for it was specifically referred to in Lord Roskill's speech, with which the other members of the Judicial Committee all agreed, without disapproval or qualification. The only comment made was that, in *Reg* v *Lawrence,* the House did not have to consider the precise meaning of "appropriation" in section 3(1) of the Act of 1968. With respect, I find this comment hard to follow in the light of the first of the questions asked in *Reg* v *Lawrence* and the answer to it, the passages from Viscount Dilhorne's speech already cited, the fact that it was specifically argued "appropriates is meant in a pejorative, rather than a neutral, sense in that the appropriation is against the will of the owner," and finally that dishonesty was common ground. I would have supposed that *the* question in *Reg* v *Lawrence* was whether appropriation necessarily involved an absence of consent.

Lord Roskill's comment on *Reg* v *Lawrence* is, however, not the only difficulty presented by his speech in *Reg* v *Morris,* but before I consider other difficulties it is necessary to set out in short form the facts of the two cases considered in that speech. In one *Anderton* v *Burnside* [1984] AC 320 the defendant (Burnside) removed a price label from a joint in a supermarket and placed it on another more expensive joint. His action was detected when he took the latter joint to the checkout point and was arrested *before he had paid.* He was convicted of theft by the justices. His appeal was dismissed by the Divisional Court and was also dismissed by the House of Lords.

In the other case, *Reg* v *Morris* [1984] AC 320 the defendant took goods from the shelves and replaced the labels on them with labels showing lesser prices. At the checkout point he was asked for and paid the lesser prices. He was thereafter arrested. He was convicted in the Crown Court of theft. No verdict was taken on a further count of obtaining property by deception contrary to section 15 of the Act of 1968. The defendant's appeal to the Court of Appeal was dismissed as also was his further appeal to the House of Lords. Against that background I can now return to Lord Roskill's speech having disagreed with the decision of the Court of Appeal that any removal of goods from the shelves of a supermarket was an appropriation he said, at p332:

"If one postulates an honest customer taking goods from a shelf put in his or her trolley to take to the checkpoint there to pay the proper price, I am unable to see that any of these actions involves any assumption by the shopper of the rights of the supermarket. In the context of section 3(1), the concept of appropriation in my view involves not an act expressly or impliedly authorised by the owner but an act by way of adverse interference with or usurpation of those rights. When the honest shopper acts as I have just described, he or she is acting with the implied authority of the owner of the supermarket to take the goods from the shelf, put them in the trolley, take them to the checkpoint and there pay the correct price, at which moment the property in the goods will pass to the shopper for the first time. It is with the consent of the owners of the supermarket, be that consent expressed or implied, that the shopper does these acts and thus obtains at least control if not actual possession of the goods preparatory, at a later stage, to obtaining the property in them upon payment of the proper amount at the checkpoint. I do not think that section 3(1) envisages any such act as an 'appropriation', whatever may be the meaning of that word in other fields such as contract or sale of goods law.

If, as I understand all your Lordships to agree, the concept of appropriation in section 3(1) involves an element of adverse interference with or usurpation of some right of the owner, it is necessary next to consider whether that requirement is satisfied in either of these cases. As I have already said, in my view mere removal from the shelves without more is not an appropriation. Further, if a shopper with some perverted sense of humour intending only to create confusion and nothing more both for the supermarket and for other shoppers, switches labels, I do not think that that act of label switching alone is without more an appropriation, though it is not difficult to envisage some cases of dishonest label-switching which could be. In cases such as the present, it is in truth a combination of these actions, the removal from the shelf and the switching of the labels, which evidences adverse interference with or usurpation of the right of the owner. Those acts, therefore, amount to an appropriation...."

With this may be compared the answer given by their Lordships, at p335, to the certified question which was in the following terms:

"There is a dishonest appropriation for the purposes of the Theft Act 1968 where by the substitution of a price label showing a lesser price on goods for one showing a greater price, a defendant either by that act alone or by that act in conjunction with another act or other acts (whether done before or after the substitution of the labels) adversely interferes with or usurps the right of the owner to ensure that the goods concerned are sold and paid for at that greater price."

In the passage at p332 Lord Roskill, as it seems to me, impliedly envisage that mere label switching could be an appropriation and that this is so is confirmed by the answer to the certified question which specifically uses the words "either by that act alone." What then is it which would make label switching alone something which adversely affects or usurps the right of the owner? At p332 it appears to be envisaged that it will depend upon the question whether the label switching was dishonest and coupled with the other elements of the offence of theft or was due to a perverted sense of humour. This, however, appears to run together the elements of dishonesty and appropriation when it is clear from *Reg* v *Lawrence (Alan)* [1972] AC 626 that they are separate. That the two elements were indeed, at any rate to some extent, run together is plain from the fact that the answer to the certified question begins with the words "There is a dishonest appropriation." Moreover, on general principles, it would in my judgment be a plain interference with or usurpation of an owner's rights by the customer if he were to remove a label which the owner had placed on goods or put another label on. It would be a trespass to goods and it would be usurping the owner's rights, for only he would have any right to do such an act and no one could contend that there was any implied consent or authority to a customer to do any such thing. There would thus be an appropriation. In the case of the customer with a perverted sense of humour there would however be no theft for there would probably be no dishonesty and certainly no intent permanently to deprive the owner of the goods themselves. The case of the customer who simply removes goods from the shelves is of course different because the basis on which a supermarket is run is that customers certainly have the consent of the owner to take goods from the shelves and take them to the checkout point there to pay the proper price for them. Suppose, however, that there were no such consent – in, for example, a shop where goods on display were to be taken from the shelves only by the attendant. In such a case a customer who took from the shelves would clearly be usurping the right of the owner. Indeed he would be doing so if he did no more than move an item from one place on a shelf to another. The only difference appears to be that in the one case there is consent and in the other there is not. Since, however, it was held in *Reg* v *Lawrence (Alan)* [1972] AC 626 that consent is not relevant to appropriation there must, one would have supposed, be no difference between the two cases on that aspect of the offence. There are further matters in *Reg* v *Morris (David)* [1984] AC 320 in which I find difficulty. I mention only two. The first is the observations made on *Reg* v *McPherson* [1973] Crim LR 191. That was a case in which the defendant took two bottles of whisky from the shelves and put them in her shopping bag. The sole question in issue was whether there had been an appropriation. It was held in the Court of Appeal that there had been. As to this Lord Roskill said, at p 333:

"That was not, of course, a label switching case, but it is a plain case of appropriation effected by the combination of the acts of removing the goods from the shelf and of concealing them in the shopping bag. *Reg* v *McPherson* is to my mind clearly correctly decided as are all the cases which have followed it. It is wholly consistent with the principles which I have endeavoured to state in this speech."

Reference to the transcript of the judgment in that case however reveals that the decision did not turn on concealment in the shopping bag but was expressly upon the ground that the goods were appropriated when they were taken from the shelves. This indeed was recognised in *Anderton* v *Wish* (Note) (1980) 72 Cr App R 23, 25, where Roskill LJ giving the judgment of the court said:

"The Court of Appeal ... held ... they were guilty of theft because when the bottles were taken there was a dishonest appropriation. If that decision is right and, with respect, it seems to me plainly right …"

Furthermore in *Reg* v *Morris (David)* [1984] AC 320 Lord Roskill said, at p334: "… I understand all your Lordships to agree that *Anderton* v *Wish* ... was rightly decided for the reasons given."

Before moving to the next matter of difficulty I refer to the judgment of Lord Lane CJ in *Reg* v *Morris* itself where he said [1983] QB 587, 597:

"As far as *Kaur (Dip)* v *Chief Constable for Hampshire* [1981] 1 WLR 568 is concerned, a decision for which I was at least partly responsible, on the facts as found by the justices theft was plainly made out and our decision was wrong. There was an appropriation when the shoes were taken from the shelf, dishonesty was found as a fact by the justices, the property then belonged to another and the intent to deprive was obvious. In retrospect the real answer to *Kaur* was that what the appellant did was probably not rightly categorised as dishonest."

This leads directly to the next matter because, with regard to *Kaur (Dip)* v *Chief Constable for Hampshire,* Lord Roskill said, at p334: "I am disposed to agree with the learned Lord Chief Justice that it was wrongly decided."

In that case the defendant had selected a pair of shoes from a rack marked £6.99. One of the shoes bore a price tag to that effect and the other a £4.99 tag. There was in fact also a £4.99 rack. She took the shoes to the checkout point without concealing either label. The attendant asked for and was paid by the defendant the lower price. The justices held that the attendant had no authority to accept the lower price and that since the defendant knew that the lower price was incorrect the contract was void and there was an appropriation. On appeal to the Divisional Court it was held that the contract was not void but voidable; the property therefore passed to the defendant and she had not appropriated property belonging to another. In addition to agreeing that *Kaur* [1981] 1 WLR 578 was wrongly decided, Lord Roskill observed in *Reg* v *Morris (David)* [1984] AC 320, 334:

"Without going into further detail I respectfully suggest that it is on any view wrong to introduce into this branch of the criminal law questions whether particular contracts are void or voidable on the ground of mistake or fraud or whether any mistake is sufficiently fundamental to vitiate a contract. These difficult questions should so far as possible be confined to those fields of law to which they are immediately relevant and I do not regard them as relevant questions under the Theft Act 1968."

After anxious consideration I have reached the conclusion that whatever *Reg* v *Morris* did decide it cannot be regarded as having overruled the very plain decision in *Reg* v *Lawrence (Alan)* [1972] AC 626 that appropriation can occur even if the owner consents and that *Reg* v *Morris* itself makes it plain that it is no defence to say that the property passed under a voidable contract. I must, before reverting to the facts of the present case, also refer to two other cases – one before and one after the decision in *Reg* v *Morris* – namely, *Reg* v *Skipp* [1975] Crim LR 114 and *Reg* v *Fritschy* [1985] Crim LR 745. In *Reg* v *Skipp* the defendant, posing as a haulage contractor, had obtained instructions to collect three loads of goods from different places in London and deliver them to customers in Leicester. In accordance with the instructions he collected the goods but instead of delivering the goods as instructed he made off with them. It was held that, up to the point when all the goods were loaded and probably up to the point when the defendant diverted the goods from their proper destination, there was no assumption of rights and therefore no appropriation. That case can in my view only be reconciled with *Reg* v *Lawrence (Alan)* [1972] AC 626 on the basis that there was much more than mere consent of the owner. There was express authority, indeed instruction to collect the goods. It could not therefore be said that the defendant was assuming any rights. Whatever his secret intentions he was, until he diverted, exercising the owner's right on his instructions and on his behalf. *Reg* v *Fritschy* was a somewhat similar case. The report in Criminal Law Review is very short but I have obtained a transcript of the judgment. The defendant was convicted of theft of a number of Krugerrands. He was the agent of a Dutch company which dealt in such coins. One H purchased 70 Krugerrands from the Dutch company and arranged for the company to hold them until they could be transferred to Switzerland. Shortly thereafter for reasons which do not matter the Dutch company sold the coins in Holland on behalf of H and with the proceeds purchased on his behalf a like number of coins from Johnson Matthey in England. H then asked the defendant to collect the coins from Johnson Matthey and take them to Switzerland. The defendant did collect the coins as instructed and went with them to Switzerland but there made off with them. He had a dishonest intention throughout. He was convicted of theft but on appeal his conviction was quashed by the Court of Appeal. The ground of the decision is shortly stated in the judgment of the court which was delivered by Skinner J. He said:

"There was here no evidence of any act by the appellant within the jurisdiction which was not expressly authorised by Mr Hoedl. That , in the light of the decision of the House of Lords in *Reg* v *Morris* [1984] AC 320, is fatal to the charge of theft. In those circumstances we are compelled to the conclusion that the learned judge's direction was wrong, and that this appeal must be allowed."

Here, as in *Reg* v *Skipp* [1975] Crim LR 114, what the defendant did was expressly authorised, ie there was more than mere consent. On this basis the decision can be reconciled with both *Reg* v *Lawrence (Alan)* [1972] AC 626 and *Reg* v *Morris (David)* [1984] AC 320.

Returning now to the present case the insurers contention that there was no theft is based on consent and the fact that there was a clear section 15(1) offence, both of which are negatived as answers to appropriation by *Reg* v *Lawrence,* and the fact that the contract of sale between the plaintiff and the rogue was voidable only and not void which is not relevant according to *Reg* v *Morris.*

If, then, the insurers are deprived of their arguments to defeat the only element of the offence of theft which was in doubt once the "belonging to another" argument has been rejected, they cannot in my judgment succeed on the basis of Lord Roskill's statement in *Reg* v *Morris* that there must be an act by way of adverse interference with or usurpation of the owner's rights. If consent and the existence of a voidable contract under which property passes are irrelevant, there was in my judgment a plain interference with or usurpation of the plaintiff's rights. I am fully conscious of the fact that in so concluding I may be said not to be applying *Reg* v *Morris.* This may be so, but in the light of the difficulties inherent in the decision, the very clear decision in *Reg* v *Lawrence (Alan)* [1972] AC 626 and the equally clear statement in *Reg* v *Morris (David)* [1984] AC 320 that the question whether a contract is void or only voidable is irrelevant, I have been unable to reach any other conclusion. I would therefore dismiss the appeal.'

Note also the obiter statements of Bingham J.

'I do not find it easy to reconcile this ruling of Viscount Dilhorne which was as I understand central to the answer which the House gave to the certified question, with the reasoning of the House in *Reg* v *Morris (David)* [1984] AC 320. Since, however, the House in *Reg* v *Morris* considered that there had plainly been an appropriation in *Reg* v *Lawrence (Alan)* [1972] AC 626, this must (I think) have been because the Italian student, although he had permitted or allowed his money to be taken, had not in truth consented to the taxi driver taking anything in excess of the correct fare. This is not a wholly satisfactory reconciliation, since it might be said that a supermarket consents to customers taking goods from its shelves only when they honestly intend to pay and not otherwise. On the facts of the present case, however, it can be said, by analogy with *Reg* v *Lawrence,* that although the plaintiff permitted and allowed his property to be taken by the third party, he had not in truth consented to the third party becoming owner without giving a valid draft drawn by the building society for the price. On this basis I conclude that the plaintiff is able to show an appropriation sufficient to satisfy section 1(1) of the Theft Act 1968 when the third party accepted delivery of the articles. On the facts here, the plaintiff has no difficulty in showing dishonesty and an intention permanently to deprive on the part of the third party. It is, however, argued for the insurers that when the third party appropriated the ring and the watch they were not property belonging to another because ownership of the goods had already, before delivery, passed to the third party under the contract of sale. The courts have been enjoined so far as possible to eschew difficult questions of contract law relating to title to goods: see *Reg* v *Morris (David)* [1984] AC 320, 334c. But whether, in the ordinary case to which section 5 of the Theft Act 1968 does not apply, goods are to be regarded as belonging to another is a question to which the criminal law offers no answer and which can only be answered by reference to civil law principles. Applying these principles, I would without much doubt impute an intention to the plaintiff and the third party that property in the watch and the ring should pass to the third party upon delivery of the goods to him and not before. That would also, as I think, be the moment of appropriation. If, therefore, it were necessary for the plaintiff to show that the goods still belonged to him at the moment of appropriation I would doubt whether he could do so, appropriation and transfer of title being simultaneous. Happily for the plaintiff, the point was raised in *Reg* v *Lawrence (Alan)* [1972] AC 626 and decided in his favour. Viscount Dilhorne said, at p 632:

"The new offence of obtaining property by deception created by section 15(1) of the Theft Act also contains the words 'belonging to another'. 'A person who by any deception dishonestly obtains property belonging to another, with the intention of permanently depriving the other of it' commits that offence. 'Belonging to another' in section 1(1) and in section 15(1) in my view signifies no more than that, at the time of the appropriation or the obtaining, the property belonged to another, with the words 'belonging to another' having the extended meaning given by section 5."

Just as it is enough to satisfy section 15 that the goods belong to the victim up to the time of obtaining, so it is enough for the plaintiff that the watch and ring belonged to him up to the time of appropriation.'

Eddy v Niman (1981) 73 Cr App R 237 Divisional Court (Ormrod LJ and Webster J)

Unauthorised acts as appropriation

Facts

The defendant had entered a self-service store intending to steal some goods. He placed some items in the wire basket provided by the store, but subsequently changed his mind and left the store. When the defendant was subsequently charged with theft of the items, the case against the him was dismissed by the justices as he had only dealt with the goods in a manner authorised by the store. On appeal by the prosecutor:

Held

The appeal would be dismissed

Webster J:

'The question therefore which the justices had to decide was whether or not on the facts found there was an assumption by the defendant of the rights of the owner, and they decided that there was not.

On behalf of the prosecutor a number of contentions are made in support of the general submission that that decision was wrong which I can conveniently summarise, without injustice I hope to Miss Swindells [counsel for the prosecutor], in this way. First of all she argues that the assumption of the rights of an owner does not involve something inconsistent with the authority of the owner and that the rights of an owner involve possession and control so that, if a person assumes possession and control of an article, then that person is assuming the rights of the owner; and the fact that that assumption may be expressly or implicitly authorised by the owner is irrelevant.

As to the relevance or irrelevance of the authorisation, Miss Swindells relies upon the decision of the House of Lords in the case of *Lawrence* v *Metropolitan Police Commissioner* (1971) 55 Cr App R 471; [1972] AC 626 where their Lordships' House decided (and I need only a few words from the headnote in [1972] AC 626) that: "Section 1 (1)" of the 1968 Act "was not to be construed as though it contained the words 'without the consent of the owner' and accordingly it was not necessary for the prosecution to prove that the taking was without his consent." For my part I accept that the authority or consent of the owner is not determinant of the question whether there has been an appropriation, although in certain circumstances it may be relevant to it.

Miss Swindells referred us to a number of other authorities which I shall mention in a moment, perhaps on the face of it the most relevant being the case of *McPherson*, which was very shortly reported in [1973] Crim App R 191 and of which we have been provided with a transcript since argument began. That was a case where one of the appellants Edna McPherson had been convicted of, in short, shoplifting in circumstances in which she, having gone into a self-service store, had taken articles from a shelf and then put them not into the wire basket of the type provided by the store but into her shopping bag.

We had thought that we might find some assistance from the judgment of the Court of Appeal (Criminal Division) in that case, but in fact it deals with the point very shortly indeed. On the question whether there was an appropriation of those articles, Lord Widgery CJ, giving the judgment of the Court, dealt with it in these short terms: "We have no hesitation whatever in saying that it is such an appropriation, and indeed we content ourselves with a judgment of this brevity because we have been unable to accept or to find any argument to the contrary, to suggest that an appropriation is not effective in those simple circumstances."   Therefore they dismissed, inter alia, the appeal of the appellant McPherson.

In the case of *Skipp* [1975] Crim LR 114, which is shortly reported, Skipp had been convicted of a count which charged the theft of a number of boxes of fruit and vegetables. Posing as a genuine haulage contractor, he obtained instructions to collect two loads of fruit and one load of onions from three different places in London and deliver them to customers in Leicester. Having collected the goods, he made off with them. In argument before the Court of Appeal (Criminal Division) it was submitted that, as he had the intention to steal the goods from the outset, the count was bad for duplicity in that there were three separate appropriations. The Court of Appeal dismissing the appeal said (and I quote from the short summarised report): "An assumption of the rights of an owner over property did not necessarily take place at the same time as an intent permanently to deprive the owner of it. There might be many cases in which a person having formed the intent was lawfully in possession of the goods and could not be said to have assumed the rights of an owner because he had not done something inconsistent with those rights."

For my part, it seems to me that, consistently with that decision, the question that one needs to ask in any ordinary case such as this where the charge is shoplifting, which may indeed be the question to be asked in all cases of theft, is whether the person charged has done some overt act (after all, the appropriation is the actus reus involved in this offence) inconsistent with the true owner's rights.

If that test is applied to the present case, it seems to me that the justices were perfectly correct in deciding that, despite the defendant's intention to steal the goods when he put them into the basket, he had not at that stage assumed the rights of the owners of them since neither then nor at any stage did he do any overt act which was inconsistent with the owner's rights.

The facts of this case are to be distinguished from the facts of *McPherson* (supra) upon which Miss Swindells relied, because there it could rightly and properly be said that taking articles from the shelf and putting them into a shopping basket rather than into the basket provided by the store was an overt act inconsistent with the rights of the owner. It seems to me that the reasons I have given for deciding as I do for my part that the justices were correct in acquitting the defendant, upon the basis that there had been no appropriation of the articles in question, are entirely consistent with the other cases to which we were referred but which I feel it unnecessary to mention more fully, namely, *Meech, Parslow and Jolliffe* (1973) 58 Cr App R 74; [1974] 1 QB 549 and *Monaghan* [1979] Crim LR 673. Nor for my part do I find it necessary to deal with the two recent decisions on the switching of price tags, namely *Anderton* v *Wish* (1981) 72 Cr App R 23 and *Oxford* v *Peers* (1981) 72 Cr App R 19. For those reasons I would dismiss this appeal.'

Ormrod LJ:

'It is important, I think, to bear in mind that the essential finding of fact in this case and in the case of *McPherson* [1973] Crim LR 191 was that there was an intent to steal which was proved by admission in both cases. It is only where the intent to steal or dishonest intent is plainly established that any of these problems arise.

The intent having been established or admitted, the question then is: Can the prosecution establish appropriation? For this purpose section 3 (1) provides the definition: "Any assumption by a person of the rights of an owner amounts to an appropriation, and this includes, where he has come by the property (innocently or not) without stealing it, any later assumption of a right to it by keeping or dealing with it as owner."

The question that the justices had to ask themselves, and asked themselves, was: did the defendant to this appeal assume the rights of the owner? To that I think there can be only one possible answer: he did not. All he did was to act like any other customer in a supermarket. He took the goods off the shelves or out of the cabinets or wherever it was, put them into the wire basket provided by the shop and later, before he had done anything else about the goods, changed his mind about stealing or attempting to steal them.

I find it most difficult to see how in those circumstances it can be said that he assumed in any way at all, technically or otherwise, the rights of the owner, and that is the answer to this case, as the magistrates held.

It is unfortunate that the judgment in *McPherson* (supra) was not more detailed because one has to assume, I think, that it was the fact of the dishonest intention coupled with the putting of the bottles into Mrs McPherson's own shopping basket which the Court in that case held to be an appropriation. I, for my part, can see quite clearly that the combination of an intention to steal coupled with the putting of the bottles into the lady's own shopping basket could amount to evidence of appropriation, but that essential fact is missing in this case.'

R v Fritschy [1985] Crim LR 745 Court of Appeal (Criminal Division) (Lord Lane CJ, Skinner and Tucker JJ)

Overt unauthorised act needed for appropriation

Facts

'The appellant was convicted of theft of a number of Krugerrands. He was a selling agent for a Dutch company dealing in such coins. Mr H bought 70 coins for around $49,000 which were to be held in Holland until they could be transferred to a Swiss safe deposit box. Soon afterwards the appellant advised Mr H to remove the coins from the Dutch company, claiming doubts about its financial standing. Eventually these Krugerrands were sold and more were bought in England with the proceeds of sale. Mr H asked the appellant to collect them from the bullion dealers and take them to Switzerland. The appellant collected them. Mr H called in the police when he was not contacted again. The prosecution contended that the appellant had appropriated the coins, within s1 of the Theft Act, when he collected the coins as he had intended at that time to steal them. The appellant gave evidence that he had merely followed Mr H's instructions. He admitted lying to the police; he had claimed that the coins were delivered to him in Switzerland. The trial judge directed that if at the time he collected the Krugerrands from the bullion dealer, the appellant had already formed a dishonest intention of keeping and dealing with them as if he were the owner, regardless of Mr H's rights, he was guilty of theft. The appellant appealed against conviction. Counsel submitted that the direction ran counter to the decision of the House of Lords in *Morris* (1983) 77 Cr App R 309. If a person is in possession of goods with the owner's consent, a secret intention to make away with them dishonestly does not amount to an appropriation. In the present case the appellant should have been charged with an offence under section 15(1) of the 1968 Act. Further on the evidence, the first time the appellant acted outside the authority given by Mr H was in Switzerland. To constitute appropriation there must be some physically observable evidence of adverse interference with, or usurpation of, some right of the owner. There was no such evidence before the appellant left this country and there was no jurisdiction in the English court.

Held

Allowing the appeal and quashing the conviction, there was no evidence of any act by the appellant within the jurisdiction which was not expressly authorised by Mr H. That was fatal to the charge of theft, in the light of *Morris* (supra) which requires an act by way of adverse interference with or usurpation of the owner's rights.

Lawrence v *Metropolitan Police Commissioner* (1971) 55 Cr App R 471 and *Eddy* v *Niman* (1981) 73 Cr App R 237 were also considered.

[*Reported by Lynne Knapman, Barrister.*]

R v Gomez (1991) 93 Cr App R 156 Court of Appeal (Criminal Division) (Lord Lane CJ, Hutchinson and Mantell JJ)

Theft - appropriation - *Lawrence* or *Morris*?

Facts

The appellant was an assistant in a shop specialising in consumer electronics. A man named Ballay, who had come into possession of two stolen building society cheques, approached him asking if he could supply electrical goods in return for the cheques. The appellant was aware that the cheques were stolen and agreed to help. The appellant consulted his manager, a Mr Gilberd, to check whether or not the store would accept such cheques (he did not of course inform Mr Gilberd that they were stolen). Gilberd instructed the appellant to check with the bank, and the appellant later informed him that the cheques were to be treated as if they was cash. Over a period of a few days the appellant provided Ballay with electrical goods to the value of £16,000. The cheques were banked and in due course dishonoured. During the course of his trial the appellant made a submission that he should not be charged with theft as there had been no appropriation of the goods. This submission was based on the proposition that any such appropriation had to be without the consent of the owner, and that the owner in this case, through its agent, had expressly consented to the delivery of the goods. The trial judge rejected this submission, and the appellant changed his plea to guilty. He appealed on the basis that the trial judge should have followed the House of Lords' decision in *R v Morris* (1983) 77 Cr App R 164.

Held

The appeal would be allowed.

Lord Lane CJ:

Lord Lane reviewed the key authorities of *Lawrence* v *MPC* [1972] AC 626, and *R v Morris* [1983] 3 WLR 697, and adverted to the widely held view that the decisions were irreconcilable to the extent that *Lawrence* did not require an unauthorised act for appropriation to be made out, but *Morris* did. He stated:

'Suffice it to say that if there is a difference between the two decisions, that was not the view taken by their Lordships in *Morris*, and that is the decision which we must follow.

It is conceded that the appellant, in carrying out his work as assistant manager for the owners, was entitled to prepare goods for collection by any customer; and if he had done that and no more, the fact that he might have formed some secret dishonest intention whilst so doing would not render him liable to conviction for theft, any more than is the shopper in the supermarket who takes goods from the shelf with a dishonest intent but does not pass the check-out point. However, contend the prosecution, the appellant has done more than that; he has allowed his employer's property to pass into the hands of a third party who, as he well knew, had no intention of paying for it, and so, it is said, is in no better position than the shopper who has dishonestly passed the check-out point without paying for the goods he has taken and has thus dishonestly appropriated them. It has been said before, and we make no apology for repeating the observation, that this is clearly a situation where an alternative charge should have lain under s15 of the Theft Act to which the appellant would have had no answer. That, however, does not answer the question which this case poses.

The way the case was presented by the prosecution was that Ballay, in a joint enterprise and acting in concert with the appellant, had stolen the electrical goods from the owners. That being the case, it seems to us that the fact that the appellant was a servant makes no difference. In order to establish the case against the appellant, it had to be proved that Ballay had appropriated goods, the property of another, in the sense of doing some act by way of "adverse interference with or usurpation" of the rights of the owner and that the appellant had actively assisted him so to do. What in fact happened was that the owner was induced by deceit to agree to the goods being transferred to Ballay. If that is the case, and if in these circumstances the appellant is guilty of theft, it must follow that anyone who obtains goods in return for a cheque which he knows will be dishonoured on presentation, or indeed by way of any other similar pretence, would be guilty of theft. That does not seem to be the law, *Morris* decides that when a person by dishonest deception induces the owner to transfer his entire proprietary interests that is not theft. There is no appropriation at the moment when he takes possession of the goods because he was entitled to do so under the terms of the contract of sale, a contract which is, it is true, voidable, but has not been avoided at the time the goods are handed over.'

His Lordship then turned his attention to the Court of Appeal's decision in *Dobson* [1989] 3 WLR 1066. Having referred to extracts from the judgments of both Parker LJ and Bingham LJ, he continued:

'Both Lords Justices imputed an intention to the plaintiff and the third party that property in the watch and ring should pass upon delivery of the articles and not before, and that that would be the moment of appropriation. We remark in passing that at least so far as the criminal law is concerned we find it difficult to draw a line between express authority and consent. Guilt or innocence should not depend upon so fine a distinction, if indeed the distinction be shown to exist. One hesitates to suggest that different legal considerations might apply according to whether the proceedings are taking place in the civil rather than the criminal courts, and we do not do so. However, one notes the passage in Lord Roskill's speech in *R* v *Morris* at p318 and p334 where he says this:

"… I respectfully suggest that it is on any view wrong to introduce into this branch of the criminal law questions whether particular contracts are void or voidable on the ground of mistake or fraud or whether any mistake is sufficiently fundamental to vitiate a contract. These difficult questions should so far as possible be confined to those fields of law to which they are immediately relevant and I do not regard them as relevant questions under the Theft Act 1968."

We do not consider that the judgment in *Dobson* requires or allows us to disregard what we have earlier in this judgment sought to extract as the ratio of the decision in *R* v *Morris*. We therefore conclude that there was a *de facto*, albeit voidable contract, between the owners and Ballay; that it was by virtue of that contract that Ballay took possession of the goods; that accordingly the transfer of the goods to him was with the consent and express authority of the owner and that accordingly there was no lack of authorisation and no appropriation. In the absence of any charge under s15 of the Theft Act 1968, this appeal must therefore be allowed and the conviction quashed.'

R v Governor of Pentonville Prison, ex parte Osman (1990) 90 Cr App R 281 Divisional Court (Lloyd LJ, and French J)

Appropriation - where acts constituting appropriation take place

Facts

The applicant sought habeus corpus. He was alleged to have dishonestly dispatched a telex instructing a New York bank to transfer funds from the bank account belonging to the company of which he was the chairman [BMFL], to the bank account of another unconnected company [one of the 'Carrian' companies], from whom he was to receive corrupt payments. One of the issues before the court was that of where the alleged theft had occurred.

Held

The act of sending the telex amounted to appropriation, therefore the offence was committed in the country from which it was transmitted.

Lloyd LJ:

'Mr Ross-Munro [for the applicant] concedes that there is jurisdiction to try charge 31, which relates to the theft of Hong Kong dollars. But he submits that the United States dollar thefts all took place in the United States, since that is where BMFL's property was appropriated. Mr Nicholls, on the other hand, submits that the property was appropriated in Hong Kong. In considering Mr Ross-Munro's argument, it is convenient to take Method A, since it was the method most frequently adopted, as well as the most straightforward. It will be remembered that under Method A BMFL would send a telex to its correspondent bank in New York, instructing it to pay the amount of the United States dollar loan to the payees' correspondent bank in the United States, for the account of one of the Carrian companies. It was common ground that the only property of BMFL capable of being stolen was the chose in action represented by the debt, if any, due to BMFL from its correspondent bank in the United States, or the contractual right, if any, to overdraw on BMFL's account. Mr Ross-Munro argued that the theft of the chose in action took place in the United States when BMFL's account was debited, and not before. That was the moment of appropriation. The dealing ticket, confirmation slip and telex were the means whereby the theft was carried out. The theft was not completed until the account was debited. Mr Nicholls argued to the contrary, that there was an appropriation when the telex instruction was sent, if not before, and that that appropriation took place in Hong Kong. In support of his argument Mr Ross-Munro referred us to the decision of the Court of Appeal Criminal Division in *Tomsett* [1985] Crim LR 369, a decision to which, as it happens, both members of the present Court were party. In that case the appellant was a telex operator employed by Credit Suisse in London. He was convicted of conspiracy to steal from the bank by diverting 7 million dollars from an account in New York to an account in Geneva. Fortunately, the dishonest plan was discovered in time. Counsel for the appellant argued that the contemplated theft would have taken place in New York or Geneva. Accordingly, the theft would not have been indictable here. We alerted the prosecution to a possible argument that the appellant appropriated the chose in action in New York, when he sent the telex from London, and that the appropriation therefore took place in England. But counsel for the prosecution declined to support the conviction on that ground. His only argument was that the theft must have taken place in England, because it was Credit Suisse's money. He dealt with that argument as follows:

"Mr Hart-Leverton's argument to the contrary was that the contemplated theft would have been a crime committed here. Alternatively, he argued that the underlying object of the conspiracy was to inflict pecuniary loss on Credit Suisse in London. On one or other or both of those grounds he submitted that the conspiracy was indictable in England. Mr Hart-Leverton did not cite any authority in support of his first argument. His sole submission was that the subject manner of the theft was, as he put it, Credit Suisse's money. We cannot accept that submission. Prima facie a theft takes place where the property is appropriated; prima facie appropriation takes place where the property is situated. The subject matter of the theft in the present case was either a debt or alternatively cash over the counter. If it was a debt then the debt was unquestionably situated in New York. If it was cash over the counter, the cash was unquestionably situated in Geneva.

It might perhaps have been argued that, though the debt was situated in New York, nevertheless, the appropriation took place in England, since this was where the appropriating telex was dispatched. But no such argument was advanced – in the absence of any argument for the Crown other than the one we have mentioned, we feel bound to accept Mr Stevens' submission that the contemplated theft would have taken place either in New York or Geneva, and would not therefore have been indictable here."

Mr Ross-Munro argued that *Tomsett* (supra) is binding on us, and that we are therefore bound to hold that the sending of the telex from Hong Kong was not an appropriation. We do not, he said, disregard the decision as per incuriam merely because the right point had not been argued. We cannot accept that argument. It would be carrying the doctrine of stare decisis beyond all reason. We could not uphold the conviction in *Tomsett* on a point which the prosecution declined to argue. On the other hand it is quite obvious, even without reading between the lines, that we were leaving the present point open for another day. We said that a theft prima facie takes place where the property is appropriated, and appropriation prima facie takes place where the property is situated. The emphasis is on prima facie. There was no acceptable argument advanced by the Crown to displace the prima facie position. The law of England cannot be made or unmade by the willingness of counsel to argue a point. The ratio of *Tomsett* stands. It was not per incuriam. But the present point was left undecided.

Mr Ross-Munro also relied on *Kohn* (1979) 69 Cr App R 395. One of the arguments in that case was that the appellant could not be liable for theft when the customer's account was overdrawn, but within the overdraft limits. The Court rejected that argument. Geoffrey Lane LJ said at p. 407:

"If the account is in credit, as we have seen, there is an obligation to honour the cheque. If the account is within the agreed limits of the overdraft facilities, there is an obligation to meet the cheque. In either case it is an obligation which can only be enforced by action. For purposes of this case it seems to us that that sufficiently constitutes a debt within the meaning of the word as explained by Lord Reid in *DPP* v *Turner* (1973) 57 Cr App R 932, 936, [1974] AC 357, 365. It is a right of property which can properly be described as a thing in action and therefore potentially a subject of theft under the provisions of the 1968 Act. The cheque is the means by which the theft of this property is achieved. The completion of the theft does not take place until the transaction has gone through to completion."

Mr Ross-Munro relied on the last two sentences of that passage. He submits that it is authority for the proposition that there can be no appropriation until the amount of the cheque has been debited to the account in question. We do not so read the passage. But in any event the observation was obiter. This appears from the subsequent case of *Navvabi* (1986) 83 Cr App R 271, [1986] 1 WLR 1311. In that case the appellant issued a cheque supported by a cheque guarantee card. The account was overdrawn, and that appellant had no overdraft facility. It was held that he could not be held liable for theft. After quoting the passage from *Kohn* (supra), already cited, Lord Lane CJ said at p275 and p1316 respectively:

"The last sentence of this passage did not affect the result in *Kohn* and was to that extent obiter. It suggests (and has been taken by Professor Griew in his article 'Stealing and Obtaining Bank Credits' [1986] Crim LR 362 to mean) that theft occurs at the time when the bank transfers the funds."

So it was clear that Lord Lane CJ himself regarded the sentence on which Mr Ross-Munro relies as obiter.

In *Chan Man-sin* v *A-G of Hong Kong* (1988) 86 Cr App R 303, [1988] 1 All ER 1 the appellant was convicted of stealing by drawing forged cheques on a company's bank account. It was argued that he could not be liable for theft, since the bank would be bound to reimburse the company's account when the forgeries came to light. The Privy Council rejected that argument. Lord Oliver said at p306 and p4 respectively:

"The owner of the chose in action consisting of a credit with his bank or a contractual right to draw on an account has, clearly, the right as owner to draw by means of a properly completed negotiable instrument or order to pay and it is, in their Lordships' view, beyond argument that one who draws, presents and negotiates a cheque on a particular bank account is assuming the rights of the owner of the credit in the account or (as the case may be) of the pre-negotiated right to draw on the account up to the agreed figure. Ownership, of course, consists of a bundle of rights and it may well be that there are other rights which an owner could exert over the chose in action in question which are not trespassed on by the particular dealing which the thief chooses to assume. In *R* v *Morris* (1983) 77 Cr App R 309, [1984] AC 320, however, the House of Lords decisively rejected a submission that it was necessary, in order to constitute an appropriation as defined by section 3(1) of the 1968 Act, to demonstrate an assumption by the accused of all the rights of an owner. Their Lordships are, accordingly, entirely satisfied that the transactions initiated and carried through by the appellant constituted an assumption of the rights of the owner and, consequently, an appropriation. It is unnecessary, for present purposes, to determine whether that occurred on presentation of the forged cheques or when the transactions were completed by the making of consequential entries in the bank accounts of the companies and the appellant or his business respectively. It is, in their Lordships' view, entirely immaterial that the end result of the transaction may be a legal nullity for it is not possible to read into section (4)(i) of the ordinance any requirement that the assumption of rights there envisaged should have a legally efficacious result."

Mr Ross-Munro relied on the reference to the transaction being "carried through" to completion. But it is clear from the passage as a whole that Lord Oliver was leaving open the question whether the presentation of the cheque was itself an appropriation. In the light of *Navvabi* (supra) and *Chan Man-sin* (supra) it is unnecessary to mention two earlier unreported cases to which we were referred, save to say that in *Doole* [1985] Crim LR 450, it does not appear to have been argued that the appellant's request to transfer the sum standing to the credit of the deposit account in question was an appropriation; and in *Wille* (1988) 86 Cr App R 296 the summing up approved by the Court of Appeal certainly suggests that the drawing and issuing of the cheque without authority would itself be an appropriation. We will not read the whole of the relevant passage of the summing up, but it concludes:

"So that in this particular case if you are sure in relation to any of the cheques in a count in the indictment, if you are sure that the defendant had no authority to draw that cheque, why then in drawing the cheque and issuing it he appropriated the debt which the bank owed to Ginarco because he assumed in relation to it the rights of an owner by taking it upon himself to direct the bank in effect to pay out money, thus lessening the debt, and it matters not that the bank were acting contrary to the mandate, that is wholly irrelevant for this purpose, it is the drawing and the issuing of the cheque without authority which constitutes the appropriation."

The Court of Appeal said that it was not possible to improve upon the terms in which the judge had summed up. In *Chan Man-sin* v *A-G for Hong Kong* (1988) 86 Cr App R 303, 307, [1988] 1 All ER 1, 4 Lord Oliver said that if *Wille* (supra) had been reported at the time when the appellant sought special leave to appeal, the probability is that leave would have been refused.

So we would hold, contrary to Mr Ross-Munro's argument, that the question whether the sending of the telex was an appropriation is fully open on the authorities. What should our answer be? We find the views expressed by Professor Smith in *Law of Theft*, 5th ed 1984) p106 and his comments on *Tomsett* [1985] Crim LR 369, 370, 371 convincing.

In R v *Morris* (1983) 77 Cr App R 309, [1984] AC 320 the House of Lords made it clear that it is not necessary for an appropriation that the defendant assume all rights of an owner. It is enough that he should assume any of the owner's rights: see per Lord Roskill at p316 and p331 and the passage cited above from *Chan Man-sin* v *A-G for Hong Kong*. If so, then one of the plainest rights possessed by the owner of the chose in action in the present case must surely have been the right to draw on the account in question. Mr Ross-Munro argues that the right to draw on an account in credit, or within an agreed overdraft limit, is not a right but a liberty or a power. He refers us in that connection to Professor Glanville Williams' *Textbook of Criminal Law* (2nd ed 1983) para 33.12 at p763. We find that hard to understand. So far as the customer is concerned, he has a right as against the bank to have his cheques met. It is that right which the defendant assumes by presenting a cheque, or by sending a telex instruction without authority. The act of sending the telex is therefore the act of theft itself, and not a mere attempt. It is the last act which the defendant has to perform and not a preparatory act. It would matter not if the account were never in fact debited. We can find no way of excluding the sending of the telex in such circumstances from the definition of appropriation contained in section 3(1) of the Act.

Professor Griew suggests that this view may raise practical problems, on the ground that it would be necessary in every case for the prosecution to prove the state of the account at the moment of appropriation, that is to say, when the telex is sent, as distinct from the moment when the account is debited. But we do not understand Professor Griew to doubt the correctness of the view in principle.

In any event, proof of the state of the account, either by direct evidence or by proper inference, will normally be available.

Mr Ross-Munro argued that until the account is debited there is no "adverse interference" with any right of the owner, and therefore, on the authority of *R* v *Morris (supra)* no appropriation. The theft of a chose in action is analogous to the theft of a chattel by destruction. See Professor Griew, *The Theft Acts 1968 and 1978* (3rd ed, 1978) at paragraph 2-13, a passage approved by the Court of Appeal in *Kohn* (1979) 69 Cr App R 395, 405.

Mr Nicholls replies that Lord Roskill's dictum in *R* v *Morris* (1983) 77 Cr App R 309, [1984] AC 320, 332 was obiter and inconsistent with the previous decision of the House of Lords in *Lawrence* v *Metropolitan Police Commissioner* (1971) 55 Cr App R 471, [1972] AC 626: obiter because the specific act of appropriation referred to in the certified question was the switching of price labels on stolen goods, not the removal of the goods from the shelf; inconsistent with *Lawrence* because that case established that absence of consent was not an essential element in the crime of theft.

It is unnecessary for us to consider the relationship between these two cases, on which, as Professor Griew sardonically observes, in The Theft Acts 1968 and 1978 (5th ed 1986) para 2-70, no two commentators (nor, we would add, any two judges) take the same view. For we regard ourselves as bound, or as good as bound, by the meaning attributed to the word "appropriation" by the unanimous decision of the House of Lords in *R* v *Morris* (supra). Applying that meaning to the facts of the instant case, we would hold that a defendant "usurp the customer's rights when he, without the customer's authority, dishonestly issues the cheque drawn on the customer's account." If "adverse interference" adds anything to usurpation, then he also thereby adversely interferes with the customer's rights. The theft is complete in law, even though it may be said that it is not complete in fact until the account is debited.

Finally, Mr Ross-Munro argued that even if the sending of the telex was the appropriation, the appropriation takes place where the telex is received, not where it is sent. He relied on the analogy of acceptance of a contractual offer by telex. It is sufficient to say that we can see no real analogy. If we are right that the act of sending the telex was the act of appropriation, then the place where that act was performed, namely, the place where the telex was despatched is the place where the chose in action was appropriated. We do not rule out the possibility that the place where the telex is received may also be regarded as the place of appropriation, if our courts were ever to adopt the view that a crime may have a dual location. But in the meantime, we would hold that Hong Kong was the place of appropriation under Method A.'

R v Hale (1978) Cr App R 415

See chapter 18.

Kaur v Chief Constable of Hampshire (1981) 72 Cr App R 359 Divisional Court (Lord Lane CJ and Lloyd J)

Selection of wrongly priced goods - whether appropriation

Facts

As stated by Lord Lane CJ:

'On September 1, 1979, the defendant went to British Home Stores at Southampton. Amongst other goods displayed, there were two racks of shoes, one alongside the other. One of the racks contained shoes which were said to be priced at £6.99 and the other, adjacent rack contained shoes marked at £4.99. The defendant took a pair of shoes from the £6.99 rack and she noticed that the pair were not identically marked; one of the shoes was marked £6.99 and the other was marked £4.99. The correct price in fact of the shoes she had selected was £6.99 and the justices found as a fact that the defendant realised this. She did not, as is regrettably sometimes done, interfere in any way with the price labels on the shoes. She took the pair of shoes to the check-out. She placed them on the desk in front of the cashier. She made no attempt to conceal either of the price labels, but she hoped that the cashier would select the wrong label and would charge her £4.99 instead of £6.99. She was going to buy the shoes whichever price was demanded. She was lucky. She must have thought so, at any rate, because the cashier rang up £4.99. That sum was handed over by the defendant to the cashier who put it in the till and, all that having happened, the shoes were then placed in a bag. They were handed to the defendant who left to go home.

The justices found as a fact "The defendant believed that it would be wrong to take the shoes out of the shop in these circumstances, but nevertheless did so, and was accosted by a store detective." These proceedings were then launched. It seems, from what we have been told, that initially the suspicion was that this lady had in fact switched the labels on the shoes, but that was not the case.

The justices came to the conclusion that the cashier had no authority to accept, on behalf of the retailer, an offer by the defendant to buy the shoes for £4.99, and, since the defendant knew that this was not the correct price, the apparent contract made at the cash point was void. Secondly, they were of the opinion that the transaction at the cash point did not convey ownership to the defendant, so that on leaving the shop she appropriated the property belonging to British Home Stores Ltd. Finally, they concluded, it was right to describe as dishonest the state of mind with which the defendant appropriated the shoes. Accordingly the justices convicted the defendant on the charge and adjudged that she be fined £25.'

On appeal by the defendant, the justices stated the case for consideration by the Divisional Court.

Held

The appeal would be allowed.

Lord Lane CJ:

'There is ample authority for the proposition that, so far as supermarkets, at any rate, are concerned, and in so far as an ordinary transaction in a supermarket is concerned, the intention of the parties, under section 18 of the Sale of Goods Act 1979, is that the ownership of the goods should pass on payment by the customer of the price to the cashier. It also seems to accord with good sense, and if any authority is needed for that, it is to be found in *Lacis* v *Cashmarts* [1969] 2 QB 400.

Prima facie, then, when the defendant picked up the shoes to take them home, she was already the owner of the shoes. They did not then belong to somebody else, and she was not intending to deprive the owner of them.

But the prosecutor contends that the apparent contract between the shop and the defendant was no contract at all, was void, and that therefore, despite the payment made by the defendant, the ownership of the shoes never passed to the defendant, and the offence was accordingly made out. Mr Mylne puts it with very great simplicity: she never paid the price, he says, and so there was never any contract at all. He went so far as to suggest that if this lady had been given 10p too much by way of change and realised that she had been given 10p too much by way of change and had walked out of the shop with the shoes, in those circumstances she would likewise have been guilty of theft of the shoes.

The first thing to note, as indeed the justices did, is that this was not a case where there was any deception at all perpetrated by the defendant. She had not switched the price labels, as happened in *Anderton* v *Wish* [1980] Crim LR 319, in which it was held that the property was appropriated when the price tickets were changed. There is no need to comment on that decision, although it has been the subject of adverse criticism.

The prosecution, before the justices, as they did here, relied upon the decision in *Hartog* v *Colin and Shields* [1939] 3 All ER 566. In that case there had been extensive negotiations between the parties, both oral and in writing, about the sale by the defendants to the plaintiffs of hare-skins. All those negotiations had been based on a price of so many pence per piece. The final offer by the defendants to sell was mistakenly quoted in so many pence per pound. Skins worth $10^3/4$d. each were on this basis being offered at $3^3/4$d. On discovering their obvious mistake, the defendants refused to deliver the skins and the plaintiffs claimed damages. The report of the extempore judgment of Singleton J is not altogether clear, but the facts are so far divorced from those on the present case that they provide little assistance. We were also referred to *Pilgram* v *Rice-Smith* [1977] 1 WLR 671. That was a case where the shop assistant and the customer agreed together to defraud the shop-owners, and likewise does not provide any guidance.

The justices based their conclusion primarily on the fact that the cashier had no authority to accept on behalf of the retailer an offer by the defendant to buy the shoes for £4.99. In my judgment they were in error. The cashier had the authority to charge the price which was marked on the ticket on the goods. The fact that there were two different prices marked and that she chose the lower one does not mean that she was acting without authority. No false representation was made by the defendant. This is not one of those cases where the true offence was really obtaining by deception under section 15, and where the prosecution should, accordingly, have alleged that offence, and have resisted the temptation to charge theft. This was either theft or nothing.

It seems to me that the court should not be astute to find that a theft has taken place where it would be straining the language so to hold, or where the ordinary person would not regard the defendant's acts, though possibly morally reprehensible, as theft. In essence here, as I have already said, the problem is, whether the ownership of the shoes passed to the defendant, or whether the apparent contract was void by reason of mistake. Where questions of mistake are involved there will always be great difficulty in deciding where the line is to be drawn and what renders a contract void and what renders a contract merely voidable.

The mistake here was the cashier's, induced by the wrong marking on the goods as to the proper price of these goods. It was not to the nature of the goods or the identity of the buyer. Speaking for myself, I find it very difficult to see how this could be described as the sort of mistake which was so fundamental as to destroy the validity of the contract. It was in essence, as Lloyd J pointed out in argument, very little, if at all, different from a mistake as to quality. A mistake as to quality has never been held sufficiently fundamental so as to avoid a contract. The cashier was in effect thinking that these were £4.99 quality shoes, when in fact they were £6.99 quality shoes. Consequently in my judgment the prosecution failed to prove that this alleged contract was void. If it was merely voidable it had certainly not been avoided when the time came for the defendant to pick up the shoes and go.

Happily in this case we are not concerned with the difficulties raised by the decision in *R* v *Lawrence (Alan)* [1972] AC 626, because here the ownership of the goods had passed on payment, and the appropriation was at a later stage, when the shoes were put in the bag and carried away by the defendant. Nor is it necessary to discuss the vexed question of whether the true owner, albeit in a voidable contract, can properly be said to "appropriate" his own property or to "assume the rights of an owner" over it when he takes possession of it. At first sight those words would appear to imply some action which was adverse to the interests of another. Nor do I pause to consider whether the justices' finding of dishonesty on the part of the defendant can be justified; whether in other words this is the sort of dishonesty which is envisaged by the Theft Act. I should also add, for the sake of completeness, that section 5(4) of the Theft Act has no application here, because the defendant was not under an obligation to make restitution of the shoes at the material time. For these various reasons I would allow this appeal and would answer the justices' question, namely whether upon the facts found by them they were right in law to conclude as they did, in the negative.'

Commentary

Note the following obiter statement from Lord Lane CJ, in *R* v *Morris* (1983) 77 Cr App R 164 at 171:

'As far as *Kaur* (supra) is concerned, a decision for which I was at least partly responsible, on the facts as found by the justices theft was plainly made out and our decision was wrong. There was an appropriation when the shoes were taken from the shelf, dishonesty was found as a fact by the justices, the property then belonged to another and the intent to deprive was obvious. In retrospect the real answer to *Kaur* (supra) was that what the appellant did was probably not rightly categorised as dishonest.[M.T.M.]'

Lawrence v Metropolitan Police Commissioner [1972] AC 626 House of Lords (Viscount Dilhorne, Lords Donovan, Pearson, Diplock and Cross)

Appropriation - whether owner's lack of consent a vital ingredient

Facts

As stated by Viscount Dilhorne:

'On September 1, 1969, a Mr Occhi, an Italian who spoke little English, arrived at Victoria Station on his first visit to this country. He went up to a taxi-driver, the appellant, and showed him a piece of paper on which an address in Ladbroke Grove was written. The appellant said that it was very far and very expensive. Mr Occhi got into the taxi, took one pound out of his wallet and gave it to the appellant who then, the wallet being still open, took a further six pounds out of it. He then drove Mr Occhi to Ladbroke Grove. The correct lawful fare for the journey was in the region of 10s 6d.

The appellant was charged with and convicted of the theft of the six pounds. In cross-examination, Mr Occhi, when asked whether he had consented to the money being taken, said that he had "permitted." He gave evidence through an interpreter and it does not appear that he was asked to explain what he meant by the use of that word. He had not objected when the six pounds were taken. He had not asked for the return of any of it. It may well be that when he used the word "permitted," he meant no more than that he had allowed the money to be taken. It certainly was not established at the trial that he had agreed to pay to the appellant a sum far in excess of the legal fare for the journey and so had consented to the acquisition by the appellant of the six pounds. The main contention of the appellant in this House and in the Court of Appeal was that Mr Occhi had consented to the taking of the six pounds and that, consequently, his conviction could not stand.'

The two points of law certified for consideration by the House of Lords were:

'(1) whether Section 1(1) of the Theft Act 1968 is to be construed as though it contained the words "without the consent of the owner" or words to that effect;

(2) whether the provisions of Section 15(1) and of Section 1(1) of the Theft Act 1968, are mutually exclusive in the sense that if the facts proved would justify a conviction under Section 15(1) there cannot lawfully be a conviction under Section 1(1) on those facts.'

Held

Both certified questions would be answered in the negative, and the appeal dismissed.

Viscount Dilhorne:

[In considering the first certified question]

'I see no ground for concluding that the omission of the words "without the consent of the owner" was inadvertent and not deliberate, and to read the subsection as if they were included is, in my opinion, wholly unwarranted. Parliament by the omission of these words has relieved the prosecution of the burden of establishing that the taking was without the owner's consent.'

[As regards the second certified question]

'There is nothing in the Act to suggest that they should be regarded as mutually exclusive and it is by no means uncommon for conduct on the part of the accused to render him liable to conviction for more than one offence. Not infrequently there is some overlapping of offences. In some cases the facts may justify a charge under Section 1(1) and also a charge under Section 15(1). On the other hand, there are cases which only come within Section 1(1) and some which are only within Section 15(1). If in this case the appellant had been charged under Section 15(1) he would, I expect, have contended that there was no deception, that he simply appropriated the money and that he ought to have been charged under Section 1(1). In my view he was rightly charged under that section.'

Commentary

See further *R* v *Morris*, below.

R v McPherson [1973] Crim LR 191 Court of Appeal (Criminal Division) (Lord Widgery CJ, Megaw LJ and Talbot J)

Unauthorised acts as appropriation

Facts

'M, C and S were convicted of theft. C and S distracted the attention of the manager of a supermarket and M took two bottles of whisky from a display stand and put them in her shopping bag. They were then apprehended. They appealed on the ground that taking the bottles at the display stand could not amount to an appropriation within section 1 of the Theft Act 1968 until the bottles had been taken past the point for payment.

Held

Dismissing the appeal, there being an intention to steal when the bottles were taken there was an appropriation.'

R v Meech (1973) 58 Cr App R 74 Court of Appeal (Criminal Division) (Roskill LJ, Thompson and Stocker JJ)

Nature of appropriation - whether cheque proceeds property belonging to another

Facts

See chapter 15.

Held

Roskill LJ:

[The following extract deals with the issue of appropriation]

'Secondly, it was argued for Parslow and Jolliffe that there was a misdirection in relation to appropriation. The judge said:

"As I direct you in law, the time of the appropriation was the time of the fake robbery. Up to that moment, although Meech had drawn the money from the bank, it was still open to him to honour the agreement which he had made with McCord and to pay it over, in due course, to McCord; but once the fake robbery had taken place, that was no longer possible."

It was argued that Meech alone had dishonestly misappropriated the proceeds of the cheque when he drew the money from the bank and that thereafter Parslow and Jolliffe were not guilty of dishonest misappropriation since Meech had already dishonestly misappropriated that money once and for all. It was said that Parslow and Jolliffe were thereafter only liable to be convicted, if at all, of dishonest handling, an offence with which neither was charged.

We think that the learned judge's direction when he said that the time of the appropriation was the time of the fake robbery was right. A dishonest intention had been formed before the money was withdrawn but the misappropriation only took place when the three men divided up the money at the scene of the fake robbery. It was then that the performance of the obligation by Meech finally became impossible by the dishonest act of these three men acting in concert together. The convictions must all be affirmed and the appeals dismissed. Meech's application for leave to appeal against sentence is formally refused.'

R v Morris; Anderton v Burnside (Consolidated Appeals) [1983] 3 WLR 697 House of Lords (Lords Fraser, Edmund-Davies, Roskill, Brandon and Brightman)

Appropriation - whether an unauthorised act required

Facts

As stated by Lord Roskill:

'Morris, the appellant from the Court of Appeal (Criminal Division), on October 30, 1981, took goods from the shelves of a supermarket. He replaced the price labels attached to them with labels showing a lesser price than the originals. At the checkout point he was asked for and paid those lesser prices. He was then arrested. Burnside, the appellant from the Division Court, was seen to remove a price label from a joint of pork in the supermarket and attach it to a second joint. This action was detected at the checkout point but before he had paid for that second joint which at that moment bore a price label showing a price of £2.73 whereas the label should have shown a price of £6.91$^1/_2$. Burnside was then arrested.

The only relevant difference between the two cases is that Burnside was arrested before he had dishonestly paid the lesser price for the joint of pork. Morris was arrested after he had paid the relevant lesser prices. Morris was tried in Acton Crown Court on two charges of theft contrary to section 1(1) of the Theft Act 1968. A third count of obtaining property by deception contrary to section 15 of that Act appeared in the indictment but the learned assistant recorder did not take a verdict upon it and ordered that count to remain on the file. Morris appealed. The Court of Appeal (Criminal Division) (Lord Lane CJ, O'Connor LJ and Talbot J) dismissed his appeal in a reserved judgment given on March 8, 1983, by the learned Lord Chief Justice.

Burnside was convicted at Manchester Magistrates' Court on January 27, 1982, on a single charge of theft contrary to section 1(1) of the Theft Act. He appealed by way of case stated. On November 5, 1982, the Divisional Court (Ackner LJ and Webster J) dismissed the appeal.

Both the Court of Appeal (Criminal Division) and the Divisional Court granted certificates. The former certificate read thus: "If a person has substituted on an item of goods displayed in a self-service store a price label showing a lesser price for one showing a greater price, with the intention of paying the lesser price and then pays the lesser price at the till and takes the goods, is there at any stage a 'dishonest appropriation' for the purposes of section 1 of the Theft Act 1968 and if so, at what point does such appropriation take place?"

The certificate in the latter case reads: "If a person has substituted on an item of goods displayed in a self-service store a price label showing a lesser price for one showing a greater price, with the intention of paying the lesser price, and then pays the lesser price at the till and takes the goods, is there at any stage a 'dishonest appropriation' for the purposes of section 1 of the Theft Act 1968?"

The two certificates though clearly intended to raise the same point of law are somewhat differently worded and, with respect, as both learned counsel ultimately accepted during the debate before your Lordships, do not precisely raise the real issue for decision, at least in the terms in which it falls to be decided.'

Held

The appeals would be dismissed.

Lord Roskill:

'My Lords, in his submission for the appellants, which were conspicuous both for their clarity and their brevity, Mr Denison QC urged that on these simple facts neither appellant was guilty of theft. He accepted that Morris would have had no defence to a charge under section 15(1) of obtaining property by deception for he dishonestly paid the lesser prices and passed through the checkpoint having done so before he was arrested. But Morris, he said, was not guilty of theft because there was no appropriation by him before payment at the checkpoint sufficient to support a charge of theft, however dishonest his actions may have been in previously switching the labels.

Mr Denison pointed out that if, as he accepted, an offence was committed against section 15(1) and if the prosecution case were right, Morris would be liable to be convicted of obtaining property by deception which he had already stolen - a situation which learned counsel suggested was somewhat anomalous.

As regards Burnside, Mr Denison submitted that for the same reason there was no appropriation before his arrest sufficient to support a charge of theft. He also submitted that Burnside's actions, however dishonest, would not support a charge of attempting to obtain property by deception contrary to section 15(1) since his dishonest act was no more than an act preparatory to obtaining property by deception.

My Lords, if these submissions be well founded it is clear that however dishonest their actions, each respondent was wrongly convicted of theft. The question is whether they are well founded. The answer must depend upon the true construction of the relevant sections of the Theft Act 1968 and it is to these that I now turn.

[His Lordship considered ss 1-4 of the 1968 Act and continued]

The starting point of any consideration of Mr Denison's submissions must, I think, be the decision of this House in *Lawrence* v *Metropolitan Police Commissioner* (1971) 55 Cr App R 471; [1972] AC 626. In the leading speech, Viscount Dilhorne expressly accepted the view of the Court of Appeal (Criminal Division) in that case that the offence of theft involved four elements, (1) a dishonest (2) appropriation (3) of property belonging to another, (4) with the intention of permanently depriving the owner of it. Viscount Dilhorne also rejected the argument that even if these four elements were all present there could not be theft within the section if the owner of the property in question had consented to the acts which were done by the defendant. That there was in that case a dishonest appropriation was beyond question and the House did not have to consider the precise meaning of that word in section 3(1).

Mr Denison submitted that the phrase in section 3(1) "any assumption by a person of *the rights* (my emphasis) of an owner amounts to an appropriation" must mean any assumption of "*all* the rights of an owner." Since neither respondents had at the time of the removal of the goods from the shelves and of the label switching assumed *all* the rights of the owner, there was no appropriation and therefore no theft. Mr Jefferies QC for the prosecution, on the other hand, contended that *the* rights in this context only meant *any* of the rights. An owner of goods has many rights - they have been described as "a bundle or package of rights." Mr Jefferies contended that on a fair reading of the subsection it cannot have been the intention that every one of an owner's rights had to be assumed by the alleged thief before an appropriation was proved and that essential ingredient of the offence of theft established.

My Lords, if one reads the words "the rights" at the opening of section 3(1) literally and in isolation from the rest of the section, Mr Denison's submission undoubtedly has force. But the later words "any later assumption of a right" in subsection (1) and the words in subsection (2) "no later assumption by him of rights" seem to me to militate strongly against the correctness of the submission. Moreover the provisions of section 2(2)(*a*) also seem to point in the same direction. It follows therefore that it is enough for the prosecution if they have proved in these cases the assumption by the respondents of *any* of the rights of the owner of the goods in question, that is to say, the supermarket concerned, it being common ground in these cases that the other three of the four elements mentioned in Viscount Dilhorne's speech in *Lawrence* (supra) had been fully established.

My Lords, Mr Jefferies sought to argue that any removal from the shelves of the supermarket, even if unaccompanied by label switching, was without more an appropriation. In one passage in his judgment in *Morris's* case, the learned Lord Chief Justice appears to have accepted the submission, for he said (1983) 77 Cr App R 164, 170; [1983] QB 587, 596 "it seems to us that in taking the article from the shelf the customer is indeed assuming one of the rights of the owner, the right to move the article from its position on the shelf to carry it to the checkout ..."

With the utmost respect, I cannot accept this statement as correct. If one postulates an honest customer taking goods from a shelf to put in his or her trolley to take to the checkpoint there to pay the proper price, I am unable to see that any of these actions involves any assumption by the shopper of the rights of the supermarket. In the context of section 3(1), the concept of appropriation in my view involves not an act expressly or impliedly authorised by the owner, but an act by way of adverse interference with or usurpation of those rights. When the honest shopper acts as I have just described, he or she is acting with the implied authority of the owner of the supermarket to take the goods from the shelf, put them in the trolley, take them to the checkpoint and there to pay the correct price, at which moment the property in the goods will pass to the shopper for the first time. It is with the consent of the owners of the supermarket, be that consent express or implied, that the shopper does these acts and thus obtains at least control if not actual possession of the goods preparatory, at a later stage, to obtaining the property in them upon payment of the proper amount at the checkpoint. I do not think that section 3(1) envisages any such act as an "appropriation," whatever may be the meaning of that word in other fields such as contract or sale of goods law.

If, as I understand all of your Lordships to agree, the concept of appropriation in section 3(1) involves an element of adverse interference with or usurpation of some right of the owner, it is necessary next to consider whether that requirement is satisfied in either of these cases. As I have already said, in my view mere removal from the shelves without more is not an appropriation. Further, if a shopper with some perverted sense of humour, intending only to create confusion and nothing more, both for the supermarket and for other shoppers, switches labels, I do not think that that act of label switching alone is without more an appropriation, though it is not difficult to envisage some cases of dishonest label-switching which could be. In cases such as the present, it is in truth a combination of these actions, the removal from the shelf and the switching of the labels which evidences adverse interference with or usurpation of the rights of the owner. Those acts, therefore, amount to an appropriation and if they are accompanied by proof of the other three elements to which I have referred, the offence of theft is established. Further if they are accompanied by other acts such as putting the goods so removed and re-labelled into a receptacle, whether a trolley or the shopper's own bag or basket, proof of appropriation within section 3(1) becomes overwhelming. It is the doing of one or more acts which individually or collectively amount to such adverse interference with or usurpation of the owner's rights which constitute appropriation under section 3(1) and I do not think it matters where there is more than one such act in which order the successive acts take place, or whether there is any interval of time between them. To suggest that it matters whether the mislabelling precedes or succeeds removal form the shelves is to reduce this branch of the law to an absurdity.

My Lords, it will have been observed that I have endeavoured so far to resolve the question for determination in these appeals without reference to any decided cases except *Lawrence* (supra) which alone of the many cases cited in argument is a decision of this House. If your Lordships accept as correct the analysis which I have endeavoured to express by reference to the construction of the relevant sections of the Theft Act, a trail through a forest of decisions, many briefly and indeed inadequately reported, will tend to confuse rather than to enlighten. There are however some to which brief reference should perhaps be made.

First, *McPherson* [1973] Crim LR 191. Your Lordships have had the benefit of a transcript of the judgment of Lord Widgery CJ. I quote from p3 of the transcript - "Reducing this case to its bare essentials we have this: Mrs McPherson in common design with the others takes two bottles of whisky from the stand, puts them in her shopping bag; at the time she intends to take them out without paying for them, in other words she intends to steal them from the very beginning. She acts dishonestly as the jury found, and the sole question is whether that is an appropriation of the bottles within the meaning of section 1. We have no hesitation whatever in saying that it is such an appropriation and indeed we content ourselves with a judgment of this brevity because we have been unable to accept or to find any argument to the contrary, to suggest that an appropriation is not effective in those simple circumstances."

That was not, of course, a label switching case, but it is a plain case of appropriation effected by the combination of the acts of removing the goods from the shelf and of concealing them in the shopping bag. *McPherson* (supra) is to my mind clearly correctly decided as are all the cases which have followed it. It is wholly consistent with the principles which I have endeavoured to state in this speech.

It has been suggested that *Meech* (1973) 58 Cr App R 74; [1974] 1 QB 549; *Skipp* [1975] Crim LR 114 - your Lordships also have a transcript of the judgment in this case - and certain other cases are inconsistent with *McPherson* (supra). I do not propose to examine these or other cases in detail. Suffice it to say that I am far from convinced that there is any inconsistency between them and other cases as has been suggested once it is appreciated that facts will vary infinitely. The precise moment when dishonest acts, not of themselves amounting to an appropriation, subsequently, because of some other and later acts combined with those earlier acts, do bring about an appropriation within section 3(1), will necessarily vary according to the particular case in which the question arises.

Of the other cases referred to, I understand all your Lordships to agree that *Anderton* v *Wish* (1981) 72 Cr App R 23 was rightly decided for the reasons given. I need not therefore refer to it further. *Eddy* v *Niman* (1981) 73 Cr App R 237 was in my view also correctly decided on its somewhat unusual facts. I think that Webster J, giving the first judgment, asked the right question at p241 of the report, though, with respect, I think that the phrase "some overt act ... inconsistent with the true owner's rights" is too narrow. I think that the act need not necessarily be "overt."

Kaur v *Chief Constable of Hampshire* (1981) 72 Cr App R 359; [1981] 1 WLR 578 is a difficult case. I am disposed to agree with the learned Lord Chief Justice that it was wrongly decided but without going into further detail I respectfully suggest that it is on any view wrong to introduce into this branch of the criminal law questions whether particular contracts are void or voidable on the ground of mistake or fraud or whether any mistake is sufficiently fundamental to vitiate a contract. These difficult questions should so far as possible be confined to those fields of law to which they are immediately relevant and I do not regard them as relevant questions under the Theft Act 1968.

My Lords, it remains briefly to consider any relationship between section 1 and section 15. If the conclusion I have reached that theft takes place at the moment of appropriation and before any payment is made at the checkpoint be correct it is wrong to assert, as has been asserted, that the same act of appropriation creates two offences one against section 1(1) and the other against section 15(1) because the two offences occur at different points of time; the section 15(1) offence is not committed until payment of the wrong amount is made at the checkpoint while the theft has been committed earlier. It follows that in cases such as *Morris* two offences were committed. I do not doubt that it was perfectly proper to add the third count under section 15(1) in this case. I think the assistant recorder was right to leave all three counts to the jury. While one may sympathise with his preventing them from returning a verdict on the third count once they convicted on the theft counts if only in the interests of simplification, the counts were not alternative as he appears to have treated them. They were cumulative and once they were left to the jury verdicts should have been taken on all of them.

My Lords, these shoplifting cases by switching labels are essentially simple in their facts and their factual simplicity should not be allowed to be obscured by ingenious legal arguments upon the Theft

Act 1968 which for some time have bedevilled this branch of the criminal law without noticeably contributing to the efficient administration of justice - rather the reverse. The law to be applied to simple cases, whether in magistrates' courts or the Crown Court, should if possible be equally simple. I see no reason in principle why, when there is clear evidence of both offences being committed, both offences should not be charged. But where a shoplifter has passed the checkpoint and quite clearly has, by deception, obtained goods either without paying or by paying only a lesser price than he should, those concerned with prosecutions may in future think it preferable in the interests of simplicity to charge only an offence against section 15(1). In many cases of that kind it is difficult to see what possible defence there can be and that course may well avoid any opportunity for further ingenious legal arguments upon the first few sections of the Theft Act. Of course when the dishonesty is detected before the defendant has reached the checkpoint and he or she is arrested before that point so that no property has been obtained by deception, then theft is properly charged and if appropriation, within the meaning I have attributed to that word in this speech, is proved as well as the other three ingredients of the offence of theft, the defendant is plainly guilty of that offence.

My Lords, as already explained I have not gone through all the cases cited though I have mentioned some. Of the rest those inconsistent with this speech must henceforth be treated as overruled.

I would answer the certified questions in this way: "There is a dishonest appropriation for the purposes of the Theft Act 1968 where by the substitution of a price label showing a lesser price on goods for one showing a greater price, a defendant either by that act alone or by that act in conjunction with another act or other acts (whether done before or after the substitution of the labels) adversely interferes with or usurps the right of the owner to ensure that the goods concerned are sold and paid for at that greater price." '

R v Navvabi (1986) 83 Cr App R 271   Court of Appeal (Criminal Division) (Lord Lane CJ, McGowan and Rose JJ)

Unauthorised drawing of cheques - whether appropriation

Facts

The defendant had opened a number of bank accounts using false names, and had subsequently used the cheques and cheque cards with which he had been provided to draw cheques on the accounts in favour of casinos at which he gambled. There were insufficient funds in the accounts to meet the cheques drawn, and the defendant had not arranged any overdraft facilities. He was convicted of theft from the banks in relation to the cheques he had drawn in favour of the casinos, on the basis that the offence occurred when the cheques were delivered to the casinos. The defendant appealed on the ground that either he had not appropriated any property by writing the cheques, or that it did not occur until such cheques were actually honoured by the paying banks.

Held

The appeal would be allowed.

Lord Lane CJ:

'Before the trial judge and again in this Court counsel for the appellant submitted that no identifiable property was appropriated, because the contractual obligation imposed on the bank was referable not to any asset which it had at the time the cheque was drawn and delivered to the casino, but to those funds which it had at the time of presentation by the casino. It was further submitted that, if there was identifiable property, its appropriation took place when the bank honoured the cheque and the funds were transferred to the casino by the bank, and not at the time the cheque was drawn and delivered to the casino. Furthermore it was contended that theft in such a way was so academic a concept that only an academically-minded person understanding such niceties would be able to form the necessary intention permanently to deprive the owner. Counsel for the appellant conceded, though this Court doubts the correctness of that concession, that if the prosecution case had been presented on the basis that the appropriation took place at the time the funds were transferred by the bank to the casino, the conviction would be unimpeachable.

On behalf of the Crown it was submitted that the sums of £50 and £100 were sufficiently identifiable notwithstanding that they were only part of the bank's assets; that when a cheque backed by a guarantee card is drawn on an account without funds, the drawer assumes the rights of the bank in their money by directing them to do something with their property which they did not want to do, the property in question being either money or other intangible property but not a chose in action; and the elements necessary for theft being dishonesty, misappropriation of the property of another and an intention permanently to deprive, the thief's knowledge of the identity of the owner and whether the drawer believed he was stealing from the bank or the casino was immaterial.

In order to test the validity of these submissions one turns to the Theft Act 1968.

[His Lordship referred to ss 1(1) - 6(1) and continued]

It is common ground between counsel that no authority directly in point is to be found in the several decisions of the Courts which have been cited. No discourtesy is intended to the diligence of counsel if we refer to only two of these decisions: *Kohn* (1979) 69 Cr App R 395, on which the appellant relies, and *Pitham and Hehl* (1977) 65 Cr App R 45, on which the prosecution rely.

Kohn was a decision of a differently constituted division of this Court. The appellant, a director of a limited company, had been convicted of theft from the company in drawing cheques for his own purposes on the company's account in amounts (i) within the credit standing to the account, (ii) within the overdraft limit on the account and (iii) in excess of the overdraft limit. The convictions in relation to situations (i) and (ii) were upheld and in relation to (iii) quashed. In relation to (i) and (ii) it was held that the company's thing in action was stolen, whereas in situation (iii) nothing in action existed.

The following is an extract from the judgment of the Court at p407, referring to the debt owed by the bank to the company:

"It is a right of property which can properly be described as a thing in action and therefore potentially a subject of theft under the provisions of the 1968 Act. The cheque is the means by which the theft of the property is achieved. The completion of the theft does not take place until the transaction has gone through to completion."

The last sentence of this passage did not affect the result in *Kohn* (supra) and was to that extent obiter. It suggests (and has been taken by Professor Griew in his article "Stealing and Obtaining Bank Credits" [1986] Crim LR 356 at 362 to mean) that theft occurs at the time when the bank transfers the funds. But Professor Smith has argued (see [1985] Crim LR 370 and *The Law of Theft*, (5th ed, 1983), paragraph 106), that the delivery of the cheque to the payee is "an assumption of the rights of an owner" and therefore the appropriation. There may, however, as Professor Griew points out, be practical difficulties with this approach, for the state of the account may be much more difficult to ascertain when the cheque is delivered to the payee than when it is presented to the bank. Such difficulties, however, do not arise, or call for resolution, in the present case.

In *Pitham and Hehl* (supra) another division of this Court upheld the appellants' convictions for handling on the basis that a third man, in purporting to sell to them someone else's furniture, had assumed the rights of the owner to the furniture when he showed it to the appellants and invited them to buy what they wanted: at that moment he appropriated the goods to himself.

We note that *Pitham and Hehl* has also been criticised by both Professor Glanville Williams (*Textbook of Criminal Law*, (2nd ed, 1983) 764) and Professor Smith (*The Law of Theft*, (5th ed, 1983), paragraph 27). It is sufficient for the purposes of the present case to say that despite the submissions of counsel before us, we see no incompatibility between the decisions in *Pitham and Hehl* and *Kohn*.

Neither of these cases however helps us to resolve the present matter which, it seems to this Court, turns essentially on the construction of section 3(1): Was use of the cheque card to guarantee payment of a cheque delivered to the casino and drawn on an account with inadequate funds an assumption of the rights of the bank and thus appropriation? In our judgment it was not. That use of the cheque card and delivery of the cheque did no more than give the casino a contractual right as against the bank to be paid a specified sum from the bank's funds on presentation of the guaranteed cheque. That was not in itself an assumption of the rights of the bank to that part of the bank's funds to which the sum specified in the cheque corresponded: there was therefore no appropriation by the drawer either on delivery of the cheque to the casino or when the funds were ultimately transferred to the casino.'

R v Philippou (1989) 89 Cr App R 290 Court of Appeal (Criminal Division) O'Connor LJ, Caulfield and Eastham JJ)

Theft Act 1968 - appropriation of company property by director shareholders - whether theft

Facts

The appellant and his co-accused were the sole director shareholders of a number of companies, including an English company, 'Sunny Tours', and a Spanish company 'Budget Espania'. The appellant, as a director of Sunny Tours, had authorised the transfer of funds from its bank account in England for the purchase of a block of flats in Spain ownership of which was transferred to Budget Espania. Sunny Tours went into liquidation with deficiencies of $11.5 million. The appellant was charged with theft, and at his trial counsel for the appellant submitted that there was no case to answer as there had been no appropriation of funds from Sunny Tours, since the company had consented, through its directors, to the transfer of the funds. The trial judge ruled against this submission, and the appellant was convicted. On appeal the the Court of Appeal on the basis that the trial judge's ruling had been wrong in law:

Held

The appeal would be dismissed. Lord Justice O'Connor expressed the view that it had been rightly conceded in the earlier Court of Appeal decision in *AG's Ref (No 2 of 1982)* [1984] QB 624, that a company could not be said to have consented to the transfer of its funds when such 'consent' was in fact provided by the dishonest intent of the sole shareholder/directors that the money should be transfered to themselves for their own purposes. Such a transaction was rightly to be regarded as an appropriation of the company's funds. Hence in the present case the appellant and his co-accused had appropriated the funds of Sunny Tours notwithstanding that company's apparent consent to the transfer.

As a general point, his Lordship did not think it necessary for the prosecution to prove that an appropriation was without the consent of the owner in any event. Lord Roskill's speech in *R v Morris* [1984] AG 320 was not to be read as in any way undermining the force of Viscount Dilhorne's observations in *R v Lawrence* [1972] AC 626.

Commentary

Since the view was expressed that the transfer of funds could not be regarded as having taken place with the consent of the owner, the comments in relation to *R v Lawrence* and *R v Morris* should, it is submitted, be regarded as obiter.

R v Pitham and Hehl (1976) 65 Cr App R 45

See chapter 22.

R v Skipp [1975] Crim LR 114 Court of Appeal (Criminal Division) (Stephenson LJ, Kilner Brown and Boreham JJ)

Appropriation - whether an unauthorised act required

Facts

'S was convicted on a count which charged the theft of 450 boxes of oranges and 50 bags of onions. Posing as a genuine haulage contractor he obtained instructions to collect two loads of oranges and one load of onions from three different places in London and deliver them to customers in Leicester. Having collected the goods he made off with them. It was submitted that as S had the intention to steal the goods from the outset the count was bad for duplicity in that there were three separate appropriations.

Held

Dismissing the appeal, whether one looked at the matter in the light of cases such as *Jemmison* v *Priddle* [1972] 1 QB 489 and considered if the different acts constituted parts of one activity, or the wording of the Theft Act, the three loads were properly included in the one count. An assumption of the rights of an owner over property did not necessarily take place at the same time as an intent permanently to deprive the owner of it. There might be many cases in which a person having formed the intent was lawfully in possession of the goods and could not be said to have assumed the rights of an owner because he had not done something inconsistent with those rights. In the present case it was proper to take the view that up to the point when all the goods were loaded, and probably up to the point when the goods were diverted from their true destination, there had been no assumption of rights, and so there was only one appropriation. There was no conceivable prejudice to S.' [*W.G.*]

17 THE MENS REA OF THEFT

R v Coffey [1987] Crim LR 498 Court of Appeal (Criminal Division) (Mustill LJ, Butler-Sloss J and Sir John Thompson)

Intention to permanently deprive - s6(1) Theft Act 1968

Facts

'The appellant was convicted of obtaining property by deception. He had obtained machinery using a worthless cheque. At his trial he explained that he had been in dispute with the victim, who refused to negotiate its resolution. He had decided to exert pressure by obtaining and keeping the machinery until he got what he wanted. It was not clear exactly what the appellant wanted or what would happen to the machinery if he did not achieve his purpose. The appellant appealed against conviction on the ground that the judge's summing up did not fully or accurately state the law as to intent and dishonesty.

Held

Allowing the appeal, the summing up was defective. The jury might reasonably have concluded that the appellant intended to keep the machinery until the victim had done what he wanted, no matter how long that might take, and if he did not comply the goods would never be returned. They should have received guidance as to the criteria to apply. There were three possible views of the law to be applied.

(1) The culpability of the appellant's act depended upon the quality of the intended detention, considered in all its aspects, including in particular the appellant's own assessment at the time as to the likelihood of the victim coming to terms and of the time for which the machinery would have to be retained. The Court preferred this view.

This was one of the rare cases where it was right for the judge to bring section 6(1) before the jury. The judge could usefully have illustrated the first part of section 6(1) by the expression "equivalent to an outright taking or disposal." If they thought that the appellant might have intended to return the goods even if the victim did not do what he wanted, they would not convict unless they were sure that he intended that the period of detention should be so long as to amount to an outright taking. Even if they did conclude that the appellant had in mind not to return the goods if the victim failed to do what he wanted, they would still have to consider whether the appellant had regarded the likelihood of this happening as being such that his intended conduct could be regarded as equivalent to an outright taking.

(2) The appellant was interested in the machinery, only as a means to an end, which if achieved would mean the return of the machinery; his intention could not be said to be to deprive permanently. That argument was unsound for it concentrated too much on the physical object which constitutes the "property" and not enough on the relationship in which the true owner stands to that property. Section 6(1) must be taken as expository of sections 1(1) and 15(1) rather than as an enlargement of their scope, but it must be recognised that it attributes to those sections a wider significance than their bare words might otherwise have suggested. The reference to "the thing itself" in s6(1) indicates that the question of deprivation will not always be confined to the tangible object itself. The reference in s6(1) to "borrowing" shows that the "deprivation" can be "permanent" even if it is meant to be temporary. *Warner* (1970) 55 Cr App R 79; *Lloyd, Buhee and Ali* (1985) 81 Cr App R 182; *Downes* (1983) 77 Cr App R 260; *Duru and Asghar* [1974] 1 WLR 2; *Easom* [1971] 2 QB 315.

(3) To create a situation in which the victim could only get his own goods back by doing something which the appellant wanted him to do was treating the machinery as the appellant's "own to dispose of." There may be cases where this argument would be correct, eg the "ransom" situation where the true

owner has to pay for the return of his goods. It will not always be so; not every wrongful conversion is theft.'

[*Reported by Lynne Knapman, Barrister.*]

R v Duru (1973) 58 Cr App R 151

See reference to this authority in *R* v *Lloyd*, below.

R v Ghosh (1982) 75 Cr App R 154 Court of Appeal (Criminal Division) (Lord Lane CJ, Lloyd and Eastham JJ)

Direction to the jury on dishonesty

Facts

As stated by Lord Lane CJ:

'On April 29, 1981 before the Crown Court in St Albans, the appellant was convicted on four counts of an indictment laid under the Theft Act 1968: on count 1, attempting to procure the execution of a cheque by deception; on count 2, attempting to obtain money by deception; on counts 3 and 4, obtaining money by deception. Count 1 was laid under section 20(2) and the remainder under section 15(1). He was fined the sum of £250 on each count with a term of imprisonment to be served in default of payment.

At all material times the appellant was a surgeon acting as *a locum tenens* consultant at a hospital. The charges alleged that he had falsely represented that he had himself carried out a surgical operation to terminate pregnancy or that money was due to himself or an anaesthetist for such an operation, when in fact the operation had been carried out by someone else, and/or under the National Health Service provisions.

His defence was that there was no deception; that the sums paid to him were due for consultation fees which were legitimately payable under the regulations, or else were the balance of fees properly payable; in other words that there was nothing dishonest about his behaviour on any of the counts.

The effect of the jury's verdict was as follows: as to count 1, that the appellant had falsely represented that he had carried out a surgical operation and had intended dishonestly to obtain money thereby; that as to count 2 he had falsely pretended that an operation had been carried out under the National Health Service; that as to count 3 he had falsely pretended that money was due to an anaesthetist; and as to count 4 that he had obtained money by falsely pretending that an operation had been carried out on a fee-paying basis when in fact it had been conducted under the terms of the National Health Service.

The grounds of appeal are simply that the learned judge misdirected the jury as to the meaning of dishonesty.'

Held

The appeal would be dismissed

Lord Lane CJ:

'What the judge had to say on that topic was as follows: "Now, finally dishonesty. There are, sad to say, infinite categories of dishonesty. It is for you. Jurors in the past and, whilst we have criminal law in the future, jurors in the future have to set the standards of honesty. Now it is your turn today, having heard what you have, to consider contemporary standards of honesty and dishonesty in the context of all that you have heard. I cannot really expand on this too much, but probably it is something rather like getting something for nothing, sharp practice, manipulating systems and many other matters which come to your mind."

The law on this branch of the Theft Act 1968 is in a complicated state and we embark upon an examination of the authorities with great diffidence.

When the case of *McIvor* (1981) 74 Cr App R 74; [1982] 1 All ER 491 came before the Court of Appeal, there were two conflicting lines of authority. On the one hand there were cases which decided that the test of dishonesty for the purposes of the Theft Act 1968 is, what we venture to call, subjective - that is to say the jury should be directed to look into the mind of the defendant and determine whether he knew he was acting dishonestly: see *Landy and Others* (1981) 72 Cr App R 237, 247; [1981] 1 WLR 355, 365 where Lawton LJ giving the reserved judgment of the Court of Appeal said: "An assertion by a defendant that throughout a transaction he acted honestly does not have to be accepted but has to be weighed like any other piece of evidence. If that was the defendant's state of mind, or may have been, he is entitled to be acquitted. But if the jury, applying their own notions of what is honest and what is not, conclude that he could not have believed he was acting honestly, then the element of dishonesty will have been established. What a jury must not do is to say to themselves: 'If we had been in his place we would have known we were acting dishonestly so he must have known he was'."

On the other hand there were cases which decided that the test of dishonesty is objective. Thus in *Green and Greenstein* (1975) 61 Cr App R 296, 301; [1975] 1 WLR 1353, the judge had directed the jury: "... there is nothing illegal in stagging. The question you have to decide and what this case is all about is whether these defendants, or either of them, carried out their stagging operations in a dishonest way. To that question you apply your own standards of dishonesty. It is no good, you see, applying the standards of anyone accused of dishonesty, otherwise everybody accused of dishonesty, if he were to be tested by his own standards, would be acquitted automatically, you may think. The question is essentially the one for a jury to decide and it is essentially one which the jury must decide by applying its own standards." The Court of Appeal, in a reserved judgment, approved that direction.

In *McIvor* (supra) the Court of Appeal sought to reconcile these conflicting lines of authority. They did so on the basis that the subjective test is appropriate where the charge is conspiracy to defraud, but in the case of theft the test should be objective. We quote from the relevant passage in full: "It seems elementary, first, that where the charge is conspiracy to defraud the prosecution must prove actual dishonesty in the minds of the defendants in relation to the agreement concerned, and, second, that where the charge is an offence contrary to section 15 of the Theft Act 1968 the prosecution must prove that the defendant knew or was reckless regarding the representation concerned. The passage in my judgment in *Landy* (supra) to which we have referred should be read in relation to charges of conspiracy to defraud, and not in relation to charges of theft contrary to section 1 of the 1968 Act. Theft is in a different category from conspiracy to defraud, so that dishonesty can be established independently of the knowledge or belief of the defendant, subject to the special cases provided for in section 2 of the Act. Nevertheless, where a defendant has given evidence of his state of mind at the time of the alleged offence, the jury should be told to give that evidence such weight as they consider right, and they may also be directed that they should apply their own standards to the meaning of dishonesty."

The question we have to decide in the present case is, first, whether the distinction suggested in *McIvor* (supra) is justifiable in theory, and secondly, whether it is workable in practice.

In *Scott* v *Metropolitan Police Commissioner* [1974] 60 Cr App R 124; (1975) AC 819, the House of Lords had to consider whether deceit is a necessary element in the common law crime of conspiracy to defraud. They held that it is not. It is sufficient for the Crown to prove dishonesty. In the course of his speech Viscount Dilhorne traced the meaning of the words "fraud," "fraudulently" and "defraud" in relation to simple larceny, as well as the common law offence of conspiracy to defraud. After referring to *Stephen, History of the Criminal Law of England* (1883), Vol 2, pp121,

122 and *East's Pleas of the Crown* (1803) p553 he continued at p128 and p836 of the respective reports as follows: "The Criminal Law Revision Committee in their Eighth Report on *Theft and Related Offences* (1966) (Cmnd 2977) in paragraph 33 expressed the view that the important element of larceny, embezzlement and fraudulent conversion was 'undoubtedly the dishonest appropriation of another person's property'; in paragraph 35 that the words 'dishonestly appropriates' meant the same as 'fraudulently converts to his own use or benefit, or the use or benefit of any other person,' and in paragraph 39 that 'dishonestly' seemed to them a better word than 'fraudulently.'

Parliament endorsed these views in the Theft Act 1968, which by section 1(1) defined theft as the dishonest appropriation of property belonging to another with the intention of permanently depriving the other of it. Section 17 of that Act replaces section 82 and 83 of the Larceny Act 1861 and the Falsification of Accounts Act 1875. The offences created by those sections and by that Act made it necessary to prove that there had been an 'intent to defraud.' Section 17 of the Theft Act 1968 substitutes the words 'dishonestly with a view to gain for himself or another or with intent to cause loss to another' for the words 'intent to defraud.'

If 'fraudulently' in relation to larceny meant 'dishonestly' and 'intent to defraud' in relation to falsification of accounts is equivalent to the words now contained in section 17 of the Theft Act 1968 which I have quoted, it would indeed be odd if 'defraud' in the phrase 'conspiracy to defraud' has a different meaning and means only a conspiracy which is to be carried out be deceit."

Later on in the same speech Viscount Dilhorne continued as follows at p130 and p839 respectively: "As I have said, words take colour from the context in which they are used, but the words 'fraudulently' and 'defraud' must ordinarily have a very similar meaning. If, as I think, and as the Criminal Law Revision Committee appears to have thought, 'fraudulently' means 'dishonestly,' then 'to defraud' ordinarily means, in my opinion, to deprive a person dishonestly of something which is his or of something to which he is or would or might but for the perpetration of the fraud be entitled."

In *Scott* v *Metropolitan Police Commissioner* (1974) 60 Cr App R 124; [1975] AC 819 the House of Lords were only concerned with the question whether deceit is an essential ingredient in cases of conspiracy to defraud; and they held not. As Lord Diplock said at p131 and p841 respectively, "dishonesty of any kind is enough." But there is nothing in the case of *Scott* which supports the view that, so far as the element of dishonesty is concerned, "theft is in a different category from conspiracy to defraud." On the contrary the analogy drawn by Viscount Dilhorne between the two offences, and indeed the whole tenor of his speech, suggests the precise opposite.

Nor is there anything in *Landy* (1981) 72 Cr App R 237; [1981] 1 WLR 355, itself which justifies putting theft and conspiracy to defraud into different categories. Indeed the Court went out of its way to stress that the test for dishonesty, whatever it might be, should be the same whether the offence charged be theft or conspiracy to defraud. This is clear from the reference to *Feely* (1972) 57 Cr App R 312; [1973] QB 530, which was a case under section 1 of the Theft Act. Having set out what we have for convenience called the subjective test, the Court in *Landy* continue at p247 and p365 of the respective reports: "In our judgment this is the way the case of *Feely* should be applied in cases where the issue of dishonesty arises. It is also the way in which the jury should have been directed in this case ..."

In support of the distinction it is said that in conspiracy to defraud the question arises in relation to an agreement. But we cannot see that this makes any difference. If "A" and "B" agree to deprive a person dishonestly of his goods, they are guilty of conspiracy to defraud: see *Scott's* case (supra). If they dishonestly and with the necessary intent deprive him of his goods, they are presumably guilty of theft. Why, one asks respectfully, should the test be objective in the case of simple theft, but subjective where they have agreed to commit a theft?

The difficulties do not stop there. The court in *McIvor* (supra) evidently regarded cases under section 15 of the Theft Act as being on the subjective side of the line, at any rate so far as proof of deception is concerned. This was the way they sought to explain *Green and Greenstein* (1975) 61 Cr App R

296; [1975] 1 WLR 1353. In that case, after directing the jury in the passage which we have already quoted, the judge continued as follows at p301 and p1360 respectively: "Now in considering whether Mr Green or Mr Greenstein had or may have had an honest belief in the truth of their representations, ... the test is a subjective one. That is to say, it is not what you would have believed in similar circumstances. It is what you think they believed and if you think that they, or either of them, had an honest belief to that effect, well then of course there would not be any dishonesty. On the other hand, if there is an absence of reasonable grounds for so believing, you might think that that points to the conclusion that they or either of them, as the case may be, had no genuine belief in the truth of their representations. In this case, applying your own standards, you may think that they acted dishonestly and it would be for you to say whether it has been established by this prosecution that they had no such honest belief ..."

The Court of Appeal in *Green and Greenstein* (supra) appear to have approved that passage. At any rate they expressed no disapproval.

In *McIvor* (1982) 74 Cr App R 74; [1982] 1 WLR 409 the Court reconciled the two passages quoted from the judge's summing up as follows at p79 and p415 of the respective reports: "It seems clear that these two passages are concerned with different points. The first, which follows and adopts the standards laid down in *Feely* (supra) is concerned with the element of dishonesty in section 15 offences, whilst the second is specifically concerned with the mental element in relation to the false representation the subject matter of the charge. Clearly, if a defendant honestly believes that the representation made was true the prosecution cannot prove that he knew of, or was reckless as to, its falsity."

The difficulty with section 15 of the Theft Act 1968 is that dishonesty comes in twice. If a person knows that he is not telling the truth he is guilty of dishonesty. Indeed deliberate deception is one of the two most obvious forms of dishonesty. One wonders therefore whether "dishonestly" in section 15(1) adds anything, except in the case of reckless deception. But assuming it does, there are two consequences of the distinction drawn in *McIvor* (supra). In the first place it would mean that the legislation has gone further than its framers intended. For it is clear from paragraphs 87-88 of the Criminal Law Revision Committee's Eighth Report that "deception" was to replace "false pretence" in the old section 32(1) of the Larceny Act 1916, and "dishonestly" was to replace "with intent to defraud." If the test of dishonesty in conspiracy to defraud cases is subjective, it is difficult to see how it could have been anything other than subjective in considering "intent to defraud." It follows that, if the distinction drawn in *McIvor* (supra) is correct, the Criminal Law Revision Committee were recommending an important charge in the law by substituting "dishonestly" for "with intent to defraud"; for they were implicitly substituting an objective for a subjective test.

The second consequence is that in cases of deliberate deception the jury will have to be given two different tests of dishonesty to apply: the subjective test in relation to deception and the objective test in relation to obtaining. This is indeed what seems to have happened in *Green and Greenstein* (supra). We cannot regard this as satisfactory from a practical point of view. If it be sought to obviate the difficulty by making the test subjective in relation to both aspects of section 15, but objective in relation to section 1, then that would certainly be contrary to what was intended by the Criminal Law Revision Committee. For in paragraph 88 they say: "The provision in clause 12(1) making a person guilty of criminal deception if he 'dishonestly obtains' the property replaces the provision in the 1916 Act, section 32(1) making a person guilty of obtaining by false pretences if he 'with intent to defraud, obtains' the things there mentioned. The change will correspond to the change from 'fraudulently' to 'dishonestly' in the definition of stealing (contained in section 1)."

We feel, with the greatest respect, that in seeking to reconcile the two lines of authority in the way we have mentioned, the Court of Appeal in *McIvor* (supra) was seeking to reconcile the irreconcilable. It therefore falls to us now either to choose between the two lines of authority or to propose some other solution.

In the current supplement to *Archbold* (40th ed), paragraph 1460, the editors suggest that the observations on dishonesty by the Court of Appeal in *Landy* (supra) can be disregarded "in view of the wealth of authority to the contrary." The matter, we feel, is not as simple as that.

In *Waterfall* (1969) 53 Cr App R 596; [1970] 1 QB 148, the defendant was charged under section 16 of the Theft Act with dishonestly obtaining a pecuniary advantage from a taxi driver. Lord Parker CJ, giving the judgment of the Court of Appeal, said this at p598 and pp150, 151 respectively: "The sole question as it seems to me in this case revolves around the third ingredient, namely, whether what was done was done dishonestly. In regard to that the deputy recorder directed the jury in this way: 'If on reflection and deliberation you came to the conclusion that this defendant never did have any genuine belief that Mr Tropp [the accountant] would pay the taxi fare, then you would be entitled to convict him ...' In other words, in that passage the deputy recorder is telling the jury they had to consider what was in this particular defendant's mind: had he a genuine belief that the accountant would provide the money? That, as it seems to this court, is a perfectly proper direction subject to this, that it would be right to tell the jury that they can use as a test, though not a conclusive test, whether there were any reasonable grounds for that belief. Unfortunately, however, just before the jury retired, in two passages the deputy recorder, as it seems to this Court, was saying: you cannot hold that this man had a genuine belief unless he had reasonable grounds for that belief."

Lord Parker then sets out the passages in question and continues at p599 and p151: " ... the court is quite satisfied that those directions cannot be justified. The test here is a subjective test, whether the particular man had an honest belief, and of course whereas the absence of reasonable ground may point strongly to the fact that that belief is not genuine, it is at the end of the day for the jury to say whether or not in the case of this particular man he did have that genuine belief."

That decision was criticised by academic writers. But it was followed shortly afterwards in *Royle* (1971) 56 Cr App R 131; [1971] 1 WLR 1764, another case under section 16 of the Theft Act. Edmund Davies LJ giving the judgment of the Court said this at pp139, 140 and pp1769, 1770 respectively: "The charges being that debts had been dishonestly 'evaded' by deception, contrary to section 16(2)(a), it was incumbent on the commissioner to direct the jury on the fundamental ingredient of dishonesty. In accordance with *Waterfall* (supra), they should have been told that the test is whether the accused had an honest belief and that, whereas the absence of reasonable ground might point strongly to the conclusion that he entertained no genuine belief in the truth of his representation, it was for them to say whether or not it had been established that the appellant had no such genuine belief."

It is to be noted that the Court in that case treated the "fundamental ingredient of dishonesty" as being the same as whether the defendant had a genuine belief in the truth of the representation.

In *Gilks* (1972) 56 Cr App R 734; [1972] 1 WLR 1341, which was decided by the Court of Appeal the following year, the appellant had been convicted of theft contrary to section 1 of the Theft Act 1968. The facts were that he had been overpaid by a book-maker. He knew that the book-maker had made a mistake, and that he was not entitled to the money. But he kept it. The case for the defence was that "book-makers are a race apart." It would be dishonest if your grocer gave you too much change and you kept it, knowing that he had made a mistake. But it was not dishonest in the case of a book-maker.

The judge directed the jury as follows: "Well, it is a matter for you to consider, members of the jury, but try and place yourselves in that man's position at that time and answer the question whether in your view he thought he was acting honestly or dishonestly."

Cairns LJ giving the judgment of the Court of Appeal at p738 and p1345 respectively, held that that was, in the circumstances of the case, a proper and sufficient direction on the matter of dishonesty. He continued (ibid.): "On the face of it the defendant's conduct was dishonest: the only possible basis on which the jury could find that the prosecution had not established dishonesty would be if they thought it possible that the defendant did have the belief which he claimed to have."

A little later *Feely* (1972) 57 Cr App R 312; [1973] QB 530 came before a Court of five judges. The case is often treated as having laid down an objective test of dishonesty for the purpose of section 1 of the Theft Act. But what it actually decided was (i) that it is for the jury to determine whether the defendant acted dishonestly and not for the judge, (ii) that the word "dishonestly" can only relate to the defendant's own state of mind, and (iii) that it is unnecessary and undesirable for judges to define what is meant by "dishonesty."

It is true that the Court said at p317 and pp537, 538 respectively: "Jurors, when deciding whether an appropriation was dishonest can be reasonably expected to, and should, apply the current standards of ordinary decent people."

It is that sentence which is usually taken as laying down the objective test. But the passage goes on: "In their own lives they have to decide what is and what is not dishonest. We can see no reason why, when in a jury box, they should require the help of a judge to tell them what amounts to dishonesty." The sentence requiring the jury to apply current standards leads up to the prohibition on judges from applying *their* standards. That is the context in which the sentence appears. It seems to be reading too much into that sentence to treat it as authority for the view that "dishonesty can be established independently of the knowledge or belief of the defendant." If it could, then any reference to the state of mind of the defendant would be beside the point.

This brings us to the heart of the problem. Is "dishonestly" in section 1 of the Theft Act 1968 intended to characterise a course of conduct? Or is it intended to describe a state of mind? If the former, then we can well understand that it could be established independently of the knowledge or belief of the accused. But if, as we think, it is the latter, then the knowledge and belief of the accused are at the root of the problem.

Take for example a man who comes from a country where public transport is free. On his first day here he travels on a bus. He gets off without paying. He never had any intention of paying. His mind is clearly honest; but his conduct, judged objectively by what he has done, is dishonest. It seems to us that in using the word "dishonestly" in the Theft Act, Parliament cannot have intended to catch dishonest conduct in that sense, that is to say conduct to which no moral obloquy could possibly attach. This is sufficiently established by the partial definition in section 2 of the Theft Act itself. All the matters covered by section 2(1) relate to the belief of the accused. Section 2(2) relates to his willingness to pay. A man's belief and his willingness to pay are things which can only be established subjectively. It is difficult to see how a partially subjective definition can be made to work in harness with the test which in all other respects is wholly objective.

If we are right that dishonesty is something in the mind of the accused (what Professor Glanville Williams calls "a special mental state"), then if the mind of the accused is honest, it cannot be deemed dishonest merely because members of the jury would have regarded it as dishonest to embark on that course of conduct.

So we would reject the simple uncomplicated approach that the test is purely objective, however attractive from the practical point of view that solution may be.

There remains the objection that to adopt a subjective test is to abandon all standards but that of the accused himself, and to bring about a state of affairs in which "Robin Hood would be no robber" (see *Green and Greenstein* (supra)). This objection misunderstands the nature of the subjective test. It is no defence for a man to say "I knew that what I was doing is generally regarded as dishonest; but I do not regard it as dishonest myself. Therefore I am not guilty." What he is however entitled to say is "I did not know that anybody would regard what I was doing as dishonest." He may not be believed; just as he may not be believed if he sets up "a claim of right" under section 2(1) of the Theft Act, or asserts that he believed in the truth of a misrepresentation under section 15 of the Theft Act. But if he *is* believed, or raises a real doubt about the matter, the jury cannot be sure that he was dishonest.

In determining whether the prosecution has proved that the defendant was acting dishonestly, a jury must first of all decide whether according to the ordinary standards of reasonable and honest people what was done was dishonest. If it was not dishonest by those standards, that is the end of the matter and the prosecution fails.

If it was dishonest by those standards, then the jury must consider whether the defendant himself must have realised that what he was doing was by those standards dishonest. In most cases, where the actions are obviously dishonest by ordinary standards, there will be no doubt about it. It will be obvious that the defendant himself knew that he was acting dishonestly. It is dishonest for a defendant to act in a way which he knows ordinary people consider to be dishonest, even if he asserts or genuinely believes that he is morally justified in acting as he did. For example, Robin Hood or those ardent anti-vivisectionists who remove animals from vivisection laboratories are acting dishonestly, even though they may consider themselves to be morally justified in doing what they do, because they know that ordinary people would consider these actions to be dishonest.

Cases which might be described as borderline, such as *Boggeln* v *Williams* (1978) 67 Cr App R 50; [1978] 2 All ER 1061, will depend upon the view taken by the jury as to whether the defendant may have believed what he was doing was in accordance with the ordinary man's idea of honesty. A jury might have come to the conclusion that the defendant in that case was disobedient or impudent, but not dishonest in what he did.

So far as the present case is concerned, it seems to us that once the jury had rejected the defendant's account in respect of each count in the indictment (as they plainly did), the finding of dishonesty was inevitable, whichever of the tests of dishonesty was applied. If the judge had asked the jury to determine whether the defendant might have believed that what he did was in accordance with the ordinary man's idea of honesty, there could have only been one answer - and that is no, once the jury had rejected the defendant's explanation of what happened.

In so far as there was a misdirection on the meaning of dishonesty, it is plainly a case for the application of the proviso to section 2(1) of the Act. This appeal is accordingly dismissed.'

R v Holden [1991] Crim LR 478 Court of Appeal (Criminal Division) (Mustill LJ, Tudor Evans and Thorpe JJ)

Dishonesty in theft

Facts

'The appellant was charged with theft of scrap tyres from Kwik Fit. He had worked for various branches of Kwik Fit, and was due to do so again, although he was not so employed at the time of the offence, and he claimed that he had seen others take tyres and had been granted permission by a supervisor to take them. The depot manager said that taking tyres or permitting others to do so would be a sackable offence. The judge directed the jury that the simple issue was dishonesty, and that it was no defence that others took tyres. She said that the test was whether he had a reasonable belief that he had a right to take them. On appeal following conviction, it was contended that such was a misdirection. Crown counsel argued that the use of the word "reasonable" was not fatal to the conviction looking at the whole summing-up, in particular the judge's direction that "If (he) believed he had authority, or would have had it if he had asked for it, then that is a defence and that is what you have to decide ..." (*Price* (1989) 90 Cr App R 409).

Held

Allowing the appeal, reasonable belief was not the relevant test of dishonesty. A man was not dishonest if he believed, reasonably or not, that he had a legal right to do that which was alleged to constitute an appropriation of property. The question was whether he had, or might have had, an honest belief, to which there was no reference in the summing-up; nor was there a reference to the twin tests of *Ghosh*. although the judge in *price* had wrongly used the word "reasonable" the Court of Appeal had concluded that he had nevertheless correctly drawn the jury's attention to the essential points which they had to decide. That was not the case here. Of the two lines of defence - express permission or honest belief that he would have got permission had he asked - the latter was certainly a real issue on the evidence. Since the honesty or otherwise of the appellant's belief was crucial, the judge should have directed the jury to that issue. Nowhere did she say that they had to consider whether he did honestly believe or might have honestly believed that he could properly take the tyres. That was a fundamental omission and, moreover, the jury were misled by the judge's direction, repeated twice, that it was the reasonableness or otherwise of the belief that was the crucial issue. The reasonableness of the belief might be relevant to the question of whether the appellant could have had an honest belief that he was entitled to take the tyres but that was not put to the jury.'

[*Reported by Veronica Cowan, Barrister.*]

R v Johnstone [1982] Crim LR 454 Newcastle-upon-Tyne Crown Court (Mr Recorder Chadwin)

Intention to permanently deprive - s6(1) Theft Act 1968

Facts

'D1 and D2 were employed by a bottling company as draymen to deliver supplies of bottled soft drinks, cider and beer to, and to collect the empties and crates from retail outlets. They were required to note down on a separate delivery sheet for each outlet the amount of empties collected so that the retailer could be credited with the deposit upon them on D1 and D2's return to the bottling company. Evidence was adduced by the prosecution that on the day in question D1 and D2 collected 28 more bottles and crates than they credited to the outlets, thereby creating a surplus of empties upon the lorry. Instead of delivering the surplus directly to their employers they dishonestly delivered it to D3, a retailer who was also a customer of the employers, with the intention of receiving a part of the deposit which D3 would himself dishonestly obtain. The Recorder accepted that this scheme only made sense if the surplus bottles were returned to the bottling company either directly or via a bottle exchange with only a short delay, since it was only in such circumstances that D3 would be able to obtain credit for the deposit. It was thus intended by D1 and D2 that the bottling company would receive their bottles back and would have to pay no more than one deposit, albeit to the wrong person.

D1 and D2 were charged with theft of the surplus bottles from the bottling company (it not being possible for the prosecution to prove from which individual retail outlet(s) the surplus had been obtained). D3 was charged with handling the surplus.

On a submission at the end of the prosecution case of no case to answer upon the argument that D1 and D2 did not intend permanently to deprive their employers of the surplus bottles the prosecution sought to rely upon the provisions of section 6(1) of the Theft Act upon the basis that D1 and D2 had treated the bottles as their own to dispose of regardless of the others rights.

Held

Referring to the case of *Holloway* (1849) 1 Den 370, the comments of Edmund Davies LJ in *Warner* (1970) 55 Cr App R 93 at pages 95-96 and the comments thereon in Smith & Hogan (4th ed), p527 and Smith's *Law of Theft* paras. 113-117.

That since on the above facts D1 and D2 contemplated and intended that the bottles should be returned to the true owners, albeit with some delay and since the object of the scheme was merely to manipulate the bottles in order to obtain the deposit, it could not be said that D1 and D2 were treating the bottles as *their* own to dispose of. A disposal which negates an intention permanently to deprive cannot be capable of providing what can be regarded as an intent permanently to deprive under section 6(1) of the Theft Act.'

[*Noted by Jeremy Hargrove, Barrister.*]

R v Lloyd (1986) 81 Cr App R 182   Court of Appeal (Criminal Division)   (Lord Lane CJ, Farquharson and Tudor Price JJ)

Intention to permanently deprive - s6(1) Theft Act 1968

Facts

The defendant was a cinema projectionist who agreed with other defendants, to make private video copies of first run feature films. The plan involved taking the print of a film at the end of an evening's public showing, and returning it after copies had been made, in time for the next day's performance. The defendants were convicted of conspiracy to steal, and appealed on the ground that there had been no intention to permanently deprive the owners of the film.

Held

The appeals would be allowed.

Lord Lane CJ:

'The complaint by the appellants is this, that the judge misdirected the jury first of all in leaving the question for them to decide whether the removal of a film in these circumstances could amount to theft, and secondly, in allowing them to consider section 6(1) of the Theft Act 1968 as being relevant at all in the circumstances of this case.

The point is a short one. It is not a simple one. It is not without wider importance, because if the judge was wrong in leaving the matter in the way in which he did for the jury to consider, it might mean, as we understand it, that the only offence of which a person in these circumstances could be convicted would be a conspiracy to commit a breach of the Copyright Act 1956. At the time when this particular case was being tried, the maximum penalties available for the substantive offence under the Copyright Act were minimal. Those penalties have now been increased by the provisions of the Copyright (Amendment) Act 1983, and in the light of that Act it can be said that although Parliament perhaps has not entirely caught up with this type of prevalent pirating offence, it is at least gaining on it.

We turn now to the provisions of the Theft Act 1968, the conspiracy alleged being a breach of that particular Act. Section 1(1) of that Act provides that "A person is guilty of theft if he dishonestly appropriates property belonging to another with the intention of permanently depriving the other of it; and 'thief' and 'steal' shall be construed accordingly."

On that wording alone these appellants were not guilty of theft or of conspiracy to steal. The success of their scheme and their ability to act with impunity in a similar fashion in the future, depended, as we have already said, upon their ability to return the film to its rightful place in the hands of the Odeon Cinema at Barking as rapidly as possible, so that its absence should not be noticed. Therefore the intention of the appellants could more accurately be described as an intention temporarily to deprive the owner of the film and was indeed the opposite of an intention permanently to deprive.

What then was the basis of the prosecution case and the basis of the judge's direction to the jury? It is said that section 6(1) of the Theft Act brings such actions as the appellants performed here within the provisions of section 1. The learned judge left the matter to the jury on the basis that they had to decide whether the words of section 6(1) were satisfied by the prosecution or not.

[His Lordship referred to s6(1), then continued]

Section 6(1) reads as follows: "A person appropriating property belonging to another without meaning the other permanently to lose the thing itself is nevertheless to be regarded as having the intention of permanently depriving the other of it if his intention is to treat the thing as his own to dispose of regardless of the other's rights; and a borrowing or lending of it may amount to so treating it if, but only if, the borrowing or lending is for a period and in circumstances making it equivalent to an outright taking or disposal."

That section has been described by JR Spencer in his article "The Metamorphosis of section 6 of the Theft Act" in [1977] Crim LR 653, as a section which "sprouts obscurities at every phrase," and we are inclined to agree with him. It is abstruse. But it must mean, if nothing else, that there are circumstances in which a defendant may be deemed to have the intention permanently to deprive, even though he may intend the owner eventually to get back the object which has been taken.

We have had the benefit of submissions by Mr Du Cann [counsel for the defendants] in this case. His first submission is that the definition of "property" in section 4 of the Theft Act does not include value, and he submits that it was on the basis of loss of value or loss of virtue of the films that the prosecution of the case proceeded. In order to substantiate that submission, he referred us to the decision of the House of Lords in *Rank Film Distributors Ltd* v *Video Information Centre* [1982] AC 380. Relying upon that case he sought to demonstrate to us that the provisions of the Theft Act 1968 do not cover the stealing of copyright or kindred matters.

We are indebted to Mr Du Cann for his careful arguments on this point, namely to the effect that copyright is probably not a subject of theft, but we are not concerned with that proposition here, so it seems to us, except perhaps incidentally, because the allegation here was one of conspiracy to steal feature films, not the copyright in them, and the allegation that the defendants conspired together to steal feature films depends upon proof by the prosecution that that is the thing that they were conspiring to steal.

Mr Du Cann next cites to us a series of helpful cases, and they are these. First of all the case of *Warner* (1970) 55 Cr App R 93. This was a case in which the judgment of the Court was delivered by Edmund Davies LJ Having cited the words in which the chairman directed the jury, Edmund Davies LJ, goes on at p96 as follows: "But unfortunately his direction later became confused by his references to section 6, the object of which he may himself have misunderstood. There is no statutory definition of the words 'intention of permanently depriving,' but section 6 seeks to clarify their meaning in certain respects. Its object is in no wise to cut down the definition of 'theft' contained in section 1. It is always dangerous to paraphrase a statutory enactment, but its apparent aim is to prevent specious pleas of a kind which have succeeded in the past by providing, in effect, that it is no excuse for an accused person to plead absence of the necessary intention if it is clear that he appropriated another's property intending to treat it as his own, regardless of the owner's rights. Section 6 thus gives illustrations, as it were, of what can amount to the dishonest intention demanded by section 1(1). But it is a misconception to interpret it as watering down section 1."

Then Mr Du Cann referred us to the case of *Duru and Asghar* (1974) 58 Cr App R 151; [1974] 1 WLR 2. That was a case involving cheques. The allegation was that the defendant had obtained certain cheques from the local authority by deception with the intention of permanently depriving the council of them. That was contrary to section 15(1) of the Theft Act 1968, but section 6(1) was equally applicable in that case as it would have been had the allegation been one simply of theft.

Megaw LJ, delivering the judgment of the Court said this, at p160 and p8 respectively: "So far as the cheque itself is concerned, true it is a piece of paper. But it is a piece of paper which changes its character completely once it is paid, because then it receives a rubber stamp on it saying it has been paid and it ceases to be a thing in action, or at any rate it ceases to be, in its substance, the same as it was before; that is, an instrument on which payment falls to be made. It was the intention of the appellants, dishonestly and by deception, not only that the cheques should be made out and handed over, but also that they should be presented and paid, thereby permanently depriving the Greater London Council of the cheque in its substance as a thing in action. The fact that the mortgagors were under an obligation to repay the mortgage loans does not affect the appellants' intention permanently to deprive the Council of these cheques. If it were necessary to look to section 6(1) of the Theft Act, this Court would have no hesitation in saying that that subsection, brought in by the terms of section 15(3), would also be relevant, since it is plain that the appellants each had the intention of causing the cheque to be treated as the property of the person by whom it was to be obtained, to dispose of, regardless of the rights of the true owner."

Finally Mr Du Cann referred us to the case of *Downes* (1983) 77 Cr App R 260. That was a case similar in essence to *Duru* (supra). The judgment in *Downes* was delivered by Nolan J who said this at p266: "It is of some interest to note in *Duru* the Court was referred to the earlier case of *Warner* (1970) 55 Cr App R 93, which Mr Lodge [counsel for the appellant in that case] cited in support of the narrower reading of section 6(1) for which he contended. *Warner* does not however appear to us, as evidently it did not appear to this Court in *Duru* to have any significant bearing on the point at issue. It follows that, for substantially the same reasons as those given by the learned judge, we consider that the charge of theft is made out, the vouchers having been dishonestly appropriated with the intention of destroying their essential character and thus depriving the owners, the Inland Revenue, of the substance of their property. In our judgment therefore the appeal must be dismissed."

In general we take the same view as Professor Griew in his work on *The Theft Acts 1968 and 1978* (4th ed, 1982), p47 at paragraph 2/73, namely that section 6 should be referred to in exceptional cases only. In the vast majority of cases it need not be referred to or considered at all.

Deriving assistance from another distinguished academic writer, namely Professor Glanville Williams, we would like to cite with approval the following passage from his *Textbook of Criminal Law* (2nd ed, 1983), at p719: "In view of the grave difficulties of interpretation presented by section 6, a trial judge would be well advised not to introduce it to the jury unless he reaches the conclusion that it will assist them, and even then (it may be suggested) the question he leaves to the jury should not be worded in terms of the generalities as applied to the alleged facts. For example, the question might be: 'Did the defendant take the article, intending that the owner should have it back only on making a payment? If so, you would be justified as a matter of law in finding that he intended to deprive the owner permanently of his article, because the taking of the article with that intention is equivalent to an outright taking.' "

Bearing in mind the observations of Edmund Davies LJ in *Warner* (supra), we would try to interpret the section in such a way as to ensure that nothing is construed as an intention permanently to deprive which would not prior to the 1968 Act have been so construed. Thus the first part of section 6(1) seems to us to be aimed at the sort of case where a defendant takes things and then offers them back to the owner for the owner to buy if he wishes. If the taker intends to return them to the owner only upon such payment, then, on the wording of section 6(1), that is deemed to amount to the necessary intention permanently to deprive: see for instance *Hall's* case (1848) 1 Den 381, where the defendant took fat from a candlemaker and then offered it for sale to the owner. His conviction for larceny was affirmed. There are other cases of similar intent: for instance, "I have taken your valuable painting. You can have it back on payment to me of £X,000. If you are not prepared to make that payment, then you are not going to get your painting back."

It seems to us that in this case we are concerned with the second part of section 6(1), namely the words after the semi-colon: "and a borrowing or lending of it may amount to so treating it if, but only if, the borrowing or lending is for a period and in circumstances making it equivalent to an outright taking or disposal." These films, it could be said, were borrowed by Lloyd from his employers in order to enable him and the others to carry out their "piracy" exercise.

Borrowing is ex hypothesi not something which is done with an intention permanently to deprive. This half of the subsection, we believe, is intended to make it clear that a mere borrowing is never enough to constitute the necessary guilty mind unless the intention is to return the "thing" in such a changed state that it can truly be said that all its goodness or virtue has gone. For example *Beecham* (1851) 5 Cox CC 181, where the defendant stole railway tickets intending that they should be returned to the railway company in the usual way only after the journeys had been completed. He was convicted of larceny. The learned judge in the present case gave another example, namely the taking of a torch battery with the intention of returning it only when its power is exhausted.

That being the case, we turn to inquire whether the feature films in this case can fall within that category. Our view is that they cannot. The goodness, the virtue, the practical value of the films to the owners has not gone out of the article. The film could still be projected to paying audiences, and, had everything gone according to the conspirators' plans, would have been projected in the ordinary way to audiences at the Odeon Cinema, Barking, who would have paid for their seats. Our view is that those particular films which were the subject of this alleged conspiracy had not themselves diminished in value at all. What had happened was that the borrowed film had been used or was going to be used to perpetrate a copyright swindle on the owners whereby their commercial interests were grossly and adversely affected in the way that we have endeavoured to describe at the outset of this judgment. That borrowing, it seems to us, was not for a period, or in such circumstances, as made it equivalent to an outright taking or disposal. There was still virtue in the film.

For those reasons we think that the submissions of Mr Du Cann on this aspect of the case are well founded. Accordingly the way in which the learned judge directed the jury was mistaken, and accordingly this conviction of conspiracy to steal must be quashed.'

R v McIvor [1982] 1 WLR 409

See references to this authority in *R* v *Ghosh*, above.

R v Small [1987] Crim LR 777 Court of Appeal (Criminal Division) (Tasker-Watkins and Mars-Jones LJJ and Henry J)

Dishonesty - belief that property had been abandoned

Facts

'On March 14, 1986 in the early hours of the morning policemen stopped a Volkswagen Passat motor car. There were three men in the motor car, all of whom decamped. A few hours later, the appellant was arrested by the police. He admitted that he had been in the motor car and that he had previously purchased it. He was released from the police station and returned both [sic] on a later date when he accepted that he had stolen it. He was charged with theft of the car.

On August 14, 1986 the appellant appeared before Croydon Crown Court. He pleaded not guilty to the charge of theft. At the Crown Court the owner of the motor car was called. He admitted under cross examination that it had been parked for some 10 days in the same place and that the keys had been lost. The appellant gave evidence that he had seen the motor car every day for two weeks. It had the keys in the ignition; it had a flat tyre, the petrol tank was empty, the wipers did not work. The value of the car had been assessed by the owner at £700 to £800. The appellant gave evidence that at the time of taking the motor car, he thought that it had been abandoned by its true owner.

During the course of the summing up the learned trial judge directed the jury as follows:

"The law says that a person's appropriation or taking of property belonging to another is not to be regarded as dishonest if he appropriates the property in the belief that he has in law the right to deprive the other of it on behalf of himself or if he appropriates the property in the belief that he would have the other's consent if the other, the owner, knew of the appropriation and the circumstances of it. Those are factors that you will have to bear in mind when you come to this question of whether or not he *reasonably* believed it had been dumped or abandoned ...

If the (appellant) reasonably believed the car had been abandoned and therefore could be taken by anyone who then desired it then he would be not guilty ...

It is a matter for you to decide whether this defendant reasonably believed the car had been abandoned by its owner ...

You will have to decide members of the jury applying the facts of this case and the evidence that I shall remind you of shortly, whether or not this (appellant) reasonably believed that this car had been abandoned. If he did members of the jury then he would not be acting dishonestly."

Held

By the Court of Appeal on May 8, 1987 as follows: The Notice of Appeal referred to cases of *R v White* (1912) 7 Cr App R (S) 266 and *Ellerman Wilson Line Limited v Webster* [1952] 1 LlLR 179. Both these cases were 40 years apart and decided by Lord Chief Justices. When examined, they can give rise to two propositions. The first, one cannot steal abandoned property and second, *an honest belief* that property is abandoned is a defence. Reference was made to *Archbold* at paragraph 18(11) and *Smith & Hogan*, and *Glanville Williams* all of whom submit that the propositions are good law. The Court assumed that the propositions remained right. It was held that in considering whether a belief was honest, there can be an honest and genuinely held belief even though it be unreasonable. Reasonableness is relevant to whether in fact such a belief was held. If the belief is unreasonable, it is a factor to be taken into account, when deciding whether it was honestly held. The case of *Ghosh* [1982] 2 All ER 689 identified two conflicting lines of authority: the subjective and objective test of dishonesty. The Court cited with approval pages 162 and 163 of the judgment as follows:

"in determining whether the prosecution had proved that the defendant was acting dishonestly, a jury must first of all decide whether according to the ordinary standards of reasonable and honest people, what was done was dishonest. If it was not dishonest by those standards, that is an end of the matter and the prosecution fails. If it was dishonest by those standards, then the jury must consider whether the defendant himself must have realised that what he was doing was by those standards dishonest."

It was held that the learned trial judge in this case had set out in his direction to the jury, the first half of the *Ghosh* direction, but not the second half.

The appeal was allowed and the conviction quashed.'

[*Reported by Richard Barraclough, Barrister.*]

R v Sobel [1986] Crim LR 261 Court of Appeal (Criminal Division) (Ackner LJ, Drake and Saville JJ)

Intention to permanently deprive - s6(1) Theft Act 1968

Facts

'The appellant was convicted of four counts of theft. As a director of a company he was alleged to have stolen cheques, using them in a dishonest manner inconsistent with his obligations. Cheques were drawn to pay the appellant's debts and obligations including the Access account used by him and his wife. The only issue at the trial was that of dishonesty.

In relation to the Access count the defence was that the appellant could not steal a cheque if he was discharging a company liability, even though the debt was unauthorised vis-à-vis the appellant and the company and had been incurred solely for the appellant's own personal purposes. The appellant appealed against conviction.

Held

Dismissing the appeal, the issue of dishonesty was clearly before the jury on the first three counts. The issue on the Access count centred on whether section 6(1) of the Theft Act 1968 applied. If a person uses a company's cheque in part, unless it is de minimis, for an unauthorised purpose (in this case his own purpose) then he demonstrates that he intends to treat the cheque as his own, to dispose of regardless of the company's rights. That left the final ingredient, of dishonesty. There may be cases where the ability to demonstrate honesty is made palpably apparent by the nature of the item which is unauthorised and in relation to the totality of the cheque; equally the subject matter and the high proportion it bears of the overall cheque may make it clear that prima facie the transaction was dishonest.'

[*Reported by Lynne Knapman, Barrister.*]

R v Warner (1970) 55 Cr App R 93

See references to this authority in *R* v *Lloyd*, above.

18 SECTIONS 8, 9, 10 AND 11 THEFT ACT 1968

R v Brown [1985] Crim LR 212 Court of Appeal (Criminal Division) (Watkins LJ, Pain J and Sir John Thompson)

Entry for the purposes of burglary

Facts

'The appellant was convicted of burglary. A witness, having heard the sound of breaking glass, saw him partially inside a shop front display. The top half of his body was inside the shop window as though he were rummaging inside it. The witness assumed that his feet were on the ground outside, although his view was obscured. He appealed on the ground that he had not "entered" the building, since his body was not entirely within it.

Held

Dismissing the appeal, that the word "enter" in section 9 of the Theft Act 1968 did not require that the whole of a defendant's body be within a building. The use by Edmund Davies LJ in *R v Collins* (1972) 56 Cr App R 554 of the words "substantial" and "effective" in relation to entry did not support the appellant's contention. "Substantial" did not materially assist in the matter, but a jury should be directed that, in order to convict, they must be satisfied that the entry was "effective." Although the trial judge had not actually used the word "effective" in his summing up, his direction gave no ground for complaint. There had clearly been an entry in the present case.'

[*Reported by Kate O'Hanlon, Barrister.*]

R v Clouden [1987] Crim LR 56 Court of Appeal (Criminal Division) (Lloyd LJ, Eastham and French JJ)

Force needed for robbery - s8(1) Theft Act 1968

Facts

'The appellant was seen to follow a woman who was carrying a shopping basket in her left hand. He approached her from behind and wrenched the basket down and out of her grasp with both hands and ran off with it. He was charged in two counts with robbery and theft respectively and convicted on the first count of robbery. He appealed on the grounds (i) that there was insufficient evidence of resistance to the snatching of the bag to constitute force on the person under section 8 of the Theft Act 1968; and (ii) that the learned judge's direction to the jury on the requirement of force on the person was inadequate and confused.

Held

Dismissing the appeal, the old cases distinguished between force on the actual person and force on the property which in fact causes force on the person but, following *Dawson and James* (1976) 64 Cr App R 170, the court should direct attention to the words of the statute without referring to the old authorities. The old distinctions have gone. Whether the defendant used force on any person in order to steal is an issue that should be left to the jury. The judge's direction to the jury was adequate. He told the jury quite clearly at the outset what the statutory definition was, though thereafter he merely used the word "force" and did not use the expression "on the person." '

R v Collins (1972) 56 Cr App R 554 Court of Appeal (Criminal Division) (Edmund Davies and Stephenson LJJ and Boreham J)

Burglary - nature of 'entry' - mens rea for trespass

Facts

As stated by Edmund Davies LJ:

'At about 2 o'clock in the early morning of Saturday July 24, of last year, a young girl of eighteen went to bed at her mother's home in Colchester. She had spent the evening with her boy-friend. She had taken a certain amount of drink, and it may be that this fact affords some explanation of her inability to answer satisfactorily certain crucial questions put to her. She had the habit of sleeping without wearing night apparel in a bed which was very near the lattice-type window of her room. At one stage in her evidence she seemed to be saying that the bed was close up against the window which, in accordance with her practice, was wide open. In the photographs which we have before us, however, there appears to be a gap of some sort between the two, but the bed was clearly quite near the window. At about 3.30 or 4 am she awoke and she then saw in the moonlight a vague form crouched in the open window. She was unable to remember, and this is important, whether the form was on the outside of the window sill or on that part of the sill which was inside the room, and for reasons which will later become clear, that seemingly narrow point is of crucial importance.

She then realised several things: first of all, that the form in the window was that of a male; secondly, that he was a naked male; and thirdly, that he was a naked male with an erect penis. She also saw in the moonlight that his hair was blond. She thereupon leapt to the conclusion that her boy-friend, with whom for some time she had been on terms of regular and frequent sexual intimacy, was paying her an ardent nocturnal visit. She promptly sat up in bed, and the man descended from the sill and joined her in bed and they had full sexual intercourse. But there was something about him which made her think that things were not as they usually were between her and her boy-friend. The length of his hair, his voice as they had exchanged what was described as "love talk," and other features led her to the conclusion that somehow there was something different. She turned on the bed-side light, saw that her companion was not her boy-friend, and slapped the face of the intruder, who was none other than the appellant. He said to her: "Give me a good time tonight," and got hold of her arm, but she bit him and told him to go. She then went into the bathroom and he promptly vanished. She said that she would not have agreed to intercourse if she had known that the person entering her room was not her boy-friend; but there was no suggestion of any force having been used upon her, and the intercourse which took place was undoubtedly effected with no resistance on her part.'

The defendant was convicted of burglary with intent to rape contrary to s9(1)(a) of the 1968 Act, and appealed on the ground that he had not entered the young woman's room as a trespasser.'

Held

Appeal allowed.

Edmund Davies LJ:

'Now, one feature of the case which remained at the conclusion of the evidence in great obscurity is where exactly the appellant was at the moment when, according to him, the girl manifested that she was welcoming him. Was he kneeling on the sill outside the window or was he already inside the room, having climbed through the window frame, and kneeling upon the inner sill? It was a crucial matter, for there were certainly three ingredients which it was incumbent upon the Crown to establish. Under section 9 of the Theft Act 1968, which renders a person guilty of burglary if he enters any building or part of a building as a trespasser and with the intention of committing rape, the entry of the accused into the building must first be proved. Well, there is no doubt about that, for it is common ground that he did enter the girl's bedroom. Secondly, it must be proved that he entered as a trespasser. We will develop that point a little later. Thirdly, it must be proved that he entered as a trespasser with intent at the time of entry to commit rape therein.

The second ingredient of the offence - that the entry must be as a trespasser - is one which has not, to the best of our knowledge, been previously canvassed in the courts. Views as to its ambit have naturally been canvassed by the textbook writers, and it is perhaps not wholly irrelevant to recall that those who were advising the Home Secretary before the Theft Bill was presented to Parliament had it in mind to get rid of some of the frequently absurd technical rules which had been built up in relation to the old requirement in burglary of a "breaking and entering." The cases are legion as to what this did or did not amount to, but happily it is not now necessary for us to consider them. But it was in order to get rid of those technical rules that a new test was introduced, namely, that the entry must be "as a trespasser."

What does that involve? According to the learned editors of Archbold's *Criminal Pleading, Evidence and Practice* (37th ed, para. 1505), "Any intentional, reckless or negligent entry into a building will, it would appear, constitute a trespass if the building is in the possession of another person who does not consent to the entry. Nor will it make any difference that the entry was the result of a reasonable mistake on the part of the defendant, so far as trespass is concerned." If that be right, then it would be no defence for the appellant to say (and even were he believed in saying), "Well, I honestly thought that this girl was welcoming me into the room and I therefore entered, fully believing that I had her consent to go in." If *Archbold* is right, he would nevertheless be a trespasser, since the apparent consent of the girl was unreal, she being mistaken as to who was at her window. We disagree. We hold that, for the purposes of section 9 of the Theft Act, a person entering a building is not guilty of trespass if he enters without knowledge that he is trespassing or at least without acting recklessly as to whether or not he is unlawfully entering.

A view contrary to that of the learned editors of *Archbold* was expressed in Professor Smith's book on *The Law of Theft* (1st ed), where, having given an illustration of an entry into premises, the learned author comments (para. 462), "It is submitted that ... D should be acquitted on the ground of lack of mens rea. Though under the civil law he entered as a trespasser, it is submitted that he cannot be convicted of the criminal offence unless he knew of the facts which caused him to be a trespasser or, at least, was reckless." The matter has also been dealt with by Professor Griew, who in para. 4-05 of his work on the Theft Act has this passage: "What if D wrongly believes that he is not trespassing? His belief may rest on facts which, if true, would mean that he was not trespassing: for instance, he may enter a building by mistake, thinking that it is the one he has been invited to enter. Or his belief may be based on a false view of the legal effect of the known facts: for instance, he may misunderstand the effect of a contract granting him a right of passage through a building. Neither kind of mistake will protect him from tort liability for trespass. In either case, then, D satisfies the literal terms of section 9(1): he 'enters ... as a trespasser.' But for the purposes of criminal liability a man should be judged on the basis of the facts as he believed them to be, and this should include making allowances for a mistake as to rights under the civil law. This is another way of saying that a serious offence like burglary should be held to require mens rea in the fullest sense of the phrase: D should be liable for burglary only if he knowingly trespasses or is reckless as to whether he trespasses or not. Unhappily it is common for Parliament to omit to make clear whether mens rea is intended to be an element in a statutory offence. It is also, though not equally, common for the courts to supply the mental element by construction of the statute."

We prefer the view expressed by Professor Smith and Professor Griew to that of the learned editors of *Archbold*. In the judgment of this Court, there cannot be a conviction for entering premises "as a trespasser" within the meaning of section 9 of the Theft Act unless the person entering does so knowing that he is a trespasser and nevertheless deliberately enters, or, at the very least, is reckless as to whether or not he is entering the premises of another without the other party's consent.

Having so held, the pivotal point of this appeal is whether the Crown established that this appellant at the moment when he entered the bedroom knew perfectly well that he was not welcome there or, being reckless as to whether he was welcome or not, was nevertheless determined to enter. That in turn involves consideration as to where he was at the time when the complainant indicated that she was welcoming him into her bedroom. If, to take an example that was put in the course of argument, her bed had not been near the window but was on the other side of the bedroom, and he (being determined to have her sexually even against her will) climbed through the window and crossed the bedroom to reach her bed, then the offence charged would have been established. But in this case, as we have related, the layout of the room was different, and it became a point of nicety which had to be conclusively established by the Crown as to where he was when the girl made welcoming signs, as she unquestionably at some stage did.

How did the learned judge deal with this matter? We have to say regretfully that there was a flaw in his treatment of it. Referring to section 9, the learned judge said: "There are three ingredients. First is the question of entry. Did he enter into that house? Did he enter as a trespasser? That is to say, was the entry, if you are satisfied there was an entry, intentional or reckless? And, finally, and you may think this is the crux of the case as opened to you by Mr Irwin [counsel for the Crown], if you are satisfied that he entered as a trespasser, did he have the intention to rape this girl?" The learned judge then went on to deal in turn with each of these three ingredients. He first explained what was involved in "entry" into a building. He then dealt with the second ingredient. But the learned judge here unfortunately repeated his earlier observation that the question of entry as a trespasser depended on "was the entry intentional or reckless?" We have to say that this was putting the matter inaccurately. This mistake may have been derived from a passage in the speech of Crown counsel when replying to the submission of "No case." Mr Irwin at one stage said, "Therefore, the first thing that the Crown have got to prove, my Lords, is that there has been a trespass which may be an intentional trespass, or it may be reckless trespass." Unfortunately the learned judge regarded the matter as though the second ingredient in the burglary charged was whether there had been an intentional or reckless entry, and when he came to develop this topic in his summing-up that error was unfortunately perpetuated. The learned judge told the jury, "He had no right to be in that house, as you know, certainly from the point of view of [the girl's parent]. But if you are satisfied about entry, did he enter intentionally or recklessly? What the prosecution say about that, is you do not really have to consider recklessness because when you consider his own evidence he intended to enter that house, and if you accept the evidence I have just pointed out to you, he, in fact did so. So, at least, you may think, it was intentional. At the least, you may think it was reckless because as he told you he did not know whether the girl would accept him."

We are compelled to say that we do not think the learned judge by these observations made sufficiently clear to the jury the nature of the second test about which they had to be satisfied before the defendant could be convicted of the offence charged. There was no doubt that his entry into the bedroom was "intentional." But what the defendant had said was "She knelt on the bed, she put her arms around me and then I went in." If the jury thought he might be truthful in that assertion, they would need to consider whether or not, although entirely surprised by such a reception being accorded to him, the appellant might not have been entitled reasonably to regard her action as amounting to an invitation to him to enter. If she in fact appeared to be welcoming him, the Crown do not suggest that he should have realised or even suspected that she was so behaving because, despite the moonlight, she thought he was someone else. Unless the jury were entirely satisfied that the appellant made an effective and substantial entry into the bedroom without the complainant doing or saying anything to cause him to believe that she was consenting to his entering it, he ought not to be convicted of the offence charged. The point is a narrow one, as narrow maybe as the window sill which is crucial to this case. But this is a criminal charge of gravity and, even though one may suspect that his *intention* was to commit the offence charged, unless the facts show with clarity that he in fact committed it, he ought not to remain convicted.

Some question arose as to whether or not the appellant can be regarded as a trespasser ab initio. But we are entirely in agreement with the view expressed in *Archbold*, again in para. 1505, that the common law doctrine of trespass ab initio has no application to burglary under the Theft Act 1968. One further matter that was canvassed ought perhaps to be mentioned. The point was raised that, the complainant not being the tenant or occupier of the dwelling-house and her mother being apparently in occupation, this girl herself could not in any event have extended an effective invitation to enter, so that, even if she had expressly and with full knowledge of all material facts invited the appellant in, he would nevertheless be a trespasser. Whatever be the position in the law of tort, to regard such a proposition as acceptable in the criminal law would be unthinkable.

We have to say that this appeal must be allowed on the basis that the jury were never invited to consider the vital question whether the appellant did enter the premises as a trespasser, that is to say knowing perfectly well that he had no invitation to enter or reckless of whether or not his entry was with permission. The certificate of the learned judge, as we have already said, demonstrated that he felt there were points involved calling for further consideration. That consideration we have given to the best of our ability. For the reasons we have stated, the outcome of the appeal is that the appellant must be acquitted of the charge preferred against him. The appeal is accordingly allowed and his conviction quashed.'

Corcoran v Anderton (1980) 71 Cr App R 104 Divisional Court (Eveleigh LJ and Watkins J)

Appropriation - whether sufficient for theft/robbery

Facts

As stated by Watkins J:

'At 7.55 p.m. on February 22, 1979, Mrs Hall was in Conran Street in Manchester. She was carrying a handbag. Two youths came along, one the defendant, Christopher Corcoran, and another his co-accused Peter Partington. They had agreed beforehand to steal Mrs Hall's handbag. They began to carry out their purpose. Partington struck her in the back, took hold of and tugged at her handbag causing her to release it. Corcoran was present and participated. Mrs Hall understandably screamed when this attack was made upon her and fell. At that these two youths ran away. So Mrs Hall managed to recover her handbag. At no time, say the justices, did Partington have sole control of the handbag. They were finally of the opinion, having been referred to a number of authorities by Mr Dowse who appeared for these two youths, that the appropriation of the bag was complete when Partington pulled at it so causing Mrs Hall to release it. Therefore they found the youths guilty and ordered the appellant to serve three months in a detention centre.

They were asked to state a case. They did and asked this Court this question: "Could the tugging at the handbag, accompanied by force, amount to robbery, notwithstanding the fact that the co-accused did not have sole control of the bag at any time?" '

Held

The appeal would be dismissed.

Watkins J:

'It has been argued very attractively before us by Mr Dowes [counsel for the defendant] that having regard to the textbook on *The Theft Acts 1968-1978* by Edward Griew, para. 2-76, an appropriation did not occur. It is sufficient I think if I read from the footnote on this page, where it is stated: "... where D's grip on the property does not give him effective control of it, however fleeting (because, eg it is attached to something from which D will have to part it), it is very likely that a court would baulk at describing his act as more than an attempt."

The word "appropriate" has also received the attention of the authors Smith and Hogan in their well-known book *Criminal Law* (4th ed). At p491 it is stated: "Appropriation therefore does not require an assumption of control over the property - 'any assumption ... of the rights of an owner' suffices. Accordingly it is arguable that a mere attempt to assume control is an appropriation. Thus if D puts his hand towards P's pocket in order to steal P's watch this might be an appropriation. Clearly the appropriation would be complete in such a case, at the latest, when D puts his hand on the watch and there would be no need of a removal of the watch to complete the appropriation. D has already taken control and thus already assumed the rights of an owner. But on a common-sense approach it seems difficult to say that D has assumed the rights of an owner where he merely puts his hand towards P's pocket; he is trying to assume control and as his act is sufficiently proximate he may be convicted of an attempt."

The differing views upon the meaning of appropriation found in these and other textbooks, are instructive and interesting. But this Court has for practical purposes to deal primarily with circumstances as found by the justices sitting in the juvenile court in the city of Manchester. These circumstances involve the use of force upon the person of Mrs Hall so that she lost her grip upon her handbag accompanied by the intention in the minds of both the appellant and his companion to steal, that is to say to take the handbag, by force if necessary, away from Mrs Hall and permanently deprive her of that handbag or its contents.

It is quite impossible for any court to delineate with precision the point at which in every conceivable kind of circumstance an appropriation begins and ends.

So confining myself to the facts as found by the justices in the instant case, I think that an "appropriation" takes place when an accused snatches a woman's handbag completely from her grasp, so that she no longer has physical control over it because it has fallen to the ground. What has been involved in such activity as that, bearing in mind the dishonest state of mind of the accused, is an assumption of the rights of the owner, a taking of the property of another. If one had to consider the definition of "theft" as contained in the Larceny Act 1916, it is inevitable, so it seems to me, that there was here a sufficient taking and carrying away to satisfy the definition of "theft" in that Act. In my judgment there cannot possibly be, save for the instance where a handbag is carried away from the scene of it, a clearer instance of robbery than that which these justices found was committed.

Turning to the actual question posed to this Court, "Could the tugging at the handbag, accompanied by force, amount to robbery, notwithstanding the fact that the co-accused did not have sole control of the bag at any time?" in my opinion, which may be contrary to some notions on what constitutes a sufficient appropriation to satisfy the definition of that word in section 3(1) of the Theft Act the forcible tugging of the handbag itself could in the circumstances be a sufficient exercise of control by the accused person so as to amount to an assumption by him of the rights of the owner, and therefore an appropriation of the property.

Accordingly if the question had been properly put, my answer would have been unequivocally and certainly in the affirmative. The question as put to us is academic. Had it been founded upon fact I feel sure I should have answered that too affirmatively.'

R v Dawson (1976) 64 Cr App R 170 Court of Appeal (Criminal Division) (Lawton LJ, MacKenna and Swanwick JJ)

Robbery - ingredients

Facts

As stated by Lawton LJ:

'On the night of July 10, 1975, a Blue Jacket in the Royal Navy on *HMS Hampshire* was on shore leave in Liverpool. Shortly before midnight he went to the Liverpool Pier Head to wait for transport to take him across to Birkenhead where his ship was berthed. He was approached by these two appellants and a third man who was never apprehended.

I turn now to the evidence. According to the Blue Jacket, two of the men came alongside him and the third was behind him. This is what he said: "There was one standing on the other side and just nudging me with the shoulder and I lost my balance. Q. Did it distract your attention, or did he stop you from being able to resist? A. I was trying to keep my balance. I was being pushed from side to side and I was trying to keep my balance. I was more interested in keeping my balance than anything else. Q. If you had been able to keep your balance what would you have been able to do when the hand was put to the wallet? A. I think I would have been able to apprehend the person. Q. Why weren't you able to apprehend them? A. I was trying to keep my balance. I was more interested in trying to keep my balance."

One of the men, almost certainly the third man who was not apprehended, managed to get his hand into the sailor's pocket, and extract a wallet which contained a fairly substantial sum of money. Once the wallet had been extracted from the sailor's pocket the three men ran off. The sailor tried to chase them, then realised he had not got a hope of catching them. Fortunately at that moment a police patrol car came along; the sailor told the police officers what had happened and the police patrol car went in pursuit of the three. They managed to apprehend two. Of the two who were apprehended they told a pack of lies as to what they had been doing. When they repeated that story at the trial they were not believed by the jury.

The question posed on their appeal was whether there was enough evidence to go before the jury on the charge of robbery, and the case is reported on the direction to be given to juries on charges under the Theft Act 1968, particularly, in the instant case, under section 8 of that Act.'

Held

The appeals would be dismissed.

Lawton LJ:

'Mr Locke, for the appellants, has been very realistic about the case. He has not sought to criticise the summing-up, although he did put forward some criticisms in his grounds of appeal. He did not pursue them here. The summing-up was a model of fairness. The learned judge was conscious of the difficulty as to whether the sailor had described what a jury would regard as "using force on him for the purposes of stealing."

Mr Locke had submitted at the end of the prosecution's case that what had happened could not in law amount to the use of force. He called the learned judge's attention to some old authorities and to a passage in *Archbold* [see now 39th ed, 1976, paragraph 1483] based on the old authorities, and submitted that because of those old authorities there was not enough evidence to go to the jury. He sought before this Court to refer to the old authorities. He was discouraged from doing so because this Court is of the opinion that in these cases what judges should now direct their attention to is the words of the statute. This has been said in a number of cases since the Theft Act 1968.

The object of that Act was to get rid of all the old technicalities of the law of larceny and to put the law into simple language which juries would understand and which they themselves would use. That is what has happened in section 8 which defines "robbery." That section is in these terms: "A person is guilty of robbery if he steals, and immediately before or at the time of doing so, and in order to do so, he uses force on any person or puts or seeks to put any person in fear of being then and there subjected to force."

The choice of the word "force" is not without interest because under the Larceny Act 1916 the word "violence" had been used, but Parliament deliberately on the advice of the Criminal Law Revision Committee changed that word to "force." Whether there is any difference between "violence" or "force" is not relevant for the purposes of this case; but the word is "force." It is a word in ordinary use. It is a word which juries understand. The learned judge left it to the jury to say whether jostling a man in the way which the victim described to such an extent that he had difficulty in keeping his balance could be said to be the use of force. The learned judge, because of the argument put forward by Mr Locke, went out of his way to explain to the jury that force in these sort of circumstances must be substantial to justify a verdict.

Whether it was right for him to put that objective before the word "force" when Parliament had not done so we will not discuss for the purposes of this case. It was a matter for the jury. They were there to use their common sense and knowledge of the world. We cannot say that their decision as to whether force was used was wrong. They were entitled to the view that force was used.

Other points were discussed in the case as to whether the force had been used for the purpose of distracting the victim's attention or whether it was for the purpose of overcoming resistance. Those sort of refinements may have been relevant under the old law, but so far as the new law is concerned the sole question is whether the accused used force on any person in order to steal. That issue in this case was left to the jury. They found in favour of the Crown.

We cannot say that this verdict was either unsafe or unsatisfactory. Accordingly the appeal is dismissed.'

R v Hale (1978) 68 Crim App R 415 Court of Appeal (Criminal Division) (Waller and Eveleigh LJJ and Tudor Evans J)

Force used at the time of stealing - duration of stealing

Facts

As stated by Eveleigh LJ:

'The prosecution alleged that the appellant and one McGuire went to the house of a Mrs Carrett. When she answered the door they rushed in. Each was wearing a stocking mask. The appellant put his hand over Mrs Carrett's mouth to stop her screaming and McGuire went upstairs to search. The appellant subsequently released his hold on Mrs Carrett and she went to the settee. He undid her dressing gown and touched her. He also exposed himself. McGuire then came downstairs with a jewellery box and asked where the rest was. The telephone rang. It was a next door neighbour who had heard Mrs Carrett scream and wanted to know if everything was all right. Under threat from the appellant she replied everything was all right. All three then went upstairs and Mrs Carrett was asked where her money was. The appellant and McGuire then used the toilet and on their return said that they would tie her up and she was not to telephone the police. They tied her ankles and hands and put socks in her mouth. They went out of the front door warning her not to telephone, saying that they would come back and do something to her little boy if she phoned the police within five minutes.

McGuire failed to appear at the trial, but in March of this year he pleaded guilty to robbery and was sentenced to four years' imprisonment.

Hale's defence was that there was no robbery or theft and no indecent assault. He said that Mrs Carrett had agreed to a mock robbery as part of an insurance fraud.

The learned judge read to the jury the definition of robbery from section 8 of the Theft Act 1968 and also correctly directed them upon the meaning of the word "steals." He also said "A person who goes into somebody else's house with or without a companion and makes the householder fear for her safety or to apprehend violence if she does not co-operate, or who ties her up at the end of the episode in order to make sure that he can get away safely with the plunder, is guilty of robbery. Do you understand that? That is what is said by the prosecution obviously took place here." He continued, "In order to be sure that a person is guilty of robbery, you have to be sure that they were stealing and the definition of stealing is that a person is guilty of stealing if he dishonestly appropriates property belonging to another with the intention of permanently depriving the other of it. Well putting it really in, I hope, equally simple and understandable words, the question for you here is whether you feel sure that this accused, by the use of force, or putting her in fear, got hold of Mrs Carrett's property without her consent, and without believing that he had got her consent, and intending to appropriate it for his own purposes without giving it back to her afterwards."

When the learned judge resumed his summing-up the following morning, he re-capitulated to the jury the matters upon which they had to feel sure before they could find the defendants guilty. He said

"First, that Mrs Carrett did not consent to her property being taken; secondly that the defendant knew that; thirdly that the defendant intended to deprive her of the property permanently and, if the matter stopped there, that would be stealing. Fourthly, for robbery, which is an aggravated form of stealing, that the appellant was a party to using or threatening force to enable him and his companion successfully to find and to take and to carry away and so steal and appropriate that property without interruption."

On behalf of the appellant it is submitted that the learned judge misdirected the jury in that the passages quoted above could indicate to them that if an accused used force in order to effect his escape with the stolen goods that would be sufficient to constitute the crime of robbery. In so far as the facts of the present case are concerned, counsel submitted that the theft was completed when the jewellery box was first seized and any force thereafter could not have been "immediately before or at the time of stealing" and certainly not "in order to steal." The essence of the submission was that the theft was completed as soon as the jewellery box was seized.'

Held

The appeal would be dismissed.

Eveleigh LJ:

'In the present case there can be little doubt that if the appellant had been interrupted after the seizure of the jewellery box the jury would have been entitled to find that the appellant and his accomplice were assuming the rights of an owner at the time when the jewellery box was seized. However, the act of appropriation does not suddenly cease. It is a continuous act and it is a matter for the jury to decide whether or not the act of appropriation has finished. Moreover, it is quite clear that the intention to deprive the owner permanently, which accompanied the assumption of the owner's rights was a continuing one at all material times. This Court therefore rejects the contention that the theft had ceased by the time the lady was tied up. As a matter of common-sense the appellant was in the course of committing theft; he was stealing.

There remains the question whether there was robbery. Quite clearly the jury were at liberty to find the appellant guilty of robbery relying upon the force used when he put his hand over Mrs Carrett's mouth to restrain her from calling for help. We also think that they were also entitled to rely upon the act of tying her up provided they were satisfied (and it is difficult to see how they could not be satisfied) that the force so used was to enable them to steal. If they were still engaged in the act of stealing the force was clearly used to enable them to continue to assume the rights of the owner and permanently to deprive Mrs Carrett of her box, which is what they began to do when they first seized it.

Taking the summing-up as a whole, and in relation to the particular facts of this case, the jury could not have thought that they were entitled to convict if the force used was not at the time of the stealing and for the purpose of stealing. The learned judge said "In order to be sure that the person is guilty of robbery you have to be sure they were stealing." While the use of the words complained of would not serve as an alternative definition of robbery and could, if standing alone, be open to the criticism that the learned judge was arriving at a conclusion of fact which the jury had to decide, those words did not stand alone and this Court is satisfied that there was no misdirection. This appeal is accordingly dismissed.'

R v Jones and Smith (1976) 63 Cr App R 47   Court of Appeal (Criminal Division)   (James and Geoffrey Lane LJJ, and Cobb J)

Trespass - burglary contrary to s9(1)(b) Theft Act 1968

Facts

The defendants, Christopher Smith and John Jones, took two television sets from the house of Alfred

Smith, the father of one of the defendants, without his knowledge or consent. The defendants were convicted of burglary contrary to s9(1)(b) of the Theft Act 1968, despite evidence given by Alfred Smith, that his son' ... would never be a trespasser in my house ...' The defendants appealed on the ground that there had been no proof of trespass by them.

Held

The appeals would be dismissed

James LJ:

'Mr Rose [counsel for the appellants] argues that a person who had a general permission to enter premises of another person cannot be a trespasser. His submission is as short and as simple as that. Related to this case he says that a son to whom a father has given permission generally to enter the father's house cannot be a trespasser if he enters it even though he had decided in his mind before making the entry to commit a criminal offence of theft against the father once he had got into the house and had entered the house solely for the purpose of committing that theft. It is a bold submission. Mr Rose frankly accepts that there has been no decision of the Court since this statute was passed which governs particularly this point. He has reminded us of the decision in *Byrne* v *Kinematograph Renters Society Ltd* [1958] 2 All ER 579, which he prays in aid of his argument. In that case persons had entered a cinema by producing tickets not for the purpose of seeing the show, but for an ulterior purpose. It was held in the action, which sought to show that they entered as trespassers pursuant to a conspiracy to trespass, that in fact they were not trespassers. The important words in the judgment of Harman J at p593D are "They did nothing that they were not invited to do, ..." That provides a distinction between that case and what we consider the position to be in this case.

Mr Rose has also referred us to one of the trickery cases, a case of *Boyle* (1954) 38 Cr App R 111; [1954] 2 QB 293, and in particular the passage on pp112-113, 295 of the respective reports. He accepts that the trickery cases can be distinguished from such a case as the present because in the trickery cases it can be said that that which would otherwise have been consent to enter was negatived by the fact that consent was obtained by a trick. We do not gain any help in the particular case from that decision.

We were also referred to *Collins* (1972) 56 Cr App R 554; [1973] QB 100 and in particular to the long passage of Edmund Davies LJ, as he then was, commencing at pp559 and 104 of the respective reports where the learned Lord Justice commenced the consideration of what is involved by the words "... the entry must be 'as a trespasser'." At p561 and pp104-105 - again it is unnecessary to cite that long passage in full, suffice it to say that this Court on that occasion expressly approved the view expressed in Professor Smith's book on the *Law of Theft* (1968) (1st ed) para. 462, and also the view of Professor Griew in his book on the *Theft Act* (1968) (1st ed) para. 4-05 upon this aspect of what is involved in being a trespasser.

In our view the passage there referred to is consonant with the passage in the well known case of *Hillen and Pettigrew* v *ICI (Alkali) Ltd* [1936] AC 65 where, in the speech of Lord Atkin these words appear at p69: "My Lords, in my opinion this duty to an invitee only extends so long and so far as the invitee is making what can reasonably be contemplated as an ordinary and reasonable use of the premises by the invitee for the purpose for which he has been invited. He is not invited to use any part of the premises for purposes which he knows are wrongfully dangerous and constitute an improper use. As Scrutton LJ has pointedly said [in *The Calgarth* [1926] P 93 at p110] 'When you invite a person into your house to use the staircase you do not invite him to slide down the banisters.' " That case of course was a civil case in which it was sought to make the defendant liable for a tort.

The decision in *Collins* (supra) in this Court, a decision upon the criminal law, added to the concept of trespass as a civil wrong only the mental element of mens rea, which is essential to the criminal offence. Taking the law as expressed in *Hillen and Pettigrew* v *ICI Ltd* (supra) and in the case of

Collins (supra) it is our view that a person is a trespasser for the purpose of section 9(1)(*b*) of the Theft Act 1968, if he enters premises of another knowing that he is entering in excess of the permission that has been given to him, or being reckless as to whether he is entering in excess of the permission that has been given to him to enter, providing the facts are known to the accused which enable him to realise that he is acting in excess of the permission given or that he is acting recklessly as to whether he exceeds that permission, then that is sufficient for the jury to decide that he is in fact a trespasser.

In this particular case it was a matter for the jury to consider whether, on all the facts, it was shown by the prosecution that the appellants entered with the knowledge that entry was being effected against the consent or in excess of the consent that had been given by Mr Smith senior to his son Christopher. The jury were, by their verdict satisfied of that. It was a novel argument that we heard, interesting but one without, in our view, any foundation.

The other ground of appeal argued by Mr Rose is that expressed in ground 2 of the forms of grounds of appeal and relates to a non-direction by the learned recorder in the summing-up. We say "non-direction" for although we have not called upon the Crown to argue to the contrary of Mr Rose's submissions it is quite clear to us that there was the omission, in this particular case, to direct the jury in the way a jury is normally directed where there is more than one accused person that statements made by one accused in the absence of the other are evidence only against the maker of the statements. The exception to that principle is when one accused goes into the witness box and confirms or reiterates a statement that he had made in the course of investigation by the police and in the absence of the other accused. In those circumstances the evidence becomes evidence in the case. Here both in respect of Smith and in respect of Jones it is said that the omission to warn the jury that answers given by Smith to the police officers were not evidence in the case of Jones and that answers given by Jones were not evidence in the case of Smith.

We do not propose to refer to the passages in the summing-up in which the judge dealt with the evidence of police officers as to the answers given by each of the appellants respectively or to the passages in the summing-up where the learned recorder dealt with the evidence of the defendants at the trial. The point can be stated quite shortly as argued for the appellants and it is a point that can be developed by reference to a number of passages; to some of which Mr Rose has invited our attention in particular to a passage at p21 of the transcript.

Mr Rose has also pointed out that at p22 of the transcript of the summing-up the learned recorder unfortunately made one error of fact when he said to the jury of Jones that in giving his evidence he had given a version of not going into the house but remaining outside. In respect of those passages of which Mr Rose has invited our attention the other passages which have the same effect, it is said that in the absence of the usual warning to the jury that is required in circumstances of this sort it may well be that the jury used the fact that Smith told lies to the police officers as evidence in the case and used the fact that Jones lied to the police officers as evidence in the case of Smith. We do not consider that that result would follow from the way in which the jury were directed in this particular case even bearing in mind there was the absence of the warning. If one looks at the nature of the defences put forward by these two appellants to which I have already referred, if one looks at the evidence in the case of the answers given by the appellants separately to the police officers and evidence of the defendants as given in the witness box in the course of the trial there is nothing there, in our view, which would be likely adversely to affect the case of either of the appellants in the absence of the warning. The position was in respect of Smith that he admitted that he had lied to the police and in evidence he gave an explanation for so lying which was an explanation peculiar to his own position. Jones admitted also in evidence that he had lied to the police and he gave an explanation of why he had lied and been obstructive which explanation was peculiar to his own situation.

Those matters were put before the jury against a background of the warning that the jury should regard the case of each of the accused separately and in those circumstances we think that the addition of the warning which the learned recorder ought to have given would in fact, in this case, have added nothing at all so far as affecting the jury and the conclusion. We would just illustrate it by reference to one of the passages which occurs on p21E. The learned recorder is recounting the answer given by Smith to the police officer in relation to the fact that Smith had not seen his father on visiting the house the answer being: "I thought he had been drinking, we decided not to bother him," and the consideration of that answer in contrast to the evidence of Smith which he had given at the trial. If the warning had been given it would have been in these terms: "Members of the jury, in respect of Jones you must not take into consideration the fact that Smith says to the police that he thought his father had been drinking and that he and Jones had decided not to bother the father in those circumstances." That warning, we feel, would have added nothing to the jury's approach to this matter. If the learned recorder had done, which everyone would concede would have been wrong, namely to say to the jury "Members of the jury, in considering Jones' case you can remember that Smith had said of the visit to the house and the non-disturbance of the father that he thought he had been drinking," it would have been quite wrong if the learned recorder had given that direction, but even if he had have done it could not have done any damage at all to the defence of Jones; all the more so is the situation where the learned recorder did not go so far as that but merely omitted to give the usual direction. That is just taking one of the passages complained about illustrative of the type of direction that is questioned in this case.

Finally, before parting with the matter, we would refer to a passage at p25 of the transcript of the summing-up to the jury. In particular the passage which I think one must read in full (from p25B to 26B). In the course of that the learned recorder said this: "I have read out the conversations they had with Detective-Sergeant Tarrant and in essence Smith said, 'My father gave me leave to take these sets and Jones was invited along to help.' If that account may be true, that is an end of the case, but if you are convinced that that night they went to the house and entered as trespassers and had no leave or licence to go there for that purpose and they intended to steal these sets and keep them permanently themselves, acting dishonestly, then you will convict them. Learned counsel for the prosecution did mention the possibility that you might come to the conclusion that they had gone into the house with leave or licence of the father and it would be possible for you to bring in a verdict simply of theft but, members of the jury, of course it is open to you to do that if you felt that the entry to the house was as a consequence of the father's leave or licence, but what counts of course for the crime of burglary to be made out is the frame of mind of each person when they go into the property. If you go in intending to steal, then your entry is burglarious, it is to trespass because no-one gave you permission to go in and steal in the house." Then the learned recorder gave an illustration of the example of a person who is invited to go into a house to make a cup of tea and that person goes in and steals the silver and he goes on: "I hope that illustrates the matter sensibly. Therefore you may find it difficult not to say, if they went in there they must have gone in order to steal because they took elaborate precautions, going there at the dead of night, you really cannot say that under any circumstances their entry to the house could have been other than trespass."

In that passage that I have just read the learned recorder put the matter properly to the jury in relation to the aspect of trespass and on this ground of appeal as upon the others we find that the case is not made out, that there was no misdirection, as I have already indicated early in the judgment, and in those circumstances the appeal will be dismissed in the case of each of the appellants.'

Norfolk Constabulary v Seekings and Gould [1986] Crim LR 167 Norfolk Crown Court (Judge Binns and local Justices)

'Building' for the purposes of burglary

Facts

'The appellants appealed against conviction for an offence of attempted burglary. They had been seen attempting to gain entry to two identical articulated lorry trailers being used by Budgens supermarket as temporary storage space during the currency of building redevelopment. Each trailer had been brought to the site by tractor, unhitched, and left supported by its own wheels and struts in a location immediately behind the supermarket on ground upon which buildings had once stood. An electric cable was attached to each trailer for the supply of lighting and, in the case of one trailer, heating; this was supported by a wire to prevent the cable blowing about in the wind; steps had been constructed and placed against each trailer; access was gained by climbing the steps, unlocking a lock at the base of ordinary trailer shutters, and the shutters then being raised; the trailers were used daily for about a year.

The court was referred to *Smith on the Law of Theft* (5th ed) paragraphs 343 et seq, and to *B and S* v *Leathley* [1979] Crim LR 314 and *Estate Products (Frozen Foods) Ltd* v *Doncaster Borough Council* [1980] Crim LR 108.

Held

By His Honour Judge Binns and L Justices that the trailer was a vehicle and not a building and accordingly allowed the appeal.'

R v Walkington (1979) 68 Cr App R 427 Court of Appeal (Criminal Division) (Geoffrey Lane LJ, Swanwick and Wien JJ)

Entry into part of a building as a trespasser

Facts

Taken from the judgment of Geoffrey Lane LJ:

'On January 20, 1977, shortly before closing time of Debenhams Store in Oxford Street, the appellant was seen in the menswear department of that store. He was kept under observation by Mr Rogers, who was a store detective, and two of his colleagues. The store closed at six o'clock. At about 20 minutes to six the various counter assistants were cashing up their tills. The evidence given by Mr Rogers was that the appellant seemed to be interested primarily, if not solely, in what was going on at the various tills in the store.

In due course he was observed to travel up on the escalator to the first floor. On that floor was an unattached till in the centre of a three-sided counter, the drawer of the till being partially opened. There was some dispute as to the precise dimensions of this three-sided rectangular counter, but what was agreed was that it was a movable counter. It was not static in the sense of being fixed to the floor. One of the descriptions of it showed that what we may call the north side of the counter was about four feet in length, the east side was about 12 feet in length and the west side was about six feet in length, the till being situated on the north side, the four feet length. Other descriptions of the counter gave different dimensions. But in each case it is to be observed that the till was in a corner formed by two of these counters. The evidence was that the area inside that rectangle or partial rectangle was reserved for the staff and it was clear, so it was suggested, that any customer seeing that area would realise that his permission to be in the store did not extend to a permission to be in that area.

The appellant, on the evidence, moved to the opening of the rectangular area described, that is to say to the part thereof which was not filled in by any counter, looked all around him, then bent down and having got to the till pulled the drawer further open. Having looked into the drawer the appellant slammed it to, said something and started making his way out of the shop, when he was stopped by the store detective.

In fact there was nothing in the drawer. The fact that the till drawer was partially open was an indication to anyone in the know that the assistant at that particular counter had cashed that particular till up.

The police were duly called in and the appellant was arrested. He was taken to Marylebone police station where he made a statement in writing, which reads as follows: "I came up the West End to do some shopping and I went into Debenhams for a tie. I walked around the store for a while and looked at some coats. I went up on the first floor to have a look at the shoes. After a while I noticed a till partly open with a drawer beneath it. I thought I might be able to steal something from it so I opened the drawer but there was nothing in it worth stealing which was my intention. I shut the drawer again and walked away. That was when the security bloke stopped me. I don't know why I did it now, it seems so stupid. I would like to take this opportunity of saying how sorry I am and apologise to the store, the police and the court."

His main ground of appeal was that the deputy circuit judge should have allowed the defence submission and withdrawn the case from the jury in that it would be wrong to divide the store artificially into "parts" in the way that would be necessary to make the case of burglary out of the situation presented by the prosecution; thus the appellant could not be said to have trespassed behind the counter.'

Held

The appeal would be dismissed.

Geoffrey Lane LJ:

[His Lordship considered s9 of the Theft Act 1968 and continued]

'What the prosecution had to prove here was that the defendant had entered a part of a building as a trespasser with intent to steal anything in that part of the building. Mr Osborne submitted that this could not be said to be a part of a building. It was a submission which we confess we found a little difficult to follow. But it transpired that what Mr Osborne was principally relying upon was a passage in a publication by Professor Griew entitled *The Theft Acts 1968 and 1978* (3rd ed, 1979). He made particular reference to paragraph 4-16 at p68, which reads: "D has the licence that all customers have in a shop to move from counter to counter. He now moves to counter 2, intending to steal at it. If in doing so he is entering a different 'part' of the shop, he may be guilty of burglary, for entry for a purpose other than that for which a licence to enter is granted is a trespassory entry. But it does not seem likely that the courts will be hasty to divide buildings artificially into 'parts' in the way that would be necessary to make a case of burglary out of the situation presented here."

With respect to Mr Osborne it seems to us that that passage is not dealing with the present situation at all. It is dealing with a situation where there is no physical demarcation at all and the only matter which may cause the man to be a trespasser is a change of intention in his own mind. This is not the situation here. Here there is a physical demarcation, and if one turns to the same publication at the passage where Professor Griew is dealing with the situation which exists here, we find this at paragraph 4-07: "A licence to enter a building may extend to part of the building only. If so, the licensee will trespass if he enters some other part not within the scope of the licence. To do so with intent to commit in that other part one of the specified offences, or to do so and then to commit or attempt to commit one of those offences therein, will be burglary." That seems to us precisely to fit the circumstances of the present case and really deals the death blow to this part of Mr Osborne's submission.

If support is required, it is to be found in Professor Smith's publication *The Law of Theft* (3rd ed 1978), at paragraph 329 (i), where he says: "... A customer in a shop who goes behind the counter and takes money from the till during a short absence of the shopkeeper would be guilty of burglary even though he entered the shop with the shopkeeper's permission. The permission did not extend to his going behind the counter ..."

There are similar passages at paragraphs 331 and 334. Paragraph 331 is the only one to which I need refer: "It would seem that the whole reason for the words 'or part of a building' is that D may enter or be in part of a building without trespass and it is desirable that he should be liable as a burglar if he trespasses in the remainder of the building with the necessary intent. It is submitted that the building need not be physically divided into 'parts.' It ought to be sufficient if a notice in the middle of a hall stated, 'No customers beyond this point.' These considerations suggest that, for the present purposes, a building falls into two parts only; first, that part in which D was lawfully present and, second, the remainder of the building. This interpretation avoids anomalies which arise if physical divisions within a building are held to create 'parts'."

One really gets two extremes, as it seems to us. First of all you have the part of the building which is shut off by a door so far as the general public is concerned, with a notice saying "Staff Only" or "No admittance to customers." At the other end of the scale you have for example a single table in the middle of the store, which it would be difficult for any jury to find properly was a part of the building into which the licensor prohibited customers from moving.

The present situation, it seems to us, was that there was a physical partition. Whether it was sufficient to amount to an area from which the public were plainly excluded was a matter for the jury. It seems to us that there was ample evidence on which they could come to the conclusion (a) that the management had impliedly prohibited customers entering that area and (b) that this particular defendant knew of that prohibition. Whether the jury came to the conclusion that the prosecution made out their case was a matter for them, but there is no dispute that the learned judge, in those two careful passages which I have read, left the matter fairly and correctly to the jury.'

R v Wilson; R v Jenkins [1983] 3 WLR 686

See chapter 5.

19 SECTIONS 12, 13, 21 AND 25 THEFT ACT 1968

R v Bevans (1988) 87 Cr App Rep 65 Court of Appeal (Criminal Division) (Watkins LJ, Jones and Leonard JJ)

Theft Act 1968 s21 - whether demand made with a view to gain

Facts (as stated by Jones J)

'Back in 1951 the appellant, who was on active service, was shot in the hip. Thereafter he became increasingly crippled by osteo-arthritis. His condition became so severe that indeed about a month after the matters which the Court is examining in this appeal, he underwent a hip replacement operation.

But before that operation took place, on the night of August 23/24, 1986, the appellant got in touch with the Medical Services. He tried in the first instance to get in touch with his own doctor. He was then complaining of severe pain in his legs. It so happened that his doctor was not available and another doctor, Dr Dias, was on call as a deputising doctor. He went to the appellant's house arriving there just after 4 o'clock in the morning.

The door was answered by the appellant who escorted the doctor into the living room. They both sat down and started to discuss the appellant's pains. Then, according to the doctor, the appellant suddenly pulled out a black handgun from his jacket and pointing it at the doctor demanded an injection of morphine to ease his pain. He told the doctor he would shoot if he was not given an injection.

The doctor explained that he did not carry morphine, but offered the appellant an injection of pethidine. The appellant accepted the offer after some deliberation, put the gun back into his pocket and the injection of pethidine was administered. After that the appellant calmed down and apologised to the doctor for the trouble he had caused. Matters ended by the doctor writing a note for the appellant to give to his own doctor recommending a strong pain killer. The appellant escorted the doctor to the door and he left.

In the course of the trial Mr Griffiths who appeared on behalf of the appellant, submitted to the learned judge that there was no case to answer. The learned judge ruled against him.

The grounds of appeal are that the learned judge was wrong in arriving at his decision and that consequently he misdirected the jury when he came to sum up to them. His misdirection, it is submitted, lies in this part of his summing up where, at p2 of the transcript, he says: "What the prosecution must prove here is really three things: first, that there was a demand for the drug," and he invited the jury to look back at the indictment, "with a view to gain for himself - 'gain' must relate to money or property; a drug clearly is an aspect of property. That is why I say the prosecution must prove there was a demand for the drug." '

Held:

The appeal would be dismissed.

Jones J:

[Mr Griffiths's (counsel for the appellant)]

'submission, put very shortly here, is that for this appellant to ask the doctor for an injection of morphine was not a demand made with a view to gain for himself.

The Act provides in section 21 that, "A person is guilty of blackmail if, with a view to gain for himself or another or with intent to cause loss to another, he makes any unwarranted demand with menaces."

Pausing there, there is no dispute here but that the appellant made a demand which was unwarranted and that it was made with menaces. The words which are highlighted by Mr Griffiths's submission are the words "with a view to gain for himself."

Section 34(2) of the Act defines "gain" and "loss," and provides thus: "For purposes of this Act - (a) 'gain' and 'loss; are to be construed as extending only to gain or loss in money or other property ... and - (i) 'gain' includes a gain by keeping what one has, as well as a gain by getting what one has not ..."

Mr Griffiths argued before the learned judge, and has repeated his argument before this Court, that the demand for an injection of morphine was not made with a view to gain for the appellant. He argues that those words, "with a view to gain for himself," involve the court in a consideration of the motive which lay behind the appellant's demand. It is said that that motive was unquestionably the relief from the pain which he was suffering at the time. Therefore what he had in mind was the gain of relief from pain, not for a gain in money or other property.

He has referred the Court to *The Law of Theft* (5th ed, 1984) of which the author is Professor Smith, a very distinguished academic lawyer. In the course of dealing particularly with that definition of gain or loss, Professor Smith said at para. 311, after having set out s34(2)(*a*) of the Act, "As has already been noted, this definition limits the offence to the protection of economic interests."

Mr Griffiths argues that in no sense of the word was there here an economic interest involved. There was not in the appellant's mind either an economic gain by him or an economic loss inflicted upon the doctor.

It may be that the difficulty has arisen in this case by importing into the Act words which are not there. Professor Smith does not suggest for a moment that the words "economic interest" or "economic loss" should be substituted for the words which appear in the statute. They appear only to be another way of referring to the gain or loss of money or property. Those are the words used in the Act. Again the word "motive" is not used anywhere in the Act. The words used are, "with a view to gain or with an intent to cause loss." As I have said, it may well be misleading to try to import those words into the Act, and then try to understand what meaning they should bear.

In the judgment of this Court the matter can be resolved quite simply and straightforwardly by reference to the Act itself. What had to be established was that the demand was made with a view to gain for the appellant; expanding those words by reference to section 34(2), that meant with a view to the appellant getting what he had not, and to getting something which consisted of money or other property.

It seems difficult, if not impossible, to argue that the liquid which constituted the substance which was to be injected into the appellant's body was not property. It clearly was. There has been no dispute but that if an ampoule containing the liquid had been handed over to the appellant instead of being transferred to a syringe and injected into his body, he would have got property in that sense. This Court can see no difference between the liquid being contained in the syringe before it is passed into his body and the liquid being contained in an ampoule. There can be no question but that that morphine was property.

Again the next question would be - did the appellant have in view the getting of that morphine (that admittedly being something which, before making the demand, he had not)? Again there seems to be only one possible answer: yes. It is nothing to the point that his ultimate motive was the relief of pain through the effect which that morphine would have upon his bodily processes.

It was pointed out in the course of argument that someone may very well demand a bottle of whisky. His ultimate motive may simply be to get drunk, that is to drink it all himself and to get drunk.

That does not detract in any way from the proposition that in fact he would be demanding property in the form of the bottle of whisky and in particular the bottle's contents.

By analogy exactly the same argument must apply here. This demand, which was a demand for an injection of morphine, involved two things: first of all it involved the passing of a drug to him, and secondly it involved the service by the doctor of actually carrying out the injection. The fact that he was gaining the service does not in any way mean that he was not gaining the property which consisted of the morphine. There is no suggestion anywhere in the Act that the gain must be exclusively directed to one particular object. Indeed Professor Smith himself at one part of his writing says precisely that in the same paragraph to which I have already referred, paragraph 311, where towards the end he says this: "No doubt it is enough that the acquisition of money or other property is one of several objects which D has in mind in making the demand." With that this Court wholly agrees.

For those reasons this Court has come to the conclusion that the learned judge's ruling was correct in law and that his consequential direction to the jury was correct in law, that on the evidence that was given, if they accepted the doctor's version, they could come only to that conclusion, namely that the demand was made with a view to gain for himself, gain of the property which consisted of the drug morphine. Accordingly this appeal will be dismissed.'

R v Bow (1976) 64 Cr App R 54 Court of Appeal (Criminal Division) (Bridge LJ, Wien and Kenneth Jones JJ)

Section 12(1) Theft Act 1968 - taking for the defendant's own use

Facts

The defendant was convicted of taking a conveyance contrary to s12(1) Theft Act 1968. He had found a vehicle (a Land Rover) parked across a roadway and had sat in the driver's seat and released the handbrake, steering the vehicle as it rolled out of the way to a safe resting place. He appealed against conviction.

Held

The appeal would be dismissed

Bridge LJ:

'Mr Toulson's [counsel for the defendant] basic submission is in these terms. He contends that if a person moves a vehicle for the sole reason that it is in his way and moves it no further than is necessary to enable him to get past the obstruction, he is not taking that vehicle for his own use. The starting point of the argument is the decision of this court in *Bogacki* (1973) 57 Cr App R 593; [1973] 1 QB 832. In that case the three defendants were charged with attempting to take without authority a motor bus. The evidence showed that they had gone to a bus garage late at night and attempted to start the engine of a bus without success. The trial judge directed the jury as follows, adverting specifically to the change of language between section 12 of the Act of 1968 and section 217 of the Act of 1960. He said: "The offence is not, I repeat, the offence is not taking and driving away, it is merely taking, and 'taking,' members of the jury, means assuming possession of an object for your own unauthorised use, however temporary that assumption of possession might be. May I give you an example. Suppose that you left your motor car parked in the car park behind a cinema, and you forgot to lock the door but you shut the door, and suppose that a man and a woman, some time later, when the motor car was unattended, came along, opened the door, got into the car, and had sexual intercourse in the car. This particular offence would then have been committed by them." Later he said with respect to the defendants before him: "The question is: Did they, without the permission of the owners, acquire possession, for however short a time, for their own unauthorised purpose? That is the question."

377

In giving the judgment of this Court in that case Roskill LJ said at pp598 and 837 of the respective reports: "The word 'take' is an ordinary simple English word and it is undesirable that where Parliament has used an ordinary simple English word elaborate glosses should be put upon it. What is sought to be said is that 'take' is the equivalent of 'use' and that mere unauthorised user of itself constitutes an offence against section 12. It is to be observed that if one treats 'takes' as a synonym for 'uses,' the subsection has to be read in this way: 'if ... he uses any conveyance for his own or another's use ...' That involves the second employment of the word 'use' being tautologous, and this court can see no justification where Parliament has used the phrase 'if ... he takes any conveyance for his own or another's use' for construing this language as meaning if he 'uses any conveyance for his own or another's use,' thus giving no proper effect to the words 'for his own or another's use.' For those reasons the court accepts Mr Lowry's submission that there is still built in, if I may use the phrase, to the word 'takes' in the subsection the concept of movement and that before a man can be convicted of the completed offence under section 12(1) it must be shown that he took the vehicle, that is to say, that there was an unauthorised taking possession or control of the vehicle by him adverse to the rights of the true owner or person otherwise entitled to such possession or control, coupled with some movement, however small ... of that vehicle following such unauthorised taking."

Basing himself on that decision, Mr Toulson submits, cogently as we think, that since the concept of taking in the definition of the offence already involves moving the vehicle taken, the words "for his own or another's use" must involve something over and above mere movement of the vehicle. What then is the concept embodied in this phrase "for his own or another's use"?

On this point the argument ranged widely, but we hope that at the end of the day it is an adequate summary of the final submission made on it by Mr Toulson to say that he contends that what is involved is that the conveyance should have been used as a conveyance, ie should have been used as a means of transport. That submission seems to us to be well-founded. Mr Toulson points out that the mischief at which this section is aimed has been appropriately defined as "stealing a ride." The interpretation of the phrase "for his own or another's use" as meaning "for his own or another's use as a conveyance" would fall into line, we think, with the discriminations suggested in *Smith and Hogan's Criminal Law*, 3rd ed (1973) at p462, where the following passage occurs: "But subject to the requirement of taking, the offence does seem, in essence, to consist in stealing a ride. This seems implicit in the requirement that the taking be for 'his own or another's *use*.' Thus if D releases the handbrake of a car so that it runs down an incline, or releases a boat from its moorings so that it is carried off by the tide this would not as such be an offence within the section."

Pausing at that point in the quotation from the textbook, the reason why neither of those examples would constitute an offence within the section would be that in neither case, although the conveyance had been moved, would it have been used as a conveyance.

The quotation from the textbook goes on: "The taking must be for D's use or the use of another and if he intends to make no use of the car or boat there would be no offence under section 12. But it would be enough if D were to release the boat from its moorings so that he would be carried downstream in the boat." In that case, since he would be carried downstream in the boat there would be a use of the boat as a conveyance, as a means of transporting him downstream.

So far the court is in agreement with Mr Toulson's submissions. But then the next step has to be taken. The next step is, as Mr Toulson submits, that merely to move a vehicle which constitutes an obstruction so that it shall be an obstruction no more cannot involve use of the vehicle as a conveyance. It is at this point that the submission requires to be carefully analysed.

Clearly one can envisage instances in which an obstructing vehicle was merely pushed out of the way a yard or two which would not involve any use of it as a conveyance. But the facts involved in the removal of the obstructing vehicle must be examined in each case.

Mr Matheson, for the Crown, meets this submission squarely by pointing to the circumstance that here the Land Rover was in the ordinary sense of the English language driven for 200 yards. Attention has already been drawn to the fact that no distinction was relied upon by Mr Toulson between a vehicle driven under its own power and a vehicle driven by being allowed to coast down hill. Mr Matheson says that again, as a matter of ordinary use of English, in the course of driving the vehicle a distance of 200 yards the appellant was inevitably using it as a conveyance and that his motive for so doing is immaterial. This submission for the Crown, it is pointed out to us, is in line with another suggestion by Professor Smith in his textbook on the *Law of Theft*, 2nd ed (1972), paragraph 317, where he says: "Probably driving, whatever the motive, would be held to be 'use.' "

In reply, Mr Toulson submits that even if it be right that the appellant had in the ordinary sense of the word to drive the Land Rover for 200 yards, and even if that did involve its use as a conveyance, nevertheless the offence was still not made out because the purpose of the taking was not to use the conveyance as a conveyance but merely to remove it as an obstruction. He emphasises that the words of the section are: "takes for his own use," not "takes and uses." This is in our judgment a very subtle and refined distinction and if it were admitted it would open a very wide door to persons who take conveyances without authority and use them as such to dispute their guilt on the ground that the motive of the taking was something other than the use of the conveyance as such.

The short answer, we think, is that where as here, a conveyance is taken and moved in a way which necessarily involves its use as a conveyance, the taker cannot be heard to say that the taking was not for that use. If he has in fact taken the conveyance and used it as such, his motive in so doing is, as Mr Matheson submits, quite immaterial. It follows, in our judgment, that the trial judge was right, not only to reject the submission of no case, but also to direct the jury, as he did, that on the undisputed facts the appellant had taken the Land Rover for his own use. Accordingly the appeal will be dismissed.'

R v Briggs [1987] Crim LR 708 Court of Appeal (Criminal Division) (Russell LJ, Hirst and Rougier JJ)

Section 12(6) Theft Act 1968 - lawful authority

Facts

'The appellant was convicted of driving a motor vehicle taken without authority. He was seen by police riding a motorcycle taken two days earlier. He told police that he was repairing the cycle for a friend; he gave the friend's name and address. The appellant did not give evidence or call witnesses at the trial. He appealed against conviction on the ground that even after the jury asked what constituted "lawful authority" the judge failed to direct the jury as to section 12(6) of the Theft Act 1968.

Held

Allowing the appeal and quashing the conviction, in circumstances such as in the present case it was incumbent upon the judge to focus on this particular aspect so that the jury could be specifically pointed to the qualification in section 12(6). The omission was a material flaw in the summing up.'

[*Reported by Lynne Knapman, Barrister.*]

R v Bundy (1977) 65 Cr App R 239 Court of Appeal (Criminal Division) (Lawton LJ, MacKenna and Gibson JJ)

Place of abode - s25(1) Theft Act 1968

Facts

The defendant appealed against his conviction under s25(1) of the Theft Act 1968, on the ground that as he lived in his car, the articles that had been found there were 'at his place of abode'.

Held

The appeal would be dismissed.

Lawton LJ:

' ... The phrase, "place of abode", as Mr Zeidman's [counsel for the defendant] researches have shown, has occurred in a number of Acts of Parliament, all dealing with entirely different subject matters. For example, the phrase occurs in section 23 of the Landlord and Tenant Act 1927 and has been construed widely by the courts. It also occurred in the Summary Jurisdiction Act 1848; in that context it was construed narrowly. This Court does not get any help from comparing constructions of the phrase in other Acts of Parliament dealing with other subject matters.

We must construe the Act [sic] in the context in which it appears in section 25(1) of the Theft Act 1968. In that context it is manifest that no offence is committed if a burglar keeps the implements of his criminal trade in his "place of abode." He only commits an offence when he takes them from his "place of abode." The phrase "place of abode," in our judgment connotes, first of all, a site. That is the ordinary meaning of the word "place." It is a site at which the occupier intends to abide. So, there are two elements in the phrase "place of abode" - the element of site and the element of intention. When the appellant took the motor car to a site with the intention of abiding there, then his motor car on that site could be said to be his "place of abode," but when he took it from that site to move it to another site where he intended to abide, the motor car could not be said to be his "place of abode" during transit.

When he was arrested by the police he was not intending to abide on the site where he was arrested. It follows that that was not then at his "place of abode." He may have had a "place of abode" the previous night, but he was away from it at the time of his arrest when in possession of articles which could be used for the purpose of theft. It follows, in our judgment, that there is no substance in the point which has been taken on behalf of the appellant. It was contended that the learned judge did not give an adequate direction to the jury as to what was the meaning of "place of abode." It is obvious why he did not. He was under the impression that there was no dispute about the matter. Mr Zeidman, in circumstances which we understand, did not disabuse the learned judge. It follows, in our judgment, that the judge cannot be criticised for having failed to direct the jury about a matter which was never in dispute at the trial.

Accordingly, the appeal will be dismissed.'

R v Clotworthy [1981] Crim LR 501 Court of Appeal (Criminal Division) (Ackner and Watkins LJJ and Davies J)

Section 12(6) Theft Act 1968- lawful authority

Facts

'The appellant worked in a garage to which a customer had brought his car for repair. In order to expedite the repair and ensure that the car was under cover at night it had to be driven to an associated garage, and the garage owner asked a mechanic to drive the car, but he had a prior appointment and asked the appellant to drive the car to the other garage. The appellant, who held no driving licence and was uninsured to drive, while driving the car was stopped by police. He was tried on a charge of contravening section 12(1) of the Theft Act 1968 by taking a conveyance without authority. His defence was that, within section 12(6), he believed that he had lawful authority to drive the car since it was common practice for garage employees to drive in the course of business whether or not they were insured and he had often done so with the garage owner's knowledge and approval. The prosecutor submitted that the appellant had no defence as the car owner would not have given consent to an unlicensed or uninsured driver, it was contrary to the garage owner's terms of bailment to allow such a person to drive and, therefore, the appellant could not rely on section 12(6) since he knew that he had no licence or insurance. The trial judge upheld that submission, the appellant thereupon changed his plea and was convicted and sentenced. He appealed against conviction.

Held

Allowing the appeal, that the submission was invalid. It was for the jury to decide what the appellant's state of mind was, whether they thought that his defence might be acceptable to them or whether they were sure that he had no genuine belief. Clearly a car owner (albeit thereby committing an offence) could authorise an unlicensed and uninsured person to drive it. Accordingly it was open to any defendant to assert his reasonable belief in having authority or consent of the owner. Whether or not such an assertion carried weight with a jury would depend on the circumstances of the case. The judge erred and the conviction would be quashed.'

[*Reported by L. Norman Williams, Barrister.*]

R v Cooke [1986] AC 909 House of Lords (Lords Bridge, Brandon, Brightman, Mackay and Goff)

Section 25 (1) Theft Act 1968 - nature of a 'cheat'

Facts

See chapter 10.

The following extracts deal with the question of whether the defendants would have committed offences contrary to s25 (1) of the Theft Act 1968 if their agreement had been carried out.

Lord Bridge:

'... the appeal also succeeds, in my opinion, on the narrower ground that there was no material before the Court of Appeal or your Lordships to justify the inference that the defendant and his fellow conspirators agreed on a course of conduct which necessarily involved the commission of offences under sections 25 and 15 of the Theft Act 1968. The nub of the matter is that, to succeed in this argument, the defendant must be in a position to say: "I could not have practised this fraud on my employers without first obtaining money by deception from passengers on the train." This issue was never raised at the trial. What would have happened if it had been is mere speculation. Upright citizens as the ordinary run of British Rail passengers may be presumed to be, I am not prepared to assume that they would necessarily refuse to take and pay for refreshments even if they knew perfectly well that the buffet staff were practising the kind of "fiddle" here involved.'

Lord Mackay:

'I turn now to consider the second submission. The defendant maintained that the evidence in this case disclosed the statutory conspiracy to commit the offence of going equipped for cheat contrary to section 25(1) of the Theft Act 1968 whereas the Crown maintained the contrary. Certain decisions of the Court of Appeal were referred to as relevant to this submission. In the first of these *R v Rashid* [1977] 1 WLR 298, Rashid, who was a British Rail steward, was stopped when about to board his train carrying with him two sliced loaves of bread and a bag of tomatoes. He was charged with an offence against section 25(1) of the Theft Act 1968 on the ground that he had intended to use his own materials to make sandwiches to sell to passengers for his own profit.

[His Lordship referred to ss25(1), 25(3) and 15(1) of the Theft Act 1968, and continued]

Rashid was convicted and appealed on the ground that the verdict of the jury was unsafe and unsatisfactory in that they had been misdirected by the trial judge saying that in effect section 25(3) of the Theft Act 1968 applied, the judge not referring specifically to section 25(5) or giving a direction as to the precise offence or offences under section 15 of the Act of 1968 which the appellant could have committed with his bread and tomatoes.

Bridge LJ, having held that the directions given were inadequate, went on, at p302:

"The only basis on which this offence could possibly be proved was on the basis that it was intended by the defendant to use his bread and tomatoes to practise an effective and operative deception upon railway passengers without which the railway passengers would not have purchased the sandwiches. The court is inclined to think, though it is unnecessary for present purposes so to decide, that this whole prosecution was really misconceived and that on a proper direction no jury would have convicted in these circumstances."

[His Lordship then considered Geoffrey Lane LJ's judgment in *R* v *Doukas*, (below)]

Finally, on this aspect of the appeal we were referred to *R* v *Corboz* (unreported), 2 July 1984. Corboz was a chief steward with British Rail who had with him at his work a small quantity of coffee which he sold, or intended to sell, to British Rail's passengers, retaining for himself the proceeds of sale. He was convicted of an offence under section 25(1) of the Theft Act 1968 and appealed against his conviction on the ground of misdirection of the jury by the trial judge. The court tested the correctness of the summing up by considering whether it accorded with the guidance given in *R* v *Doukas* [1978] 1 WLR 372. Having concluded that the summing up did meet this standard the appeal was dismissed, the court indicating that in future it would be well if in directing juries with regard to an offence of this kind judges should use a direction strictly in accordance with the terms of the judgment of the court in *Doukas*.

I respectfully agree, that the elements necessary to establish the offence are correctly described in the judgment of Geoffrey Lane LJ in *R* v *Doukas*. I do not, however, agree with the prosecution's way of putting their case on the element of dishonesty as described in the judgment. The dishonesty in question is the lying to or misleading the guests so that there is a deception of the guests.

Although the court in *R* v *Rashid* [1977] 1 WLR 298 indicated doubt whether in the circumstances of that case a jury could properly have convicted, the only question to be decided by the Court of Appeal in that case was whether there had been a misdirection by the trial judge and the court held that there had. Therefore the conviction was set aside. In my opinion the question whether the necessary ingredients for the offence have been established in any particular case is one for the jury, and whether they have been will depend on the detail of the evidence particularly that relating to the attitude and understanding of those receiving the supplies.

I consider it quite impossible to say that the evidence led in the present case, and we do not have a full record of it before us, would inevitably have produced, had the jury been required to consider the matter, a verdict that the defendant was guilty of a conspiracy to breach section 25, and indeed this was the reason that the Court of Appeal did not substitute a conviction of a statutory conspiracy to breach that section for the verdict of guilty of conspiracy to defraud which the jury actually returned.

The final submission for the defendant, if it were correct, would give him an answer to the conviction for conspiracy to defraud in the present case for the same reason as led to the decision in *Ayres* [1984] AC 447. The submission is that the conduct by which it was agreed that British Rail should be defrauded was theft of British Rail money contrary to section 1 of the Theft Act 1968 or was false accounting contrary to section 17 of the Theft Act 1968. As I have already said this submission was not put in the Court of Appeal and we do not have the transcript of evidence available to us, but on the basis of the information which has been put before your Lordships I am of opinion that this submission of the defendant has not been made out. *Attorney-General's Reference (No. 1 of 1985)* [1986] QB 491 negatives the contention that the conduct here in question could amount to theft. As to false accounting, your Lordships were informed that the method of accounting required by British Rail from an employee in the position of the defendant is that all British Rail stock on the restaurant car at the beginning of the journey is detailed and then the stock which remains after the journey is detailed and the difference between these discloses the transactions, the proceeds of which have to be accounted for to British Rail by the employee. On what we know of the position in the present case that account that the defendant intended to make to British Rail would be perfectly in order since the fraud alleged is based upon using not British Rail supplies which would show up in the account, but private supplies which do not show up in the accounts.

While this submission might well require reconsideration in a case where a full record of the evidence was available, on the basis of the information put before your Lordships in the present appeal, I am of opinion that it fails. Even if it were to succeed it would be difficult to avoid the conclusion that the proviso should be applied.'

R v Doukas (1978) 66 Cr App R 228 Court of Appeal (Criminal Division) (Geoffrey Lane LJ, Milmo and Watkins JJ)

Section 25(1) Theft Act 1968 - nature of a 'cheat'

Facts

The defendant was a wine waiter at an hotel. He was arrested whilst bringing his own wine into the hotel intending to sell it to customers as the hotel's, and keep the proceeds. He was convicted under s25(1) Theft Act 1968, and appealed on the ground that had the customers purchased his wine there would have been no 'cheat' as required by s25(1), since they were indifferent as to whose wine they were buying.

Held

The appeal would be dismissed.

Geoffrey Lane LJ:

'Combining those two sections of the Theft Act - section 25 and section 15 - which are apposite, one reaches this result: "A person shall be guilty of an offence if, when not in his place of abode, he has with him any article for use in the course of or in connection with, any deception, whether deliberate or reckless, by words or conduct, as to fact or as to law, for purposes of dishonestly obtaining property belonging to another with the intention of permanently depriving the other of it."

If one analyses that combined provision, one reaches the situation that the following items have to be proved: first of all that there was an article for use in connection with the deception: here the bottles. Secondly, that there was a proposed deception: here the deception of the guests into believing that the proffered wine was hotel wine and not the waiter's wine. Thirdly, an intention to obtain property by means of deception, and the property here is the money of the guests which he proposes to obtain to keep. Fourthly, dishonesty. There is twofold dishonesty in the way the prosecution put the case. First of all the dishonesty in respect of his employers, namely putting into his pocket the money which really should go to the hotel and, more important, the second dishonesty, vis-à-vis the guests, the lying or misleading the guests into believing that the wine which had been proffered was the hotel wine and not the waiter's wine. Fifthly, there must be proof that the obtaining would have been, wholly or partially, by virtue of the deception.

The prosecution must prove that nexus between the deception and obtaining. It is this last and final ingredient which, as we see it in the present case, is the only point which raises any difficulty. Assuming, as we must, and indeed obviously was the case, the jury accepted the version of the police interviews and accepted that this man had made the confession to which I have referred, then the only question was, would this obtaining have in fact been caused by the deception practised by the waiter?

We have, as in the notice of appeal, been referred to the decision in *Rashid* (1976) 64 Cr App R 201; [1977] 1 WLR 298, which was a decision by another division of this Court. That case concerned not a waiter in a hotel, but a British Railways waiter who substituted not bottles of wine for the Railway wine but his own tomato sandwiches for the Railway tomato sandwiches; and it is to be observed in that case the basis of the decision was that the summing up of the learned judge was inadequate. On that basis the appeal was allowed. But the Court went on to express its views obiter on the question whether in these circumstances it could be said that the obtaining was by virtue of deception and it came to the conclusion, as I say obiter, that the answer was probably no.

Of course each case of this type may produce different results according to the circumstances of the case and according, in particular, to the commodity which is being proffered. But, as we see it, the question has to be asked of the hypothetical customer, "Why did you buy this wine?" or "If you had been told the truth, would you or would you not have bought the commodity?" It is, at least in theory, for the jury in the end to decide that question.

Here, as the ground of appeal is simply the judge's action in allowing the case to go to the jury, we are answering that question, so to speak, on behalf of the judge rather than the jury. Was there evidence of the necessary nexus fit to go to the jury? Certainly so far as the wine is concerned, we have no doubt at all that the hypothetical customer, faced with the waiter saying to him: "This of course is not hotel wine, this is stuff which I imported into the hotel myself and I am going to put the proceeds of the wine, if you pay, into my own pocket," would certainly answer, so far as we can see, "I do not want your wine, kindly bring me the hotel carafe wine." Indeed it would be a strange jury that came to any other conclusion, and a stranger guest who gave any other answer, for several reasons. First of all the guest would not know what was in the bottle which the waiter was proffering. True he may not know what was in the carafe which the hotel was proffering, but he would at least be able to have recourse to the hotel if something was wrong with the carafe wine, but he would have no such recourse with the waiter; if he did, it would be worthless.

It seems to us that the matter can be answered on a much simpler basis. The hypothetical customer must be reasonably honest as well as being reasonably intelligent and it seems to us incredible that any customer, to whom the true situation was made clear, would willingly make himself a party to what was obviously a fraud by the waiter upon his employers. If that conclusion is contrary to the obiter dicta in *Rashid* (supra), then we must respectfully disagree with those dicta.

It is not necessary to examine the question any further as to whether we are differing from *Rashid* (supra) or not. But it seems to us, beyond argument, that the learned judge was right in the conclusion he reached and was right to allow the matter to go to the jury on the basis which he did.

There are two other matters which are raised on behalf of the appellant. The first is the question of the gin, whisky, brandy and Cointreau which was found in the appellant's car, which was also included in the indictment as being part of the articles which were being used for cheating. The jury were invited, if they wished, to come to a separate conclusion on the spirits from that which they reached on the wine. They did not make any distinction and Mr Adams [counsel for the defendant] suggests that they must have been wrong so far as the spirits were concerned on the basis that any customer who was proffered a sealed bottle of a proprietary brand of spirits, either brandy, whisky or gin, would be certain, or might reasonably be expected to say "Yes" to the waiter's offer, although he may have said "No" so far as the wine was concerned. We think that the same reasoning can be applied to that. No reasonable customer would lend himself to such a swindle, whether the basis of the swindle was wine or spirits.'

R v Dunn and Derby [1984] Crim LR 367 Snaresbrook Crown Court (Judge Birkett-Barker)

Section 12(1) Theft Act 1968 - no offence unless conveyance used as such

Facts

'The two defendants were seen by police officers at about 7.15 pm holding a motor bike and apparently tampering with it. On being questioned they allegedly denied touching it, but later admitted to having wheeled the bike a distance of about 40 yards to look at it by a porch light. At the close of the prosecution case it was submitted on behalf of the defendants that there was no case to answer. It was submitted that, takes any conveyance "for his own or another's use" means for use as a conveyance, ie as a means of transport. The mischief aimed at was stealing a ride. *Bow* (1977) 64 Cr App R 54 cited. Although the defendants had taken unauthorised possession of the conveyance, and wheeled it 40 yards, it had not been used as a means of transport. To move from A to B, to look at it out of curiosity was no offence. The Crown conceded these submissions, and accordingly the learned judge directed the jury to enter a verdict of not guilty.'

[*Reported by Lalith de Kauwe, Barrister.*]

R v Ellames (1974) 60 Cr App R 7 Court of Appeal (Criminal Division) (Megaw LJ, Browne and Wien JJ)

Section 25(1) Theft Act 1968 - no liability where offence already committed

Facts

The defendant was convicted under s25(1) Theft Act 1968, and appealed on the ground that the articles in question had been used in the commission of offences, but were not intended for use in the immediate future.

Held

The appeal would be allowed.

Browne J:

'In our judgment, the words in subsection (1) "has with him any article for use" means "has with him for the purpose" (or "with the intention") "that they will be used." The effect of subsection (3) is that if the article is one "made or adapted for use in committing a burglary, theft or cheat" that is evidence of the necessary intention, though not of course conclusive evidence. If the article is not one "made or adapted" for such use, the intention must be proved on the whole of the evidence - as it must be in the case of an article which is so made or adapted, if the defendant produces some innocent explanation. We agree with the learned editors of Smith and Hogan, *Criminal Law*, 3rd ed (1973), p484-485, that section 25 is directed against acts preparatory to burglary, theft or cheat; that "questions as to D's knowledge of the nature of the thing can hardly arise here, since it must be proved that he intended to use it in the course of or in connection with" burglary, theft or cheat; and that the mens rea for this offence includes "an intention to use the article in the course of or in connection with any of the specified crimes."

An intention to use must necessarily relate to use in the future. If any support is needed for this view, we think it is found in the recent decision of this Court in *Allamby and Medford* (1974) 59 Cr App R 189, decided under the Prevention of Crime Act 1953. It seems to us impossible to interpret section 25(1) as if it read "has with him any article for use or *which has been used* in the course of or in connection with any burglary, theft or cheat." Equally, it is impossible to read subsection (3) as if it said "had it with him for *or after* such use."

In our judgment, the words "for use" govern the whole of the words which follow. The object and effect of the words "in connection with" is to add something to "in the course of." It is easy to think of cases where an article could be intended for use "in connection with" though not "in the course of" a burglary etc - eg articles intended to be used while doing preparatory acts or while escaping after the crime (see Smith and Hogan, 3rd ed (1973), pp485-486).

In our view, to establish an offence under section 25(1) the prosecution must prove that the defendant was in possession of the article, and intended the article to be used in the course of or in connection with some future burglary, theft or cheat. But it is not necessary to prove that he intended it to be used in the course of or in connection with any specific burglary, theft or cheat; it is enough to prove a general intention to use it for some burglary, theft or cheat; we think that this view is supported by the use of the word "any" in section 25(1). Nor, in our view, is it necessary to prove that the defendant intended to use it himself; it will be enough to prove that he had it with him with the intention that it should be used by someone else. For example, if in the present case it had been proved that the defendant was hiding away these articles, which had already been used for one robbery, with the intention that they should later be used by someone for some other robbery, he would be guilty of an offence under section 25(1).'

R v Gannon (1988) 87 Cr App Rep 254 Court of Appeal (Criminal Division) (Watkins LJ, Jones and Leonard JJ)

Theft Act 1968 s12(6) - belief in lawful authority - relevance of self-induced intoxication

Facts (as stated by Jones J):

'The evidence for the prosecution here was that on October 31 1986 a Mr Anwar Ali parked his white Ford Cortina motor car in Harley Grove in E3 at about 10.30 at night. He later found that it had been taken without his authority.

At about 10.40 the car was seen to go sideways on to the footpath of West Ham Lane, then driven into the front of a fish and chip shop demolishing the shop front. The appellant was the only person in the car. He smelt strongly of drink. In the car was a set of keys with the name tag "Kevin" in the ignition. Kevin was the Christian name of the appellant.

The appellant was detained in hospital for some four days. On 8 November he went into West Ham police station, where he was arrested. He was interviewed on that same day.

In that interview he said that he had been to a dance and had been drinking a lot. He did not remember leaving the dance and remembered nothing after being at the dance until he woke up in hospital. So obviously he had no memory of taking the car, driving it, or the crash in which he was involved.

He himself owned a white Ford Cortina motor car. In the course of the interview the police officer put to him this: "Would it be reasonable to say that you being so drunk you could have left the party, forgotten you hadn't brought your car, mistaken this car for yours and tried to drive home in it? The appellant answered, "Well, I've never done anything like that before and I've been that drunk before, but it's a possibility."

He gave evidence consistently with what he had said in the interview. He added that he deliberately went to the party by the Underground intending to drink but not to drive. He agreed that he had accepted the possibility to which I have just referred. In re-examination he said he would not have done so, meaning making the mistake of taking the car in question, if he had been sober. He also went on to say, "I accept I took the car in which I crashed in order to get home." He stated he had to take his car keys to the party as his front door key was on the same ring. It was wholly accepted on the evidence that this car which he had driven away had a similarity to his own white Ford Cortina and that he had been able to drive it by using his own key.

At the end of his evidence the learned judge invited submissions in law, and gave a ruling. That ruling is set out in the learned judge's certificate, where he says this: "I have ruled that if a belief arises as a result of self-induced intoxication, it is not a belief that affords a defence under section 12(6) of the Theft Act 1968. If such an issue is raised, it is for the jury to decide whether the belief arises from self-induced intoxication."

Immediately following that ruling, and obviously as a result of it, the appellant changed his plea to one of guilty.'

Held: The appeal would be dismissed.

Jones J:

'Before this Court Mr Philips on behalf of the appellant has argued that the learned judge's ruling was wrong in law, that if it had not been given the appellant would not have pleaded guilty, and the issue would have been left to the jury. That issue would have been whether the prosecution had satisfied the jury that the taking was not done in the belief that he had lawful authority to do it, that is that it was his own car.

The onus was of course on the prosecution to prove the absence of the belief - *MacPherson* [1973] RTR 157. But before that stage was reached, it was of course for the appellant to raise the issue. That means that he was required to call evidence or at least be able to point to some evidence which tended to show that he did hold the belief referred to in section 12(6). This he did not do. He was of course wholly unable to say anything about his own state of mind at the material time, because he had no memory relating to such time.

He might have pointed to the similarity of make and colour of his own car and Mr Ali's, and that his car key fitted the lock on Mr Ali's car. But those facts were equivocal. They did not establish a belief in him that the car was his. It would have been equally consistent with the appellant having in his drunken state decided to take someone else's car, having selected a car similar to his own, and found that his key fitted it.

He certainly accepted the police officer's suggestion as a possibility. That was no more than mere specification. Finally of course it is really impossible to argue that simply because he was drunk, the appellant must have believed, or may simply on that basis have believed, that Mr Ali's car was his. That would amount in effect to replacing the defence provided by section 12(6) by some simple defence of drunkenness.

It follows that there was no evidential basis whatsoever upon which the defence of belief that he had authority to take the car could have been based. The appellant having proffered no proof, there was nothing for the prosecution to disprove, and there was no issue to be left to the jury. The learned judge would therefore have to have directed them in law that the only verdict open to them was one of guilty.

There was therefore no occasion for the learned judge to examine and rule upon the law as to the effect, if any, which self-induced intoxication might have upon the belief referred to in section 12(6). It follows therefore that there is no occasion for this Court to express any views as to whether his ruling was correct or not in law. Even if it were wrong, he should have ruled that no defence had been raised on the evidence. The result would have been the same. The appellant would probably have pleaded guilty in that event. If not, there would inevitably have been a verdict of guilty from the jury.

For all these reasons the appeal against conviction is dismissed.'

R v Garwood [1987] 1 WLR 319 Court of Appeal (Criminal Division) (Lord Lane CJ, Caulfield and McGowan JJ)

Section 21(1) Theft Act 1968 - meaning of menaces

Facts

As stated by Lord Lane CJ:

'On 12 September 1986 in the Crown Court at Acton the appellant, Patrick Augustus Garwood, was convicted of blackmail and was sentenced to $2^1/_2$ years' imprisonment. In addition a suspended sentence of four months' imprisonment, imposed at Willesden Magistrates' Court on 22 May 1986 for theft, was activated in full and ordered to run consecutively, making a total of 34 months' imprisonment.'

He now appeals against conviction and sentence by leave of the single judge.

The charge arose out of events on 3 June 1986. On that date a conversation took place between the appellant and the victim, an Indian youth called Sayed, aged 18, as a result of which Sayed went home and fetched £10 which he gave to the appellant. So much was not in dispute.

Sayed gave evidence that, as he was passing through the flats where he lived on the way to the library, carrying a bag full of books, the appellant - whom he knew by sight - called out to him from behind. The appellant then indicated to Sayed that he should follow him into a secluded area in the vicinity of the flats. Having arrived there the appellant accused Sayed of having "done over" his house. He asked Sayed if he or his family had a television or jewellery; he asked where they were kept; he stated that he wanted something "to make it quits" for what he alleged Sayed had done.

He then became aggressive, seizing Sayed by the shirt and pushing him up against a girder. He eventually demanded £10 and some jewellery saying that if the victim had been white he would have beaten him up by then. At that Sayed went home and got £10 which he gave to the appellant. He told the appellant that he could not get any jewellery. The appellant then said to him, "Don't tell the police or your parents or I'll get you." He demanded that Sayed should give him a further £20 three days later; if he did this, he would be protected. On 7 June the appellant met Sayed at a bus stop and reminded him that the £20 had not been forthcoming.

When the appellant was interviewed by the police, he denied any threats or aggression towards Sayed. He denied asking Sayed anything about the television or jewellery. He said that the two of them had had a conversation about sport and that he had asked Sayed if he could lend him £5. Sayed agreed and brought back £10. So he asked if he could borrow the £10, to which Sayed had agreed. He admitted that he had seen Sayed on 7 June. He was then simply apologising for not having paid back the money. The appellant gave evidence along the lines of his statement to the police, except that he said he only ever asked the victim for £10; the mention of £5 was a mistake.'

The defendant appealed against conviction, contending that the trial judge had misdirected the jury as to the meaning of 'menaces', under s21(1).

Held

The appeal would be dismissed.

Lord Lane CJ:

'In our judgment it is only rarely that a judge will need to enter upon a definition of the word menaces. It is an ordinary word of which the meaning will be clear to any jury. As Cairns LJ said in *R* v *Lawrence (Rodney)* (1971) 57 Cr App R 64, 72:

"In exceptional cases where because of special knowledge in special circumstances what would be a menace to an ordinary person is not a menace to the person to whom it is addressed, or where the converse may be true, it is no doubt necessary to spell out the meaning of the word."

It seems to us that there are two possible occasions upon which a further direction on the meaning of the word menaces may be required. The first is where the threats might affect the mind of an ordinary person of normal stability but did not affect the person actually addressed. In such circumstances that would amount to a sufficient menace: see *R* v *Clear* [1968] 1 QB 670.

The second situation is where the threats in fact affected the mind of the victim, although they would not have affected the mind of a person of normal stability. In that case, in our judgment, the existence of menaces is proved providing that the accused man was aware of the likely effect of his actions upon the victim.

If the recorder had told the jury that Sayed's undue timidity did not prevent them from finding "menaces" proved, providing that the appellant realised the effect his actions were having on Sayed, all would have been well. The issue before the jury was clear-cut. If they felt sure that Sayed's version of events was true, there were plainly menaces. If they thought that the appellant's version might be true, there were equally plainly no menaces. There was no need for the recorder to have embarked upon any definition of the word. It only served to confuse, as the jury's question showed.

However, if he had given a proper and full answer to the jury's question in the terms which we suggested earlier, the jury could have been in no doubt at all that if Sayed's version was correct -

which they must have felt that it was - the appellant must have realised from the moment that the conversation started the effect which his actions and words were having upon Sayed.'

R v Hargreaves [1985] Crim LR 243 Court of Appeal (Criminal Division) (Robert Goff LJ, Mars-Jones and Drake JJ)

Section 25(1) Theft Act 1968 - where article 'might be used' by defendant

Facts

'The appellant was found by police to be in possession of a piece of "strimmer" wire adapted for the purpose of clocking up credits on a gaming machine without payment. When asked by the police whether he intended to use the piece of wire, he replied "I don't know." He was charged with going equipped for theft, and was convicted. He appealed on the ground, inter alia, that the trial judge had wrongly directed the jury that they could convict him if they were satisfied that he might have used the wire even though they were not satisfied that he had a firm intention to do so.

Held

Allowing the appeal, that it was clear that in order for a defendant to be convicted of the offence of going equipped, the prosecution must satisfy the jury that he had intended to use the article in question in the course of or in connection with theft. An intention so to do, given a suitable opportunity, would be sufficient. Where a defendant had not decided whether to use the article should an opportunity present itself, he did not have the necessary intention. It was quite clear that the jury might have understood the judge's direction to mean that the appellant would be guilty if his frame of mind had been such that he might have used the wire although he had not formed a firm intention to do so. This quite clearly constituted a misdirection, and the conviction must be quashed.'

[*Reported by Kate O'Hanlon, Barrister.*]

R v Harvey and Others (1980) 72 Cr App R 139 Court of Appeal (Criminal Division) (Shaw LJ, Wien and Bingham JJ)

Section 21(1) Theft Act 1968 - whether demand 'unwarranted'

Facts

The defendants had paid a man named Scott £20,000 for a consignment of cannabis. When delivery took place it was discovered that the consignment contained rubbish, not cannabis. The defendants made threats to Scott and his family indicating that they would be killed or injured if the £20,000 was not returned. The defendants were convicted, inter alia, of blackmail, and appealed on the ground that the demands made to Scott and his family had been warranted for the purposes of s21(1) Theft Act 1968.

Held

The appeals would be dismissed.

Bingham J:

'For the appellants it was submitted that the learned judge's direction, and in particular the earlier of the passages quoted, was incorrect in law because it took away from the jury a question properly falling within their province of decision, namely, what the accused in fact believed. He was wrong to rule as a matter of law that a threat to perform a serious criminal act could never be thought by the person making it to be a proper means. While free to comment on the unlikelihood of a defendant believing threats such as were made in this case to be a proper means, the judge should nonetheless (it was submitted) have left the question to the jury. For the Crown it was submitted that a threat to perform a criminal act can never as a matter of law be a proper means within the subsection, and that the learned judge's direction was accordingly correct. Support for both these approaches is to be found in academic works helpfully brought to the attention of the Court.

The answer to this problem must be found in the language of the subsection, from which in our judgment two points emerge with clarity: (1) The subsection is concerned with the belief of the individual defendant in the particular case: "... a demand with menaces is unwarranted unless *the person making it* does so in the belief ..." (added emphasis). It matters not what the reasonable man, or any man other than the defendant, would believe save in so far as that may throw light on what the defendant in fact believed. Thus the factual question of the defendant's belief should be left to the jury. To that extent the subsection is subjective in approach, as is generally desirable in a criminal statute. (2) In order to exonerate a defendant from liability his belief must be that the use of the menaces is a "proper" means of reinforcing the demand. "Proper" is an unusual expression to find in a criminal statute. It is not defined in the Act, and no definition need be attempted here. It is, however, plainly a word of wide meaning, certainly wider than (for example) "lawful." But the greater includes the less and no act which was not believed to be lawful could be believed to be proper within the meaning of the subsection. Thus no assistance is given to any defendant, even a fanatic or a deranged idealist, who knows or suspects that his threat, or the act threatened, is criminal, but believes it to be justified by his end or his peculiar circumstances. The test is not what he regards as justified, but what he believes to be proper. And where, as here, the threats were to do acts which any sane man knows to be against the laws of every civilised country no jury would hesitate long before dismissing the contention that the defendant genuinely believed the threats to be a proper means of reinforcing even a legitimate demand.

It is accordingly our conclusion that the direction of the learned judge was not strictly correct. If it was necessary to give a direction on this aspect of the case at all (and in the absence of any evidence by the defendants as to their belief we cannot think that there was in reality any live issue concerning it) the jury should have been directed that the demand with menaces was not be to regarded as unwarranted unless the Crown satisfied them in respect of each defendant that the defendant did not make the demand with menaces in the genuine belief both - (a) that he had had reasonable grounds for making the demand; and (b) that the use of menaces was in the circumstances a proper (meaning for present purposes a lawful, and not a criminal) means of reinforcing the demand.

The learned judge could, of course, make appropriate comment on the unlikelihood of the defendants believing murder and rape or threats to commit those acts to be lawful or other than criminal.

On the facts of this case we are quite satisfied that the misdirection to which we have drawn attention could have caused no possible prejudice to any of the appellants. Accordingly, in our judgment, it is appropriate to apply the proviso to section 2(1) of the Criminal Appeal Act 1968, and the appeals are dismissed.'

Low v Blease [1975] Crim LR 513 Divisional Court (Lord Widgery CJ, Milmo and Wien JJ)

Section 13(1) Theft Act 1968 - whether electricity can be appropriated

Facts

'The defendant entered premises as a trespasser and made a telephone call from those premises. He was subsequently charged before justices with stealing electricity while using the telephone, contrary to section 9(1)(*b*) of the Theft Act 1968. The justices accepted the prosecution's submission that electricity was "property" within the meaning of section 4 of the Act and was capable of being stolen and convicted the defendant of burglary. He appealed by case stated to the Queen's Bench Divisional Court.

Held

Allowing the appeal, that electricity was not appropriated by switching on a current and could not be described as "property" within the meaning of section 4 of the Theft Act 1968. Parliament recognised the difficulty inherent in the concept that electricity could be "appropriated," and section 13 of the Act of 1968 dealt with the offence of dishonestly using electricity. The defendant was not guilty of burglary under section 9(1)(*b*) of the Act and the conviction would be quashed.'

[*Reported by A. G. B. Helm, Barrister.*]

McKnight v Davies [1974] RTR 4 Divisional Court (Lord Widgery CJ, Bridge and May JJ)

Section 12(1) Theft Act 1968 - taking without the consent of the owner

Facts

The defendant, a lorry driver, failed to return his vehicle to his employer's premises at the end of the working day as he was required to do. Instead he used the lorry to go on a 'pub-crawl', eventually driving it into a low bridge. He appealed against his conviction under s12(1) of the Theft Act 1968, on the ground that there had been no 'taking' without the owner's consent.

Held

The appeal would be dismissed.

Lord Widgery CJ:

'... It is, therefore, not in itself an answer in the present case for the defendant to say that he was lawfully put in control of the vehicle by his employers. The difficulty which I feel is in defining the kind of unauthorised activity on the part of the driver, whose original control is lawful, which will amount to an unlawful taking for the purpose of section 12. Not every brief, unauthorised diversion from his proper route by an employed driver in the course of his working day will necessarily involve a "taking" of the vehicle for his own use. If, however, as in *R* v *Wibberley* he returns to the vehicle after he has parked it for the night and drives it off on an unauthorised errand, he is clearly guilty of the offence. Similarly, if in the course of his working day, or otherwise while his authority to use the vehicle is unexpired, he appropriates it to his own use in a manner which repudiates the rights of the true owner, and shows that he has assumed control of the vehicle for his own purposes, he can properly be regarded as having taken the vehicle within section 12.'

R v Peart (1970) 54 Cr App R 374 Court of Appeal (Criminal Division) (The Lord Chief Justice, Sachs LJ and Eveleigh J)

Section 12(1) Theft Act 1968 - taking without the consent of the owner

Facts

The defendant induced the owner of a vehicle, a man named Mr Black, to allow him to borrow it on the pretext that he had urgent business in Alnwick. Mr Black agreed to the vehicle being taken there, provided it was returned that evening. In fact, the defendant drove the vehicle to Burnley, where he was stopped by the police because of a defective exhaust. The defendant was convicted under s12(1) of the Theft Act 1968, and appealed on the ground that the owner had consented to his 'taking' the vehicle.

Held

The appeal would be allowed.

Sachs LJ:

[After relating the facts of the case, and having referred to s12(1) of the Theft Act 1968, his Lordship continued:]

'... That provision is the successor of section 217(1) of the Road Traffic Act 1960, which itself was the successor of section 28(1) of the Road Traffic Act 1930. So far as any issue relevant to the present case is concerned, this Court is of the clear opinion that there are no relevant differences between the currently operating subsection of the 1968 Theft Act and those of the Road Traffic Acts 1930 and 1960, which have just been mentioned.

It is, of course, well known that section 28 of the 1930 Act was introduced to provide a simple criminal remedy for the spate of occasions when cars were taken against the wishes of owners from the street or from a garage without permanently intending to deprive the owner of that vehicle. It was intended in its very nature to deal with takings made without any reference to the owner. Forty years have gone by since the 1930 Act was passed, and this is, so far as this Court is aware, the first time that it has been suggested that it should be applied to occasions when consent was obtained by false pretences.

The direction of the learned Deputy Chairman in regard to this particular offence read as follows: "What is consent here? I am going to say, members of the jury - and here I do not hide from you that I may be wrong; it may be that it can be put in a different way from this - that consent induced by dishonest statements is not a real consent; though it may be an apparent one. I am using certain words that have been used in textbooks, that have been used for offences of obtaining by using trickery, in the law on larceny: Was the consent obtained by Mr Peart obtained by the result of false statements made by Mr Peart?" It is to be observed that this was the sole issue in effect left to the jury; there was no issue left to them as to whether in this particular case there could have been a fresh taking within the meaning of the Act of this particular van at some time after it was originally driven away at 2.30 pm The consent which has to be considered is thus a consent, at that time, to taking possession of the van with licence to drive and use it.

Whether fraudulent representations vitiate consent was the subject of considerable discussion in the days when there was a distinction between larceny by a trick and obtaining goods by false pretences. That discussion and the resulting decision must have been known to those who framed and passed the 1930 Act. The principles applicable to consent in relation to obtaining property - and I use "property" in the technical sense - thus seem to this Court to be in general applicable to consent to obtaining possession with licence to take and drive.

An example of a fraudulent representation which did not vitiate the consent is to be found in *London Jewellers Ltd* v *Attenborough* [1934] 2 QB 206 decided after the passing of the 1930 Act. There have been other decisions since, but it is not necessary to cite them. In substance these decisions can be said to establish that there may well be a distinction between fraudulent representations of facts that are regarded as fundamental and of facts that are not: those regarded as fundamental fall within a somewhat narrow category, for example, fraudulent representations as to identity or as to the nature of a transaction. These distinctions are of a kind which it would be unfortunate to introduce into the particular provisions under consideration, which were clearly intended to apply to offences of quite a simple type.

Whilst, however, reserving the point as to whether in regard to section 1(1) of the Theft Act a fundamental misrepresentation can vitiate consent, this Court has today to deal with a false pretence of the most usual category no different in principle from the false pretences which come before the courts on a very great variety of occasions. If this Court acceded to the submission put forward by the Crown, it would have some far reaching consequences which can hardly have been within the intention of the legislature. If, for instance, the false representation induced someone to enter into a hiring agreement or a hire-purchase agreement by reason of which alone the representor obtained possession of and licence to take away a vehicle, that would then result in an offence which fell within the ambit of section 12(1).

That does not however appear to this Court to be the mischief aimed at by the legislature. So to hold would in effect be inventing a fresh crime of obtaining possession by false pretences - an offence unknown to the law except when accompanied by intent to deprive the owner *permanently* of possession. It is a feature of the law of this country that unless there is an intent permanently to deprive of possession, temporary deprivation of an owner of his property is in general no offence. It may perhaps be apposite to refer to what the Criminal Law Revision Committee on Theft and

Related Offences (May 1966) at p27 said when considering whether such temporary deprivation should in general be made a crime: "Quarrelling neighbours and families would be able to threaten one another with prosecution; students and young people sharing accommodation who might be tempted to borrow one another's property in disregard of a prohibition by the owner would be in danger of acquiring a criminal record. Further it would be difficult for the police to avoid being involved in wasteful and undesirable investigation into alleged offences which had no social importance." To introduce the offence of obtaining possession by false pretences as regards motor vehicles would obviously tend to produce disadvantages of the types recited and to induce considerable confusion into what has so far been an uncomplicated crime. For those reasons this Court is not prepared to hold that section 12(1) extends to cases where consent is obtained by the type of misrepresentation here under review.

So far as the facts of the instant case are concerned, the essential false pretence relied upon was that the car was going to be used to make a journey to Alnwick and not one to Burnley. There was also a pretence, which was false, as to the purpose for which this car was going to be used. Neither of those pretences can by any reasoning be made to fall within the concept of a fundamental misrepresentation within the narrow category to which reference has been made. In those circumstances the sole issue left to the jury being that which has already been related, it seems to this Court that there is no alternative but to quash the conviction, allowing the appeal.'

Commentary

See *Whittaker* v *Campbell*, below.

R v Phipps and McGill (1970) 54 Cr App R 300 Court of Appeal (Criminal Division) (Fenton Atkinson LJ, Donaldson and Talbot JJ)

Section 12(1) Theft Act 1968 - taking without the consent of the owner

Facts

As stated by Fenton Atkinson LJ:

'The appellants were convicted at the Central Criminal Court on May 15, 1969, McGill of taking a motor vehicle without authority, contrary to section 217 of the Road Traffic Act 1960 [now replaced by section 12 of the Theft Act 1968] larceny and forgery, and Phipps of allowing himself to be carried in the same vehicle contrary to the same section.

The car in question belonged to a Mr Larking, who lived at Dagenham. He said that on November 25, 1968, at about 9.45 pm the appellant McGill came to his house and asked if he could borrow Larking's motor car because he wanted to take his wife to Victoria Station in order to get a train to Hastings. Larking said that he agreed, but only on the express condition that the appellant brought the car straight back after dropping his wife off at the station. He said that McGill failed to keep his promise as he did not return the car that night, and, in fact, at about 3.45 the following morning the police came round to Larking's house to inquire about this car, which they said had been stopped with both the appellants inside it. Larking explained that he had lent it only on the understanding that it would be returned the previous evening after a journey to Victoria Station, and shortly after the police had gone he received a telephone call from McGill apologising for keeping the car and saying that he would be back in five minutes, but in fact, he never turned up.

The appellant McGill did not return the car next morning. Larking went off to the police and reported the matter. In fact, at some time before 4 o'clock that morning a constable had seen the car stationary. McGill was in the driving seat, Phipps was sitting next to him and there were two other men sitting in the back seat. He questioned them and they told him about the car belonging to Larking, who had lent it to them, and that is why he made inquiries of Larking later during that night.

The car was not returned until some time on November 28, and it was quite clear from the evidence that, having failed to return the car on the night of the 25th, on the 26th McGill with Phipps as a passenger took the car and drove off down to Hastings. They said that there it developed some mechanical trouble and it had to be left at a garage, and that explained the late delivery.'

The defendants appealed against conviction.

Held

The appeals would be dismissed.

Fenton Atkinson LJ:

'The question which was raised in the notice of appeal and on which the Court gave leave was whether the original taking and using of the car being with the permission of Mr Larking, it could be said that McGill was guilty of the offence of taking and driving away the car because afterwards he failed to return it at the appropriate time and continued using it without authority? The same point arose, of course, in the case of Phipps, who was a passenger being carried in that vehicle

The point that Miss Pearlman takes on their behalf is that, so long as the original taking and driving away was with the consent of the owner, it really does not matter for how long they kept it thereafter, or what they did with it short of actually stealing it, and that if they decided the next day to drive off or to take it to the Continent on a holiday, they could not have been taking and driving away without authority, even though they knew perfectly well that the owner would object strongly to what they were doing.

In our view, that is an impossible submission, with respect to Miss Pearlman, who has said everything possible in support of this appeal.

The learned Common Serjeant put it to the jury in this way: "The allegation against him is that having lawfully borrowed the car with Mr Larking's consent for a particular purpose and for a particular purpose only, he" - referring here, of course, to McGill - "thereafter did not return the car, and if that is the position, then as from the time he decided not to return the car and drove it off on his own business after having taken his wife to Victoria Station, or rather brought her back again because she had missed the train, as from then, as a matter of law, and common sense, if he did not have Mr Larking's permission, he took it and drove it away, and it is that subsequent taking and driving that the Crown allege constitutes the offence in this matter."

He went on to give the direction required by what was then section 217(2) of the Road Traffic Act 1960 and he said: "If McGill reasonably believed that Mr Larking would in all the circumstances have agreed to him keeping the car for that extra period until it was ultimately returned, if he had asked Mr Larking this, members of the jury, he is not guilty of taking it without Mr Larking's consent."

In our view, the direction of the learned Common Serjeant was perfectly proper and accurate. On the facts there was really an overwhelming case from the time when McGill drove the car away to Hastings that following day, and he had no reason whatever to think that Mr Larking would approve of what he was doing and he really knew very well that he would have objected.'

R v Rashid (1977) 64 Cr App R 201

See references to this authority in *R v Doukas* and *R v Cooke*, above.

R v Stokes [1982] Crim LR 695 Court of Appeal (Criminal Division) (O'Connor LJ, Purchas and Farquarson JJ)

Section 12(1) Theft Act 1968 - whether conveyance used as such

Facts

'The appellant and two friends were driving past the home of a former girl friend of one of them. The girl's car was parked outside. As a practical joke the men moved it round the corner so that she would think it had been stolen. The appellant was charged, inter alia, with taking a vehicle for his/another's use, contrary to section 12 of the Theft Act 1968. At his trial there was a conflict of evidence as to whether anyone was in the car when it was being moved. The appellant was convicted and sentenced to seven days' imprisonment and his licence was endorsed. He appealed on the ground, inter alia, that there was no evidence that the vehicle had been taken for his own or another's use.

Held

Allowing the appeal and quashing the conviction, that on the authority of *Bow* (1977) 64 Cr App R 54 "use" of a vehicle necessarily involved use as a conveyance. The trial judge had failed specifically to emphasise the importance of establishing that someone was being conveyed inside the car or riding in it as an element of its use as a conveyance, and there was a danger that the jury had convicted on an interpretation of section 12 of the Theft Act 1968 which involved the use of the car as a conveyance even if no-one was inside it but merely if one or other of the men involved was pushing it from outside.'

[*Reported by Eira Caryl-Thomas, Barrister.*]

R v Whiteside and Antoniou [1989] Crim LR 436 Court of Appeal (Criminal Division) (Watkins LJ, Popplewell and Auld JJ)

Going equipped for cheating

Counterfeit cassette tapes - obtaining by deception - no direct evidence from purchasers - obtaining wholly by defendant's deception - direction to jury

Facts

'The appellants were convicted of going equipped for cheating. They were seen selling counterfeit cassette tapes outside an underground station. When uniformed police arrived the appellants ran off but were arrested. They did not deny that they were selling counterfeit tapes at a much lower price than the average retail price. In evidence they said that they had never claimed the tapes were originals and if asked they told customers that they were good quality copies. They appealed against conviction on the grounds, inter alia, that (1) there was no direct evidence from any prosecution witness that he had bought a tape believing it to be original and that the prosecution were unable to establish an intention to cheat; (2) the recorder erred in directing the jury that the obtaining could be wholly or partly as a result of the appellants' deception; (3) the recorder erred in introducing, for the first time, in his summing up the question of breach of copyright from which dishonesty might be inferred.

Held

Allowing the appeals and quashing the convictions, (1) although ordinarily the fact that the deception operated on the mind of the person deceived should be proved by direct evidence, the proposition is not of universal application: *R v Sullivan* (1945) 30 Cr App R 132, approved in *R v Lambie* (1981) 73 Cr App R 294. At the end of the prosecution case the evidence was clear that the tapes were counterfeit and the appellants knew them to be. They did nothing to disabuse any of the crowd from believing that they were genuine and the appearance of the tapes was such as to indicate, or might indicate, that they were in fact genuine. It was open to the jury to draw the inference that any purchaser was relying upon a representation that they were genuine.

(2) The recorder had based his direction on R v Doukas (1978) 66 Cr App R 228. That direction had been approved in *R v Cook* (1986) 83 Cr App R 339. Those cases had concerned deception of guests and of employers by staff seeking to sell their own food to their employer's customers. As explained in *Cook* (supra) the dishonesty in question was the lying to or misleading the guests. It therefore follows

that the direction that the obtaining must have been wholly or partially by virtue of the deception is not apposite to every case. If there is only one factor capable of acting as an operative cause the word 'partially' is an inappropriate direction.

(3) The question of copyright had not been relied upon as part of the prosecution case. Had the recorder invited observations from counsel before beginning his summing up, the prosecution would have so indicated. The direction was wholly irrelevant and clouded the simple issue which the jury had to decide.'

[*Reported by Lynn Knapman, Barrister.*]

Whittaker and Whittaker v Campbell (1983) 77 Cr App R 267 Divisional Court (Robert Goff LJ and Glidewell J)

Section 12(1) Theft Act 1968 - taking without the consent of the owner

Facts

As stated by Robert Goff LJ:

'(1) In about June 1981 the defendants, who are brothers aged 27 and 25 years, and who live in St Helens Auckland, County Durham, had an opportunity to obtain some coal at an advantageous price from a private colliery quite lawfully.

(2) In order to remove the said coal the defendants required their own means of transport. At all material times, the defendant Wilson Coglan Whittaker had no driving licence whatsoever and the defendant Stewart Whittaker had a provisional licence only and neither defendant had a vehicle of his own.

(3) In about June 1981 the defendants came into possession of a full driving licence belonging to one Derek Dunn. The defendant Wilson Coglan Whittaker said that he had found it near Mr Dunn's place of work. The defendants decided to use the licence to hire a van to remove the coal.

(4) On June 24, 1981 the defendants went to a local vehicle hire firm called Stangarths Ltd in Leazes Lane, St Helens Auckland and there hired from a director, one Duncan Stuart Robson, aged 23 years, a Ford Transit van for a day. The defendant Wilson Coglan Whittaker represented himself as being Derek Dunn of the address shown on the driving licence which he produced to Mr Robson. The same defendant also signed the name "D Dunn" on the hire agreement form No. 0309 (Exhibit 1). The appropriate hire charge was paid by the defendants and the defendant Wilson Coglan Whittaker drove away the Ford Transit van.

(5) On five subsequent occasions the defendants did the same thing - on July 2, 1981, July 16, 1981, July 22, 1981, October 8 and October 15, 1981, on each occasion the defendant Wilson Coglan Whittaker signing the hire agreement form "D Dunn." On the later occasions the driving licence was not produced to Mr Robson, who acted in reliance on what had happened on earlier occasions. On each occasion the defendants paid the appropriate hire charge.

(6) On October 16, 1981, the defendant Stewart Whittaker was driving the hire van when it was stopped and checked by police officers. The van was found to have an incorrect excise licence displayed. The defendants were questioned and their true identities were established.

(7) According to Mr Robson, the hire company's director, on the occasion of each hire, he was deceived by the defendants into believing that the defendant Wilson Coglan Whittaker was Derek Dunn and that he was the holder of a full driving licence, and had he known that that was not the case the defendant Wilson Coglan Whittaker would not have been allowed to hire any of his (Robson's) vehicles or drive any of his vehicles.

(8) By summonses dated January 21, 1982 it was alleged that the defendants jointly on October 16 without the consent of the owner or other lawful authority, took a certain conveyance, namely a

motor van for their own use, contrary to section 12(1) of the Theft Act 1968. The offence alleged referred to the last occasion of hire. They were convicted by the justices of the said offence following a submission that there was no case to answer in law. The defendants pleaded guilty to various related road traffic offences, including driving with no licence, no insurance, no "L" plates and fraudulent use of a driving licence. The appeals related solely to the offence of taking a conveyance without the owner's consent.'

Held

The appeals would be allowed.

Robert Goff LJ:

'Before the Crown Court, it was contended by the defendants that they had the consent of the owner to take the conveyance, that consent having been given by Mr Robson to the persons with whom he was dealing, namely the defendants, and that consent not having been vitiated by the misrepresentation of Wilson Coglan Whittaker that he was in fact Derek Dunn and the holder of a full driving licence. The misrepresentation as to identity and the holding of a full driving licence were not fundamental so as to vitiate the consent given, but were merely misrepresentations as to the representor's attributes, such as to render a contract voidable and not void ab initio. The mere fact that Mr Robson would not have consented to parting with possession of the vehicle if he had known the true position was not conclusive against the defendants, nor was the fact that the defendants would not be insured to drive the vehicle.

The prosecution on the other hand, contended that the defendants were guilty of the offence because in law and in fact they did not have the consent of the vehicle owner or other lawful authority to take the vehicle in question. Although the vehicle owner gave his de facto consent to the defendants taking the vehicle, that consent was not a true consent or a consent at all in law or in fact because it was vitiated by the fraudulent misrepresentations as to identity and the holding of a full driving licence made by the defendants which induced the owner to part with possession of his vehicle. These misrepresentations were fundamental to the transaction in that the owner would not have parted with possession had he known of the true position because the hirer would not have been insured to drive the vehicle.

These arguments were repeated and developed in the submissions made by counsel before this Court. We, like the Crown Court, were referred to certain authorities, some of which we shall consider later in this judgment. The conclusion of the Crown Court was that the defendant's misrepresentations were fundamental in that the vehicle owner would not have contemplated handing over the vehicle had he known the true position, and that his consent was therefore vitiated by the fraudulent misrepresentation of the defendants. We quote from the case: "The question in the present appeals was whether the vehicle owner gave his consent to the defendants taking the vehicle. In my opinion he did not. He consented to someone called Derek Dunn with a full driving licence taking the vehicle. I accordingly held that in law the defendants were guilty of the offence under section 12(1) of the Theft Act 1968."

The following questions were stated for the opinion of the Court by the Crown Court judge:

"(1) Whether in law the de facto consent to take a conveyance, namely a motor vehicle given by the vehicle owner to a person hiring that vehicle, is vitiated by reason of its being induced by the false representation of the person hiring the vehicle as to his identity and the holding of a full driving licence, so that the person taking the vehicle under the contract of hire is guilty of taking a conveyance without the owner's consent or other lawful authority contrary to section 12(1) of the Theft Act 1968.

(2) Whether, on the facts found by me and having regard to the cases cited, the Crown Court was wrong in law in rejecting the appeals of the defendants."

We are concerned in the present case with the construction of certain words, viz "without having the consent of the owner," in their context in a particular subsection of a criminal statute. But the concept of consent is relevant in many branches of the law, including not only certain crimes but also the law of contract and the law of property. There is, we believe, danger in assuming that the law adopts a uniform definition of the word "consent" in all branches of the law.

Furthermore there is, in our opinion, no general principle of law that fraud vitiates consent. Let us consider this proposition first with reference to the law of contract. In English law, every valid contract presupposes an offer by one party which has been accepted by the offeree. Plainly, there can be no such acceptance unless offer and acceptance correspond: so the offer can only be accepted by the offeree, the acceptance must relate to the same subject-matter as the offer, and must also be in all material respects, in the same terms as the offer. But the test whether there has been correspondence between offer and acceptance is not subjective but objective. If there is objective agreement, there may be a binding contract, even if in his mind one party or another has not consented to it - a principle recently affirmed by the Court of Appeal in *Centrovincial Estates PLC* v *Merchant Investors Assurance Co Ltd, The Times*, March 8, 1983. Furthermore, putting on one side such matters as the ancient doctrine of non est factum and relief from mistake in equity, there is no principle of English law that any contract may be "avoided," ie not come into existence, by reason simply of a mistake, whether a mistake of one or both parties. The question is simply whether objective agreement has been reached and, if so, upon what terms. If objective agreement has been reached, in the sense we have described, then the parties will be bound, unless on a true construction the agreement was subject to a condition precedent, express or implied, failure of which has in the event prevented a contract from coming into existence.

What is the effect of fraud? Fraud is, in relation to a contract, a fraudulent misrepresentation by one party which induces the other to enter into a contract or apparent contract with the representor. Apart from the innocent party's right to recover damages for the tort of deceit, the effect of the fraud is simply to give the innocent party the right, subject to certain limits, to rescind the contract. These rights are similar to (though not identical with) the rights of a party who has been induced to enter into a contract by an innocent, as opposed to a fraudulent, misrepresentation; though there the right to recover damages derives from statute, and the limits to rescission are somewhat more severe. It is plain, however, that in this context fraud does not "vitiate consent," any more than an innocent misrepresentation "vitiates consent." Looked at realistically, a misrepresentation, whether fraudulent or innocent, induces a party to enter into a contract in circumstances where it may be unjust that the representor should be permitted to retain the benefit (the chose in action) so acquired by him. The remedy of rescission, by which that unjust enrichment of the representor is prevented, though for historical and practical reasons treated in books on the law of contract, is a straightforward remedy in restitution subject to limits which are characteristic of that branch of the law.

The effect of rescission of a contract induced by a misrepresentation is that property in goods transferred under it may be revested in the transferor (the misrepresentee). But this may not be possible if the goods have been transferred to a third party, for the intervention of third party rights may preclude rescission. In such a case, especially if the misrepresentor has disappeared from the scene or is a man of straw so that damages are an ineffective remedy, the misrepresentee's only practical course may be to seek to establish that there never was any contract (ie that the supposed contract was "void"), so that he never parted with the property in the goods and he can claim the goods or their value from the third party. To succeed in such a claim, he has generally to show that there was no objective agreement between him and the representor. For that purpose, however, the misrepresentation (fraudulent or innocent) is simply the origin of a set of circumstances in which it may be shown that there was no objective agreement, eg that the offer was, objectively speaking, made to one person and (perhaps as a result of fraud) objectively speaking, accepted by another. Again, it cannot be said that fraud "vitiates consent"; fraud was merely the occasion for an apparent contract which was, in law, no contract at all.

Similar criteria to those applied in order to ascertain whether property in goods had passed in circumstances such as these, were at one time of particular relevance in criminal law. This was because, under the old law of larceny, the crime of larceny as the result of a mistake was only committed if the mistake was sufficient to prevent the property from passing to the accused: and the crime of larceny by a trick was only committed if the accused, having the relevant mens rea, induced the owner to transfer possession of the goods to him; though the owner did not intend to convey the property to the accused. If the owner was induced to convey the property to the accused, the latter could not be guilty of larceny but could be guilty of obtaining by false pretences. The nature of the mistake in cases of larceny as the result of a mistake, and the distinction between larceny by a trick and obtaining by false pretences, were, not surprisingly, fruitful sources of dispute and of nice distinctions. But one purpose of the Theft Act 1968 was to avoid, as far as possible, problems of this kind. And even under the old law of larceny it could not be said that fraud "vitiated consent"; for the existence of the crime of larceny as the result of a mistake demonstrates that the "vitiating" of the consent of the owner to part with the property in the goods was not dependent on fraud on the part of the accused.

It is against this background that we turn to the problem in the instant case. There being no general principle that fraud vitiates consent, we see the problem simply as this: can a person be said to have taken a conveyance for his own or another's use "without having the consent of the owner or other lawful authority" within those words as used in section 12(1) of the Theft Act 1968, if he induces the owner to part with possession of the conveyance by a fraudulent misrepresentation of the kind employed by the defendants in the present case?

Now there is no doubt about the mischief towards which this provision (like its predecessors, sections 28(1) and 217(1) of the Road Traffic Acts 1930 and 1960, respectively) is directed. It is directed against persons simply taking other persons' vehicles for their own purposes, for example, for use in the commission of a crime, or for a joyride, or just to get home, without troubling to obtain the consent of the owner but without having the animus furandi necessary for theft. In the vast majority of circumstances, no approach is made to the owner at all; the vehicle is just taken. But is the crime committed when the owner is approached, and when he is compelled to apart with his possession by force, or when he is induced to part with his possession by fraud?

Now it may be that, if the owner is induced by force to part with possession of his vehicle, the offence is committed, because a sensible distinction may be drawn between consent on the one hand, and submission to force on the other. This is a point which, however, we do not have to decide, though we comment that, in the generality of such cases, the accused is likely to have committed one or more other offences with which he could perhaps be more appropriately charged.

But where the owner is induced by fraud to part with the possession of his vehicle, no such sensible distinction can be drawn. In common sense terms, he has consented to part with the possession of his vehicle, but his consent has been obtained by the fraud. In such a case no offence under this subsection will have been committed unless, on a true construction, a different meaning is to be placed upon the word "consent" in the subsection. We do not however consider that any such construction is required.

It is to be observed, in the first instance, that the presence or absence of consent would be as much affected by innocent as by fraudulent misrepresentation. We do not however regard this point as persuasive, for the answer may lie in the fact that, where the misrepresentation is innocent, the accused would lack the mens rea which, on the principle in *Tolson* (1889) 23 QBD 168, may well be required as a matter of implication (a point which, once again, we do not have to decide). It is also to be observed that the owner's consent may, to the knowledge of the accused, have been self-induced, without any misrepresentation, fraudulent or innocent, on the part of the accused. More compelling, however, is the fact that it does not appear sensible to us that, in cases of fraud, the commission of the offence should depend not upon the simple question whether possession of the vehicle had been obtained by fraud, but upon the intricate question whether the effect of the fraud had been such that it precluded the existence of objective agreement to part with possession of the car, as

399

might for example be the case where the owner was only willing to part with possession to a third party, and the accused fraudulently induced him to do so by impersonating that third party.

We find it very difficult to accept that the commission of an offence under this subsection should depend upon the drawing of such a line which, having regard to the mischief to which this subsection is directed, appears to us to be irrelevant. The judge in the Crown Court felt it necessary to inquire, on the appeal before him, whether this line had been crossed before he could hold that the defendants had committed the offence. An inquiry of this kind is by no means an easy one, as is demonstrated by, for example, the disagreement on a similar point among the members of the Court of Appeal in *Ingram* v *Little* [1961] 1 QB 31, and by the subsequent preference by the Court of Appeal in *Lewis* v *Averay* [1972] 1 QB 198, for the dissenting judgment of Devlin LJ (as he then was) in the earlier case. Indeed, we would (had we thought it necessary to do so) have reached a different conclusion on the point from that reached by the judge in the Crown Court in the present case, considering that the effect of the defendants' fraud was not that the owner parted with possession of his vehicle to a different person from the one to whom he intended to give possession, but that the owner believed that the person to whom he gave possession had the attribute, albeit a very important attribute, of holding a driving licence. However, on our view of the subsection, the point does not arise.

In circumstances such as those of the present case, the criminality (if any) of the act would appear to rest rather in the fact of the deception, inducing the person to part with the possession of his vehicle, rather than in the fact (if it be the case) that the fraud has the effect of inducing a mistake as to, for example, "identity" rather than "attributes" of the deceiver. It would be very strange if fraudulent conduct of this kind has only to be punished if it happened to induce a fundamental mistake; and it would be even more strange if such fraudulent conduct has only to be punished where the chattel in question happened to be a vehicle. If such fraudulent conduct is to be the subject of prosecution, the crime should surely be classified as one of obtaining by deception, rather than an offence under section 12(1) of the Act of 1968, which appears to us to be directed to the prohibition and punishment of a different form of activity. It was suggested to us in argument that, in the present case, the defendants could have been accused of dishonestly obtaining services by deception contrary to section 1(1) of the Theft Act 1978; the submission was that, having regard to the broad definition of "services" inherent in section 1(2) of the Theft Act, the hiring of a vehicle could, untypically, be regarded as a form of services. Since we did not hear full argument upon the point, we express no opinion upon it, commenting only that, in a comprehensive law of theft and related offences, a decision of policy has to be made whether a fraudulent obtaining of temporary possession of a vehicle or other goods should be punishable, irrespective of any of the nice distinctions which the Crown Court felt required to consider in the present case.

We are fortified in our conclusion by the opinion expressed by Sachs LJ in *Peart* (1970) 54 Cr App R 374; [1970] 2 QB 672. In that case, on comparable facts, the Court of Appeal held that no offence had been committed under section 12(1) of the Act of 1968, because the fraudulent misrepresentation did not relate to a fact which was sufficiently fundamental. But Sachs LJ, in delivering the judgment of the Court, expressly reserved the question whether, in any case where consent had been induced by fraud, an offence would be committed under the subsection; and it is plain from his comments that he had serious misgivings whether any such offence would be committed in those circumstances. These misgivings we share in full measure, and it is our conclusion that the subsection on its true construction contemplates no such offence.

We wish to add that our judgment is confined to the construction of section 12(1) of the Theft Act 1968. We are not to be understood to be expressing any opinion upon the meaning to be attached to the word "consent" in other parts of the criminal law, where the word must be construed in its own particular context.

It follows that we answer the first question posed for our decision in the negative, and the second question in the affirmative; and that the convictions of the defendants under section 12(1) of the Theft Act 1968 will be quashed.'

20 SECTIONS 15, 16, 17 AND 20 THEFT ACT 1968

R v Bevan [1987] Crim LR 129 Court of Appeal (Criminal Division) (Neill LJ, Tudor Evans and Staughton JJ)

Section 16(1) Theft Act 1968 - unauthorised use of cheque card

Facts

'The appellant was convicted of obtaining a pecuniary advantage by deception contrary to section 16(1) of the Theft Act 1968. He had been issued with a cheque card but had no arrangement for an overdraft. The cheque card did not entitle him to overdraw without such an arrangement. The counts alleged that on three occasions abroad and once in England he had presented a cheque supported by his cheque card while his account was overdrawn. His bank was obliged to honour the cheques. The charges were said to be sample counts. He appealed against conviction on the ground that he had not been allowed to borrow by way of overdraft and that in relation to the counts concerning cheques presented abroad there was no jurisdiction in the English courts.

Held

Dismissing the appeal, (1) a bank card transaction is a borrowing by way of overdraft: *Kovacs* (1974) 58 Cr App R 412; *Commissioner of Police for the Metropolis* v *Charles* [1977] AC 177; *Waites* [1982] Crim LR 369. When the appellant's bank received a request by the paying bank for reimbursement in respect of a cheque drawn by the appellant, it complied. Its motive was no doubt the protection of its own reputation as well as its contractual obligation owed directly to the paying bank, but the reimbursement was nevertheless an act of will. The overdraft was consensual since the appellant had impliedly requested it and the bank had, albeit reluctantly, agreed. (2) The basic principle is stated in *Archbold* (42nd ed) at para. 2-28 but it is clear from *Treacy* v *DPP* [1971] AC 537, *Baxter* [1972] 1 QB 1 and *DPP* v *Stonehouse* [1978] AC 55 that where a particular result is part of the definition of a crime, then the crime may be tried here, even if only the result occurred in England and Wales. By his conduct abroad the appellant obtained a pecuniary advantage in England, a borrowing by way of overdraft.'

[Reported by Lynne Knapman, Barrister.]

R v Bolton [1991] Crim LR 57 Court of Appeal (Criminal Division) (Woolf LJ, McCullough and Turner JJ)

Meaning of 'valuable security'

Facts

'The appellant was convicted of two counts of conspiracy to procure the execution of valuable securities representing mortgage advances by deception. He was a branch manager of an insurance company; in November 1986 he, his wife and an employee and his wife established a mortgage brokerage company. The case for the Crown was that he and his co-conspirators had caused building societies and other institutions to enter into mortgages and make mortgage advances to members of the public on the basis of false information. Thirty-four transactions were relied upon and the conspiracies were said to have been designed to achieve commission on those transactions. In relation to first count N gave evidence that he had prepared false letters and accounting documents giving a false and inflated picture of the financial standing of applicants for mortgages; the documents were attached to the applications without the knowledge of the applicants. On the second count, B gave evidence that as manager of a building society he had supplied the appellant with the names of persons in arrears with mortgage payments.

Those people were then approached with proposals for re-mortgaging their properties with other building societies. B would then provide false satisfactory references to enable the re-mortgage transaction to be concluded. The appellant and his wife were also indicted, but not tried, on specific counts alleging offences contrary to s20(2) of the Theft Act 1968. At the conclusion of the prosecution case counsel for the appellant submitted that on the evidence before the court it was possible that the mortgage advances would not be made by cheque but by electronic or telegraphic transfer and thus no valuable security would come into existence; there was no evidence that the defendants knew or believed that a particular method would be used for making the mortgage advance; that unless the Crown could demonstrate that the agreed course of conduct necessarily amounted to or involved the execution of a document by the building society the case must fail; that if the conspirators agreed merely to procure or obtain mortgage advances there was no criminal conspiracy because there was no offence of procuring or obtaining a mortgage advance by deception.

Held

Allowing the appeal and quashing the convictions. (1) The appellant's submission was flawed because it failed to distinguish between the manner in which a conspiracy was intended to operate and the way in which it in fact operated. There can be a distinction between the manner in which conspirators intend to achieve their objective and how that objective is in fact achieved. On the evidence called on behalf of the prosecution it could properly be inferred that while it was possible at the time of the offences for some sophisticated electronic method of transfer of funds to be used the usual method of transferring funds at that time for the purpose of making a mortgage advance was by cheque and the appellant and the other alleged conspirators must have contemplated the transactions or some of them to be carried out by cheque and therefore they had the intention to procure building societies to execute valuable securities, cheques, for this purpose. The fact that it was possible for some transactions to take place without the use of cheques was not critical.

(2) Obtaining a mortgage advance by deception dishonestly for another could amount to an offence under s15 of the Theft Act 1968. Dishonestly by deception procuring the execution of a mortgage, however the money was transferred, could be an offence in relation to a valuable security contrary to s20(2). Having regard to the wide language of s20(3) there was no reason why procuring dishonestly and by deception the execution of a mortgage deed which is almost inevitably part of any mortgage transaction should not be an offence against s20(2) even though the mortgagor is not party to the offence.

(3) The trial judge had erred in ruling against the appellant by inferring that it sufficed that there must have been a bank statement informing the building society's solicitors that the money had been paid into their account for the purpose of providing the mortgage advance if some form of electronic or telegraphic transfer was used. A bank statement is not a valuable security, notwithstanding the wide definition contained in s20(3).

(4) The Court did not accept the submission of the Crown that "document" should be widely interpreted and include a telegraphic transfer within the definition of valuable security in s20(3). Despite the wide terms of the subsection it cannot include as a document all possible forms of electronic authority for a mortgage transaction between a building society and its solicitors.

(5) The jury were not left to determine the question whether it was part of the purpose of the conspiracy to procure the building societies to execute "valuable securities representing mortgage advances." The drafting of the counts meant that that was an essential element which had to be proved. In the light of the judge's ruling (and direction to the jury) that as a matter of law a building society advance by cheque or telegraphic transfer was capable of constituting a valuable security, it would not be proper to apply the proviso.

(6) The case illustrated the need to draw a count alleging conspiracy so that the particulars of the offence reflect what would have been the actual objective of the conspirators if they had committed a substantive offence.'

[*Reported by Lynne Knapman, Barrister.*]

Commissioner of the Police for the Metropolis v Charles [1977] AC 177 House of Lords (Lords Diplock, Salmon, Edmund-Davies and Fraser and Viscount Dilhorne)

Unauthorised use of cheque card - whether an offence contrary to s16(1) Theft Act 1968

Facts

The defendant drew cheques on his current account for amounts in excess of his agreed overdraft. The cheques had been supported by the cheque guarantee card provided by the defendant's bank. The defendant was convicted on a number of counts alleging that he had obtained a pecuniary advantage (being allowed to borrow by way of overdraft) by deception, contrary to s16(1) of the Theft Act 1968. The defendant's conviction was upheld by the Court of Appeal, and he appealed further to the House of Lords.

Held

The appeal would be dismissed.

Lord Edmund-Davies:

'What representation, if any, did the accused make when he cashed each of those cheques? It was against the background of his knowledge of his limited overdraft facilities that he drew each for £30 in favour of Mr Cersell, the club manager, and on each occasion produced his cheque card so that its number could be endorsed on the back of each cheque. The essence of the defence consists in Mr Comyn's [counsel for the defendant] submissions that by such conduct the only representation made was that "This cheque, backed by the card, will be honoured without question"; that such representation was true; that there was accordingly no deception of the club staff; and that therefore no offence was committed even though as a result the accused's account became overdrawn substantially beyond the permitted limit in consequence of his bank doing precisely what he had represented they would do on presentation of each of the cheques.

Both in the Court of Appeal and before your Lordships there was considerable discussion as to what representation is to be implied by the simple act of drawing a cheque. Reference was made to *R v Page (Note)* [1971] 2 QB 330, where the Court of Appeal (Criminal Division) adopted with apparent approval the following passage which (citing *R v Hazelton* (1874) LR 2 CCR 134 in support) has appeared in *Kenny, Outlines of Criminal Law* ever since the 1st edition appeared in 1902, see pp246-247:

"Similarly the familiar act of drawing a cheque - a document which on the fact of it is only a command of a future act - is held to imply at least three statements about the present: (1) That the drawer has an account with that bank; (2) That he has authority to draw on it for that amount; (3) That the cheque, as drawn, is a valid order for the payment of that amount (ie that the present state of affairs is such that, in the ordinary course of events, the cheque will on its future presentment be duly honoured). It may be well to point out, however, that it does not imply any representation that the drawer now has money in this bank to the amount drawn for; inasmuch as he may well have authority to overdraw, or may intend to pay in (before the cheque can be presented) sufficient money to meet it."

My noble and learned friend, Lord Fraser of Tullybelton, rightly pointed out that representations (1) and (2) were supererogatory in the light of representation (3), which embraced both of them. My noble and learned friend, Lord Diplock, also criticised representation (2) on the ground that the representation made by the simple act of drawing a cheque does not relate to or rest upon "authority" but is rather a representation that the drawer had contracted with his bank to honour his cheques. Notwithstanding the antiquity of the quoted passage, it accordingly appears right to restrict the representation made by the act of drawing and handing over a cheque to that which has been conveniently labelled "Page (3)." The legal position created by such an act was even more laconically described by Pollock B in *R v Hazelton*, LR 2 CCR 134, 140 in this way:

"I think the real representation made is that the cheque will be paid. It may be said that that is a representation as to a future event. But that is not really so. It means that the existing state of facts is such that in ordinary course the cheque will be met."

With understandable enthusiasm, Mr Comyn submitted that this was correct and that such representation was manifestly true when made, as was demonstrated by the later honouring of all the accused's cheques. But it has to be remembered that we are presently concerned to inquire what was the *totality* of the representations; with whether they were true or false to the accused's knowledge; whether they deceived; and whether they induced the party to whom they were addressed to act in such a manner as led to the accused obtaining "increased borrowing by way of overdraft." What of the production and use of the cheque card when each of the 25 cheques in the new cheque book was drawn on the night of January 2-3, 1973? Is Mr Comyn right in submitting that the only representation made by its production was the perfectly correct one that, "This cheque, backed by this card, will be honoured without question"? In my judgment, he is not. The accused knew perfectly well that he would not be able to get more chips at the club simply by drawing a cheque. The cheque alone would not have been accepted; it had to be backed by a cheque card. The card played a vital part, for (as my noble and learned friend, Lord Diplock, put it during counsel's submission) in order to make the bank liable to the payee there must be knowledge on the payee's part that the drawer has the bank's authority to bind it, for in the absence of such knowledge the all-important contract between payee and bank is not created; and it is the representation by the drawer's production of the card that he has that authority that creates such contractual relationship and estops the bank from refusing to honour the cheque. By drawing the cheque the accused represented that it would be met, and by producing the card so that the number thereon could be endorsed on the cheque he in effect represented, "I am authorised by the bank to show this to you and so create a direct contractual relationship between the bank and you that they will honour this cheque." The production of the card was the badge of the accused's ostensible authority to make such a representation on the bank's behalf. And this emerges with clarity from the evidence of the club manager, Mr Cersell, who repeatedly stressed during his lengthy testimony that the accused's cheque would not have been accepted unless accompanied by a cheque card the signature on which corresponded with that of the accused when making out the cheque.

If, indeed, such was the representation made by the production of the cheque card, I did not understand Mr Comyn to dispute that it was false, and, though he withdrew (as he was perfectly entitled to do) an earlier concession that it was false to the knowledge of the accused, that must inevitably have been his state of mind. For by the time he drew the twentieth cheque (count 9) he had already drawn 19 cheques, each for £30 and totalling £570, and when he drew the twenty-fifth cheque (count 10) he had previously drawn 24 cheques, each for a like amount and totalling £720. He therefore clearly knew that he was using the cheque card in circumstances and for a purpose for which it was wholly unwarranted.

There remains to be considered the vitally important question of whether it was established that it was as a result of such dishonest deception that the club's staff were induced to give chips for cheques and so, in due course, caused the accused's bank account to become improperly overdrawn. This point exercised the Court of Appeal, though they were not troubled by the fact that, whereas the deception alleged was said to have induced the club servants to accept the cheques, the pecuniary advantage was obtained from and damnified only the bank. In that they were, in my judgment, right, for *R v Kovacks* [1974] 1 WLR 370 correctly decided (as, indeed, appellant's counsel accepted) that, in the words of Lawton LJ, at p373:

"Section 16(1) does not provide either expressly or by implication that the person deceived must suffer any loss arising from the deception. What does have to be proved is that the accused by deception obtained for himself or another a pecuniary advantage. What there must be is a causal connection between the deception used and the pecuniary advantage obtained."

What had troubled the Court of Appeal, however, was the question of inducement, and this after hearing Mr Tabachnik, learned counsel for the accused, submit that in a cheque card case there is no such implied representation as that conveniently labelled "Page (2)":

"for the simple reason that the payee is not, in the slightest degree, concerned with the question of the drawer's credit-worthiness. The state of the drawer's account at the bank, the state of the contractual relationship between the bank and the drawer is ... a matter of complete indifference to the payee of the cheque; it is a matter to which he never needs to apply his mind ... where the recipient of the cheque has the bank's express undertaking held out in the form of a cheque card to rely on, there is no necessity, in order to give business efficacy to the transaction, that there should be any collateral representation implied on the part of the drawer of the cheque as to the state of his account with the bank or the state of his authority to draw on that account. Still less is there any basis for an inference that any such representation operates on the mind of the recipient of the cheque as an inducement persuading him to accept it. He relies, ... and relies exclusively, on the bank's undertaking embodied in the cheque card." (per Bridge LJ [1976] 1 WLR 248, 255C-F).

Whether a party was induced to act as he did because of the deception to which he was dishonestly subjected is a question of fact to be decided on the evidence adduced in each case. In the present case the Court of Appeal were apparently led to reject - with some reluctance - the foregoing trenchant submissions on behalf of the accused because in what the court regarded as the virtually indistinguishable case of *R* v *Kovacks* [1974] 1 WLR 370, 373 Lawton LJ had said:

"The railway booking clerk and the pet shop owner had been deceived because the appellant in presenting the cheque card with her cheque had represented that she was entitled to be in possession of it and to use it ... The next question is: how did she obtain this pecuniary advantage? On the facts the answer is clear, namely, by inducing the railway booking clerk and the pet shop owner to believe that she was entitled to use the cheque card when she was not."

Then is there room for coming to a different conclusion on the similar, though not identical, facts of the present case? In my judgment, it again emerges clearly from the evidence of Mr Cersell that there is not. He accepted that:

"with a cheque card, so long as the conditions on the back are met, the bank will honour the card irrespective of the state of the drawer's account or the authority, or lack of it, which he has in drawing on the account,"

and that "All those matters, in fact, once there is a cheque card, are totally irrelevant." But in this context it has again to be borne in mind that the witness made clear that the accused's cheques were accepted *only* because he produced a cheque card, and he repeatedly stressed that, had he been aware that the accused was using his cheque book and cheque card "in a way in which he was not allowed or entitled to use [them]" no cheque would have been accepted. The evidence of that witness, taken as a whole, points irresistibly to the conclusions (a) that by this dishonest conduct the accused deceived Mr Cersell in the manner averred in the particulars of the charges and (b) that Mr Cersell was thereby induced to accept the cheques because of his belief that the representations as to both cheque and card were true. These and all other relevant matters were fully and fairly dealt with in the admirable summing up of His Honour Judge Finestein QC, the jury showed by their verdicts that they were fully alive to the nature of the issues involved, and in my judgment there was ample evidence to entitle them to arrive at their "guilty" verdicts on the two charges with which we are concerned in this appeal. I would therefore dismiss it.

Something finally needs to be said about the point of law of public importance certified as fit to be considered by this House. It was expressed in this way [1976] 1 WLR 248, 259:

"When the holder of a cheque card presents a cheque in accordance with the conditions of the card which is accepted in exchange for goods, services or cash, does this transaction provide evidence of itself from which it can or should be inferred (a) that the drawer represented that he then had authority, as between himself and the bank, to draw a cheque for that amount, and (b) that the recipient of the cheque was induced by that representation to accept the cheque?"

I have to say that (b) is not a point of law at all. It raises a question of pure fact. As such, it is unanswerable in general terms (which is the object of certifying points for consideration by this House), for whether people were induced must depend on all the circumstances and, above all, upon what the recipient of cheques in those circumstances has to say. In the vase majority of cases the recipient will be a witness, and it becomes a question for the jury who have seen and heard him to determine whether inducement has been established.

The underlying aim of (a), too, is capable of being more accurately expressed, albeit by the change of only a few words in the certified question. The preferable form is that suggested by my noble and learned friend, Viscount Dilhorne, viz:

"When the holder of a cheque card presents it together with a cheque made out in accordance with the conditions of the card, which cheque is accepted in exchange for goods, services or cash, does this transaction provide evidence of itself from which it can be inferred that the drawer represented that he then had authority as between himself and the bank to use the card in order to oblige the bank to honour the cheque?"

In my judgment, the proper answer to that revised question is "Yes." '

Lord Diplock:

'When a cheque card is brought into the transaction, it still remains the fact that all the payee is concerned with is that the cheque should be honoured by the bank. I do not think that the fact that a cheque card is used necessarily displaces the representation to be implied from the act of drawing the cheque which has just been mentioned. It is, however, likely to displace that representation at any rate as the main inducement to the payee to take the cheque, since the use of the cheque card in connection with the transaction gives to the payee a direct contractual right against the bank itself to payment on presentment, provided that the use of the card by the drawer to bind the bank to pay the cheque was within the actual or ostensible authority conferred upon him by the bank.

By exhibiting to the payee a cheque card containing the undertaking by the bank to honour cheques drawn in compliance with the conditions indorsed on the back, and drawing the cheque accordingly, the drawer represents to the payee that he has actual authority from the bank to make a contract with the payee on the bank's behalf that it will honour the cheque on presentment for payment.

It was submitted on behalf of the accused that there is no need to imply a representation that the drawer's authority to bind the bank was actual and not merely ostensible, since ostensible authority alone would suffice to create a contract with the payee that was binding on the bank; and the drawer's possession of the cheque card and the cheque book with the bank's consent would be enough to constitute his ostensible authority. So, the submission goes, the only representation needed to give business efficacy to the transaction would be true. This argument stands the doctrine of ostensible authority on its head. What creates ostensible authority in a person who purports to enter into a contract as agent for a principal is a representation made to the other party that he has the actual authority of the principal for whom he claims to be acting to enter into the contract on that person's behalf. If (1) the other party has believed the representation and on the faith of that belief has acted upon it and (2) the person represented to be his principal has so conducted himself towards that other party as to be estopped from denying the truth of the representation, then, and only then, is he bound by the contract purportedly made on his behalf. The whole foundation of liability under the doctrine of ostensible authority is a representation, believed by the person to whom it is made, that the person claiming to contract as agent for a principal has the actual authority of the principal to enter into the contract on his behalf.'

R v Doukas [1978] 1 All ER 1061

See chapter 19.

DPP v Ray [1974] AC 370 House of Lords (Lords Reid, MacDermott, Morris, Hodson and Pearson)

Deception by conduct

Facts

The defendant was one of a number of men who had entered a restaurant and ordered a meal. At the end of the meal they decided not to pay, and ran out of the restaurant whilst the attention of the waiters was distracted. The defendant's conviction under s16(1) of the Theft Act 1968 was quashed on appeal to the Divisional Court. The prosecution now appealed to the House of Lords.

Held (Lords Reid and Hodson dissenting)

The appeal would be allowed.

Lord MacDermott:

'To prove the charge against the respondent the prosecution had to show that he (i) by a deception (ii) had dishonestly (iii) obtained for himself (iv) a pecuniary advantage. The last of these ingredients no longer raises, on the facts of this appeal, the problems of interpretation which were recently considered by this House in *R v Turner* [1974] AC 357. By that decision a debt is "evaded" even if the evasion falls short of being final or permanent and is only for the time being; and a pecuniary advantage has not to be proved in fact as it is enough if the case is brought within section 16(2)(*a*) or (*b*) or (*c*).

On the facts here, this means that the respondent's debt for the meal he had eaten was evaded for the purposes of subsection (2)(*a*); and that in consequence he obtained a pecuniary advantage within the meaning of subsection (1). No issue therefore arises on the ingredients I have numbered (iii) and (iv). Nor is there any controversy about ingredient (ii). If the respondent obtained a pecuniary advantage as described he undoubtedly did so dishonestly. The case is thus narrowed to ingredient (i) and that leaves two questions for consideration. First, do the facts justify a finding that the respondent practised a deception? And secondly, if he did, was his evasion of the debt obtained by that deception?

The first of these questions involves nothing in the way of words spoken or written. If there was deception on the part of the respondent it was by his conduct in the course of an extremely common form of transaction which, because of its nature, leaves much to be implied from conduct. Another circumstance affecting the ambit of this question lies in the fact that, looking only to the period *after* the meal had been eaten and the respondent and his companions had decided to evade payment, there is nothing that I can find in the discernible conduct of the respondent which would suffice in itself to show that he was then practising a deception. No doubt he and the others stayed in their seats until the waiter went into the kitchen and while doing so gave all the appearance of ordinary customers. But, in my opinion, nothing in this or in anything else which occurred *after* the change of intention went far enough to afford proof of deception. The picture, as I see it, presented by this last stage of the entire transaction, is simply that of a group which had decided to evade payment and were awaiting the opportunity to do so.

There is, however, no sound reason that I can see for restricting the inquiry to this final phase. One cannot, so to speak, draw a line through the transaction at the point where the intention changed and search for evidence of deception only in what happened before that or only in what happened after that. In my opinion the transaction must for this purpose be regarded in its entirety, beginning with the respondent entering the restaurant and ordering his meal and ending with his running out without paying. The different stages of the transaction are all linked and it would be quite unrealistic to treat them in isolation.

Starting, then, at the beginning one finds in the conduct of the respondent in entering and ordering his meal evidence that he impliedly represented that he had the means and the intention of paying for it before he left. That the respondent did make such a representation was not in dispute and in the absence of evidence to the contrary it would be difficult to reach a different conclusion. If this representation had then been false and matters had proceeded thereafter as they did (but without any change of intention) a conviction for the offence charged would, in my view, have had ample material to support it. But as the representation when originally made in this case was not false there was therefore no deception at that point. Then the meal is served and eaten and the intention to evade the debt replaced the intention to pay. Did this change of mind produce a deception?

My Lords, in my opinion it did. I do not base this conclusion merely on the change of mind that had occurred for that in itself was not manifest at the time and did not amount to "conduct" on the part of the respondent. But it did falsify the representation which had already been made because that initial representation must, in my view, be regarded not as something then spent and past but as a continuing representation which remained alive and operative and had already resulted in the respondent and his defaulting companions being taken on trust and treated as ordinary, honest customers. It covered the whole transaction up to and including payment and must therefore, in my opinion, be considered as continuing and still active at the time of the change of mind. When that happened, with the respondent taking (as might be expected) no step to bring the change to notice, he practised, to my way of thinking, a deception just as real and just as dishonest as would have been the case if his intention all along had been to go without paying.

Holding for these reasons that the respondent practised a deception, I turn to what I have referred to as the second question. Was the respondent's evasion of the debt obtained by that deception?

I think the material before the justices was enough to show that it was. The obvious effect of the deception was that the respondent and his associates were treated as they had been previously, that is to say as ordinary, honest customers whose conduct did not excite suspicion or call for precautions. In consequence the waiter was off his guard and vanished into the kitchen. That gave the respondent the opportunity of running out without hindrance and he took it. I would therefore answer this second question in the affirmative.'

Lord Morris:

'It is clear that the respondent went into the restaurant in the capacity of an ordinary customer. Such a person by his conduct in ordering food impliedly says: "If you will properly provide me with that which I order, I will pay you the amount for which I will become liable." In some restaurants a customer might have a special arrangement as to payment. A customer might on occasion make a special arrangement. Had there been any basis for suggesting that the respondent was not under obligation to discharge his debt before he left the restaurant that would have been recorded in the case stated. All the facts as found make it unlikely that it would have been possible even to contend that in this case the debt incurred was other than one which was to be discharged by a cash payment made before leaving.

If someone goes to a restaurant and, having no means whatsoever to pay and no credit arrangement, obtains a meal for which he knows he cannot pay and for which he has no intention of paying he will be guilty of an offence under section 15 of the Theft Act. Such a person would obtain the meal by deception. By his conduct in ordering the meal he would be representing to the restaurant that he had the intention of paying whereas he would not have had any such intention. In the present case when the respondent ordered his meal he impliedly made to the waiter the ordinary representation of the ordinary customer that it was his intention to pay. He induced the waiter to believe that that was his intention. Furthermore, on the facts as found it is clear that all concerned (the waiter, the respondent and his companions) proceeded on the basis that an ordinary customer would pay his bill before leaving. The waiter would not have accepted the order or served the meal had there not been the implied representation.

The situation may perhaps be unusual where a customer honestly orders a meal and therefore indicates his honest intention to pay but thereafter forms a dishonest intention of running away without paying if he can. Inherent in an original honest representation of an intention to pay there must surely be a representation that such intention will continue.

In the present case it is found as a fact that when the respondent ordered his meal he believed that he would be able to pay. One of his companions had agreed to lend him money. He therefore intended to pay. So far as the waiter was concerned the original implied representation made to him by the respondent must have been a continuing representation so long as he (the respondent) remained in the restaurant. There was nothing to alter the representation. Just as the waiter was led at the start to believe that he was dealing with a customer who by all that he did in the restaurant was indicating his intention to pay in the ordinary way, so the waiter was led to believe that that state of affairs continued. But the moment came when the respondent decided and therefore knew that he was not going to pay: but he also knew that the waiter still thought that he was going to pay. By ordering his meal and by his conduct in assuming the role of an ordinary customer the respondent had previously shown that it was his intention to pay. By continuing in the same role and behaving just as before he was representing that his previous intention continued. That was a deception because his intention, unknown to the waiter, had become quite otherwise. The dishonest change of intention was not likely to produce the result that the waiter would be told of it. The essence of the deception was that the waiter should not know of it or be given any sort of clue that it (the change of intention) had come about. Had the waiter suspected that by a change of intention a secret exodus was being planned, it is obvious that he would have taken action to prevent its being achieved.

It was said in the Divisional Court that a deception under section 16 should not be found unless an accused has actively made a representation by words or conduct which representation is found to be false. But if there was an original representation (as, in my view, there was when the meal was ordered) it was a representation that was intended to be and was a continuing representation. It continued to operate on the mind of the waiter. It became false and it became a deliberate deception. The prosecution do not say that the deception consisted in not informing the waiter of the change of mind; they say that the deception consisted in continuing to represent to the waiter that there was an intention to pay before leaving.

On behalf of the respondent it was contended that no deception had been practised. It was accepted that when the meal was ordered there was a representation by the respondent that he would pay but it was contended that once the meal was served there was no longer any representation but that there was merely an obligation to pay a debt: it was further argued that thereafter there was no deception because there was no obligation in the debtor to inform his creditor that payment was not to be made. I cannot accept these contentions. They ignore the circumstance that the representation that was made was a continuing one: its essence was that an intention to pay would continue until payment was made: by its very nature it could not cease to operate as a representation unless some new arrangement was made.

A further contention on behalf of the respondent was that the debt was not in whole or in part evaded. It was said that on the facts as found there was an evasion of the payment of a debt but no evasion of the debt and that a debt (which denotes an obligation to pay) is not evaded unless it is released or unless there is a discharge of it which is void or voidable. I cannot accept this contention. Though a "debt," as referred to in the section does denote an obligation to pay, the obligation of the respondent was to pay for his meal before he left the restaurant. When he left without paying he had, in my view, evaded his obligation to pay before leaving. He dodged his obligation. Accordingly he obtained a "pecuniary advantage."

The final question which arises is whether, if there was deception and if there was pecuniary advantage, it was by the deception that the respondent obtained the pecuniary advantage. In my view, this must be a question of fact and the magistrates have found that it was by his deception that the respondent dishonestly evaded payment. It would seem to be clear that if the waiter had thought that if he left the restaurant to go to the kitchen the respondent would at once run out, he (the waiter) would not have left the restaurant and would have taken suitable action. The waiter proceeded on the basis that the implied representation made to him (ie of an honest intention to pay) was effective. The waiter was caused to refrain from taking certain courses of action which but for the representation he would have taken. In my view, the respondent during the whole time that he was in the restaurant made and by his continuing conduct continued to make a representation of his intention to pay before leaving. When in place of his original intention he substituted the dishonest intention of running away as soon as the waiter's back was turned, he was continuing to lead the waiter to believe that he intended to pay. He practised a deception on the waiter and by so doing he obtained for himself the pecuniary advantage of evading his obligation to pay before leaving. That he did so dishonestly was found by the magistrates who, in my opinion, rightly convicted him.'

Lord Reid (dissenting):

'If a person induces a supplier to accept an order for goods or services by a representation of fact, that representation must be held to be a continuing representation lasting until the goods or services are supplied. Normally it would not last any longer. A restaurant supplies both goods and services: it supplies food and drink and the facilities for consuming them. Customers normally remain for a short time after consuming their meal, and I think that it can properly be held that any representation express or implied made with a view of obtaining a meal lasts until the departure of the customers in the normal course.

In my view, where a new customer orders a meal in a restaurant, he must be held to make an implied representation that he can and will pay for it before he leaves. In the present case the accused must be held to have made such a representation. But when he made it it was not dishonest: he thought he would be able to borrow money from one of his companions.

After the meal had been consumed the accused changed his mind. He decided to evade payment. So he and his companions remained seated where they were for a short time until the waiter left the room and then ran out of the restaurant.

Did he thereby commit an offence against section 16 of the Theft Act 1968? It is admitted, and rightly admitted, that if the waiter had not been in the room when he changed his mind and he had immediately run out he would not have committed an offence. Why does his sitting still for a short time in the presence of the waiter make all the difference?

The section requires evasion of his obligation to pay. That is clearly established by his running out without paying. Secondly, it requires dishonesty: that is admitted. There would have been both evasion and dishonesty if he had changed his mind and run out while the waiter was absent.

The crucial question in this case is whether there was evasion "by any deception." Clearly there could be no deception until the accused changed his mind. I agree with the following quotation from the judgment of Buckley J in *In re London and Globe Finance Corporation Ltd* [1903] 1 Ch 728, 732:

"To deceive is, I apprehend, to induce a man to believe that a thing is true which is false, and which the person practising the deceit knows or believes to be false."

So the accused, after he changed his mind, must have done something intended to induce the waiter to believe that he still intended to pay before he left. Deception, to my mind, implies something positive. It is quite true that a man intending to deceive can build up a situation in which his silence is as eloquent as an express statement. But what did the accused do here to create such a situation? He merely sat still.

It is, I think apparent from the case stated that the magistrates accepted the prosecution contention that:

"... as soon as the intent to evade payment was formed and the appellant still posed as an ordinary customer the deception had been made."

The magistrates stated that they were of opinion that:

"... having changed his mind as regards payment, by remaining in the restaurant for a further 10 minutes as an ordinary customer who was likely to order a sweet or coffee, the appellant practised a deception."

I cannot read that as finding that after he changed his mind he intended to deceive the waiter into believing that he still intended to pay. And there is no finding that the waiter was in fact induced to believe that by anything the accused did after he changed his mind. I would infer from the case that all that he intended to do was to take advantage of the first opportunity to escape and evade his obligation to pay.

Deception is an essential ingredient of the offence. Dishonest evasion of an obligation to pay is not enough. I cannot see that there was, in fact, any more than that in this case.

I agree with the Divisional Court [1973] 1 WLR 317, 323:

"His plan was totally lacking in the subtlety of deception and to argue that his remaining in the room until the coast was clear amounted to a representation to the waiter is to introduce an artificiality which should have no place in the Act."

I would therefore dismiss this appeal.'

Halstead v Patel (1972) 56 Cr App R 334 Divisional Court (The Lord Chief Justice, Melford Stevenson and Forbes JJ)

Section 15(1) Theft Act 1968 - cheque drawn without authority

Facts

As stated by the Lord Chief Justice:

'The respondent was employed by the Post Office for some time, and on October 30, 1970, he opened a National Giro Account, the National Giro Headquarters being at Bootle, which was not where he was serving at that time. The account was duly opened; he arranged to have his wages paid into the account, and so they were paid until, unhappily for him, there was a strike of Post Office employees, which meant that he received no wage for a substantial period, and the money being fed into the account was cut off for that reason. He knew that he was not allowed to overdraw. The justices find that he read and understood a booklet issued to him when the account was opened, which told him that he could not overdraw. The money coming into the account consisted of his wages when they were paid, and the money going out of the account was always withdrawn by him in the form of cheques payable to cash which he presented at a Post Office, the Giro system allowing the account holder to withdraw a sum not exceeding £20 in cash on demand at any Post Office, and this was the way in which the respondent operated his account.

On January 14, 1971, his account was overdrawn by a small sum, £7 6s 11d, and he was sent a letter which the justices find he received, pointing out this overdraft, and asking him to clear the account immediately. However, despite the receipt of that letter, he went on drawing cheques. There was a credit in respect of wages which momentarily brought his account into credit to the tune of about £21, but during January and early February, when no further credits were coming into the account, he proceeded to draw cheques. By January 30 his account was overdrawn to the extent of £48; on February 4 he cashed a further cheque, raising the overdraft to £68. The same thing happened again on February 17. In due course the respondent was interviewed by representatives of the Giro Office, if I may so describe it, and his explanation of what happened became perfectly clear. He was receiving no wages because of the strike; he had to have money to live, so he knowingly and quite deliberately overdrew his account, knowing that the money was not there to meet these cheques, and knowing that he had no business to overdraw. His explanation was that he needed the money to live, and that he intended to make good to the National Giro the amount which he had overdrawn as soon as the Post Office strike was over and as soon as he was in funds to achieve that.'

The justices dismissed the charges against the defendant on the basis that there was insufficient evidence of his intention to permanently deprive the Post Office of the sums involved. The prosecutor appealed by way of case stated.

Held

The appeal would be allowed.

The Lord Chief Justice:

[His Lordship referred to s15 and continued:]

'Taking the essentials of that section separately, it is necessary to show that the obtaining was by deception. One goes back to authority on the earlier law to remind oneself of what representation is made by a person who draws a cheque which is to be cashed by a third party and not the banker on whom it is drawn. We find that conveniently stated in the report of *Page* (1971) 55 Cr App R 184, where the extract from *Kenny's Outlines of Criminal Law* adopted by the court on that occasion is set out at p190. The extract is this: "The familiar act of drawing a cheque (a document which on the face of it is only a command of a future act) is held to imply at least three statements about the present: (a) [sic] that the drawer has an account with that bank; (2) that he has authority to draw on it for that amount; (3) that the cheque, as drawn, is a valid order for the payment of that amount (ie that the present state of affairs is such that, in the ordinary course of events, the cheque will on its future presentment be duly honoured)." There was here clearly a deception within the meaning of that definition. When the respondent drew these cheques he knew there was no money in the account; he knew he had no business to draw them, yet he made what on Kenny's interpretation of the law was a false representation to the effect the cheque would be duly honoured in the ordinary course of events. So much for the deception.

The next question is whether it was done with the intention of permanently depriving the Post Office of the money. It is here, I think, with deference to the justices, that they went wrong. There can be no doubt in this case that the actual notes or coins which were handed over the counter to this respondent were leaving the control of the Post Office for ever. There was no doubt at all of an intention permanently to deprive the Post Office of the actual coins or notes which were transferred. Accordingly, the only remaining feature of the offence which justified consideration is the requirement of dishonesty.

So far as dishonesty is concerned, it is quite clearly established on authority that a man who passes a cheque in respect of an account in which there are no immediate funds to meet the cheque does not necessarily act dishonestly if he genuinely believes on reasonable grounds that when the cheque is presented to the paying bank there will be funds to meet it. For example the man who, overdrawn on Saturday, draws a cheque in favour of a third party in the honest and well-founded belief that funds will be put into his bank on a Monday, is a man whom many juries would undoubtedly acquit of any dishonesty, because he has a genuine and honest belief that the cheque will be met in the ordinary course of events. But that is not this case; this case is the more common case in which there is no suggestion that the drawer of the cheque thought that funds would be available when the cheque in the ordinary course reached Bootle for payment. This is a case of a man who knows perfectly well that there are no funds and that there will not be funds to meet the cheque on presentation, but who has the hope, and as the justices find, honest intention of repaying the money another day when he acquires funds for the purpose.

What is the situation in regard to that defence in the context of the requirement of section 15 that the action shall be dishonest? For this I go to *Cockburn* (1968) 52 Cr App R 134, where the headnote says: "If money belonging to another person is dishonestly taken by the defendant against the will of the owner and without any claim of right and with intention at the time of taking permanently to deprive the owner of the property in the notes and coins concerned, the defendant is guilty of larceny. The fact that he intended soon to replace the money taken with its currency equivalent and reasonably expected to be able to do so may be a matter of strong mitigation, but it does not constitute a defence to the charge." That headnote is fully justified by the reference on p138 by Winn LJ to a dictum of Lord Goddard CJ in the case of *Williams* (1953) 37 Cr App R 71; [1953] 1 QB 660 there mentioned. What Lord Goddard CJ had said at pp74 and 668 of the respective reports was this: "It seems to the Court in this case that, by taking the coins and notes and using them for their own purposes, the appellants intended to deprive the Postmaster General of the property in those notes and coins, and in so doing they acted without a claim of right, and they acted fraudulently, because they knew what they were doing. The knew they had no right to take the money which they knew was not their money. The fact that they may have had a hope or expectation in the future of repaying that money is a matter which at most can go to mitigation, and does not amount to a defence."

To my mind those authorities make the whole situation in this case crystal clear. When the cheques were presented for payment, the respondent knew that he had no right to overdraw, that he had no funds in the Giro account to meet these cheques, and that he had no sort of prospect of providing such funds before the cheques were presented in the ordinary course. He had at best the pious hope of repaying this money at some uncertain future date when the Post Office strike was over, and that, as Lord Goddard CJ pointed out (supra), although it may be a matter in mitigation, is no defence to this charge. The element of dishonesty is satisfied on proof that he had no belief based on reasonable grounds that the money would be there when the cheque was presented. It is not enough to meet the allegation of dishonesty to say: "I honestly meant to pay the money back some day." '

R v Hamilton [1990] Crim LR 806 Court of Appeal (Criminal Division) (Neill LJ, Waterhouse and Evans JJ) 1990.6

Credit balance consisting of the proceeds of forged cheques - demand to withdraw cash using standard withdrawal slip - whether representation

Facts

'H forged the authorising signature on stolen company cheques drawn on a "Nat West" bank account (counts 1, 3, 4), paid them into accounts with the TSB, and withdrew cash against them by signed withdrawal slips (counts 2, 5, 6). Following conviction, he appealed only on counts 2, 5 and 6, which were charges of obtaining or attempting to obtain property by deception by false representations that the balance in the TSB account/s was genuine and that he was entitled to withdraw the sum/s therefrom. His counsel argued that there had been no representation. There were no dealings involving third parties such as the payee of the cheque, so the cheque cases did not apply. The slip merely said "give me the money" and no representations had been made as to the genuineness of the credit balance, nor as to his lawful entitlement to the sum claimed. The position was analogous to that of a person depositing stolen bank-notes, when the receiving bank must restore either them or an equivalent amount and was not concerned with how they had been come by, nor with the depositor's entitlement to them. A mere demand for the return of the money was not a representation.

Held

Dismissing the appeal, the credit balance represented the proceeds of forged cheques, and the jury's verdicts on counts 1, 3 and 4 meant that the appellant had dishonestly induced the bank to make the credit entries in his favour using the cheques. He thus sought to take advantage of an entry in the bank's records which he knew was dishonestly obtained. Those facts could not be ignored when deciding what representation, if any, should be inferred from his act of making a cash demand from the account.

The authorities on representations made by an account-holder to the payee of a cheque could be summarised as being that: (i) the cheque would be met in the ordinary course (*Hazelton* (1874) LR 2

CCR 134); (ii) a post-dated cheque would be met on or after the date specified (*Gilmartin* [1983] QB 953); (iii) those and other representations are made on behalf of the bank when the cheque is accompanied by a cheque card (*Charles* [1977] AC 177) or a credit card (*Lambie* [1982] AC 449). No cheques were involved here but that H had made some representation was clear. Even if the withdrawal slip meant no more than "give me the money" that was meaningless unless "the money" or, more strictly, the account was identified, which it was by means of the number on the slip, and A's presentation of it was a statement to the bank that he was the person whose account it was. But, did he also represent that the credit balance was genuine; that he was legally entitled to demand the money? The legal relationship between a bank and its customers, in regard to deposit and current accounts, was that of debtor and creditor, with a condition that the debt only became payable by the bank upon a proper demand being made at the branch where the amount was held (see *Joachimson* v *Swiss Bank Corp* [1921] 3 KB 110 at p127).

Inferentially, the proceeds of the forged cheques had been credited to H's account so the legal position was as follows: The TSB presented the forged cheques to "Nat West" and received payment against them, made under a mistake of fact that the forged signatures were genuine. On discovery of the mistake, the money became repayable to "Nat West" and any claim by H against the TSB would have no reasonable chance of success (see *Commissioner for the Lord High Admiral* v *National Provincial Bank* (1922) 127 LT 452 at p452). He had no right to demand payment of the sums sought on the basis of ex turpi causa ... A representation that he was so entitled could be inferred from his conduct in presenting the written demand for cash – the withdrawal slip. By identifying the account, he represented that he was the person to whom the bank was indebted in respect of the account, and by demanding withdrawal of a stated sum he necessarily represented that the bank owed him that amount. That was the substance of the representation alleged, the falsity and dishonesty of which had been found by the jury to be proven. Whilst counsel had correctly distinguished the cheque cases, the facts of the present case were indistinguishable from those which would exist if the account holder made his demand in the form of a cheque payable to self or cash without using a withdrawal slip.'

[*Reported by Veronica Cowan, Barrister.*]

R v Kassim (1991) 93 Cr App R 391 House of Lords (Lord Bridge, Lord Brandon, Lord Ackner, Lord Jauncey and Lord Lowry)

Theft Act 1968 s20 - meaning of 'execution' in relation to a valuable security

Facts (as stated by Lord Ackner)

'On 26 November 1986, in the Crown Court at Southwark the appellant was convicted on all counts of a 21 count indictment and was sentenced to four years' imprisonment. Counts 1, 3, 5, 7, 9, 11, 13, 15 and 17 alleged obtaining property by deception, contrary to s15 of the Theft Act 1968, the particulars being that the appellant had in each case dishonestly obtained from Lloyds Bank a cheque book by falsely representing that he was one Michael Scott with an address at 10 Sandringham Road, London E8 and, in effect, that he intended to conduct an account with Lloyds Bank in the ordinary manner. The corresponding even numbered counts, namely, 2, 4, 6, 8, 10, 12, 14, 16 and 18, each charged the appellant with procuring the execution of a valuable security by deception contrary to s20(2) of the Theft Act 1968. The particulars to count 2 alleged that the appellant:

"dishonestly, with a view to gain for himself or another, or with intent to cause loss to another, procured the execution by Lloyds Bank plc of a certain valuable security, namely, a cheque No 023543, in the sum of £50 by deception, namely, by false representations that he was one Michael Scott, his address was 10 Sandringham Road, London E8 2LR, that he was able and intended to conduct a current account in accordance with any agreement made with that bank, and that he was able and intended to pay any debt to that bank which he incurred by reason of the conduct of that account."

This was a specimen count concerning the use of the cheque book allegedly obtained by deception as laid in count 1.

The remaining even numbered counts similarly charged procuring the execution of a valuable security by deception contrary to s20(2), each again being a specimen charge in relation to the use by the appellant of the other eight cheque books. Counts 19 and 20 charged obtaining property by deception, these counts being related to withdrawals made by the appellant by means of two Cashpoint cards. Count 21 charged procuring the execution of a valuable security by deception, the valuable security being an Access voucher in the sum of £450.

The case for the Crown was that during the months of January-March 1986 a number of bank accounts were opened with Lloyds Bank, and a Lloyds Bank Access card was issued, all in the name of Michael Scott of 10 Sandringham Road, London E8. It was only shortly after the appellant was arrested on April 19, 1986, that these accounts gave rise to concern after a large number of cheques drawn on the account were presented through the clearing system and a large number of withdrawals were processed. All the cheques and withdrawals represented transactions made in the space of one week prior to the date of the appellant's arrest. Over the same period a large number of transactions were carried out using the Access card. By April 1986 the accounts in the name of Michael Scott were overdrawn by a total of £8,338 and there was an outstanding balance on the Access card of £943.

The prosecution alleged that the appellant was the person who opened the accounts and obtained the Access card under a false name and address and that it was he who had carried out the various transactions laid in the indictment. The evidence was that the cashier at a Bureau de Change near Victoria Station became suspicious when the appellant attempted to cash one of the relevant cheques and produced a cheque guarantee card in the name of "M Scott." The police were telephoned and the appellant was arrested. In his possession were four Lloyds Bank cheque books, an Access card and a Eurocheque card all in the name of M Scott. He also produced a rent book giving the address of 10 Sandringham Road, London E8 and showing Mr Scott as the name of the tenant. Subsequent investigation showed that the appellant had no connection with 10 Sandringham Road, and after much prevarication and one attempt to escape from police custody, the appellant admitted his true name and his real address which was in West Ferry Road, London E14. On searching that address there was found a number of Access vouchers and statements relating to the Access card in the name of M Scott, also cheque counterfoils in the same name.

The appellant did not give evidence but, through his counsel, asserted that the entire case was a "frame up" by the police who had chosen the appellant as a victim, being someone who had previously been convicted of offences very similar to those presently charged, and that the police, together with an immigration officer, had conspired to pervert the course of justice by 'pinning' unsolved bank and credit card frauds on him.

At the trial the sole issue was whether the person who had conducted the fraudulent activities in question was the appellant or some other person. The issue as to the true construction of the word "execution" in s20(2) was not raised until the notice of appeal, as settled by counsel, was filed. Leave to appeal was granted only against the convictions on the even numbered counts 2-18 and on count 21. On 12 February 1988, the Court of Appeal (Criminal Division), while acknowledging the attraction and force of the argument advanced by Mr Rowe QC on behalf of the appellant, dismissed the appeal in the light of two previous decisions of that Court, viz, *Beck (Brian)* (1984) 80 Cr App R 355; [1985] 1 WLR 22 and *Nanayakkara and Others* (1987) 84 Cr App R 125; [1987] 1 WLR 265. The Court certified the following point of law to be of general public importance:

> "Is there an 'execution' of a valuable security, within the meaning of s20(2) of the Theft Act 1968, when a bank upon which a cheque is drawn, or a credit card company which receives a credit voucher as a result of a credit transaction, gives effect to it by paying it?"

In anticipation that leave to appeal might be given by your Lordships' House (it was in fact given on 13 February 1989) the Court recommended that when the Crown has evidence to prove an offence under s15 of the Act and when no problem as to jurisdiction arises, charges should be brought under s15 (obtaining property by deception) and not under s20(2).'

Held

The appeal would be allowed.

Lord Ackner:

Lord Ackner gave a lengthy account of the legislative history of s20, concluding that:

'The Theft Act 1968 repealed the Larceny Act 1916. Section 20(1) re-enacts s32(1). Section 20(2) is not in precisely the same terms as those to be found in s32(2) of the Larceny Act 1916. The offence consists of dishonestly procuring the execution of the valuable security with the requisite intent and the subsequent words of the subsection ("... and this subsection shall apply ...") clearly indicate that the word "execution" is, as pointed out by Professor Griew in his book "*The Theft Acts 1968 and 1978*" 6th ed (1990), p194, a shorthand expression for an extensive range of acts spelt out in this subsection itself. They include "the making, acceptance, indorsement, alteration, cancellation or destruction" of a valuable security, the two activities "alteration" and "cancellation" being the only new ones. These are all words peculiarly apt to describe acts in connection with, that is, done to bills of exchange and other negotiable instruments. The question is: - did the legislature intend by the terms of s20(2) to expand the meaning of "execute" so that it included "give effect to?"

The Act was the product of the Criminal Law Revision Committee and was annexed as a draft Bill to its Eighth Report "*Theft and Related Offences*" (Cmnd 2977). Clause 16(2) of the Bill was accepted by Parliament without alteration and became s20(2) of the 1968 Act. In paragraph 107 of their Report, the Committee state:

"Clause 16(2) reproduces the substance of the offence under 1916 s32(2) of fraudulently procuring the execution of a valuable security. The language has been altered so as to accord with the other provisions of the Bill relating to offences of deception."

There was apparently no intention to make any alteration. All that appears to have happened is the use of the drafting technique of deeming a particular activity to extend to and include other activities.'

Lord Ackner then turned to consider the relevant case law. It was necessary for his Lordship to deal with two particular decisions at length: *R v Beck* (1985) 80 Cr App R 355; [1985] 1 WLR 22; and *R v Nanayakkara* (1987) 84 Cr App R 125; [1987] 1 WLR 265.

R v Beck

'The appellant obtained cash or goods in the south of France by forging stolen travellers' cheques issued by the Bank of England or by using a Diners Club card that had been stolen in England. Both Barclays Bank in respect of the travellers' cheques and the Diners Club in respect of the charge card reimbursed the French traders for the money which they had paid out, although it was known to both organisations that the cheques on the one hand, and the card on the other, had been stolen. This was because the French traders had complied with all the necessary conditions. The appellant was convicted of three counts of procuring the execution of a valuable security by deception, contrary to s20(2). He appealed on the ground, *inter alia*, that the trial judge was wrong in law in ruling that the final acceptance of a valuable security, when it was a travellers' cheque, was when it was paid. Watkins LJ giving the judgment of the Court said (1984) 80 Cr App R 355, 359; [1985] 1 WLR 22, 26:

"We heard much argument about the definition properly to be given to the word 'execution'. It is a term of art, Mr Hytner [for the appellant] contended. It bears the meaning it would bear in relation to a legal instrument. It means the due performance of all formalities necessary to give validity to a document ... Mr Price [for the respondent] argued that execution in this context means no more than giving effect to. The terms of s20(2) envisage more than one kind of execution. A shopkeeper executes, in other words gives effect to, a valuable security, namely, a bill arising out of the use of a Diners Club card, by demanding payment of the bill."

The Court of Appeal who were not addressed as to the legislative history of s20(2) understandably took the view that "execution" was not to be construed in a restricted sense. It considered that it had an extended meaning by reason of the later words used in the subsection which provides, *inter alia*, that the "alteration, cancellation or destruction" of a valuable security can amount to an "execution" of it. Accordingly the court held that when a travellers' cheque is accepted as genuine by a payer who pays the monetary value of it to the holder, he executes it. Likewise, when Diners Club (France) accepts a bill for payment signed by the actual or ostensible holder of a Club card and pays it, execution takes places.'

R v Nanayakkara

'A number of United States Treasury Social Security orders for payment of money drawn on the United States Treasury and payable only in America, were stolen in California. The first appellant accompanied S to the latter's bank in London, the Indo-Suez Bank, where S endorsed a number of stolen orders and handed them over to a cashier for monies to be credited to his bank account in America. The orders were passed to the bank's head office in London and the police were informed that the bank had the stolen orders in its possession. The appellants and others were charged with conspiracy to procure the execution of valuable securities by deception and the particulars alleged they had conspired to procure the execution of valuable securities by the acceptance of the orders. The judge ruled, *inter alia*, that "acceptance" in s20(2) of the Theft Act 1968 meant "taking into possession" and was not restricted to its technical meaning as used in the Bills of Exchange Act 1882.

It was contended by the prosecution that it could choose any of the activities set but in the second half of s20(2) to found their allegation of "dishonest execution." It chose to rely upon "acceptance" and argued that it had its ordinary colloquial meaning of "receiving" or "taking into possession." The appellants, however, submitted that "acceptance" has its technical meaning derived from the Bills of Exchange Act 1882, that there was no acceptance when the documents were handed over to the bank of England and therefore no execution. It was contended that the second half of s20(2) sets out in chronological order all the stages in the life of a bill of exchange.

Lord Lane CJ giving the judgment of the Court, traced the history of s20(2), and concluded that the term "acceptance" had without doubt been used in its technical sense in s32(2) of the Larceny Act 1916 and that s20(2) was not using the term in any different sense. Accordingly, "acceptance" has in relation to valuable securities, no other meaning than its proper commercial meaning. It is a term of art having acquired a special and restricted meaning. However, having considered the Court's decision in *Beck* (supra) he distinguished it (1987) 84 Cr App R 125, 130, 131; [1987] 1 WLR 265, 270, 271, because the facts of that case "included the payment out of money in the United Kingdom on the basis of the stolen valuable securities," whereas in the case the Court was considering, all that had happened in the United Kingdom was that the orders were handed to the bank. The mere handing over of the valuable securities to the bank in England could not possibly have amounted to an "acceptance." Accordingly the appeal was allowed, the prosecution having failed to establish that which was admittedly the whole basis of their case, namely, that the appellants had executed a valuable security by procuring its "acceptance" by the bank in England.'

Lord Ackner expressed his agreement with the Court of Appeal's decision in *Nanayakkara*, to the effect that the word 'acceptance' in relation to valuable securities had a narrower, more technical meaning than that attributed to it in *Beck*. His view was that it referred to the drawee's act of writing on the bill or relevant document and signing his assent to the order of the drawer. He continued:

'It is however also clear from the legislative history of s20(2) that "execution" which is deemed to cover the various activities detailed in the subsection has as its object a wide variety of documents including bills of exchange and other negotiable instruments. The subsection contemplates acts being done to or in connection with such documents. It does not contemplate and accordingly is not concerned with giving effect to the documents by the carrying out of the instructions which they may contain, such as the delivery of goods or the payment out of money.

Both Mr Richard du Cann QC and Mr Curtis on behalf of the Crown sought to place reliance on the word "cancellation" or "destruction," as being frequently the ultimate fate of the stolen valuable security, the value of which has been paid out. This final result, it was argued, was brought about by the conduct of the appellant and in this respect it can be properly said, so it is argued, that he has "procured the execution" of a negotiable instrument.

This argument, however, confuses consequences with intention. What the appellant set out to achieve was a gain for himself. The dishonest means by which he intended to achieve this was not by the cancellation or destruction of the cheque. He achieved the profit he sought prior to the cheque's destruction or cancellation. He had done so by falsely representing that he was one Michael Scott, his address was 10 Sandringham Road, etc, etc, as particularised in count 2 quoted above. Hence the advice of the Court of Appeal, also quoted above, that in circumstances like the present case, resort should be had to s15 - obtaining by false pretences - and not to s20(2).

My Lords, I fully appreciate that the current use of cheque guarantee cards and credit cards does give rise to problems where charges are brought under s15 in cases where the representation alleged is that the defendant was authorised to use his card, when he knew he was not because, for example, his account is overdrawn. However, since the whole object of the card is to relieve the tradesman from concerning himself with the relationship between the customer and his own bank, the tradesman may well not care whether or not the customer was exceeding the authority accorded to him by his own bank. All he will be concerned with is that the conditions on the card are satisfied. Such cases obviously give rise to the difficulty of establishing an operative deception. This problem cannot, however, be overcome by overstraining the meaning of the word "execution" as used in s20(2). Obviously such problems could not have been within the contemplation of the legislature over a hundred years ago when s90 of the Larceny Act 1861 was passed. Similar observations must equally apply to the problems of jurisdiction which were highlighted in *Beck*'s case. The remedy must lie in bringing the relevant legislation up to date.

For the sake of completeness I should add that a few days following the conclusion of the argument, there appeared in *The Times* newspaper a report of the judgment of the Court of Appeal, Criminal Division, in the case *King*, The Times, 26 June 1991 in which the court gave its reasons for dismissing on 21 June the appeals against conviction. The case concerned Clearing House Automated Payment System orders ("CHAPS" orders) and their use in perpetrating an extensive fraud on the National Westminster Bank by means of dishonest applications for mortgage facilities. The appellants had been convicted of dishonestly procuring the execution of these "CHAPS" orders contrary to s20(2) of the Act. The two questions raised by the appeal were whether the CHAPS orders were "valuable securities" and whether they had been "executed" within the meaning of s20(2). The court in dismissing the appeals gave affirmative answers to both questions.

Having considered the transcript of the judgment it is apparent that neither the Court nor counsel involved in that appeal were aware of these proceedings in your Lordships' House, Lord Lane CJ, in giving the judgment of the Court, referred to *Beck (Brian)* and *Nanayakkara* and concluded that even giving the word "execution" its narrower meaning (the meaning for which the appellant has contended in this appeal) the CHAPS orders were executed by the bank officials when, in order to give them validity, they signed them. The case of *King* provides, therefore, no further or additional support for the Crown's arguments.

I would accordingly answer the certified question in the negative and quash the convictions on those counts in the indictment, the subject matter of this appeal.'

R v King; R v Stockwell [1987] 2 WLR 746 Court of Appeal (Criminal Division) (Neill LJ, Waterhouse and Saville JJ)

Operative deception for s15(1) Theft Act 1968

Facts

As stated by Neill LJ:

'On 5 March 1985 the appellants went to the house of Mrs Mitchell, in New Milton. Mrs Mitchell, who had lived in the house all her life, was a widow of 68 years of age. The appellants told her that they were from Streets, a firm of tree surgeons. She knew of the firm, and in answer to her question one of the appellants claimed to be Mr Street. They told her that a sycamore tree in her garden was likely to cause damage. They purported to carry out a test, with a plastic strip placed against the tree, and one of the appellants then said that the tree was dangerous.

They told her that the roots of the tree were growing into the gas main and could cause thousands of pounds in damage. They told her that it would cost £150 to fell the tree, which Mrs Mitchell agreed to pay. They then looked at other trees and told her that another sycamore was dangerous as well as one of her conifers. In addition they told her that the roots of her bay tree were causing damage to the foundations of the house. Mrs Mitchell asked the appellants about the cost of doing all the work, and they told her that to remove the four trees including the bay tree would cost about £500. When Mrs Mitchell told them that she was going to telephone her brother, one of the appellants informed her that they would do the work for £470 if paid in cash. Mrs Mitchell then said that she would have to go and get the money from the bank. In fact, she decided to draw some money from her two building society accounts. From one account she withdrew £100, and she was in the process of withdrawing £200 from her account with a second building society, intending at that stage to go to her bank to draw the balance, when the cashier at the second building society noticed that she seemed very distressed.

Following a conversation between Mrs Mitchell and the cashier, the police were informed. Police officers then went to Mrs Mitchell's house and found the appellants there. The appellants were arrested, and on 17 February 1986 they appeared at the Crown Court at Southampton on an indictment charging them with attempting to obtain property by deception, contrary to section 1(1) of the Criminal Attempts Act 1981.'

The defendants were convicted of attempting to obtain property by deception, contrary to s1(1) of the Criminal Attempts Act 1981, and s15(1) of the Theft Act 1968, and appealed on the ground that there was no operative deception on their part.

Held

The appeals would be dismissed.

Neill LJ:

'In support of the appeal against conviction counsel for the appellants argued that the judge erred in rejecting the motion to quash the indictment, or alternatively the submission that there was no case to answer. The argument was developed on the following lines: (1) that, as the appellants were charged with an attempt, it was incumbent on the prosecution to prove that if the relevant conduct had been completed it would have constituted a criminal offence. (2) That if the appellants had received £470 for cutting down the trees they would have been paid by reason of the work they had done, and not by reason of any representation they had made to secure the work. (3) That since the decision in *R v Lewis* (unreported), Somerset Assizes January 1922 it had been generally recognised that conduct of the kind complained of in the present case did not constitute the criminal offence of obtaining property by false pretences or by deception because, as a matter of causation, the relevant property was obtained by reason of the work carried out rather than by reason of any representation or deception. Our attention was directed to statements on the subject in some leading textbooks. (4) That the offence of obtaining a pecuniary advantage by deception contrary to section 16 of the Theft

Act 1968 had no relevance in the present case: (*a*) because the appellants were not given the opportunity to earn the remuneration "in an office or employment"; on the facts of this case the appellants were independent contractors; and (*b*) because during the course of the argument at the trial the prosecution stated in terms that they were not relying on the provisions of section 16.

In order to examine these arguments it is necessary to start by setting out the particulars of offence as stated in the indictment, as amended. The particulars read:

"David King and Jimmy Stockwell on 5 March 1985 in Hampshire, dishonestly attempted to obtain from Nora Anne Mitchell, £470 in money with the intention of permanently depriving the said Nora Anne Mitchell thereof by deception, namely by false oral representations that they were from J. F. Street, Tree Specialists, Pennington, that essential work necessary to remove trees in order to prevent damage to the gas supply and house foundations would then have to be carried out."

It will be remembered that the word "then" towards the end of the particulars was added by way of amendment on 18 February.

The argument advanced on behalf of the appellants on causation or remoteness was founded on the decision in *R* v *Lewis*, and on commentaries on that decision by academic writers. The report of the decision in *R* v *Lewis* is scanty and, as far as we are aware, is contained only in a footnote in *Russell on Crime*, 12th ed (1964), vol 2, p1186, note 66. In that case (which was a decision at Somerset Assizes in January 1922) a schoolmistress obtained her appointment by falsely stating that she possessed a teacher's certificate. She was held to be not guilty of obtaining her salary by false pretences, on the ground that she was paid because of the services she rendered, and not because of the false representation.

It was submitted on behalf of the appellants that the principle underlying the decision in *R* v *Lewis* could be applied in the present case. It was further submitted that the authority of *R* v *Lewis* was implicitly recognised by the enactment of section 16(2)(*c*) of the Theft Act 1968. Section 16 is concerned with the obtaining of a pecuniary advantage by deception; section 16(2) provides:

"a pecuniary advantage is to be regarded as obtained for a person ... where ... (*c*) he is given the opportunity to earn remuneration or greater remuneration in an office or employment ..."

It is to be observed, however, that Professor Glanville Williams in his *Textbook of Criminal Law*, 1st ed (1978), p751 has this to say of the decision in *R* v *Lewis*:

"Yet Lewis would not have got the job, and consequently her salary, if it had not been for the pretence. Her object in making the pretence was to get the salary. Assuming, as is likely, that the employer would not have made her any payment of salary if the lie had not been operating on his mind, there was certainly a factual causal connection between the lie and the obtaining of salary. Why should it not be a causal connection in law? We have seen that when the defendant produces a consequence intentionally, this is generally regarded as imputable to him. Why should it not be so here?"

Furthermore, the author of *Russell on Crime*, p1187 (immediately after footnote 66 already referred to) states:

"But it is submitted that cases of this kind could be placed beyond doubt if the indictment were worded carefully. The essential point in this crime is that in making the transfer of goods the prosecutor must have been influenced by the false pretence as set out in the indictment."

We have given careful consideration to the argument based on causation or remoteness and have taken account of the fact that some support for the argument may be provided by the writings of a number of distinguished academic lawyers. Nevertheless, we have come to the conclusion that on the facts of the present case the argument is fallacious.

In our view, the question in each case is: was the deception an operative cause of the obtaining of the property? This question falls to be answered as a question of fact by the jury applying their common sense.

Moreover, this approach is in accordance with the decision of the Court for Crown Cases Reserved in *R* v *Martin* (1867) LR 1 CCR 56, where it was held that a conviction for obtaining a chattel by false pretences was good, although the chattel was not in existence at the time that the pretence was made, provided the subsequent delivery of the chattel was directly connected with the false pretence. Bovill CJ said, at p60:

"What is the test? Surely this, that there must be a direct connection between the pretence and the delivery - that there must be a continuing pretence. Whether there is such a connection or not is a question for the jury."

The decision in *R* v *Martin* was referred to with approval in *R* v *Moreton* (1913) 8 Cr App R 214, where Lord Coleridge J said, at p217:

"*Martin* leaves the law in no doubt; it was held there that the fact that the goods are obtained under a contract does not make the goods so obtained goods not obtained by a false pretence, if the false pretence is a continuing one and operates on the mind of the person supplying the goods."

In the present case there was, in our judgment, ample evidence upon which the jury could come to the conclusion that had the attempt succeeded the money would have been paid over by the victim as a result of the lies told to her by the appellants. We consider that the judge was correct to reject both the motion to quash the indictment and the submission that there was no case to answer.'

R v Lambie [1982] AC 449 House of Lords (Lords Diplock, Fraser, Russell, Keith and Roskill)

Unauthorised use of credit card - whether deception

Facts

As stated by Lord Roskill:

'... on April 20, 1977, the respondent was issued by Barclays Bank Ltd ("the bank") with a Barclaycard ("the card"). That card was what today is commonly known as a credit card. It was issued subject to the Barclaycard current conditions of use, and it was an express condition of its issue that it should be used only within the respondent's credit limit. That credit limit was £200 as the respondent well knew, since that figure had been notified to her in writing when the card was issued. The then current conditions of use included an undertaking by the respondent, as its holder, to return the card to the bank on request. No complaint was, or indeed could be, made of the respondent's use of the card until November 18, 1977. Between that date and December 5, 1977, she used the card for at least 24 separate transaction, thereby incurring a debt of some £533. The bank became aware of this debt and thereupon sought to recover the card. On December 6, 1977, the respondent agreed to return the card on December 7, 1977. She did not, however, do so. By December 15, 1977, she had used the card for at least 43 further transactions, incurring a total debt to the bank of £1,005.26.

My Lords, on December 15, 1977, the respondent entered into the transaction out of which this appeal arises. She visited a Mothercare shop in Luton. She produced the card to a departmental manager at Mothercare named Miss Rounding. She selected goods worth £10.35. Miss Rounding completed the voucher and checked that the card was current in date, that it was not on the current stop list and that the respondent's signature on the voucher corresponded with her signature on the card. Thereupon, the respondent took away the goods which she had selected. In due course, Mothercare sent the voucher to the bank and were paid £10.35 less the appropriate commission charged by the bank. On December 19, 1977, the respondent returned the card to the bank.

My Lords, at her trial at Bedford Crown Court, on August 1 and 2, 1979, before Judge Counsell and a jury, the respondent faced two charges of obtaining a pecuniary advantage by deception contrary to section 16(1) of the Theft Act 1968. These were specimen charges. The first related to an alleged offence on December 5, 1977, and the second to the events which took place at the Mothercare shop at Luton which I have just related.'

The defendant was convicted of the second charge, obtaining a pecuniary advantage contrary to s16(1) Theft Act 1968, and appealed successfully to the Court of Appeal where it was held that the use of the credit card by the defendant had not involved any operative deception. The prosecution appealed.

Held

The appeal would be allowed.

Lord Roskill:

'My Lords, at the close of the case for the prosecution, learned counsel for the respondent invited the learned judge to withdraw both counts from the jury on, it seems from reading the learned judge's clear ruling upon this submission, two grounds, first, that as a matter of law there was no evidence from which a jury might properly draw the inference that the presentation of the card in the circumstances I have described was a representation by the respondent that she was authorised by the bank to use the card to create a contract to which the bank would be a party, and secondly, that as a matter of law there was no evidence from which a jury might properly infer that Miss Rounding was induced by any representation which the respondent might have made to allow the transaction to be completed and the respondent to obtain the goods. The foundation for this latter submission was that it was the existence of the agreement between Mothercare and the bank that was the reason for Miss Rounding allowing the transaction to be completed and the goods to be taken by the respondent, since Miss Rounding knew of the arrangement with the bank, so that Mothercare was in any event certain of payment. It was not, it was suggested, any representation by the respondent which induced Miss Rounding to complete the transaction and to allow the respondent to take the goods.

My Lords, the learned judge rejected these submissions. He was clearly right to do so, as indeed was conceded in argument before your Lordships' House, if the decision of this House in *R* v *Charles* [1977] AC 177 is of direct application. In that appeal this House was concerned with the dishonest use, not as in the present appeal of a credit card, but of a cheque card. The appellant defendant was charged and convicted on two counts of obtaining a pecuniary advantage by deception, contrary to section 16 of the Act of 1968. The Court of Appeal (Criminal Division) and your Lordships' House both upheld those convictions. Your Lordships unanimously held that where a drawer of a cheque which is accepted in return for goods, services or cash uses a cheque card he represents to the payee that he has the actual authority of the bank to enter on its behalf into the contract expressed on the card that it would honour the cheque on presentation for payment.

My Lords, I quote in their entirety three paragraphs from the speech of my noble and learned friend, Lord Diplock [1977] AC 177, 182-183, which, as I venture to think, encapsulate the reasoning of all those members of your Lordships' House who delivered speeches:

[His Lordship referred to passages from Lord Diplock's speech which are set out above under *Commissioner of the Police for the Metropolis* v *Charles*]

'If one substitutes ... the words "to honour the voucher" for the words "to pay the cheque," it is not easy to see why mutatis mutandis the entire passages are not equally applicable to the dishonest misuse of credit cards as to the dishonest misuse of cheque cards.

But the Court of Appeal in the long and careful judgment delivered by Cumming-Bruce LJ felt reluctantly impelled to reach a different conclusion. The crucial passage in the judgment which the learned Lord Justice delivered reads thus [1981] 1 WLR 78, 86-87:

"We would pay tribute to the lucidity with which the judge presented to the jury the law which the House of Lords had declared in relation to deception in a cheque card transaction. If that analysis can be applied to this credit card deception, the summing up is faultless. But, in our view, there is a relevant distinction between the situation described in *R* v *Charles* [1977] AC 177 and the situation devised by Barclays Bank for transactions involving use of their credit cards. By their contract with the bank, Mothercare had bought from the bank the right to sell goods to Barclaycard holders without regard to the question whether the customer was complying with the terms of the contract between the customer and the bank. By her evidence Miss Rounding made it perfectly plain that she made no assumption about the defendant's credit standing at the bank. As she said, 'the company rules exist because of the company's agreement with Barclaycard.' The flaw in the logic is, in our view, demonstrated by the way in which the judge put the question of the inducement of Miss Rounding to the jury: 'Is that a reliance by her, Miss Rounding of Mothercare, upon the presentation of the card as being due authority *within the limits as at that time* as with count one?' In our view, the evidence of Miss Rounding could not found a verdict that necessarily involved a finding of fact that Miss Rounding was induced by a false representation that the defendant's credit standing at the bank gave her authority to use the card."

I should perhaps mention, for the sake of clarity, that the person referred to as the appellant in that judgment is the present respondent.

It was for that reason that the Court of Appeal (Criminal Division) allowed the appeal, albeit with hesitation and reluctance. That court accordingly certified the following point of law as of general public importance, namely:

"In view of the proved differences between a cheque card transaction and a credit card transaction, were we right in distinguishing this case from that of *R* v *Charles* [1977] AC 177 upon the issue of inducement?"

My Lords, as the appellant says in paragraph 9 of his printed case, the Court of Appeal (Criminal Division) laid too much emphasis upon the undoubted, but to my mind irrelevant, fact that Miss Rounding said she made no assumption about the respondent's credit standing with the bank. They reasoned from the absence of assumption that there was no evidence from which the jury could conclude that she was "induced by a false representation that the defendant's credit standing at the bank gave her authority to use the card." But, my Lords, with profound respect to the learned Lord Justice, that is not the relevant question. Following the decision of this House in *R* v *Charles*, it is in my view clear that the representation arising from the presentation of a credit card has nothing to do with the respondent's credit standing at the bank but is a representation of actual authority to make the contract with, in this case, Mothercare on the bank's behalf that the bank will honour the voucher upon presentation. Upon that view, the existence and terms of the agreement between the bank and Mothercare are irrelevant, as is the fact that Mothercare, because of that agreement, would look to the bank for payment. That being the representation to be implied from the respondent's actions and use of the credit card, the only remaining question is whether Miss Rounding was induced by that representation to complete the transaction and allow the respondent to take away the goods. My Lords, if she had been asked whether, had she known the respondent was acting dishonestly and, in truth, had no authority whatever from the bank to use the credit card in this way, she (Miss Rounding) would have completed the transaction, only one answer is possible - no. Had an affirmative answer been given to this question, Miss Rounding would, of course, have become a participant in furtherance of the respondent's fraud and a conspirator with her to defraud both Mothercare and the bank. Leading counsel for the respondent was ultimately constrained, rightly as I think, to admit that had that question been asked of Miss Rounding and answered, as it must have been, in the negative, this appeal must succeed. But both he and his learned junior strenuously argued that, as my noble and learned friend, Lord Edmund-Davies, pointed out in his speech in *R* v *Charles* [1977] AC 177, 192-193, the question whether a person is or is not induced to act in a particular way by a dishonest representation is a question of fact, and since what they claimed to be the crucial question had not been asked of Miss Rounding, there was no adequate proof of the requisite inducement. In her deposition, Miss Rounding stated, no doubt with complete truth, that she only remembered this particular transaction with the respondent because some one subsequently came and asked her about it after it had taken place. My Lords, credit card frauds are all too frequently perpetrated, and if conviction of offenders for offences against sections 15 or 16 of the Act of 1968 can only be obtained if the prosecution are able in each case to call upon the person upon whom the fraud was immediately perpetrated to say that he or she positively remembered the particular transaction and, had the truth been known, would never have entered into that supposedly well-remembered transaction, the guilty would often escape conviction. In some cases, of course, it may be possible to adduce such evidence if the particular transaction is well remembered. But where as in the present case no one could reasonably be expected to remember a particular transaction in detail, and the inference of inducement may well be in all the circumstances quite irresistible, I see no reason in principle why it should not be left to the jury to decide, upon the evidence in the case as a whole, whether that inference is in truth irresistible as to my mind it is in the present case. In this connection it is to be noted that the respondent did not go into the witness box to give evidence from which that inference might conceivably have been rebutted.

My Lords, in this respect I find myself in agreement with what was said by Humphreys J giving the judgment of the Court of Criminal Appeal in *R v Sullivan* (1945) 30 Cr App R 132, 136:

"It is, we think, undoubtedly good law that the question of the inducement acting upon the mind of the person who may be described as the prosecutor is not a matter which can only be proved by the direct evidence of the witness. It can be, and very often is, proved by the witness being asked some question which brings the answer: 'I believed that statement and that is why I parted with my money'; but it is not necessary that there should be that question and answer if the facts are such that it is patent that there was only one reason which anybody could suggest for the person alleged to have been defrauded parting with his money, and that is the false pretence, if it was a false pretence."

It is true that in *R v Laverty* (1970) 54 Cr App R 495, Lord Parker CJ said, at p498, that the Court of Appeal (Criminal Division) was anxious not to extend the principle in *R v Sullivan* further than was necessary. Of course, the Crown must always prove its case and one element which will always be required to be proved in these cases is the effect of the dishonest representation upon the mind of the person to whom it is made. But I see no reason why in cases such as the present, where what Humphreys J called the direct evidence of the witness is not and cannot reasonably be expected to be available, reliance upon a dishonest representation cannot be sufficiently established by proof of facts from which an irresistible inference of such reliance can be drawn.

My Lords, I would answer the certified question in the negative and would allow the appeal and restore the conviction of the respondent upon the second count in the indictment which she faced at Bedford Crown Court.'

R v Laverty (1970) 54 Cr App R 495 Court of Appeal (Criminal Division) (The Lord Chief Justice, Karminski LJ and Stephenson J)

Deception must operate on the victim's mind

Facts

The defendant sold a Hillman Imp car bearing the registration plates DUV 111C to a man named Bedborough. The car had originally borne the registration number JPA 945C, but the registration plates had been changed by the defendant when he was renovating the car for sale. The defendant was convicted of obtaining property by deception from Bedborough. The defendant appealed on the ground that any deception exercised by him had not induced Bedborough to purchase the car, and had thus not been operative.

Held

The appeal would be allowed.

The Lord Chief Justice:

'Although it was contested at the trial, it was conceded in this Court that there was a representation by conduct that the car being sold to Mr Bedborough was the original Hillman Imp to which the chassis plate and rear plate which it bore had been assigned. It is conceded that such a representation was made by conduct; it is clear that that was false, and false to the knowledge of the appellant. The sole question was whether this false representation operated on Mr Bedborough's mind so as to cause him to hand over this cheque.

As sometimes happens, Mr Bedborough did not give the answers which were helpful to the prosecution and no leading questions could be put. The nearest he got was: "I bought this because I thought the appellant was the owner." In other words, he was saying: what induced me to part with my money was the representation by conduct that the appellant had a title to sell. It was in those circumstances that at the end of the case for the prosecution a submission was made that there was no case to answer. The Deputy Chairman did not accede to that submission. The trial proceeded, and when he came to sum up to the jury, he said this: "There is no evidence at all that anything was said by Mr Laverty to that effect, but the prosecution is entitled to say that that representation can be made by conduct, and it is a matter for you whether you feel, in the circumstances of this case, a representation was made by conduct that the motor car in question was the original Hillman Imp, bearing in mind that there had been put upon it number plates with the registration number DUV 111C, one of which indeed had come off the original car, and that in due course a log book was produced; but it does not appear in the evidence that the log book was seen or relied on by Mr Bedborough at the time when he handed over the cash and the cheque. What is meant by 'the original Hillman Imp' in this case? You may think that that means the car which was originally so registered, and it is a matter for you whether or not it is a necessary inference that a car offered for sale with the registration number upon it is the car for which that number was originally issued; if you think the answer to that is 'yes' then you will have to consider: Is that an inference which must have been in the mind of the purchaser; is it something that must have operated on the mind of Mr Bedborough and played its part in inducing him to hand over the cash and the cheque?" The jury apparently were satisfied that that was the true inference and convicted the appellant.

The real point is whether there was any evidence here which enabled the jury to draw that inference. It is axiomatic that it is for the prosecution to prove that the false representation acted on the mind of the purchaser, and in the ordinary way, and the Court emphasises this, the matter should be proved by direct evidence. However, it was said in *Sullivan* (1945) 30 Cr App R 132 that the inducement need not be proved by direct evidence, and I quote from the headnote "If the facts are such that the alleged false pretence is the only reason that could be suggested as having been the operative inducement." In the special facts of that case the Court held that the prosecution had given sufficient proof, although they made it very clear that the proper way and the ordinary way of proving the matter was by direct evidence.

Mr Wadsworth submits that when the Court in *Sullivan* (supra) referred to the only reason that could be suggested, they were not emphasising that it was the only reason, but that it was the only inference that could be drawn. He is saying here that the only inference here is that this false representation did operate on Mr Bedborough's mind and the jury were fully entitled to come to the conclusion to which they came.

This Court is very anxious not to extend the principle in *Sullivan* (supra) more than is necessary, The proper way of proving these matter is through the mouth of the person to whom the false representation is conveyed, and further it seems to the Court in the present case that no jury could say that the only inference here was that Mr Bedborough parted with his money by reason of this false representation. Mr Bedborough may well have been of the mind which he stated, namely that what operated on his mind was the belief that the appellant was the owner. Provided that the appellant was the owner, it may well be that Mr Bedborough did not mind that the car did not bear its original number plates. At any rate as it seems to the Court it cannot be said that the only possible inference here is that that fact actuated upon Mr Bedborough's mind.

In those circumstances, though with some reluctance, this Court feels that the proper course here is to allow the appeal and quash the conviction.'

R v Price (1990) 90 Cr App R 409 Court of Appeal (Criminal Division) (Lord Lane CJ, Hutchinson and Rougier JJ)

Dishonesty in deception offences

Facts

The appellant opened a number of bank accounts, depositing small amounts of money in each account. He subsequently drew cheques for much larger sums on three accounts to pay for goods and services supplied on credit, or in advance of payment. When interviewed by police, the appellant insisted that he had acted in good faith as he was the beneficiary of a trust fund and that he would in due course be receiving £100,000 from the fund. He was charged on five counts of obtaining services by deception, two counts of evading liability by deception, one count of forgery, and one count of attempting to obtain property by deception. Following conviction the appellant sought to challenge his convictions on the ground that the trial judge had failed to direct the jury in accordance with the 'Ghosh' guidelines.

Held

The appeal would be dismissed.

Per Lord Lane CJ:

'Mr Barton who has pursued the appeal in this Court makes a number of complaints about the way in which the learned recorder dealt with the case. First of all he complains that no *Ghosh* (1982) 75 Cr App R 154, [1982] QB 1053, direction was given so far as dishonesty was concerned.

It has been said more than once in this Court, and in particular in *Roberts (William)* (1987) 84 Cr App R 117, that it is by no means in every case involving dishonesty that a *Ghosh* direction is necessary. Indeed in the majority of such cases, of which this was one, it is unnecessary and potentially misleading to give such a direction. It need only be given in cases where the defendant might have believed that what he is alleged to have done was in accordance with the ordinary person's idea of honesty.

Here the simple question was this: Did the defendant honestly believe that he was the beneficiary of a £100,000 trust fund? If he did not, and the jury were sure of it, he was guilty; otherwise he was not.

As the learned recorder said in his summing up, the question for the jury to decide was this:

"Dishonesty; there is no need for me to explain it to you. You all know what honesty is and dishonesty is the opposite side of the coin. So that is the issue that you have to decide on that count, and, similarly, when you come to count 3 when he booked in at the Railway Hotel. Again, did he falsely purport that he had the means to pay for that? Was he dishonest at that time? When he booked in with Mrs Cumming, in count 8, and again with Paragon Laundry, Mrs Fox and Mrs Gilchrist. Again, was he falsely purporting that he had the means to pay?

That was a simple direction. It was an accurate direction and it was a direction which was correct in law, and it is not a proper subject of complaint.

The next ground of appeal is broadly that the learned recorder did not set out the case for the defence fairly. Mr Barton has referred us to a number of instances where he complains that the recorder was unfair in the way he dealt with the matter. The first passage about which complaint is made is at p11E:

"But essentially in this case, as indeed Mr Barton has said, you will have to decide at any stage in this matter did the accused have any reasonable belief that he had prospects of funds coming from Coutts or the family or wherever it may be, or was this a total farce?"

It might have been better if he had used the word "honest" instead of "reasonable" in that passage. But the jury cannot have been misled, in the light of the earlier direction already referred to, as to the true nature of that direction.

Complaint is made by Mr Barton of the use of the words "total farce". That is exactly what the jury had to decide. They had to decide, before they could convict this man, whether the trust fund of £100,000 was a total farce. If they came to that conclusion, then the verdict would be one of guilty. If not, then the verdict would be one of not guilty.

There are a number of other passages to which reference has been made. At p13D is this passage:

"Another example, you see, of unchallenged evidence, because the suggestion put by counsel that he was paid is not supported by any evidence at all but you heard Mr Woodhouse say: 'I was never paid for that cheque,' and that may help you in relation to other cheques that were issued."

We see no proper ground of complaint so far as that is concerned.

There have been a variety of other complaints which we do not think it is necessary for us to examine in detail, save to say that, read against the summing up as a whole, and read against the evidence in the case, which incidentally did not include any evidence on oath from the defendant himself who did not go into the box, we do not think proper complaint can be made.

It is only necessary perhaps to refer to two other points of complaint. One of them is to be found at p18 and reads as follows:

"As Mr O'Doire [a bank employee] said, the cheque for £22,000 odd was of course presented and sent straight back by the bank. You see, if on that very day, the 22nd June, Mr Price was telling Mr Winton: 'I have purchase money immediately available, seven days' notice,' does that give a clue as to what has been going on all the time, what this trust money was - was it a figment of this man's imagination and just being told to people to, as they say in the old fashioned way, 'con' people into thinking he had money he did not have? But it is a matter for you to decide, as I have told you."

There again was a perfectly proper expression by the learned judge of the problem which faced the jury.

Then comes the Billy Bunter passage at p20 EF, which figures largely in the notice of appeal. It reads as follows:

"I do not know whether any of you remember the stories of Greyfriars School by Frank Richards, but in those stories there was a boy called Billy Bunter, and Billy Bunter was always expecting a postal order the next day. The only trouble with Billy Bunter was that the postal order had never arrived the next day and it went on and on never arriving (and the funds go on and on in this case never arriving) because Billy Bunter tried to persuade people to lend him money on the strength of the postal order that was due to arrive."

Mr Barton suggests that that was an unfair comment. We disagree. Although Mr Barton suggests that it is factually incorrect, in that Billy Bunter's postal order, he tells us, did eventually arrive, the fact remains that it was a homely illustration which could not have done any harm to the defendant, and would no doubt interest the jury as being an accurate illustration of how they were to approach the case.

We do not think in the upshot that these comments made by the learned judge did in any way render this conviction unsafe or unsatisfactory.'

R v Rashid [1977] 2 All ER 237

See chapter 19.

R v Silverman [1987] Crim LR 574 Court of Appeal (Criminal Division) (Watkins LJ, Bush and Ian Kennedy JJ)

Overcharging - whether obtaining property by deception

Facts

'The appellant was convicted of a number of offences of obtaining property by deception, by representing that the sum charged for work was a fair and proper charge. It was agreed that he had charged two elderly sisters grossly excessive prices for work done on their property by his firm. The appellant was known to the sisters from work previously done for their family. He appealed against conviction on the grounds:

(1) that the judge had failed to put the appellant's defence to the jury and

(2) that an excessively high quotation did not amount to a false representation under section 15(1) of the Theft Act 1968.

Held

Allowing the appeal,

(1) the judge did not adequately deal with the defence, misdirecting them that the explanation adverted to in the appellant's interview with the police was of no evidential value - *Hamand* (1986) 82 Cr App R 65 followed.

(2) Whether a quotation amounts to false representation must depend upon the circumstances. In these circumstances of mutual trust, one party depending upon the other for fair and reasonable conduct, the criminal law may apply if one party takes dishonest advantage of the other by representing as a fair charge that which he, but not the other, knows is dishonestly excessive. The situation of mutual trust in the present case had been built up over a long time. The appellant's silence on any matter other than the sums to be charged was as eloquent as if he had said that he was going to make no more than a modest profit.'

[*Reported by Lynne Knapman, Barrister.*]

R v Staines (1974) 60 Cr App R 160 Court of Appeal (Criminal Division) (James LJ, Phillips and May JJ)

Reckless deception

Facts

As stated by James LJ:

'On July 23, 1973 the appellant went with her friend, Mrs Gehr, to one shop where she selected lamps and shades to the value of some £14, and although the appellant had a bank pass book of her own which was in credit to the sum of £20, she used a cheque from a bank book belonging to Mrs Gehr and which related to a bank account with Barclays Bank that had been closed as from October 16 in the previous year. She signed a cheque from that bank book in the name of E. A. Gehr and she dated it August 23, not July 23. She put an address on the back of the cheque, 25 Howard Road, South Norwood. That was not her address. When the shop proprietor asked for proof of address, she indicated the back of the cheque.

Having made purchases in that way the appellant, with Mrs Gehr, went to another shop in Tooting and obtained articles to the value of something over £13. She asked the assistant if she could pay by cheque because she did not have sufficient cash with her. She was allowed to do so. She used another cheque from Mrs Gehr's book. She signed that one in the same way. Again the cheque was dated August 23 and a different address, 85 Longley Road, was written on the back of that cheque. She produced to support the cheque and the address on the cheque a document which had the appearance of coming from the Gas Board, and apparently did come from the Gas Board, which had that address on it. That address, 85 Longley Road, was not the appellant's address nor had it been, but Mrs Gehr had in fact previously lived at that address.

Both cheques were dishonoured and on August 3 the appellant was seen by the police and asked questions. She was asked if she had bought the goods from the hardware shop and paid by cheque and she immediately replied, "Yes, I've had a row with her about it. I didn't know she had no money in the account until Wednesday," which would be August 1, "I've thrown her out." That referred to Mrs Gehr. So right at the outset she was saying that she did not know the account upon which the cheque had been drawn was a closed account or an account in which there were no funds with which the cheque would be met on due presentation. She admitted signing the cheque in Mrs Gehr's name and explained that she had done so because Mrs Gehr had some injury to her hand, which was bandaged, and therefore it was difficult for her to write. She told the police that the property that she had bought was at her other flat where Mrs Gehr had been living, and indeed the property was recovered from that flat at 30 Stretton Road, where the appellant was about to take up residence. She made a statement later in which she said, "If I'd known she hadn't any money in the bank, I'd have taken it out of my account." In fact her account was not sufficiently in credit to meet both the cheques at the time, but she was then maintaining that she did not know there was insufficient money in the account of Mrs Gehr at that time to meet the cheques.'

The defendant was convicted of two offences of obtaining property by deception, contrary to s15(1) Theft Act 1968, and appealed.

Held

The appeal would be dismissed.

James LJ:

[His Lordship referred to s15 of the Theft Act 1968, and continued:]

'The important words for present purposes are "any deception (whether deliberate or reckless)." There is no dispute between the appellant and the Crown through their counsel that the word "reckless" in that subsection should be given the construction of meaning "without caring," being indifferent to whether the statement is true or false; "reckless" means something more than carelessness or negligence.

In support of his argument that that is the proper construction to be placed on the statute Mr Forbes [counsel for the defendant] has referred us to the old authority in civil law of *Derry* v *Peek* (1889) 14 App Cas 337, and also invited our attention to Professor Smith's current book on the Theft Act and the law of theft in which he deals with that particular statutory provision. This Court accepts the contention put forward that in this section "reckless" does mean more than being careless, does mean more than being negligent, and does involve an indifference to or disregard of the feature of whether a statement be true or false. From that basis Mr Forbes proceeds to argue that in the present case when summing-up to the jury the judge introduced the concept of recklessness in words that may have resulted in the jury misunderstanding the proper construction to be placed upon the word and reaching a conclusion of guilt on the basis of a decision on their part that the appellant had been careless or negligent.

The passages which are used to support this argument appear at page 3 and then at page 18 of the summing-up. At page 3 the judge said: "Mr Forbes for the defence, just now in what he was telling you about the law was indicating, to put it at its lowest, that the accused had to have been acting deliberately. That is not quite the law as far as deception goes. Because deception in law means any deception whether deliberate or reckless, by words or conduct, as to fact or as to law ..." Mr Forbes said that in his address to the jury he had not raised the issue of reckless deception. He had submitted to the jury that they should acquit unless they were made sure by the evidence that there was deliberate dishonesty in what was done by the accused in relation to the cheques. Whatever counsel's words were, it is quite clear that the learned judge felt that he must invite the jury's attention to the fact that acting deliberately was only one part of the definition of deception in the Act and so it came about that he introduced the concept of recklessness in that passage. But there is nothing of which complaint is made in relation to that passage.

So one comes to page 18 where ... the judge again refers to this aspect: "The accused said: 'I would not have drawn the cheques for Mrs Gehr if I'd known the money was not in her account.' Well, I told you that in law deception means 'any deception whether deliberate or reckless, by words or conduct, as to fact or as to law.' 'Reckless' we have heard very little about - in fact we have heard absolutely nothing about inquiries made by the accused as to whether she really did have any reason to suppose there was money in the account. There she was drawing cheques on an account which could not honour the cheques and does not seem to have done much to be satisfied that the cheques would not bounce, and indeed they did bounce."

Mr Forbes contended that there is a strong invitation to the jury to look at the situation and decide whether there had been a lack of care, or negligence, in failing to make elementary inquiries as to the state of the account upon which the cheques were drawn and that in those words a risk was introduced into the case that the jury might convict this appellant on a wrong basis of law. But those words have to be read in relation to the summing-up as a whole and in relation to the facts disclosed by the evidence as to which there was very little, if any, in dispute - the signing of the cheques in Mrs Gehr's name, the putting of the wrong address on the cheque and so forth to which reference has already been made. What the judge was in effect saying in the passage complained of, as we read it, was this: the accused is saying "I would not have drawn those cheques if I had known there was no money." Well, deception can include deliberate acts and recklessness and in this case you have heard very little about recklessness. We have heard nothing about inquiries. Let us get on with the rest of the case.

Indeed, the case had not been put forward on the basis of recklessness, and recklessness was introduced only by this side wind. We do not accept as valid the contention that by these words at page 18, the jury may have been diverted from the true point that they had to consider. The word "recklessness," is not used at all. In its ordinary meaning it would convey to the jury something more than mere carelessness and the argument advanced on this first point that is taken in our judgment fails.'

R v Thompson (1984) 79 Cr App R 191 Court of Appeal (Criminal Division) (May LJ, Bristow and MacPherson JJ)

Theft Act 1968 s15 - where obtaining takes place

Facts

The defendant was employed as a computer operator at a bank in Kuwait. He opened a number of savings accounts there, and programmed his employer's computer to re-direct funds intended for clients' accounts into his own savings accounts. On his return to England, he telexed the Kuwait bank to transfer the funds from his savings accounts there to accounts in England. The defendant was convicted of obtaining property by deception contrary to s15(1) of the Theft Act 1968, and he appealed on the ground that the English courts lacked jurisdiction since, in his view, the obtaining of property occurred in Kuwait.

Held

The appeal would be dismissed.

May LJ:

'It will thus be apparent, and it has been the Crown's case throughout, that the *obtaining* in the six offences under section 15 of the Theft Act alleged against the appellant in this case occurred in England, within the jurisdiction, at the time when in each instance he received into a particular bank account the sterling equivalent of the credit balance in an account in Kuwait, which he had fraudulently created and which the bank transferred by telex as the result of the request in the appellant's letters. One might have thought that any other contention about the place where the relevant obtaining in each of the six offences in this case occurred was unarguable. However, Mr Caplan [counsel for the defendant] has attractively argued before us that the relevant obtaining in each of the six instances occurred as the result of fraud committed by this appellant, and occurred in Kuwait on each occasion when the corresponding debit and credit entries in the respective savings accounts were made as the result of his dishonest manipulation of the bank's computer.

Mr Caplan has submitted that section 15 is not concerned with questions of lawful title to any relevant property but, as the section itself specifically provides, with the ownership, possession or control of such property. He submits that when one asks the question whether at any material time - that is to say at any time before the bank in Kuwait was asked to remit to England - the appellant had control of what seemed to be his credit balance, the answer must be "yes, he did" - at least until the bank discovered the fraud. Until they were so put on inquiry it would not have been possible for them to have said that this appellant had no such credit balance. Mr Caplan went on to argue that the proof of the pudding was in the eating because the bank in Kuwait in fact acted upon the letters which the appellant wrote asking for the transfers of his credit balances; it is thus difficult to say, Mr Caplan contends, that the appellant did not have control of a credit balance when the bank acted upon the basis that he did. In this connection he referred us to the case of *Kohn* (1979) 69 Cr App R 395. That was a case in which the defendant had been an accountant for various companies and in that capacity had used company cheques to draw sums of money from the bank accounts of the companies concerned, which he thereafter pocketed and used for himself. He was charged with nine counts of theft. It was contended that the property which he had stolen by the company cheques used in that way were choses in action, the property of the bank's customer, his employer, and that in those circumstances, having regard to the definition of "property" in section 4 of the Theft Act, the indictment was properly drawn and the offences properly charged.

When *Kohn's* case came before this Court on appeal, it held that in respect of those accounts from which he had drawn money where the defendant's employer was in credit, the bank had owed the employer a debt, and therefore by obtaining the money in that way the defendant had obtained a chose in action or property and the conviction could be sustained. A similar situation obtained, so it was held, where the account of the relevant employing company was in overdraft, but in overdraft within the extent of a facility which had previously been granted by the bank. There was however one count in respect of which Kohn was charged where the company's account was overdrawn to an extent in excess of any facility which had been granted by the bank. In those circumstances, as the employer/customer would not have been in a position to sue the bank for any debt, and no money was legitimately owed by the bank on the cheque as drawn - because all that was needed was for the bank to return it marked "return to drawer" - there was no chose in action, there was thus no theft by Kohn, and consequently that count could not be substantiated. In relation to that count the only passage in the judgment of the court, which was delivered by Geoffrey Lane LJ (as he then was), to which we think it is necessary to refer is on p405, where in considering the submissions by Mr Tyrrell on behalf of the appellant in that case the Court said this:

"It seems to us that the argument is quite untenable. First of all, is there a thing in action, and the answer is undoubtedly yes. Secondly, has the appellant appropriated it? The answer is yes. Was the intention permanently to deprive the owner, and again there was ample evidence upon which the jury properly directed could come to the conclusion that it was. Was it dishonest? Again there was ample evidence on which the jury could come to that conclusion. A submission was made at the close of the prosecution case similar to that made to us, which the judge rejected. We think he was right to reject it. Mr Tyrrell has frankly said that his researches have brought to light no authorities which give any support to his proposition. In so far as there is authority it is against his contentions. It is contained in the writings of two eminent academic lawyers: first of all Professor Griew in his book *The Theft Acts 1968 and 1978* (3rd ed 1978, paras. 2-11) where one finds this:

'The case of an employee (D) who has authority to draw on his employer's (P's) bank account and who dishonestly draws on it for unauthorised purposes seems also to be theft (assuming the account to be in credit). D has in some manner appropriated the debt owed by the bank to P. Although nothing in the transaction operates as an assignment of that debt to D, it would seem that D has appropriated the debt or part of it by causing P's credit balance to be diminished, or at the very least taking the risk of such diminution. The case is analogous to the theft of a chattel by destruction.'

The whole of that passage, and particularly the last sentence, if it is correct, as we think it is, sounds the death knell to this particular submission on behalf of the appellant."

Death knell it may have been in the case of *Kohn*: in the instant appeal Mr Caplan fastens upon the last part of the approved passage from Professor Griew's book where he wrote: "... or at the very least taking the risk of such diminution." He submits that when the appellant acted as he did in programming the computer in Kuwait with the result that in addition to it appearing to give him credit on his savings accounts it also diminished the amounts standing to the credit of the other five substantial but dormant accounts, there was at the very least the risk of the diminution in the credit balances on those accounts. Consequently he submitted that we ought to hold that for the purposes of the relevant provisions of the Theft Act the obtaining of the property, the chose in action, occurred in Kuwait at the time that the computer went into action as the appellant's plane was in the air over the Mediterranean.

We think, however, that one may legitimately ask: of what property did this appellant in that way obtain control in Kuwait? What was the nature of that property? Mr Caplan's reply, as we understand it, was that the appellant obtained the control of those credit balances on his savings accounts, which were effectively choses in action, and were such until the bank discovered his fraud. With all respect to Mr Caplan's persuasive argument, we think that when it is examined it is untenable. We do not think that one can describe as a chose in action a liability which has been brought about by fraud, one where the action to enforce that liability is capable of immediate defeasance as soon as the fraud is pleaded. It is neither here nor there, we think, that the person defrauded, in this case the bank, may not have been aware that one of its employees had been fraudulent in this way until a later time. The ignorance of the bank in no way, in our view, breathes life into what is otherwise a defunct situation brought about entirely by fraud. One has only to take a simple example. Discard for the moment the modern sophistication of computers and programs and consider the old days when bank books were kept in manuscript in large ledgers. In effect all that was done by the appellant through the modern computer in the present case was to take a pen and debit each of the five accounts in the ledger with the relevant sums and then credit each of his own five savings accounts in the ledger with corresponding amounts. On the face of it his savings accounts would then have appeared to have in them substantially more than in truth they did have as the result of his forgeries; but we do not think that by those forgeries any bank clerk in the days before computers would in law have thus brought into being a chose in action capable either of being stolen or of being obtained by deception contrary to section 15 of the Theft Act 1968.

In so far as the customers whose accounts had been fraudulently debited and who had to be reimbursed by the bank, as Mr Caplan submitted, are concerned, we prefer the approach of Mr Walsh. He submitted that properly considered it was not a question of reimbursement: it was merely a question of correcting forged documents, forged records, to the condition in which they ought to have been but for the fraud.

In those circumstances and for those reasons we agree with the learned judge in the court below that the only realistic view of the undisputed facts in this case is that the six instances of obtaining charged in the indictment each occurred when the relevant sums of money were received by the appellant's banks in England. Further it seems to us quite clear (as it was to the learned judge below) that those sums of money were obtained as the result of the letters which the appellant wrote to the bank in Kuwait. The only proper construction to be put upon those letters is that they contain the representations pleaded in the particulars of offences in the indictment. Those representations were the effective cause of each and every one of the obtainings. However, Mr Caplan submits and we agree that each of those matters, that is to say where did the obtaining take place and of what did it consist, were the representations made, and were they the effective cause of each of the particular obtainings, were matters of fact to be determined by the jury. It may be, Mr Caplan accepts, that in the circumstances of the instant case any verdict on any of the counts by a jury other than one of guilty would have been perverse. Nevertheless he contends that the appellant was on those issues of fact entitled to have the jury's verdict.'

R v Woolven (1983) 77 Cr App R 231 Court of Appeal (Criminal Division) (Lord Lane CJ, Ackner LJ and Leonard J)

Dishonesty - claim of right - s15(1) Theft Act 1968

Facts

As stated in the judgment of Leonard J:

'The appellant's co-defendant Roberts, was the owner of a hotel in North Devon. The appellant worked for him as a head waiter during the 1980 and 1981 seasons. By the end of 1981 Roberts was substantially in debt. The appellant also had financial difficulties.

According to Roberts's evidence he devised a plan to get him out of his difficulties. He discussed the plan with the appellant and they decided to put it into operation. The appellant was to get £1,000 for his part. In January 1982 Roberts rented a room in Birmingham giving the name "P Williams." He acquired an "Off the shelf" company called Cutlerbrook Ltd.

On February 16, 1982, the appellant and Roberts travelled to Birmingham. The appellant went to a branch of Barclays Bank where he arranged to open an account in the name of Cutlerbrook Ltd. He was given a bank mandate form. Later that day the appellant posted off the completed form, bearing the name of a referee. The form was signed by the appellant in the name of "Peter Williams" and by Roberts in the name of "Jane Williams."

Roberts had worked until 1979 as finance manager for Imperial Metal Industries Finance Ltd (IMI Finance). He therefore knew that it was the company's practice to transfer money to subsidiary companies by telephoning the company's bank. Confirmatory documentation would follow the telephone call. On February 23, Roberts telephoned the branch of Lloyds Bank at Birmingham, where IMI Finance had its account. He gave the name of a genuine member of the company's staff and asked the bank to transfer £20,000 to Cutlerbrook Ltd. In order no doubt to camouflage what he was doing, he also arranged the transfer of a similar amount to a genuine subsidiary of IMI Finance.

That afternoon the appellant went to Barclays Bank branch and asked to withdraw £16,200 from Cutlerbrook's account. The bank confirmed that the £20,000 had arrived shortly before. It appears that the reference had not yet been taken up and, more importantly, the bank wanted confirmation that the appellant was "P Williams". They declined to pay out the money.

The appellant left the bank and telephoned Roberts. That evening Roberts telephoned the appellant suggesting a plan. As a result they met next morning. Roberts gave the appellant a letter addressed to P Williams and signed in a fictitious name. There was also the rent book for the room which Roberts had rented. It was in the name of P Williams. The letter bore a telephone number in case the bank wanted to get in touch with its writer. The number was that of a telephone box where Roberts was to wait.

After these arrangements had been made the appellant returned to the bank. By that time the fraud had been discovered and he was arrested. Roberts was arrested at the telephone box.

The ground of appeal was that the trial judge should have directed the jury that section 2(1)(*a*) of the

Theft Act 1968 (claim of right not to be regarded as dishonest) applied to dishonesty under section 15 of the Act. "Dishonesty" in section 15 should have the same meaning as dishonesty in section 1.'

Held

The appeal would be dismissed

Leonard J:

'In the grounds of appeal and in his careful submission to the Court, Mr Hotten [counsel for the defendant] has argued that the partial definition of "dishonest" which appears in section 2(1)(*a*) of the Act must be applied to section 15. Section 2 provides: "(1) A person's appropriation of property belonging to another is not to be regarded as dishonest - (*a*) if he appropriates the property in the belief that he has in law the right to deprive the other of it, on behalf of himself or of a third person ..." It follows, Mr Hotten says, that where, as in the present case, a defendant raises the issue of claim of right, the trial judge must incorporate into his direction of the meaning of "dishonestly" in section 15 a specific direction based on the words of section 2(1)(*a*). On the present facts such a direction would be to the effect that if the jury concluded that the appellant might have attempted to obtain the money from Barclays Bank in the belief that he had in law the right to deprive them of it on behalf of Roberts, whom he understood to be its owner, they should acquit.

Mr Webb, who appeared for the Crown in this Court, submitted that section 2(1)(*a*) was specifically limited to theft by section 1(3) of the Act. Section 1(1) contains the basic definition of theft. Sections 2 to 6 inclusive focus their attention on specific parts of that basic definition. Section 2 is concerned with the word "dishonestly". Section 1(3) provides as follows: "The five following sections of this Act shall have effect as regards the interpretation and operation of this section (and, except as otherwise provided by this Act, shall apply only for purposes of this section)."

The Act does not provide for the application of any part of section 2 for the purposes of the Act as a whole or of any particular section of it. By contrast sections 4(1) and 5(1) are applied to the Act generally by section 34(1). Section 6, which is concerned with the words "with the intention of permanently depriving the other of it", is applied for the purposes of section 15 with the necessary adaptation of the reference to "appropriating" which appears in section 6(1). Therefore, said Mr Webb, the learned judge had only to give the jury the necessary direction on dishonesty in accordance with the decision of this Court in *Ghosh* (1982) 75 Cr App R 154; [1982] QB 1053. He did so fully and nothing further was required.

Mr Hotten conceded that section 1(3) prevented the application of section 2(1)(*a*) to section 15; but nevertheless asked this Court to read its effect into the definition of obtaining by deception. In support of his argument he invited us to look at the eighth report of the Criminal Law Revision Committee, which was the framework upon which the Theft Act was built.

Paragraph 88 adverts to the reason for not repeating the effect of section 2(1)(*a*) in the definition of obtaining by deception, and adds the following words: "It would be only partly applicable to the offence of criminal deception, and it seems unnecessary and undesirable to complicate the Bill by including a separate definition in clause 12" (which was to become section 15). "The fact that a claim of right will be a defence to a charge under clause 12(1) is probably in accordance with the present law of obtaining by false pretences; for the existence of a claim of right to the property obtained is regarded as inconsistent with that of 'intent to defraud' for the purpose of section 32(1) of the Larceny Act 1916."

Our attention was also drawn to Professor Smith on "*The Law of Theft*." In chapter IV, which deals with criminal deception, paragraph 181 accepts that section 2(1)(*a*) only applies to theft and that therefore a judge would be reluctant to direct a jury in accordance with its terms. The passage continues: "It is thought that it is reasonable to assume that one who obtains property, a service, or a pecuniary advantage by deception but under a claim of right made in good faith is not guilty." See also Professor Griew on *The Theft Act*, paragraph 6-47, and Smith and Hogan on *The Criminal Law*, (4th ed), p545.

In the absence of authority which bears on this topic subsequent to the Theft Act, Mr Hotten referred us to *Williams* (1836) 7 C & P 354, which was a case of obtaining by false pretences. Coleridge J directed the jury in terms which required them to acquit if the prisoner did not intend to defraud but had a claim of right.

Commenting on that case in *Hamilton* (1845) 1 Cox's CC 244, Pollock CB at p247 said: "In *Williams* (supra) the defendant believed, however erroneously, that he had some sort of right to do as he did, and this was probably the ground on which the jury acquitted him." The cases of *Parker* (1910) 74 JP 208 and *Bernhard* (1938) 28 Cr App R 137; [1938] 2 KB 264 were also cited by Mr Hotten, who submitted that they were no decisive authority against his argument. This Court agrees.

The question which arises for our decision i[s] whether the learned judge's direction as to the element of dishonesty was adequate to do justice i[n] the present case. At an early stage in the summing up he directed the jury in accordance with the judgment of the Court in *Ghosh* (1982) 75 Cr App R 154; [1982] QB 1053. In giving the judgment of the Court the Lord Chief Justice said at pp162-163 and p1064 respectively: "In determining whether the prosecution has proved that the defendant was acting dishonestly, a jury must first of all decide whether according to the ordinary standards of reasonable and honest people what was done was dishonest. If it was dishonest by those standards, then the jury must consider whether the defendant himself must have realised that what he was doing was by those standards dishonest."

The learned judge in the present case said to the jury at page 3F of the transcript: "So the final ... and the determining question ... is whether on the evidence you are satisfied that [the appellant] was acting dishonestly." He told them to ask themselves first what the appellant had done. Then they were to consider whether his actions were dishonest, measured by the standards of any ordinary honest man. Finally they had to decide whether they were satisfied that the appellant must have realised his conduct would be condemned as dishonest by any other ordinary person. He added the following words at p4D: "If, having heard all the evidence in the case, your final conclusion is that notwithstanding what he did he may not have regarded it as dishonest, that is an answer to this charge."

Towards the end of the summing up the learned judge again returned to the issue of dishonesty, leaving it to the jury in these words: "If you think in the face of those facts, members of the jury, that he may at the time have regarded his conduct as being perfectly honest, then he is entitled to be acquitted by your hand. If, having looked at the whole of the facts that he himself admits, if your conclusion is that he must have known at the time when he did these things that judged by ordinary standards of ordinary men he was acting dishonestly, then he is guilty of this offence. That is the issue for your consideration."

In the judgment of this Court any direction based on the concept of claim of right as set out in section 2(1)(a), or otherwise, would have added nothing to what the learned judge in fact said. Indeed a direction based on *Ghosh* (supra) seems likely to us to cover all occasions when a section 2(1)(*a*) type direction might otherwise have been desirable.'

21 THE THEFT ACT 1978

R v Allen [1985] AC 1029 House of Lords (Lord Hailsham LC, Lords Scarman, Diplock, Bridge and Brightman)

Section 3(1) Theft Act 1978 - intent to avoid payment

Facts

The defendant had stayed at an hotel for nearly a month and left without paying the bill outstanding of £1,286. He contacted the hotel a few days later and explained he was in financial difficulties but would return to the hotel to collect his belongings and leave his passport as security. When he did so he was arrested and charged with an offence contrary to s3(1) of the Theft Act 1978. The defendant claimed that he was not acting dishonestly and he had genuinely expected to be able to pay the bill from the proceeds of various business ventures. The trial judge directed the jury that the intent to avoid payment merely referred to the time when payment should have been made 'on the spot'. The jury returned a guilty verdict. The Court of Appeal quashed the conviction and allowed the accused's appeal.

The Crown appealed to the House of Lords.

Held

The appeal would be dismissed.

Lord Hailsham LC:

'After a fairly lengthy summing up by the trial judge to which, in the light of what happened, I need make no special reference, the jury retired at 1 pm and came back at 2.18 pm with a note containing the following specific question for guidance by the judge:

"Regarding count 2 of the indictment, the words 'and with intent to avoid payment of the £1,286.94', do you refer to permanent intention or one applying only to the dates mentioned in the charge?"

To this question the judge gave the following explicit answer:

"The answer is: one applying to 8 and 11 February 1983. You see it says in count 2: 'knowing that payment on the spot for goods supplied and services done was required or expected from him ...' 'On the spot' means the day you leave. There was no payment on the spot when he should have paid. It contrasts sharply with count 1 where the intent there is permanent; that is not so in count 2 where he was required to pay on the spot; and there has been a failure to do that. Will you please, once more, retire to consider your verdict?"

The original summing up had contained the same direction, but in view of what happened there is no need to refer to it separately, for the effect on the jury of this specific reply was immediate and decisive. Within five minutes they returned the verdict of guilty.

Despite some (though not unanimous) textbook opinions in an opposite sense (see Smith *The Law of Theft* (5th ed, 1984) para. 250, p130, Griew *The Theft Acts 1968 and 1978* (4th ed, 1982) para. 11-14, p155 and, less strongly, Glanville Williams *Textbook of Criminal Law* (2nd ed, 1983) p878), I consider this answer to be clearly erroneous.

[His Lordship referred to s3 of the Theft Act 1978, and continued]

The Crown's contention was that the effect of this section is to catch not only those who intend permanently to avoid payment of the amount due, but also those whose intention is to avoid payment on the spot, which, after all, is the time at which, ex hypothesi, payment has been "expected or required", and the time, therefore, when the "amount" became "due".

The judgment of the Court of Appeal, with which I agree, was delivered by Boreham J. He said ([1985] 1 All ER 148 at 154, [1985] 1 WLR 50 at 57):

"To secure a conviction under s3 of the 1978 Act the following must be proved: (1) that the defendant in fact made off without making payment on the spot; (2) the following mental elements: (a) knowledge that payment on the spot was required or expected of him; and (b) dishonesty; and (c) intent to avoid payment [sc 'of the amount due']."

I agree with this analysis. To this the judge adds the following comment:

"If (c) means, or is taken to include, no more than an intention to delay or defer payment of the amount due, it is difficult to see what it adds to the other elements. Anyone who knows that payment on the spot is expected or required of him and who then dishonestly makes off without paying as required or expected must have at least the intention to delay or defer payment. It follows, therefore, that the conjoined phrase 'and with intent to avoid payment of the amount due' adds a further ingredient: an intention to do more than delay or defer, an intention to evade payment altogether."

My own view, for what it is worth, is that the section thus analysed is capable only of this meaning. But counsel for the Crown very properly conceded that, even if it were equivocal and capable of either meaning, in a penal section of this kind any ambiguity must be resolved in favour of the subject and against the Crown. Accordingly, the appeal falls to be dismissed either if on its true construction it means unambiguously that the intention must be permanently to avoid payment, or if the clause is ambiguous and capable of either meaning. Even on the assumption that, in the context, the word "avoid" without the addition of the word "permanently" is capable of either meaning, which Boreham J was inclined to concede, I find myself convinced by his final paragraph, which reads:

"Finally, we can see no reason why, if the intention of Parliament was to provide, in effect, that an intention to delay or defer payment might suffice, Parliament should not have said so in explicit terms. This *might* have been achieved by the insertion of the word 'such' before payment in the phrase in question. It *would* have been achieved by a grammatical reconstruction of the material part of s3(1) thus, 'dishonestly makes off without having paid and with intent to avoid payment of the amount due as required or expected'. To accede to the Crown's submission would be to read the section as if it were constructed in that way. That we cannot do. Had it been intended to relate the intention to avoid 'payment' to 'payment as required or expected' it would have been easy to say so. The section does not say so. At the very least it contains an equivocation which should be resolved in favour of [the respondent]."

There is really no escape from this argument. There may well be something to be said for the creation of a criminal offence designed to protect, for instance, cab drivers and restaurant keepers against persons who dishonestly abscond without paying on the spot and without any need for the prosecution to exclude an intention to pay later, so long as the original act of "making off" could be described as dishonest. Unlike that in the present section, such an offence might very well as with the railway ticket offence, be triable summarily, and counsel for the Crown was able to call in aid the remarks of Cumming-Bruce LJ in *Corbyn* v *Saunders* [1978] 2 All ER 697 at 699, [1978] 1 WLR 400 at 403 which go a long way to support such as view. But, as the Court of Appeal remarked, that decision was under a different statute and a differently worded section which did not contain both the reference to "dishonestly" and the specific intention "to avoid payment" as two separate elements in the mens rea of the offence. In order to give the section now under consideration the effect required the section would have to be remodelled in the way suggested by Boreham J in the passage quoted above, or the word "and" in the ultimate phrase would have to be read as if it meant "that is to say" so that the required intent would be equated with "dishonestly" in the early part of the subsection.

Apart from the minor matter not relevant to the judgment there is nothing really to be added to the judgment delivered by Boreham J.

The minor matter to which I have just referred was the disinclination of the Court of Appeal to consider the Criminal Law Revision Committee's Thirteenth Report (Section 16 of the Theft Act 1968) (Cmnd 6733 (1977)) which led to the passing of the 1978 Act. In accordance with the present practice, this, for the purpose of defining the mischief of the Act but not to construe it, their Lordships in fact have done. The "mischief" is covered by paras. 18 to 21 of the report and it is significant that the report was accompanied by a draft Bill, 3 of which is in terms identical with s3 of the Act, save that the proposed penalty was three years instead of two. Though we did not use it as an aid to construction, for the purpose of defining the mischief to be dealt with by the section, I consider it to be relevant. The discussion had originated from the decision in *DPP* v *Ray* [1973] 3 All ER 131, [1974] AC 370 and the committee defined the mischief in the following terms (para. 18):

"... there was general support for our suggestion that where the customer knows that he is expected to pay on the spot for goods supplied to him or services done for him it should be an offence for him dishonestly to go away without having paid *and intending never to pay*." (My emphasis.)

From this it is plain beyond doubt that the mischief aimed at by the authors of the report was precisely that which the Court of Appeal, construing the section without reference to the report, attributed to the section by the mere force of grammatical construction.

In the result I agree with the judgment of the Court of Appeal and apart from my reference to the Criminal Law Revision Committee report can add nothing usefully to it ...'

R v Brooks and Brooks (1982) 76 Cr App R 66   Court of Appeal (Criminal Division)   (Watkins LJ, Kilner Brown and Taylor JJ)

Section 3(1) Theft Act 1978 - mens rea

Facts

The defendants, father and daughter, had consumed a meal at a restaurant with another man named Smith. The defendants were convicted of making off without payment contrary to s3(1) of the Theft Act 1978. The daughter appealed against her conviction on the ground that the trial judge had not directed the jury adequately as to her defence that she honestly believed Smith would be paying for the meal.

Held

The appeal would be allowed. (The father's appeal against conviction was dismissed.)

Kilner Brown J:

'The appeal raises interesting questions as to which there appears to be no reported decision of this court, the only reported case being that of *McDavitt* [1981] Crim LR 843, in which the words of the subsection were considered by Mr Recorder Mann, QC (as he then was). Even that case concerned only part of the words and concentrated upon the meaning to be given to "on the spot."

We have been referred to a fuller examination of the definition of the offence which has been made in the academic field, notably by Professor Smith in "The Law of Theft" (4th ed 1979) paragraph 242 and Mr JR Spencer in an article entitled "The Theft Act 1978," [1979] Crim LR 24, in particular at p37 thereof. Thus Professor Smith comments that the words "makes off" should be construed in a pejorative sense and includes both a sudden and secret departure but excludes departure consented to by means of a deception. Mr Spencer relies upon one meaning given to the term "makes off" in the Shorter Oxford Dictionary, namely "to depart suddenly, often with a disparaging implication, to hasten away; to decamp."

Pausing there, it is plain that the learned compilers do not suggest that the words must always be construed in the pejorative sense. In any case it is an unnecessary construction, for the words do not stand alone. The making off must be dishonest.

Mr Spencer is of the opinion that the term suggests a sudden and unexpected departure. In so doing he fails to consider one of the alternatives given in the dictionary, namely to "decamp," which may be an exercise accompanied by the sound of trumpets or a silent stealing away after the folding of tents. Obviously, the term covers a wide variety of modes of departure. Nevertheless, we strongly deprecate the involvement of a jury in any philosophic study, however interesting it may be to lawyers and academics. Nor do we adopt the attitude feared by Mr Spencer of simply saying it is "all a question of fact for the jury."

In our opinion, the words "dishonestly makes off" are words easily understandable by any jury which, in the majority of cases, require no elaboration in a summing-up. The jury should be told to apply the words in their ordinary natural meaning and to relate them to the facts of the case. We agree with the decision in *McDavitt* (supra) that "making off" involves a departure from the spot where payment is required.

It is convenient shortly to recite the facts, before considering the submissions made by Mr Pleming in admirably cogent fashion.

[His Lordship stated the facts and continued]

At the trial, the prosecution case was that the appellants jointly and severally intended to avoid payment and separately made off from the spot which, so it was said, was the restaurant as a whole. The jury found them both guilty.

The first submission on behalf of both appellants is that the jury should have been directed as to the meaning of the words "makes off" and that the direction given was so inadequate that it amounted to a misdirection.

The recorder said this at page 4A to D of the transcript of the summing-up: "Your attention was directed by the defence to the question of making off. That is not a term of art. There is no particular significance, or particular requirements. You all know what 'making off' means and there is no question of any special requirements. The whole essence of the offence is that it is done dishonestly. If you walk out of a restaurant thinking that somebody else was paying your bill you would have made off but you would not have done so dishonestly, if you did it by mistake thinking that somebody else was paying. That would not be an offence. Here, the whole essence of the offence is that the people left intending, if they could, to get away without paying. It is suggested that they did this together, but it would be open to you, if you were so minded, to find that it had been done by one but not the other; that they were not party to any joint plan."

For the reasons already given, we are of the opinion that on the facts of this case no further elaboration was necessary and that the summing-up was entirely adequate on this point. This submission, therefore, fails.

The second ground put forward is that the recorder failed adequately or at all to direct the jury that the prosecution had to prove that the accused had either made off or was about to do so when challenged, and second that the making off was with intent to avoid payment.

But the recorder had, immediately before the passage previously cited, read out in full the words of the subsection which are remarkably clear and simple. He then summarised the effect of the subsection in succinct fashion in the sentence: "Here, the whole essence of the offence is that the people left intending, if they could, to get away without paying." The matter could not have been put any better than that. So the jury could not have been left in any doubt.

On the facts of this case, it was not necessary to elaborate on the necessity to establish that there was a departure from the spot. The evidence of this was there. Both went outside the premises.

However, in a case where the accused is stopped before passing the spot where payment is required, a jury should be directed that that may constitute an attempt to commit the offence, rather than the substantive offence, provided that the other ingredients are established.

In so far as the appellant Edward George Brooks is concerned, the appeal against conviction is dismissed. There is no appeal against the sentence of a fine of £25 and an order for compensation in the sum of £8.52.

In the case of the appellant Julie Brooks, there is a further and different consideration. It is submitted on her behalf that a clear direction was required to the effect that it must be proved that at the time she left the premises she knew that no payment was intended and that there was an intention on her part to participate in a dishonest evasion of the cost of the meal.

All that the judge said as to this was the general direction which was given in the passage previously cited and, earlier to that, he had directed the jury in these words: "There are two defendants and you will bring in separate verdicts in respect of each. You may find one guilty and one not guilty or both not guilty. Their cases must be considered separately."

That was all right as far as it went, but the jury were never told that upon the evidence that she left earlier and in haste and her defence that she went to the restaurant at the other man's invitation believing that he would pay, they would have to draw the inference that at the time she left she intended dishonestly to evade payment, before she could be convicted. If the jury had been alerted to this necessity, it is quite possible that they may not have been satisfied of her guilt.

In the opinion of this Court, this failure to direct the jury more fully in her case makes her conviction unsafe and unsatisfactory and her appeal is allowed.'

R v Firth (1990) 91 Cr App R 217 Court of Appeal (Criminal Division) (The Lord Chief Justice, Mr Justice Rose and Mr Justice Morland)

Evasion of a liability by deception - s2(1)(a) Theft Act 1978

Facts

The appellant was a consultant gynaecologist/obstetrician who dealt with both National Health Service and private patients. The prosecution alleged that he had failed to inform the hospital treating several of his patients that they were receiving private medical treatment, and hence he had not been billed for the treatment that they had received. He was charged, inter alia, with four counts (hereinafter referred to as counts 4 to 7) of evading a liability by deception contrary to s2(1)(c) of the Theft Act 1978. The appellant was convicted and appealed (inter alia), on the following ground:

'That the learned recorder erred in not acceding to the submission made by the defence at the close of the Crown's case that counts 4, 5, 6 and 7 were wrongly laid in law in that the allegations to be proved required proof of acts of commission whereas the evidence disclosed only acts of omission.'

Held

The appeal would be dismissed.

Lord Lane CJ:

'It is not altogether clear what [ground 1 of the ground of appeal] means. We take it to mean that the counts laid under section 2(1)(c) of the Theft Act cannot be brought home against the defendant unless the prosecution prove that the dishonest obtaining was achieved by acts of commission, that is to say the deception must be by commission, and not by omission.

One turns to the Act itself to see what the draftsman of the statute in fact says. Section 2 reads as follows:

[His Lordship recited sections 2(1)(c) and 2(2) of the 1978 Act and continued]

That would cover, for instance, if it were the case, this appellant obtaining an exemption on behalf of a patient whom he was treating.

The prosecution allegation in these various counts was that the appellant, by failing dishonestly to inform the hospital of the private patient status of the women ... had caused either them or himself not to be billed for services which should have been charged against them.

If, as was alleged, it was incumbent upon him to give the information to the hospital and he deliberately and dishonestly refrained from doing so, with the result that no charge was levied either upon the patients or upon himself, in our judgment the wording of the section and subsection which I have just read is satisfied. It matters not whether it was an act of commission or an act of omission. Providing those matters were substantiated the prosecution had made out their case. That means, in brief, that the recorder was right to reject any submission to the contrary.

But before us Mr Rogers [counsel for the appellant] enlarged upon that ground of appeal and the second limb of the argument was this. He submitted to us that the words "legally enforceable" in the section mean that in order to proceed under that subsection the prosecution has to establish an existing liability at the time when the alleged deception is made. I hope I do his submission justice: I think that is the proposition which he advanced. If, accordingly, goes on the submission, the defendant is asking for a service to be performed, the liability only arises when the service has been performed. Consequently, goes the submission, one must find the liability and then go on to prove that the deception was practised when the liability had arisen. In the present case, he submits, if the deception was practised before the liability to pay had come into existence, then no offence was committed.

It seems to us that that overlooks the wording not only of section 2(1)(c), but also the wording of the two previous paragraphs, because both in 2(1)(a) and 2(1)(b) the words "existing liability" are to be found. Let me read paragraph (a): "... where a person by any deception – (a) dishonestly secures the remission of the whole or any part of any existing liability to make a payment, whether his own or another's." There is similar wording in (b).

It is immediately to be remarked that in paragraph (c) the word "existing" is omitted. It seems to us that that is indicative of what the draftsman of the Act really meant. The argument put forward by Mr Rogers might very well have something to command it if section 2(1)(c) had contained the word "existing", but the word in that paragraph is conspicuous by its absence. The words as they stand are apt to cover an expected liability or future liability, even if the deception alleged is not in truth a continuing deception. The omission of the word "existing" was, it seems clear to us, purposeful and not a matter of chance.

Consequently in our judgment the second limb to ground 1 of the notice of appeal fails and that part of the appeal cannot be successful.'

R v Halai [1983] Crim LR 624

See *R* v *Widdowson*, below.

R v Holt and Lee (1981) 73 Cr App R 96   Court of Appeal (Criminal Division)   (Griffiths LJ, Lawson and Balcombe JJ)

Section 2(1)(b) Theft Act 1978 - forgoing payment of a liability.

Facts

As stated by Lawson J:

'... in the evening of December 9, 1979, the appellants consumed meals costing £3.65 in the Pizzaland Restaurant in Southport. There was a police officer off-duty also feeding in the restaurant and he overheard the appellants planning to evade payment for their meals by the device of pretending that a waitress had removed a £5 note which they had placed on the table. When presented with their bill, the appellants advanced this deception and declined payment. The police officer concerned prevented them from leaving the restaurant and they were shortly afterwards arrested and charged.'

The defendants were convicted of attempting to commit an offence contrary to s2(1)(b) of the Theft Act 1978, and appealed on the basis that if they had not been apprehended they would in fact have committed an offence contrary to s2(1)(a) of the 1978 Act.

Held

The appeals would be dismissed.

Lawson J:

'At the close of the prosecution case in the Crown Court, Mr Reid [counsel for the defendant], who has also conducted this appeal, made a submission which was overruled, the main point of which was that assuming the facts as we have recounted them to be correct, the attempt to evade thus emerging was an attempt to commit an offence not under section 2(1)(*b*) as charged but under section 2(1)(*a*) of the 1978 Act since, he submitted, had the attempt succeeded, the appellants' liability to pay for their meals would have been "remitted" and not just "forgone," to use the contrasting terms contained in the respective subsections.

Mr Reid further developed his submission before us. As we understand it, he submits that the vital differences between the two offences defined in the first two paragraphs of section 2(1) of the Act are that "remission" involves that, first, the creditor who "remits" the debtor's existing liability must communicate his decision to the debtor and, secondly, the legal consequence of the "remission" is to extinguish the debt, whereas the "forgoing of an existing liability," to use the words of section 2(1)(*b*), need not be communicated to the debtor and has not the consequence in law of extinguishing such liability. We find great difficulty in introducing these concepts into the construction of the subsection. We will later return to the matter.

Mr Reid further submitted that the effect of section 2(1) of the Act was to create three different offences but conceded that there could be situations in which the conduct of the debtor or his agent could fall under more than one of the three paragraphs of section 2(1).

The elements of the offence defined by section 2(1)(*b*) of the Act relevant to the present case are clearly these: first, the defendant must be proved to have the intent to make permanent default on the whole or part of an existing liability. This element is unique to section 2(1)(*b*); it has no application to the offences defined in section 2(1)(*a*) or (*c*). Secondly, given such intent, he must use deception. Thirdly, his deception must be practised dishonestly to induce the creditor to forgo payment.

It must always be remembered that in the present case, whatever offence was being attempted, the attempt failed. The creditor was not induced by the dishonest deception and did not forgo payment. It is clear on the evidence that the appellants' conduct constituted an attempt to evade liability be deception, and the jury, who were properly directed, clearly concluded that the appellants' conduct was motivated by the intent to make permanent default on their supper bill. Thus, all the elements needed to enable an attempt to commit the offence defined in section 2(1)(*b*) were found to be present, so that the appellants were rightly convicted and charged.

Reverting to the construction of section 2(1) of the Act, as to which the commentators are not at one, we are not sure whether the choice of expressions describing the consequences of deception employed in each of it s paragraphs, namely, in paragraph (*a*) "secures the remission of an existing liability," (*b*) "induces a creditor to forgo payment" and (*c*) "obtains any exemption from liability" are simply different ways of describing the same end result or represent conceptual differences.

Whilst it is plain that there are substantial differences in the elements of the three offences defined in section 2(1), they show these common features: first, the use of deception to a creditor in relation to a liability, secondly, dishonesty in the use of deception, and thirdly, the use of deception to gain some advantage in time or money. Thus the differences between the offences relate principally to the different situations in which the debtor-creditor relationship has arisen.

The practical difficulty which Mr Reid's submission failed to confront is strikingly illustrated by cases of attempting to commit an offence under section 2(1)(*a*) or section 2(1)(*b*). If, as he submits, section 2(1)(*a*) requires communication of remission to the debtor, whereas section 2(1)(*b*) does not require communication of the "forgoing of payment" but, as the case is a mere attempt, the matter does not *end* in remission of liability or forgoing of payment, then the prosecution would be in a dilemma since it would either be impossible to charge such an attempt or the prosecution would be obliged to charge attempts in the alternative in which case, since any attempt failed, it would be quite uncertain which of the alternatives it was.'

R v Jackson [1983] Crim LR 617 Court of Appeal (Criminal Division) (Purchas LJ, Jones and Drake JJ)

Section 2(1)(a) Theft Act 1978 - securing the remission of a liability

Facts

'A stolen Access credit card was presented by occupants of the appellant's car at petrol stations and accepted in satisfaction of payment for petrol and other goods. The appellant was charged, inter alia, with handling stolen goods (count 3) and evading liability by deception by dishonestly securing the remission of an existing liability, contrary to section 2(1)(*a*) of the Theft Act 1978 (counts 5 and 8). At the close of the prosecution evidence the defence submitted that counts 5 and 8 should have been charged under section 2(1)(*b*), and should be withdrawn from the jury. The trial judge ruled that the case should proceed as charged. The appellant was convicted and appealed on the ground, inter alia, that the judge had failed properly to rule on the defence submission.

Held

Dismissing the appeal, that although in *Holt* [1981] 1 WLR 1000 it was held that the element under section 2(1)(*b*) of an intent to make permanent default on the whole or part of an existing liability was unique to sub-paragraph (*b*), that judgment was not authority for the proposition that the elements in sub-paragraphs (*a*), (*b*) and (*c*) of section 2(1) were mutually exclusive. The transaction of tendering a stolen credit card and having it accepted by a trader who forthwith would look to the authority issuing the card for payment and not to the person tendering the card, meant that that person had dishonestly secured the remission of an existing liability. It was not necessary to consider whether a charge in respect of that transaction could be brought under section 2(1)(*b*). In the circumstances the matter was not wrongly charged under section 2(1)(*a*).'

[*Reported by Eira Caryl-Thomas, Barrister.*]

R v Lambie [1982] AC 449

See chapter 20.

R v Modupe [1991] Crim LR 530 Court of Appeal (Criminal Division) (Lord Lane CJ, Henry and Hidden JJ)

Theft Act 1978 s2(1)(b) - whether an existing liability

Facts

'M was charged with obtaining financial assistance to enable him to buy cars, by giving false information to companies with whom he was negotiating. He traded in one car for another, and obtained finance by falsifying application forms until there was around £50,000 outstanding. In relation to a hire-purchase agreement for a Mercedes he gave a false name and address, exaggerated his employment status and indicated that he owned property which he did not. Two county court judgments were registered against him for large sums of money. He was convicted, *inter alia*, of the evasion of liability by deception contrary to the Theft Act 1978, s2(1)(b).

Section 61(1) of the Consumer Credit Act 1974 provided that a regulated agreement was not properly executed unless it contained all the prescribed terms in conformity with the regulations made thereunder (SI 1983 No 1553) schedule 1, paragraph 11 of which required information of the total amount payable to be entered on the documents which embodied the agreement. The person completing the form of agreement had failed to add the cash and balance sums together to get the total amount payable, leaving the "total amount payable" box blank. The result was that the agreement was improperly executed. Under s65(1) and (2) of the 1974 Act it was enforceable against the debtor or hirer by court order only, and a retaking of goods was an enforcement of the agreement. On appeal it was submitted for M that the fact that the agreement was enforceable against him only on an order of the court meant that there was no existing liability to make payment.

Held

Dismissing the appeal, the fact that the agreement was not enforceable without an order of the court did not mean that there was no existing liability. There was an existing liability, albeit enforceable only by an order of the court. The plain object of s65 was that, if the agreement was not properly completed, one of the remedies of a disappointed contractor for enforcing his liability was removed because he could not help himself by retaking the vehicle if it was a hire-purchase type of agreement. But the argument that no legal liability existed in the light of those matters was not tenable.'

[*Reported by Veronica Cowan, Barrister.*]

R v Sibartie [1983] Crim LR 470 Court of Appeal (Criminal Division) (Lord Lane CJ, McGowan and Nolan JJ)

Section 2(1) (c) Theft Act 1978 - exemption from a liability

Facts

'The appellant, a law student who lived in Acton and attended college in Hendon, bought two season tickets on the Underground, one ticket covering the beginning of his journey on one line for two stations and the other ticket covering the end of his journey on another line for two stations; in between were 14 stations including an interchange station between the two lines. At the interchange station, on passing a ticket inspector, the appellant held aloft a wallet containing the season ticket - according to the inspector, "flashing it" so that she could not see what was on it - and on being challenged said that he was going to the first of the two stations at the end of his journey. The appellant's version was that he was going out at the interchange station and was intending to pay. He was charged on counts 1 and 2 with evasion of a liability by deception, contrary to section 2(1)(c) of the Theft Act 1978 and on count 3 of an attempted evasion of a liability by deception. The jury acquitted him on counts 1 and 2 but convicted him on count 3. He appealed against conviction.

Held

Dismissing the appeal, that the correct method of approach was to ask whether, taking the words of section 2(1)(c) in their ordinary meaning, one would say that what the appellant was attempting to do fell within the ambit of the words. The jury by their verdict must have been satisfied that the appellant dishonestly used his season tickets, which did not in fact cover the journey he was making, in an attempt to persuade the ticket inspector that they did cover the journey. Did that amount to an attempt to obtain exemption from liability to make a payment for the journey he was making or had made? He was saying, albeit tacitly, by waving the supposed season ticket in the air that he was the holder of a ticket authorising him to be making the journey without further payment and consequently he was not under any liability to pay any more. In the ordinary meaning of words that was dishonestly obtaining an exemption from the liability to pay the excess which, had he been honest, he would have had to pay. There might be a degree of overlap between section 2(1)(*a*), (*b*) and (*c*), and the fact that what the appellant did might also have been an attempt to commit an offence under section 2(1)(*b*) was neither here nor there.'

[*Reported by L. Norman Williams, Barrister.*]

Troughton v The Metropolitan Police [1987] Crim LR 138 Divisional Court (Watkins LJ, Mann and Nolan JJ)

Section 3(3) Theft Act 1978 - intent to avoid payment of the amount due.

Facts

'The appellant was convicted before the magistrates of making-off without payment of a taxi-fare contrary to section 3 of the Theft Act 1978. His appeal against conviction was dismissed by the Crown Court. The findings of fact were as follows. A taxi driver agreed to take the appellant to his home somewhere in Highbury. The appellant, having had a great deal to drink, had not told the driver his address. The driver had to stop to obtain directions from the appellant at some point. There was an argument, the appellant accusing the driver of making an unnecessary diversion. The taxi driver, being unable to get an address from the appellant, drove to the nearest police station to see if someone else could help. The evidence concerning what occurred there was unclear. The Crown Court left unresolved the conflicting evidence as to whether or not the appellant left the police station to go to the taxi and steal from the driver's pouch. There was also difficulty in resolving the appellant's allegation that he had tendered money to the driver at the police station. The Crown Court having dismissed the appeal the appellant appealed by case stated to the High Court.

Held

Allowing the appeal and quashing the conviction (the prosecutor not contesting the appeal), that *R* v *Brooks and Brooks* (1983) 76 Cr App R 66; [1983] Crim LR 188 would have shed some light on this case but not necessarily determined it. It was not referred to in the Magistrates' or Crown Court. The basis for allowing this appeal was that the journey had not been completed and the consequence of that was a breach of contract by the taxi driver. Instead of resolving the argument about further instructions during the journey the driver broke away from the route which would have taken the appellant home in order to go to the police station. The driver being in breach of contract was not lawfully able to demand the fare at any time thereafter. For that reason, among others, the appellant was never in a situation in which he was bound to pay or even tender the money for the journey, and thus it could not be contended that he made off without payment.'

[*Reported by Maggy Piggot, Barrister.*]

R v Widdowson (1986) 82 Cr App R 314

Section 1(1) Theft Act 1978 - 'services'

Facts

See chapter 11.

Held

Saville J:

'The learned judge also rejected a further submission that the obtaining of a hire purchase agreement could not, as a matter of law, amount to the obtaining of services, which had been put forward on the basis that such an agreement is indistinguishable from a mortgage advance and so is covered by the decision of the Court in *Halai* [1983] Crim LR 624 ...

… we reject the suggestion that the obtaining of a hire purchase agreement cannot amount to the obtaining of services. In *Halai* (supra) this Court held that a mortgage advance cannot be described as a service. It is suggested that a hire purchase agreement is indistinguishable. We disagree. As we have just said, a hire purchase agreement (at least in the ordinary form) is the hiring of goods with various options given to the hirer, who in return agrees to pay the instalments, maintain the vehicle and so on. In our view the hire purchasing of a vehicle on some such terms can be regarded as the conferring of some benefit by doing some act, or causing or permitting an act to be done, on the understanding that the benefit has been or will be paid for, this being the definition of services in section 1(2) of the Theft Act 1978. The finance company confers a benefit by delivering possession of the vehicle to the hirer (or by causing or permitting the garage to do so) on the understanding that the hirer has paid or will pay a deposit and subsequent instalments.'

22 HANDLING STOLEN GOODS

Atwal v Massey (1971) 55 Cr App R 6 Divisional Court (The Lord Chief Justice, O'Connor and Lawson JJ)

Knowing or believing goods to be stolen

Facts

The defendant was convicted of handling a stolen electric kettle, contrary to s22(1) Theft Act 1968. He appealed on the ground that the justices had erred in law by finding that he ought to have known that the kettle was stolen.

Held

The appeal would be allowed

The Lord Chief Justice:

'The position can be stated quite simply. If when the justices said that the appellant ought to have known that the kettle was stolen they meant that any reasonable man would have realised that it was stolen, then that was not the right test. It is not sufficient to establish an offence under section 22 that the goods were received in circumstances which would have put a reasonable man on his enquiry. The question is a subjective one: was the appellant aware of the theft or did he believe the goods to be stolen or did he, suspecting the goods to be stolen, deliberately shut his eyes to the consequences? It may be that the justices meant the word "ought" to have the second meaning, namely that he suspected but closed his eyes, but we do not think that we ought to speculate on such a possibility, but rather that we ought to deal with the matter on the words used by the justices in the case.

Counsel for the respondent sensibly recognise that it is too small a case to justify us sending it back for further investigation, and in those circumstances the only alternative is to treat the matter on the footing that the justices were wrong and applied the wrong test, and thus that the appeal should be allowed and the conviction quashed.'

R v Bloxham [1983] 1 AC 109 House of Lords (Lords Diplock, Scarman, Bridge and Brandon)

Innocent receipt of stolen goods - subsequent disposal with mens rea

Facts

As stated by Lord Bridge:

'... in January 1977 the appellant purchased a motor car for £1,300. He paid the seller £500 in cash and was to pay the balance when the seller produced the car's registration document, but in the event this never happened. The car had in fact been stolen. It is accepted by the Crown that the appellant did not know or believe this when he acquired the car. In December 1977 he sold the car for £200 to an unidentified third party who was prepared to take the car without any registration document.

The appellant was charged under section 22(1) of the Theft Act 1968 with handling stolen goods, the particulars of the relevant count in the indictment alleging that he

"dishonestly undertook or assisted in the disposal or realisation of certain stolen goods, namely a Ford Cortina motor car registered number SJH 606M, by or for the benefit of another, namely the unknown purchaser knowing or believing the same to be stolen goods."

At the trial it was submitted that the count disclosed no offence in that the disposal or realisation of

447

the car had been for the appellant's own benefit, not for the benefit of the unknown purchaser, and that in any event the purchaser was not within the ambit of the categories of "other person" contemplated by section 22(1). The judge ruled that the purchaser derived a benefit from the transaction, in that, although he got no title, he had the use of the car; that there was no reason to give any restricted construction to the words "another person" in the subsection; that, accordingly, on the undisputed facts, the appellant had undertaken the disposal or realisation of the car for the benefit of another person within the meaning of section 22(1). In face of this ruling the appellant entered a plea of guilty, thereby, it may be noted, confessing both his guilty knowledge and his dishonesty in relation to the December transaction.

On appeal against conviction to the Court of Appeal, the court affirmed the trial judge's ruling and dismissed the appeal. The court certified the following point of law of general public importance as involved in their decision:

"Does a bona fide purchaser for value commit an offence dishonestly undertaking the disposal or realisation of stolen property for the benefit of another if when he sells the goods on he knows or believes them to be stolen?"

The present appeal is brought by leave of your Lordships' House.'

Held

The appeal would be allowed.

Lord Bridge:

[His Lordship referred to s22(1) of the Theft Act 1968, and continued:]

'It is, I think, now well settled that this subsection creates two distinct offences, but no more than two. The first is equivalent to the old offence of receiving under section 33 of the Larceny Act 1916. The second is a new offence designed to remedy defects in the old law and can be committed in any of the various ways indicated by the words from "undertakes" to the end of the subsection. It follows that the new offence may and should be charged in a single count embodying in the particulars as much of the relevant language of the subsection, including alternatives, as may be appropriate to the circumstances of the particular case, and that such a count will not be bad for duplicity. It was so held by Geoffrey Lane J delivering the judgment of the Court of Appeal in *R* v *Willis* [1972] 1 WLR 1605, and approved by the Court of Appeal in *R* v *Deakin* [1972] 1 WLR 1618. So far as I am aware, this practice has been generally followed ever since.

The critical words to be construed are "undertakes ... their ... disposal or realisation ... for the benefit of another person." Considering these words first in isolation, it seems to me that, if A sells his own goods to B, it is a somewhat strained use of language to describe this as a disposal or realisation of the goods for the benefit of B. True it is that B obtains a benefit from the transaction, but it is surely more natural to say that the disposal or realisation is for A's benefit than for B's. It is the purchase, not the sale, that is for the benefit of B. It is only when A is selling as agent for a third party C that it would be entirely natural to describe the sale as a disposal or realisation for the benefit of another person.

But the words cannot, of course, be construed in isolation. They must be construed in their context, bearing in mind, as I have pointed out, that the second half of the subsection creates a single offence which can be committed in various ways. I can ignore for present purposes the concluding words "or if he arranges to do so," which throw no light on the point at issue. The preceding words contemplate four activities (retention, removal, disposal, realisation). The offence can be committed in relation to any one of these activities in one or other of two ways. First, the offender may himself undertake the activity *for the benefit of* another person. Secondly, the activity may be undertaken *by* another person and the offender may assist him. Of course, if the thief or an original receiver and his friend act together in, say, removing the stolen goods, the friend may be committing the offence in both ways. But this does not invalidate the analysis and if the analysis holds good, it must follow, I think, that the category of other persons contemplated by the subsection is subject to the same limitations in whichever way the offence is committed. Accordingly, a purchaser, as such, of stolen goods, cannot, in my opinion, be "another person" within the subsection, since his act of purchase could not sensibly be described as a disposal or realisation of the stolen goods *by* him. Equally, therefore, even if the sale to him could be described as a disposal or realisation for his benefit, the transaction is not, in my view, within the ambit of the subsection. In forming this opinion I have not overlooked that in *R* v *Deakin* [1972] 1 WLR 1618, 1624, Phillimore LJ said of the appellant, a purchaser of stolen goods who was clearly guilty of an offence under the first half of section 22(1) but had only been charged under the second half, that he was "involved in the realisation." If he meant to say that a purchase of goods is a realisation of those goods by the purchaser, I must express my respectful disagreement.

If the foregoing considerations do not resolve the issue of construction in favour of the appellant, at least they are, I believe, sufficient to demonstrate that there is an ambiguity. Conversely it is no doubt right to recognise that the words to be construed are capable of the meaning which commended itself to the learned trial judge and to the Court of Appeal. In these circumstances, it is proper to test the question whether the opinion I have expressed in favour of a limited construction of the phrase "for the benefit of another person" is to be preferred to the broader meaning adopted by the courts below, by any available aids to construction apt for the resolution of statutory ambiguities.

As a general rule, ambiguities in a criminal statute are to be resolved in favour of the subject, sc in favour of the narrower rather than the wider operation of an ambiguous penal provision. But here there are, in my opinion, more specific and weightier indications which point in the same direction as the general rule.

First, it is significant that the Theft Act 1968, notwithstanding the wide ambit of the definition of theft provided by sections 1 and 3(1), specifically protects the innocent purchaser of goods who subsequently discovers that they were stolen, by section 3(2) which provides:

"Where property or a right to interest in property is or purports to be transferred for value to a person acting in good faith, no later assumption by him of rights which he believed himself to be acquiring shall, by reason of any defect in the transferor's title, amount to theft of the property."

It follows that, though some might think that in this situation honesty would require the purchaser, once he knew the goods were stolen, to seek out the true owner and return them, the criminal law allows him to retain them with impunity for his own benefit. It hardly seems consistent with this that, if he deals with them for the benefit of a third party in some way that falls within the ambit of the activities referred to in the second half of section 22(1), he risks prosecution for handling which carries a heavier maximum penalty (14 years) than theft (10 years). The force of this consideration is not, in my view, significantly weakened by the possibility that the innocent purchaser of stolen goods who sells them after learning they were stolen may commit the quite distinct offences of obtaining by deception (if he represents that he has a good title) or, conceivably, of aiding and abetting the commission by the purchaser of the offence of handling by receiving (if both know the goods were stolen).

Secondly, it is clear that the words in parenthesis in section 22(1) "otherwise than in the course of the stealing" were designed to avoid subjecting thieves, in the ordinary course, to the heavier penalty provided for handlers. But most thieves realise the goods they have stolen by disposing of them to third parties. If the judge and the Court of Appeal were right, all such thieves are liable to prosecution as principals both for theft and for handling under the second half of section 22(1).

Finally, we have the benefit of the report of the Criminal Law Revision Committee, 8th Report, Theft and Related Offences (1966) (Cmnd 2977), which led to the passing of the Theft Act 1968 including the provisions presently under consideration in the same form as they appeared in the draft Bill annexed to the report, to assist us in ascertaining what was the mischief which the Act, and in particular the new offence created by section 22(1), was intended to cure. We are entitled to consider the report for this purpose to assist us in resolving any ambiguity, though we are not, of course, entitled to take account of what the committee thought their draft Bill meant: *Black-Clawson International Ltd* v *Papierwerke Waldhof-Aschaffenburg AG* [1975] AC 591.

There is a long section in the report headed "Handling stolen goods, etc" from paragraphs 126 to 144. The committee, after drawing attention to the limitations of the existing offence of receiving, say in paragraph 127:

"... we are in favour of extending the scope of the offence to certain other kinds of meddling with stolen property. This is because the object should be to combat theft by making it more difficult and less profitable to dispose of stolen property. Since thieves may be helped not only by buying the property but also in other ways such as facilitating its disposal, it seems right that the offence should extend to these kinds of assistance."

This gives a general indication of the mischief aimed at. The ensuing paragraphs, after setting out the proposed new provision in the terms which now appear in section 22(1) of the Act, give numerous illustrations of the activities contemplated as proper to attract the same criminal sanction as that previously attaching to the old offence of receiving. Throughout these paragraphs there is no hint that a situation in any way approximating to the circumstances of the instant case lay within the target area of the mischief which the committee intended their new provision to hit.

For these reasons I have reached the conclusion that any ambiguity in the relevant language of section 22(1) should be resolved in favour of the narrower meaning suggested earlier in this opinion.'

R v Brown [1970] 1 QB 105   Court of Appeal (Criminal Division) (Lord Parker CJ, Winn LJ and Eveleigh J)

Assisting in the retention of stolen goods - failure to inform the police

Facts

As stated by Lord Parker CJ:

'The short facts were that on a night in January a café at Weymouth was broken into and a quantity of cigarettes and foodstuff was stolen. The next morning, January 19, police went to the flat of which the defendant was the tenant and found him in bed, and in that flat they found a quantity of the stolen goods. He was asked if he knew anything about the theft, and he said that he did not. He did not impede a search and some of the stolen goods, namely ham, bacon and other perishable foodstuffs were found in a refrigerator. The police did not find any quantity of the cigarettes which had been stolen. When he was about to be arrested, or indeed had been arrested, the defendant said to the officer "Get lost" and he was thereupon taken to the police station. It was only later that the cigarettes were found; they had been taken out of their packets, put into a plastic bag and were in fact at the foot of a wardrobe in which some of the defendant's clothes were hanging.'

The defendant was subsequently convicted of handling stolen goods contrary to s22(1) of the Theft Act 1968, by dishonestly assisting in their retention, and appealed.

Held

The appeal would be dismissed.

Lord Parker CJ:

'The point of law arises on a direction given by the chairman in regard to the handling of stolen goods. In fact the defendant had been charged on three counts; the first was the breaking in. The prosecution did not pursue that and the jury at the direction of the chairman acquitted him. The second and third counts both alleged offences of handling the goods, but they were divided into two parts, count 2 relating to a handling by way of receiving, getting the goods into his possession or control, and on that likewise he was acquitted. But the third count alleged a handling of goods by dishonestly assisting in the retention of the stolen goods. It is in regard to the direction on that count upon which he was convicted that this appeal arises.

This conviction must clearly have been on the basis that the jury were satisfied that, at some stage before the police arrived, the defendant knew that these cigarettes had been stolen, and indeed that the rest of the property had been stolen. It was on the assumption that the jury were so satisfied that the chairman gave this direction:

"So far as the other count of dishonestly assisting in the retention of the goods is concerned, it appears to me that the matter for you to consider is whether, assuming that you are satisfied that Brown knew that these stolen cigarettes were in the wardrobe when Detective Constable Chatterley came, he was dishonestly assisting in their retention by not telling the constable that they were there."

He goes on to embroider that:

"Remember that when Constable Chatterley went there, having found the perishable goods but not the cigarettes, he went and spoke to the defendant whose reply merely was, "Get lost!" The defendant was thereupon arrested. Well, instead of saying "Get lost!," it would have been open to the defendant, assuming that he knew all about it, to have said to the constable, "You will find that the rest of the goods, which are cigarettes, are hidden behind the drawer in that wardrobe there."

Later he said much the same:

"The matters to which you ought to apply your minds are the hiding of the cigarettes behind the drawer of the wardrobe and assisting in their retention, if you think he did, by not telling Detective Constable Chatterley that the cigarettes were there."

Finally, just before the jury retired he said:

"Well, members of the jury, it may well be that if Brown had kept his mouth completely shut it might on that be possible to say he was not guilty, but he did not keep his mouth completely shut, he told the police constable to get lost, and it is for you, members of the jury, to consider whether in saying 'Get lost' instead of helping the police constable he was dishonestly assisting in the retention of stolen goods."

It is urged here that the mere failure to reveal the presence of the cigarettes, with or without the addition of the spoken words "Get lost," was incapable in itself of amounting to an assisting in the retention of the goods within the meaning of section 22(1). The court has come to the conclusion that that is right. It does not seem to this court that the mere failure to tell the police, coupled if you like with the words "Get lost," amounts in itself to an assisting in their retention. On the other hand, those matters did afford strong evidence of what was the real basis of the charge here, namely that, knowing that they had been stolen, he permitted them to remain there or, as it has been put, provided accommodation for these stolen goods in order to assist Holden to retain them. To that extent, it seems to this court, that the direction was incomplete. The chairman should have gone on to say:

"But the fact that he did not tell the constable that they were there and said 'Get lost' is evidence from which you can infer if you think right that this man was permitting the goods to remain in his flat, and to that extent assisting in their retention by Holden."

It may be thought to be a matter of words, but in the opinion of the court some further direction was needed. On the other hand it is a plain case in which the proviso should be applied. It seems to the court that the only possible inference in these circumstances, once Holden was believed, is that the defendant was assisting in their retention by housing the goods and providing accommodation for them, by permitting them to remain there. In those circumstances the court is satisfied that the appeal fails and should be dismissed.'

R v Grainge (1973) 59 Cr App R 3 Court of Appeal (Criminal Division) (Scarman LJ, Chapman and Eveleigh JJ)

Handling stolen goods - mens rea

Facts

As stated by Eveleigh J:

'On March 7, 1973, the appellant, his co-defendant a man named O'Connor, and a third man entered a shop in Sheffield which sold office machinery and stationery. During the course of the visit O'Connor stole a pocket calculating machine valued at £59. The loss of the machine was soon noticed and the salesman went out of the shop into the street to search for the three men. Having seen them, he noticed that one of the men passed the calculator to the appellant. Eventually the salesman reported the matter to a police officer, who then cautioned and arrested all three men and told them that he was taking them to the offices of the Criminal Investigation Department. On the way the officer noticed the appellant pass the calculator across towards the direction of O'Connor's pocket. In evidence the appellant said, "I never gave it a second thought. He is a friend of mine. I have known him two or three years. He has never been dishonest. I never even asked him about it. I just put it in my pocket. I thought it was a radio." '

The defendant was convicted of handling stolen goods, and appealed on the ground that the trial judge had misdirected the jury as to the mens rea required.

Held

The appeal would be allowed.

Eveleigh J:

'The appeal against conviction is based upon grounds which may be summarised as follows: (A) The learned Recorder misdirected the jury to the effect that suspicion that the goods were stolen was an alternative to knowledge or belief as an essential mental element, and failed to direct them that the test thereof was subjective and not objective. (B) The learned Recorder failed to direct the jury that knowledge or belief must be proved at the time when the goods were received.

The Recorder said, "... you have got to decide whether there was any element of dishonesty about it and that ... he handled it dishonestly, that at the time he knew or believed or suspected that the article had been stolen. That is what is referred to as guilty knowledge." He then referred to the circumstances from which knowledge could be inferred and continued, "... so those are the three elements, the theft, the dishonest handling and the guilty knowledge, the knowledge or belief or suspicion that the property was stolen when it was handled."

In our judgment, this passage in its reference to suspicion was a misdirection. Before the Theft Act 1968 it was necessary for the prosecution to prove that the accused knew that the goods were "stolen or obtained in any way whatever under circumstances which amount to felony or misdemeanour" (Larceny Act 1916, s33(1)). It is understandable that members of the jury might have different views as to the degree of certainty in the mind of an accused necessary to constitute knowledge. Furthermore, they might well have had difficulty in evaluating the evidence upon which proof of knowledge rested, and have asked, "How can I know what was in the accused's mind?"

These two considerations naturally led to directions being given with a view to indicating that absolute certainty was not necessary (*White* (1859) 1 F & F 665), and to indicating the appropriate facts in a given case which might lead to an inference of knowledge. Negligence or even recklessness did not amount to knowledge: see *Havard* (1914) 11 Cr App R 2. Knowledge might be inferred from evidence that the accused wilfully shut his eyes to facts from which ordinary men would realise that the goods were stolen, but the inference is a process of reasoning based on the circumstances of the case and not a presumption of law.

Section 22 of the Theft Act 1968 has clarified the law. It provides, inter alia, that if "knowing or believing" goods to be stolen a person dishonestly receives them he is guilty of the offence of handling stolen goods. The section does not say that suspicion is enough. *Atwal* v *Massey* (1971) 56 Cr App R 6 illustrates the scope of the section. At p7 Lord Widgery CJ said in relation to the facts of the Case Stated, "Of course the whole case reeked with suspicion ... but it was for the justices to decide as a matter of fact whether the appellant at the time when he received the kettle knew that it was stolen or believed it to be stolen and took it dishonestly under the terms of the section."

At the close of the summing-up counsel for the prosecution drew the Recorder's attention to the direction he had given the jury as to the relevance of suspicion. The Recorder then sought to put the matter right in the following way: "What counsel wishes me to clarify to you, if I misled you, was, if a man suspects that property is stolen, he then cannot shut his eyes to the suspicion but must be put on inquiry as to whether or not it was stolen. It is not enough to have suspicion. He cannot say 'I am going to forget about it.' He has got to do something about it. In other words, when he suspects property is stolen he is on inquiry, he must be on his guard. He cannot shut his eyes to the fact that it may be stolen."

The Recorder had previously dealt with the question of guilty knowledge when he dealt with the elements of the offence using the words set out at the beginning of this judgment. He said, "you can infer guilty knowledge from the surrounding circumstances of the transaction, or if a man shuts his eyes and does not make an inquiry. A person is not entitled to shut his eyes if circumstances look suspicious and from suspicion such as that you can infer guilty knowledge."

The various expressions used by the Recorder went some way to eradicating the error introduced when he had spoken of suspicion as an actual ingredient in the offence. In all the circumstances, however, this Court does not think that he completely succeeded. The summing-up as a whole could well have left the jury with the impression that suspicious circumstances, irrespective of whether the accused himself appreciated they were suspicious, imposed a duty as a matter of law to act and inquire and that a failure so to do was to be treated as knowledge or belief.

In *Atwal* v *Massey* (supra) the justices had asked "whether the fact that the appellant ought to have known that the kettle was stolen is sufficient to render him guilty of an offence under section 22 of the Theft Act 1968." The Lord Chief Justice said at p7, "If when the justices say that the appellant ought to have known that the kettle was stolen they mean that any reasonable man would have realised that it was stolen, then that is not the right test. It is not sufficient to establish an offence under section 22 that the goods were received in circumstances which would have put a reasonable man on his inquiry. The question is a subjective one: was the appellant aware of the theft or did he believe the goods to be stolen or did he, suspecting the goods to be stolen, deliberately shut his eyes to the consequences? It may be that the justices meant the word 'ought' to have the second meaning, namely that he suspected but closed his eyes, but we do not think that we ought to speculate on such a possibility, but rather that we ought to deal with this matter on the words used by the justices in the case." The Lord Chief Justice was not seeking to introduce another definition of the offence, but was examining the possible approaches made by the justices to the question which they had to decide and he was emphasising at the same time that the mental element was subjective.

No doubt the learned Recorder was seeking to explain the position to the jury along the lines indicated by the Lord Chief Justice. It is, however, impossible to be satisfied that the jury did interpret the words in a manner consistent with the definition of the offence laid down by section 22 of the Act.

In an appellate Court's judgment there are frequently found possible alternative expressions which accurately embrace the definition of a criminal offence. The danger of treating them as alternative definitions lies in the fact that they are often formulated to deal with the particular facts before the Court and to meet the arguments in the case. There is the further risk that repetition will not be precise - as happened in this case. Where the words of a statute are in simple language in common use it is better to adhere to those words when actually defining the case to the jury: see *Feely* (1973) 57 Cr App R 312; [1973] 2 WLR 201.

As to the second ground of appeal the Recorder used the word "handled" and not the word "received" when he said it was "at that time," ie when it was handled, that knowledge had to be proved. Counsel for the defence submitted that the jury were not clearly directed that upon an indictment, as in this case, which charged a receiving, guilty knowledge had to be shown to exist at the time of the receipt. We think there is substance in the point.

In the judgment of this Court the Recorder ought to have made plain that it was at that moment of receipt and not at any time during the handling thereafter that guilty knowledge had to be proved.

For those reasons the appeal is allowed.'

R v Griffiths (1974) 60 Cr App R 16   Court of Appeal (Criminal Division)   (James and Ormrod LJJ and Waller J)

Handling stolen goods - mens rea

Facts

As stated by James LJ:

'On October 3, 1973, at the Crown Court at Gloucester, Leslie George Griffiths, the appellant, was convicted of an offence of handling a pair of stolen candlesticks. On a second indictment he was convicted of an offence of burglary committed on April 28, 1973. He was sentenced to consecutive terms of two years' imprisonment. He appeals against the conviction of handling by way of certificate granted by the Recorder under section 1(1) of the Criminal Appeal Act 1968. He also applies for leave to appeal against the sentences.

The candlesticks were stolen from a church in Cheltenham on May 31, 1973. The appellant, who lived in Cheltenham, was arrested on June 4 in Cirencester. He had tried to sell the candlesticks that afternoon to two dealers to whom he admittedly told lies as to how he came into possession of the candlesticks. He first told the police that he had bought them that afternoon from a dealer. He later said he had purchased them from a man he could not describe in the High Street in Cheltenham that morning. When asked if he had asked the man where they came from, he replied, "You don't ask questions like that, do you?" When it was suggested that he must have realised they were stolen he replied, "Yes, I suppose so." In a written statement he repeated the story of buying the candlesticks from the man in the High Street and said, "I did not ask him where he got them, you don't do things like that, do you?" The defence was the same as the account in his written statement. He denied making answer to the police in terms that he knew the candlesticks were stolen. He said in evidence that he might have had suspicions, but the suspicions were not related to any criminal offence.'

Held

The appeal would be dismissed.

James LJ:

[After stating the facts, the learned Lord Justice continued:]

'There was no evidence tending to show that the appellant was the thief. It was not suggested to or by any witness, including the appellant, that the appellant was the thief or that the candlesticks were in his possession, to use the words of section 22(1) of the Theft Act, "in the course of the stealing." But at the close of the evidence, in the absence of the jury, Mr Keane - who appeared for the appellant at the trial and who has conducted the appeal in this Court - submitted to the Recorder that the burden lay on the Crown to prove the positive factor that the candlesticks were in the appellant's possession otherwise than in the course of the stealing, and that on the evidence the Crown had not established that the appellant was not the thief. Mr Keane indicated that he proposed to address the jury on those lines and the Recorder, in rejecting the submission, said he proposed to direct the jury that there was no evidence that the appellant was the thief.

Mr Keane also raised at this stage of the trial a question as to what the Crown must establish to prove an offence under section 22(1) of the Theft Act 1968 in relation to "knowing or believing" the goods to be stolen goods. He invited the Recorder's attention to *Atwal* v *Massey* (1972) 56 Cr App R 6. It is significant to observe that the Recorder in discussion with counsel expressed the view that "The jury have to get inside the mind and they can decide, taking into account the circumstances, whether the man did know or believe."

In this appeal Mr Keane takes the same two points, the first alone being the subject of the Recorder's certificate. Upon the first point the argument is that, in the state of the evidence, the Recorder should have directed the jury that they should first decide whether they believed or rejected the appellant's version as to the receipt of the goods, and, if they rejected his version as to receipt, they should convict only if they were sure that the Crown had established that his receipt was otherwise than in the course of the stealing. Mr Keane relied on *Stapylton* v *O'Callaghan* [1973] 2 All ER 782. In that case the magistrate dismissed both informations, one alleging dishonestly receiving a stolen driving licence and the other alleging theft of the same licence, because he found the evidence inconclusive as to how the defendant came into possession of the licence and the prosecution had failed to satisfy him which offence had been committed. The facts found by the magistrate were that the defendant dishonestly possessed himself of the licence, which was a stolen licence, and intended to keep that licence. On the appeal by case stated to the Divisional Court, Lord Widgery CJ pointed out, at p784, that on those findings the defendant was one who had appropriated property belonging to another within the definition of "appropriated" in section 3(1) of the Theft Act 1968 and therefore the offence of theft was committed. The judgment continued: "Of course, if one looks on to section 22, which is the section charging handling, one finds that activities such as described here if committed otherwise than in the course of stealing may be caught by section 22, and understandably attract a more severe penalty, but if the facts justify the conclusion that the offence of stealing was committed, the right course in my judgment is to convict of stealing and not to go on to consider the possible additional hazard of convicting the accused of handling with the added penalty which might arise." Mr Keane also referred to *Seymour* (1954) 1 WLR 678 but we derive no assistance in the present matter from that authority which is concerned with the circumstances in which an indictment should contain counts for theft and receiving (under the old law) and the procedure appropriate to the return of the jury's verdict where that is done.

The Recorder directed the jury in terms which made no reference to "otherwise than in the course of the stealing" in relation to the ingredients of the offence charged. He did not give the direction which Mr Keane has argued should have been given. In the judgment of this Court the Recorder was absolutely right to deal with this aspect of the case as he did. There was no issue as to whether the receipt of the candlesticks was otherwise than in the course of the stealing. In a case in which there is, on the evidence, an issue as to whether the receipt of stolen goods was in the course of the stealing or otherwise a direction would be necessary. To give such a direction in this case, in which there was no issue to which counsel's submission could relate, would have been both confusing and wrong.

The second point taken has caused us more difficulty. Mr Keane argues that the Recorder misdirected the jury in that he told them that they could convict if they were satisfied that the appellant was in one of three states of mind as to the stolen nature of the candlesticks, (i) that he knew, (ii) that he believed, or (iii) that he suspected and deliberately chose not to ask any questions as to the circumstances. The passage in the summing-up upon which Mr Keane particularly relies is, "there is a third possibility which you may think is a matter of common sense although it is a matter of good law, and that is this, that a man suspects that goods are stolen and then deliberately shuts his eyes to the circumstances and doesn't want to know. You may have in those circumstances a man with real suspicion - not grounds for suspicion, but really suspecting - who really closes his eyes to the circumstances - a man in law in those circumstances knows or believes the goods were stolen."

Taken in isolation, those words are capable of being construed as directing the jury that *as a matter of law* they must find that the appellant knew or believed the goods to be stolen if they found that he suspected they were stolen and he deliberately shut his eyes to the circumstances. Such a direction would be wrong in that it removes from the jury's consideration the essential ingredient which it is for the jury to decide. Whether the jury seized upon this particular part of the summing-up and construed it in that way is a matter for speculation. But if it is open to that construction and there is a possibility that the jury approached their task on the basis of a misdirection, then we should have to consider the application of the proviso to Section 2(1) of the Criminal Appeal Act 1968. The passage cited is not to be read in isolation. It follows the direction which commences earlier: "At the time when he acquired possession of the candlesticks, what was his state of mind? Now, you have got here a difficult task, and every jury has to do it. You have got to enter into the mind of this particular man. It is no use saying, 'Well, we think a reasonable man would be suspicious in these circumstances.' That is something which arises in the civil court, it does not arise in the criminal court at all. You convict a man on what he thought, and not on what somebody else thought. It is because you cannot naturally open his skull and look inside and see what he is thinking, and you have got to do the best you can, in accordance with your oath, on the evidence you have got. What you have got to say is, 'In the circumstances of what we are given on the evidence, are we sure, are we satisfied that Mr Griffiths dishonestly received these goods? Has he dishonestly received them knowing or believing the same to have been stolen?' Now what is meant by knowing or believing is not all that difficult, and would you please be very careful about this. You can, in law, know or believe something to have been stolen in three different ways. The first is that you know about the theft - either because you saw the theft or you know about the theft, or the thief told you and you believed it. The second is that without actually knowing anything about the theft instinctively you can believe that they were stolen, and there may be plenty of circumstances in which way that things come (into) your possession you know and could not help but believe that they were stolen. Although it is not the charge as laid ..." then follow the words already cited and the Recorder continues: "That is the way you have got to approach Mr Griffiths in this case. Did he know? Perhaps there is no evidence at all that he knew the goods were actually stolen, but did he believe? You will have to consider the circumstances of how he said the goods came into his possession, and if he knew they were stolen. Did he know they were stolen? Did he know they were stolen or did he have the real suspicion that they were stolen and shut his eyes to the circumstances of the case, and that they were stolen, and the way the things came into his possession?"

Then later there is another passage, "It is a matter for you whether you think it is an indication that he either knew the goods were stolen or believed they were stolen, or was closing his eyes to circumstances where he was really suspicious about it. It is a matter for you entirely to judge ..." And later: "It is a matter for you, but he said that 'If I said that I bought them off a chap in the High Street, then that is so suspicious that I wouldn't expect them to pay over money,' if that is what Mr Griffiths suspected that the shopkeepers might think, does it now follow that he himself has also thought that buying off someone in the High Street was a bit suspicious? It is a matter for you."

Finally the Recorder said: "... what do you believe about what Mr Griffiths thought about where these candlesticks came from really? Do you suppose that Mr Griffiths thought about it? If you decided that he did not think about it at all, then you decide things in his favour. But if you do decide that he did think about it on this basis, that it was a stranger coming up to him in the market place and offering him goods at half price, members of the jury, it is a matter for you whether you decide that Mr Griffiths came at that moment into the category of someone who did have real suspicion that the goods were stolen and deliberately shut his eyes to the circumstances. It is a matter for you to decide what you think."

It appears to this Court that the Recorder in giving his directions on this aspect of the case was seeking to follow what was said by Lord Widgery, the Lord Chief Justice, in *Atwal* v *Massey* (supra). In that case the justices convicted the appellant of an offence of handling a stolen kettle. The facts found by the justices were that the appellant received the stolen kettle and obtained possession of it after it had been stolen by one Mott, who had left it by a gate to be collected by the appellant. The appellant paid Mott for it. The justices found that the appellant, from the circumstances in which he had collected the kettle, ought to have known that it was stolen. The question for the Divisional Court was whether the fact that the appellant ought to have known it was stolen was sufficient to render him guilty of an offence under section 22. In his judgment, with which O'Connor and Lawson JJ agreed, the Lord Chief Justice said at (p7): "It was for the justices to decide as a matter of fact whether the appellant at the time he received the kettle knew it was stolen or believed it to have been stolen and took it dishonestly under the terms of the section," and having pointed out that the test was not whether the circumstances in which the goods received would have put a reasonable man on inquiry, he continued: "The question is a subjective one, was the appellant aware of the theft or did he believe the goods to be stolen or did he, suspecting the goods to be stolen, deliberately shut his eyes to the consequences?" The conviction was quashed on the basis that, on the words of the justices in the case "ought to have known", the justices applied the wrong test.

Mr Keane argues that the words in the judgment "or did he suspecting that the goods were stolen deliberately shut his eyes to the consequences," if they are to be taken as adding a third state of mind to those of knowing or believing, are an extension of the definition of the offences contained in the statute. In *Grainge* (1973) 59 Cr App R 3; [1974] 1 WLR 619, the appellant was convicted of handling a stolen calculating machine after a direction of the Recorder that the requirement of guilty knowledge in the offence was satisfied by proof of "knowledge or belief or suspicion that the property was stolen when it was handled." On appeal this was held to be a misdirection which was not wholly corrected in other passages of the summing-up. The relevance of the judgment to the present matter is that Eveleigh J, giving the judgment of the Court, said at pp5 and 623 of the respective reports, after citing the judgment in *Atwal* v *Massey* (supra): "Lord Widgery CJ was not seeking to introduce another definition of the offence but was examining the possible approaches made by the justices to the question they had to decide and he was emphasising at the same time that the mental element was subjective." We understand the judgment in *Atwal* v *Massey* (supra) in the same way. It is inconceivable that the Lord Chief Justice would have sought to introduce an additional alternative mental element into the statutory definition which is restricted to "knowing or believing." *Atwal* v *Massey* (supra) is to be read as the judgment of the Divisional Court dealing with the approach which justices, as judges of fact, may adopt in order to arrive at their decision as to the knowledge or belief of the defendant.

There is a danger in the adoption of the passage cited from the judgment in *Atwal* v *Massey* (supra) as the direction to a jury unless great care is taken to avoid confusion between the mental element of knowledge or belief and the approach by which the jury may arrive at a conclusion as to knowledge or belief. To direct the jury that the offence is committed if the defendant, suspecting that the goods were stolen, deliberately shut his eyes to the circumstances as an alternative to knowing or believing the goods were stolen is a misdirection. To direct the jury that, in common sense and in law, they may find that the defendant knew or believed the goods to be stolen, because he deliberately closed his eyes to the circumstances, is a perfectly proper direction.

Taking this summing up as a whole, we are satisfied that the jury were left in the understanding that it was their province to decide the state of mind of the appellant at the time when he received the candlesticks and that that issue was not removed from their consideration. Further, although the direction at page 10 could have been better expressed than in the words "a man in law in those circumstances knows or believes," we are satisfied that the direction read in its entirety is that the jury had to be satisfied of either knowledge or belief and that one approach to that issue on the facts was to decide whether the appellant suspected the candlesticks were stolen and adopted an attitude of wilful blindness to the circumstances of receipt. We, therefore, conclude, after some doubt, that there was no misdirection and that the appeal fails on this point as it does upon the first point raised. We would add that had we decided that there was in this respect a misdirection, we would have had no hesitation in applying the proviso. The evidence was overwhelming and no reasonable jury on this evidence could have arrived at a conclusion other than that the appellant believed the goods were stolen.'

R v Kanwar [1982] 1 WLR 845 Court of Appeal (Criminal Division) (Dunn LJ, Cantley and Sheldon JJ)

Assisting in the retention of stolen property

Facts

As stated by Cantley J:

'In counts 7 and 9 of an indictment on which she was tried with others, the appellant was charged with dishonestly assisting in the retention of stolen goods for the benefit of Maninder Singh Kanwar, who was her husband. She was convicted and by way of sentence was given a conditional discharge. She now appeals against her conviction.

Her husband had brought the stolen goods to their house where the goods were used in the home. It was conceded that the appellant was not present when the goods were brought to the house. She was in hospital at the time. On November 2, 1978, police officers, armed with a search warrant, came to the house to look for and take away any goods which they found there which corresponded with a list of stolen goods in their possession. The appellant arrived during the search and was told of the object of the search. She replied: "There's no stolen property here."

She was subsequently asked a number of questions with regard to specific articles which were in the house and in reply to those questions, she gave answers which were lies. It is sufficient for present purposes to take two examples. She was asked about a painting which was in the living room and she replied: "I bought it from a shop. I have a receipt." The officer said: "That's not true." She said: "Yes, I have." He said: "If you can find a receipt, please have a look." She made some pretence of looking for the receipt but none was produced and ultimately she at least tacitly admitted there was none. The painting is one of the articles in the particulars to count 9.

She was also asked about a mirror which was in the kitchen. This is one of the articles in the particulars to count 7. The officer said: "What about the mirror?" She said: "I bought it from the market." The officer asked: "When?" She said: "Sometime last year." There is no dispute that that answer was a lie as was the answer about the painting. Later on, she was warned that she was telling lies and that the property was stolen. She said: "No, it isn't. We're trying to build up a nice home." Ultimately, although the officer had had no intention of arresting her when he came to the house, he did arrest her and she was subsequently charged.

The appellant did not give evidence and the evidence of the police officer stood uncontradicted.'

The defendant was convicted on two counts of handling stolen goods contrary to s22(1) Theft Act 1968, by assisting in their retention, and appealed.

Held

The appeal would be dismissed.

Cantley J:

'In *R v Thornhill* (unreported), May 15, 1981, and *R v Sanders*, The Times, March 1, 1982, decided in this court on February 25, 1982, it was held that merely using stolen goods in the possession of another does not constitute the offence of assisting in their retention. To constitute the offence, something must be done by the offender, and done intentionally and dishonestly, for the purpose of enabling the goods to be retained. Examples of such conduct are concealing or helping to conceal the goods, or doing something to make them more difficult to find or to identify. Such conduct must be done knowing or believing the goods to be stolen and done dishonestly and for the benefit of another.

We see no reason why the requisite assistance should be restricted to physical acts. Verbal representations, whether oral or in writing, for the purpose of concealing the identity of stolen goods may, if made dishonestly and for the benefit of another, amount to handling stolen goods by assisting in their retention within the meaning of section 22(1) of the Theft Act 1968.

The requisite assistance need not be successful in its object. It would be absurd if a person dishonestly concealing stolen goods for the benefit of a receiver could establish a defence by showing that he was caught in the act. In the present case, if, while the police were in one part of the house, the appellant, in order to conceal the painting had put it under a mattress in the bedroom, it would not alter the nature of her conduct that the police subsequently looked under the mattress and found the picture because they expected to find it there or that they caught her in the act of putting it there.

The appellant told these lies to the police to persuade them that the picture and the mirror were not the stolen property which they had come to take away but were her lawful property which she had bought. If that was true, the articles should be left in the house. She was, of course, telling these lies to protect her husband, who had dishonestly brought the articles there but, in our view, she was nonetheless, at the time, dishonestly assisting in the retention of the stolen articles.

In his summing up, the judge directed the jury:

"It would be quite wrong for you to convict this lady if all she did was to watch her husband bring goods into the house, even if she knew or believed that they were stolen because, no doubt, you would say to yourselves: What would she be expected to do about it? Well, what the Crown say is that she knew or believed them to be stolen and that she was a knowing and willing party to their being kept in the house in those circumstances. The reason the Crown say that - and we shall be coming to the evidence - is that when questioned about a certain number of items, Mrs Kanwar gave answers which the Crown say were not true and that she could not possibly have believed to be true and that she knew perfectly well were untruthful. So, say the prosecution, she was not just an acquiescent wife who could not do much about it, she was, by her conduct in trying to put the police officers as best she could off the scent, demonstrating that she was a willing and knowing party to those things being there and that she was trying to account for them. Well, it will be for you to say, but you must be satisfied, before you can convict her on either of these counts, not only that she knew or believed the goods to be stolen, but that she actively assisted her husband in keeping them there; not by just passive acquiescence in the sense of saying: 'What can I do about it?,' but in the sense of saying: 'How nice to have these things in our home, although they are stolen goods.' "

In so far as this direction suggests that the appellant would be guilty of the offence if she was merely willing for the goods to be kept and used in the house and was thinking that it was nice to have them there, although they were stolen goods, it is a misdirection. We have considered whether on that account the conviction ought to be quashed. However, the offence was established by the uncontradicted evidence of the police officer which, looked at in full, clearly shows that in order to mislead the officer who had come to take away stolen goods, she misrepresented the identity of the goods which she knew or believed to be stolen. We are satisfied that no miscarriage of justice has occurred and the appeal is accordingly dismissed.'

R v Pitchley (1973) 57 Cr App R 30 Court of Appeal (Criminal Division) (Cairns LJ, Nield and Croom-Johnson JJ)

Assisting in the retention of stolen property

Facts

The defendant was asked by his son to look after £150, which he did by placing the money in his own Post Office savings account. The defendant subsequently discovered that his son had stolen the money, but allowed the money to remain in his account until questioned by the police. The defendant was convicted of assisting in the retention of stolen property contrary to s22(1) of the Theft Act 1968, and appealed.

Held

The appeal would be dismissed.

Cairns LJ:

'The main point that has been taken by Mr Kalisher, who is appearing for the appellant in this Court, is that, assuming that the jury were not satisfied that the appellant received the money knowing it to have been stolen, and that is an assumption which clearly it is right to make, then there was no evidence after that, that from the time when the money was put into the savings bank, that the appellant had done any act in relation to it. His evidence was, and there is no reason to suppose that the jury did not believe it, that at the time when he put the money into the savings bank he still did not know or believe that the money had been stolen - it was only at a later stage that he did. That was on the Saturday according to his evidence, and the position was that the money had simply remained in the savings bank from the Saturday, to the Wednesday when the police approached the appellant. It is fair to say that from the moment when he was approached he displayed the utmost frankness to the extent of correcting them when they said it was £100 to £150 and telling them where the post office savings book was so that the money could be got out again and restored to its rightful owner.

But the question is: Did the conduct of the appellant between the Saturday and the Wednesday amount to an assisting in the retention of his money for the benefit of his son Brian? The Court has been referred to the case of *Brown* (1969) 53 Cr App R 527, [1970] 1 QB 105 [see above].

In this present case there was no question on the evidence of the appellant himself, that he was permitting the money to remain under his control in his savings bank book, and it is clear that this Court in the case of *Brown* (supra) regarded such permitting as sufficient to constitute retention within the meaning of retention. That is clear from the passage I have already read, emphasised in the next paragraph, the final paragraph of the judgment, where the Lord Chief Justice said (at p531): "It is a plain case in which the proviso should be applied. It seems to this Court that the only possible inference in these circumstances, once Holden was believed is that this man was assisting in their retention by housing the goods and providing accommodation for them, by permitting them to remain there." It is important to realise that that language was in relation to a situation where there was no evidence that anything active had been done by the appellant in relation to the goods.

In the course of the argument, Nield J cited the dictionary meaning of the word "retain" - keep possession of, not lose, continue to have. In the view of this Court, that is the meaning of the word "retain" in this section. It was submitted by Mr Kalisher that, at any rate, it was ultimately for the jury to decide whether there was retention or not and that even assuming that what the appellant did was of such a character that it could constitute retention, the jury ought to have been directed that it was for them to determine as a matter of fact, whether that was so or not. The Court cannot agree with that submission. The meaning of the word "retention" in this section is a matter of law in so far as the construction of the word is necessary. It is hardly a difficult question of construction because it is an ordinary English word and in the view of this Court, it was no more necessary for the Deputy Chairman to leave to the jury the question of whether or not what was done amounted to retention, than it would be necessary for a judge in a case where goods had been handed to a person who knew that they had been stolen for him to direct the jury it was for them to decide whether or not that constituted receiving.

We are satisfied that no complaint of the summing-up which was made can be sustained and that there is no other ground on which this verdict could be said to be unsafe or unsatisfactory. The appeal is therefore dismissed.'

R v Pitham and Hehl (1976) 65 Cr App R 45   Court of Appeal (Criminal Division)   (Lawton and Waller LJJ and Bristow J)

Handling otherwise than in the course of stealing

Facts

The defendants had met a man named Millman at the house of another man, named McGregor, who was in prison. Millman told the defendants that McGregor's furniture was for sale, and the defendants agreed to buy it from him. Millman was convicted of theft of McGregor's furniture, and the defendants were convicted of handling stolen goods by agreeing to buy it. The defendants appealed against their convictions on the ground that the handling alleged against them had not taken place 'otherwise than in the course of stealing'.

Held

The appeal would be dismissed.

Lawton LJ:

'The third way [in which the prosecution put its case] and the one the jury in the end accepted, was that Millman was the man who had stolen the property and these two had bought from the thief Millman, knowing it to have been stolen. This third way was reflected in counts 4 and 5. Now, stated in that way, the issues would appear to be easy for a jury to understand. Mr Murray, with much ingenuity and persistence, for which he is to be congratulated, has urged upon the Court that this simple case goes to the very heart of what seems to be an academic difference of opinion between the professor of law at Nottingham University, Professor Smith, and the professor of law at Leicester University, Professor Griew, as to the construction of a few words in section 22 of the Theft Act 1968.

Section 22(1) of the Theft Act provides: "A person handles stolen goods if (otherwise than in the course of the stealing)" - I emphasise the words "otherwise than in the course of the stealing" - "knowing or believing them to be stolen goods he dishonestly receives the goods, or dishonestly undertakes or assists in their retention, removal, disposal, or realisation by or for the benefit of another person, or if he arranges to do so." Now, the two conflicting academic views can be summarised in this way. Professor Smith's view in his book on *The Theft Act 1968* (2nd ed, 1974), para. 400, seems to be that "in the course of the stealing" can be a very short time or it can be a very long period of time. Professor Griew in his book *The Law of Theft* (3rd ed, 1977) paras. 8-18, 8-19, seems to be of the opinion that, "in the course of the stealing," embraces not only the act of stealing as defined by section 1 of the Theft Act 1968, but in addition making away with the goods. In the course of expounding their differing views in their books on the Theft Act the two professors have both referred to ancient authorities. Both are of the opinion that the object of the words, "otherwise than in the course of the stealing," was to deal with the situation where two men are engaged in different capacities in a joint enterprise. In those circumstances, unless some such limiting words as those to which I have referred were included in the definition of handling, a thief could be guilty of both stealing and receiving. An illustration of the sort of problem which arises is provided by Professor Smith's reference to the old case of *Coggins* (1873) 12 Cox CC 517. In his book on the Theft Act at paragraph 400, he summarises the facts of *Coggins* (supra) in these terms: "If a servant stole money from his master's till and handed it to an accomplice in his master's shop, the accomplice was guilty of larceny and not guilty of receiving." He added another example. It was the case of *Perkins* (1852) 5 Cox CC 554. He summarises that case as follows: "Similarly, if a man committed larceny in the room in which he lodged and threw a bundle of stolen goods to an accomplice in the street, the accomplice was guilty of larceny and not guilty of receiving."

In our judgment the words to which I have referred in section 22(1), were designed to make it clear that in those sorts of situations a man could not be guilty under the Theft Act of both theft and handling. As was pointed out to Mr Murray by my brother, Bristow J, in the course of argument, the Theft Act in section 1 defines theft. It has been said in this Court more than once that the object

461

of that definition was to make a fresh start so as to get rid of all the subtle distinctions which had arisen in the past under the old law of larceny. Subsection (1) of section 1 has a side heading, "Basic definition of theft." That definition is in these terms: "A person is guilty of theft if he dishonestly appropriates property belonging to another with the intention of permanently depriving the other of it; and 'thief' and 'steal' shall be construed accordingly." What Parliament meant by "appropriate" was defined in section 3(1): "Any assumption by a person of the rights of an owner amounts to an appropriation, and this includes, where he has come by the property (innocently or not) without stealing it, any later assumption of a right to it by keeping or dealing with it as owner."

Mr Murray's submission - a very bold one - was that the general words with which section 3(1) opens, namely, "Any assumption by a person of the rights of an owner amounts to an appropriation," are limited by the words beginning "and this includes." He submitted that those additional words bring back into the law of theft something akin to the concept of asportation, which was one of the aspects of the law of larceny which the Theft Act 1968 was intended to get rid of. According to Mr Murray, unless there is something which amounts to "coming by" the property there cannot be an appropriation. We disagree. The final words of section 3(1) are words of inclusion. The general words at the beginning of section 3(1) are wide enough to cover *any* assumption by a person of the rights of an owner.

What was the appropriation in this case? The jury found that the two appellants had handled the property *after* Millman had stolen it. That is clear from their acquittal of these two appellants on count 3 of the indictment which had charged them jointly with Millman. What had Millman done? He had assumed the rights of the owner. He had done that when he took the two appellants to 20 Parry Road, showed them the property and invited them to buy what they wanted. He was then acting as the owner. He was then, in the words of the statute, "assuming the rights of the owner." The moment he did that he appropriated McGregor's goods to himself. The appropriation was complete. After this appropriation had been completed there was no question of these two appellants taking part, in the words of section 22, in dealing with the goods "in the course of the stealing."

It follows that no problem arises in this case. It may well be that some of the situations which the two learned professors envisage and discuss in their books may have to be dealt with at some future date, but not in this case. The facts are too clear.

Mr Murray suggested the learned judge should have directed the jury in some detail about the possibility that the appropriation had not been an instantaneous appropriation, but had been one which had gone on for some time. He submitted that it might have gone on until such time as the furniture was loaded into the appellant's van. For reasons we have already given that was not a real possibility in this case. It is not part of a judge's duty to give the jury the kind of lecture on the law which may be appropriate for a professor to give a class of undergraduates. We commend the judge for not having involved himself in a detailed academic analysis of the law relating to this case when on the facts it was as clear as anything could be that either these appellants had helped Millman to steal the goods, or Millman had stolen them and got rid of them by sale to these two appellants. We can see nothing wrong in the learned judge's approach to this case and on that particular ground we affirm what he did and said.'

R v Sainthouse [1980] Crim LR 506 Court of Appeal (Criminal Division) (Lord Lane CJ, Phillips and Woolf JJ)

Handling - otherwise than in the course of stealing

Facts

'The appellant was present while another man stole from the boot of an unattended car a box full of tools, a can of petrol and a brief-case. The appellant, who was admittedly dishonest, sold the box and tools, forced open the brief-case and took some part in putting the petrol from the can into the vehicle used by him and the other man. Later on the same day the appellant put the brief-case inside a suitcase stolen by the other man, which the appellant knew was to be thrown away. The appellant was arraigned at the Crown Court on two counts of theft of the property, contrary to section 1(1) of the Theft Act 1968. He offered to plead guilty to handling but the prosecution would not accept the plea and he pleaded not guilty as charged. The recorder questioned the appellant when giving evidence in chief and then ruled that, on the appellant's own account in the witness box, he was guilty; the jury were directed to return verdicts of guilty, which they did. He appealed on the grounds, inter alia, that the recorder was wrong in ruling that the appellant could be said to have appropriated the property at a time when the property had already been appropriated by the other man and the legislature could not have intended to provide that a person might (subject to the exception in s22) be guilty of both stealing and handling goods by the same actions.

Held

Allowing the appeal, that the legislature's intention was to be sought from the words used in the statute. There was no need to go further than section 1(1) and section 3(1), from which it followed that, when the actions of the handler amounted to a dishonest assumption by him of the rights of an owner with the intent permanently to deprive, the handler would also be guilty of theft; eg *Stapylton* v *O'Callaghan* [1973] 2 All ER 782, DC. Nothing in section 22, apart from the words in parenthesis ("otherwise than in the course of the stealing") indicated that handling was to be treated as an offence separate and apart from theft. Difficult questions might arise as to what was or was not done "in the course of stealing" eg *Pitham and Hehl* (1976) 65 Cr App R 45, but they were irrelevant, for the use of "the" made clear that the reference was to the previous stealing, namely, the theft by the other man. The recorder was technically correct in deciding that the appellant's handling actions were capable of amounting to the dishonest appropriation necessary for establishing theft; it would have been better to have left the matter to the jury. However, he had taken too active a part in the prosecution of the case, the convictions were unsatisfactory and they had to be quashed.'

[*Reported by L. Norman Williams, Barrister.*]

23 FORGERY AND COUNTERFEITING ACT 1981

R v Campbell (Mary) (1985) 80 Cr App 47 Court of Appeal (Criminal Division) Ackner LJ, Bristow and Popplewell JJ

False endorsement of a cheque - whether any intention to prejudice

Facts

The defendant endorsed a cheque for her friend by forging the payee's signature on the reverse, and paying it into her own account. She then withdrew from her account an equivalent amount in cash, and gave this to the friend. The defendant was convicted under s1 of the 1981 Act, and appealed on the basis that she had not intended that another person (the paying bank) should be 'prejudiced' by her action, as that term was understood within s10 of the 1981 Act.

Held

The appeal would be dismissed.

Ackner LJ:

'The offence of forgery under section 1 of the Forgery and Counterfeiting Act 1981 arises "... if [a person] makes a false instrument, with the intention that he or another shall use it to induce somebody to accept it as genuine, and by reason of so accepting it to do or not to do some act to his own or any other person's prejudice." It is common ground that the intention which the statute requires contains two ingredients. One is the intention that the false instrument shall be used to induce somebody to accept it as genuine and the other is the intention to induce somebody by reason of so accepting it to do or not to do some act to his own or any other person's prejudice. It is common ground, as it has to be on these facts, that the appellant did make a false instrument because she endorsed the fictitious name on the back of the cheque thereby giving the impression that the cheque had been properly made out to G. N. Croydon, and that G. N. Croydon had endorsed the cheque over to her. It is conceded that she did that with the intention to induce somebody – that is the bank – to accept it as genuine. So the first of the ingredients of the intention was properly made out by the prosecution. In fact it was not in issue.

That which is in issue is whether the prosecution on the facts which we have recounted have established the second ingredient, namely that the intention was to induce somebody by reason of so accepting that false document to do some act to his own or any other person's prejudice. Again so far as the law is concerned it is common ground that section 10 of the Act exhaustively defines "induce" and "prejudice" for the purpose of this second ingredient. It is a lengthy section. We need only read that part of the section which relates to the facts of this case. Subsection (1): "Subject to subsections (2) and (4) below, for the purpose of this Part of this Act an act or omission intended to be induced is to a person's prejudice if, and only if, it is one which, if it occurs – ... (c) will be the result of his having accepted a false instrument as genuine ... in connection with his performance of any duty."

It is common ground that in the context of this case "his" means "the bank," so it will read: "will be the result of the bank having accepted a false instrument as genuine in connection with the bank's performance of any duty."

Mr Tabor [counsel for the defendant] seeks to rely before us, though he did not before the learned judge, on subsection (2). Again we read only those words that can relate to this case: "An act which a person has an enforceable duty to do ... shall be disregarded for the purpose of this Part of this Act." In our judgment, that subsection provides no assistance to the appellant for this simple reason, that it was the bank's duty to pay out only on a valid instrument and it is common ground in this case that that which was presented to the bank, and which was accepted by the bank, was a false instrument which it was not part of the bank's duty to honour. On the contrary, had the bank known of the true status of that document, they would have wholly rejected it. In these circumstances it seems plain to us that the offence was properly established. It would be remarkable if such a situation was not covered one way or another by this far-embracing, recent piece of legislation.

Accordingly the appeal against conviction is dismissed.'

R v Donnelly (1984) 79 Cr App R 76   Court of Appeal (Criminal Division)   (Lawton LJ, Kilner Brown and Beldam JJ)

Meaning of falsity within s9 of the 1981 Act

Facts

The defendant, a jeweller, drew up a valuation certificate in relation to some jewellery that did not in fact exist, in order to enable another man to make fraudulent claims against an insurance company in respect of the jewellery. The defendant was convicted under s1(1) of the 1981 Act, and appealed on the ground that his drawing up of the valuation certificate was not the making of a 'false' instrument for the purposes of the 1981 Act.

Held

The appeal would be dismissed.

Lawton LJ:

'The point of law is this: did what the appellant was proved to have done, namely making in writing what purported to be a jewellery valuation certificate, when there was no jewellery to be valued, with intent to induce somebody to accept it as genuine, amount in law to forgery contrary to section 1 of the 1981 Act?

[The learned Lord Justice stated the facts and continued:]

Mr Peddie, on behalf of the appellant, accepted that this valuation was an instrument within the meaning of sections 1 and 8 of the 1981 Act but submitted that it was not a false one, just a lying one, and that an instrument was not a forgery if it did no more than on its face tell a lie, not being a lie as to what it was.

Mr Bevan for the prosecution conceded that both at common law and under the Forgery Act 1913 this valuation would not have been a forgery. He submitted, however, that the 1981 Act made new law and specifically enacted in section 9 what made an instrument a false one. There can be no doubt that in 1981 Parliament intended to make new law. The long title of the Act starts with these words: "An Act to make fresh provision ... with respect to forgery and kindred offences." The trial judge was of the opinion that this valuation was a false instrument within the meaning of section 9(1)(*g*) which is in these terms: "An instrument is false for the purposes of this part of this Act – ... (*g*) if it purports to have been made or altered on a date on which, or at a place at which, or otherwise in circumstances in which, it was not in fact made or altered."

Following the wording of paragraph (*g*) the judge directed the jury as follows: "An instrument can be false if it purports to be made in circumstances in which it was not in fact made."

In our judgment the words coming at the end of paragraph (*g*) "otherwise in circumstances ..." expand its ambit beyond dates and places to *any* case in which an instrument purports to be made when it was not in fact made. This valuation purported to be made *after* the appellant had examined the items of jewellery set out in the schedule. He did not make it after examining these items because they did not exist. That which purported to be a valuation after examination of the items was nothing of the kind: it was a worthless piece of paper. In our judgment the trial judge's direction was correct. This purported valuation was a forgery. The appeal is dismissed.'

Commentary

The decision has been roundly condemned as an unacceptable extension of the law beyond the limits envisaged by the legislature. The valuation certificate contained lies, but it does not purport to have been made or altered by someone who did not in fact do so. If the expression '… other circumstances …' is held to cover the situation where a valuation certificate is drawn up without any jewellery actually having been valued, then it would equally cover the situation where D fills in an application form for a job, and claims to have qualifications which he does not have. The decision offends the common law principle as expounded in *R v Windsor* (below), that the instrument must tell a lie about itself in order to come within the scope of forgery. If this sub-section has the wide meaning that this decision suggests, then there was no need for Parliament to have gone to the length of setting out all the other grounds of falsity in s9 (M.T.M.).

(See *R v More*, below.)

R v Garcia [1988] Crim LR 115 Court of Appeal (Criminal Division) (Russell LJ, Leggatt and Alliot JJ)

Mens rea of forgery under the 1981 Act

Facts

'Trans World Airlines (TWA) were members of the International Air Traffic Association (IATA), which body controlled fares. Their authorised agents were issued with validation stamps for use on TWA tickets. Upon the sale of a ticket, an audit coupon should be despatched to TWA headquarters, together with the appropriate fares, less the agent's commission. The appellant was a travel agent in Saudi Arabia, but was not an authorised agent for TWA tickets. However, it was well known that international air tickets could be obtained through agents not authorised by IATA and, as a result, "bucket shops" existed in the United Kingdom. One such "shop" bought some tickets issued by the appellant's agency. The tickets had not been paid for and a large number of passengers had travelled on TWA aircraft, using tickets that were forged in the sense that they purported to be genuine tickets whereas in fact no payment had been made to TWA in respect of them, and no authority for their sale and distribution had been given by the airline. The appellant was convicted, with another, of conspiracy to use false instruments and appealed, inter alia, on the ground that the trial judge had erred in his direction of intention in section 3 of the 1981 Act. His counsel submitted that a double intention had to be present, ie the intention to induce somebody to accept the tickets and orders as genuine, and an intention that that "somebody" should act or omit to act to his own or someone else's prejudice.

Held

Allowing the appeal and quashing the conviction, sections 3 and 10 of the 1981 Act had to be read together. Thus, in order to prove prejudice in section 3, it was necessary to prove an intention to induce the recipient of the false instrument to act or to omit to act to his prejudice as provided by section 10. The only "person" whom the appellant could conceivably have intended to prejudice, as a matter of certainty as required by section 10, was the corporate body, TWA, which had not been paid for the tickets and had clearly been prejudiced. However, the question for the jury should have been whether the appellant was aware of such prejudice and whether he intended it. Prejudice to those who had used, or would use, the tickets, namely passengers, was less certain; a passenger would not inevitably suffer temporary or permanent loss of property. Potential prejudice was not enough: section 10 contained the words "will result" [in temporary or permanent loss].' (*R v Tobierre* [1986] 1 All ER 346 applied).

[*Reported by Veronica Cowan, Barrister.*]

R v Gold [1988] 2 WLR 985 House of Lords (Lords Keith, Brandon, Templeman, Oliver and Goff)

Computer 'hacking' - whether forgery

Facts

The defendants had used the customer identification numbers (CINs) of authorised 'Prestel' users to gain access to the system's database. The CINs input by the defendants were received by the user segment of the computer, which consisted of three 'segments', the 'Input Buffer', the 'Control Area', and the 'Output Buffer'. The CINs would be held briefly in the computer's 'Control Area' whilst verification took place. The defendants were charged with nine specimen counts of making false instruments (the computer's 'Control Area'), contrary to s1(1) of the Forgery and Counterfeiting Act 1981. They appealed successfully to the Court of Appeal, and the Crown now appealed to the House of Lords.

Held

The appeal would be dismissed.

Lord Brandon:

'On the defendants' appeal to the Court of Appeal (Criminal Division) it was contended for them, on various grounds, that what they had been proved to have done could not, as a matter of law, amount to the offence of forgery under the Act of 1981. The court, which had been referred during the course of the argument to the Law Commission. (Law Com No. 55) Criminal Law Report on Forgery and Counterfeit Currency of 1973, accepted most of the contentions put forward for the defendants. Lord Lane CJ, giving the judgment of the court, said [1987] QB 1116, 1124:

"In our judgment the user segment in the instant case does not carry the necessary two types of message to bring it within the ambit of forgery at all. Moreover, neither the report nor the Act, so it seems to us, seeks to deal with information that is held for a moment whilst automatic checking takes place and is then expunged. That process is not one to which the words 'recorded or stored' can properly be applied, suggesting as they do a degree of continuance.

There is a further difficulty. The prosecution had to prove that the appellants intended that someone should accept as genuine the false instrument which they had made. The suggestion here is that it was a machine (under section 10(3)) which the appellants intended to induce to respond to the false instrument. But the machine (ie, the user segment) which was intended, so it was said, to be induced seems to be the very thing which was said to be the false instrument (ie, the user segment) which was inducing the belief. If that is a correct analysis, the prosecution case is reduced to an absurdity.

We have accordingly come to the conclusion that the language of the Act was not intended to apply to the situation which was shown to exist in this case. The submissions at the close of the prosecution case should have succeeded. It is a conclusion which we reach without regret. The Procrustean attempt to force these facts into the language of an Act not designed to fit them produced grave difficulties for both judge and jury which we would not wish to see repeated. The appellants' conduct amounted in essence, as already stated, to dishonestly gaining access to the relevant Prestel data bank by a trick. That is not a criminal offence. If it is thought desirable to make it so, that is a matter for the legislature rather than the courts. We express no view on the matter. Our decision on this aspect of the case makes it unnecessary to determine the other issues raised by the appellants, in particular the submission that they should be found guilty of forgery when there was no evidence that either of them had any inkling that what they were doing might amount to a contravention of the Act."

The reference in the first paragraph of the passage set out above to the user segment not carrying the two types of message necessary to bring it within the ambit of forgery is a reference to paragraph 22 of the Law Commission Report. In that paragraph it was pointed out that, in the straightforward case of forgery, a document contains two messages of two distinct kinds, first, a message about the document itself (eg that it is a cheque), and secondly, a message to be found in the words of the document that is to be accepted and acted upon (eg that a banker is to pay £x); and that it is only documents which contain both types of message that require protection by the law of forgery.

My Lords, the points of law of general public importance certified by the Court of Appeal (Criminal Division) as being involved in its decision to allow the appeals were these:

"1. Whether on a true construction of sections 1, 8, 9 and 10 of the Forgery and Counterfeiting Act 1981, a false instrument is made in the following circumstances – (a) a person keys into part of a computer (the user segment) a customer identification number and password of another, without the authority of that other, (b) with the intention of causing the same computer to allow unauthorised access to its database, and (c) the user segment, upon receiving such information (in the form of electronic impulses), stores or records it for a very brief period whilst it checks it against similar information held in the user file of the database of the same computer.

2. Whether, in order to constitute a false instrument within the meaning of the said Act, an instrument must contain – (a) a message about the instrument itself, and (b) a message to be found in the words of the instrument that is to be accepted and acted upon.

3. Whether, in order for a person to be found guilty of forgery within the meaning of the said Act, he must be proved to have been aware of the relevant facts which constitute the making of the false instrument.

4. Whether the offence is made out if the 'somebody' whom the appellants allegedly intended should accept the false instrument as genuine (in this case – under section 10(3) – a machine) is the same machine as that which was said to be the false instrument, namely the user segment."

Point 1 comprises, potentially at least, two questions. The first question, which has to be answered in any case, is whether, in the circumstances specified in paragraphs (a) (b) and (c), an instrument as defined in section 8(1) of the Act is made at all. The second question, which only arises if an affirmative answer is given to the first, is whether the instrument so made is a false instrument as defined in section 9(1).

The case for the Crown on the first question was this. The relevant instrument was the control area of the user segment of the relevant Prestel computer whilst it had recorded and/or stored within it the electronic impulses purporting to be a CIN and a password. That control area of the user segment consisted of semi-conductor chips and/or magnetic cores, either or both of which are devices "on or in which information is recorded or stored by ... electronic means" within the meaning of section 8(1)(d) of the Act. Such an instrument was made by each respondent when he keyed into the control area of the user segment through a telephone line the electronic impulses which constituted the CIN and the password.

The case for the respondents on the first question was this. The recording and storage of information referred to in section 8(1) (d) are processes of a lasting and continuous nature. The process relied on by the Crown involved no more than the CIN and the password being held momentarily in the control area of the user segment while the checking of them was carried out, and then being totally and irretrievably expunged. The process did not, therefore, amount to the recording or storage of the CIN and the password within the meaning of the section 8(1)(d).

My Lords, section 8(1)(d) contemplates that information may be recorded or stored by electronic means on or in (i) a disc, (ii) a tape, (iii) a sound track (presumably of a film) and (iv) devices other than these three having a similar capacity. The words "recorded" and "stored" are words in common use which should be given their ordinary and natural meaning. In my opinion both words in their ordinary and natural meaning connote the preservation of the thing which is the subject matter of them for an appreciable time with the object of subsequent retrieval or recovery. Further, in relation to information recorded or stored on or in a disc, tape or sound track, that is the meaning of the two expressions which appears to me to be clearly intended. For both these reasons I have reached the conclusion that the respondents' case on the first question is right and that the Crown's case on it is wrong. Moreover I share the view of the Court of Appeal (Criminal Division) as expressed by Lord Lane CJ, that there is no reason to regret the failure of what he aptly described as the Procrustean attempt to force the facts of the present case into the language of an Act not designed to fit them.

On the footing that the respondents' act did not amount to the making of any instruments as defined in section 8(1) at all, point 1 of the certified points of law must be answered in the negative; and it is unnecessary to consider whether, if they had done so, the instruments so made would have been false instruments as defined in section 9(1).

Once point 1 of the certified points has been answered in the negative, points 2, 3 and 4 become academic. That being so, it is unnecessary to give answers to them either.

I would dismiss the appeal.'

Commentary

The decision seems to suggest that to make a plastic card which gives access to a cash machine would be within the scope of the Act, but simply to use someone else's number in conjunction with their card to obtain their money would not be. This latter situation is merely analogous to a safecracker discovering the combination of a safe (M.T.M)

R v More [1988] 1 WLR 1578 House of Lords (Lords Keith, Elwyn-Jones, Brandon, Templeman and Ackner)

Signing cheques in another's name – whether forgery

Facts

The defendant intercepted a cheque made out to Mark Richard Jessell for £5,303.23 and opened a building society savings account using that name (MRJ). A few days later he withdrew £5,000 from the account, signing the withdrawal form 'MRJ'. He was charged under s1 of the 1981 Act on the basis that he had made a false instrument, namely the withdrawal form. He appealed unsuccessfully against conviction to the Court of Appeal. On appeal to the House of Lords:

Held

The appeal would be allowed.

Lord Ackner:

[His Lordship referred to ss1 and 9(1) of the 1981 Act and continued]

'It is common ground that the consistent use of the word "purports" in each of the paragraphs *(a)* to *(h)* inclusive of section 9(1) of the Act imports a requirement that for an instrument to be false it must tell a lie about itself, in the sense that it purports to be made by a person who did not make it (or altered by a person who did not alter it) or otherwise purports to be made or altered in circumstances in which it was not made or altered.

The assistant recorder accepted the submission of counsel for the prosecution that the withdrawal form came within section 9(1)*(c)* because the appellant purported to be not only the MR Jessell who opened the account but also the MR Jessell in whose favour the stockbrokers' cheque was drawn, which cheque was used to fund the account and from which it was sought to withdraw a similar, slightly smaller sum. The withdrawal form was accordingly a forgery. It had been submitted by counsel for the prosecution at the trial that the withdrawal form was caught by section 9(1)*(a)* in that it purported to have been made in the form in which it was made by the "MR Jessell" the payee of the stockbroker's cheque, who did not, in fact, make it. The Court of Appeal (Criminal Division), in my judgment, rightly concluded, however, that the withdrawal form could not be brought within either *(a)* or *(c)*. Hodgson J, giving the judgment of the court said that the document "was undoubtedly made by the appellant and it was undoubtedly made in the form of a withdrawal form. It was undoubtedly signed by the person making it, and that signature was undoubtedly the signature of the holder of the account in the name 'Mark Richard Jessell.' "

The Court of Appeal might well have added that the document did not purport to have been made by the Mr Jessell in whose name a cheque had been drawn to open the account, since the withdrawal form made no mention on the face of it of that cheque.

The Court of Appeal, however, decided that the withdrawal form came within section 9(1)(h) since it purported to have been made by an existing person but he did not, in fact, exist. But the appellant was a real person. It was he who was the holder of the account and in that capacity had signed the withdrawal form. The withdrawal form clearly purported to be signed by the person who originally opened the account and in this respect it was wholly accurate. Thus, in my judgment, it cannot be validly contended that the document told a lie about itself ...'

Commentary

Although neither case was specifically cited in the course of Lord Ackner's speech, it would appear that both *R v Hassard and Devereux* (above), and *R v Donnelly* (above) are overruled by this decision (M.T.M).

R v Tobierre (1985) 82 Cr App R 212 Court of Appeal (Criminal Division) (O'Connor LJ, Tudor Evans and Eastham JJ)

Mens rea for forgery under the 1981 Act

Facts

The defendant signed his wife's family allowance book in her name, failing to reveal the fact that both she and their children were living in St Lucia. The defendant was convicted under s3 of the 1981 Act of using a false instrument, but appealed on the ground that the trial judge had failed to direct the jury on the need to prove an intention on the part of the defendant that 'another person' (in this case the Secretary of State) should be induced to act to his prejudice.

Held

The appeal would be allowed.

Tudor Evans J:

'The appellant accepted that he had signed the vouchers in his wife's name and that he had received the payments. His defence was that he genuinely believed that he was entitled to draw the money. He said in evidence that he understood that the purpose of the scheme for child allowance was to ensure that children were properly maintained and that, to this end, deductions were made from an employee's wages and put into a fund from which the benefit was drawn at a post office. Moreover, on occasions in the past when his wife and children were in this country but the wife, through illness, had been unable to collect the money, she had asked him to collect it and to sign her name. Finally, the appellant said that he had in fact sent the money or some of it to his wife for which there was supporting evidence.

The appellant maintained that he had not read the instructions in the book, although how he could have failed to have read the declaration we do not know since it was printed immediately above the place where he had signed his wife's name. In effect, the defence was that the appellant had no intention of inducing the Secretary of State to accept the vouchers as genuine and that he did not intend to induce him to act to his detriment by paying out the benefits because the appellant believed that he was fully entitled to the money he had drawn even though his wife and children were abroad. These were the only live issues at the trial, although it became clear on the evidence that the appellant intended the Secretary of State to accept the vouchers as genuine.

The question which we have to consider in the appeal is whether, upon a proper construction of section 3 of the Act of 1981, it is a defence available to a defendant that he did not intend the Secretary of State to act to his prejudice. If it is a defence, Mr Nash, counsel for the respondent, rightly accepts that the defence was not put, that the summing-up is in this respect defective and that the convictions cannot stand.

Before we refer to the language of section 3, we must consider the criticisms which Miss Maharaj, counsel for the appellant, makes of the summing-up. This was a short case. The evidence lasted a day. The recorder summed-up on the next morning and the jury retired at 11.38 am. At 12.55 pm they sent a note to the recorder in these words:

"Does intention mean in this case (a) to defraud, because of not knowing the rules in the yellow pages or (b) to defraud because of signing someone else's name or (c) both? ie is ignorance of the law (the yellow pages in this case) an excuse?"

The reference to the yellow pages was a reference to the instructions printed in the book and to which we have referred. The recorder asked counsel to agree an appropriate direction. There then followed a lengthy discussion and further directions were not given until 2.46 pm. A majority direction was given at 4 pm. The jury then retired but they then sent a further note in these terms:

"If, by writing another's name on, in this case, the voucher, does this fact make the voucher a false document, even though the defendant believes that he is not doing anything wrong, ie is there a necessity to find out if the defendant intended, by the act, to obtain payment falsely?"

The recorder directed the jury that in fact the vouchers were false instruments for the purpose of the trial. The jury retired again at 5.32 pm and returned with their verdict at 5.45 pm.

Miss Maharaj makes numerous criticisms of the summing-up. First, she points to evidence that the appellant was an alternative payee in that his name appeared on the outside of the book and it is said that this was evidence that the appellant believed that he was entitled to draw the benefits even though his family were abroad. The point was never put forward by the appellant as one of the factual bases for his belief and we do not see how the recorder can be criticised for not having dealt with the point as part of the defence. The question of the appellant being an alternative payee was raised by the Crown to show that if the appellant genuinely believed that he was entitled to draw the benefit, he would have signed his own name and not that of his wife.

Secondly, it is said that the recorder misdirected the jury and withdrew from them the issue whether the instrument was false. Miss Maharaj relies upon the evidence to which we have referred that the appellant believed that he had been authorised by his wife to sign the vouchers and to draw the benefits. Counsel relies upon section 9(1)(b) of the Act as showing that if a person in fact authorises the making of the relevant document, it cannot be a false instrument. She therefore submits that the recorder should have left this issue to the jury which he clearly did not. Section 9 of the Act provides:

"(1) An instrument is false for the prosecution of this Part of the Act ... (b) if it purports to have been made in the form in which it is made on the authority of a person who did not in fact authorise its making in that form."

In our opinion, the Act envisages that there may be cases in which formal authority is given by the holder of the book to another who is thereby authorised to collect the benefits. We have been shown the original vouchers on the reverse side of which there is provision for the holder of the book to indicate that he or she is unable to collect the benefit and authorising a named person to do so as agent. There is also provision for the agent to acknowledge and to sign for receipt of the benefit. This is fully keeping with the Act. There is not the slightest evidence to suggest that the appellant was properly authorised to sign the vouchers on his wife's behalf and to collect the benefit. It is clear on the evidence that the vouchers were false instruments and that the appellant knew that they were false. He knew perfectly well that the signatures on the vouchers were not his wife's and it was not disputed that he used the instruments within the meaning of section 3. It is also clear that the appellant intended the Secretary of State to accept the vouchers as genuine.

Miss Maharaj submitted that the recorder erred in directing the jury that the Crown must prove that the appellant had the intention to induce the Secretary of State to accept the vouchers as genuine at the time when he signed them instead of directing that such intention must be proved at the time when he cashed them. It is true that the recorder did not direct the jury only to consider the appellant's state of mind at the time of signing but counsel for the Crown corrected him and pointed out that the relevant time was when the vouchers were cashed. The recorder merely indicated that counsel was right. Miss Maharaj complains that the recorder should have given a specific direction and that it was not enough simply to indicate his consent to what counsel had said. We think there is nothing in this point. It is apparent from their notes and the length of their deliberations that the jury were fully attentive to the proceedings and we see no reason to conclude that they did not understand what counsel had said.

Finally, Miss Maharaj submits that the summing-up was defective in that there was an inadequate direction on the essential issue of the appellant's state of mind, that is whether he intended the Secretary of State to accept the vouchers as genuine and whether he intended the Secretary of State to act to his prejudice by paying out on the false instruments. When the recorder was summing-up, having correctly told the jury that the defence was that the appellant thought that he was entitled to draw the benefits, he continued at page 5 of the transcript:

"You have to consider, members of the jury, whether the prosecution have proved that part of the indictment, in particular, which, if you can follow in count 1, starts with the words: 'Had the intention of inducing the Secretary of State for Social Services to accept the false child allowance order as genuine and by reason of so accepting it to pay out the sum of £17.55'. That, you may think, is the aspect of the case that you will have to give your substantial and principal attention to, not forgetting that it is for you to decide that the other elements making up that offence under section 3 have to be proved by the prosecution."

This seems to us to be a clear direction that the Crown had to prove that the appellant had the intention to induce the Secretary of State to accept the vouchers as genuine. The recorder subsequently gave an adequate review of the evidence on that and other issues and we do not consider that the summing-up is open to the criticism which Miss Maharaj has advanced. There was, in our view, overwhelming evidence that the appellant intended the Secretary of State to accept the vouchers as genuinely containing the wife's signature.

As to the remainder of the summing-up, when the recorder directed the jury with respect to the first note, he correctly told them that the word "defraud" which was used in the note was not a word which appeared in the statute and that the yellow pages, that is the reference to the instructions, were relied upon by the Crown only as evidence of the appellant's knowledge that he was not entitled to the benefits. What the recorder did not do was to direct the jury that the Crown had to prove that the appellant intended the Secretary of State to act to his prejudice. The question is to whether the language of section 3 requires such a direction. Section 3 provides:

"It is an offence for a person to use an instrument which is, and which he knows or believes to be, false, with the intention of inducing somebody to accept it as genuine, and by reason of so accepting it to do or not to do some act to his own or any other person's prejudice."

There are two possible constructions of the section: first, that the only intention which has to be proved is an intention to induce someone to accept the instrument as genuine. On this construction, once such an intention is proved, it is simply an objective question whether that person, by accepting the instrument as genuine, in fact acted or omitted to act to his own or some other person's prejudice. The alternative construction requires proof of a double intention, the intention to induce and an intention that the other person shall act or omit to act to his own or someone else's prejudice. Sections 1, 2, 4 and 5 which are the other offence creating sections, do not assist upon the construction of section 3. Mutatis mutandis, the same language is used. But, in our view, sections

3 and 10 of the Act, when read together, make it clear that proof of a double intention is necessary. Section 10 provides:

"Subject to subsections (2) and (4) below, for the purposes of this Part of this Act, an act or omission intended to be induced is to a person's prejudice if, and only if, it is one which, if it occurs - *(a)* will result - (i) in his temporary or permanent loss of property ... "

There follows provision for a number of other species of results to which we need not refer.

We must read sections 3 and 10 together and, doing so, it is clear, in our view, that in order to prove prejudice in section 3, it is necessary to prove an intention to induce the recipient of the document to act or to omit to act to his prejudice as provided by section 10. Prejudice is the result of an act or omission intended to be induced. Putting the matter another way, if one looks to see what is meant by prejudice in section 3, one finds in section 10 that it involves an intention to induce the act or omission to act. This conclusion inevitably follows from the words in section 10, "... an act or omission intended to be induced ..." The act or omission in section 10 is a mirror of the words, "... to do or not to do some act ... " in section 3. The same construction must apply to the same language in sections 1, 2, 4 and 5, reading those sections together with section 10.

It follows from the construction we have placed on section 3 that the recorder did not direct the jury to consider whether the appellant intended to induce the Secretary of State to act to his prejudice and for this reason the convictions must be quashed.'

R v Utting [1987] 1 WLR 1375 Court of Appeal (Criminal Division) (Parker LJ, Bush and Kennedy JJ)

Mens rea for forgery under the 1981 Act

Facts

The defendant was a solicitor. A client of his, a man named Rudkin, was awarded £45,000 damages in a personal injury action. The defendant paid the money into his private account to clear his own overdraft. The defendant, when questioned by the police, produced a photocopy of a loan agreement which he claimed had been signed by Rudkin, under which Rudkin had agreed to loan the defendant the money. The original was never produced, and the copy was incomplete as Rudkin's signature had been missed from the bottom of the document. The defendant was convicted under s1 of the 1981 Act of making a false instrument (the photocopy) with the intention that he should use it to induce someone to accept it as genuine and, by reason of so accepting it, induce them not to do some act to the prejudice of himself. He appealed on the ground, inter alia, that the trial judge had misdirected the jury as to the meaning of the phrase 'to his own or another's prejudice' within s10 of the 1981 Act.

Held

The appeal would be allowed.

Parker LJ:

'We now turn to the first two grounds of appeal which are of more general importance. It is convenient to begin by returning to the particulars of the offence which were that exhibit 9 was made by the appellant

"with the intention that he, John Benjamin Utting, should use it to induce somebody to accept it as genuine and by reason of so accepting it not to do some act to the prejudice of himself, John Benjamin Utting."

Assuming that exhibit 9 was false and that the appellant had the intention that he should use exhibit 9 to induce the police to accept it as genuine, and by reason of so accepting it not to prosecute him, does that constitute an offence under section 1?

The prosecution say "Yes." To prosecute the appellant is to do an act to the appellant's prejudice.

The appellant is a person. Section 1 is therefore satisfied. The appellant's intention was within the words of the section "not to do some act to ... any other person's prejudice."

For the defence Mr Alun Jones submits that this is to misread the section which, if not by itself, certainly when read with other provisions, covers acts or omissions which prejudice either the victim of the deceit or anyone else other than the deceiver himself.

In our judgment this submission is well founded for a number of reasons. If the person making the false instrument (the forger) is included in "any other person" at the end of the section it would be an offence for the forger to make a false instrument with the intention of using it to induce someone to accept it as genuine and thereby do an act to the prejudice or harm of the forger himself. That anyone should so act seems unlikely. That, if he did, Parliament should have intended to make his conduct a crime we regard as absurd.

Next, on a fair reading of the words it is the doing or not doing of the act which must cause the prejudice. If it were otherwise there would be an offence if the victim were intended to refrain from doing an act prejudicial to himself or anyone else.

Thirdly, the structure of the section is such that the forger himself cannot have been intended to be included in the words "any other person" at the end. It plainly envisages the maker of the instrument ("A") having the intention that either he himself or another (who cannot of course be "A") shall use the instrument to induce somebody ("B") to accept it as genuine and, as a result, do or refrain from doing some act, the doing or omission to do which will harm himself or any other person. There can be no possible reason to suppose that the words "any other person," which naturally point to someone other than those already mentioned, should be read as if there were included in brackets immediately after them the words "including the maker of the instrument." We can see no basis on which such an intention can be imputed to Parliament. It would be, in effect, making it a crime to make a false instrument intending to procure harm to yourself by act or omission.

If there were any doubt about the meaning of the words "to do or not to do some act" it is set at rest by section 10(1) of the Act of 1981 which begins:

"Subject to subsections (2) and (4) below, for the purpose of this Part of this Act an act or omission intended to be induced is to a person's prejudice if, and only if, it is one which, if it occurs – ..."

Even supposing, however, that this is wrong, section 10 provides an exhaustive definition of what acts or omissions are to be regarded as being to a person's prejudice. The act or omission which it is said the appellant intended to be induced was the omission to prosecute or delay in prosecuting him. It would be remarkable it this was to be regarded as to his prejudice. It was suggested by the prosecution that it fell within section 10(1)*(a)(i)*, ie that non-prosecution or delay in prosecuting would, if it occurred, result in the appellant's "temporary or permanent loss of property." This suggestion is in our judgment quite untenable.

In the result the appeal succeeded on the first two grounds also. It was at a late stage in the argument suggested that the case might fall within section 10(1)*(c)* which provides that an act or omission is to a person's prejudice which if it occurs "will be the result of his having accepted a false instrument as genuine, or a copy of a false instrument as a copy of a genuine one, in connection with his performance of any duty."

It may well be that if the charge had been that the act or omission intended to be induced had been to the prejudice of the police, such a charge could have been made out, but that was not the charge made. It may also be that the appellant could have been successfully prosecuted under section 2 of the Act of 1981, but he was not.'

24 STRICT, VICARIOUS AND CORPORATE LIABILITY – BIGAMY – PERJURY

R v Bradish (1990) 90 Cr App R 271 Court of Appeal (Criminal Division) (Watkins LJ, Tudor Evans and Auld JJ)

Section 5(1) Firearms Act 1968 - whether an offence of strict liability

Facts [As stated by Auld J]

'On July 18, 1988, before Mr Assistant Recorder R J Pearse-Wheatley sitting in the Crown Court at Acton, the appellant pleaded guilty to burglary and not guilty to possessing a prohibited weapon contrary to section 5(1) of the Firearms Act 1968. Counsel for the defence and for the prosecution sought a ruling from the assistant recorder at the outset of the trial on the question whether section 5 of the 1968 Act created an absolute offence or one that required proof of mens rea. The assistant recorder ruled that it created an absolute offence. The appellant thereupon upon changed his plea to guilty. He was subsequently sentenced, on August 1, 1988, to three months' imprisonment suspended for that offence, the sentence to be served consecutively to a 12 months' suspended prison sentence for the burglary and another offence.

He now appeals against his conviction by reference from the Registrar of Criminal Appeals, on a point of law, on the ground that the assistant recorder erred ruling that section 5 of the Firearms Act 1968 creates an offence of strict liability. On December 21, 1987 the appellant was arrested in connection with another matter and taken to the police station. When he was searched, there was found in his jacket pocket a metal spray canister, marked in prominent letters "Force 10 Super Magnum CS". As that description indicated, it contained CS gas. He was asked, "Is this a CS gas aerosol," and he is alleged to have replied, "Yes, it is." He was then asked, "Do you know you are not meant to have this?" to which he is alleged to have replied, "Yes, I do." When he was interviewed later he told the police that he knew it was illegal to carry the CS gas canister in the street and explained that he had found it in a public house. It was accepted for the purpose of the ruling sought that CS gas was a noxious gas and that, with the canister, it was a prohibited weapon within the meaning of section 5(1)(b) of the Act.

After the assistant recorder's ruling and the appellant's change of plea, there was a *Newton* hearing to determine the appellant's state of knowledge of the canister [see (1983) 77 Cr App R 13]. The assistant recorder found, contrary to the appellant's contention, that he had known the canister contained CS gas.

The issue for decision is whether section 5(1) of the Firearms Act 1968, creates an offence of strict liability.

It provides as follows:

"5(1) A person commits an offence if, without the authority of the Defence Council, he has in his possession, or purchases or acquires, or manufactures, sells or transfers – (a) any firearm which is so designed or adapted that, if pressure is applied to the trigger, missiles continue to be discharged until pressure is removed from the trigger or the magazine containing the missiles is empty; (b) any weapon of whatever description designed or adapted for the discharge of any noxious liquid, gas or other thing; (c) any ammunition containing, or designed or adapted to contain any such noxious thing."

The ambit of the offence is extended by section 57(1) of the 1968 Act, which provides as follows:

"In this Act, the expression 'firearm' means a lethal barrelled weapon of any description from which any shot, bullet or other missile can be discharged and includes – (a) any prohibited weapon, whether it is such a lethal weapon as aforesaid or not; and (b) any component part of such a lethal or prohibited weapon; and (c) any accessory to any such weapon designed or adapted to diminish the noise or flash caused by firing the weapon ..." '

Following the trial judge's ruling that s5(1) created an offence of strict liability, the appellant changed his plea to one of guilty, and subsequently appealed against his conviction.

Held

The appeal would be dismissed.

Per Auld J:

'In *Clarke (Frederick)* (1986) 82 Cr App R 308, CA, the Court of Appeal held that the words of section 57(1) are to be read into section 5(1). In that case, which concerned an incomplete sub-machine gun, the Court held that it was nevertheless a prohibited weapon for two reasons, one of which was that the words of section 57(1)(b) were to be read into section (1)(a) with the result that it was an offence to possess any component part of a weapon designed or adapted for automatic fire. Whilst this appeal relates to an alleged offence under section (l)(b), which concerns weapons for the discharge of noxious liquid or gas, our decision as to whether the offence is absolute or requires *mens rea* covers all three categories in section (1)(a), (b) and (c). In the case of a firearm, the subject of section (1)(a), the question may arise in relation to some small part of an automatic weapon, perhaps not readily identifiable as such on its own.

The Firearms (Amendment) Act 1988 has now, by section 1, considerably extended the categories of prohibited weapons falling within section 5.

The maximum penalty on indictment for an offence under section 5 is five years' imprisonment, or a fine, or both. It is also triable summarily.

There is no authority on the question whether an offence under section 5 of the 1968 Act is one of strict liability or requires mens rea. There is, however, authority on the same question in relation to the lesser offence under section 1(1) of the Act which makes it an offence for a person to possess, purchase or acquire a firearm unless he or she is authorised to do so by a current firearm certificate. That subsection, so far as material, provides as follows:

"1(1) ... it is an offence for a person – (a) to have in his possession, or to purchase or acquire a firearm to which this section applies without holding a firearm certificate in force at the time, or otherwise than as authorised by such a certificate – (b) to have in his possession, or to purchase or acquire, any ammunition to which this section applies without holding a firearm certificate in force at the time, or otherwise than as authorised by such a certificate, or in quantities in excess of those so authorised."

The maximum penalty on indictment for an offence under section 1 of the 1968 Act is three years' imprisonment and/or a fine or, where committed in an aggravated form within section 4(1) of the Act, ie shortening the barrel of a shot gun, five years and/or a fine. It, too, is triable summarily.

Any consideration of an issue such as this must start with the frequently approved words of R S Wright J in *Sherras* v *De Rutzen* [1895] 1 QB 918, 921:

"There is a presumption that mens rea, an evil intention, or a knowledge of the wrongfulness of the act, is an essential ingredient in every offence; but that presumption is liable to be displaced either by the words of the statute creating the offence or by the subject-matter with which it deals, and both must be considered."

In *Warner* v *Metropolitan Police Commissioner* (1968) 52 Cr App R 373 [1969] 2 AC 256, the House of Lords held by a majority (Lords Morris of Borth-y-Gest, Guest, Pearce and Wilberforce; Lord Reid dissenting) that section 1 of the Drugs (Prevention of Misuse) Act 1964 created an absolute offence. That provision read: "(1) it shall not be lawful for a person to have in his possession a substance ... specified in the Schedule to this Act ...."

The case concerned a parcel of drugs which the appellant claimed he had assumed contained scent. At his trial at the Inner London Sessions the chairman directed the jury that if he had control of the parcel which in fact turned out to be full of drugs, the offence had been committed, and the fact that he had not known what the contents were would be relevant only in mitigation.

In Lord Morris's view, which he expressed at p412 and p283 respectively, and with which Lord Guest agreed, it was sufficient for the prosecution to prove that a person knowingly had in his possession something which in fact was a prohibited substance and that it was not necessary for the prosecution to prove he knew the nature and quality of what he had. According to Lord Pearce, with whom Lords Reid and Wilberforce agreed, there was "a half-way house" in the form of a rebuttable inference of possession. He said at p480 and p307:

"There is a very strong inference of fact in any normal case that a man who possesses a parcel also possesses its contents, an inference on which a jury would in a normal case be justified in finding possession .... But that inference can be disproved or shaken by evidence that, although a man was in possession of a parcel, he was completely mistaken as to its contents and would not have accepted possession had he known what kind of thing the contents were. A mistake as to the qualities of the contents, however, does not negative possession."

A recurring theme in their Lordships' speeches was that the dangerous subject matter of the criminal legislation being construed – drugs – in conjunction with the plain words of the section creating the offence, indicated that the intention of the legislature was to relieve the prosecution of the need to prove guilty knowledge. The same can be said about legislation creating offences in relation to firearms. Thus, Lord Guest said, at p421 and p301:

"Absolute offences are by no means unknown to our law and have been created inter alia in relation to firearms (Firearms Act 1937), and shotguns (Criminal Justice Act 1967, s85), which Acts create serious offences. A common feature of these Acts and the Drugs Act is that they all deal with dangerous substances and where the object is to prevent unauthorised possession and illegal trafficking in these articles."

It is interesting to see Lord Guest's reference to section 85 of the Criminal Justice Act 1967. It provided:

"85(1) Subject to any exemption having effect by virtue of this section any person who has in his possession or purchases or acquires a shot gun without holding a certificate authorising him to possess shot guns shall be guilty of an offence. "

The statutory successor of this provision is section 2 of the Firearms Act 1968 which is in very similar terms, and is comparable with the offence creating provisions of sections 1 and 5 of that Act.

The House of Lords, in *Sweet* v *Parsley* (1969) 53 Cr App R 221, [1970] AC 132, construed a quite different type of provision in section 5 of the Dangerous Drugs Act 1965, creating the offence of permitting premises to be used for the purpose of smoking cannabis, as requiring proof of mens rea. The speeches in that case indicate that the adjective "absolute," when applied to a statutory offence, may be a convenient shorthand, but it can also be misleading. Thus, in *Warner,* the word "possession" connoted "some degree of awareness of that which was within the possessor's physical control." (See per Lord Diplock in *Sweet* v *Parsley* at p245 and p162.

Returning to *Warner,* it is important to note that it was decided before (although only just) the enactment of the Firearms Act 1968. If the implications of construing a similarly worded prohibition in the field of drugs were apparent to the Legislature when passing that Act, it made no provision clarifying the position as to the need or not to prove mens rea or to provide for it by means of "the half-way house" approach of certain of their Lordships in that case. Nor has it since, despite the recent comprehensive extension and tightening up of the control of firearms in the Firearms (Amendment) Act 1988. This lack of legislative attention to the problem may be contrasted with the following express provision made in section 28(3) of the Misuse of Drugs Act 1971, which replaced the Drugs (Prevention of Misuse Act) 1964, section 1 of which was the subject of *Warner* and the Dangerous Drugs Act 1965, section *S(b)* of which was the subject of *Sweet* v *Parsley*. It provides:

"Where in any proceedings for an offence to which this section applies it is necessary, if the accused is to be convicted of the offence charged, for the prosecution to prove that some substance or product involved in the alleged offence was the controlled drug which the prosecution alleges it to have been, and it is proved that the substance or product in question was that controlled drug, the accused (a) shall not be acquitted of the offence charged by reason only of proving that he neither knew nor suspected nor had reason to suspect that the substance or product in question was the particular controlled drug alleged; (b) but shall be acquitted thereof –

(i) if he proves that he neither believed nor suspected nor had reason to suspect that the substance or product in question was a controlled drug; or (ii) if he proves that he believed the substance or product in question to be a controlled drug, or a controlled drug of a description, such that, if it had in fact been that controlled drug or a controlled drug of that description, he would not at the material time have been committing any offence to which this section applies."

This Court has recently considered, in *McNamara* (1988) 87 Cr App R 246, another drugs "container" case, the ratio decidendi of the House of Lords' decision in *Warner* and the effect upon it of the above provision. Lord Lane CJ, giving the judgment of the Court, said, at p250, that the following propositions seem to emerge:

"First of all a man does not have possession of something which has been put into his pocket or into his house without his knowledge: ... Secondly, a mere mistake as to the quality of a thing under the defendant's control is not enough to prevent him being in possession. For instance, if a man is in possession of heroin, believing it to be cannabis or believing it perhaps to be aspirin.

Thirdly, if the defendant believes that the thing is of a wholly different nature from that which in fact it is, then the result ... would be otherwise. Fourthly, in the case of a container or a box, the defendant's possession of the box leads to the strong inference that he is in possession of the contents or whatsoever it is inside the box. But if the contents are quite different in kind from what he believed, he is not in possession of it."

As to section 28 of the Misuse of Drugs Act 1971, the Lord Chief Justice commented (at p251) that its purpose appeared to have been to elucidate some of the problems which arose out of the speeches in *Warner* v *Metropolitan Police Commissioner* and he continued, at p252:

"Once the prosecution have proved that the defendant had control of the box, knew that he had control and knew that the box contained something which was in fact the drug alleged, the burden, in our judgment, is cast upon him to bring himself within those provisions."

So much for the authorities concerned with unlawful possession of drugs. We must now look at such relevant authorities as there are in relation to the unlawful possession of firearms, and consider the application, if any, of *Warner* and *McNamara* to the same question there.

Our attention has been drawn to three cases under the firearms legislation in which offences created by that legislation have been held to be absolute. The first, *Pierre* [1963] Crim LR 513, concerned an offence of using a firearm to resist arrest contrary to what is now section 17 of the 1968 Act. The other two, *Howells* (1977; 65 Cr App R 86, [1977] QB 614, CA and *Hussain* (1981) 72 Cr App R 143 CA, both concerned the possession of a firearm without a firearm certificate, contrary to section 1 of the 1968 Act.

In *Pierre* it was submitted on behalf of the appellant on his appeal against conviction that the prosecution had to prove he had known that the weapon in question was prohibited. Gorman J, giving the judgment of the Court, dismissed his appeal in these terms:

"This Court is clearly of the view that the submission of the appellant is wrong. It arrives at its view on three considerations: the words of the section; the mischief in fact aimed at by the section; and by the third matter of less importance, the difficulty of proving in certain cases where the issues are so great and so important that the defendant did in fact know that it was a weapon prohibited by the Act."

In *Howells* (1977) 65 Cr App R 86, [1977] QB 614, CA this Court held that section 1 of the Firearms Act 1968 had to be construed strictly and that proof of mens rea was unnecessary. The issue arose in this way. Section 58(2) exempts from the prohibition in section 1 any antique firearm sold, transferred, purchased, acquired or possessed as a curiosity or ornament. The defendant's case was that revolvers, the subject of charges under section 1(1), were antiques, but that, if they were not, he had honestly and reasonably believed them to be antiques. Browne LJ, giving the judgment of the Court, at p93 and p625 reviewed the authorities, in particular *Warner v MPC* (supra) and *Sweet v Parsley* (supra), and observed that they lead to the view:

" ... that in construing a penal statute it is vitally important to remember the presumption of mens rea as a necessary ingredient, but that Parliament may, by the wording of the Act and the nature of the matter dealt with, intend that the conduct forbidden should be penalised without proof of a guilty mind."

Adopting that approach, Browne LJ went on to rule that section 1 created an offence of absolute liability. His reasoning, at pp94 and 626 respectively, is of considerable relevance to the interpretation which we should give to section 5, and we set it out in full:

"This Court has reached the decision that section 1 should be construed strictly. First, the wording would on the face of it, so indicate. Secondly, the danger to the community resulting from the possession of lethal firearms is so obviously great that an absolute prohibition against their possession without proper authority must have been the intention of Parliament when considered in conjunction with the words of the section. Thirdly, to allow a defence of honest and reasonable belief that the firearm was an antique and therefore excluded would be likely to defeat the clear intentions of the Act.

There are two other matters which have influenced the Court in reaching its decision. The House of Lords in *Warner* (supra) ... strictly construed section 1 of the Drugs (Prevention of Misuse) Act 1964, so that possession without lawful authority, for whatever reason, was an offence, but by section 28 of the Misuse of Drugs Act 1971 (an Act repealing the Act of 1964) Parliament has alleviated the strictness by permitting a defence of proof of lack of knowledge. This would seem to indicate that Parliament accepted the interpretation in *Warner's* case. In addition the Court has noted that section 17(2) of the Firearms Act 1968 permits a defence of possession for a lawful object to a charge under that subsection, and by section 19, a defence of lawful authority or reasonable excuse is permitted to a charge of possession in a public place. By section 24(5), reasonable belief is a defence to a charge under that section."

The Court certified that a point of law of general public importance was involved in its decision, but refused leave to appeal to the House of Lords. The appellant's petition to the Appeal Committee of the House of Lords for leave to appeal was also refused.

In *Hussain* (1981) 72 Cr App R 143, [1981] 1 WLR 416, this Court again held that section 1 created an absolute offence. The case concerned an eight inch metal tube with a striker pin activated by a spring capable of firing .32 cartridges. The trial judge directed the jury that if they found that article to be a firearm as defined in section 57(1) of the Act the defendant would be guilty even though he did not know it was a firearm. On appeal it was argued that to constitute the offence it was necessary for the prosecution to prove that the defendant knew the nature of the article. Eveleigh LJ, as he then was, giving the judgment of the Court, rejected that argument on two grounds, at p145 and p418:

(1) He held that the reasoning of the House of Lords in *Warner v Metropolitan Police Commissioner* (1968) 52 Cr App R 373, [1969] 2 AC 256 applied, and, paraphrasing the words of Lord Morris of Borth-y-Gest at p412 and p295, said that all that the prosecution had to prove was that the appellant knowingly had in his possession an article which was in fact a lethal barrelled weapon from which a

missile could be discharged, in other words, a firearm, and that it was not necessary for the prosecution to prove that the appellant knew the nature and quality of the article.

(2) He pointed out that section 1(1), in contrast to other provisions in the Act, such as sections 24(5) and 25, makes no reference to the state of knowledge of the accused.

Having set out the principal authorities bearing on the question, we turn now to the assistant recorder's ruling and the arguments advanced before us in support of and against the appeal.

The assistant recorder ruled, at pp8G to 9A of the transcript:

" ... I can see no argument for distinguishing, in respect of this particular case, from section 1 and section 5.1, therefore, feel bound to follow the judgments of *Howells* (supra) and... *Hussain* (supra), which is that it is an offence of strict liability and the prosecution need not prove mens rea; ...."

The principal submission of Mr Jenkins on behalf of the appellant is that this is a "container" case of the sort considered by the House of Lords in *Warner* (supra) and that, therefore, the "half-way house" approach adopted by Lords Pearce, Reid and Wilberforce in that case applies. He argues that once the prosecution have proved a person was knowingly in possession of an item and that that item was in fact a prohibited weapon, it is a defence for him to show, on a balance of probabilities, that he neither knew nor suspected nor should be deemed to have known that it was a prohibited weapon. He added that, in practice, this defence will only be available in a "container" case; that is, where the nature of the item is concealed by the container.

In his submission that this is a "container" case Mr Jenkins treats the canister as the container and the noxious gas the thing contained. He suggests that the Court should not assume that the appellant had read the marking on the canister, "Force 10 Super Magnum CS". He distinguishes the cases of *Howells* (supra) and *Hussain* (supra) on the basis that they were not "container" cases. He pointed out that in each case the nature of the weapon was evident to its possessor; Howells knew that he had a firearm although he may have believed it to be an antique; Hussain knew what sort of article he had although he claimed that he thought it was a small gun in the nature of a toy, not a firearm which required a certificate. As Mr Jenkins put it in argument, both knew that they had a weapon of some sort, but they had made a mistake in law. Mr Birch, on behalf of the respondent, submits that section 5 of the 1968 Act creates an offence of strict liability. He argues that all the prosecution have to prove is that a person knowingly had possession of an article which was in fact a prohibited weapon. He relies upon the authorities of *Howells* (supra) and *Hussain* (supra), decided upon the very similar formula in section 1, and says that the "half-way house" approach of certain of their Lordships in *Warner,* now enshrined in section 28(3) of the Misuse of Drugs Act 1971, does not apply to firearms, there being no comparable provision in relation to sections 1 or 5 of the 1968 Act. By contrast, he refers to certain provisions in other sections of the Act where specific reference has been made to the state of mind of the accused. In addition, he maintains that this is not a "container" case, since the canister is itself the weapon, in the words of section s(l)(b), "designed or adapted for the discharge of... noxious... gas ... ," and therefore it could not come within the "half-way house" rule in *Warner* (supra) even if that applied to unlawful possession of firearms.

We start with the presumption of statutory interpretation that Parliament intends there to be a mental element in offences of a truly criminal nature. However that presumption may be rebutted, and it is conceded on behalf of the appellant that it is rebutted in the case of an offence under section 5 to the extent that all the prosecution have to do is prove that an accused knowingly had in his possession an article which was in fact a prohibited weapon. The only issue is whether, if the prosecution prove that, it is a defence for an accused to show on a balance of probabilities that he did not know and could not have been expected to know that the article was a prohibited weapon.

The justification for the concession on behalf of the appellant, which we agree has been properly made, that the offence created by section 5 is one of strict liability, at least in the absence of a defence of ignorance, may be summarised as follows:

First, the words of the section themselves, "A person commits an offence if without ... authority ... he has in his possession ... " any firearm, weapon or ammunition of the type defined, makes plain that this is an offence of strict liability.

Secondly, the comparable words and structure of section 1 of the 1968 Act have been held by this Court in *Howells* (supra) and *Hussain* (supra) to create an offence of strict liability.

Thirdly, the clear purpose of the firearms legislation is to impose a tight control on the use of highly dangerous weapons. To achieve effective control and to prevent the potentially disastrous consequences of their misuse, strict liability is necessary, just as it is in the equally dangerous field of drugs. See per Lord Guest in *Warner*, at p421 and p301, (supra). Given that section 1 has been held to create an offence of strict liability, this consideration applies a fortiori to section 5, which is concerned with more serious weapons, such as automatic handguns and machine guns, and imposes a higher maximum penalty.

On the question whether the approach adopted by certain of their Lordships in *Warner* v *MPC* (supra) applies to a "container" case under section 5, and presumably section 1 too, of the 1968 Act, so as to enable an accused to raise a defence that he did not know what was in the container, we are of the view that it does not. We say that for the following reasons:

First, whilst neither *Howells* (1977) 65 Cr App R 86, [1977] QB 614, nor *Hussain* (1981) 72 Cr App R 143, [1981] 1 WLR 416, was a "container" case, the Court of Appeal in each case adopted the much stricter line of Lord Morris in Warner than the "half-way house" approach of Lords Pearce, Reid and Wilberforce. See *Howells*, per Browne LJ at pp91, 92, and p626F-H; and *Hussain*, per Eveleigh LJ at p145 and p418 respectively.

Secondly, as noted by Browne LJ in *Howells*, there are a number of provisions creating offences in the 1968 Act where there is specific reference to the accused's state of mind as an ingredient of the offence or express provision of a defence where the accused can show that he did not have a particular state of mind. Neither section 1 nor section 5 is so drafted.

Thirdly, the scheme in the Firearms legislation of specifically providing where intended a defence based on the absence of a particular state of mind has been continued in the Firearms Act 1982. Section 1 of that Act subjects imitation firearms to the control of the 1968 Act, but provides in subsection (S) that it is a defence for the accused to show that he did not know and had no reason to suspect that the imitation firearm was constructed or adapted so as to be readily convertible into a firearm to which section 1 of the 1968 Act applies.

Fourthly, no provision corresponding to section 28(3) of the Misuse of Drugs Act 1971 has been introduced to the Firearms legislation so as to import the *Warner* "half-way house" concept into offences aimed at controlling the possession or use of firearms. In particular, the recent comprehensive extension of that control in the Firearms (Amendment) Act 1988 contains no such provision in relation to offences under section 1 or 5 of the 1968 Act.

Fifthly, the possibilities and consequences of evasion would be too great for effective control, even if the burden of proving lack of guilty knowledge were to be on the accused. The difficulty of enforcement, when presented with such a defence, would be particularly difficult where there is a prosecution for possession of a component part of a firearm or prohibited weapon, as provided for by sections 1 and 5 when read with section 57(1) of the 1968 Act. It would be easy for an accused to maintain, lyingly but with conviction, that he did not recognise the object in his possession as part of a firearm or prohibited weapon. To the argument that the innocent possessor or carrier of firearms or prohibited weapons or parts of them is at risk of unfair conviction under these provisions there has to be balanced the important public policy behind the legislation of protecting the public from the misuse of such dangerous weapons. Just as the Chicago-style gangster might plausibly maintain that he believed his violin case to contain a violin, not a sub-machine gun, so it might be difficult to meet a London lout's assertion that he did not know an unmarked plastic bottle in his possession contained ammonia rather than something to drink.

Accordingly, we are of the view that, whether or not this case is regarded as a "container" case, and even if the canister had not been clearly marked "Force 10 Super Magnum CS," this was an absolute offence, and it would have been no defence for the appellant to maintain that he did not know or could not reasonably have been expected to know that the canister contained CS gas. It follows that, in our view, the assistant recorder was correct in the ruling that he gave, so far as it went, that section 5 creates an offence of strict liability. He was not asked to consider the further question that we have just resolved against the appellant, whether, if the prosecution established possession of the prohibited weapon, it was open to the defence to raise and to prove on a balance of probabilities that he did not know that he had a prohibited weapon.

We would add that, on the facts of this case, it is a surprising vehicle for the arguments of law that have been advanced to us on behalf of the appellant, even if we had accepted them. It is clearly not a "container" case. As we have already observed section (1)(b) refers to a "weapon ... designed or adapted for the discharge of any noxious liquid, gas or other thing." It is the combination of canister and contents that makes the weapon; the noxious gas in this case cannot be regarded as the contents of a container in the sense that drugs were the contents of a box in the *Warner* (supra) and *McNamara* (supra) cases. Given the clear marking on the canister of what it contained, we cannot see the beginnings of a defence for the appellant, even if one had existed in law, that he took possession of the canister without realising what it was.

For the reasons that we have given, this appeal is dismissed.'

R v Coroner for East Kent, ex parte Spooner (1989) 88 Cr App R 10 Queens Bench (Divisional Court) (Bingham LJ, Mann and Kennedy JJ)

Corporate manslaughter

Facts

On 6 March 1987, the ferry ship 'Herald of Free Enterprise' capsized outside Zeebrugge harbour resulting in nearly 200 deaths. A public inquiry into the sinking was held under Mr Justice Sheen, which resulted in the publication of a report. The public inquiry was followed by an inquest into the deaths of some of those who had been aboard the ferry. During the course of the inquest the coroner ruled, inter alia, that a body corporate could not be guilty of manslaughter. A number of relatives of the deceased sought judicial review of the coroner's ruling.

Held

The applications would be dismissed.

Bingham LJ:

'On September 22 Messrs Kingsley Napley wrote to the coroner, drawing his attention to a further authority on the question whether manslaughter could be committed by a corporation. The authority referred to was a case tried at the Glamorgan Assizes in February 1965, when a contracting company was indicted for manslaughter and the trial proceeded before Streatfield J. The prosecution were represented by Mr Philip Wien QC as he then was, and the Corporation represented by Mr Mars-Jones QC as he then was. The company was acquitted but the significance attached by Kingsley Napley to the report of the case is that the prosecution failed on its facts, and neither of those distinguished counsel nor the extremely experienced judge evidently considered that a company could not in principle be indicted for manslaughter.

The case having been drawn to the coroner's attention - and no possible criticism is to be made of the fact that it was not drawn to his attention before because the earlier submissions had been made at short notice - the Coroner replied by a letter of September 23. He said: "I am very grateful to you for drawing my attention to the case of *Northern Strip Mining Construction Co Ltd* (unreported, 1956). It is not clear whether the question of corporate liability was argued. However, as I said in my ruling of September 18 at pp5 and 6, the acts of the company would have to be those of an individual (and I should have said an individual director) who was himself guilty of unlawful killing. I made it clear there was no prima facie evidence that any of the three relevant directors had done any act or been guilty of any omission which could be said to be a direct or substantial cause of the capsize and that therefore the question of corporate manslaughter did not in any event arise."

At the time when that letter was written, on September 23, 340 witnesses had given evidence orally and 400 statements had been read to the jury. The matter was re-argued before the coroner on October 1, the argument before him being, I think it is fair to say, no doubt more elaborate but to substantially the same effect as before. He gave a further ruling in these terms: "As I have said, Mr Forrest submitted that the actus reus and the mens rea may be found in the hands and brain of the company, respectively. Had the facts been, as in the *Glamorgan Assizes* case, ie *Northern Strip Mining Construction Co Ltd*, (where the instruction alleged, which had been given by the Managing Director, was to demolish a bridge starting in the middle) that the company brains had given instructions to go out to sea with the bow doors open, at full speed, when trimmed by the head, that would be a wholly different set of facts. The submission might then have been relevant. It has not been suggested by anyone that that is what happened here. I have considered all the evidence given by the Directors of the Sheen Inquiry, and that, incidentally, is 467 pages of transcript and not 367 as I mistakenly said on a previous occasion, when I gave these rulings, and I have now also considered the evidence given by one former director to this inquest, and I can see nothing in any of that evidence to support such a suggestion. It accordingly seems to me to be irrelevant to the issues before the jury. Quite apart from anything else, a failure to act would only ground manslaughter if it was that person's duty to act. The jury would need evidence of the extent of the duties of each of the directors concerned. It would also need evidence of the powers which each director had to take action. And, for example, would he have had to persuade the whole Board, or some other director, to agree with the proposal. It is obvious, as a matter of ordinary common sense, that the whole subject goes far beyond the proper scope of an Inquest, which is essentially a fact finding and not a fault finding enquiry. For these reasons I intend to tell the jury that they are not concerned with corporate manslaughter, whether it exists or not, and that in this inquest, when considering the possible verdict of unlawful killing, they are only concerned with the acts or omissions of those individuals who could be said to have caused the deaths."

The arguments which were deployed and elaborated before the coroner have, in substance, been repeated with great cogency and skill before us. The first question is whether a corporation can be indicted for manslaughter. The coroner originally ruled that it could not. In the course of argument in this Court we indicated at an early stage that we were prepared to assume for the purposes of this hearing that it could. As a result the question has not been fully argued and I have not found it necessary to reach a final conclusion. I am, however, tentatively of opinion that on appropriate facts the mens rea required for manslaughter can be established against a corporation. I see no reason in principle why such a charge should not be established. I am therefore tentatively of opinion that the coroner's original ruling was wrong, and indeed I would need considerable persuasion to reach the conclusion that it was correct.

But that is not the end of the matter because the coroner clearly adhered to his substantial ruling even on the assumption that a company could in principle be guilty of manslaughter. The coroner made it clear that he was of opinion that the evidence which he had considered was not capable of supporting the conclusion that those who represented the directing mind and will of the company and controlled what it did had been guilty of conduct amounting to manslaughter.

I am not persuaded that this is a conclusion which is or may be wrong. Nothing was, in my judgment, said by Sheen J or by way of concession before him which undermines that conclusion. It is important to bear in mind an important distinction. A company may be vicariously liable for the negligent acts and omissions of its servants and agents, but for a company to be criminally liable for manslaughter - on the assumption I am making that such a crime exists - it is required that the mens rea and the actus reus of manslaughter should be established not against those who acted for or in the name of the company but against those who were to be identified as the embodiment of the company itself. The coroner formed the view that there was no such case fit to be left to the jury against this company. I see no reason to disagree. I would add that I see no sustainable case in manslaughter against the directors who are named either.

I do not think the aggregation argument assists the applicants. Whether the defendant is a corporation or a personal defendant, the ingredients of manslaughter must be established by proving the necessary mens rea and actus reus of manslaughter against it or him by evidence properly to be relied on against it or him. A case against a personal defendant cannot be fortified by evidence against another defendant. The case against a corporation can only be made by evidence properly addressed to showing guilt on the part of the corporation as such. On the main substance of his ruling I am not persuaded that the coroner erred.'

Commentary

See *R* v *P & O European Ferries* (below).

Cundy v Le Cocq (1884) 13 QBD 207 Divisional Court (Stephens and Matthew JJ)

Imposition of strict liability

Facts

The defendant was convicted of unlawfully selling alcohol to an intoxicated person, contrary to s13 of the Licensing Act 1872. On appeal to the Divisional Court, the defendant contended that he had been unaware of the customer's drunkenness and thus should have been acquitted.

Held

The conviction would be affirmed.

Stephen J:

'I am of opinion that this conviction should be affirmed. Our answer to the question put to us turns upon this, whether the words of the section under which this conviction took place, taken in connection with the general scheme of the Act, should be read as constituting an offence only where the licensed person knows or has means of knowing that the person served with intoxicating liquor is drunk or whether the offence is complete where no such knowledge is shown. I am of the opinion that the words of the section amount to an absolute prohibition of the sale of liquor to a drunken person, and that the existence of a bona fide mistake as to the condition of the person served is not an answer to the charge, but is a matter only for mitigation of the penalties that may be imposed. I am led to that conclusion both by the general scope of the Act, which is for the repression of drunkenness, and from a comparison of the various sections under the head "offences against public order." Some of these contain the word "knowingly", as for instance section 14, which deals with keeping a disorderly house, and section 16, which deals with the penalty for harbouring a constable. Knowledge in these and other cases is an element in the offence; but the clause we are considering says nothing about the knowledge of the state of the person served. I believe the reason for making this prohibition absolute was that there must be a great temptation to a publican to sell liquor without regard to the sobriety of the customer, and it was thought right to put upon the publican the responsibility of determining whether his customer is sober. Against this view we have had quoted the maxim that in every criminal offence there must be a guilty mind; but I do not think that maxim has so wide an application as it is sometimes considered to have. In old time, and as applicable to the common law or to earlier statutes, the maxim may have been of general application; but a difference has arisen owing to the greater precision of modern statutes. It is impossible now, as illustrated by the cases of *R* v *Prince* and *R* v *Bishop*, to apply the maxim generally to all statutes, and the substance of all the reported cases is that it is necessary to look at the object of each Act that is under consideration to see whether and how far knowledge is of the essence of the offence created.

Here, as I have already pointed out, the object of this part of the Act is to prevent the sale of intoxicating liquor to drunken persons, and it is perfectly natural to carry that out by throwing on the publican the responsibility of determining whether the person supplied comes within that category.

I think, therefore, the conviction was right and must be affirmed.'

R v Gould [1968] 2 QB 65 Court of Appeal (Criminal Division) (Diplock LJ, Widgery and Blain JJ)

Mistake as a defence to bigamy

Facts

The defendant was convicted of bigamy contrary to s57 of the Offences Against the Person Act 1861. He appealed on the ground that he had honestly and reasonably believed that his marriage to his first wife, who was still alive, had been dissolved.

Held

The appeal would be allowed

Diplock LJ:

'The question of law in this appeal is whether on a charge of bigamy under section 57 of the Offences against the Person Act 1861, a defendant's honest belief upon reasonable grounds that at the time of his second marriage his former marriage has been dissolved is a good defence to the charge. In *Wheat and Stocks* (1921) 15 Cr App R 134; [1921] 2 KB 119), the Court of Criminal Appeal decided that it was not. The learned Deputy Chairman rightly regarded himself as bound by the decision, but we are not.

[His Lordship then considered a number of authorities, including *R* v *Wheat and Stocks* (above) and *R* v *Tolson* (see chapter 14) and continued]

In *King* (1964) 48 Cr App R 17; [1964] 1 QB 285, the Court of Criminal Appeal in England followed the decision of the High Court of Australia. The mistake of fact there was that at the time of his former marriage the defendant's own previous marriage to another person had not been dissolved. Had this been so, the former marriage would have been void ab initio and his second marriage in respect of which he was charge with bigamy would not have been bigamous. In this respect the case was on all fours with *Thomas* v *R* (supra). The Court of Criminal Appeal, however, expressed the view not only that their own decision did not conflict with the decision in *Wheat and Stocks* (supra), but that the Australian High Court themselves felt that *Thomas* v *R* (supra) was clearly distinguishable from *Wheat and Stocks* (supra). With great respect, this latter view must have been formed per incuriam. We have already referred to the passages in the judgments of Latham CJ and Dixon J which show the contrary.

If there is a distinction in principle between *Wheat and Stocks* (supra) and *King* (supra) wherein does that distinction lie and how is it to be extracted from the wording of the section? In *King* (supra) the court approved and followed the direction of the Common Serjeant in *Thomson* (1906) 70 JP 6, of which Avory J had said in *Wheat and Stocks* (at pp141 and 127 of the respective reports): "We doubt if it can be supported consistently with our present decision." This, as the court pointed out in *King* (supra) was obiter, but where does the distinction lie? The mistake in both cases was of the same kind: whether or not a court of competent jurisdiction had made a decree dissolving a marriage. No-one, apart from Starke J, has ever suggested that this is not a mistake of fact. In both cases the fact mistakenly believed to have been true would, if true, have had the legal consequence that at the relevant time for seeing whether element (b) of the offence existed, ie the date of the second marriage ceremony, element (a) was absent - ie, the defendant was not married. The legal consequences differ in one respect only, that in *King* (supra) the defendant would never have been married to his former reputed wife, whereas in *Wheat and Stocks* (supra) he would at some time previous to the relevant time have been married to his former wife.

But what construction could be placed upon the words of the section which would result in this distinction between the legal consequences of the supposed fact being relevant to the guilt or innocence of the honest and reasonable believer of the fact? There might perhaps be a plausible argument, based on the second part of the proviso, that the expression "being married" in the enacting words should be construed as "having been married." This would have the effect of making the provisions of the proviso relating to dissolution and declarations of nullity of the previous marriage true exceptions to the enacting words instead of surplusage as they are if "being married" is construed in the present tense, in which grammatically it is. We doubt if in any event it would be permissible to let the tail in the proviso wag the dog in the enacting words. But even if it were, the only effect would be that the fact mistakenly believed to have been true in *King* (supra) would, if true, have made the second marriage innocent because the defendant did not come within the expression "having been married" in the enacting words, whereas the corresponding fact in *Wheat and Stocks* (supra) would, if true, have made the second marriage innocent because the defendant did come within the exception in the proviso as being a "person who at the time of such second marriage shall have been divorced from the bond of the first marriage."

Once it is accepted, as it has been in *King* (supra), that the offence is not an absolute one and that honest and reasonable belief in a fact affecting the matrimonial status of the defendant which, if true, would make his second marriage lawful and innocent can constitute a defence, there can, in our view, be no possible ground in justice or in reason for drawing a distinction between facts the result of which would be that he was innocent because he did not come within the enacting words at all, and facts the result of which would be that he was excluded from the enacting words by the proviso.

Given that the belief is formed honestly and upon reasonable grounds, there can be no difference on grounds of moral blameworthiness or of public policy between a mistaken belief that a decree absolute has been granted as in *Wheat and Stocks* (supra) and one that it has not as in *King* (supra). Indeed it needs little ingenuity to postulate circumstances in which the existence of a decree absolute would make the defendant's first purported marriage void ab initio as the absence of a decree absolute would have done in *King* (supra) and *Thomas* v *R* (supra). To draw such fine distinctions would we think, in the words of Dixon J (at p811 of the report) "lead to consequences which would not only be contrary to principle but which would be discreditable to our system of criminal law."

We think that *Wheat and Stocks* (supra) was wrongly decided. We agree with the High Court of Australia that it conflicts with *Tolson* (supra). In this respect we respectfully differ from the opinion expressed by the Court of Criminal Appeal in *King* (supra), but our decision is in conformity with the result arrived at in *King* (supra) and those parts of the reasoning which led to that result.

The prosecution accept that the appellant at the time of the second marriage did honestly believe that his former marriage had been dissolved and that he had reasonable grounds for that belief. This appeal is, accordingly, allowed and the conviction quashed.'

R v Larsonneur (1933) 24 Cr App R 74

See chapter 2.

R v Lewis [1988] Crim LR 517, Court of Appeal (Criminal Division) (May LJ, Mars-Jones and Turner JJ)

Possession or control of drugs - whether knowledge can be imputed

Facts

'The appellant was the sole tenant of a house in Troedyrhiw, in which amphetamines and cannabis were found. He was not present during the search, but agreed that he had seen the endorsed warrant which the police had left behind. His defence was that the tenancy was a device which he used to obtain DHSS benefits to which he was not entitled. Although others went to the house, he had never intended to live there and visited the premises only occasionally; his wife and landlord testified that his visits were infrequent. When there, he never looked in the cupboards and took little notice of what was on the premises; he never suspected the presence of drugs. He was convicted and appealed, inter alia, on the ground that the judge, relying on a direction in *Warner* v *MPC* (1968) 52 Cr App R 373, had misdirected the jury on the meaning of "possession". Counsel sought to distinguish *Warner* from the present case. He argued, inter alia, that: the mere fact that the appellant might have had an opportunity of discovering the drugs was not sufficient to support a finding of his possession of them; the question of investigation was material only when there was something to put one on inquiry; on a proper approach, *Warner's* case had laid down that there had to be actual knowledge of the fact of control before there could be said to be possession of the articles in issue.

Held

Dismissing the appeal on this ground (allowed on another point), it was not necessary to direct the jury that they had to be satisfied that the defendant had actual knowledge that the articles were under his control before they could convict. Whilst *Warner* was the leading authority on the particular question here, the speeches in that case seemed to reflect a number of different shades of meaning and approach as to what constituted "possession," from which it was not easy to distil a majority conclusion relevant to the present appeal. It was proposed to follow the approach of Lord Scarman in *R* v *Boyensen* (1982) 75 Cr App R 51 (in adopting and applying Lord Wilberforce's description of "possession" in *Warner*) when he said: "The question, to which an answer is required, and in the end a jury must answer it, is whether ... the accused should be held to have possession of the substance, rather than mere control ... the jury should be invited to consider all the circumstances ... by which the custody commences and the legal incident in which it is held ... what knowledge or means of knowledge or guilty knowledge as to the presence of the substance, or as to the nature of what has been received, the accused had at the time of receipt or thereafter up to the moment when he is found with it ... On such matters ... they must make the decision whether, in addition to physical control, he has, or ought to have imputed to him the intention to possess, or knowledge that he does possess ... a prohibited substance. If he has this intention or knowledge it is not additionally necessary that he should know the nature of the substance." Thus, the question in the end was whether, on the facts, the defendant had been proved to have, or ought to have imputed to him, either the intention or the knowledge that he possessed what was in fact a prohibited substance.'

[*Reported by Veronica Cowan, Barrister.*]

Lim Chin Aik v R [1963] AC 160 Privy Council (Viscount Radcliffe, Lord Evershed and Lord Devlin)

Purpose in imposing strict liability

Facts

The defendant had been convicted of contravening an order prohibiting, in absolute terms, his entry into Singapore, despite his ignorance of the order's existence. He appealed, ultimately, to the Privy Council.

Held

The appeal would be allowed.

Lord Evershed:

'That proof of the existence of a guilty intent is an essential ingredient of a crime at common law is not at all in doubt. The problem is of the extent to which the same rule is applicable in the case of offences created and defined by statute or statutory instrument. Their Lordships were very properly referred to a number of cases, including the often-cited *Nichols* v *Hall* (1873) LR 8 CP 322 and *Cundy* v *Le Cocq* [above] and covering a considerable period ending with the decision last year of the Court of Criminal Appeal in *R* v *Cugullere* [1961] 1 WLR 858. As was observed by Wright J at the beginning of his judgment in the case of *Sherras* v *De Rutzen* [below] to which their Lordships will presently make further reference, the difficulty of the problem is enhanced by the face that many of the cases are not easy to reconcile. Thus it has been held that a licensee of a public-house commits an offence under the licensing legislation of serving alcoholic liquor to a drunken man even though he was unaware of the customer's condition (*Cundy* v *Le Cocq*): but that a licensee does not commit the offence under the same legislation of serving drinks to a police constable on duty if he reasonably supposed that the constable was in fact off duty ... : and in the latest case above cited the Court of Criminal Appeal held that the terms of section 1 of the Prevention of Crime Act 1953, "Any person who without lawful authority or reasonable excuse, the proof whereof shall lie on him, has with him in any public place any offensive weapon shall be guilty of an offence" must be read as if the word "knowingly" were written before the word "has".

Mr Gratiaen founded his argument upon the formulation of the problem contained in the judgment of Wright J in *Sherras's* case. The language of that learned and experienced judge was as follows: "There is a presumption that mens rea, or evil intention or knowledge of the wrongfulness of the act, is an essential ingredient in every offence, but that presumption is liable to be displaced either by the words of the statute creating the offence or by the subject-matter with which it deals, and both must be considered."

It is to be observed that in that case the court held the presumption not to be displaced even though the word "knowingly" which was not found in the subsection involved in the case did appear in another subsection of the same section. Their Lordships add that the circumstance last mentioned was regarded by Day J in his judgment in the same case as shifting the onus of proof to the defendant (which onus the learned judge held to have been discharged). The question of onus does not, as already stated, arise in the present case. Their Lordships think it right, however, to say that they should not be thought to assent to Day J's proposition ...

Their Lordships accept as correct the formulation cited from the judgment of Wright J. They are fortified in that view by the fact that such formulation was expressly accepted by Lord du Parcq in delivering the judgment of the Board in the case in 1947 of *Srinivas Mall Bairoliya* v *King-Emperor* (1947) ILR 26 Pat 460, a case which unfortunately has not found its way into the Law Reports. That was a case in which one of the appellants had been charged with an offence under the rules made by virtue of the Defence of India Act, 1939, consisting of the sale of salt at prices exceeding those prescribed under the rules, the sale having in fact been made without that appellant's knowledge by one of his servants. The Indian High Court had held the appellant to be nonetheless liable upon the terms of the rules; but the Board rejected the view of the High Court. Lord du Parcq, after citing with approval the judgment already quoted of Lord Wright J, also adopted the language of Lord Goddard CJ in the case of *Brend* v *Wood* (1946) 62 TLR 462, DC: "It is in my opinion of the utmost importance for the protection of the liberty of the subject that a court shall always bear in mind that unless a statute either clearly or by necessary implication rules out mens rea as a constituent part of a crime a defendant should not be foundguilty of an offence against the criminal law unless he has got a guilty mind."

The adoption of these formulations of principle does not, however, dispose of the matter ... The difficulty remains of their application. What should be the proper inferences to be drawn from the language of the statute or statutory instrument under review - in this case of sections 6 and 9 of the Immigration Ordinance? More difficult perhaps still, what are the inferences to be drawn in a given case from the "subject-matter with which [the statute or statutory instrument] deals"?

Where the subject-matter of the statute is the regulation for the public welfare of a particular activity - statutes regulating the sale of food and drink are to be found among the earliest examples - it can be and frequently has been inferred that the legislature intended that such activities should be carried out under conditions of strict liability. The presumption is that the statute or statutory instrument can be effectively enforced only if those in charge of the relevant activities are made responsible for seeing that they are complied with. When such a presumption is to be inferred, it displaces the ordinary presumptions of mens rea. Thus sellers of meat may be made responsible for seeing that the meat is fit for human consumption and it is no answer for them to say that they were not aware that it was polluted. If that were a satisfactory answer, then as Kennedy LJ pointed out in *Hobbs* v *Winchester Corporation* [1910] 2 KB 471, the distribution of bad meat (and its far-reaching consequences) would not be effectively prevented. So a publican may be made responsible for observing the condition of his customers, *Cundy* v *Le Cocq* [above].

But it is not enough in their Lordships' opinion merely to label the statute as one dealing with a grave social evil and from that to infer that strict liability was intended. It is pertinent also to inquire whether putting the defendant under strict liability will assist in the enforcement of the regulations. That means that there must be something he can do, directly or indirectly, by supervision or inspection, by improvement of his business methods or by exhorting those whom he may be expected to influence or control, which will promote the observance of the regulations. Unless this is so, there is no reason in penalising him, and it cannot be inferred that the legislature imposed strict liability merely in order to find a luckless victim. This principle has been expressed and applied in *Reynolds* v *G H Austin & Sons Ltd* [[1951] 2 KB 135] and *James & Son Ltd* v *Smee* [1955] 1 QB 78. Their Lordships prefer it to the alternative view that strict liability follows simply from the nature of the subject-matter and that persons whose conduct is beyond any sort of criticism can be dealt with by the imposition of a nominal penalty. This latter view can perhaps be supported to some extent by the dicta of Kennedy LJ in *Hobbs* v *Winchester Corporation*, and of Donovan J in *R v St. Margaret's Trust Ltd* [1958] 1 WLR 522. But though a nominal penalty may be appropriate in an individual case where exceptional lenience is called for, their Lordships cannot, with respect, suppose that it is envisaged by the legislature as a way of dealing with offenders generally. Where it can be shown that the imposition of strict liability would result in the prosecution and conviction of a class of persons whose conduct could not in any way affect the observance of the law, their Lordships consider that, even where the statute is dealing with a grave social evil, strict liability is not likely to be intended.

Their Lordships apply these general observations to the Ordinance in the present case. The subject-matter, the control of immigration, is not one in which the presumption of strict liability has generally been made. Nevertheless, if the courts of Singapore were of the view that unrestricted immigration is a social evil which it is the object of the Ordinance to control most rigorously, their Lordships would hesitate to disagree. That is a matter peculiarly within the cognisance of the local courts. But Mr Le Quesne was unable to point to anything that the appellant could possibly have done so as to ensure that he complied with the regulations. It was not, for example, suggested that it would be practicable for him to make continuous inquiry to see whether an order had been made against him. Clearly one of the objects of the Ordinance is the explusion of prohibited persons from Singapore, but there is nothing that a man can do about it if, before the commission of the offence, there is no practical or sensible way in which he can ascertain whether he is a prohibited person or not.

Mr Le Quesne, therefore, relied chiefly on the text of the Ordinance and their Lordships return, accordingly, to the language of the two material sections. It is to be observed that the Board is here concerned with one who is said (within the terms of section 6 (3) to have "contravened " the subsection by "remaining" in Singapore (after having entered) when he had been "prohibited" from entering by an "order" made by the Minister containing such prohibition. It seems to their Lordships that, where a man is said to have contravened an order or an order of prohibition, the common sense of the language presumes that he was aware of the order before he can be said to have contravened it. Their Lordships realise that this statement is something of an over-simplification when applied to the present case; for the "contravention" alleged is of the unlawful act, prescribed by subsection (2) of the section, of remaining in Singapore after the date of the order of prohibition. Nonetheless it is their Lordships' view that, applying the test of ordinary sense to the language used, the notion of contravention here alleged is more consistent with the assumption that the person charged had knowledge of the order than the converse. But such a conclusion is in their Lordships' view much reinforced by the use of the word "remains" in its context. It is to be observed that if the respondent is right a man could lawfully enter Singapore and could thereafter lawfully remain in Singapore until the moment when an order of prohibition against his entering was made; that then, instanter, his purely passive conduct in remaining - that is, the mere continuance, quite unchanged, of his previous behaviour, hitherto perfectly lawful - would become criminal. These considerations bring their Lordships clearly to the conclusion that the sense of the language here in question requires for the commission of a crime thereunder mens rea as a constituent of such crime; or at least that there is nothing in the language used which suffices to exclude the ordinary presumption. Their Lordships do not forget the emphasis placed by Mr Le Quesne on the fact that the word "knowingly" or the phrases "without reasonable cause" or "without reasonable excuse" are found in various sections of the Ordinance (as amended) but find no place in the section now under consideration - see, for example, sections 16 (4), 18 (4), 19 (2), 29, 31 (2) and 56 (d) and (e) of the Ordinance. In their Lordships' view the absence of such a word or phrase in the relevant section is not sufficient in the present case to prevail against the conclusion which the language as a whole suggests. In the first place, it is to be noted that to have inserted such words as "knowingly" or "without lawful excuse" in the relevant part of section 6 (3) of the Act would in any case not have been sensible. Further, in all the various instances where the word or phrase is used in the other sections of the Ordinance before-mentioned the use is with reference to the doing of some specific act or the failure to do some specific act as distinct from the mere passive continuance of behaviour theretofore perfectly lawful. Finally, their Lordships are mindful that in the *Sherras* case itself the fact that the word "knowingly" was not found in the subsection under consideration by the court but was found in another subsection of the same section was not there regarded as sufficient to displace the ordinary rule.'

R v McNamara (1988) 87 Cr App R 246 Court of Appeal (Criminal Division) (Lord Lane CJ, Drake and Henry JJ)

Proof of knowledge of possession of drugs

Facts

As stated by the Lord Chief Justice:

'On December 3 1986, police officers went to the house of a co-defendant of this appellant with a warrant to search for drugs. Three of the co-defendants - the men charged with the conspiracy - were present at the house. Shortly after the police arrived, the appellant rode up to the premises on his motorcycle. According to the prosecution evidence he knocked at the door and announced to those inside that he had the stuff.

When confronted by one of the officers, the appellant started to run away. He was brought back to the house. He was said to have been shaking. He would not say what the stuff was, but said that it was on the back of his motorcycle. So out went the police to the motorcycle, and on the back of it they found a cardboard box, which they said was unsealed, containing about 20 kilogrammes of cannabis resin.

The appellant was arrested. Again according to the police, after caution he said that he was not the dealer but was only the carrier. He admitted that it was cannabis, but would not say where he had got it from because it was more than his life was worth to tell. He was simply told by someone, whom he refused to identify, to deliver the cannabis resin as instructed.

The appellant gave evidence. He said that he did delivery on his motorcycle for a man called John. He declined to give any further information about that individual. He said that he thought the material which he was delivering in the box on the back of his motorcycle was pornographic or pirated video films. He never thought for a moment that he was carrying any drugs. He had simply been told by John to take the box from one public house to another. He had by chance decided to call at the co-defendant's house where the police happened to be on his way because he wanted to pick up his boots.

The appellant was convicted under s5(3) Misuse of Drugs Act 1971, of possession of a controlled drug with intent to supply. The trial judge had directed the jury that 'they should convict if satisfied so as to be sure that the appellant had possession of the contents of the box, which admittedly was cannabis resin, and he knew the box contained something, unless on the balance of probabilities he neither knew, suspected or had reason to suspect the box contained any controlled drug. However, they should acquit the appellant, notwithstanding they were satisfied that he was in possession of the cannabis resin if they concluded that he probably did not know, nor did he suspect, nor did he have reason to suspect that the box contained a controlled drug. The appellant was convicted and appealed on the ground that the judge's direction was wrong and that the prosecution had to prove knowledge on the part of the appellant of the contents of the box.'

Held

The appeal would be dismissed.

Lord Lane CJ:

'Mr Kamlish in his submission on behalf of the appellant in this Court ... submits that the prosecution must prove, as part of their duty, knowledge on the part of the defendant what the nature of the contents of the box were. He is forced to concede however that if his argument is correct, then the words of section 28(3), which we will read fully in a moment, are otiose. He is unable on his argument to prove those words with a sensible meaning.

The operation of section 28 of the Misuse of Drugs Act 1971, to say the least, is not free from difficulty. For instance subsection (2) reads as follows:

"Subject to subsection (3) below, in any proceedings for an offence to which this section applies it shall be a defence for the accused to prove that he neither knew of not suspected nor had reason to suspect the existence of some fact alleged by the prosecution which it is necessary for the prosecution to prove if he is to be convicted of the offence charged"

If one reads those words literally, they seem in effect to cast upon the defendant the burden of disproving all facts adduced by the prosecution in support of the charges. This, one imagines, cannot possibly have been the intention of the draftsman.

We have had our attention drawn by Mr Kamlish to the decision of this Court in the case of *Ashton-Rickhardt* (1977) 65 Cr App R 67, [1978] 1 All ER 173. The view of the Court in that case was certainly that subsection (2) of section 28 did not have that extraordinary effect.

There are certain passages in the judgment of Roskill LJ, in that case which prima facie seem to support the arguments of Mr Kamlish. However when one examines the facts of that case, the judge went a good deal further in his direction to the jury than did Judge Stable in the present case, because in that case the Judge was inviting the jury to find possession proved from the fact that the "thing" was in the defendant's car without more, and that thereafter the burden rested on the defendant to disprove possession. That is not the case here, as has already been made clear.

In so far as the judgment in *Ashton-Rickhart* (supra) deals with that point, of course we are bound by it. However when Roskill LJ at p72 and p178 of the respective reports, goes on to consider a passage which he reads from Smith and Hogan's *Criminal Law* (3rd ed 1973), p73, he seems to us to go a good deal further than was necessary for the point in issue in that case, and his remarks in that respect are obiter.

One therefore starts off with the proposition that the prosecution must prove basic possession. That sounds simple. It is not, because the concept of possession is itself an extremely difficult one to understand.

In the well known case of *Warner v Metropolitan Police Commissioner* (1968) 52 Cr App R 373, [1969] 2 AC 256, Lord Wilberforce at p433 and p309 respectively put the matter thus:

"The Act refers to possession, a concept which is both central in many areas of our legal system, and also lacking in definition. As Earl Jowitt has said of it, 'the English law has never worked out a completely logical and exhaustive definition of possession' (*United States of America and Republic of France v Dolfus Mieg et Cie SA and Bank of England* [1952] AC 582, 605). In relation to it we find English law, as so often, working by description rather than by definition. Ideally, a possessor of a thing has complete physical control over it; he has knowledge of its existence, its situation and its qualities: he has received it from a person who intends to confer possession of it and he has himself the intention to possess it exclusively of others. But these elements are seldom all present in situations with which the courts have to deal, and where one or more of them is lacking, or incompletely present, it has to be decided whether the given approximation is such that possession may be held sufficiently established to satisfy the relevant rule of law. As it is put by Pollock and Wright, possession 'is defined by modes or events in which it commences or ceases and by the legal incidents attached to it' (*Possession in the Common Law* Part III, Chap 1 (1888) p119 - per RS Wright)."

The situation in the present case with which we are dealing is, to pick up Lord Wilberforce's words, a non-deal form of possession, namely, holding by the defendant of a box and its contents, which perhaps it is convenient to refer to as box-possession, observing, as we do, that we appreciate the danger of begging the question altogether by the use of the word "possession." The defendant admittedly has control of a box which he knows contains a "thing" which he has not seen. If he knows what the thing is, no problem arises. But what if the defendant knows that the box contains something, but is mistaken as to the nature of that thing? That is to say, in terms of the present case, what if he knew that the box contained something, but he thought it was pornographic or pirated video films, whereas in fact it was undoubtedly cannabis resin?

Prior to the passing of the 1971 Act, the House of Lords, in *Warner v Metropolitan Police Commissioner* (1968) 52 Cr App 373, [1969] 2 AC 256, tackled this question. Unhappily it is not altogether easy to extract from the speeches of their Lordships the ratio decidendi. But doing the best we can, and appreciating that we may not have done full justice to the speeches, the following propositions seem to us to emerge.

First of all a man does not have possession of something which has been put into his pocket or into his house without his knowledge: in other words something which is "planted" on him, to use the current vulgarism. Secondly, a mere mistake as to the quality of a thing under the defendant's control is not enough to prevent him being in possession. For instance, if a man is in possession of heroin, believing it to be cannabis or believing it perhaps to be aspirin.

Thirdly, if the defendant believes that the thing is of a wholly different nature from that which in fact it is, then the result, to use the words of Lord Pearce, would be otherwise. Fourthly, in the case of a container or a box, the defendant's possession of the box leads to the strong inference that he is in possession of the contents of whatsoever it is inside the box. But if the contents are quite different in kind from what he believed, he is not in possession of it.

"... the prima facie assumption is discharged if he proves (or raises a real doubt in the matter) either (a) that he was a servant or bailee who had no right to open it and no reason to suspect that its contents were illicit or were drugs or (b) that although he was the owner he had no knowledge of (including a genuine mistake as to) its actual contents or of their illicit nature and that he received them innocently and also that he had had no reasonable opportunity since receiving the package of acquainting himself with its actual contents."

We have had our attention drawn by counsel to two passages in those speeches: one in the speech of Lord Reid at p389 and p280, and two passages in the speech of Lord Wilberforce at pp434, 435 and p310 and 312 respectively which we have not overlooked.

But turning back to Lord Pearce, at p428 and p306 he had this to observe about the conclusion:

"[This view] would leave some unfortunate victims of circumstance who move innocently but rashly in shady surroundings and who carry packages or tablets for strangers or unreliable friends. But I think even they would have an opportunity of ventilating their story and in some cases, if innocent of any knowledge and bad motives, obtaining an acquittal. Some of the person in some of the rather far-fetched circumstances which have been envisaged in argument would still be left in difficulties. But I do not think that Parliament intended to cater for them in its efforts to stop a serious evil."

It seems to us that it was with a view to elucidating some of the problems which arise from the speeches in that case that the 1971 Act was passed. First of all the preamble to the Act reads as follows: "An Act to make new provision with respect to dangerous or otherwise harmful drugs and related matters, and for purposes connected therewith." No doubt Parliament was stimulated to make this enactment by reason, partially at any rate, of what Lord Pearce said at p307 of the report, which reads as follows: "It would, I think, be an improvement of a difficult position if Parliament were to enact that when a person has ownership or physical possession of drugs he shall be guilty unless he proves on a balance of probabilities that he was unaware of their nature or had reasonable excuse for their possession."

It seems to us, in order to make sense of the provisions of section 28, and also to make as clear as can be possible the decision in *Warner v MPV* (supra), the draftsman of the Act intended that the prosecution should have the initial burden of proving that the defendant had, and knew that he had, in these circumstances the box in his control and also that the box contained something. That, in our judgment, establishes the necessary possession. They must also of course prove that the box in fact contained the drug alleged, in this case cannabis resin. If any of those matters are unproved, there is no case to go to the jury.

The speeches in *Warner v MPC* (supra) then seem to have qualified that comparatively simple concept by saying that the defendant has the burden thereafter to show or suggest that he had no right or opportunity to open the box or reason to doubt the legitimacy of the contents and that he believed the contents were different in kind, and not merely quality, than what they actually were.

To implement those considerations as they stood, and explain them so the jury can understand them, would have been a daunting task for a judge. Accordingly, in our view, it is to those matters that the words of section 28, and particularly section 28(3)(*b*)(i) are directed.

Let me read those words: "28(1) This section applies to offences under any of the following provisions of this Act, that is to say section 4(2) and (3), section 5(2) and (3), section 6(2) and section 9." That is to say, one of the sections under which this charge was laid, namely section 5(3). The side-note to section 5 is "Restriction of possession of controlled drugs."

Section 28(3) reads as follows:

"Where in any proceedings for an offence to which this section applies it is necessary, if the accused is to be convicted of the offence charged, for the prosecution to prove that some substance or product involved in the alleged offence was the controlled drug which the prosecution alleges it to have been and it is proved that the substance or product in question was that controlled drug, the accused - (*a*) shall not be acquitted of the offence charged by reason only of proving that he neither knew nor suspected nor had reason to suspect that the substance or product in question was the particular controlled drug alleged, but (*b*) shall be acquitted thereof - (i) if he proves that he neither believed nor suspected nor had reason to suspect that the substance or product in question was a controlled drug..."

Once the prosecution have proved that the defendant had control of the box, knew that he had control and knew that the box contained something which was in fact the drug alleged, the burden, in our judgment, is cast upon him to bring himself within those provisions. Thus in our judgment the direction of the judge in the present case was correct.

We now turn to deal with the other grounds of appeal.

Complaint is made of a passage in the summing up which runs as follows:

"Members of the jury, you may think it is stupid and wrong headed for a solicitor, or his representative, to advise a person who is innocent and has an explanation for his suspicious behaviour to give a 'no reply interview,' but you really must try not to hold it against any defendant who said he would not answer any questions, and did not, and that applies to Mr Wheatley. Nor should you hold it against Mr Kiernan who having been reminded by his solicitor he need not make a reply, and Mr McNamara was advised by his solicitor to his second interview not to comment, proceeded to say nothing to a number of questions but to say something to some of the other questions, and you may think to advise an innocent man with an explanation not to make his explanation as early as he can to the police, simply because he has a right to remain silent is about as silly advice as can be given. The only sound advice you may think if you are innocent and have an explanation is give it to the police and answer their questions, and if you have no explanation you are better saying nothing until you know what the strength of the case against you is. This unfortunately is advice which was not apparently given on this occasion. When a man is given advice and says nothing in consequence you must not hold it against him for saying nothing. To hold it against him would be to turn the caution, which is meant to be a warning, into a trap, and it ignores the fact he may have been given bad advice if he is innocent, and could have explained."

However illogical it may seem, it is not proper for a judge to invite a jury to form an adverse opinion against a defendant by reason of the defendant exercising his right to remain silent. The judge here did not do that. Juries however are apt to draw their own conclusions. There is therefore no objection to a judge mentioning to a jury the conclusions which that jury might perhaps reach, basing themselves upon the silence of a defendant, and then to tell the jury that despite those immediate reactions which they may have had, they must not hold it, that is to say the silence, against him, because that would have the effect of nullifying the words of the caution which had been administered to the defendant at an earlier stage. That is exactly what the judge in the present case did, and he added as an additional bonus to the appellant in this case the comment that the stupidity or the wrong-headedness of a solicitor is not to be visited upon the head of the solicitor's client.

The ground of appeals fails, and with it so does the appeal, which is dismissed.'

R v Millward (1985) 80 Cr App R 280 Stafford Crown Court (Mr Justice Drake)

Materiality of a defendant's statement for the purposes of perjury

Facts

At the close of the prosecution case at his trial for perjury the defendant made a submission of 'no case' on the grounds that the untrue statements he had made under oath, which were the subject of the charge, had not been material in the proceedings in which they had been made, and that he had not inteneded to make untrue statements which were material to those proceedings.

Mr Justice Drake gave the following ruling:

[Having considered the facts His Lordship turned to consider the issues of law]

'Mr Tucker's [counsel for the defendant] first submission is that the evidence does not show a prima facie case that the false statements, made by this police officer, were made with the necessary mens rea to support a conviction for the offence of perjury under section 1 of the Perjury Act 1911. Section 1 of the Perjury Act, so far as it is relevant to the present proceedings, provides: "(1). If any person lawfully sworn as a witness … in a judicial proceeding wilfully makes a statement material in that proceeding which he knows to be false or does not believe to be true, he shall be guilty of perjury …"

Mr Tucker submits, first, that, in the present case, the evidence does not show a prima facie case that the defendant made any false statement or statements *wilfully*, within the meaning of that word as used in that section of the Perjury Act. He submits that the evidence shows that, at the time he told the lies, this police officer believed they were immaterial to the proceedings, and the word "wilfully" governs not only the making of a statement, but also the maker's belief as to the materiality.

I do not accept those submissions. I was referred, in support of them to a passage in the fifth edition of *Smith and Hogan Criminal Law*, at p697, and to a short passage in the judgment of McNeill J sitting as a single judge of the Queen's Bench Divisional Court, in *R* v *Inland Revenue Commissioners, ex parte Chisholm* [1981] 2 All ER 602, 605F. In the latter case, McNeill J said, in the passage referred to, "I also accept, and it is not really in dispute between the parties, that the word 'wilfully' means 'intentionally' or 'deliberately' ..."

McNeill J was there considering the meaning of the word "wilfully" where it appears in a regulation, (SI 1973 No. 334) made under the provisions of section 204 of the Income and Corporation Taxes Act 1970.

I readily accept that the word "wilfully" has a similar meaning and effect in section 1 of the Perjury Act 1911. But, I do not think it helps Mr Tucker's submission that the word "wilfully" also governs the defendant's belief in the materiality of the statement. In my judgment, the word "wilfully" requires the prosecution to prove that the defendant who made the statement did so deliberately and intentionally, when knowing it was false. If the false statement was made accidentally, or if the falsity of the statement was made accidentally or unintentionally, that is to say, with the defendant not appreciating, at the time, that he was telling a deliberate lie, then the offence of perjury, under this section, would not be made out. The passage in *Smith and Hogan* also appears to me to support this interpretation of the meaning of the word.

In the present case, this defendant clearly knew he was telling a lie, when he replied to each one of the three questions to which he did, in fact, answer with lies. Each of these lies were told wilfully, and, in my judgment, it is immaterial whether or not the defendant considered the question asked and the answers he gave to be immaterial to the case against the two Indian defendants. It would, indeed, open the floodgates to lies told under oath, if a person telling those lies could defend a prosecution for perjury by stating that he considered the questions asked and, hence, the answers he gave to be immaterial to the hearing before the court. So, I am pleased that what I believe to be the true meaning of the word "wilfully" in this section, does not, in effect, provide a charter for lies to be told under oath.

The second submission on behalf of the defendant is that each of the false statements he made was not (and, I now refer back to section 1 of the Perjury Act) " ... a statement material in that proceeding ... " Mr Tucker says the matter can be tested thus: if Constable Millward had, in fact, told the truth would his answer, or any of the three answers relied on by the prosecution, have had any affect at all on the case proceeding against Manjit Singh or Parshan Singh? He says, "Clearly not, and, therefore, each of the lies told was not a statement material in that proceeding."

I am not convinced that Mr Tucker's test is the correct one to apply, for I think it may well be that the proper test is to ask whether the false statement made is material, not whether the statement would have been material if it had been true. However, even on Mr Tucker's own suggested test, I reject his submission because I think that, had Constable Millward given true answers to the three questions asked, they would have been highly material to the proceeding.

The relevant questions put to Constable Millward, in cross-examination, were, quite clearly, directed to the main issue alive in the proceedings, that is to say, that of identity or recognition of the driver. More specifically, they were aimed at testing Constable Millward's evidence that he knew one Manjit Singh by sight, and had been able to recognise him as the driver of the motor vehicle when he stopped it in June 1982. The context in which the questions were asked clearly shows this. They were, clearly, material questions. Were the answers material? Again, I think, clearly, so.

Applying Mr Tucker's suggested test of materiality, I ask myself, "Would the magistrates have considered it material to learn that, outside the court, just before the case against these two men was started, the principal prosecution witness, whose evidence of identity or recognition was vital, had sent a fellow police officer to ask the men questions which might have the effect of assisting him to identify them?" I bear in mind that in answer to a question put to him in cross-examination by Mr Tucker, Constable Revelle, in evidence in *this* case, said that PC Millward had not asked him to identify the two Indian men for him; but, the effect of Constable Millward's inquiries of PC Revelle was to help identify the men.

If the defendant had told the magistrates he had asked Constable Revelle to check the men's driving licences, and had spoken to Constable Revelle after he had done so, that would have laid the foundation for a suggestion by the defence solicitor that PC Millward was unsure of his recognition of Manjit Singh. I fully appreciate that Constable Millward could have gone on to explain to the magistrates that he had a proper motive in asking PC Revelle to check the licences - namely, a reasonable suspicion that they might be about to practise a further deception by again switching identities before the court. I also think, on the evidence, that the magistrates might very well have accepted that explanation as true, or possibly true; but, in my judgment, that does not show that the answers, if truly given, would not have been material. They would have been answers to relevant and proper questions - relevant to an enquiry into Constable Millward's ability to identify and recognise Manjit Singh.

So, even on Mr Tucker's test, I rule that the statements were material in that proceeding. But, I think that the proper test is, to ask whether the statement in fact made, that is to say, the lie told, was material in that proceeding, and, in my judgment, each of the lies told by Police Constable Millward was material.

Let me test it this way: suppose that, at the end of the proceedings, but before announcing their decision, the magistrates had decided to accept Police Constable Millward's vital evidence of identification and recognition of Manjit Singh, and convict the two Indian men. Next, suppose that they somehow learned, at that stage, perhaps by being called back to court and informed by the prosecution, that Constable Millward had told lies - the three lies in question. Would it have affected the decision that the magistrates had thus far reached? I think it would, and the reason it would do so is because the lies, and each of them, were highly material. Even, had the magistrates, at the same time, been told of Constable Millward's motive for asking PC Revelle to see the men's driving licences, and that he had told lies because he panicked, would they not have reconsidered their decision to find the men guilty on the evidence of a witness who had told lies, even in a panic? I think they would have re-considered their decision, and, again, they would have done so because the statements made, that is to say, the lies, were material.

At one stage during Mr Tucker's submission it was suggested - and I joined in the suggestion - that the questions which the defence solicitor put to Constable Millward, in cross-examination, went to his credit. But, on reflection, I do not think that is right. They went to his ability to recognise and identify Manjit Singh. However, I would also rule that, if the questions *did* go to credit and resulted in quite deliberate lies about something which had occurred that same morning outside the court and affecting the two defendants in the case, then the answers (the lies) would be material in that proceeding.

In the course of Mr Tucker's submissions and the reply by Mr Stretton, for the prosecution, I was referred to a number of authorities, as well as certain passages in *Archbold, Smith and Hogan* (41st ed and 5th ed) and *Russell on Crime*. The textbooks give general guidance on the meaning of the word "materiality," but none of the passages is very directly relevant to the particular issue I have to decide in the present case.

I was also referred to a decision of Lawton J as he then was, at first instance at the Devonshire Assizes, in the case of *Sweet-Escott* (1971) 55 Cr App R 316; and older cases under earlier statutes, particularly *Baker* (1895) 1 QB 793, where Lord Russell of Killowen CJ gave a judgment with which the other four judges sitting with him concurred.

Again, these older decisions are of somewhat limited assistance in dealing with the particular point I have to decide under the 1911 statute in the present case. Certainly, the textbooks and authorities all agree that a false answer which would affect a man's credit, may be material.

In *Sweet-Escott* (supra), the defendant was indicted for perjury arising from false answers given to magistrates sitting on committal proceedings. He had lied when asked if he had certain criminal convictions which at the time were over 20 years old, since when he had had a clean record, and grown from youth to maturity. The questions in that case, clearly, concerned the credit of the defendant, who, when he told the lies, was a prosecution witness who was the victim of an alleged blackmail. Lawton J held that the lies were immaterial because, had the defendant told the truth and revealed his old convictions, it was inconceivable that the magistrates, sitting on the proceedings, would have considered his evidence so tainted that they would have refused to commit the accused's alleged blackmailer.

This ruling, from a judge so highly respected in matters of criminal as well as other matters of law, has a highly persuasive effect. Mr Tucker argues that it supports his suggested test, namely - would the answers have made any difference to the proceedings had they been answered truthfully?

In my view, the test adopted by Lawton J was entirely appropriate for the facts of that particular case, but I do not think it follows that the same test must, or should, be applied to all other cases.

Lawton J in his judgment, also said (p321) that he considered the questions put to the witness, in cross-examination, were not material. This was because the cross-examination purported to relate to credit, and the man's convictions, over 20 years earlier, could not reasonably affect the man's credit 20 years later, and after leading a blameless life.

I think it could also have been held, in that case, that had the committing magistrates discovered that the witness had falsely concealed stale convictions, after that length of time, that they would not have considered the lie told before them as materially affecting the man's credit.

In this case, of Constable Millward, the facts are easily distinguishable. He told lies about matters which had taken place that same morning, affecting the defendants in the case, in which he was the principal witness. They were matters which, at first sight - even if not after full investigation - would appear to be directly relevant to the vital issue of his ability to identify the accused.

Therefore, whatever test is adopted, I rule against Mr Tucker's submissions. At the end of the day, it comes back to my judgment that the statements admittedly made by Police Constable Millward, and known by him to be lies, were material in the proceedings in which they were made.

As a matter of law, under the provisions of section 1(6) of the Perjury Act 1911, I shall, therefore, direct the jury that the relevant statements, relied on by the prosecution, were material to the proceedings in which they were made.'

The defendant then changed his plea to one of guilty.

R v P & O European Ferries (Dover) Ltd (1991) 93 Cr App R 72 Central Criminal Court (Mr Justice Turner)

Corporate liability for manslaughter

Facts

On 6 March 1987 the ferry 'Herald of Free Enterprise' capsized whilst leaving Zeebrugge harbour. The owners and operators of the ferry P & O European Ferries (Dover) Ltd were charged, along with seven other defendants, with the manslaughter of the passengers and crew that died as a result of the capsizing. During the trial, the question arose as to whether or not an indictment would lie against a corporation for the offence of manslaughter.

Held

A body corporate could be indicted for the offence of manslaughter.

Mr Justice Turner:

Mr Justice Turner began by looking at the historical origins of incorporation, and the development of the company as an independent legal personality in English law. He concluded:

'In my view, therefore, the question: what natural persons are to be treated in law as being the company for the purpose of acts done in the course of its business, including the taking of precautions and the exercise of due diligence to avoid the commission of a criminal offence, is to be fund by identifying those natural persons who by the memorandum and articles of association or as a result of action taken by directors, or by the company in general meeting pursuant to the articles, are entrusted with the exercise of the powers of the company.

This test is in conformity with the classic statement of Viscount Haldane LC in *Lennard's Carrying Co Ltd* v *Asiatic Petroleum Co Ltd* [1915] AC 705. The relevant statute in that case, although not a criminal statute, was in *pari materia*, for it provided for a defence to a civil liability which excluded the concept of vicarious liability of a principal for the physical acts and state of mind of his agent.

There has been in recent years a tendency to extract from Denning LJ's judgment in *H L Bolton (Engineering) Co Ltd* v *T J Graham & Sons Ltd* [1957] 1 QB 159, 172, 173 his vivid metaphor about the 'brains and nerve centre' of a company as contrasted with its hands, and to treat this dichotomy, and not the articles of association, as laying down the test of whether or not a particular person is to be regarded in law as being the company itself when performing duties which a statute imposes on the company.

In the case in which this metaphor was first used Denning LJ was dealing with acts and intentions of directors of the company in whom the powers of the company were vested under its articles of association.'''

His Lordship then turned to the issue of corporate liability for manslaughter:

'Since the nineteenth century there has been a huge increase in the numbers and activities of corporations whether nationalised, municipal or commercial, which enter the private lives of all or most of "men and subjects" in a diversity of ways. A clear case can be made for imputing to such corporations social duties including the duty not to offend all relevant parts of the criminal law. By tracing the history of the cases decided by the English Courts over the period of the last 150 years, it can be seen how first tentatively and, finally confidently the Courts have been able to ascribe to corporations a "mind" which is generally one of the essential ingredients of common law and statutory offences. Indeed, it can be seen that in many Acts of Parliament the same concept has been embraced. The parliamentary approach is, perhaps, exemplified by s18 of the Theft Act 1968, which provides for directors and managers of a limited company to be rendered liable to conviction if an offence under s15, 16 or 17 of the Act are proved to have been committed - and I quote: "with the consent, connivance of any director, manager, secretary ... purporting to act in such capacity, then such director, manager or secretary shall be guilty of the offence." Once a state of mind could be effectively attributed to a corporation, all that remained was to determine the means by which that state of mind could be ascertained and imputed to a non-natural person. That done, the obstacle to the acceptance of general criminal liability of a corporation was overcome. *Cessante ratione legis, cessat ipsa lex.* As some of the decisions in other common law countries indicate, there is nothing essentially incongruous in the notion that a corporation should be guilty of an offence of unlawful killing. I find unpersuasive the argument of the company that the old definitions of homicide positively exclude the liability of a non-natural person to conviction of an offence of manslaughter. Any crime, in order to be justiciable must have been committed by or through the agency of a human being. Consequently, the inclusion in the definition of the expression "human being" as the author of the killing was either tautologous or, as I think more probable, intended to differentiate those cases of death in which a human being played no direct part and which would have led to forfeiture of the inanimate, or if animate non-human, object which caused the death (*deodand*) from those in which the cause of death was initiated by human activity albeit the instrument of death was inanimate or if animate non-human. I am confident that the expression "human being" in the definition of homicide was not intended to have the effect of words of limitation as might have been the case had it been found in some Act of Parliament or legal deed. It is not for me to attempt to set the limits of corporate liability for criminal offences in English Law. Examples of other crimes which may or may not be committed by corporations will, no doubt, be decided on a case by case basis in conformity with the manner in which the common law has adapted itself in the past. Suffice it that where a corporation, through the controlling mind of one of its agents, does an act which fulfils the prerequisites of the crime of manslaughter, it is properly indictable for the crime of manslaughter.

In arriving at this decision, which may be thought by some to have increased the scope of English criminal law, but which I believe merely reflects the extent of developments which have already occurred, I have borne fully in mind the warning shot put across my bows by Mr Kentridge when he referred me to the passage in *Withers* v *Director of Public Prosecutions* (1974) 60 Cr App R 85; [1975] AC 842, in the course of which Lord Simon of Glaisdale, p95 and at p863, had said:

"The first principle is that it is not open to the courts nowadays either to create new offences or so to widen existing offences as to make punishable conduct of a type hitherto not subject to punishment (*Newland* (1953) 37 Cr App R 154, 153, [1954] 1 QB 158, 167; *Shaw* v *Director of Public Prosecutions* (1961) 45 Cr App R 113, 157, [1962] AC 220, 267; *R* v *Knuller (Publishing, Printing and Promotions) Limited* (1972) 56 Cr App R 633, [1973] AC 435)."

As it seemed to me, however, the decision that manslaughter is an offence which may be committed by corporations involves neither the widening of any existing offence nor the making punishable conduct of a type hitherto not subject to punishment. Counsel for the Crown, in his admirable reply, reminded me of the second of Lord Simon's principles in *Withers* case which is that "the courts cannot refuse to apply a legal rule deducible from an authoritative decision to circumstances analogous to those inherent in such decision." In support of which Lord Simon referred to *Mirehouse* v *Rennell* (1833) 1 Cl & F 527, 546, which was approved in *Shaw* v *Director of Public Prosecutions* and *Knuller*, already referred to. My decision in the present case is, I believe, in accord with the second rather than the first of these principles.

It would not be respectful to the industry and skill of counsel who have argued the issue of corporate manslaughter not to refer to some of the decisions of courts of other common law jurisdictions which bear upon the present issue to which I was referred.

It is at once necessary to record that in some of those jurisdictions the opportunity has been taken to codify parts at least of their criminal law. As in the case of New Zealand, by way of example, the original criminal code was enacted in 1893 using as its origin the draft criminal code proposed by Sir James Fitzjames Stephen. It is no surprise that the definition follows the Digest.

The Crimes Act 1961 closely followed the 1893 Act, so that for all practical purposes the definition of manslaughter remained the same in both Acts. As it happens, a case from New Zealand is much relied upon by this company was *Murray Wright Ltd* [1970] NZLR 476, in the Court of Appeal. The report in that case helpfully includes citations from certain State Courts in the United States which demonstrate a diversity of approach. As has already been noted, the definition in question was the codified version of Stephen, as above. It is of interest, however, to trace *Murray Wright's* case from its first instance decision, which was a decision of Henry J reported in [1969] NZLR 1069. The argument for the company in that case was identical to that made in the present case, and I quote from p1070, of the report, line 33: "The argument is first that these words," - the words "definition in the statute" - "clearly exclude a corporate entity," and that was a submission with which Henry J agreed. However, he went on to say at p1071 that he considered that the proper approach be a different one:

"The only type of killing of which the law takes cognizance is a killing of one human being by another directly or indirectly by any means whatsoever, but this does not wholly dispose of the question... The killing referred to [in s160(2)(a), (b) and (c) of the Crimes Act 1961 (NZ)] is *ex facie* a killing by a human agency. There is nothing in that fact which would necessarily exclude a corporation because in all cases of corporate criminal responsibility the responsibility is for the act of some human being. But it is a special kind of human activity which constitutes an unlawful act or an omission ... to perform or observe a legal duty ... Corporate activities ... are acts or omissions of a human being or beings, but if such acts or omissions can also properly be held to be the acts or omissions of the corporate body which is the alter ego of the ... persons who do those acts or are guilty of those omissions then there is no reason why the corporate body should not be held to be responsible ..."

For myself, with the substitution of the word "embodiment" for the expression "alter ego" in this passage, and the addition of the word "also" after the word "should," although related as it is to a statutory provision as I recognise, I would readily embrace the reasoning in this passage. But in the Court of Appeal [1970] NZLR 476 the reasoning was not approved. In giving his judgment, at p479, line 20 of the report, the President, North J said:

"The question we are called upon to determine is a narrow one and depends essentially on the definition of what constitutes culpable homicide as laid down in ss 158 and 160 of the Crimes Act 1961.

In this Court, Mr Davison, senior counsel for the appellant company, made it perfectly plain that his argument did not depend on the broad question of the circumstances in which a company may be convicted of a crime. He said that he did not rely on the opinion expressed by Finlay J in *Cory Brothers and Co Ltd* [1927] 1 KB 810, that in England an indictment will not lie against a corporation for manslaughter. Counsel conceded that whatever the law may have been at that point of time, subsequent decisions plainly showed that there is nothing in the ingredients of the crime of manslaughter standing in the way of a company, in a suitable case, being indicated for this crime. He drew our attention to a number of cases and particularly to *ICR Haulage Ltd* [1944] KB 551; [1944] 1 All ER 691, where a Court of Criminal Appeal consisting of Humphreys, Croom-Johnson and Stable JJ reviewed the way the law had developed in the more recent years, even in cases where mens rea was an essential ingredient of the crime. In discussing *Cory Brothers and Co Ltd*, Stable J who delivered the judgment of the Court said at p556 and p694:

'It is sufficient in our judgment to say that, in as much as that case was decided before the decision in *Director of Public Prosecutions* v *Kent and Sussex Contractors Ltd* [1944] KB 146 and that *Chuter* v *Freeth & Pocock Ltd* [1911] 2 KB 832 was not cited at all, if the matter came before the Court today, the result might well be different.'"

And then the citation continues, and in order to avoid repetition, I continued that defence counsel submitted at p481:

"that the words in our s158 'the killing of a human being by another' clearly meant that 'Homicide' was the killing of one human being by another human being which, in his submission, made all the difference. So far as I am aware, this question has never before been considered in New Zealand but Mr Davison was able to point to a judgment of the Court of Appeals of New York, *People* v *Rochester Railway and Light Co* (1909) 195 NY 102; [1909] 88 NE Re 22, where the precise point argued by him had been considered by that Court and determined in a way favourable to his submission. The judgment of the Court of Appeals of New York was delivered by Hiscock J, who had this to say:

'Within the principles thus and elsewhere declared, we have no doubt that a definition of certain forms of manslaughter might have been formulated which would be applicable to a corporation, and make it criminally liable for various acts of misfeasance and nonfeasance when resulting in homicide, and amongst which very probably might be included conduct in its substance similar to that here charged against the respondent. But, this being so, the question still confronts us whether corporations have been so made liable for the crime of manslaughter as now expressly defined, in the section alone relied on by the people, and this question we think must be decisively answered in the negative. Section 179 of the Panel Code defines homicide as "the killing of one human being by the act, procurement or omission of another." We think that this final word "another" naturally and clearly means a second or additional member of the same kind or class alone referred to by the preceding words, namely, another human being, and that we should not interpret it as the appellant asks us to, as meaning another "person," which might then include corporations. It seems to us that it would be a violent strain upon a criminal statute to construe this word as meaning an agency of some kind other than that already mentioned or referred to, and is bridging over a radical transition from human beings to corporations. Therefore we construe this definition of homicide as meaning the killing of one human being by another human being ... Thus we have the underlying and fundamental definition of homicide as the killing of one human being by another human being, and out of this basic act thus defined and according to the circumstances which accompany it are established crimes of varying degree including that of manslaughter for which the respondent has been indicated.' "

We were also referred to another American case by Mr Davison, *State* v *Lehigh Valley Railway Co* 90 NJ Law 372, a judgment of the Supreme Court of New Jersey. In that case Swayze J found himself able to distinguish the earlier case, that is the *Rochester* case on the ground that he was not bound by a statutory definition. The following extract from that learned Judge's opinion is, I think, worth citing. He said:

"We have examined the authorities in other jurisdictions to which we were referred. The decision of *People* v *Rochester Railway and Light Co* (1909) 195 NY 102 was based entirely upon the construction of the exact language of the Penal Code, which defined homicide as "the killing of one human being by the act, procurement or omission of another," and the Court necessarily, we think, held that "another" meant "another human being." But Judge Hiscock, now the eminent Chief Judge, who spoke for the Court, was at some pains to show that there was nothing essentially incongruous in holding a corporation aggregate criminally liable for manslaughter. The case is a good illustration of the way in which the proper growth and development of the law can be prevented by the hard and fast language of a statute, and of the advantage of our own system by which the way is open for a Court to do justice by the proper application of legal principles."

I have given careful consideration to Henry J's thoughtful judgment, but, in the end I find myself unable to accept his reasoning or his conclusion. The passage I have cited from *People* v *Rochester Railway and Light Co* clearly shows that the situation in the New York statute was expressed in very similar terms to our s160.

As I have earlier mentioned, the plain fact is that those responsible for the drafting of the Crimes Act 1961 failed to appreciate that in defining 'Homicide" as the killing of a human being by another of necessity they excluded a company which cannot possibly be described as another human being."

Turner J in his judgment said at p483:

"Mr Davison cited in support a decision, of the Court of Appeals of New York State, *People* v *Rochester Railway and Light Co* (1909) 195 NY 102; [1909] 88 NE Rep 22, in which the same reasoning was adopted. [And then continued:] while manslaughter must always involve the killing of one human being *by another*, yet if a company omits to perform a legal duty of care resting upon it, and this omission *causes one human being to kill another*, is not the result manslaughter for which the company must be criminally liable as a principal? It itself has omitted to do what the law has enjoined upon it to do.

For myself I was for a time attracted by this argument, but reflection has convinced me that it cannot succeed, for the reasons which I shall now set out. Manslaughter is culpable homicide. Homicide is the killing of one human being by another. No act or omission of a company which causes death can itself amount to manslaughter, because the act or omission which kills must ex-hypothesi be the act or omission of a human being. On the other hand, if the act or omission of the company is relied on, not as directly causing death, but as causing some human being to cause death, the chain of causation is broken in law; what has in law caused death in such a case is not the act or omission of the company, but the act or omission of the human being concerned, for which the company cannot be held vicariously criminally responsible, except under the provisions of s66 ..."

That has to be compared to the provision of accessories and abetters under our law. It is of note that the Courts in those jurisdictions in which the crime of manslaughter was the subject of statutory definition have not felt able to depart from the strict wording of the statute whereas those in which the common law still defines the offence have had the freedom to: "apply a legal rule deducible from an authoritative decision to circumstances analogous to those inherent in such decisions" *pace* Lord Simon as above.'

His Lordship then considered the decision of the Division Court in *ex parte Spooner* and stated:

'In conclusion, if my primary reason for this ruling were incorrect in law, I would be minded to follow a route close to that adopted by Henry J in *Murray Wright*'s case (supra) in New Zealand who ruled that if it be accepted that manslaughter in English law is the unlawful killing of one human being by another human being (which must include both direct and indirect acts) and that a person who is the embodiment of a corporation and acting for the purposes of the corporation is doing the act or omission which caused the death, the corporation as well as the person may also be found guilty of manslaughter.'

Pharmaceutical Society of Great Britain v Storkwain [1986] 1 WLR 903 House of Lords (Lords Bridge, Brandon, Templeman, Ackner and Goff)

Imposition of strict liability

Facts

The defendants were retail chemists charged with supplying controlled medicines on invalid prescriptions, contrary to s58(2)(a) of the Medicines Act 1968. The case against the defendants was dismissed at first instance because they had acted in good faith, ignorant of the fact that the prescriptions were in fact forgeries. The prosecutor appealed successfully to the Divisional Court, and the defendants now appealed to the House of Lords.

Held

The appeal would be dismissed

Lord Goff:

'For the defendants, Mr Fisher submitted that there must, in accordance with the well-recognised presumption, be read into section 58(2)(*a*) words appropriate to require mens rea in accordance with *R v Tolson* 23 QBD 168; in other words, to adopt the language of Lord Diplock in *Sweet v Parsley* [1970] AC 132, 163, the subsection must be read subject to the implication that a necessary element in the prohibition (and hence in the offence created by the subsection together with section 67(2) of the Act of 1968) is the absence of belief, held honestly and upon reasonable grounds, in the existence of facts which, if true, would make the act innocent. He further submitted, with reference to the speech of Lord Reid in *Sweet v Parsley,* at p149, that the offence created by section 58(2)(*a*) and section 67(2) of the Act of 1968 was not to be classified as merely an offence of a quasi-criminal character in which the presumption of mens rea might more readily be rebutted, because in his submission the offence was one which would result in a stigma attaching to a person who was convicted of it, especially as Parliament had regarded it as sufficiently serious to provide that it should be triable on indictment, and that the maximum penalty should be two years' imprisonment. He also submitted that, if Parliament had considered that a pharmacist who dispensed under a forged prescription in good faith and without fault should be convicted of the offence, it would surely have made express provision to that effect; and that the imposition of so strict a liability could not be justified on the basis that it would tend towards greater efficiency on the part of pharmacists in detecting forged prescriptions. Finally, he referred your Lordships to the Misuse of Drugs Act 1971. Under section 4(1) and (3) of that Act, it is an offence to supply a controlled drug to another; but it is provided in section 28 that (subject to an immaterial exception) it shall be a defence for the accused to prove that he neither knew of nor suspected nor had reason to suspect the existence of some fact alleged by the prosecution which it is necessary for the prosecution to prove if he is to be convicted of the offence charged. Mr Fisher submitted that it would be anomalous if such a defence were available in the case of the more serious offence of supplying a controlled drug to another, but that the presumption of mens rea should be held inapplicable in the case of the offence created by section 58(2)(a) and 67(2) of the Act of 1968.

I am unable to accept Mr Fisher's submission, for the simple reason that it is, in my opinion, clear from the Act of 1968 that Parliament must have intended that the presumption of mens rea should be inapplicable to section 58(2)(a). First of all, it appears from the Act of 1968 that, where Parliament wishes to recognise that mens rea should be an ingredient of an offence created by the Act, it has expressly so provided. Thus, taking first of all offences created under provisions of Part II of the Act of 1968, express requirements of mens rea are to be found both in section 45(2) and in section 46(1)(2) and (3) of the Act. More particularly, in relation to offences created by Part III and Parts V and VI of the Act of 1968, section 121 makes detailed provision for a requirement of mens rea in respect of certain specified sections of the Act, including sections 63 to 65 (which are contained in Part III), but significantly not section 58, nor indeed sections 52 and 53. I have already set out the full text of section 121 and need not repeat it. It is very difficult to avoid the conclusion that, by omitting section 58 from those sections to which section 121 is expressly made applicable, Parliament intended that there should be no implication of a requirement of mens rea in section 58(2)(a). This view is fortified by subsections (4) and (5) of section 58 itself. Subsection (4)(a) provides that any order made by the appropriate ministers for the purposes of section 58 may provide that section 58(2)(a) or (b), or both, shall have effect subject to such exemptions as may be specified in the order. From this subsection alone it follows that the ministers, if they think it right, can provide for exemption where there is no mens rea on the part of the accused. Subsection (5) provides that any exemption conferred by an order in accordance with subsection (4)(a) may be conferred subject to such conditions or limitations as may be specified in the order. From this it follows that if the ministers, acting under subsection (4), were to confer an exemption relating to sales where the vendor lacked the requisite mens rea, they may nevertheless circumscribe their exemption with conditions and limitations which render the exemption far narrower than the implication for which Mr Fisher contends should be read into the statute itself. I find this to be very difficult to reconcile with the proposed implication.

It comes as no surprise to me, therefore, to discover that the relevant order in force at that time, the Medicines (Prescriptions only) Order 1980, is drawn entirely in conformity with the construction of the statute which I favour. It is unnecessary, in the present case, to consider whether the relevant articles of the Order may be taken into account in construing section 58 of the Act of 1968; it is enough, for present purposes, that I am able to draw support from the fact that the ministers, in making the Order, plainly did not read section 58 as subject to the implication proposed by Mr Fisher. So, for example, article 11 of the Order (which is headed "Exemption in cases involving another's default") reads as follows:

"The restrictions imposed by section 58(2)(a) (restrictions on sale and supply) shall not apply to the sale or supply of a prescription only medicine by a person who, having exercised all due diligence, believes on reasonable grounds that the product sold or supplied is not a prescription only medicine, where it is due to the act or default of another person that the product is a product to which section 58(2)(a) applies."

This provision which, by including the words "having exercised due diligence," provides for a narrower exemption than that which Mr Fisher has submitted should be read by implication into the statute, in the limited circumstances specified in the concluding words of the paragraph, is plainly inconsistent with the existence of any such implication. Likewise, article 13(1) provides that, for the purposes of section 58(2)(*a*), a prescription only medicine shall not be taken to be sold or supplied in accordance with a prescription given by a practitioner unless certain specified conditions are fulfilled. Those conditions, which are very detailed, are set out in article 13(2); and they all presuppose the existence of a valid prescription. Furthermore article 13(3) provides:

"The restrictions imposed by section 58(2)(*a*) (restrictions on sales and supply) shall not apply to a sale or supply of a prescription only medicine which is not in accordance with a prescription given by an appropriate practitioner by reason only that a condition specified in paragraph (2) is not fulfilled, where the person selling or supplying the prescription only medicine, having exercised all due diligence, believes on reasonable grounds that that condition is fulfilled in relation to that sale or supply."

So here again we find a provision which creates an exemption in narrower terms than that which Mr Fisher submits is to be found, by implication, in section 58(2)(*a*) itself. It follows that article 13, like article 11, of the Order is inconsistent with the existence of any such implication.

For these reasons, which are substantially the same as those which are set out in the judgments of Farquharson and Tudor Price JJ in the Divisional Court [1985] 3 All ER 4, I am unable to accept the submissions advanced on behalf of the defendants. I gratefully adopt as my own the following passage from the judgment of Farquharson J, at p10:

"it is perfectly obvious that pharmacists are in a position to put illicit drugs and perhaps other medicines on the market. Happily this rarely happens but it does from time to time. It can therefore be readily understood that Parliament would find it necessary to impose a heavier liability on those who are in such a position, and make them more strictly accountable for any breaches of the Act."

I would therefore answer the certified question in the negative, and dismiss the appeal with costs.'

Readhead Freight Ltd v Shulman [1988] Crim LR 696 Divisional Court (Woolf LJ, Hutchinson J)

Corporate liability

Facts

The appellant company was convicted on two counts of offences contrary to s97(1) of the Transport Act 1968, in relation to causing an employee to use a goods vehicle fitted with a tachograph. The evidence was that the company's transport manager had deliberately shut his eyes to the fact that drivers were not filling in their records as required. The company appealed by way of case stated.

Held

The appeal would be allowed. The transport manager could be described as the alter ego of the company, through whom it had known of what the drivers were doing, but 'causing' the commission of the offence required proof of some instruction or mandate from the company to the drivers, to the effect that they should falsify their records in some way, and there was no evidence of any such instruction in the present case.

Richmond upon Thames LBC v Pinn & Wheeler Ltd (1989) The Times 14 February Divisional Court (Glidewell LJ, and Pill J)

Corporate liability

Facts

Richmond upon Thames LBC (the authority), had laid informations before magistrates at Barking which led to the conviction of Pinn & Wheeler Ltd, (the company), for breaches of Article 3 of the Greater

London Council (Restriction of Goods Vehicles) Traffic Order 1985, which prohibited the driving of certain goods vehicles in restricted streets during proscribed hours. The company appealed successfully to the Crown Court, a decision from which the authority now appealed by way of case stated.

Held

As the act of driving could only be viewed as a physical act carried out by a natural, as opposed to artificial, legal person, a limited company could not incur liability for the offence charged.

Commentary

See *Griffiths* v *Studebaker Ltd* [1924] 1 KB 102. Does it make any difference in this situation whether or not the company's senior management are aware of the fact that drivers are ignoring such restrictions? [MTM]

Sherras v De Rutzen [1895] 1 QB 918 Divisional Court (Day and Wright JJ)

Imposition of strict liability

Facts

The defendant was convicted of selling alcohol to a police officer whilst on duty, contrary to s16(2) of the Licensing Act 1872. He appealed to the Divisional Court on the ground that he could not have known that the police officer was on duty as he had not been wearing the arm band that would have indicated this.

Held

The conviction would be quashed.

Wright J:

'There is a presumption that mens rea, an evil intention, or a knowledge of the wrongfulness of the act, is an essential ingredient in every offence; but that presumption is liable to be displaced either by the words of the statute creating the offence or by the subject-matter with which it deals, and both must be considered: *Nichols* v *Hall* (1873) LR 8 CP 322. One of the most remarkable exceptions was in the case of bigamy. It was held by all the judges, on the statute 1 Jac 1, c 11, that a man was rightly convicted of bigamy who had married after an invalid Scotch divorce, which had been obtained in good faith, and the validity of which he had no reason to doubt: *Lolly's Case* (1812) R & R 237. Another exception, apparently grounded on the language of a statute, is *Prince's Case* (1875) LR 2 CCR 154, where it was held by fifteen judges against one that a man was guilty of abduction of a girl under sixteen, although he believed, in good faith and on reasonable grounds, that she was over that age. Apart from isolated and extreme cases of this kind, the principal classes of exceptions may perhaps be reduced to three. One is a class of acts which, in the language of Lush J in *Davies* v *Harvey* (1874) LR 9 QB 433, are not criminal in any real sense, but are acts which in the public interest are prohibited under a penalty. Several such instances are to be found in the decision on the Revenue Statutes, eg, *Att-Gen* v *Lockwood* (1842) 9 M & W 378, where the innocent possession of liquorice by a beer retailer was held to be an offence. So under the Adulteration Acts, *R* v *Woodrow* (1846) 15 M & W 404 as to innocent possession of adulterated tobacco; *Fitzpatrick* v *Kelly* (1873) LR 8 QB 337, and *Roberts* v *Egerton* (1874) LR 9 QB 494, as to the sale of adulterated food. So under the Game Acts, as to the innocent possession of game by a carrier: *R* v *Marsh* (1824) 2 B & C 717. So as to the liability of a guardian of the poor, whose partner, unknown to him, supplied goods for the poor: *Davies* v *Harvey* (1874) LR 9 QB 433. To the same head may be referred *R* v *Bishop* (1880) 5 QBD 259, where a person was held rightly convicted of receiving lunatics in an unlicensed house, although the jury found that he honestly and on reasonable grounds believed that they were not lunatics. Another class comprehends some, and perhaps all, public nuisances: *R* v *Stephens* (1866) LR 1 QB 702, where the employer was held liable on indictment for a nuisance caused by workmen without his knowledge and contrary to his orders; and so in *R* v *Medley* (1834)

6 C & P 292, and *Barnes* v *Akroyd* (1872) LR 7 QB 474. Lastly, there may be cases in which, although the proceeding is criminal in form, it is really only a summary mode of enforcing a civil right: see per Williams and Willes JJ in *Morden* v *Porter* (1860) 7 CB (NS) 641, as to unintentional trespass in pursuit of game; *Lee* v *Simpson* (1847) 3 CB 871, as to unconscious dramatic piracy; and *Hargreaves* v *Diddams* (1875) 10 QB 582, as to a bona fide belief in a legally impossible right to fish. But, except in such cases as these, there must in general be guilty knowledge on the part of the defendant, or of someone whom he has put in his place to act for him, generally, or in the particular matter, in order to constitute an offence. It is plain that if guilty knowledge is not necessary, no care on the part of the publican could save him from a conviction under section 16, subsection (2), since it would be as easy for the constable to deny that he was on duty when asked, or to produce a forged permission from his superior officer, as to remove his armlet before entering the public-house. I am, therefore, of opinion that this conviction ought to be quashed.'

Sweet v Parsley [1970] AC 132 House of Lords (Lords Reid, Morris, Pearce, Wilberforce and Diplock)

Strict liability for serious criminal offences

Facts

The defendant was convicted under s5(b) of the Dangerous Drugs Act 1965, of 'being concerned in the management of premises used for the smoking of cannabis', following a police raid on a house owned by the defendant which she had let to tenants. The defendant had had no knowledge that drugs were being consumed there. Her appeal to the Divisional Court was dismissed, and she appealed further to the House of Lords.

Held

The appeal would be allowed

Lord Reid:

'Where it is contended that an absolute offence has been created, the words of Alderson B. in *Attorney-General* v *Lockwood* (1842) 9 M & W 378, have often been quoted: "The rule of law, I take it, upon the construction of all statutes, and therefore applicable to the construction of this, is, whether they be penal or remedial, to construe them according to the plain, literal, and grammatical meaning of the words in which they are expressed, unless that construction leads to a plain and clear contradiction of the apparent purpose of the Act, or to some palpable and evident absurdity."

That is perfectly right as a general rule and where there is no legal presumption. But what about the multitude of criminal enactments where the words of the Act simply make it an offence to do certain things but where everyone agrees that there cannot be a conviction without proof of mens rea in some form? This passage, if applied to the present problem, would mean there there is no need to prove mens rea unless it would be "a plain and clear contradiction of the apparent purpose of the Act" to convict without proof of mens rea. But that would be putting the presumption the wrong way round: for it is firmly established by a host of authorities that mens rea is an essential ingredient of every offence unless some reason can be found for holding that that is not necessary.

It is also firmly established that the fact that other sections of the Act expressly require mens rea, for example because they contain the word "knowingly", is not in itself sufficient to justify a decision that a section which is silent as to mens rea creates an absolute offence. In the absence of a clear indication in the Act that an offence is intended to be an absolute offence, it is necessary to go outside the Act and examine all relevant circumstances in order to establish that this must have been the intention of Parliament. I say "must have been" because it is a universal principle that if a penal provision is reasonably capable of two interpretations, that interpretation which is most favourable to the accused must be adopted.

What, then, are the circumstances which it is proper to take into account? In the well-known case of *Sherras* v *De Rutzen* [above] Wright J only mentioned the subject-matter with which the Act deals. But he was there dealing with something which was one of a class of acts which "are not criminal in any real sense, but are acts which in the public interest are prohibited under a penalty". It does not in the least follow that when one is dealing with a truly criminal act it is sufficient merely to have regard to the subject-matter of the enactment. One must put oneself in the position of a legislator. It has long been the practice to recognise absolute offences in this class of quasi-criminal acts, and one can safely assume that, when Parliament is passing new legislation dealing with this class of offences, its silence as to mens rea means that the old practice is to apply. But when one comes to acts of a truly criminal character, it appears to me that there are at least two other factors which any reasonable legislator would have in mind. In the first place a stigma still attaches to any person convicted of a truly criminal offence, and the more serious or more disgraceful the offence the greater the stigma. So he would have to consider whether, in a case of this gravity, the public interest really requires that an innocent person should be prevented from providing [sic] his innocence in order that fewer guilty men may escape. And equally important is the fact that fortunately the Press in this country are vigilant to expose injustice and every manifestly unjust conviction made known to the public tends to injure the body politic by undermining public confidence in the justice of the law and of its administration. But I regret to observe that, in some recent cases where serious offences have been held to be absolute offences, the court has taken into account no more than the wording of the Act and the character and seriousness of the mischief which constitutes the offence.

The choice would be much more difficult if there were no other way open than either mens rea in the full sense or an absolute offence; for there are many kinds of case where putting on the prosecutor the full burden of proving mens rea creates great difficulties and may lead to many unjust acquittals. But there are at least two other possibilities. Parliament has not infrequently transferred the onus as regards mens rea to the accused, so that, once the necessary facts are proved, he must convince the jury that on balance of probabilities he is innocent of any criminal intention. I find it a little surprising that more use has not been made of this method: but one of the bad effects of the decision of this House in *Woolmington* v *Director of Public Prosecutions* [1935] AC 462, may have been to discourage its use. The other method would be in effect to substitute in appropriate classes of cases gross negligence for mens rea in the full sense as the mental element necessary to constitute the crime. It would often be much easier to infer that Parliament must have meant that gross negligence should be the necessary mental element than to infer that Parliament intended to create an absolute offence. A variant of this would be to accept the view of Cave J in *R* v *Tolson* [see chapter 15]. This appears to have been done in Australia where authority appears to support what Dixon J said in *Proudman* v *Dayman* (1941) 67 CLR 536, 540: "As a general rule an honest and reasonable belief in a state of facts which, if they existed, would make the defendant's act innocent affords an excuse for doing what would otherwise be an offence." It may be that none of these methods is wholly satisfactory but at least the public scandal of convicting on a serious charge persons who are in no way blameworthy would be avoided.

If this section means what the Divisional Court have held that it means, then hundreds of thousands of people who sublet part of the premises or take in lodgers or are concerned in the management of residential premises or institutions are daily incurring a risk of being convicted of a serious offence in circumstances where they are in no way to blame. For the greatest vigilance cannot prevent tenants, lodgers or inmates or guests whom they bring in from smoking cannabis cigarettes in their own rooms. It was suggested in argument that this appellant brought this conviction on herself because it is found as a fact that when the police searched the premises there were people there of the "beatnik fraternity." But surely it would be going a very long way to say that persons managing premises of any kind ought to safeguard themselves by refusing accommodation to all who are of slovenly or exotic appearance, or who bring in guests of that kind. And unfortunately drug taking is by no means confined to those of unusual appearance.

Speaking from a rather long experience of membership of both Houses, I assert with confidence that no Parliament within my recollection would have agreed to make an offence of this kind an absolute offence if the matter had been fully explained to it. So, if the court ought only to hold an offence to be an absolute offence where it appears that that must have been the intention of Parliament, offences of this kind are very far removed from those which it is proper to hold to be absolute offences.

I must now turn to the question what is the true meaning of section 5 of the 1965 Act. It provides: "If a person (*a*) being the occupier of any premises, permits those premises to be used for the purposes of smoking cannabis or cannabis resin or of dealing in cannabis or cannabis resin (whether by sale or otherwise); (*b*) is concerned in the management of any premises used for any such purpose as aforesaid; he shall be guilty of an offence against this Act." We are particularly concerned with paragraph (*b*), and the first question is what is meant by "used for any such purpose". Is the "purpose" the purpose of the smoker or the purpose of the management? When in *Warner's* case, I dealt briefly with *Yeandel's* case, I thought it was the purpose of the smoker, but fuller argument in this present case brought out that an identical provision occurs in section 8 (*d*) which deals with opium. This latter provision has been carried on from the Dangerous Drugs Act 1920, and has obviously been copied into the later legislation relating to cannabis. It would require strong reasons - and there are none - to justify giving this provision a new meaning in section 5 different from that which it had in the 1920 Act and now has in section 8 of the 1965 Act. I think that in section 8 it is clear that the purpose is the purpose of the management. The first purpose mentioned is the purpose of the preparation of opium for smoking which can only be a purpose of the management. I believe that opium cannot be smoked casually anywhere at any time as can a cannabis cigarette. The section is dealing with "opium dens" and the like when the use of opium is the main purpose for which the premises are used. But it is a somewhat strained use of language to say that an ordinary room in a house is "used for the purpose" of smoking cannabis when all that happens is that some visitor lights a cannabis cigarette there. Looking to the origin and context of this provision, I have come to the conclusion that it cannot be given this wide meaning. No doubt this greatly reduces the scope of this provision when applied to the use of cannabis. But that is apt to happen when a draftsman simply copies an existing provision without regard to the different circumstances in which it is to operate. So, if the purpose is the purpose of the management, the question whether the offence with regard to opium in 1920, and now with regard to cannabis, is absolute can hardly arise. It could only arise if, although the manager not only knew about cannabis smoking and conducted the premises for that purpose, some person concerned in the management had no knowledge of that. One would first have to decide whether a person who is not actually assisting in the management can be regarded as being "concerned in the management," although ignorant of the purpose for which the manager was using the premises. Even if such a person could be regarded as "concerned in the management," I am of opinion that, for the reasons which I have given, he could not be convicted without proof of mens rea.

I would allow the appeal and quash the appellant's conviction.'

Tesco Supermarkets Ltd v Nattrass [1972] AC 153 House of Lords (Lords Reid, Morris, Pearson and Diplock and Viscount Dilhorne)

Corporate liability

Facts

The defendant company was convicted, under s11(2) of the Trade Descriptions Act 1968, of displaying a misleading price notice. Posters had been placed in a store window advertising packets of washing powder for sale at 2s 11d, when in fact those in stock were being retailed at 3s 11d. The company sought to rely on the defence provided by s24 of the Act, in that they had taken all reasonable steps to prevent the commission of the offence, which had resulted from the act of default of 'another person', namely one of its store managers. The defendants were convicted at first instance and, having appealed unsuccessfully to the Divisional Court, appealed to the House of Lords.

Held

The appeal would be allowed.

Lord Diplock:

'… My Lords, a corporation incorporated under the Companies Act 1948 owes its corporate personality and its powers to its constitution, the memorandum and articles of association. The obvious and only place to look to discover by what natural persons its powers are exercisable, is in its constitution. The articles of association, if they follow Table A, provide that the business of the company shall be managed by the directors and that they may "exercise all such powers of the company" as are not required by the Act to be exercised in general meeting. Table A also vests in the directors the right to entrust and confer upon a managing director any of the powers of the company which are exercisable by them. So it may also be necessary to ascertain whether the directors have taken any action under this provision or any other similar provision providing for the co-ordinate exercise of the powers of the company by executive directors or by committees of directors and other persons, such as are frequently included in the articles of association of companies in which the regulations contained in Table A are modified or excluded in whole or in part.

In my view, therefore, the question: what natural persons are to be treated in law as being the company for the purpose of acts done in the course of its business, including the taking of precautions and the exercise of due diligence to avoid the commission of a criminal offence, is to be found by identifying those natural persons who by the memorandum and articles of association or as a result of action taken by the directors, or by the company in general meeting pursuant to the articles, are entrusted with the exercise of the powers of the company.

This test is in conformity with the classic statement of Viscount Haldane LC in *Lennard's Carrying Co Ltd* v *Asiatic Petroleum Co Ltd* [1915] AC 705. The relevant statute in that case, although not a criminal statute, was in pari materia, for it provided for a defence to a civil liability which excluded the concept of vicarious liability of a principal for the physical acts and state of mind of his agent.

There has been in recent years a tendency to extract from Denning LJ's judgment in *H L Bolton (Engineering) Co Ltd* v *T J Graham & Sons Ltd* [1957] 1 QB 159, 172, 173 his vivid metaphor about the "brains and nerve centre" of a company as contrasted with its hands, and to treat this dichotomy, and not the articles of association, as laying down the test of whether or not a particular person is to be regarded in law as being the company itself when performing duties which a statute imposes on the company.

In the case in which this metaphor was first used Denning LJ was dealing with acts and intentions of directors of the company in whom the powers of the company were vested under its articles of association. The decision in that case is not authority for extending the class of persons whose acts are to be regarded in law as the personal acts of the company itself, beyond those who by, or by action taken under, its articles of association are entitled to exercise the powers of the company. In so far as there are dicta to the contrary in *The Lady Gwendolen* [1965] P 294, they were not necessary to the decision and, in my view, they were wrong …'

R v Tolson (1889) 23 QBD 168

See chapter 14.

Vane v Yiannopoullos [1965] AC 486 House of Lords (Lords Reid, Evershed, Morris, Hodson and Donovan)

Vicarious liability

Facts

The defendant was licensed to sell alcohol to those of her patrons who ordered meals. She was charged under s22(1) of the Licensing Act 1961 with the offence of knowingly selling alcohol to persons to whom she was not permitted to sell, after one of her waitresses had sold alcohol to two youths in contravention of the terms of the licence. The magistrates had dismissed the case against the defendant on the basis that she had not had any mens rea, and the prosecutor appealed to the House of Lords.

Held

The appeal would be dismissed.

Lord Morris:

'... My Lords, the principle "respondeat superior" finds no place in our criminal law. If a master tells or authorises his servant to do some particular act any criminal liability in the master that might result, either as a principal or as an accessory, springs from the authorisation and not simply from the relationship of master and servant. Parliament may, however, in an infinite variety of ways provide that there is to be criminal liability in one who has personally no mens rea or in one who personally has not committed an actus reus. The question is whether Parliament has done this in section 22(1) (a). It is open to Parliament to provide that a particular act is wrongful and that a person who does the act is guilty of an offence. In general our criminal law requires that there should be mens rea in order to establish guilt. Parliament may, however, enact that mens rea is not necessary. There may be strict liability. So also it might be enacted that a person is guilty of an offence if his servant or agent does some act and does it with *mens rea*. It might be enacted that a person is guilty of an offence if some other person not his servant or agent does some act and does it with mens rea. It might be enacted that a person is guilty of an offence if there is mens rea either in him or in the person doing the act. It might be enacted that a person is guilty of an offence if an act is done by some other person even though there is no mens rea in anyone. My Lords, the cases cited by Mr Buzzard in his careful argument provide illustrations of the ways in which courts have interpreted particular sections of particular Acts. I do not propose to refer to them in detail. I do not feel that they ought to determine the construction of the section of the Act of 1961 now being considered. The decisions may seem to be divergent. There is, however, no present need to express a preference for some of them rather than for others. The section of the Act of 1961 now under consideration had no ancestry in earlier Licensing Acts. Even if it had, I am not prepared to accept that there are any canons of construction which are specially applicable to legislation dealing with licensing, or that in such legislation the principle "respondeat superior" commands some exceptional yet general acceptance. If in some of the decided cases there are words suggesting that evil consequences would flow if conclusions were reached different from those pronounced, such words must be read (for otherwise they could hardly be justified) as denoting that in the process of construing the words used by Parliament in particular contexts the purpose that was in the mind of Parliament was not be to forgotten. In *Mousell Brothers Ltd* v *London & North Western Railway Co* [1917] 2 KB 836, 845, Atkin J (as he then was) said: "I think that the authorities cited ... make it plain that while prima facie a principal is not to be made criminally responsible for the acts of his servants, yet the legislature may prohibit an act or enforce a duty in such words as to make the prohibition or the duty absolute; in which case the principal is liable if the act is in fact done by his servants. To ascertain whether a particular Act of Parliament has that effect or not regard must be had to the object of the Statute, the words used, the nature of the duty laid down, the person upon whom it is imposed, the person by whom it would in ordinary circumstances be performed, and the person upon whom the penalty is imposed."

I do not find it necessary to express any opinion in regard to the cases which distinguish between what has been called total and partial delegation. I know of no statutory wording which while pointing to "delegation" distinguishes between servants and agents with major responsibility and those with lesser responsibility. The holder of a licence, it is said, may be criminally liable in some circumstances for the acts of a manager of licensed premises (who may or may not be his own servant) if the manager is in control but will not be liable for what is done by a servant who is not in control. I think that further consideration of these matters need not now arise. While finding myself in agreement with the conclusion of the learned magistrate I base my agreement merely upon an interpretation of the wording of section 22(1) (a) of the Act of 1961. That Act contained new provisions as to licences for restaurants and guest houses and it amended the Licensing Act of 1953. The Act of 1953, which was an Act that consolidated a number of licensing enactments, contained many variations of wording.

... In section 21 (of the 1961 Act) it is provided that "the holder of the licence or his servant shall not knowingly sell" to a person under 18. The section now to be interpreted is the section which follows. The words of section 22(1) (a) include the word "knowingly". There is no express mention of any servant or agent of the holder of the licence. As a matter of construction it seems to me that in the context of section 22(1) the presence of the word "knowingly" requires knowledge in the holder of the licence: it requires that he should know that there is a sale to someone to whom (as he knows) he is not permitted to sell. The contention of the appellant is that an offence is committed by the holder of the licence if there is a sale either personally by him or by someone acting on his behalf, provided that either he or such other person knows that the sale is to someone to whom he is not permitted to sell. Having regard to the wording of other sections, I consider that different and much clearer wording was needed in section 22(1) to convey the meaning contended for by the appellant. In a penal section there should be certainty. The interpretation urged by the appellant involves reading words into the subsection which are not there. I would dismiss the appeal.'

R v Winson [1969] 1 QB 371 Court of Appeal (Criminal Division) (Lord Parker CJ, Salmon LJ and Widgery J)

Vicarious liability

Facts

The defendant held a justices' on-licence in respect of a bar under which he was prohibited from selling alcohol to persons who had been members of the club for less than 48 hours. He visited the bar infrequently, and had effectively delegated the running of the bar to a manager. Following evidence that alcohol had been sold at the club in breach of the terms of the licence, the defendant was convicted under s161(1) of the Licensing Act 1964 of knowingly selling liquor to persons to whom he was not permitted to sell. The defendant appealed.

Held

The appeal would be dismissed

Lord Parker CJ:

'It is therefore necessary to look a little further back into the inception of this doctrine. It is to be observed in the first instance that this doctrine is something quite independent of the principles which come into play when Parliament has created an absolute offence; when an absolute offence has been created by Parliament, then the person on whom a duty is thrown is responsible, whether he has delegated or whether he has acted through a servant; he is absolutely liable regardless of any intent or knowledge or mens rea. The principle of delegation comes into play, and only comes into play, in cases where, although the statute uses words which import knowledge or intent such as in this case "knowingly" or in some other cases "permitting" or "suffering" and the like, cases to which knowledge is inherent, nevertheless it has been held that a man cannot get out of his responsibilities which have been put upon him by delegating those responsibilities to another.

Though not the first case by any means on the subject, the first case to which attention is drawn is that of *Allen* v *Whitehead* [1930] 1 KB 211, DC. The offence in question there was knowingly permitting or suffering prostitutes to meet together on premises contrary to section 44 of the Metropolitan Police Act, 1839. In that case the occupier and licensee of a refreshment house did not manage the refreshment house himself but employed a manager for that purpose. A number of women known to the manager to be prostitutes resorted to the refreshment house. In that case, as here, the occupier and licensee said, "It was not knowingly on my part, I was not there, I had appointed a manager". Lord Hewart CJ said (at p220):

"I think that this provision in this statute would be rendered nugatory if the contention raised on behalf of this respondent were held to prevail. That contention was this, that as the respondent did not himself manage the refreshment house and had no personal knowledge that prostitutes met together and remained therein, and had not been negligent in failing to notice these facts, and had not wilfully closed his eyes to them, he could not in law be held responsible."

He went on to say (at p221)

"He had transferred to the manager the exercise of discretion in the conduct of the business, and it seems to me that the only reasonable conclusion is, regard being had to the purposes of this Act, that the knowledge of the manager was the knowledge of the keeper of the house."

Branson J put the matter very succinctly. He said (at p221)

"I agree. The essence of the respondent's case was that he had no personal knowledge of the fact that prostitutes were meeting and remaining upon these premises. It is found that his manager knew, and Lord Coleridge CJ said in *Somerset* v *Hart* (1884) 12 QBD 360, DC 'that a man may put another in his position so as to represent him for the purpose of knowledge.' I think that is what the respondent has done here and that, consequently, the contention set up by the respondent fails."

It is just worth referring to *Somerset* v *Hart* itself, if only because that was decided on the basis that there had been no valid delegation. The offence there concerned gaming, that the licensee of premises had suffered gaming to take place on the premises. In fact he had not delegated the management to anybody else, but a servant of his employed on the premises, without any connivance or wilful blindness on the part of the licensee, had suffered gaming to take place. In the course of the argument Lord Coleridge said (at p362)

"How can a man suffer a thing done when he does not know of it? It is true that a man may put another in his position so as to represent him for the purpose of knowledge, but there is no evidence of such delegation here."

In his judgment Lord Coleridge said (at p364)

"I quite agree that the provisions of an Act which is passed in the interests of public morality and order should receive a reasonably liberal construction. I do not say that proof of actual knowledge on the part of the landlord is necessary. Slight evidence might be sufficient to satisfy the magistrates that the landlord might have known what was taking place if he had pleased, but where no actual knowledge is shown there must, as it seems to me, be something to show either that the gaming took place with the knowledge of some person clothed with the landlord's authority, or that there was something like connivance on his part, that he might have known but purposely abstained from knowing."

Finally, of the more important authorities on this point there is the case of *Linnett* v *Metropolitan Police Commissioner*, [1946] KB 290, DC. The offence there was "knowingly permitting disorderly conduct contrary to section 44 of the Metropolitan Police Act". In fact the licensee of the premises had absented himself from the premises and left the control to another man. It was held that although he, the licensee, had no knowledge, the man he had appointed manager or controller did have knowledge and on the principle of delegation he, the licensee, was liable.

Lord Goddard CJ said (at p294)

"The principle underlying these decisions does not depend upon the legal relationship existing between master and servant or between principal and agent; it depends on the fact that the person who is responsible in law, as for example, a licensee under the Licensing Acts, has chosen to delegate his duties, powers and authority to another."

He goes on to refer to *Somerset v Hart* and points out that in that case there had been no delegation of control, but that it was merely a case, as indeed was *Vane v Yiannopoullos* of a servant acting behind the back of the licensee. He ends up by saying (at p295)

"Where there is such delegation, [that is, true delegation] then the knowledge of the servant or agent becomes that of the master or principal.

In this case there was no relationship of master and servant between the appellant and Baker. They were joint licensees. If one licensee chooses to say to his co-licensee, although not his servant: "We are both licensees and both keepers of this house, but I am not going to take any part in the management of this house, I leave the management to you", he is putting his co-licensee into his own place to exercise his own powers and duties and he must, therefore, accept responsibility for what is done or known by his co-licensee in that exercise. That is the principle which underlies all the cases to which I have referred. I am far from saying, and I do not wish it to be thought that I am saying, that where a statute provides that in any business a certain act permitted by the manager shall be an offence on the part of the manager if it is done with his knowledge, that if that act takes place whilst the manager himself is carrying on that business and is in charge of that business but without his knowledge, so that he was powerless to prevent it, that person necessarily commits the offence. But if the manager chooses to delegate the carrying on of the business to another, whether or not that other is his servant, then what that other does or what he knows must be imputed to the person who put the other into that position."

That is the doctrine of delegation which does form part of our law and no one in the House of Lords has said that it does not.'

HLT PUBLICATIONS

All HLT Publications have two important qualities. First, they are written by specialists, all of whom have direct practical experience of teaching the syllabus. Second, all Textbooks are reviewed and updated each year to reflect new developments and changing trends. They are used widely by students at polytechnics and colleges throughout the United Kingdom and overseas.

A comprehensive range of titles is covered by the following classifications.

- **TEXTBOOKS**
- **CASEBOOKS**
- **SUGGESTED SOLUTIONS**
- **REVISION WORKBOOKS**

The books listed overleaf should be available from your local bookshop. In case of difficulty, however, they can be obtained direct from the publisher using this order form. Telephone, Fax or Telex orders will also be accepted. Quote your Access, Visa or American Express card numbers for priority orders. To order direct from publisher please enter cost of titles you require, fill in despatch details and send it with your remittance to The HLT Group Ltd. **Please complete the order form overleaf.**

DETAILS FOR DESPATCH OF PUBLICATIONS
Please insert your full name below

Please insert below the style in which you would like the correspondence from the Publisher addressed to you
TITLE Mr, Miss etc.   INITIALS   SURNAME/FAMILY NAME

Address to which study material is to be sent (please ensure someone will be present to accept delivery of your Publications).

POSTAGE & PACKING
You are welcome to purchase study material from the Publisher at 200 Greyhound Road, London W14 9RY, during normal working hours.

If you wish to order by post this may be done direct from the Publisher. Postal charges are as follows:

UK   - Orders over £30: no charge. Orders below £30: £2.60. Single paper (last exam only): 55p
OVERSEAS   - See table below

The Publisher cannot accept responsibility in respect of postal delays or losses in the postal systems.
DESPATCH All cheques must be cleared before material is despatched.

SUMMARY OF ORDER

Date of order:

Add postage and packing:

Cost of publications ordered:
UNITED KINGDOM:

£

OVERSEAS:	TEXTS		Suggested Solutions (Last exam only)	
	One	Each Extra		
Eire	£5.00	£0.70	£1.00	
European Community	£10.50	£1.00	£1.00	
East Europe & North America	£12.50	£1.50	£1.50	
South East Asia	£12.00	£2.00	£1.50	
Australia/New Zealand	£14.00	£3.00	£1.70	
Other Countries (Africa, India etc)	£13.00	£3.00	£1.50	

Total cost of order: £

Please ensure that you enclose a cheque or draft payable to
THE HLT GROUP LTD for the above amount, or charge to ☐ Access ☐ Visa ☐ American Express

Card Number

Expiry Date...   Signature ....

LLB PUBLICATIONS	TEXTBOOKS		CASEBOOKS		REVISION WORKBOOKS		SUG. SOL 1986/91		SUG. SOL 1992	
	Cost £	£	Cost £	£	Cost £	£	Cost £	£	Cost £	£
Administrative Law	£18.95		£19.95				£9.95		£3.00	
Commercial Law Vol I	£18.95		£19.95		£9.95		£9.95		£3.00	
Commercial Law Vol II	£17.95		£19.95							
Company Law	£19.95		£19.95		£9.95		£9.95		£3.00	
Conflict of Laws	£18.95		£17.95		£9.95					
Constitutional Law	£16.95		£17.95		£9.95		£9.95		£3.00	
Contract Law	£16.95		£17.95		£9.95		£9.95		£3.00	
Conveyancing	£19.95		£17.95							
Criminal Law	£16.95		£18.95		£9.95		£9.95		£3.00	
Criminology	£17.95						£4.95†		£3.00	
English Legal System	£16.95		£14.95		£9.95		£8.95*		£3.00	
European Community Law	£17.95		£19.95		£9.95		£4.95†		£3.00	
Equity and Trusts	£16.95		£17.95		£9.95					
Evidence	£19.95		£18.95		£9.95		£9.95		£3.00	
Family Law	£18.95		£19.95		£9.95		£9.95		£3.00	
Jurisprudence	£16.95				£9.95		£9.95		£3.00	
Land Law	£16.95		£17.95		£9.95		£9.95		£3.00	
Law of Trusts							£9.95		£3.00	
Public International Law	£18.95		£18.95		£9.95		£9.95		£3.00	
Revenue Law	£19.95		£19.95		£9.95		£9.95		£3.00	
Roman Law	£14.95									
Succession	£19.95		£18.95		£9.95		£9.95		£3.00	
Tort	£16.95		£17.95		£9.95		£9.95		£3.00	

BAR PUBLICATIONS

	TEXTBOOKS		CASEBOOKS				SUG. SOL		SUG. SOL	
Conflict of Laws	£18.95		£17.95				£9.95§		£4.50	
Civil & Criminal Procedure	£21.95		£20.95				£14.95		£4.50	
European Community Law & Human Rights	£17.95		£19.95				£9.95§		£4.50	
Evidence	£19.95		£18.95				£14.95		£4.50	
Family Law	£18.95		£19.95				£14.95		£4.50	
General Paper I	£21.95		£20.95				£14.95		£4.50	
General Paper II	£21.95		£20.95				£14.95		£4.50	
Law of International Trade	£17.95		£19.95				£14.95		£4.50	
Practical Conveyancing	£19.95		£17.95				£14.95		£4.50	
Revenue Law	£19.95		£19.95				£14.95		£4.50	
Sale of Goods & Credit	£18.95		£18.95				£14.95		£4.50	

LAW SOCIETY FINALS	TEXTBOOKS		REVISION WORKBOOKS		SUGGESTED SOLUTIONS to Summer & Winter Examinations for all 7 Papers	
Accounts	£14.95		£9.95		Final Exam Papers (Set) (All Papers) Summer 1989	£9.95
Business Organisations & Insolvency	£14.95				Final Exam Papers (Set) (All Papers) Winter 1990	£9.95
Consumer Protection & Employment Law	£14.95				Final Exam Papers (Set) (All Papers) Summer 1990	£9.95
Conveyancing I & II	£14.95					
Family Law	£14.95				Final Exam Papers (Set) (All Papers) Winter 1991	£9.95
Litigation	£14.95					
Wills, Probate & Administration	£14.95		£9.95		Final Exam Papers (Set) (All Papers) Summer 1991	£9.95

CPE PUBLICATIONS	TEXTBOOKS		CASEBOOKS	
Criminal Law	£16.95		£18.95	
Constitutional & Administrative Law	£16.95		£17.95	
Contract Law	£16.95		£17.95	
Equity & Trusts	£16.95		£17.95	
Land Law	£16.95		£17.95	
Tort	£16.95		£17.95	

INSTITUTE OF LEGAL EXECUTIVES	TEXTBOOKS	
Company & Partnership Law	£18.95	
Constitutional Law	£13.95	
Contract Law	£13.95	
Criminal Law	£13.95	
Equity & Trusts	£13.95	
European Law & Practice	£17.95	
Evidence	£17.95	
Land Law	£13.95	
Tort	£13.95	

*1987-1991
†1990-1991
§1988-1991